SHONEN JUMP

NARUTO

THE MOVIE

GUARDIANS OF THE CRESCENT MOON KINGDOM

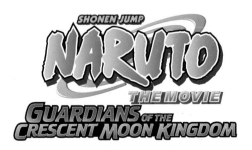

SHONEN JUMP
NARUTO
THE MOVIE
GUARDIANS OF THE CRESCENT MOON KINGDOM

Original Concept by Masashi Kishimoto
Edited by Jump Comics

English Adaptation/Katy Bridges
Touch-up Art & Lettering/Hudson Yards
Cover and Interior Design/Sean Lee
Editor/Shaenon K. Garrity

Editor in Chief, Books/Alvin Lu
Editor in Chief, Magazines/Marc Weidenbaum
VP, Publishing Licensing/Rika Inouye
VP, Sales and Product Marketing/Gonzalo Ferreyra
VP, Creative/Linda Espinosa
Publisher/Hyoe Narita

NARUTO GEKIJOBAN ANIME COMICS – DAIKOFUN! MIKAZUKIJIMA
NO ANIMAL PANIC DATTEBAYO – © 2002 MASASHI KISHIMOTO
© NMP 2006 All rights reserved. First published in Japan in 2007 by
SHUEISHA Inc., Tokyo. English translation rights arranged by
SHUEISHA Inc.

Printed in Singapore

Published by VIZ Media, LLC
P.O. Box 77010
San Francisco, CA 94107

SHONEN JUMP Manga Edition
10 9 8 7 6 5 4 3 2 1
First printing, November 2008

www.viz.com

THE WORLD'S MOST POPULAR MANGA
SHONEN JUMP ANI-MANGA
www.shonenjump.com

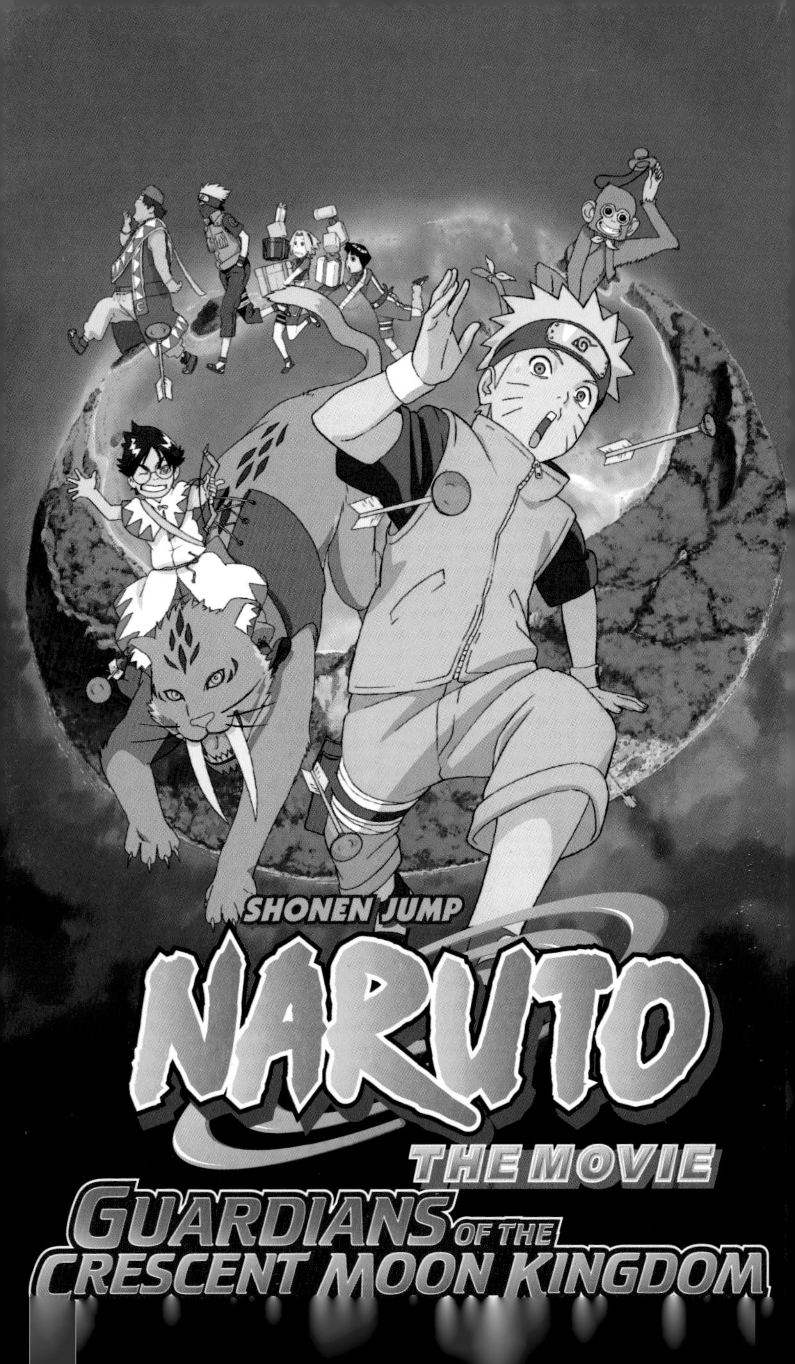
SHONEN JUMP
NARUTO
THE MOVIE
GUARDIANS OF THE
CRESCENT MOON KINGDOM

Main Characters

Here's the cast of our story! Naturally, there are both Hidden Leaf ninja and characters original to the movie…

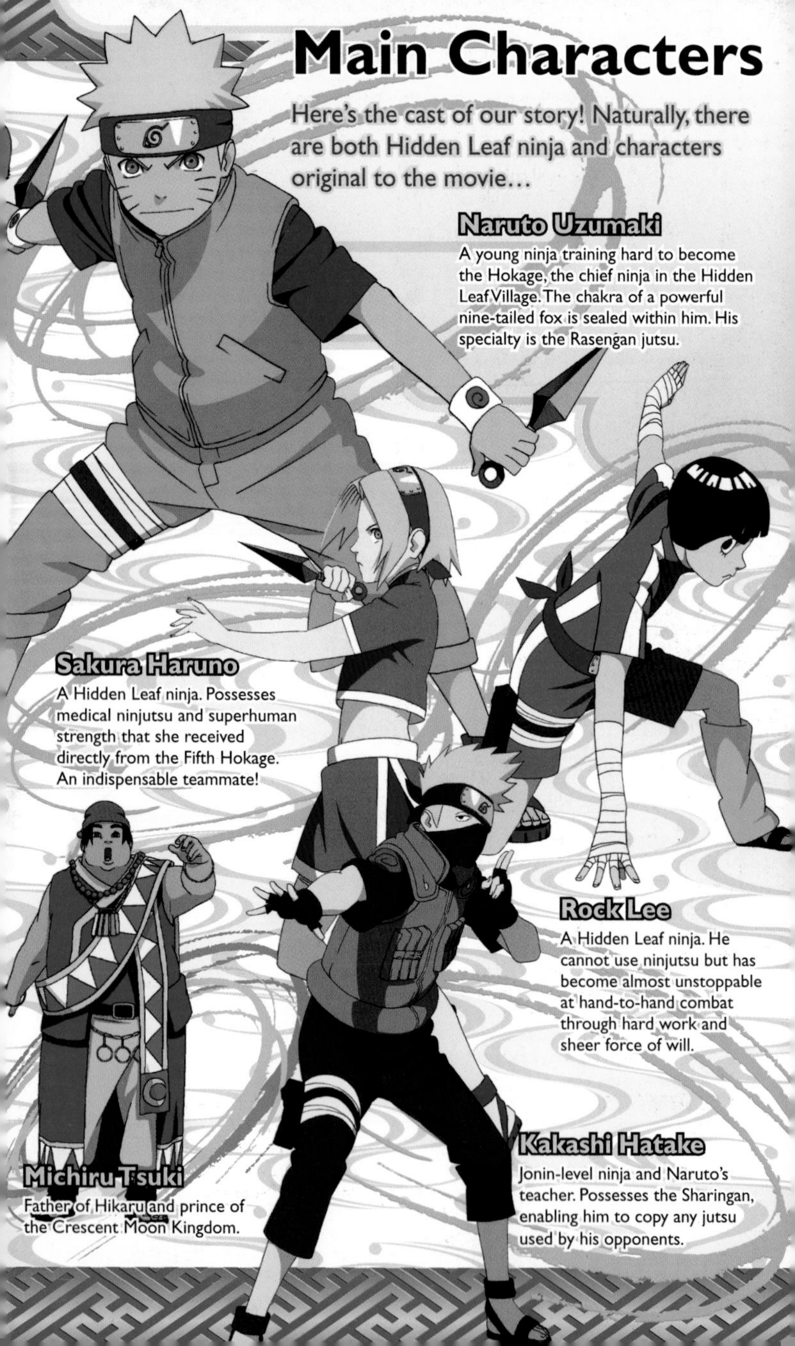

Naruto Uzumaki

A young ninja training hard to become the Hokage, the chief ninja in the Hidden Leaf Village. The chakra of a powerful nine-tailed fox is sealed within him. His specialty is the Rasengan jutsu.

Sakura Haruno

A Hidden Leaf ninja. Possesses medical ninjutsu and superhuman strength that she received directly from the Fifth Hokage. An indispensable teammate!

Rock Lee

A Hidden Leaf ninja. He cannot use ninjutsu but has become almost unstoppable at hand-to-hand combat through hard work and sheer force of will.

Michiru Tsuki

Father of Hikaru and prince of the Crescent Moon Kingdom.

Kakashi Hatake

Jonin-level ninja and Naruto's teacher. Possesses the Sharingan, enabling him to copy any jutsu used by his opponents.

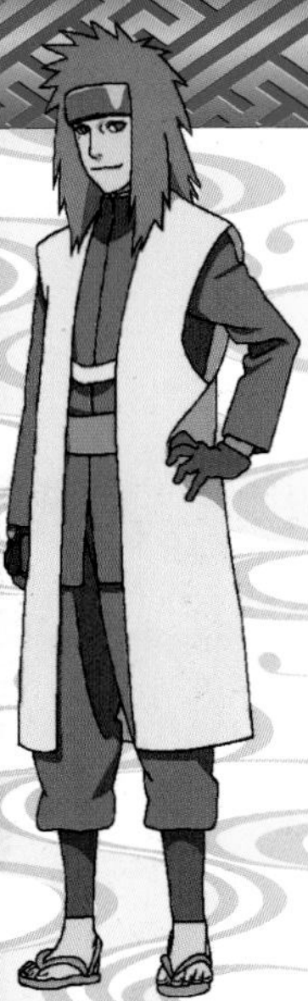

Ishidate

Leader of the shinobi hired by Shabadaba. Cool and collected, he's a formidable fighter with the power to change anything he touches into stone.

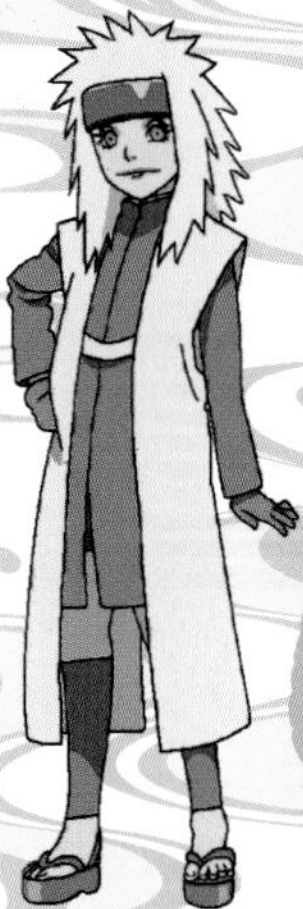

Karenbana

Uses poison gas to disorient her enemies. Looks younger than she is.

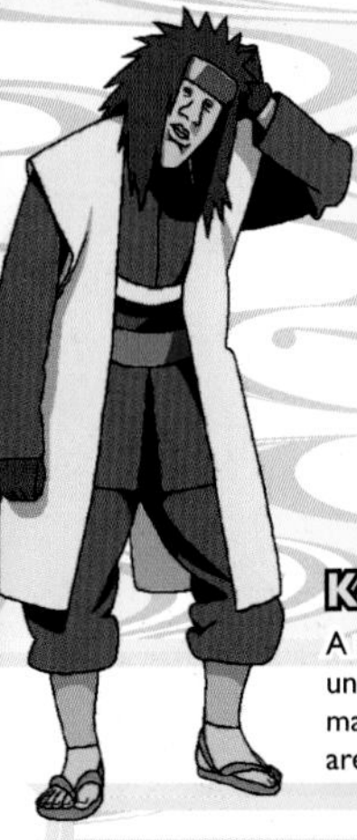

Kongou

A ninja who works under Ishidate. His massive size and strength are his weapons.

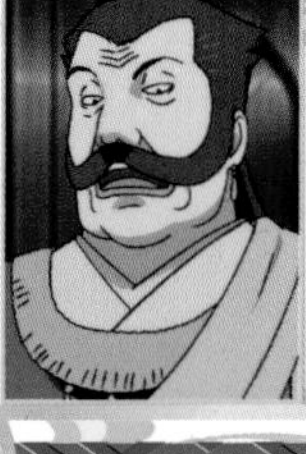

Shabadaba

Minister of the Crescent Moon Kingdom. Is plotting to seize the throne.

Hikaru Tsuki

Son of the prince of the Crescent Moon Kingdom. Skilled with the bow and arrow.

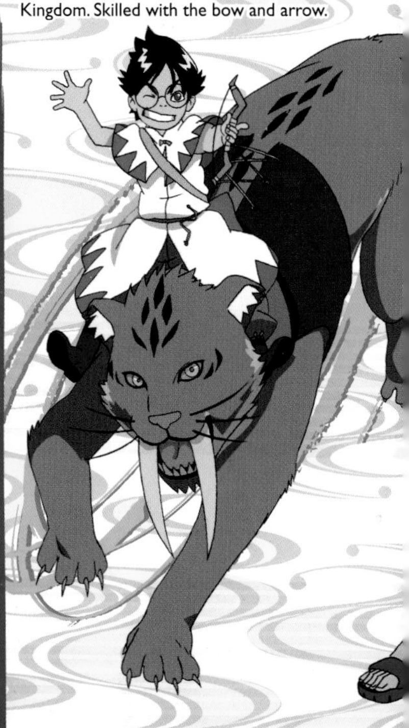

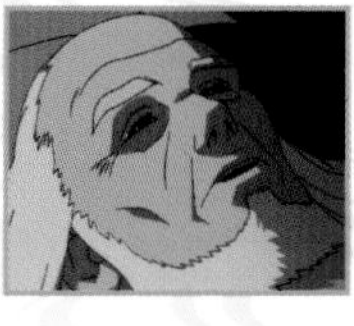

King Tsuki

King of the Crescent Moon Kingdom. His dream is to build a government that will help his people.

Amayo

Hikaru's mother. She returned to her parents after she grew tired of living with the prince.

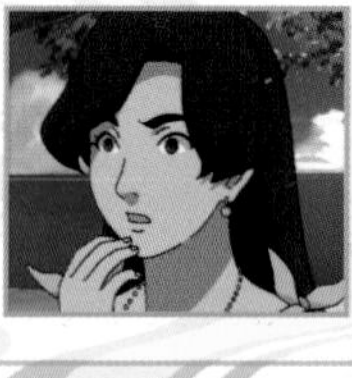

SHONEN JUMP

NARUTO THE MOVIE GUARDIANS OF THE CRESCENT MOON KINGDOM

ANI-MANGA

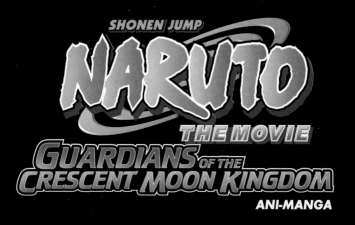

Contents

🐾 Chapter 1: The Princes of the Crescent Moon Kingdom

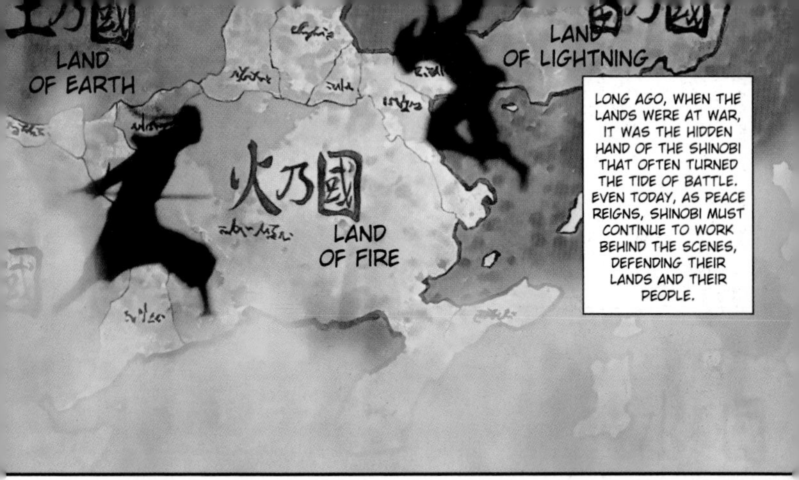
LAND OF LIGHTNING
LONG AGO, WHEN THE LANDS WERE AT WAR, IT WAS THE HIDDEN HAND OF THE SHINOBI THAT OFTEN TURNED THE TIDE OF BATTLE. EVEN TODAY, AS PEACE REIGNS, SHINOBI MUST CONTINUE TO WORK BEHIND THE SCENES, DEFENDING THEIR LANDS AND THEIR PEOPLE.
LAND OF EARTH
火乃國
LAND OF FIRE

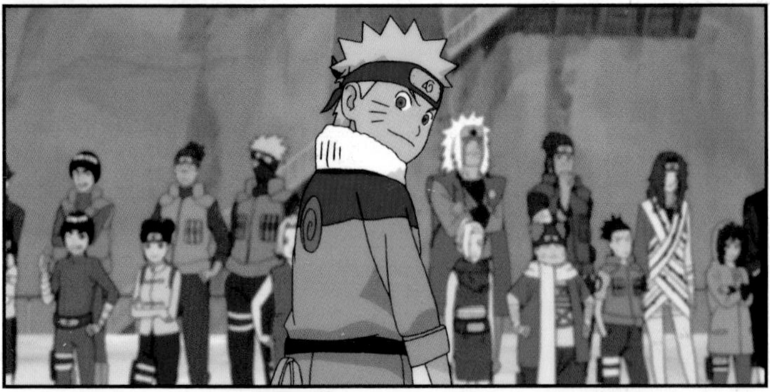

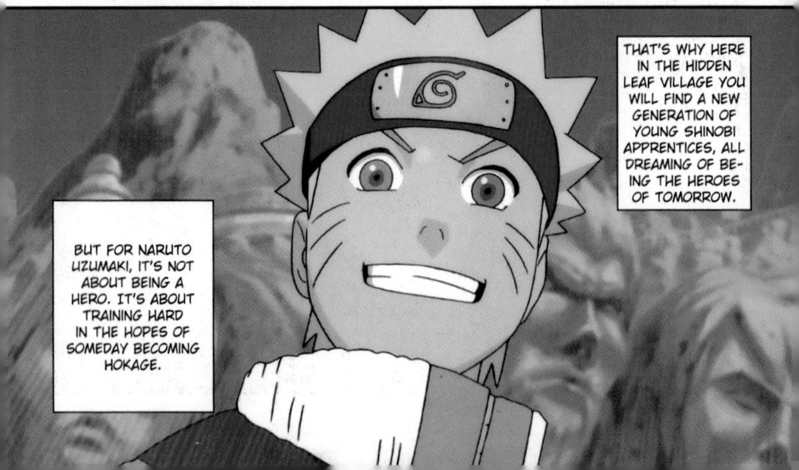
THAT'S WHY HERE IN THE HIDDEN LEAF VILLAGE YOU WILL FIND A NEW GENERATION OF YOUNG SHINOBI APPRENTICES, ALL DREAMING OF BEING THE HEROES OF TOMORROW.
BUT FOR NARUTO UZUMAKI, IT'S NOT ABOUT BEING A HERO. IT'S ABOUT TRAINING HARD IN THE HOPES OF SOMEDAY BECOMING HOKAGE.

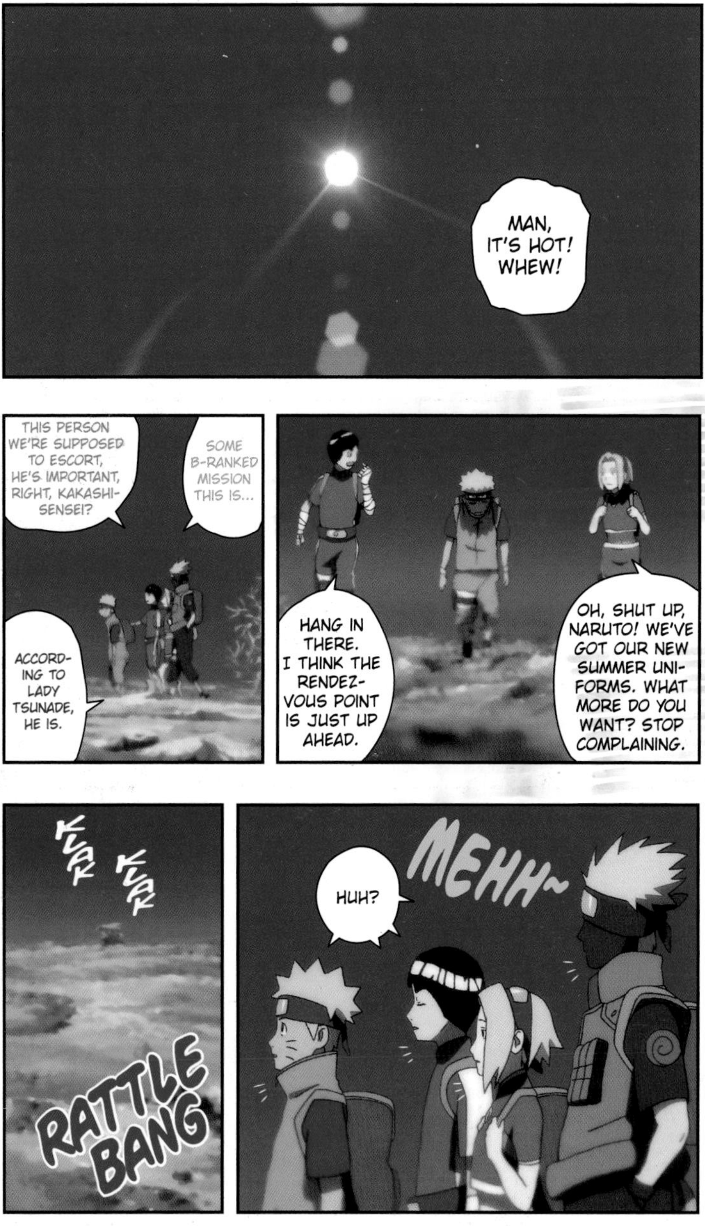
MAN, IT'S HOT! WHEW!
OH, SHUT UP, NARUTO! WE'VE GOT OUR NEW SUMMER UNIFORMS. WHAT MORE DO YOU WANT? STOP COMPLAINING.
HANG IN THERE. I THINK THE RENDEZVOUS POINT IS JUST UP AHEAD.
SOME B-RANKED MISSION THIS IS...
THIS PERSON WE'RE SUPPOSED TO ESCORT, HE'S IMPORTANT, RIGHT, KAKASHI-SENSEI?
ACCORDING TO LADY TSUNADE, HE IS.
MEHH~
HUH?
KLAK KLAK
RATTLE BANG

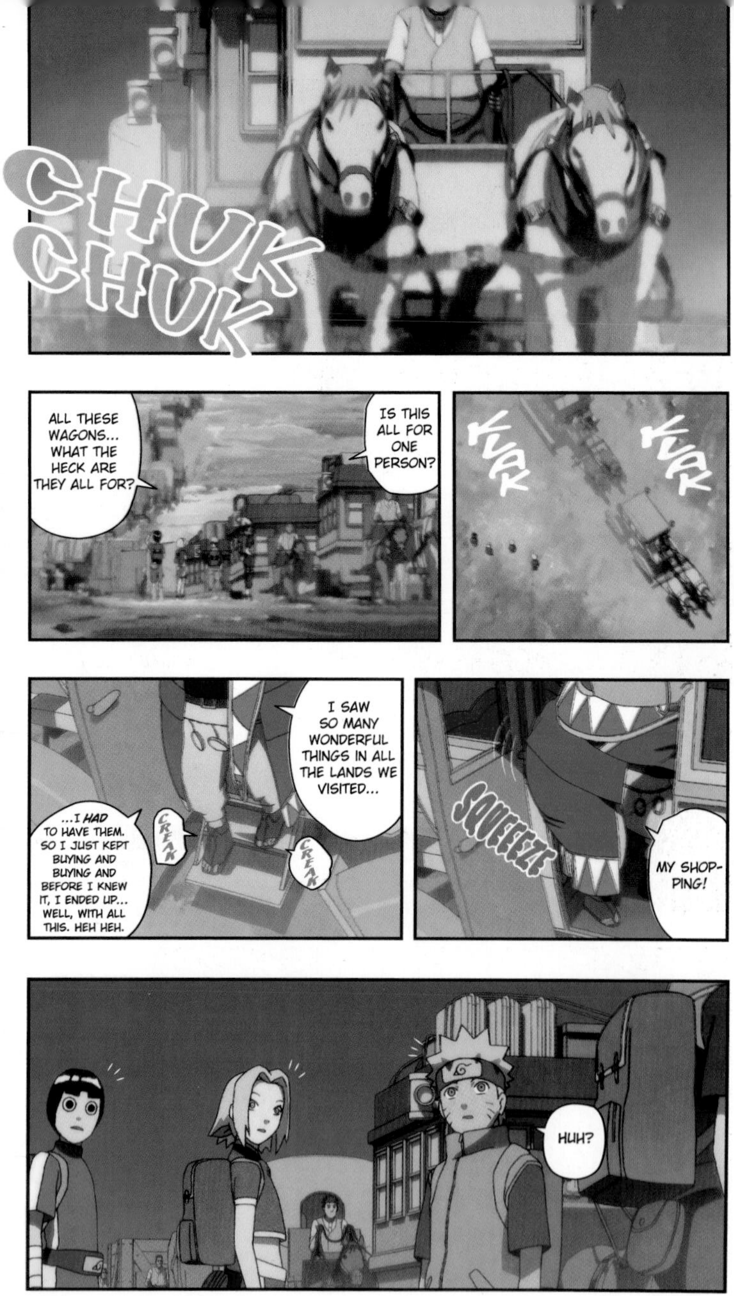
CHUK CHUK
KLAK
KLAK
IS THIS ALL FOR ONE PERSON?
ALL THESE WAGONS... WHAT THE HECK ARE THEY ALL FOR?
SQUEEEZE
MY SHOPPING!
I SAW SO MANY WONDERFUL THINGS IN ALL THE LANDS WE VISITED...
CREAK
CREAK
...I *HAD* TO HAVE THEM. SO I JUST KEPT BUYING AND BUYING AND BEFORE I KNEW IT, I ENDED UP... WELL, WITH ALL THIS. HEH HEH.
HUH?

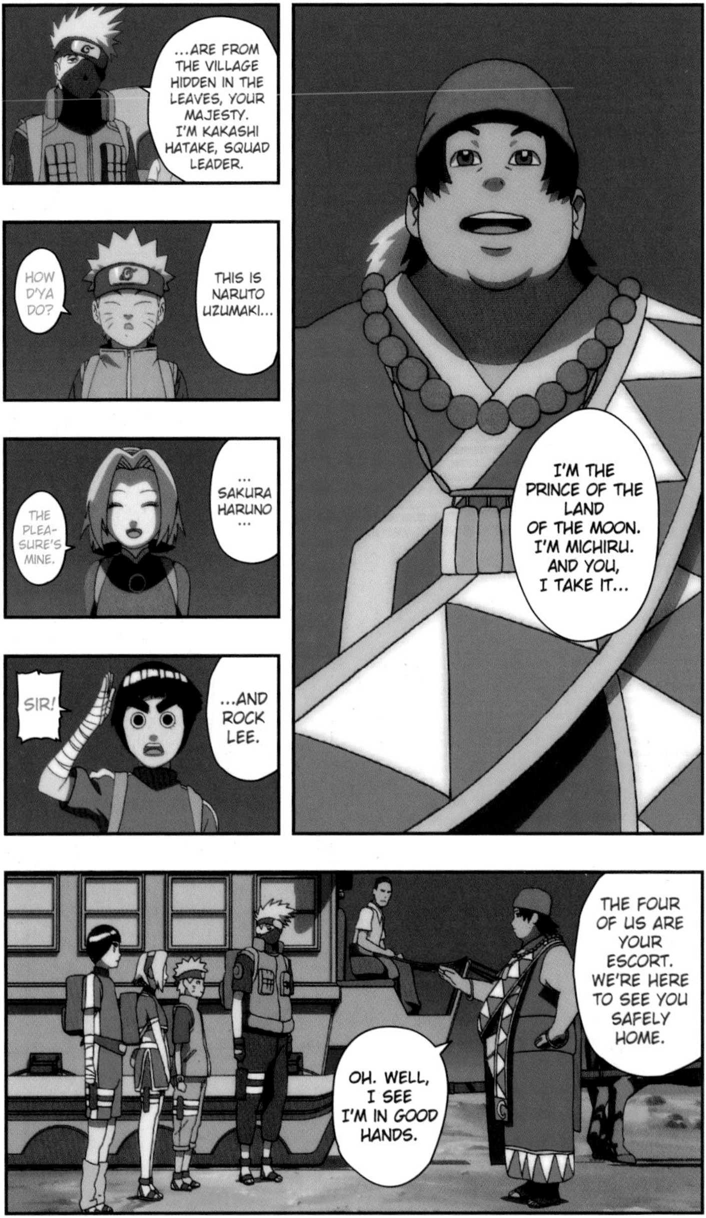
I'M THE PRINCE OF THE LAND OF THE MOON. I'M MICHIRU. AND YOU, I TAKE IT...
...ARE FROM THE VILLAGE HIDDEN IN THE LEAVES, YOUR MAJESTY. I'M KAKASHI HATAKE, SQUAD LEADER.
THIS IS NARUTO UZUMAKI...
HOW D'YA DO?
...SAKURA HARUNO...
THE PLEA-SURE'S MINE.
...AND ROCK LEE.
SIR!
THE FOUR OF US ARE YOUR ESCORT. WE'RE HERE TO SEE YOU SAFELY HOME.
OH. WELL, I SEE I'M IN GOOD HANDS.

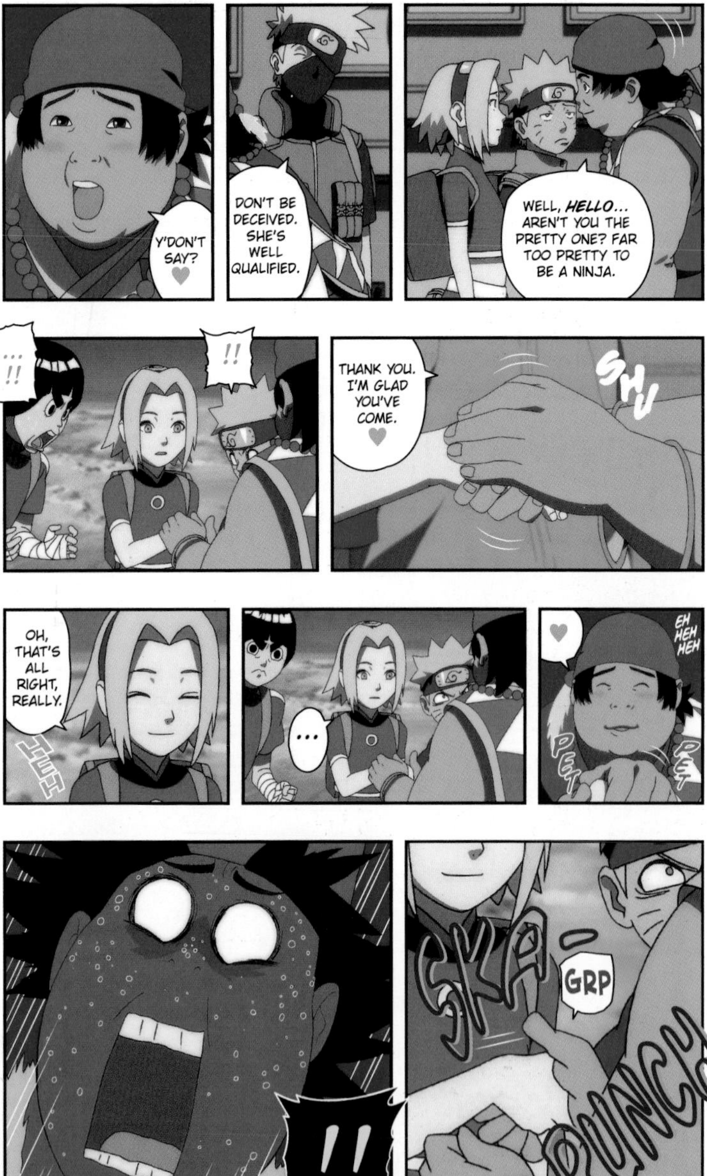
WELL, *HELLO*... AREN'T YOU THE PRETTY ONE? FAR TOO PRETTY TO BE A NINJA.
DON'T BE DECEIVED. SHE'S WELL QUALIFIED.
Y'DON'T SAY? ♥
SHU
THANK YOU. I'M GLAD YOU'VE COME. ♥
!!
...!!
EH HEH HEH
♥
PET PET
...
OH, THAT'S ALL RIGHT, REALLY.
HEH
SKA-RUNCH
GRP
!!

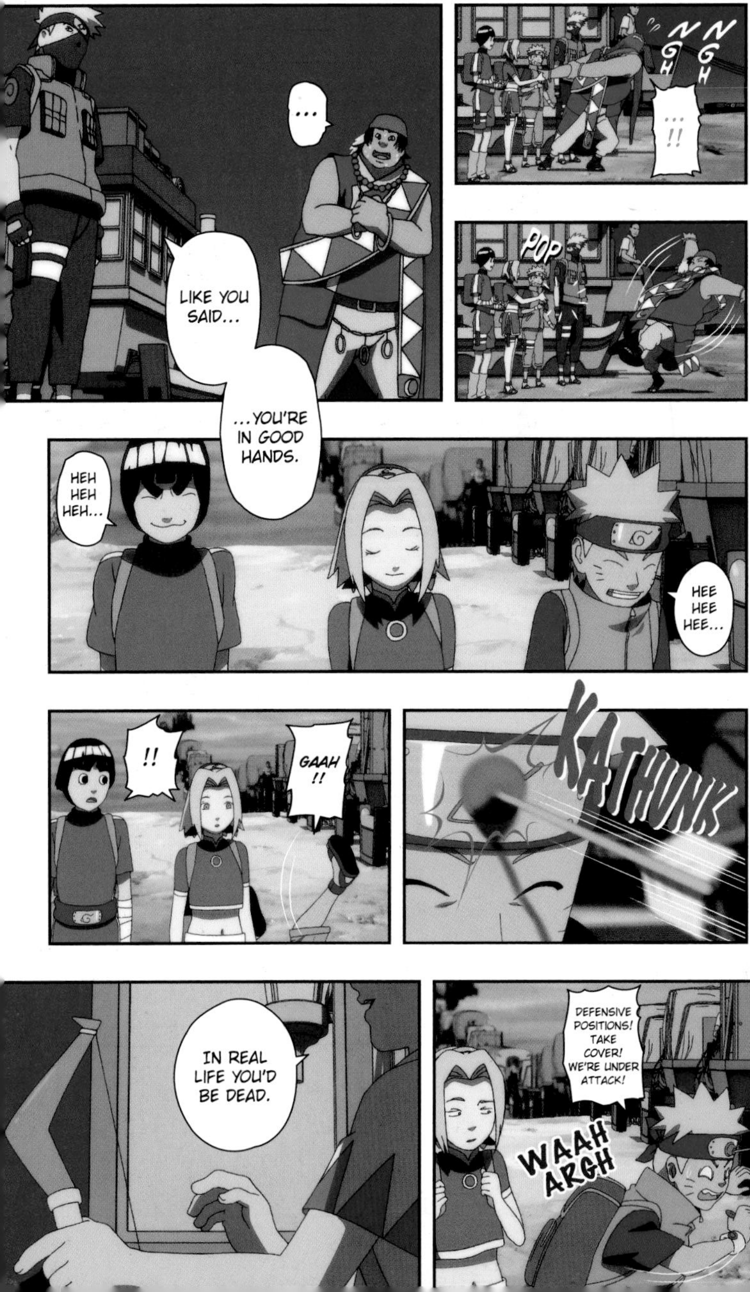
NNGH NNGH
...!!
POP
...
LIKE YOU SAID...
...YOU'RE IN GOOD HANDS.
HEE HEE HEE...
HEH HEH HEH...
KA THUNK
GAAH!!
!!
DEFENSIVE POSITIONS! TAKE COVER! WE'RE UNDER ATTACK!
WAAH ARGH
IN REAL LIFE YOU'D BE DEAD.

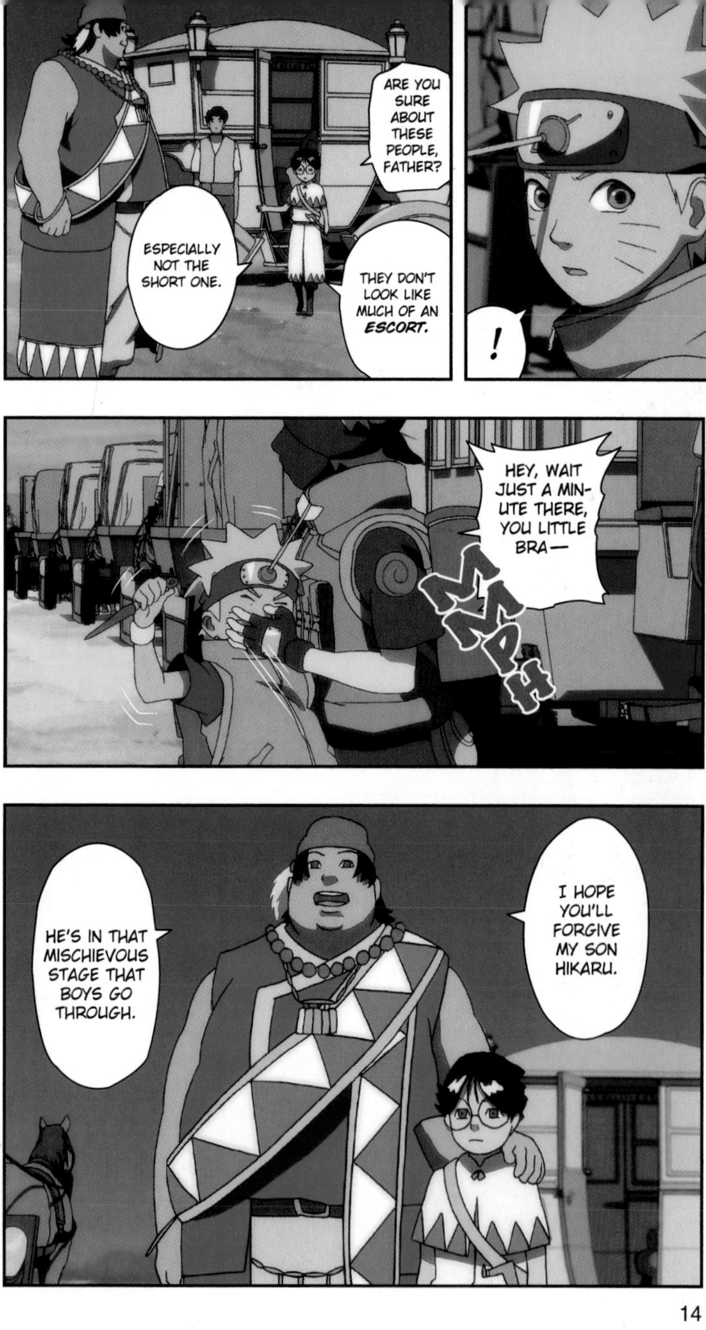
!
ARE YOU SURE ABOUT THESE PEOPLE, FATHER?
THEY DON'T LOOK LIKE MUCH OF AN ESCORT.
ESPECIALLY NOT THE SHORT ONE.
HEY, WAIT JUST A MIN-UTE THERE, YOU LITTLE BRA—
MMMPH
I HOPE YOU'LL FORGIVE MY SON HIKARU.
HE'S IN THAT MISCHIEVOUS STAGE THAT BOYS GO THROUGH.

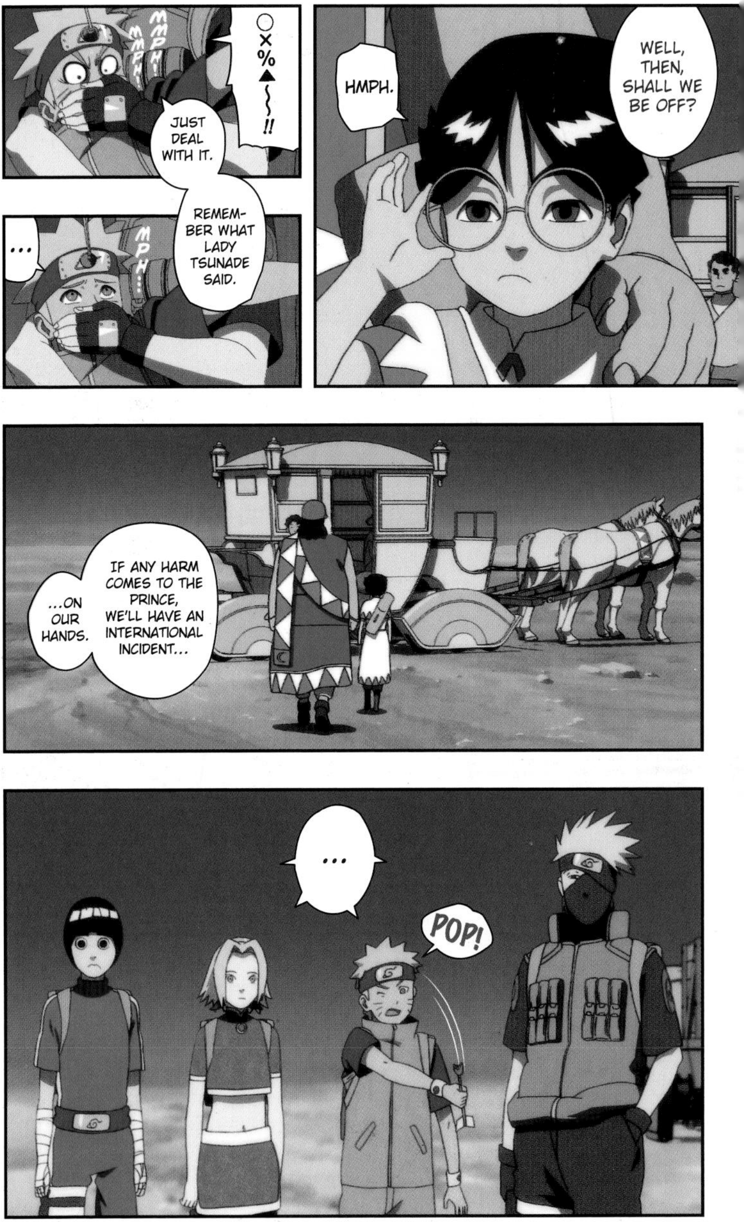
WELL, THEN, SHALL WE BE OFF?
HMPH.
○×%▲~~!!
MMPH! MMPH!
JUST DEAL WITH IT.
REMEM-BER WHAT LADY TSUNADE SAID.
MPH...
...
IF ANY HARM COMES TO THE PRINCE, WE'LL HAVE AN INTERNATIONAL INCIDENT...
...ON OUR HANDS.
...
POP!

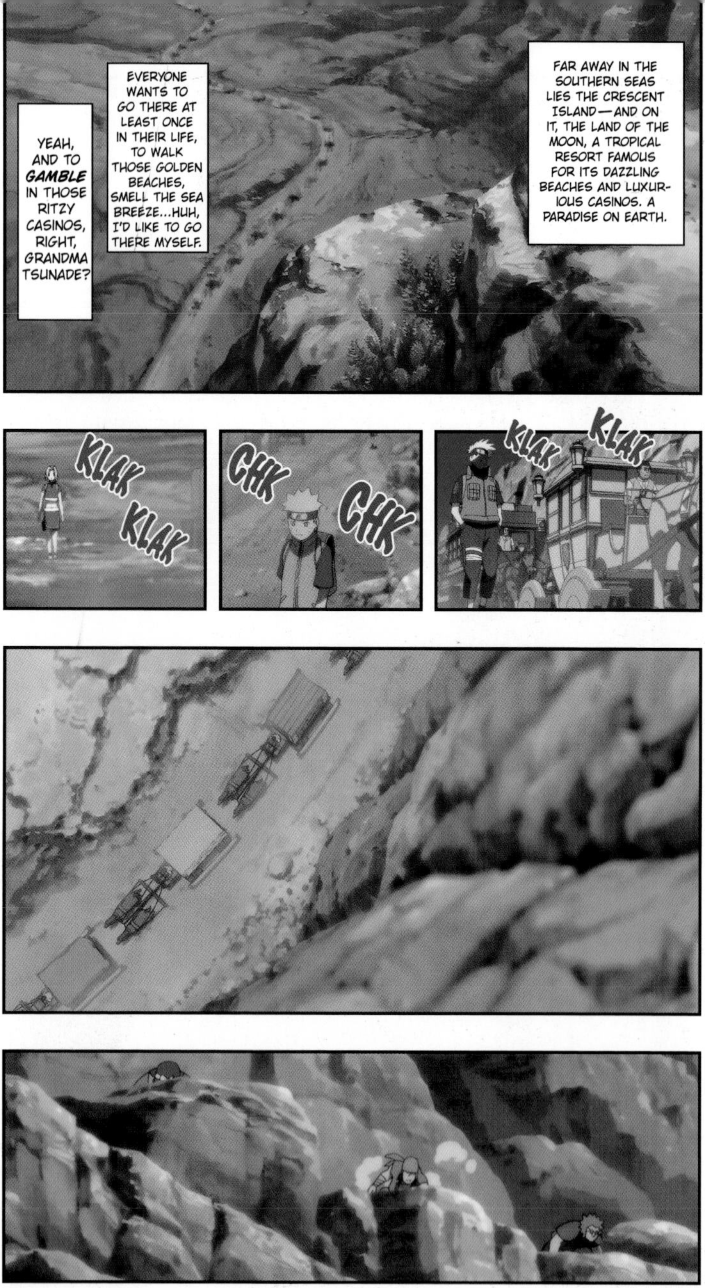
FAR AWAY IN THE SOUTHERN SEAS LIES THE CRESCENT ISLAND—AND ON IT, THE LAND OF THE MOON, A TROPICAL RESORT FAMOUS FOR ITS DAZZLING BEACHES AND LUXURIOUS CASINOS. A PARADISE ON EARTH.
EVERYONE WANTS TO GO THERE AT LEAST ONCE IN THEIR LIFE, TO WALK THOSE GOLDEN BEACHES, SMELL THE SEA BREEZE...HUH, I'D LIKE TO GO THERE MYSELF.
YEAH, AND TO *GAMBLE* IN THOSE RITZY CASINOS, RIGHT, GRANDMA TSUNADE?
KLAK
KLAK
CHK
CHK
KLAK
KLAK

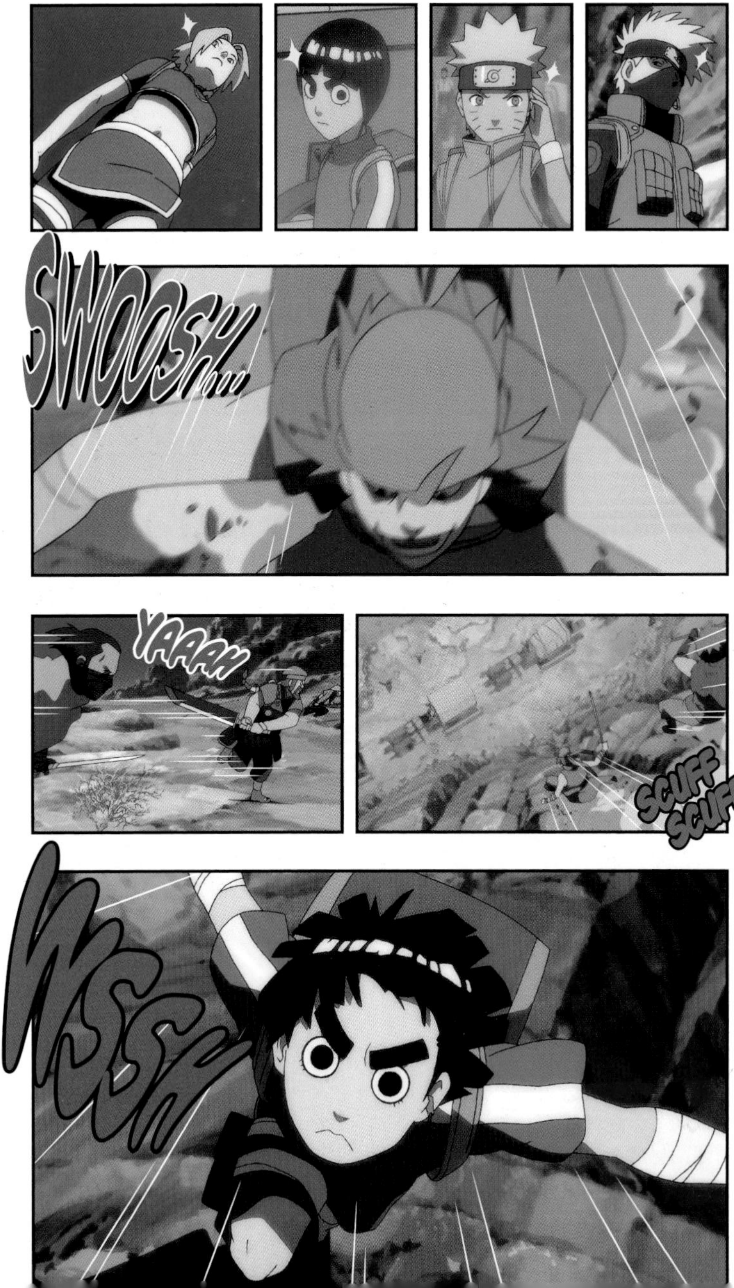
SWOOSH...
SCUFF SCUFF
YAAAH
WSSH

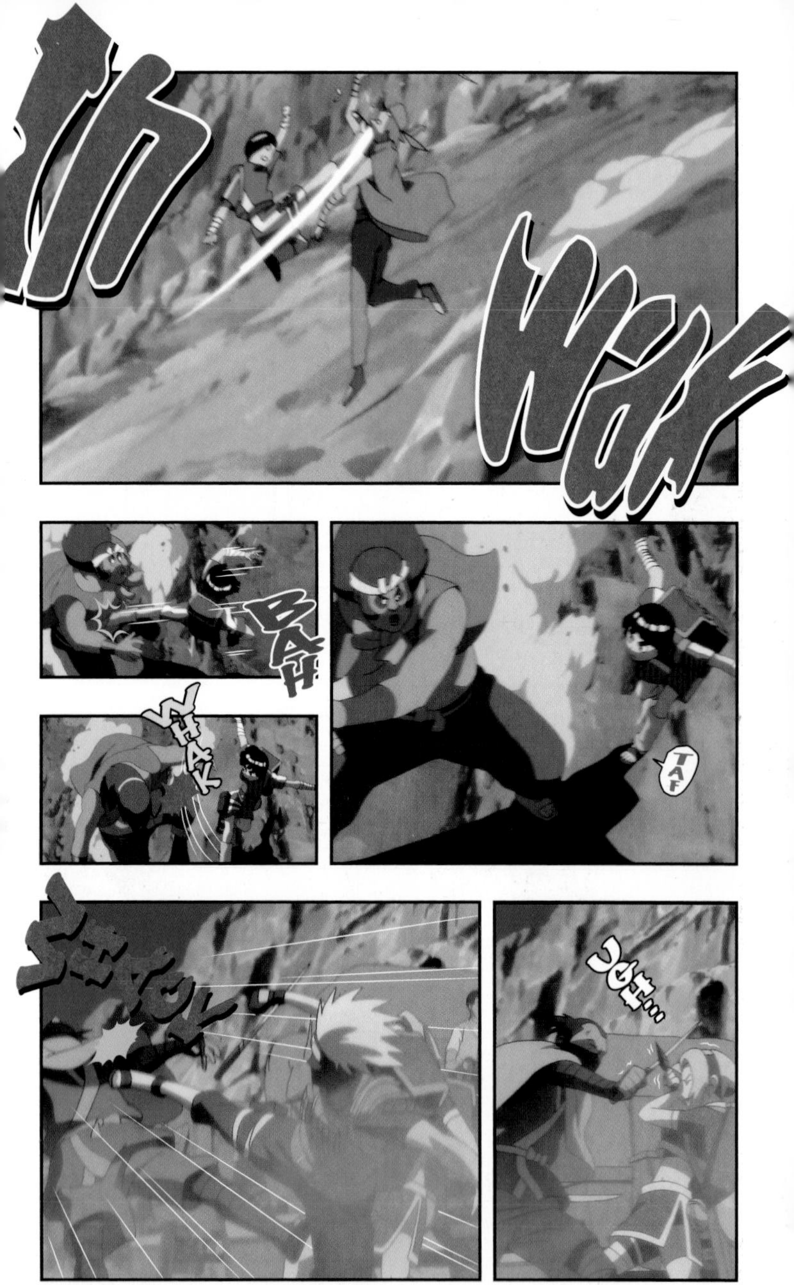
TAF
BAH!
WHAK

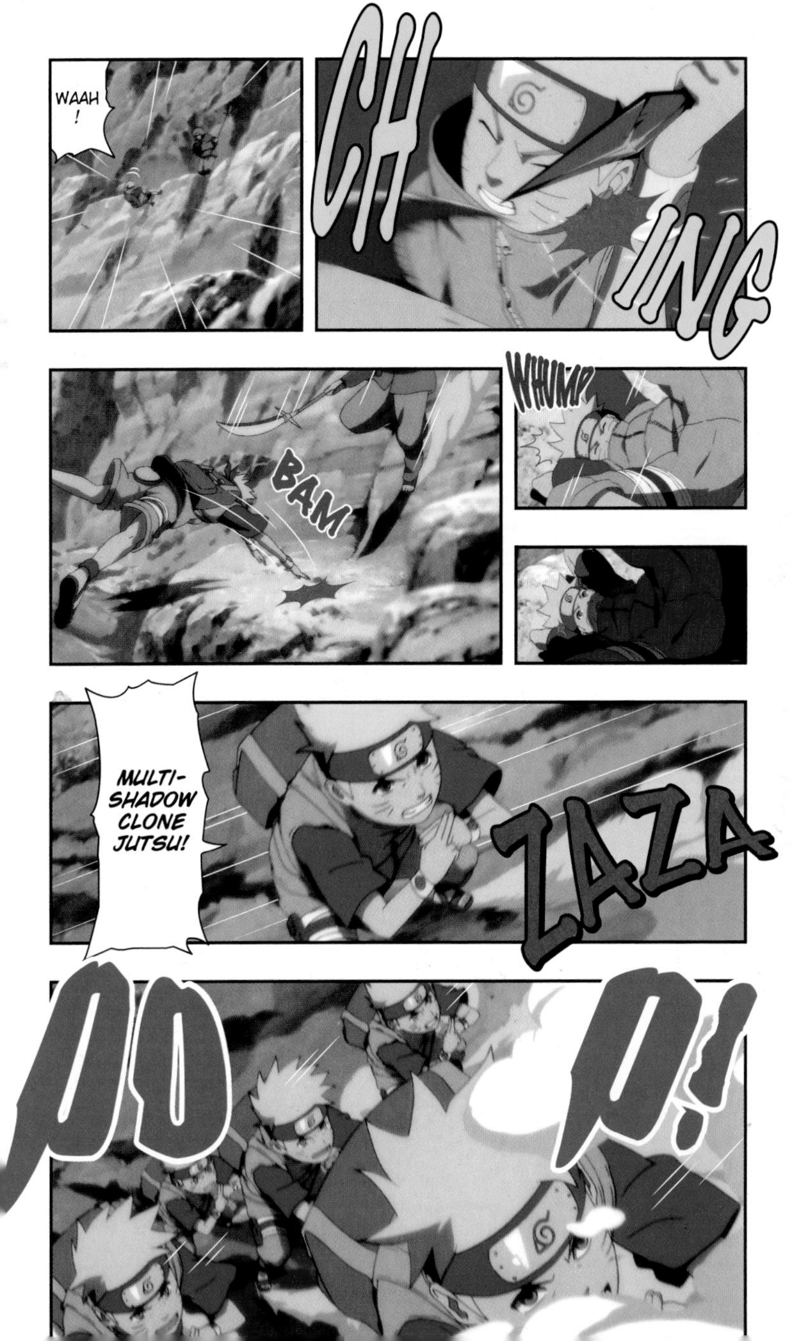
CHING
WAAH!
WHUMP
BAM
MULTI-SHADOW CLONE JUTSU!
ZAZA
PO
P!

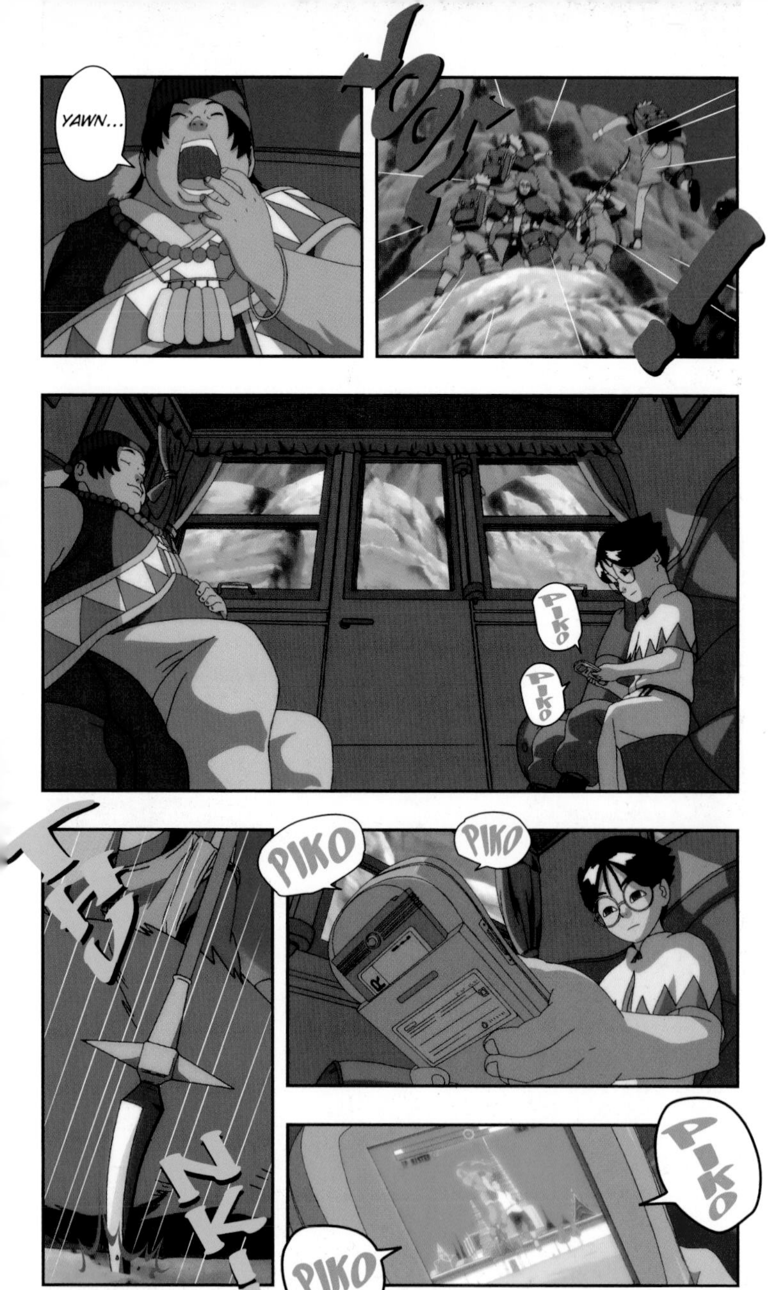
JOLT!
YAWN...
PIKO
PIKO
PIKO
PIKO
PIKO
PIKO
TEENK!

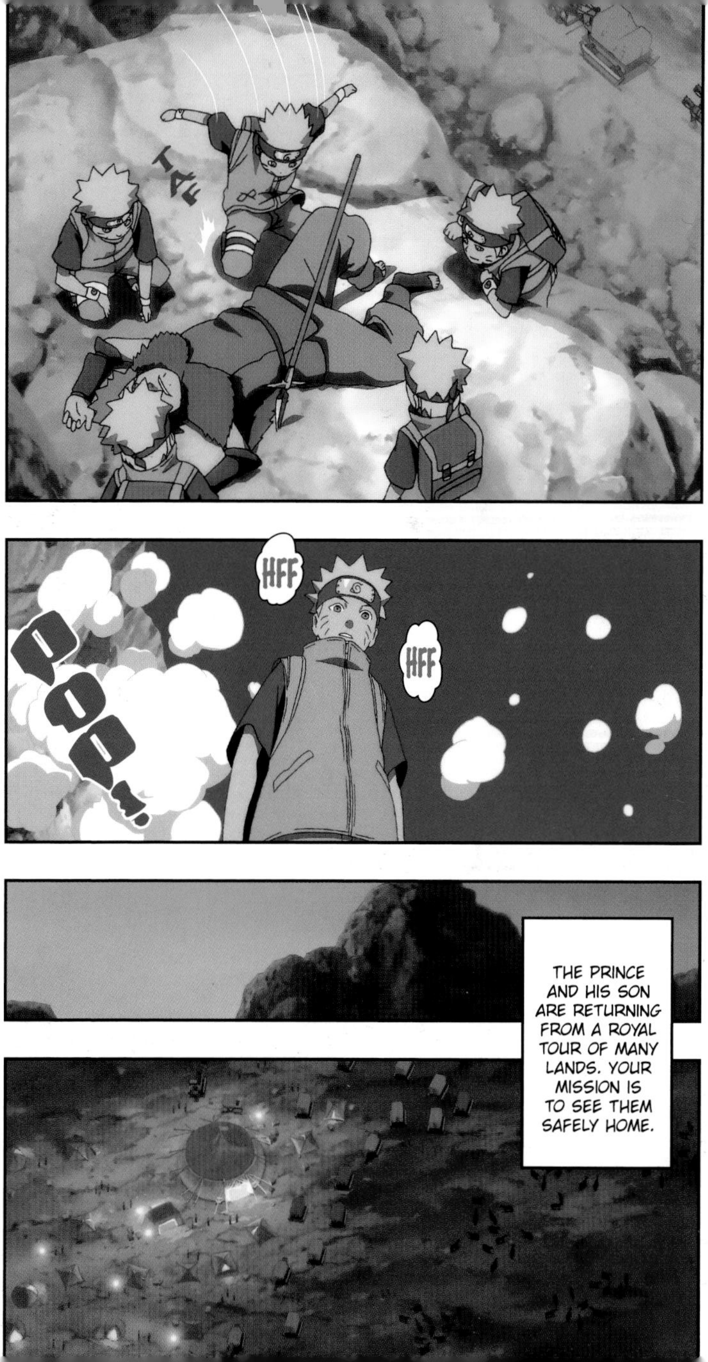
TAF
HFF
HFF
POOF!
THE PRINCE AND HIS SON ARE RETURNING FROM A ROYAL TOUR OF MANY LANDS. YOUR MISSION IS TO SEE THEM SAFELY HOME.

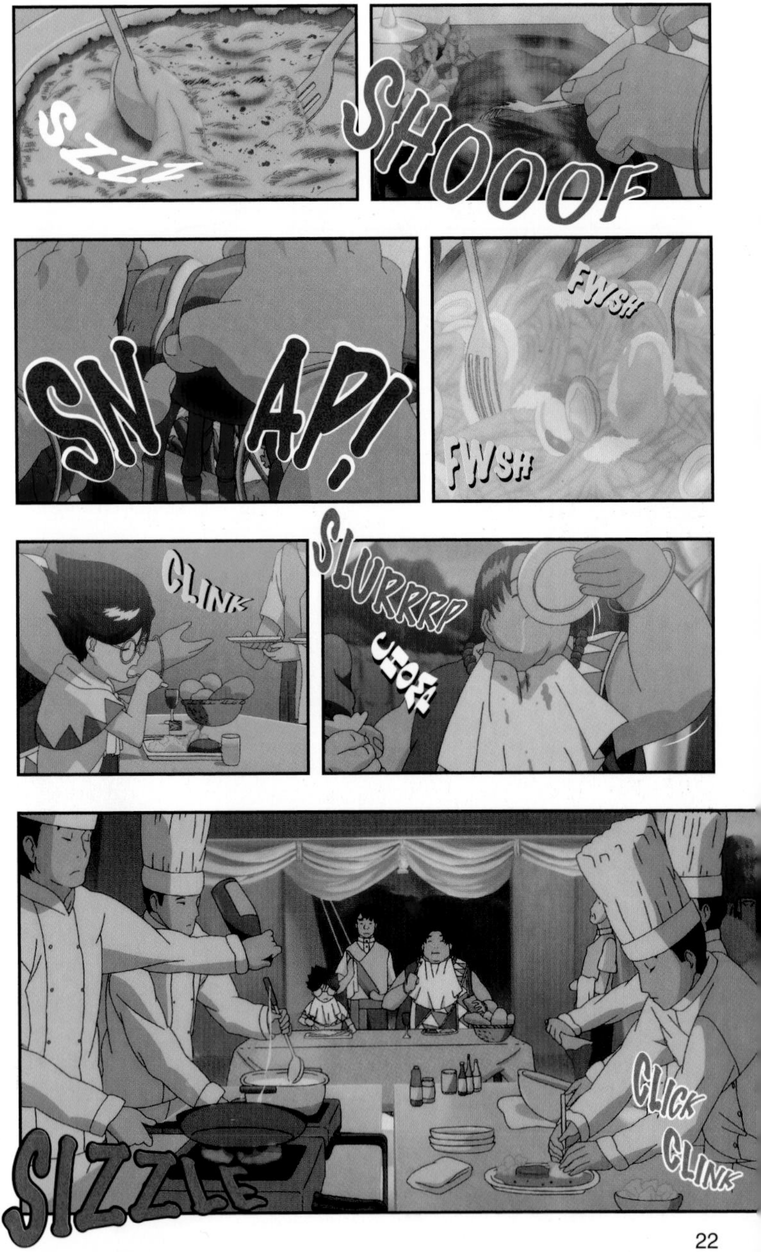
SHOOOF
SZZZ
FWSH
FWSH
SNAP!
SLURRRP
CLINK
CLICK
CLINK
SIZZLE

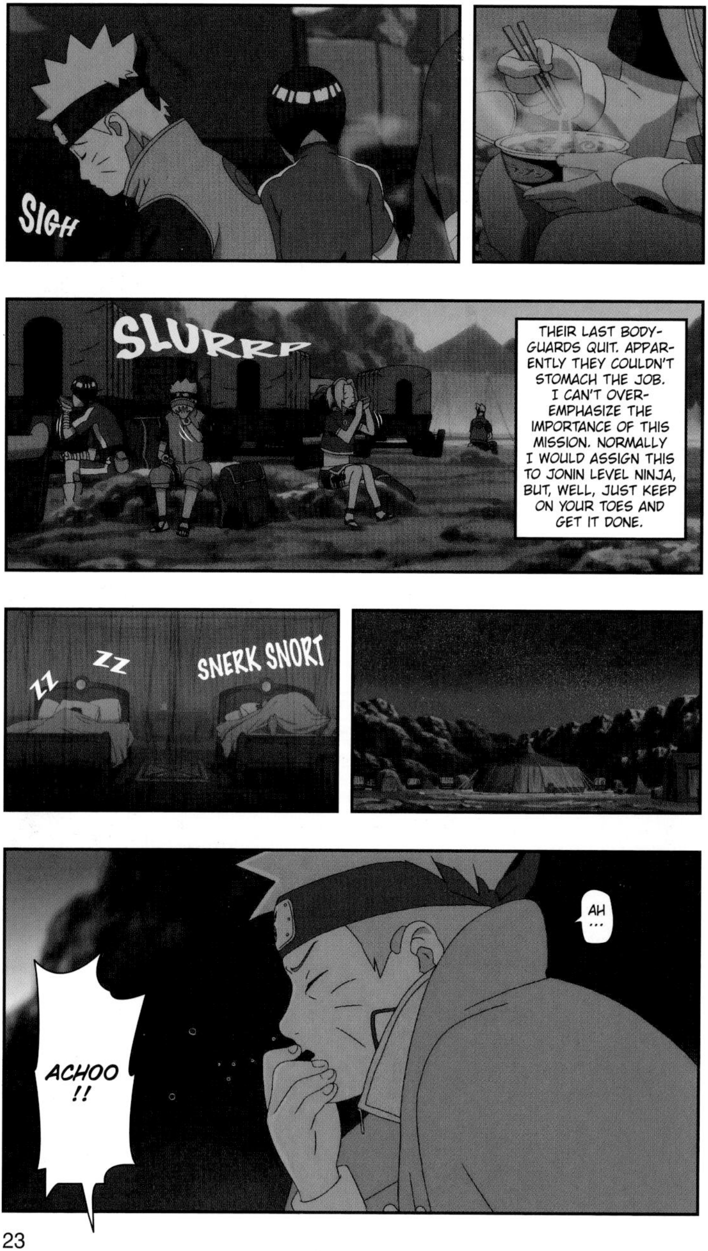
SIGH
THEIR LAST BODY-GUARDS QUIT. APPARENTLY THEY COULDN'T STOMACH THE JOB. I CAN'T OVER-EMPHASIZE THE IMPORTANCE OF THIS MISSION. NORMALLY I WOULD ASSIGN THIS TO JONIN LEVEL NINJA, BUT, WELL, JUST KEEP ON YOUR TOES AND GET IT DONE.
SLURRP
SNERK SNORT
ZZ
ZZ
AH...
ACHOO!!

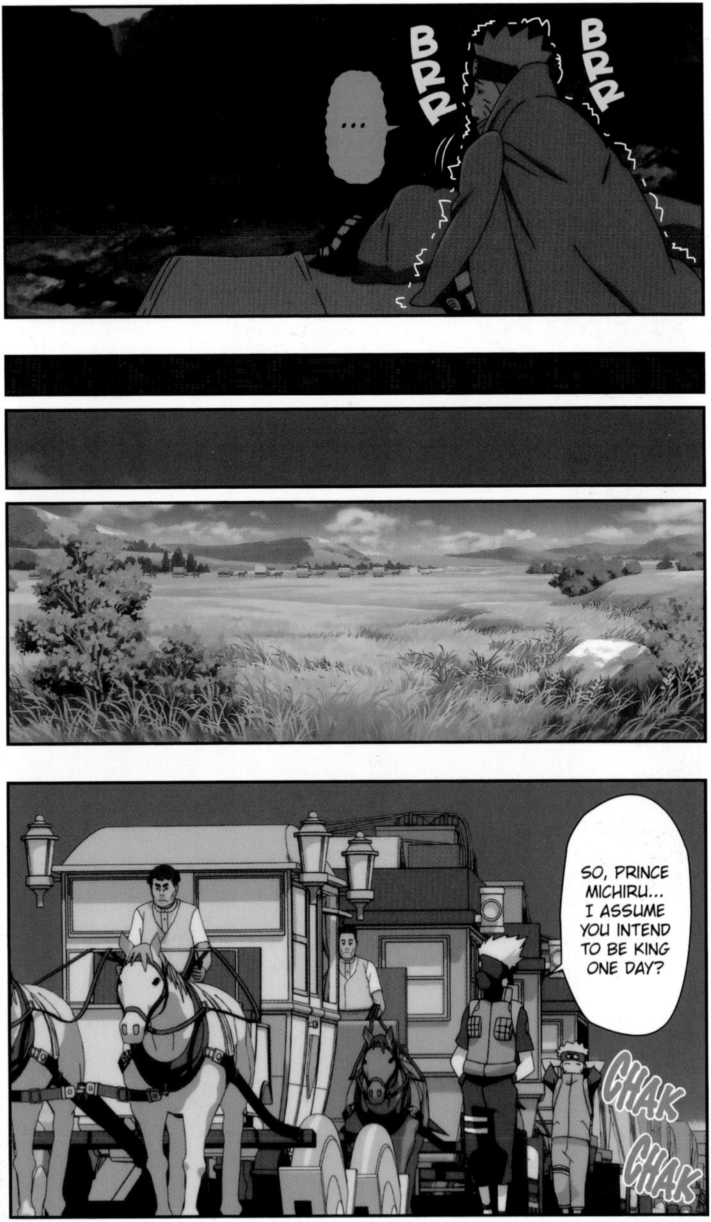
BRRR
BRRR
...
SO, PRINCE MICHIRU... I ASSUME YOU INTEND TO BE KING ONE DAY?
CHAK
CHAK

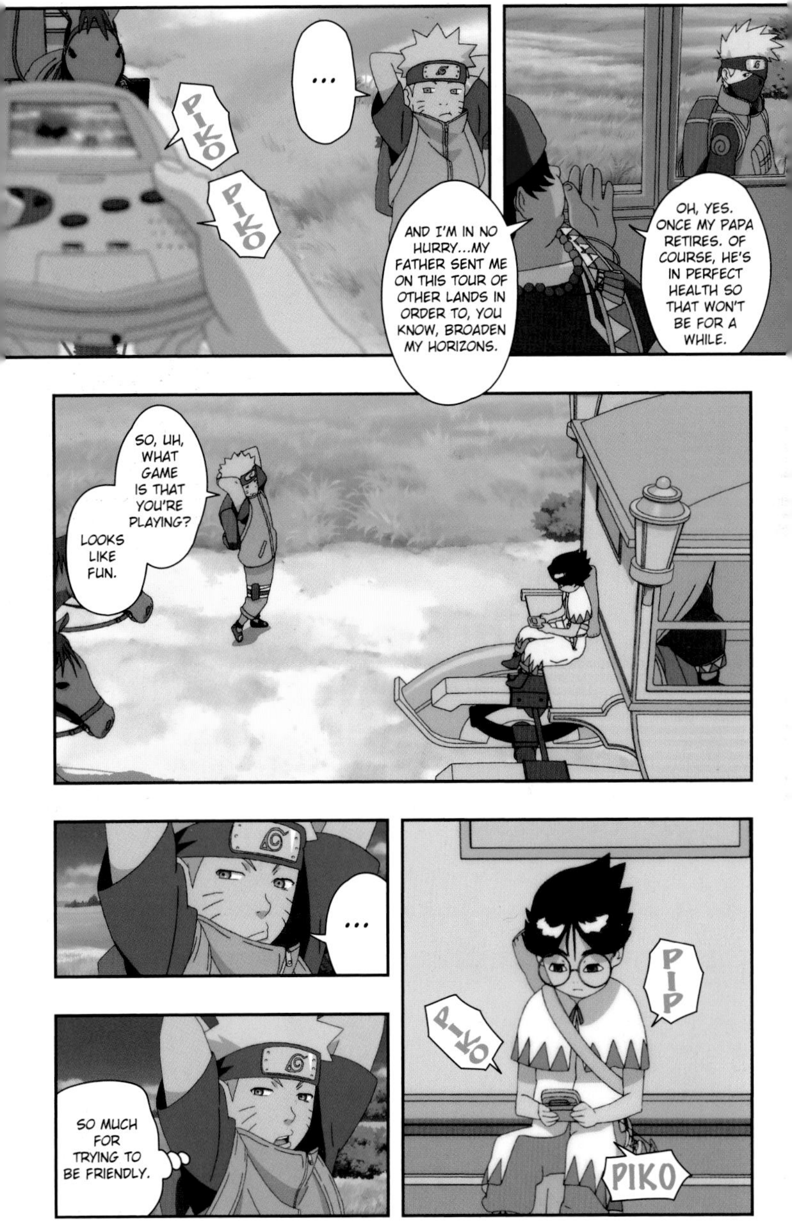
OH, YES. ONCE MY PAPA RETIRES. OF COURSE, HE'S IN PERFECT HEALTH SO THAT WON'T BE FOR A WHILE.
AND I'M IN NO HURRY...MY FATHER SENT ME ON THIS TOUR OF OTHER LANDS IN ORDER TO, YOU KNOW, BROADEN MY HORIZONS.
...
PIKO
PIKO
SO, UH, WHAT GAME IS THAT YOU'RE PLAYING?
LOOKS LIKE FUN.
PIP
PI-KO
PIKO
...
SO MUCH FOR TRYING TO BE FRIENDLY.

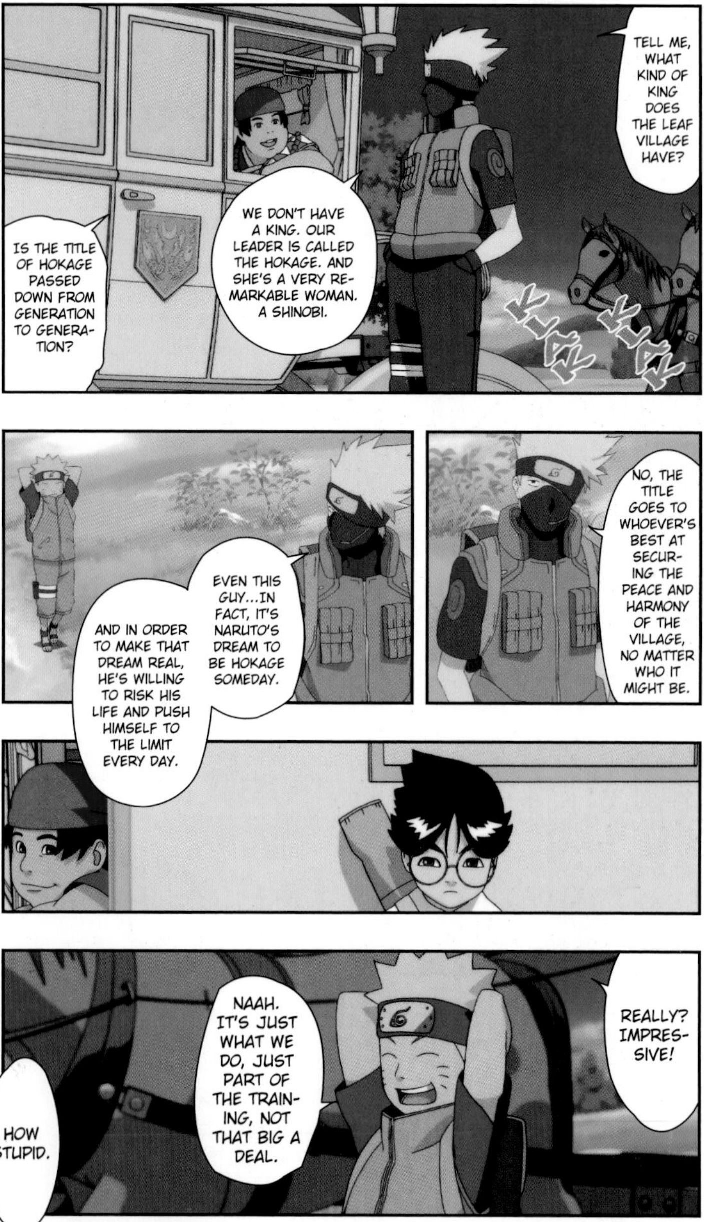
TELL ME, WHAT KIND OF KING DOES THE LEAF VILLAGE HAVE?
WE DON'T HAVE A KING. OUR LEADER IS CALLED THE HOKAGE. AND SHE'S A VERY RE-MARKABLE WOMAN. A SHINOBI.
IS THE TITLE OF HOKAGE PASSED DOWN FROM GENERATION TO GENERA-TION?
NO, THE TITLE GOES TO WHOEVER'S BEST AT SECUR-ING THE PEACE AND HARMONY OF THE VILLAGE, NO MATTER WHO IT MIGHT BE.
EVEN THIS GUY...IN FACT, IT'S NARUTO'S DREAM TO BE HOKAGE SOMEDAY.
AND IN ORDER TO MAKE THAT DREAM REAL, HE'S WILLING TO RISK HIS LIFE AND PUSH HIMSELF TO THE LIMIT EVERY DAY.
REALLY? IMPRES-SIVE!
NAAH. IT'S JUST WHAT WE DO, JUST PART OF THE TRAIN-ING, NOT THAT BIG A DEAL.
HOW STUPID.

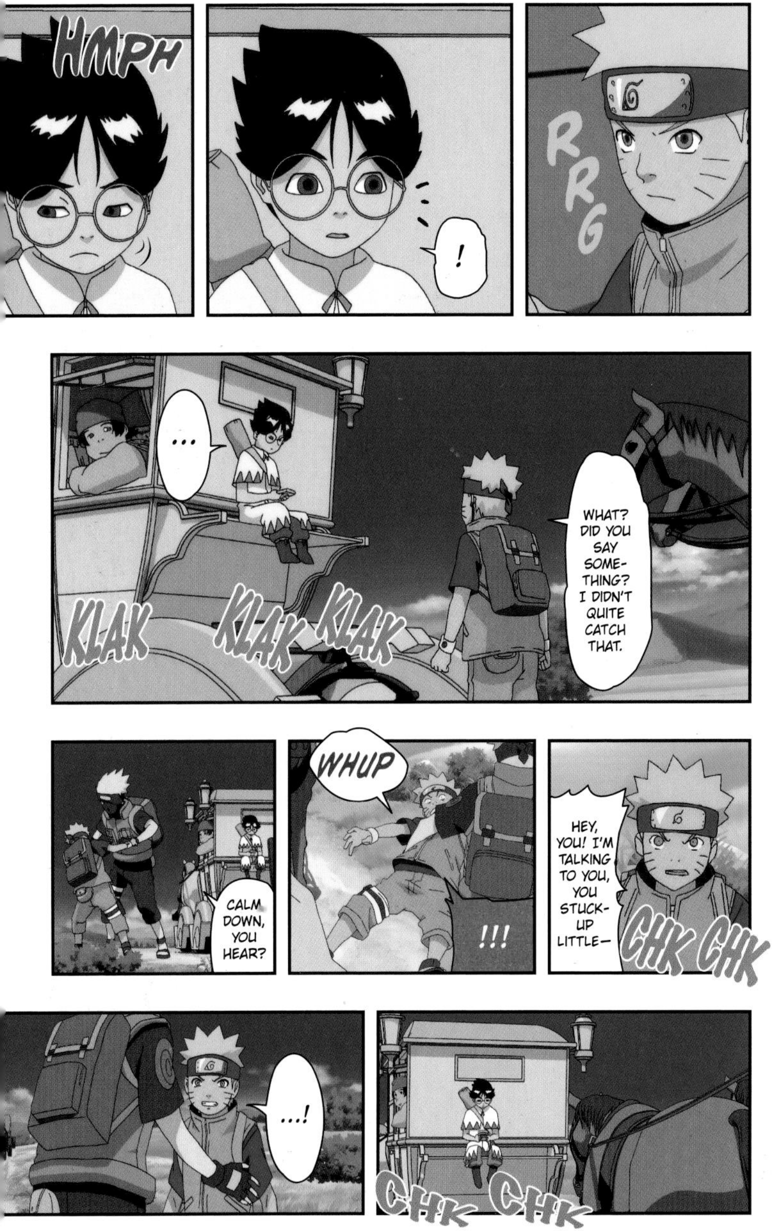
RRG
!
HMPH
WHAT? DID YOU SAY SOME-THING? I DIDN'T QUITE CATCH THAT.
...
KLAK
KLAK
KLAK
HEY, YOU! I'M TALKING TO YOU, YOU STUCK-UP LITTLE—
CHK CHK
WHUP
!!!
CALM DOWN, YOU HEAR?
CHK CHK
...!

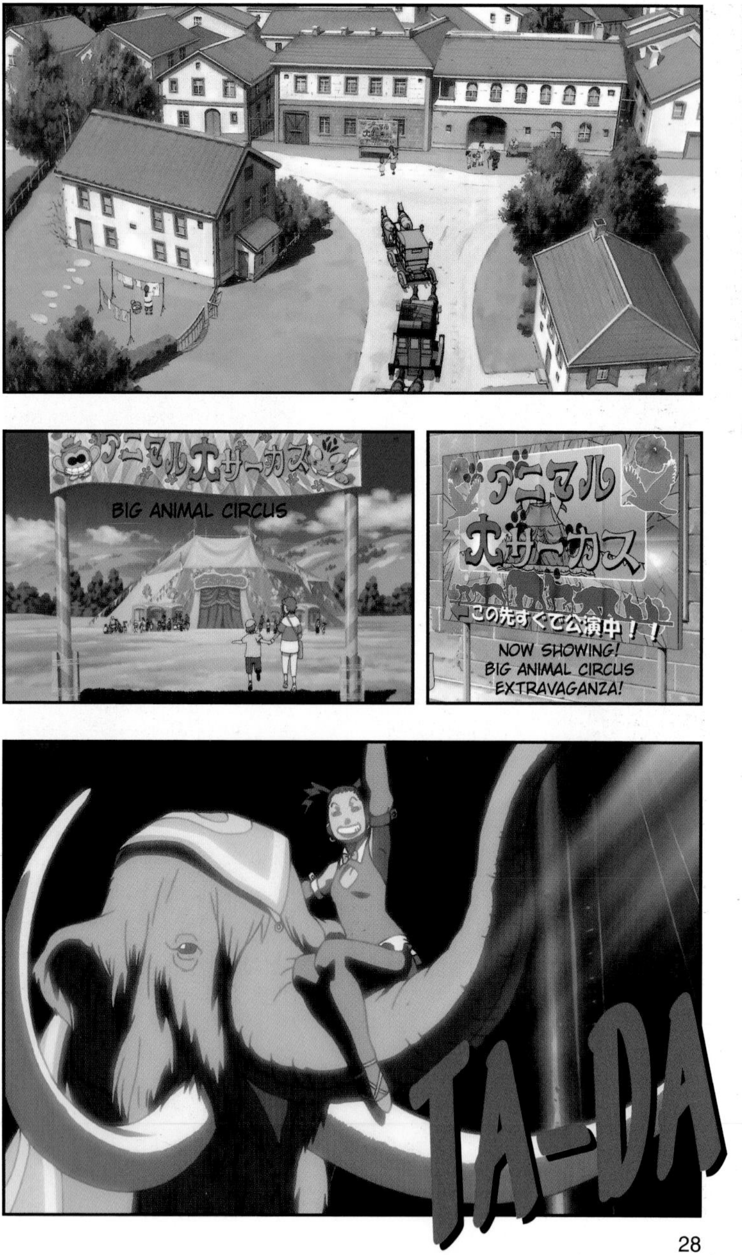
アニマル大サーカス
この先すぐで公演中！！
NOW SHOWING! BIG ANIMAL CIRCUS EXTRAVAGANZA!
アニマル大サーカス
BIG ANIMAL CIRCUS
TA-DA

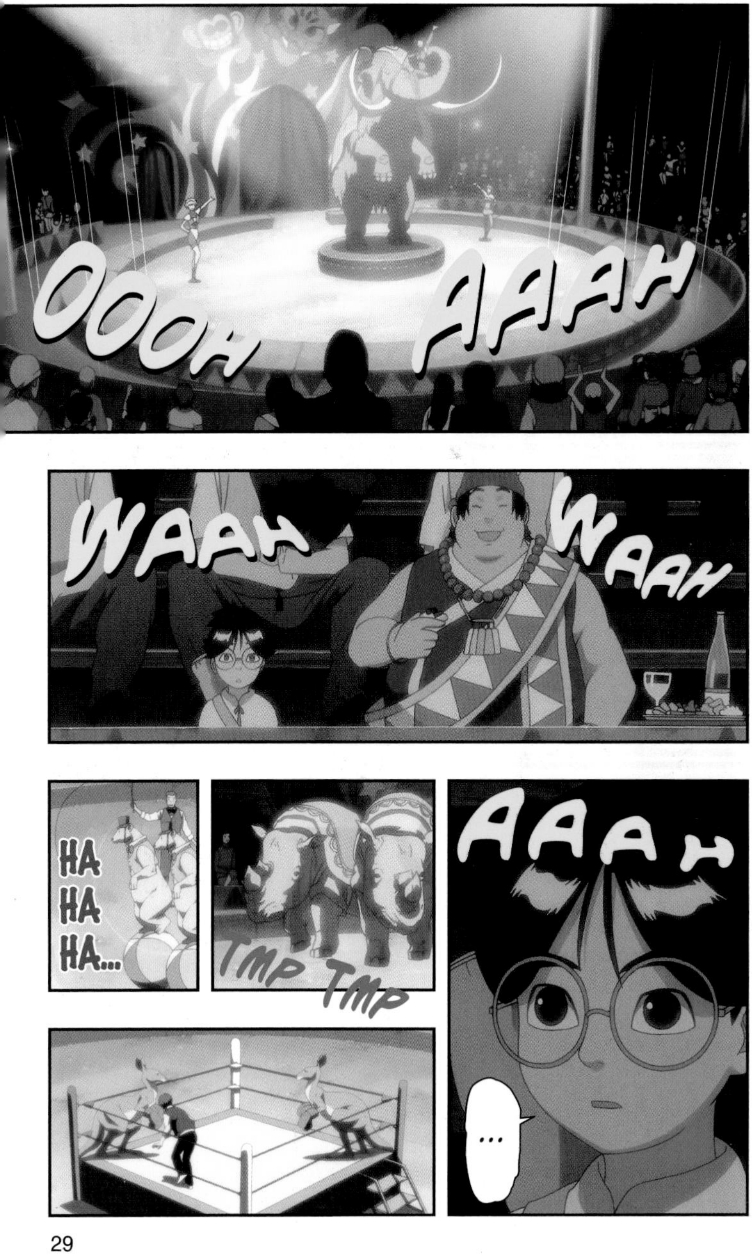
AAAH
OOOH
WAAH
WAAH
AAAH
...
TMP TMP
HA
HA
HA...

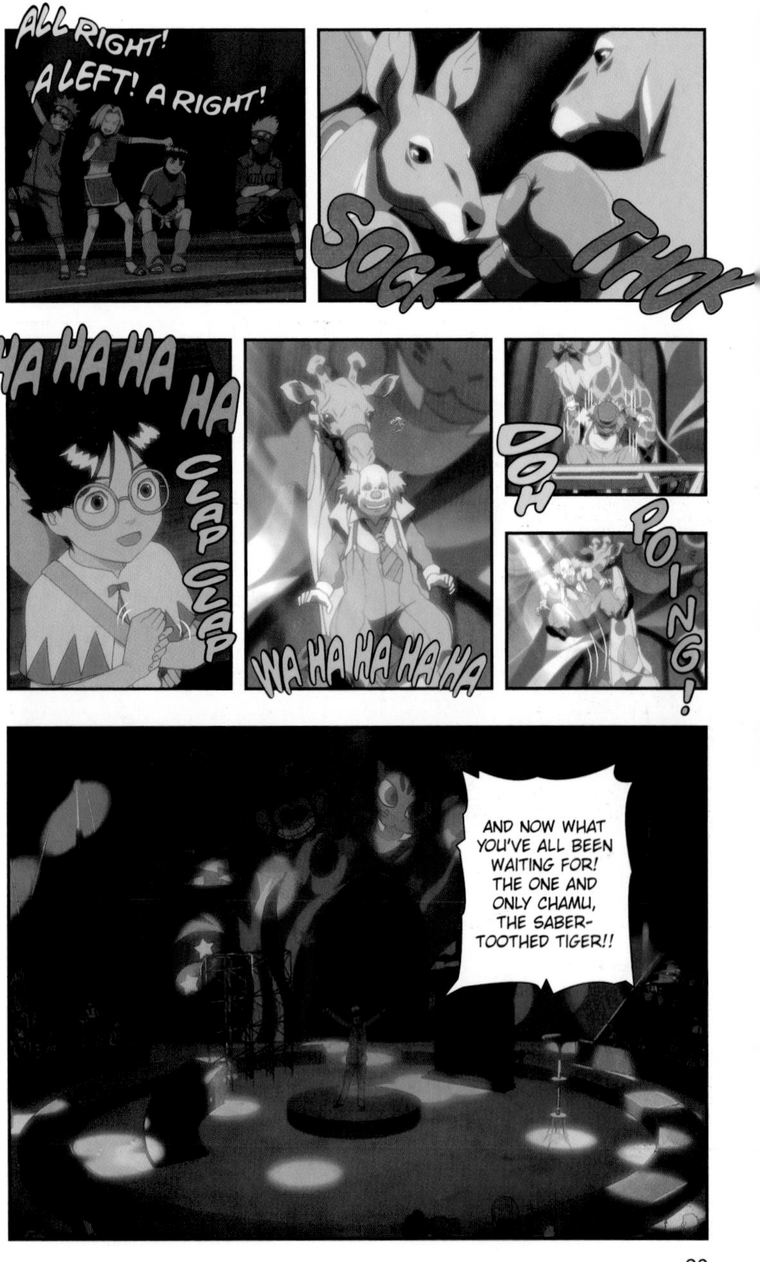
THOK
SOCK
ALL RIGHT!
A LEFT! A RIGHT!
DOOH
POING!
WA HA HA HA HA HA
HA HA HA HA HA
CLAP CLAP
AND NOW WHAT YOU'VE ALL BEEN WAITING FOR! THE ONE AND ONLY CHAMU, THE SABER-TOOTHED TIGER!!

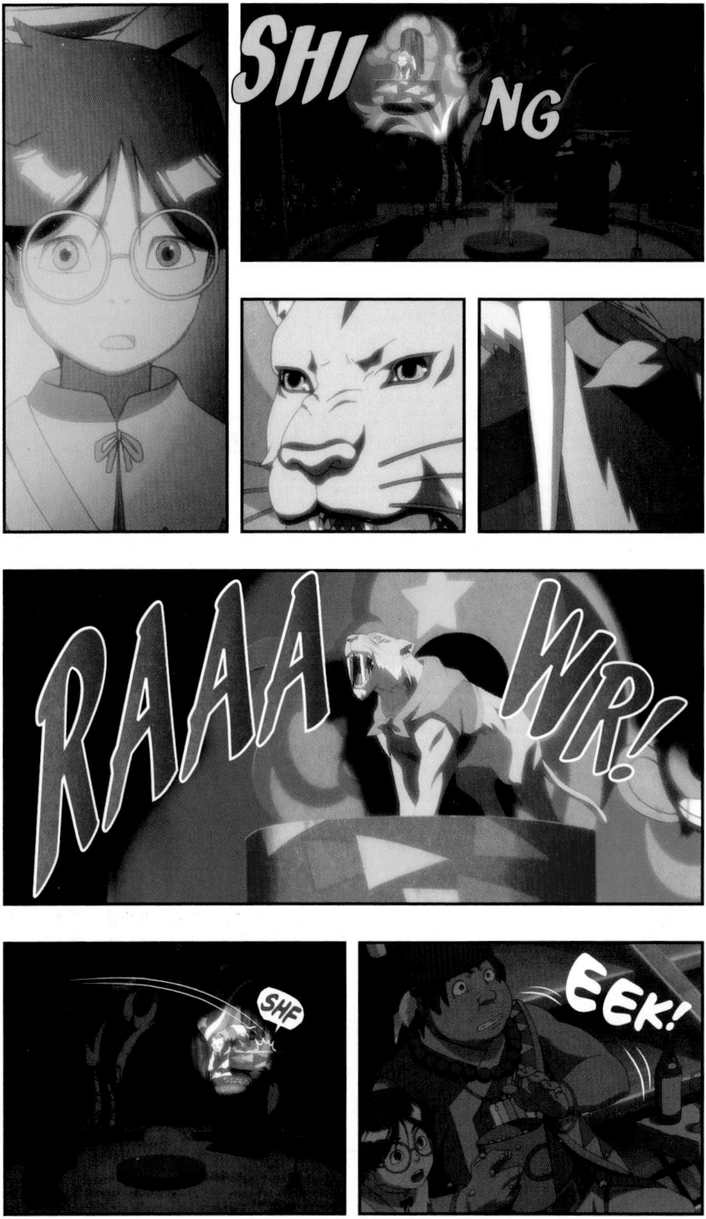
SHING
RAAAWR!
EEK!
SHF

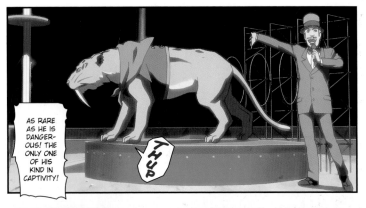

AS RARE AS HE IS DANGEROUS! THE ONLY ONE OF HIS KIND IN CAPTIVITY!

THUP

THP

KII

AND HERE'S CHAMU'S FRIEND AND PARTNER, KIKKI!

AND NOW, CHAMU AND KIKKI HAVE A VERY SPECIAL TREAT FOR YOU!

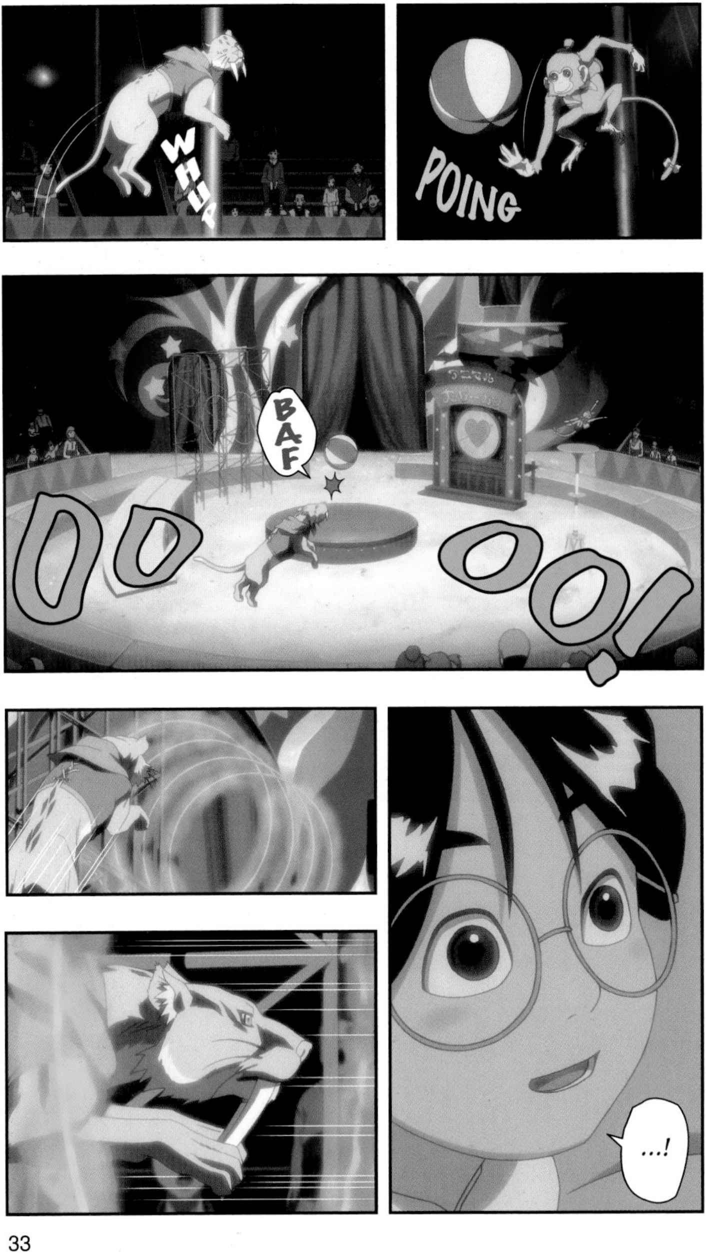
POING
WHUP
BAF
OOOOO!
...!

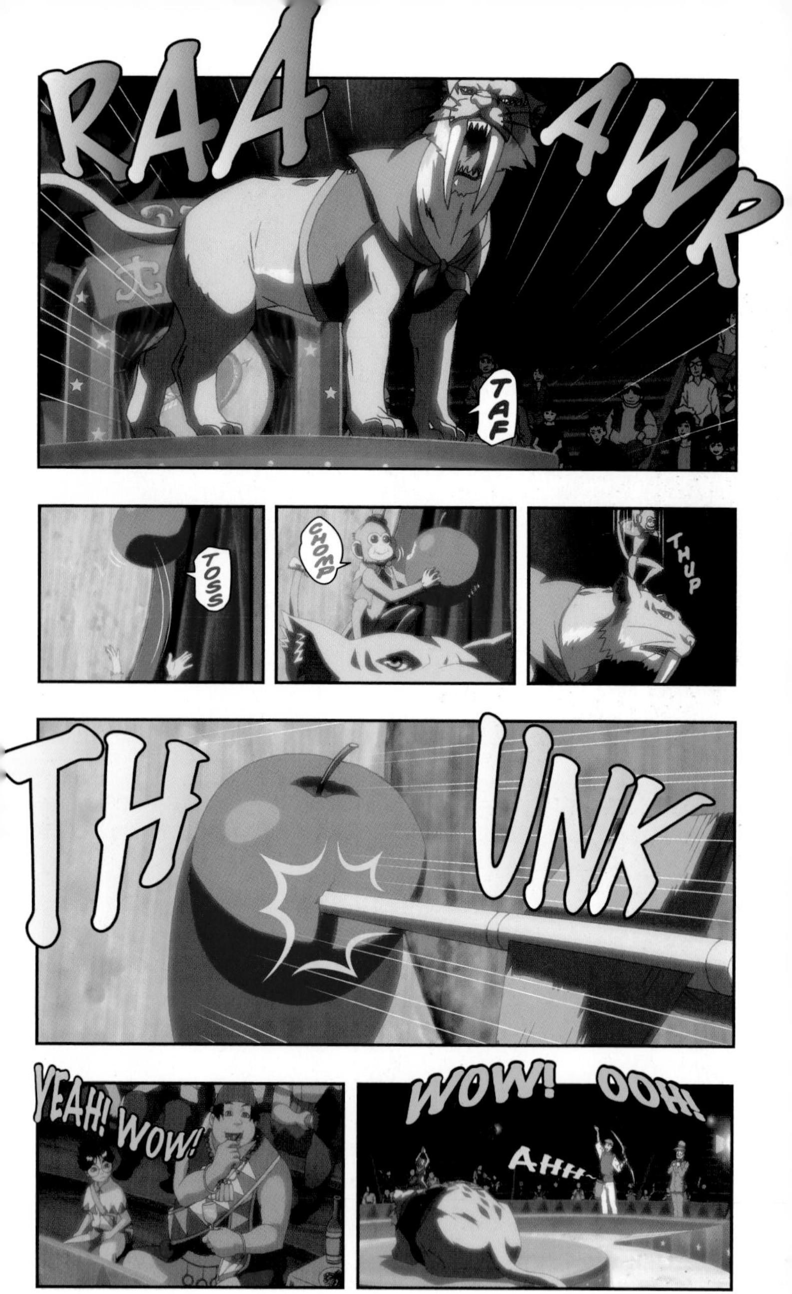
RAAAWR
TAF
THUP
CHOMP
TOSS
THUNK
WOW! OOH!
AHH~
YEAH! WOW!

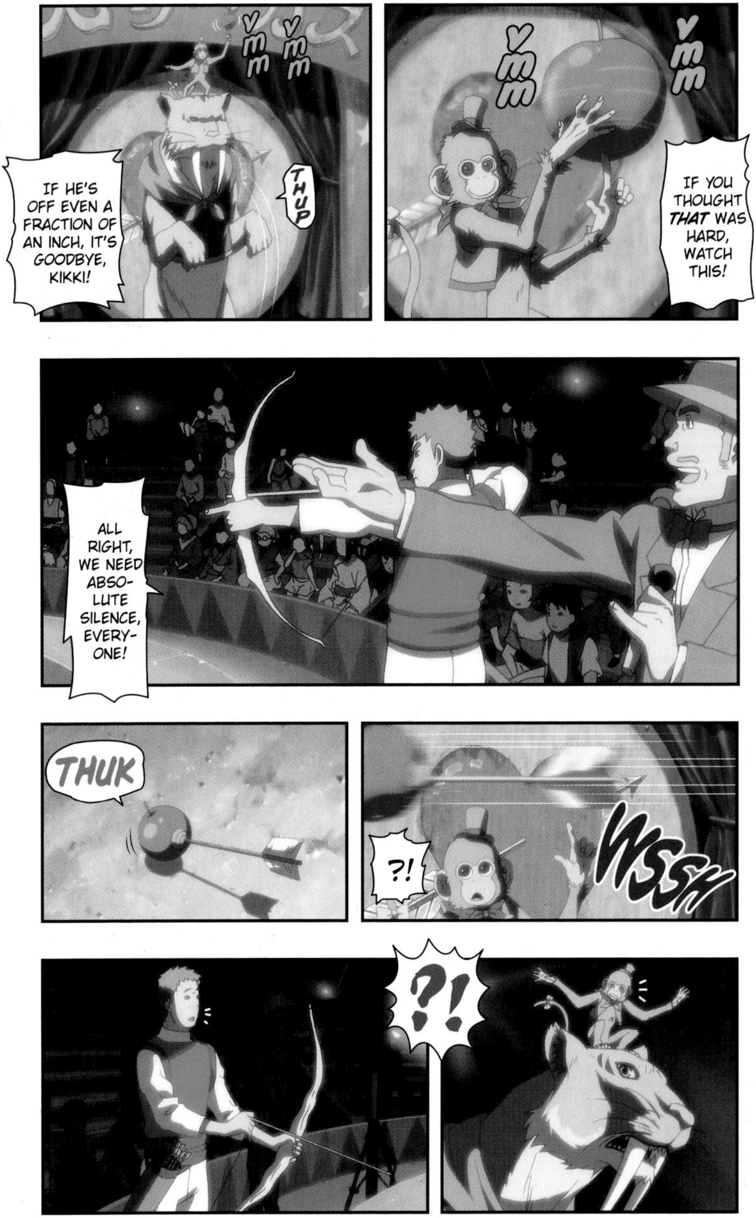

VMM
VMM
IF YOU THOUGHT *THAT* WAS HARD, WATCH THIS!
VMM
VMM
IF HE'S OFF EVEN A FRACTION OF AN INCH, IT'S GOODBYE, KIKKI!
THUP
ALL RIGHT, WE NEED ABSO-LUTE SILENCE, EVERY-ONE!
?!
WSSH
THUK
?!

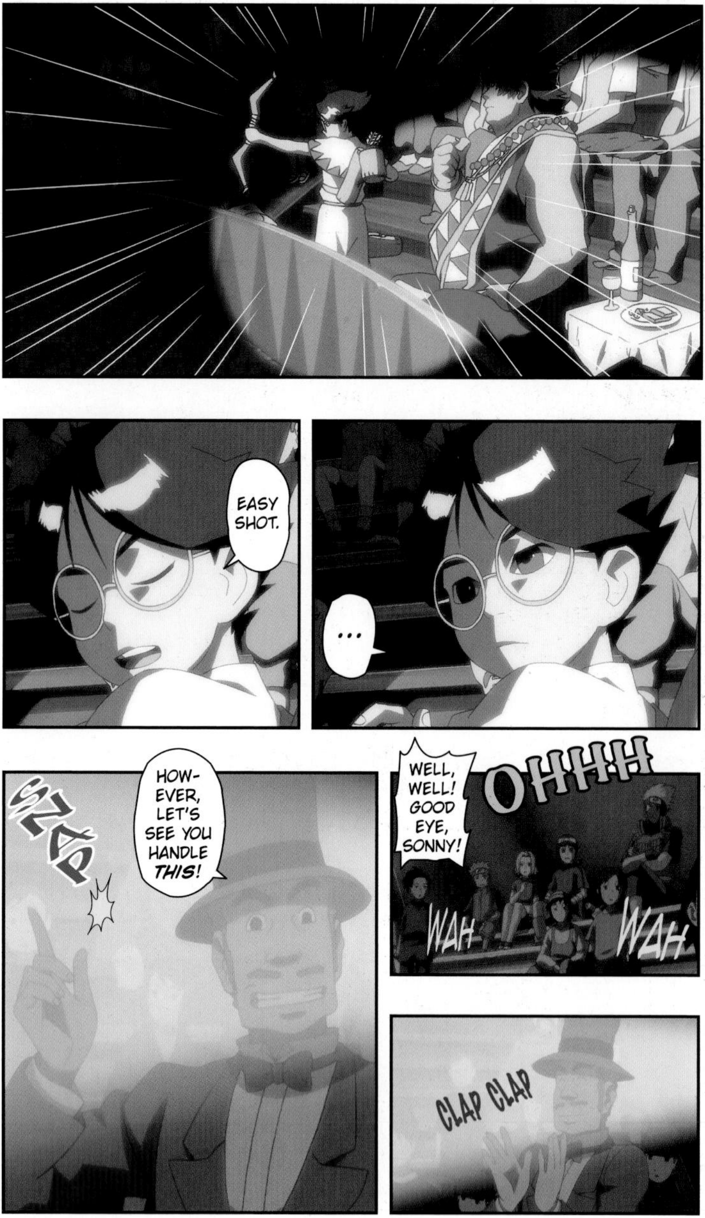
...
EASY SHOT.
WELL, WELL! GOOD EYE, SONNY!
OHHH
WAH
WAH
CLAP CLAP
HOW-EVER, LET'S SEE YOU HANDLE *THIS*!
SZAP

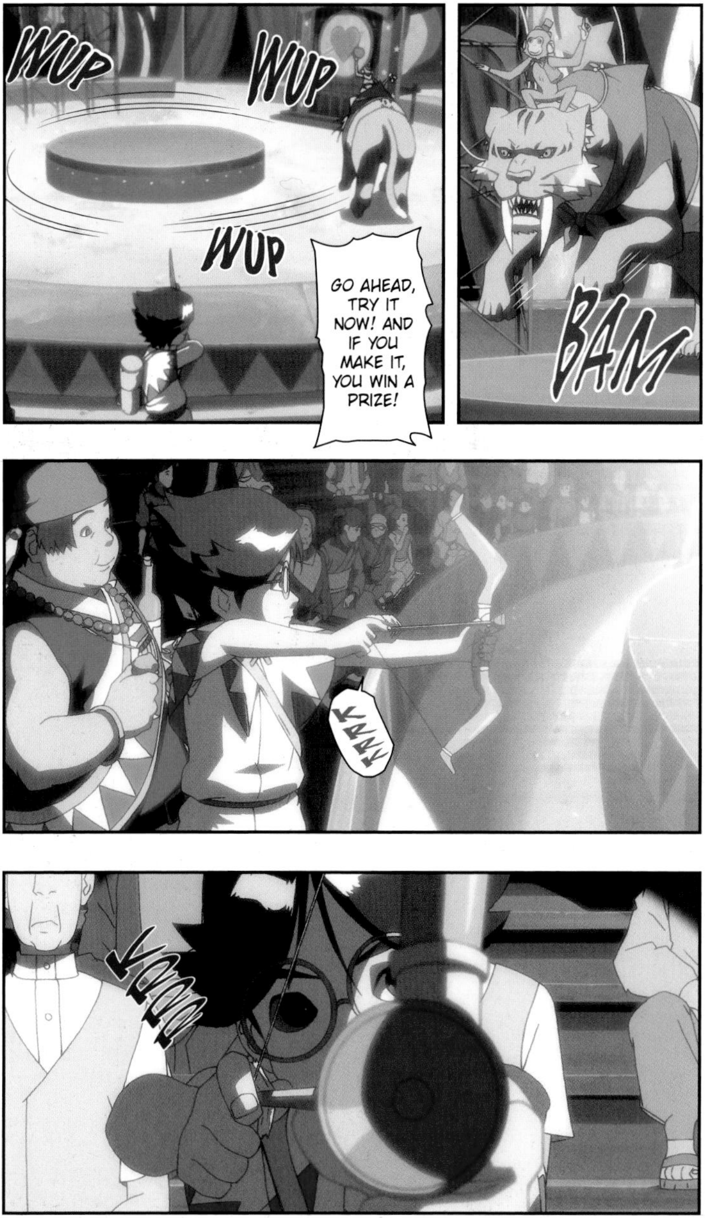
BAM
WUP
WUP
WUP
GO AHEAD, TRY IT NOW! AND IF YOU MAKE IT, YOU WIN A PRIZE!
KRRK

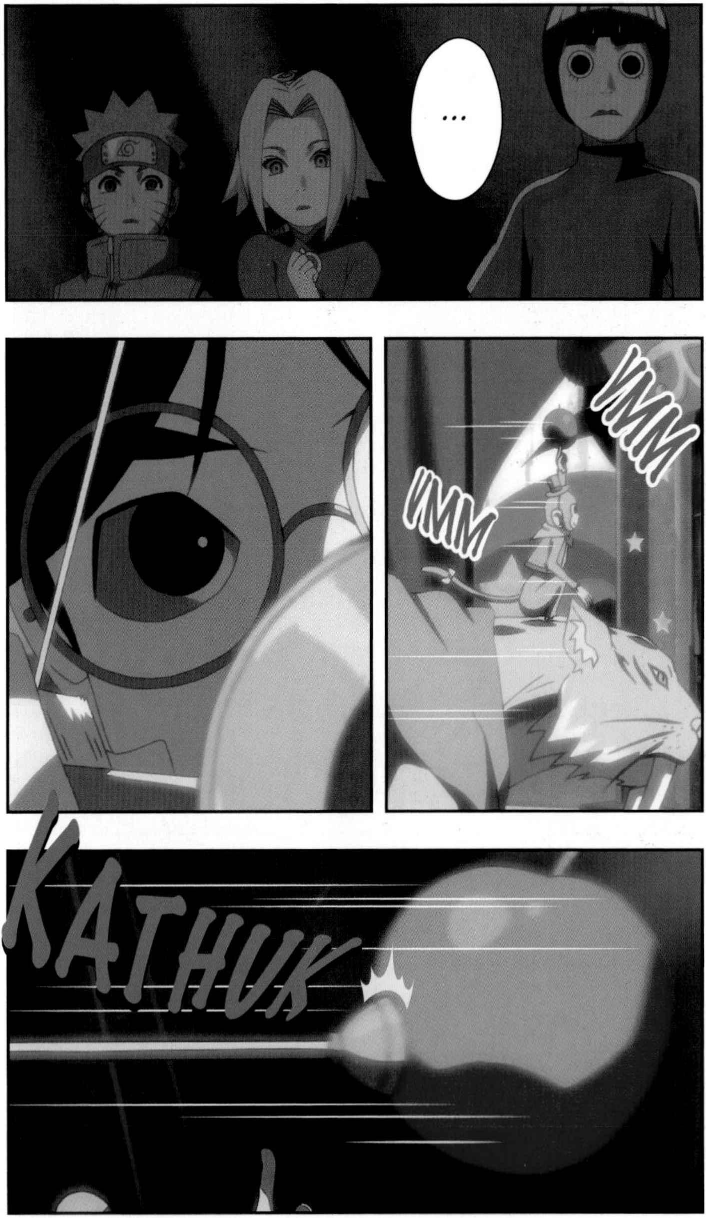
...
VMM
VMM
KATHUK

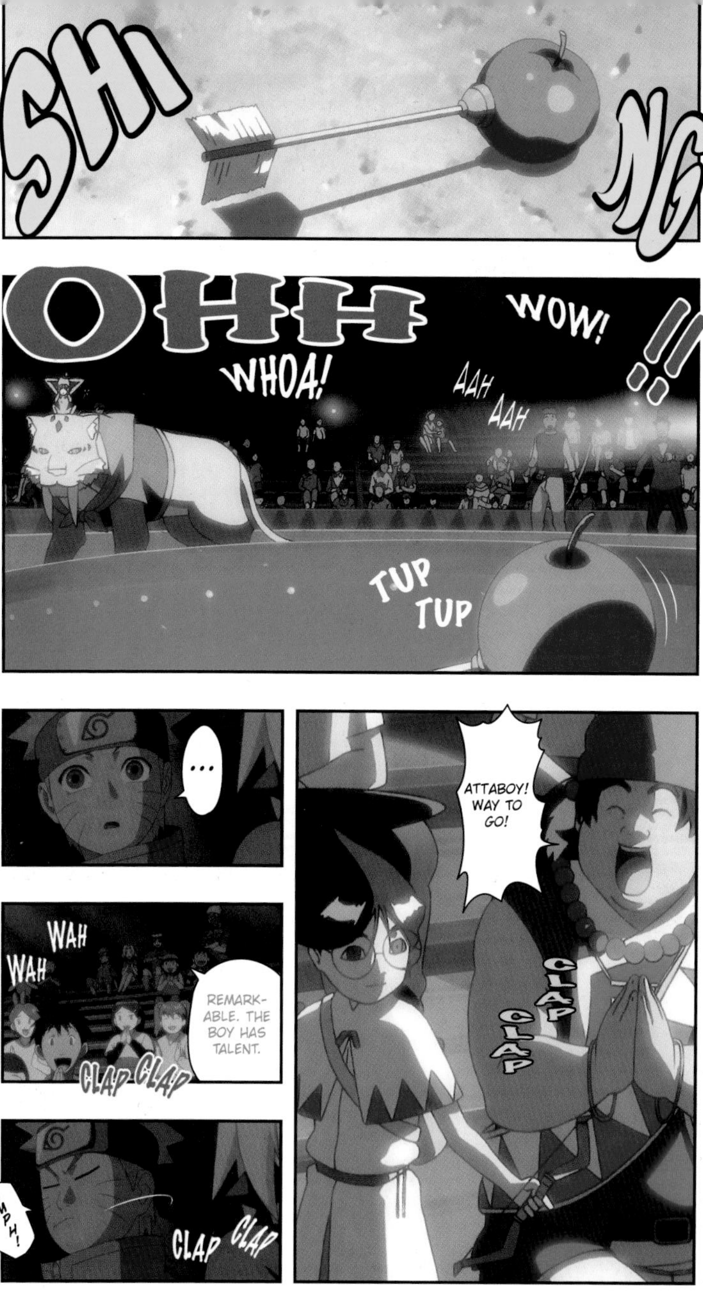
SHI NG
!!
WOW!
AAH AAH
WHOA!
OHH
TUP TUP
ATTABOY! WAY TO GO!
CLAP CLAP
...
WAH WAH
REMARKABLE. THE BOY HAS TALENT.
CLAP CLAP
HMPH!
CLAP CLAP

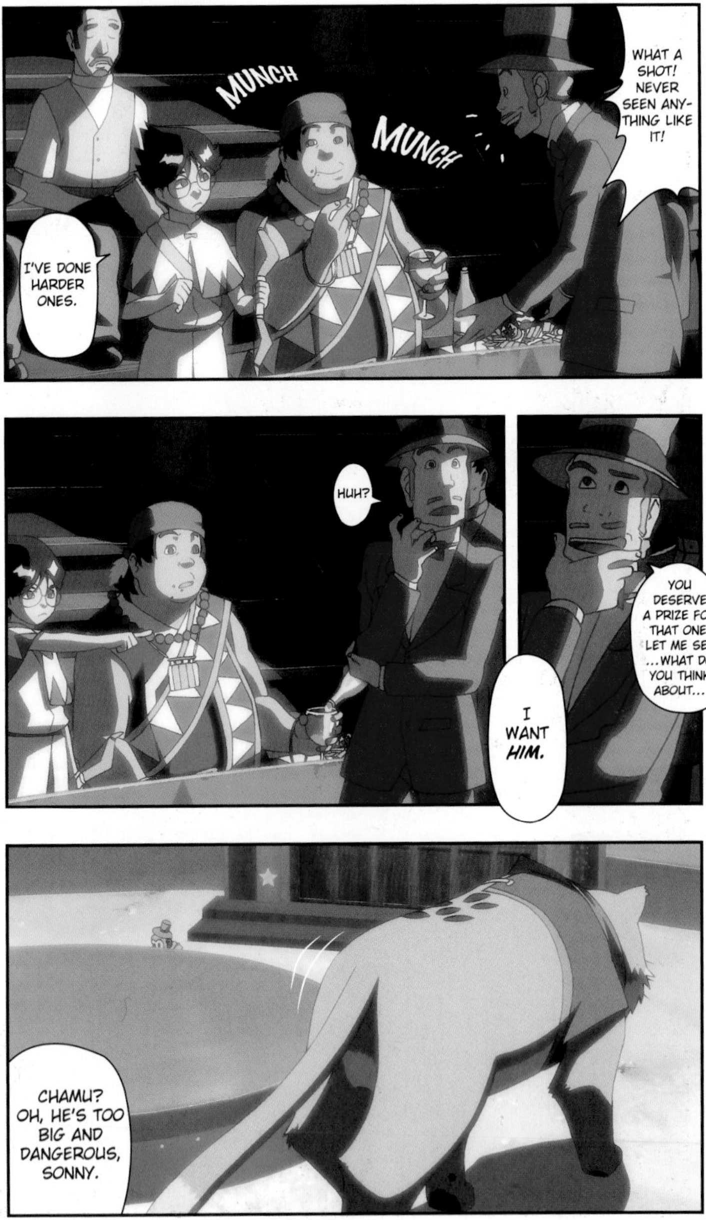
WHAT A SHOT! NEVER SEEN ANYTHING LIKE IT!
MUNCH
MUNCH
I'VE DONE HARDER ONES.
YOU DESERVE A PRIZE FOR THAT ONE. LET ME SEE ...WHAT DO YOU THINK ABOUT...
I WANT *HIM.*
HUH?
CHAMU? OH, HE'S TOO BIG AND DANGEROUS, SONNY.

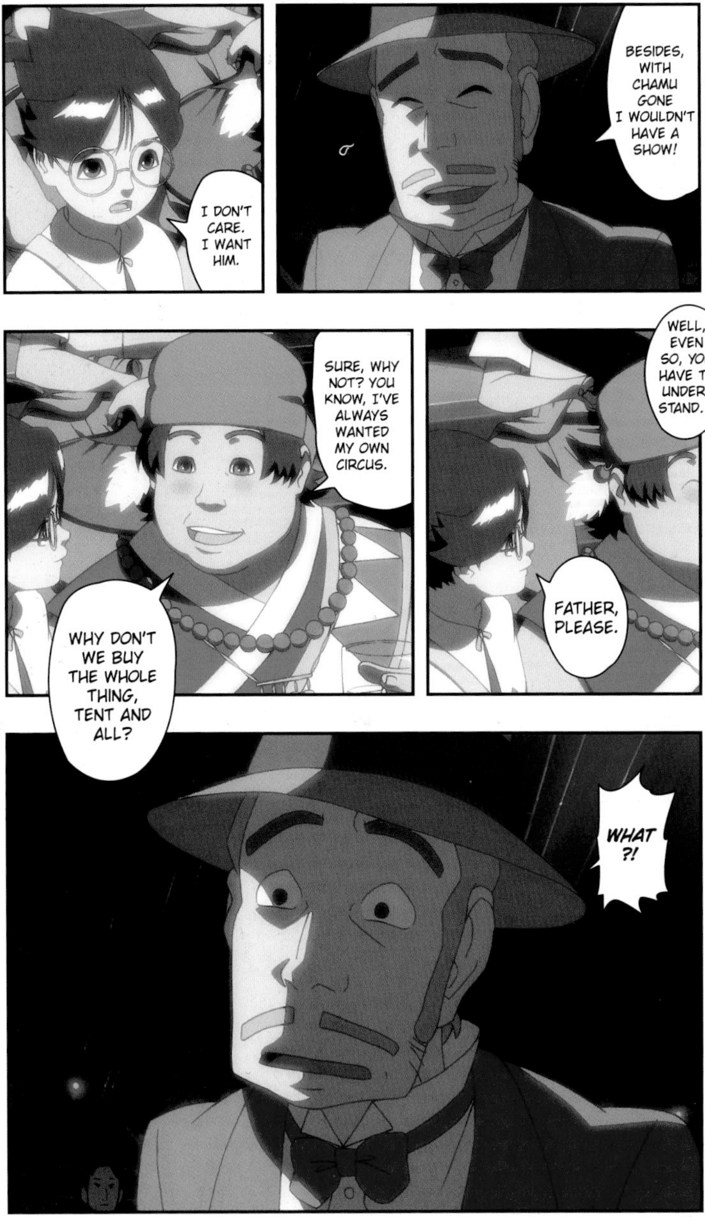
BESIDES, WITH CHAMU GONE I WOULDN'T HAVE A SHOW!
I DON'T CARE. I WANT HIM.
WELL, EVEN SO, YOU HAVE TO UNDER-STAND...
FATHER, PLEASE.
SURE, WHY NOT? YOU KNOW, I'VE ALWAYS WANTED MY OWN CIRCUS.
WHY DON'T WE BUY THE WHOLE THING, TENT AND ALL?
WHAT ?!

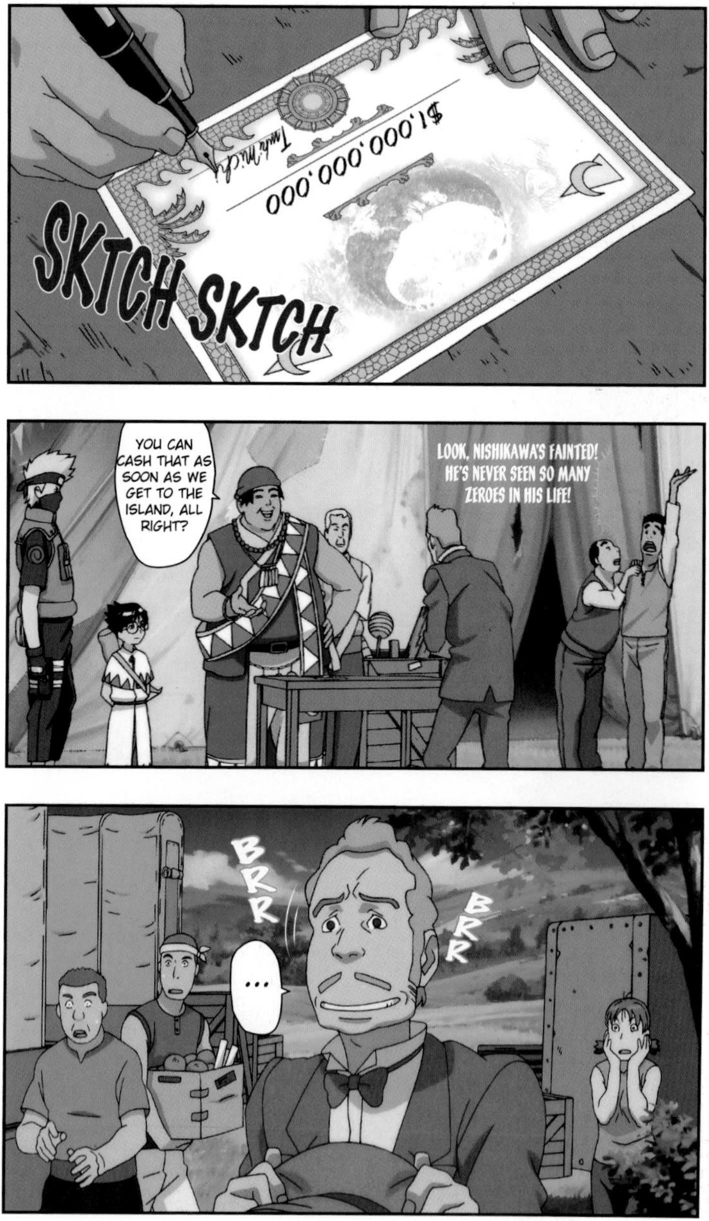
SKTCH SKTCH
LOOK, NISHIKAWA'S FAINTED! HE'S NEVER SEEN SO MANY ZEROES IN HIS LIFE!
YOU CAN CASH THAT AS SOON AS WE GET TO THE ISLAND, ALL RIGHT?
BRR BRR
BRR
...

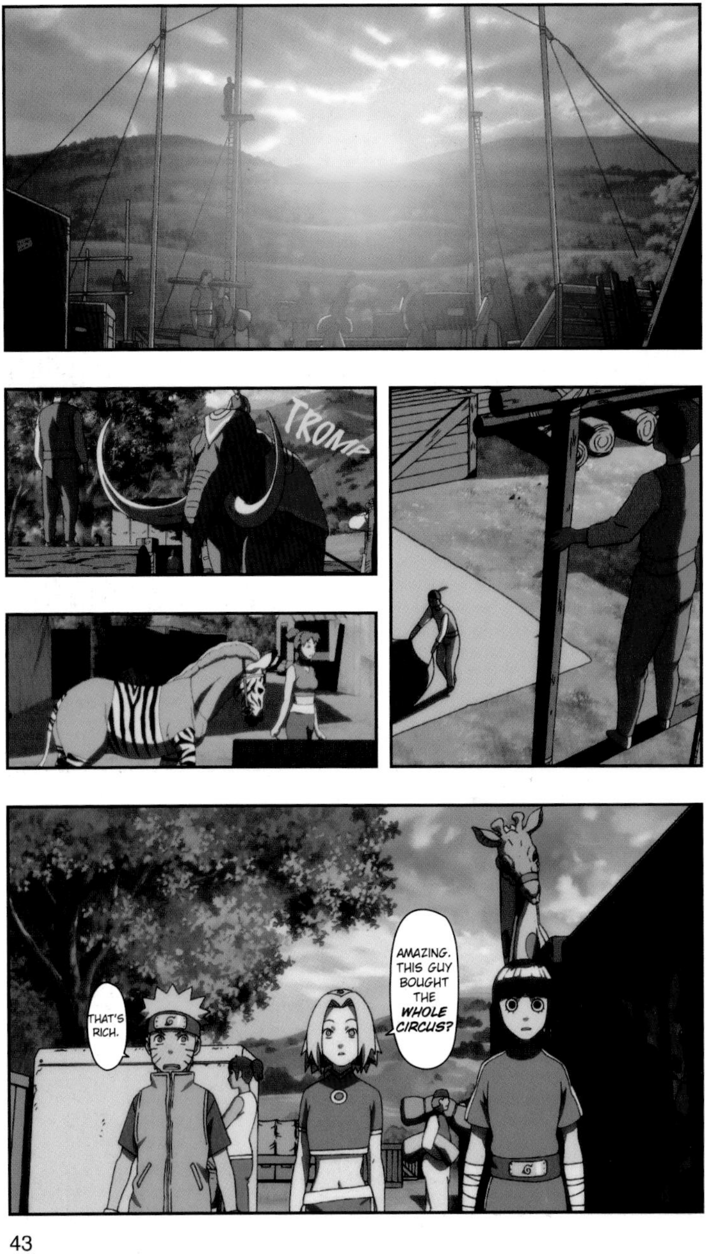
TROMP
AMAZING. THIS GUY BOUGHT THE **WHOLE CIRCUS?**
THAT'S RICH.

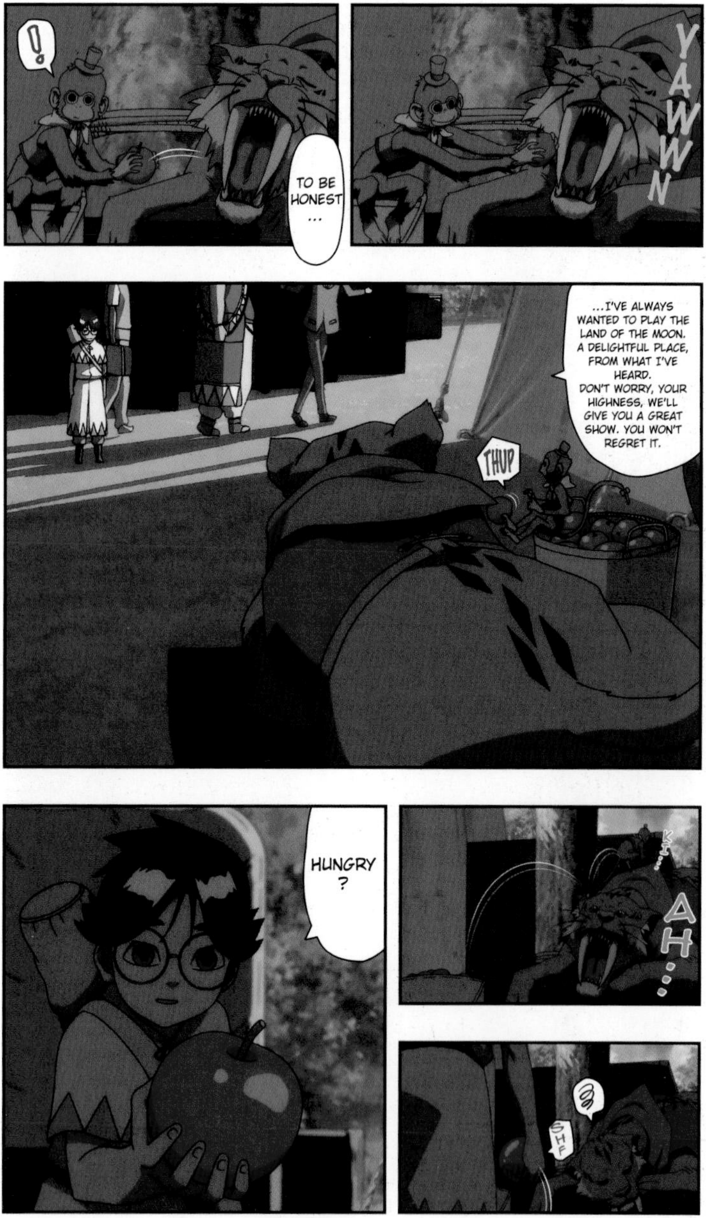
YAWWN
!
TO BE HONEST ...
...I'VE ALWAYS WANTED TO PLAY THE LAND OF THE MOON. A DELIGHTFUL PLACE, FROM WHAT I'VE HEARD. DON'T WORRY, YOUR HIGHNESS, WE'LL GIVE YOU A GREAT SHOW. YOU WON'T REGRET IT.
THUP
KI...
AH...
SHF
HUNGRY ?

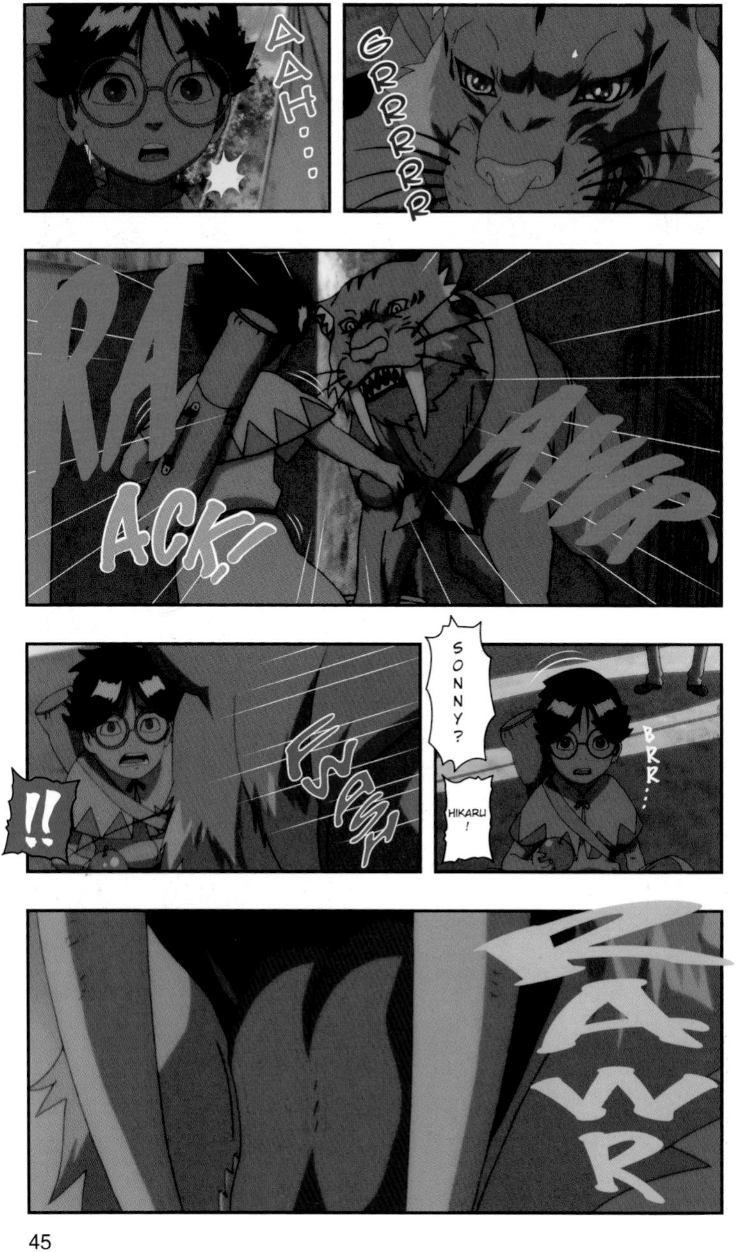
GRRRRR
AAH...
AWR
RA
ACK!!
SONNY?
HIKARU!
BRR...
FWASH
!!
RAWR

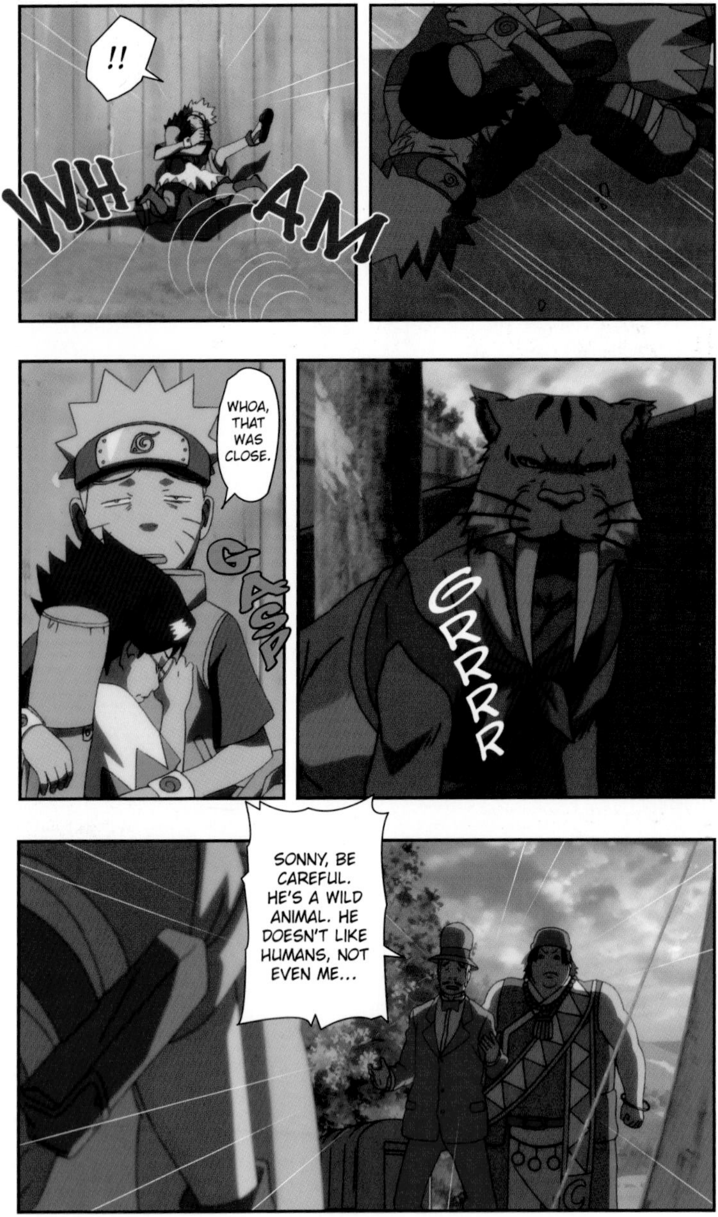

!!
WHAM
GRRRR
WHOA, THAT WAS CLOSE.
GASA
SONNY, BE CAREFUL. HE'S A WILD ANIMAL. HE DOESN'T LIKE HUMANS, NOT EVEN ME...

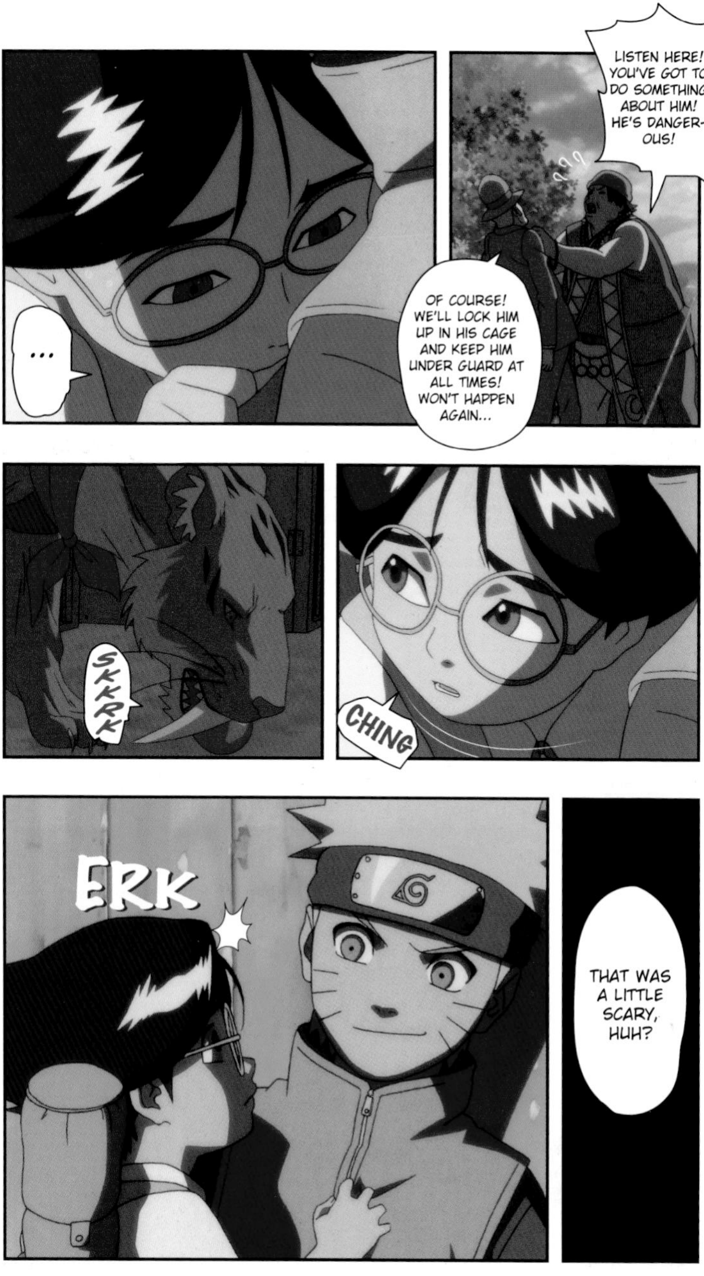
LISTEN HERE! YOU'VE GOT TO DO SOMETHING ABOUT HIM! HE'S DANGER-OUS!
???
OF COURSE! WE'LL LOCK HIM UP IN HIS CAGE AND KEEP HIM UNDER GUARD AT ALL TIMES! WON'T HAPPEN AGAIN...
...
CHING
SKKRK
THAT WAS A LITTLE SCARY, HUH?
ERK

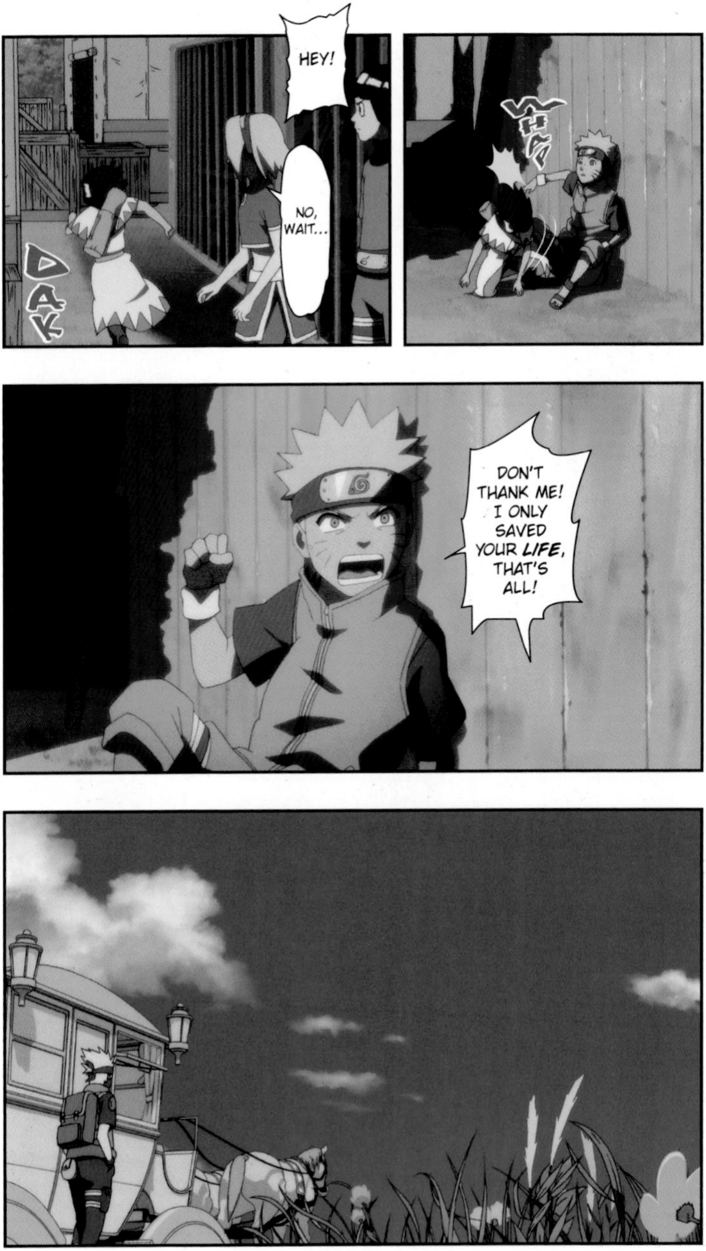
WHAP
HEY!
NO, WAIT...
DAK
DON'T THANK ME! I ONLY SAVED YOUR *LIFE*, THAT'S ALL!

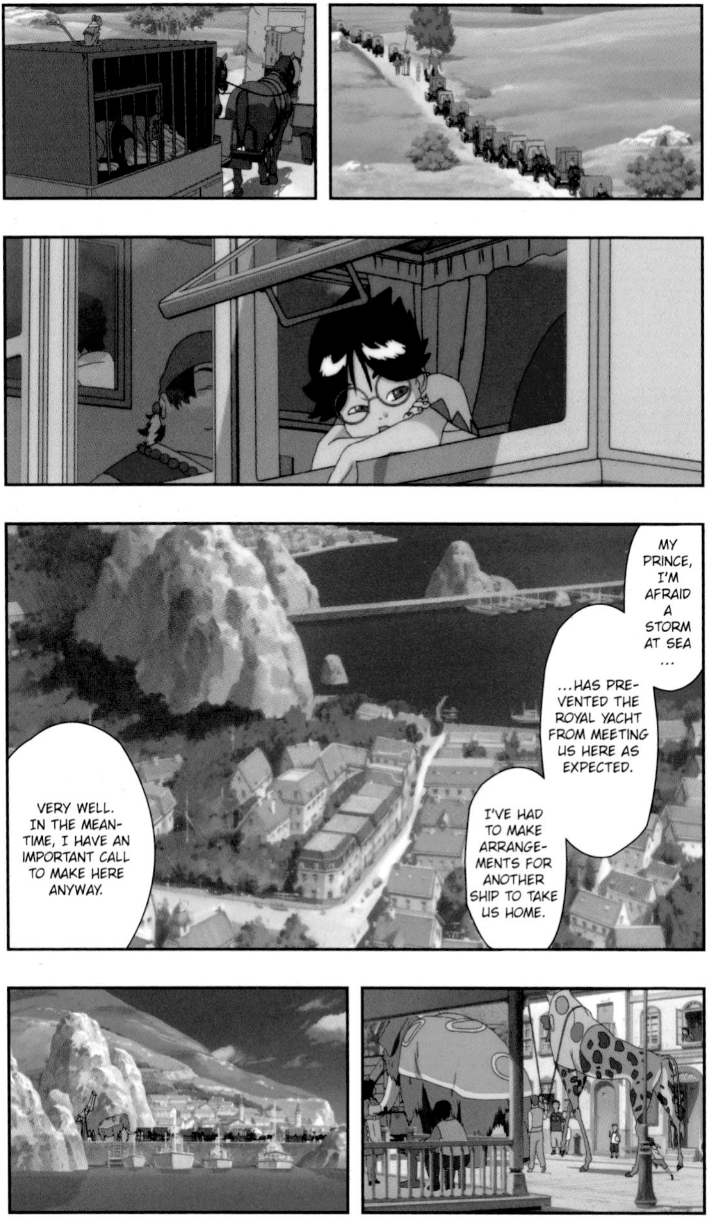
MY PRINCE, I'M AFRAID A STORM AT SEA...
...HAS PREVENTED THE ROYAL YACHT FROM MEETING US HERE AS EXPECTED.
I'VE HAD TO MAKE ARRANGEMENTS FOR ANOTHER SHIP TO TAKE US HOME.
VERY WELL. IN THE MEANTIME, I HAVE AN IMPORTANT CALL TO MAKE HERE ANYWAY.

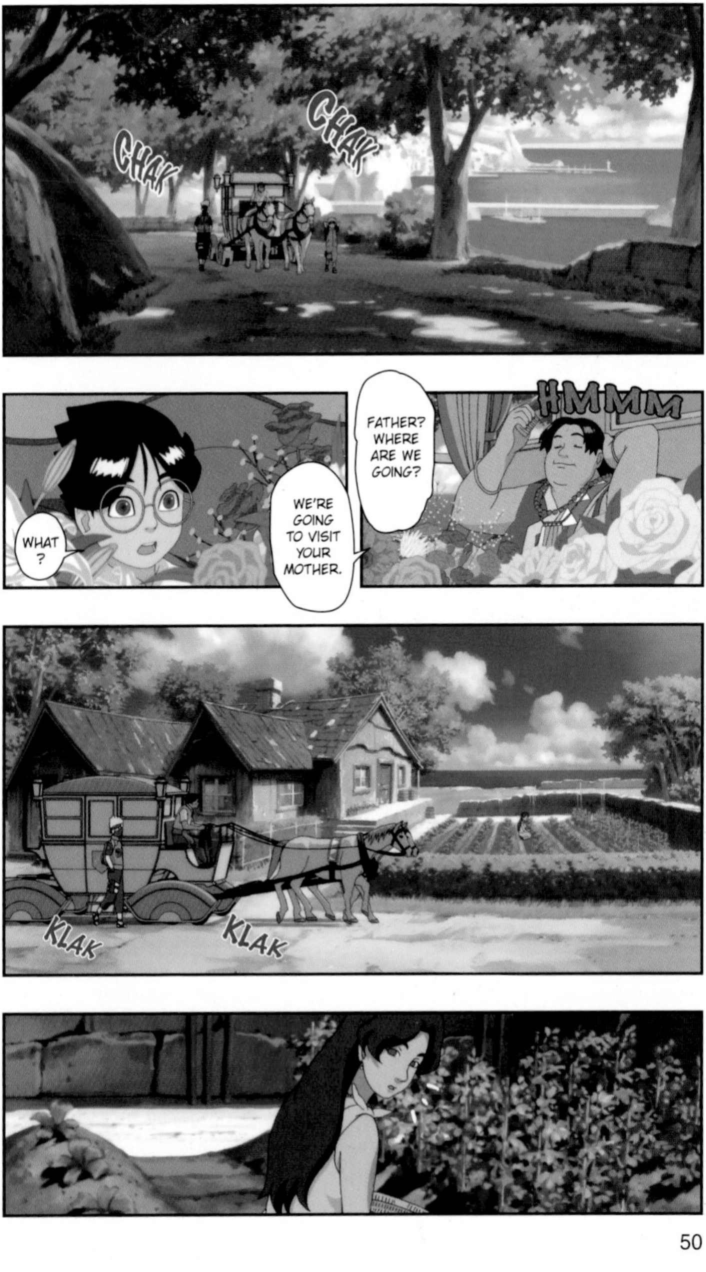
CHAK
CHAK
HMMMM
FATHER? WHERE ARE WE GOING?
WE'RE GOING TO VISIT YOUR MOTHER.
WHAT?
KLAK
KLAK

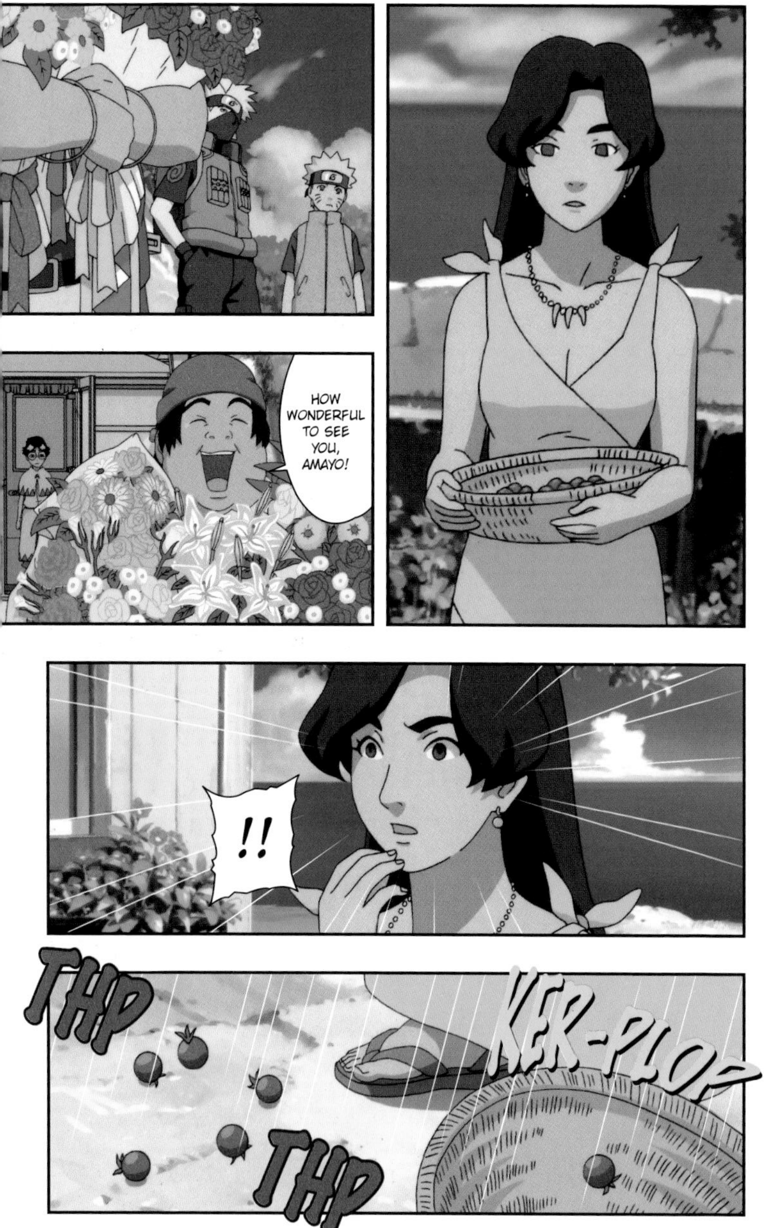
HOW WONDERFUL TO SEE YOU, AMAYO!
!!
KER-PLOP
THP
THP

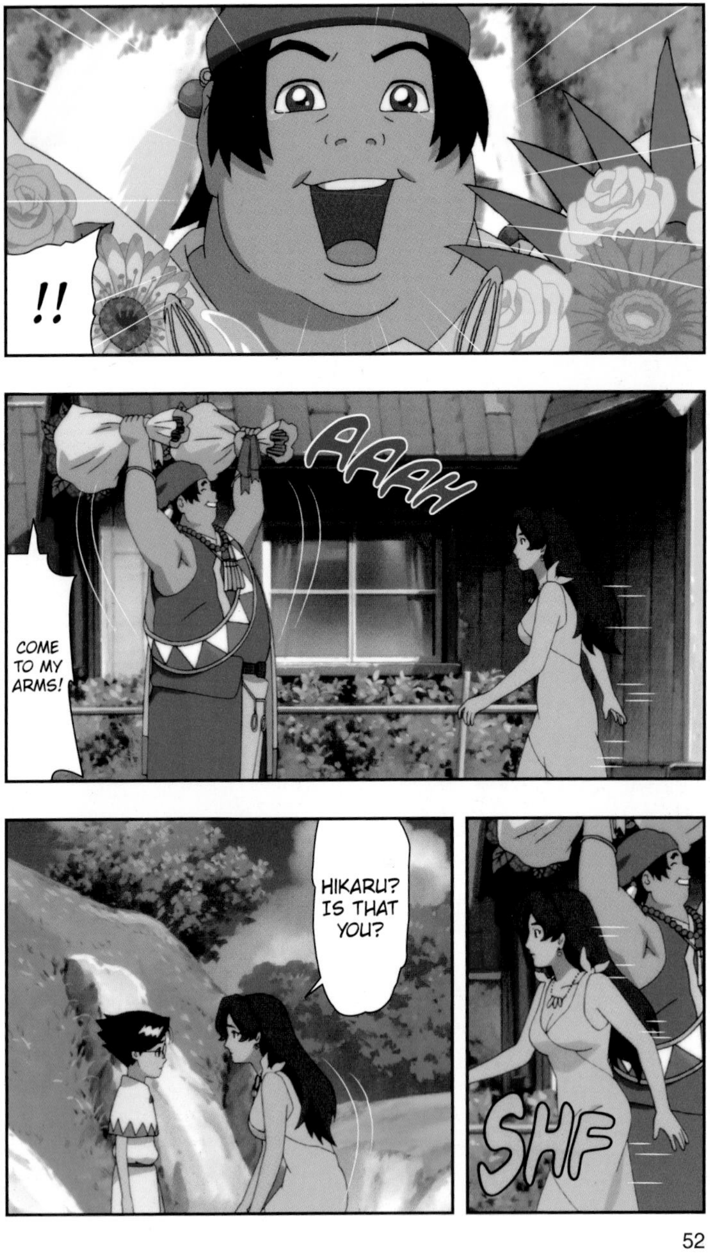
!!
AAAH
COME TO MY ARMS!
SHF
HIKARU? IS THAT YOU?

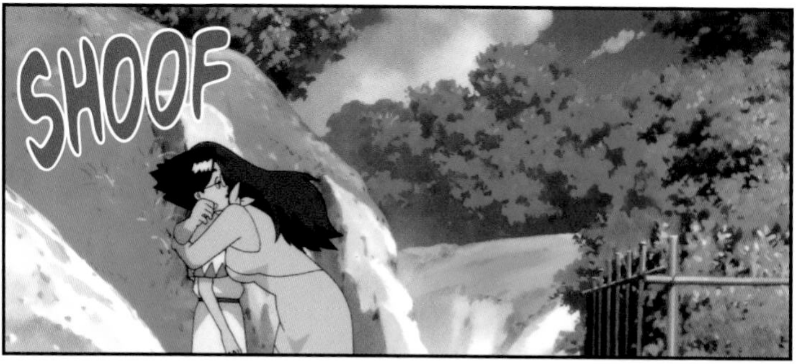
SHOOF
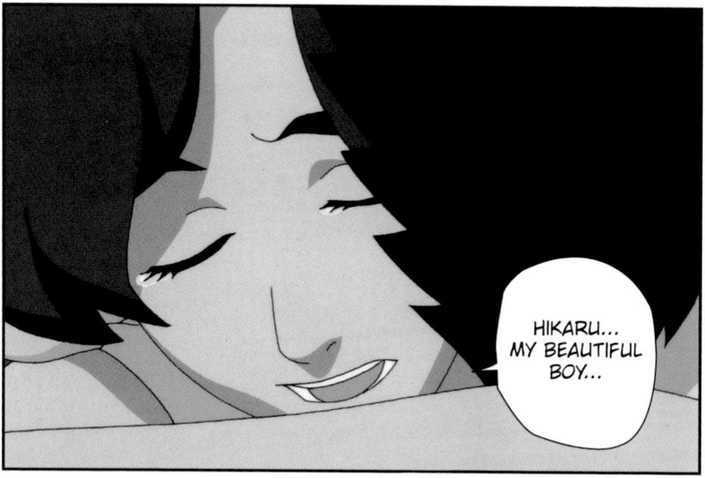
HIKARU... MY BEAUTIFUL BOY...
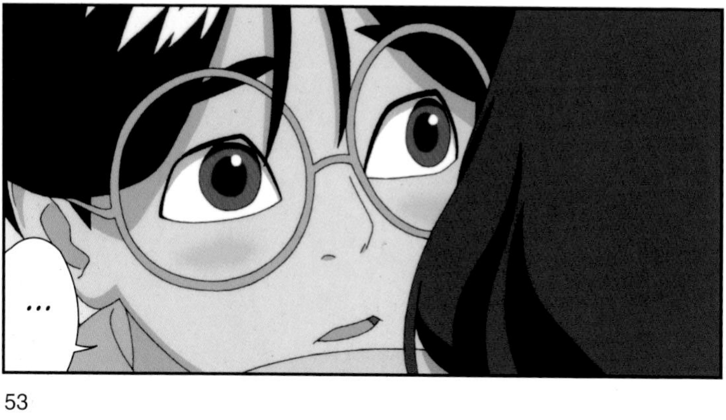
...

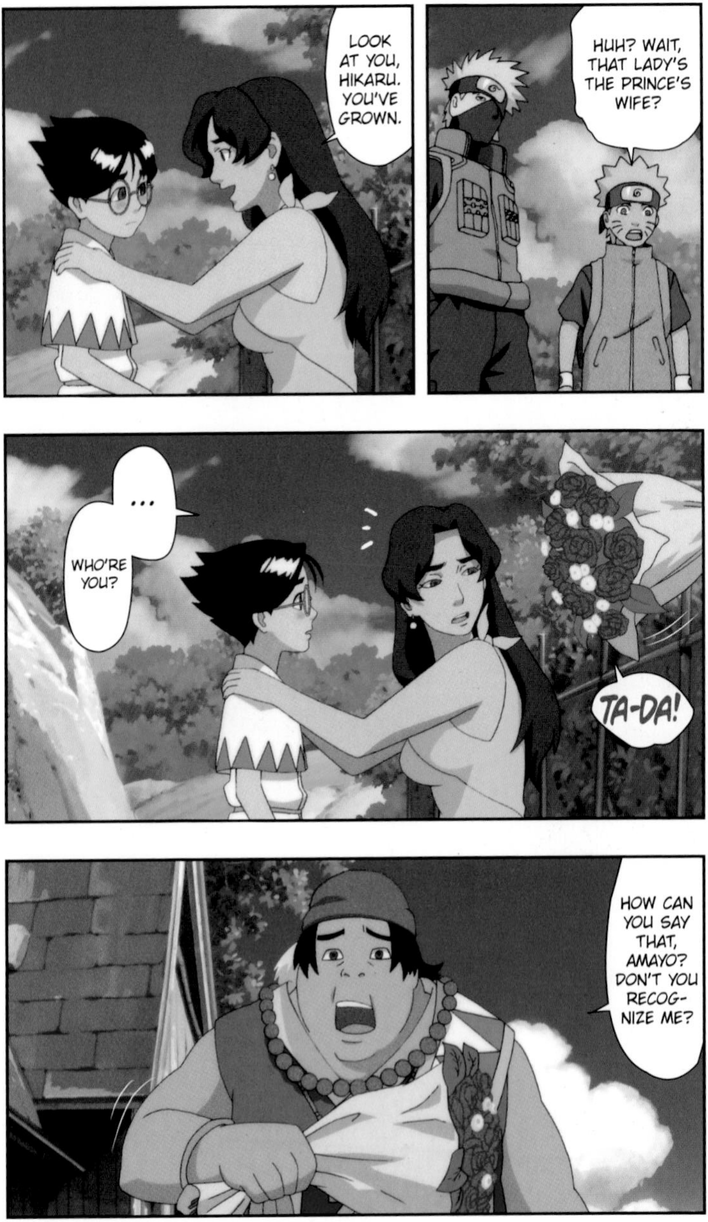
HUH? WAIT, THAT LADY'S THE PRINCE'S WIFE?
LOOK AT YOU, HIKARU. YOU'VE GROWN.
...
WHO'RE YOU?
TA-DA!
HOW CAN YOU SAY THAT, AMAYO? DON'T YOU RECOG-NIZE ME?

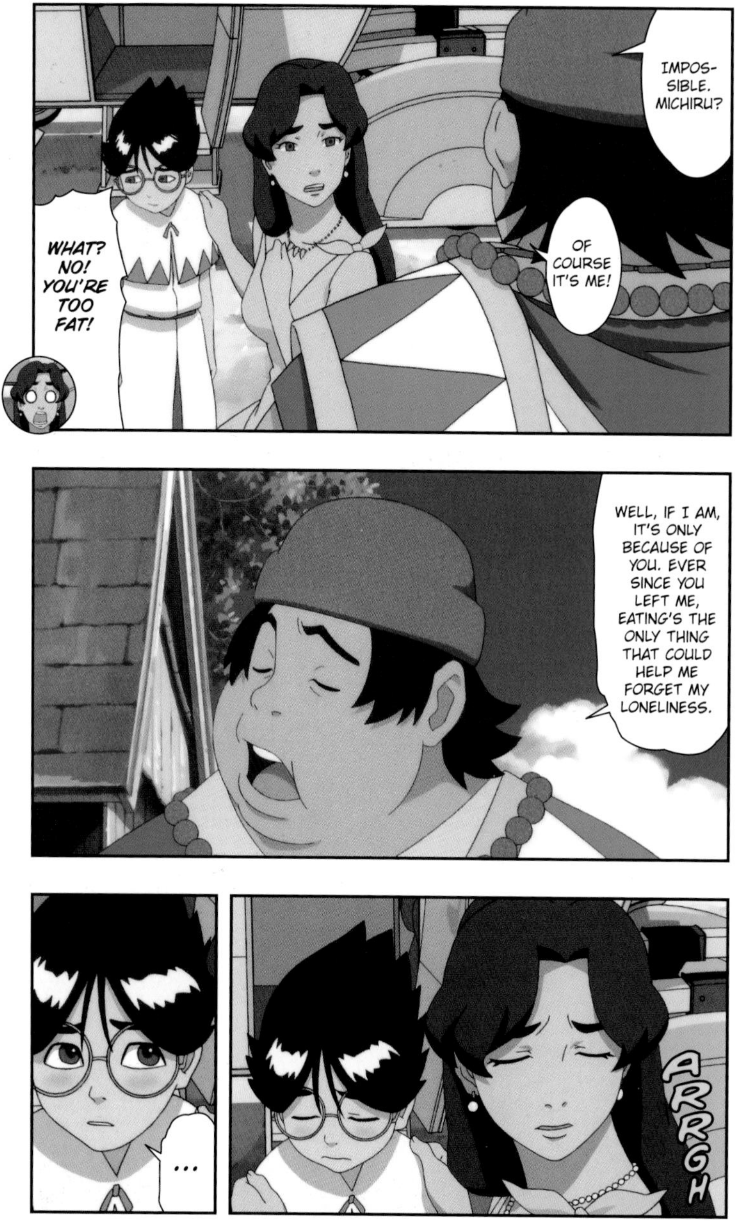
IMPOS-
SIBLE.
MICHIRU?
OF COURSE IT'S ME!
WHAT? NO! YOU'RE TOO FAT!
WELL, IF I AM, IT'S ONLY BECAUSE OF YOU. EVER SINCE YOU LEFT ME, EATING'S THE ONLY THING THAT COULD HELP ME FORGET MY LONELINESS.
ARRGH
...

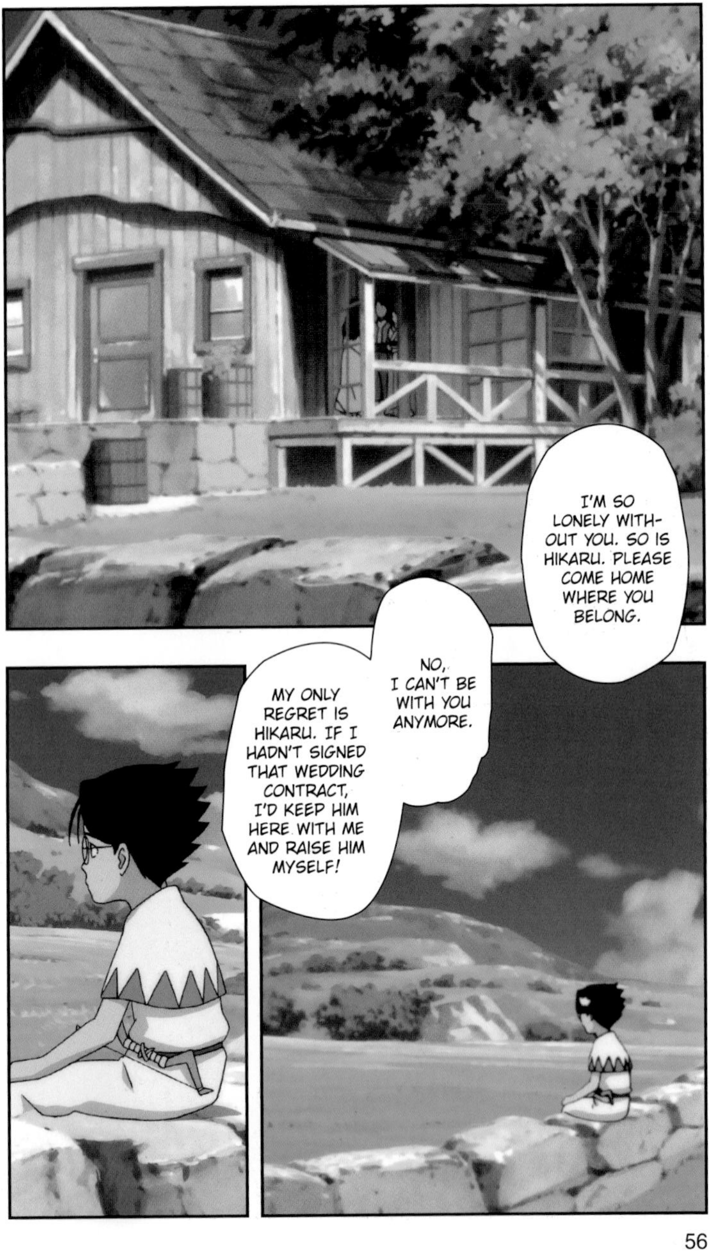
I'M SO LONELY WITHOUT YOU. SO IS HIKARU. PLEASE COME HOME WHERE YOU BELONG.
NO, I CAN'T BE WITH YOU ANYMORE.
MY ONLY REGRET IS HIKARU. IF I HADN'T SIGNED THAT WEDDING CONTRACT, I'D KEEP HIM HERE WITH ME AND RAISE HIM MYSELF!

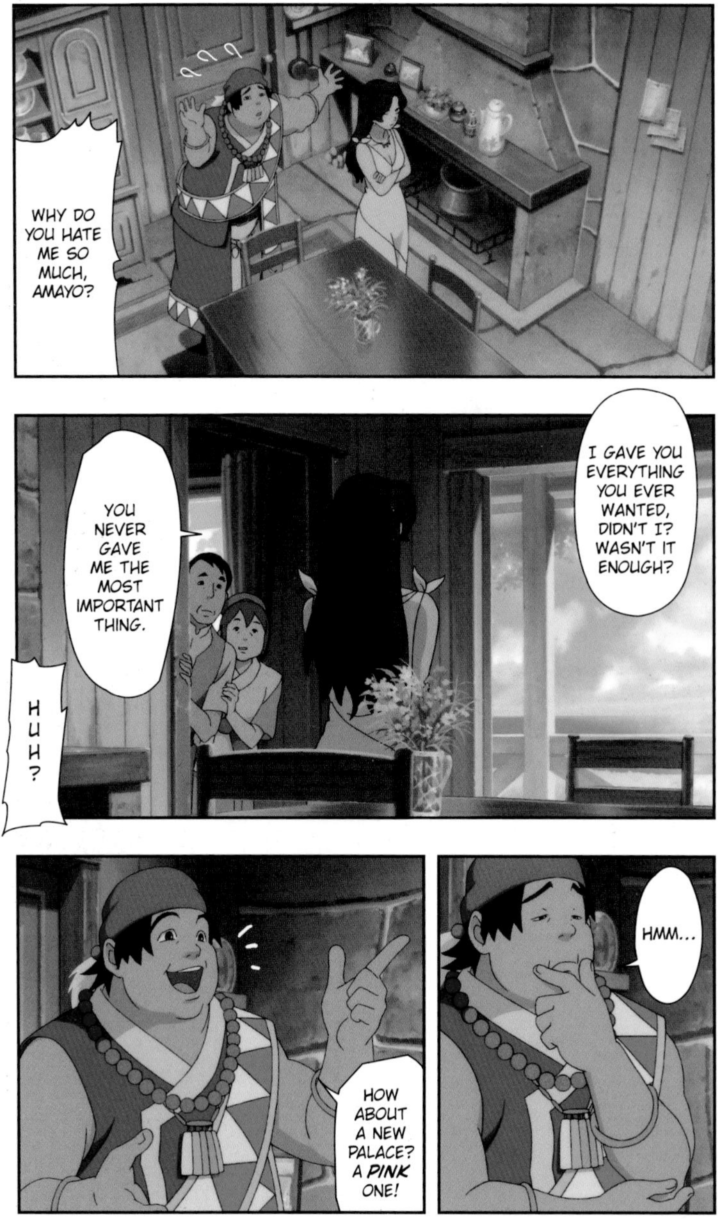
WHY DO YOU HATE ME SO MUCH, AMAYO?
I GAVE YOU EVERYTHING YOU EVER WANTED, DIDN'T I? WASN'T IT ENOUGH?
YOU NEVER GAVE ME THE MOST IMPORTANT THING.
HUH?
HMM...
HOW ABOUT A NEW PALACE? A PINK ONE!

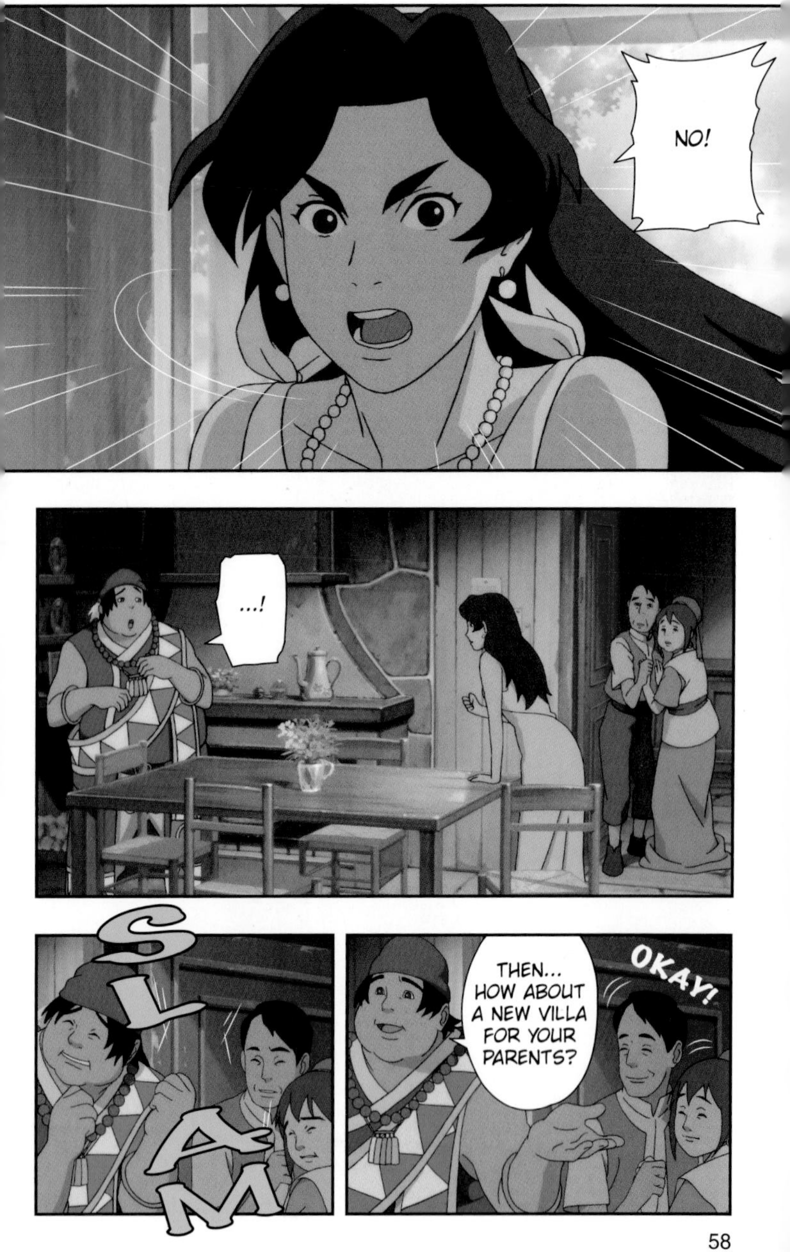
NO!
...!
THEN... HOW ABOUT A NEW VILLA FOR YOUR PARENTS?
OKAY!
SLAM

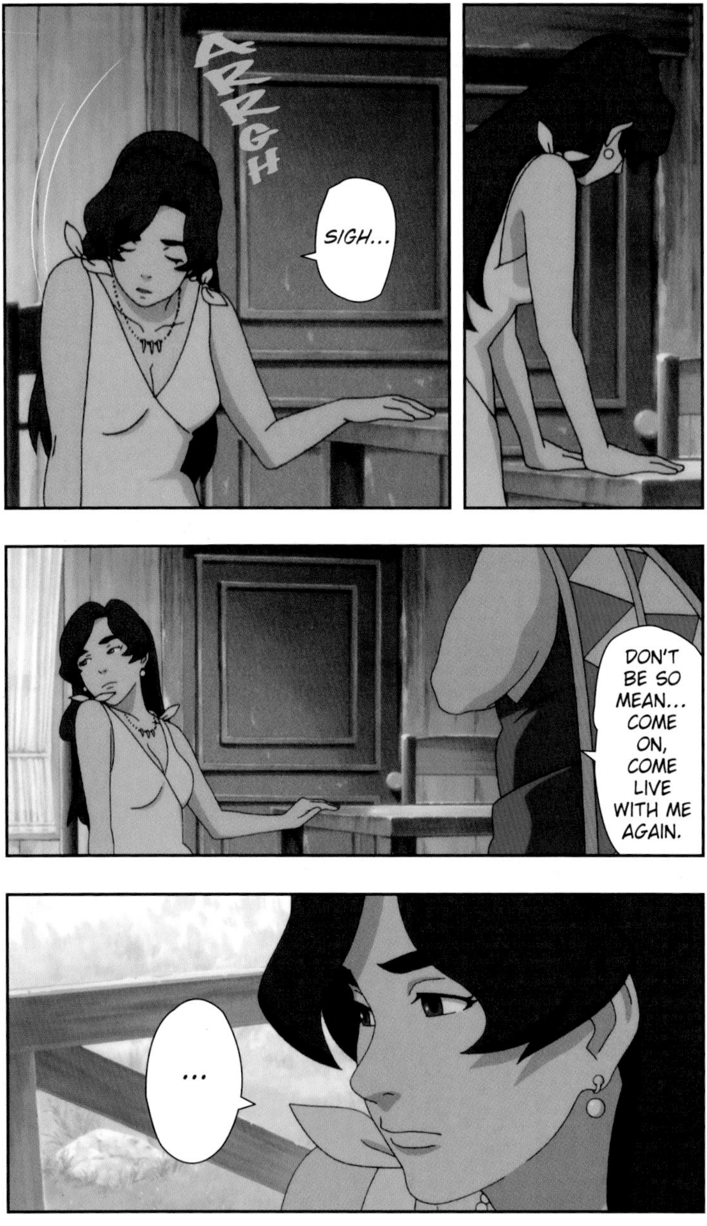
ARRGH
SIGH...
DON'T BE SO MEAN... COME ON, COME LIVE WITH ME AGAIN.
...

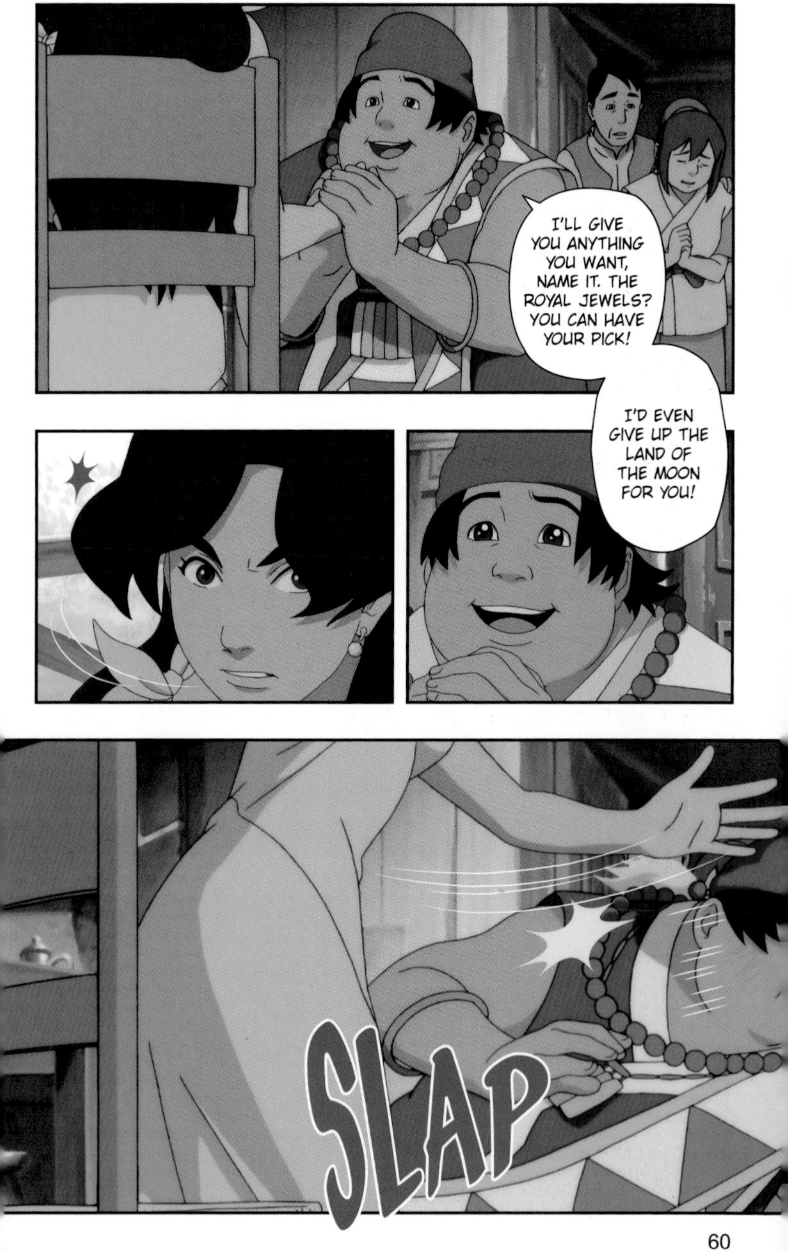
I'LL GIVE YOU ANYTHING YOU WANT, NAME IT. THE ROYAL JEWELS? YOU CAN HAVE YOUR PICK!
I'D EVEN GIVE UP THE LAND OF THE MOON FOR YOU!
SLAP

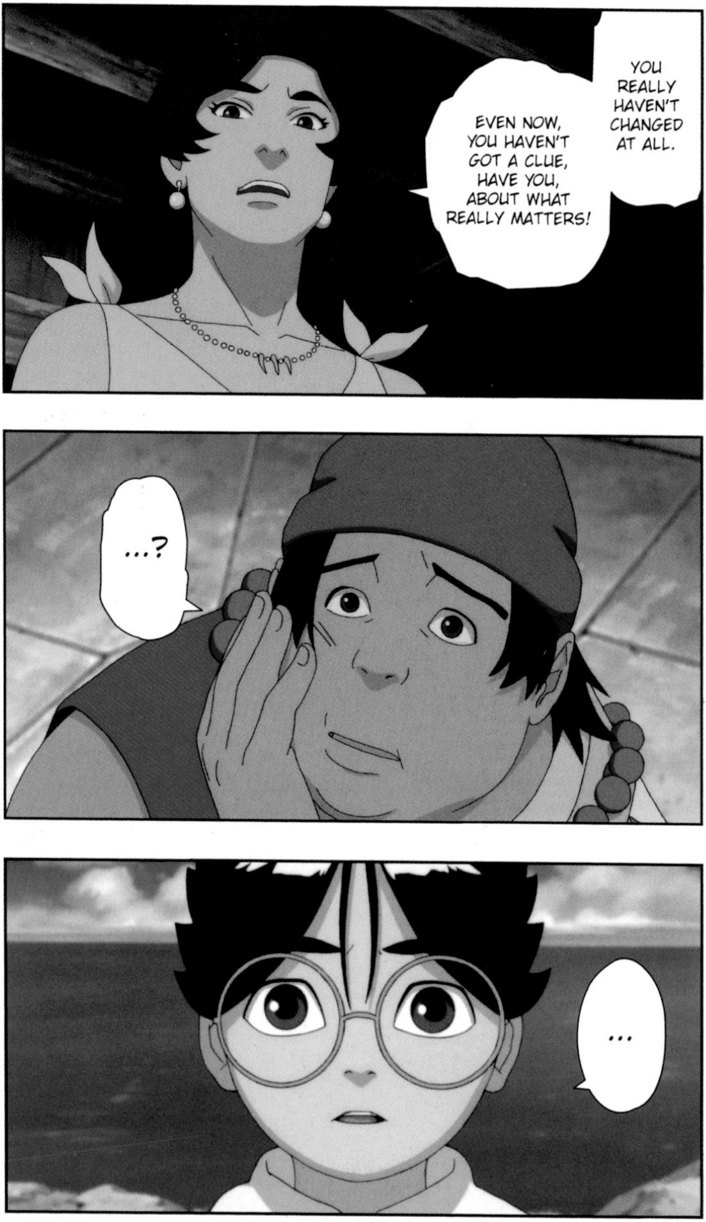
YOU REALLY HAVEN'T CHANGED AT ALL.
EVEN NOW, YOU HAVEN'T GOT A CLUE, HAVE YOU, ABOUT WHAT REALLY MATTERS!
...?
...

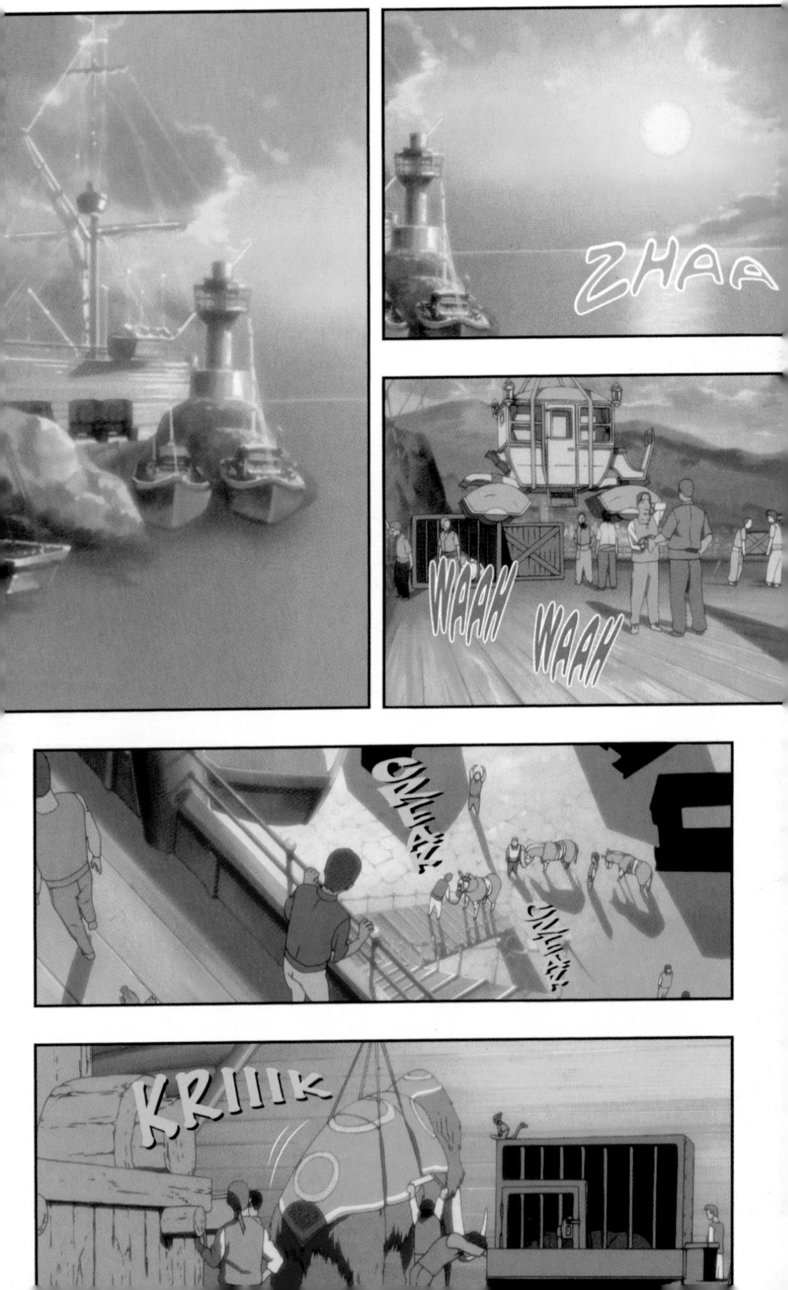
ZHAA
WAAH
WAAH
KRIIIK

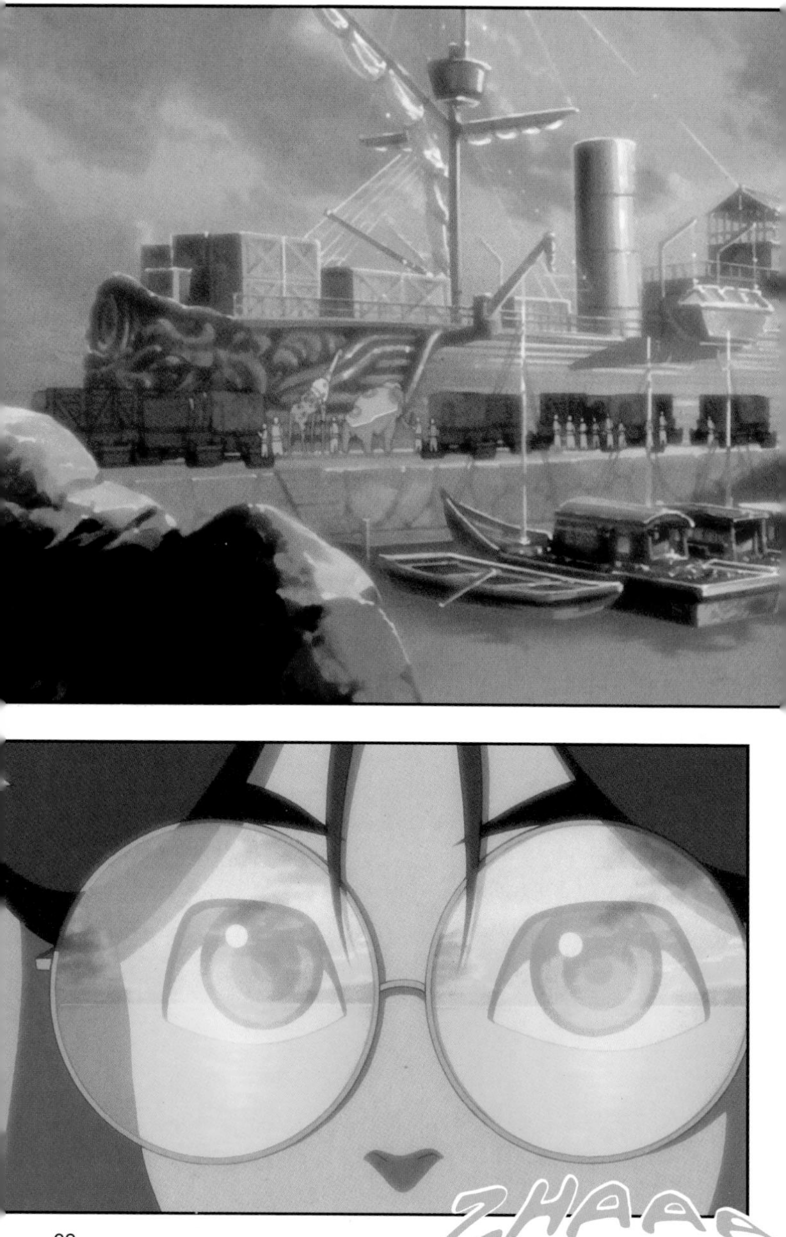
ZHAAA

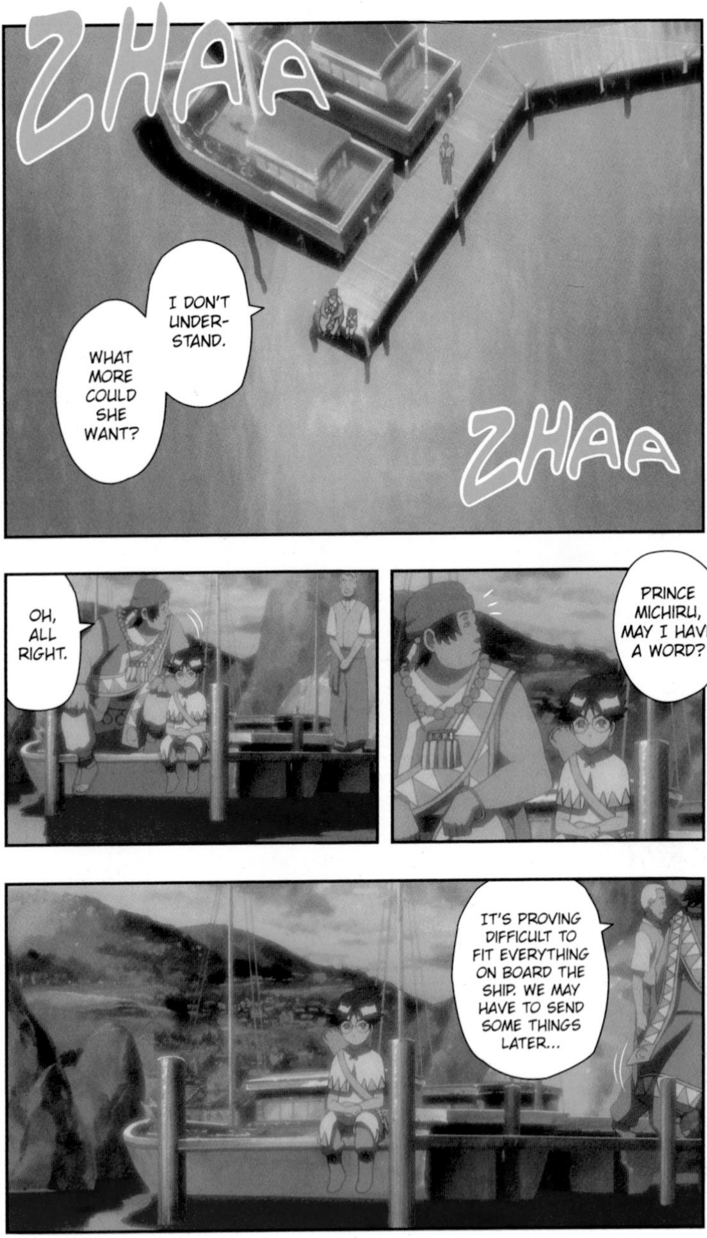
ZHAA
I DON'T UNDER-STAND.
WHAT MORE COULD SHE WANT?
ZHAA
PRINCE MICHIRU, MAY I HAVE A WORD?
OH, ALL RIGHT.
IT'S PROVING DIFFICULT TO FIT EVERYTHING ON BOARD THE SHIP. WE MAY HAVE TO SEND SOME THINGS LATER...

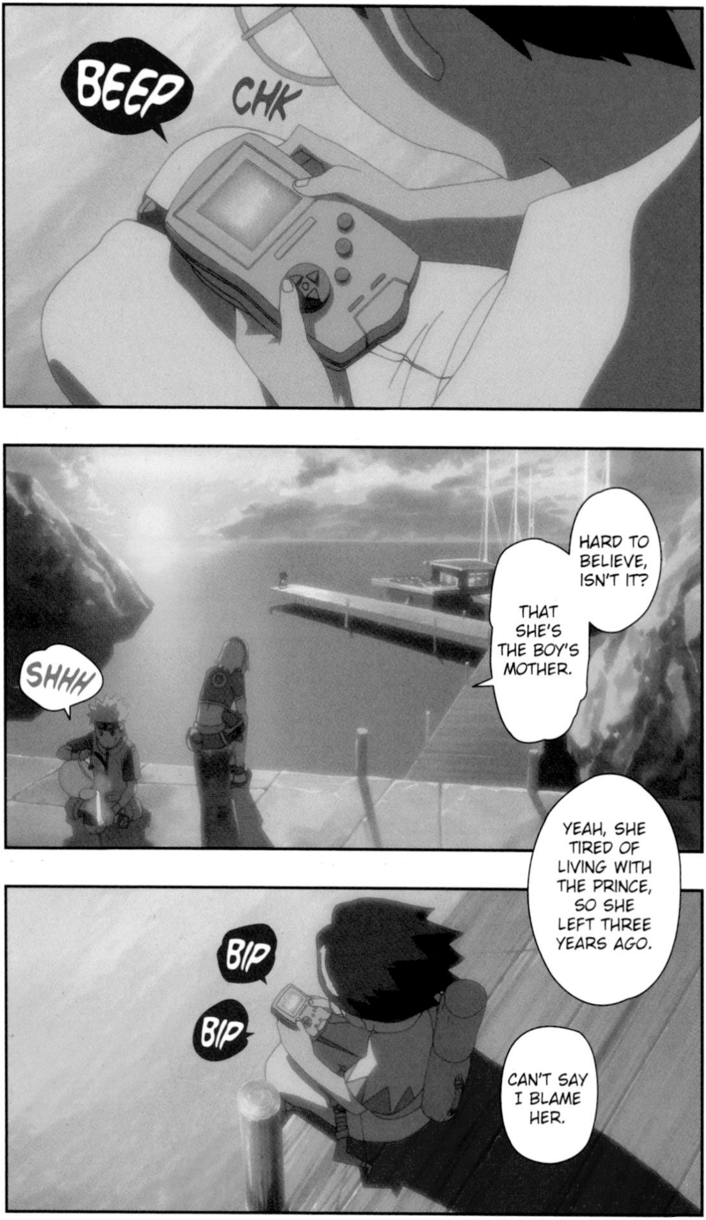
BEEP
CHK
HARD TO BELIEVE, ISN'T IT?
THAT SHE'S THE BOY'S MOTHER.
SHHH
YEAH, SHE TIRED OF LIVING WITH THE PRINCE, SO SHE LEFT THREE YEARS AGO.
BIP
BIP
CAN'T SAY I BLAME HER.

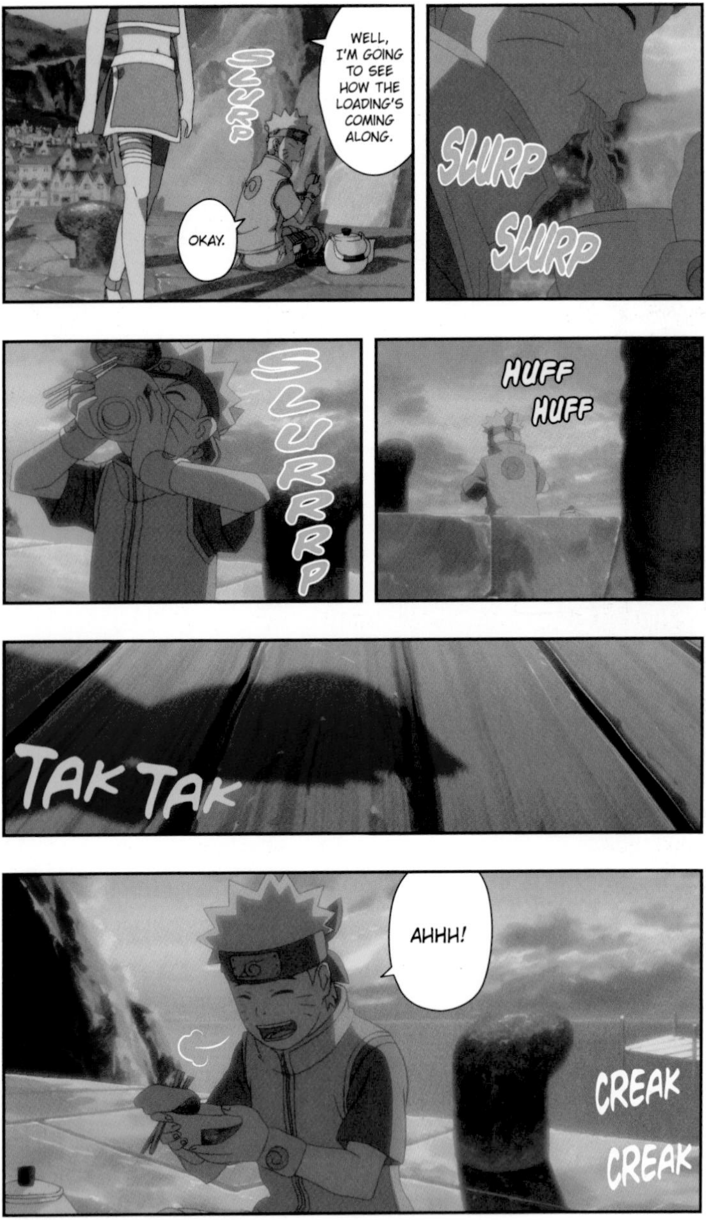
SLURP
SLURP
WELL, I'M GOING TO SEE HOW THE LOADING'S COMING ALONG.
SLURP
OKAY.
HUFF
HUFF
SLURRRP
TAK TAK
AHHH!
CREAK
CREAK

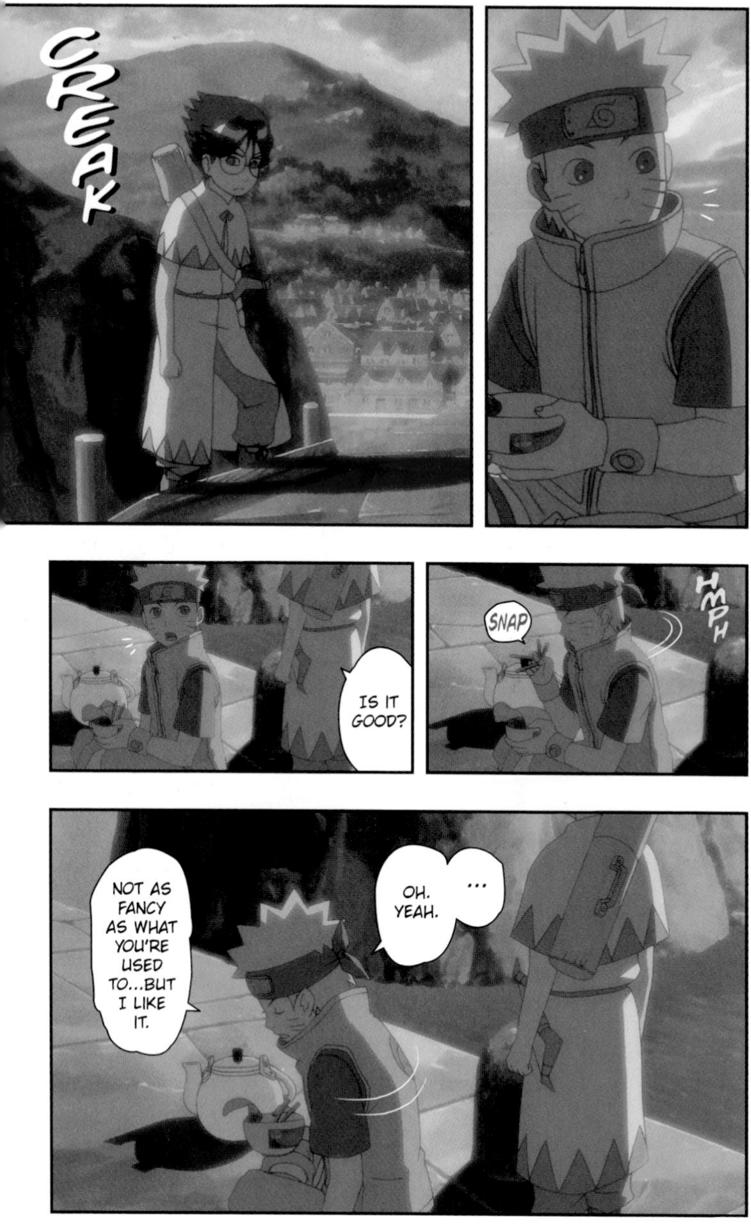
CREAK
HMPH
SNAP
IS IT GOOD?
...
OH. YEAH.
NOT AS FANCY AS WHAT YOU'RE USED TO...BUT I LIKE IT.

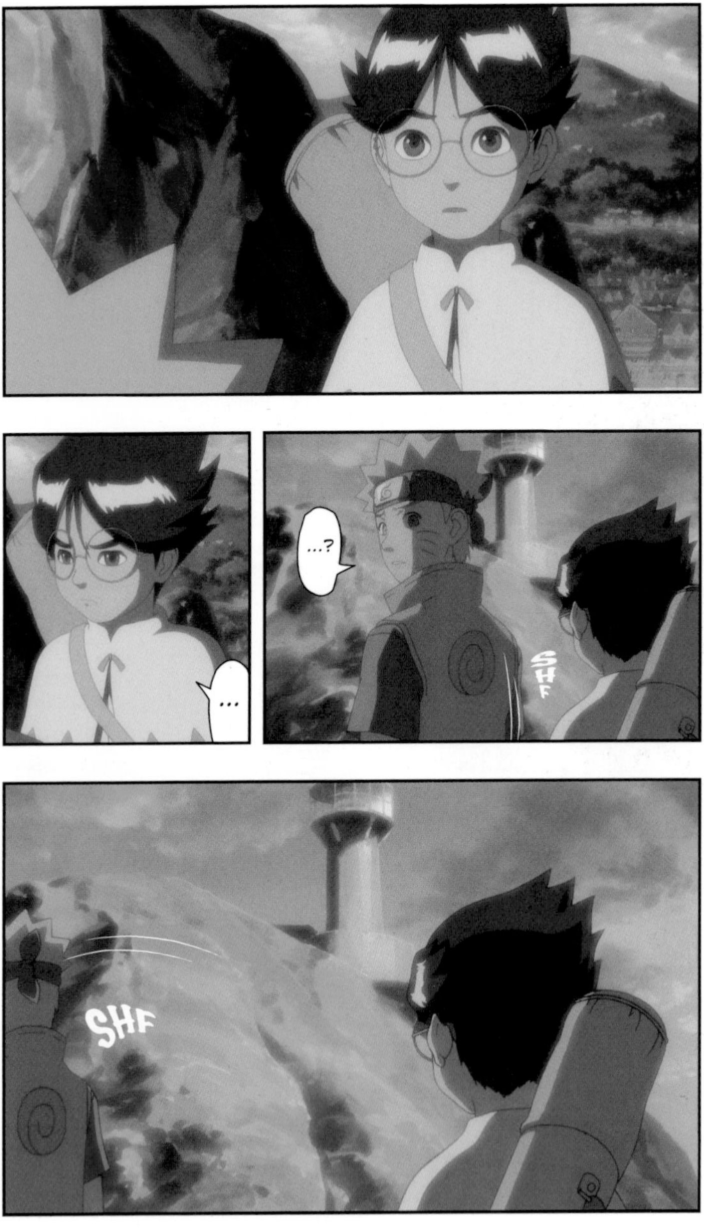
...?
SHF
...
SHF

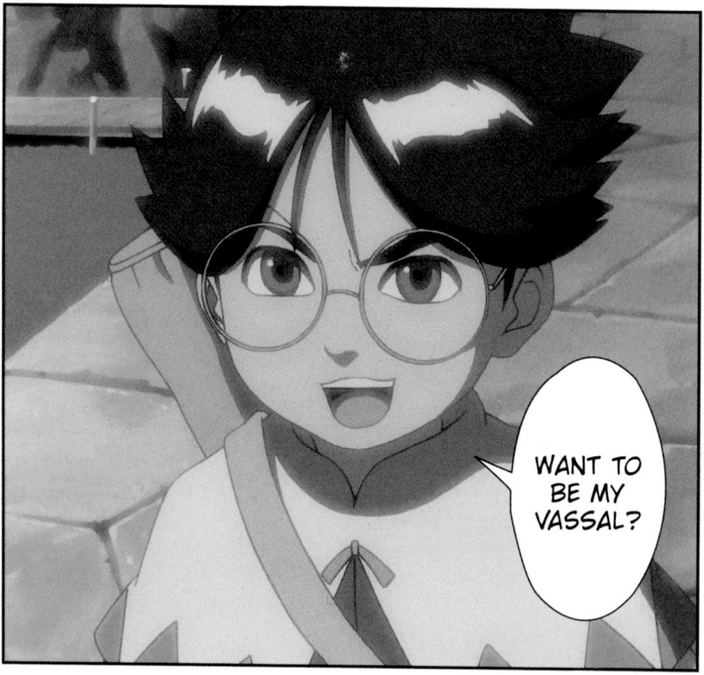
WANT TO BE MY VASSAL?

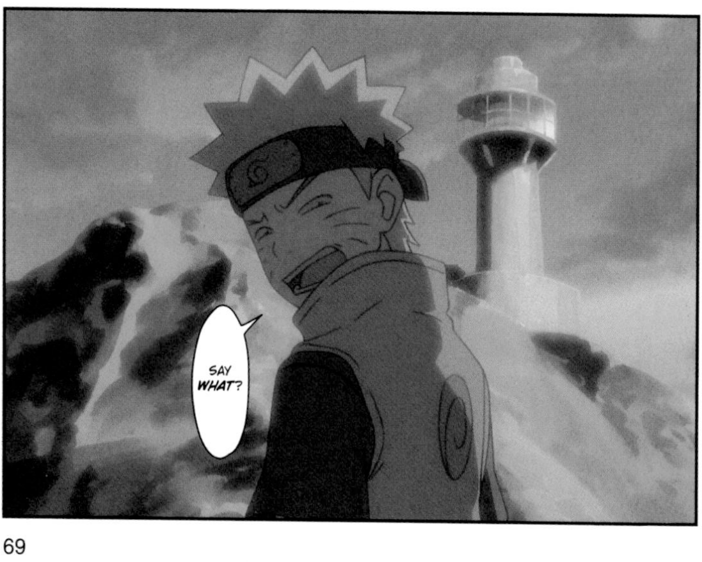
SAY *WHAT*?

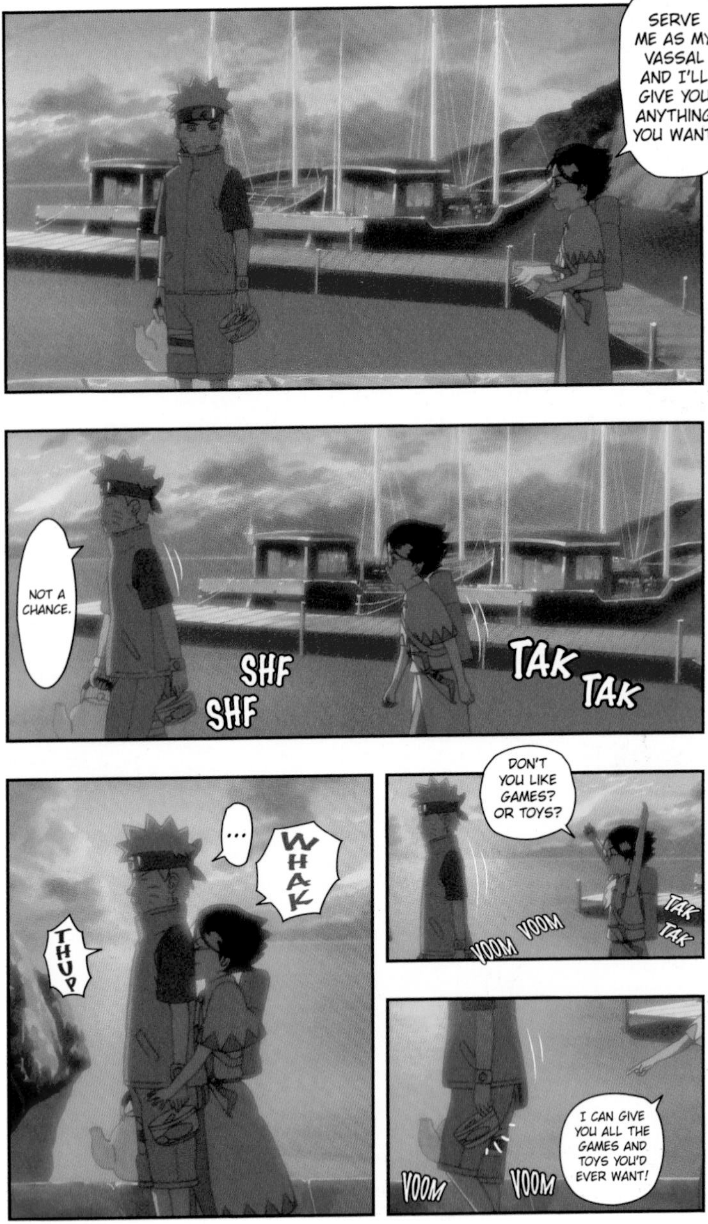
SERVE ME AS MY VASSAL AND I'LL GIVE YOU ANYTHING YOU WANT.
NOT A CHANCE.
TAK TAK
SHF SHF
DON'T YOU LIKE GAMES? OR TOYS?
TAK TAK
VOOM VOOM
I CAN GIVE YOU ALL THE GAMES AND TOYS YOU'D EVER WANT!
VOOM VOOM
...
WHAK
THUP

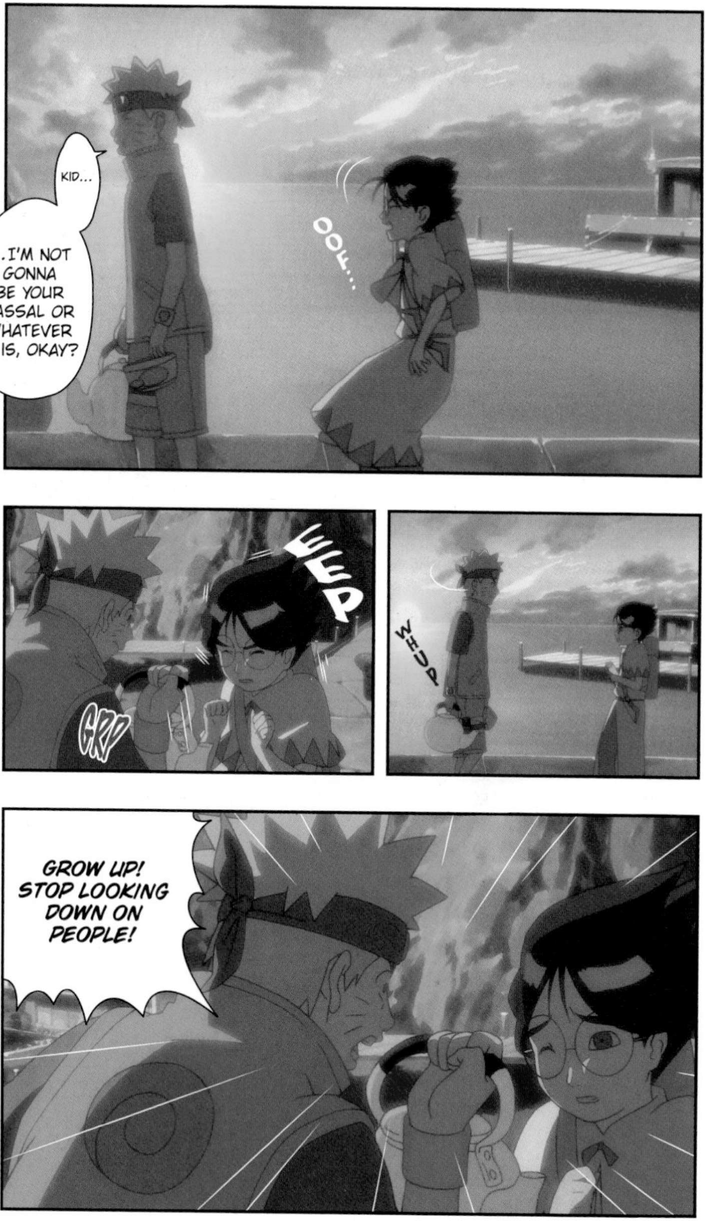
OOF...
KID...
...I'M NOT GONNA BE YOUR VASSAL OR WHATEVER IT IS, OKAY?
WHUP
EEP
GRP
GROW UP! STOP LOOKING DOWN ON PEOPLE!

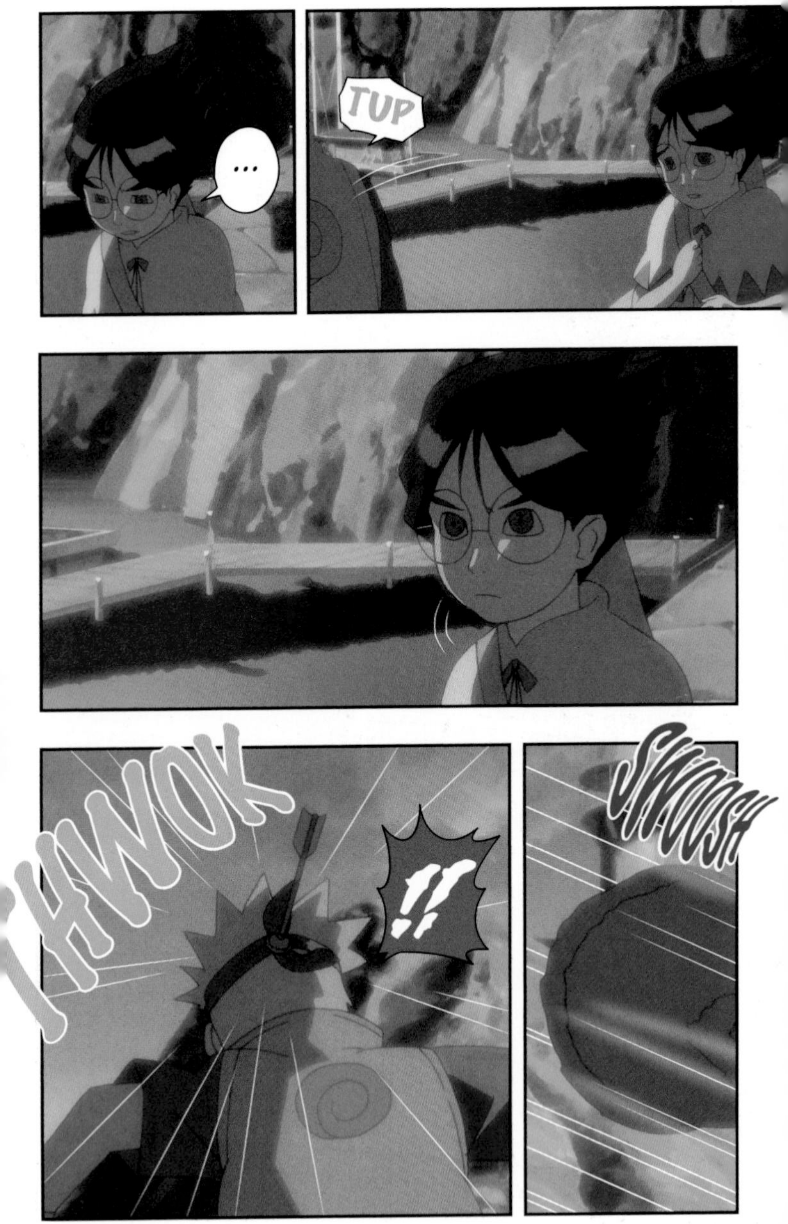
TUP
...
SWOOSH
THWOK
!!

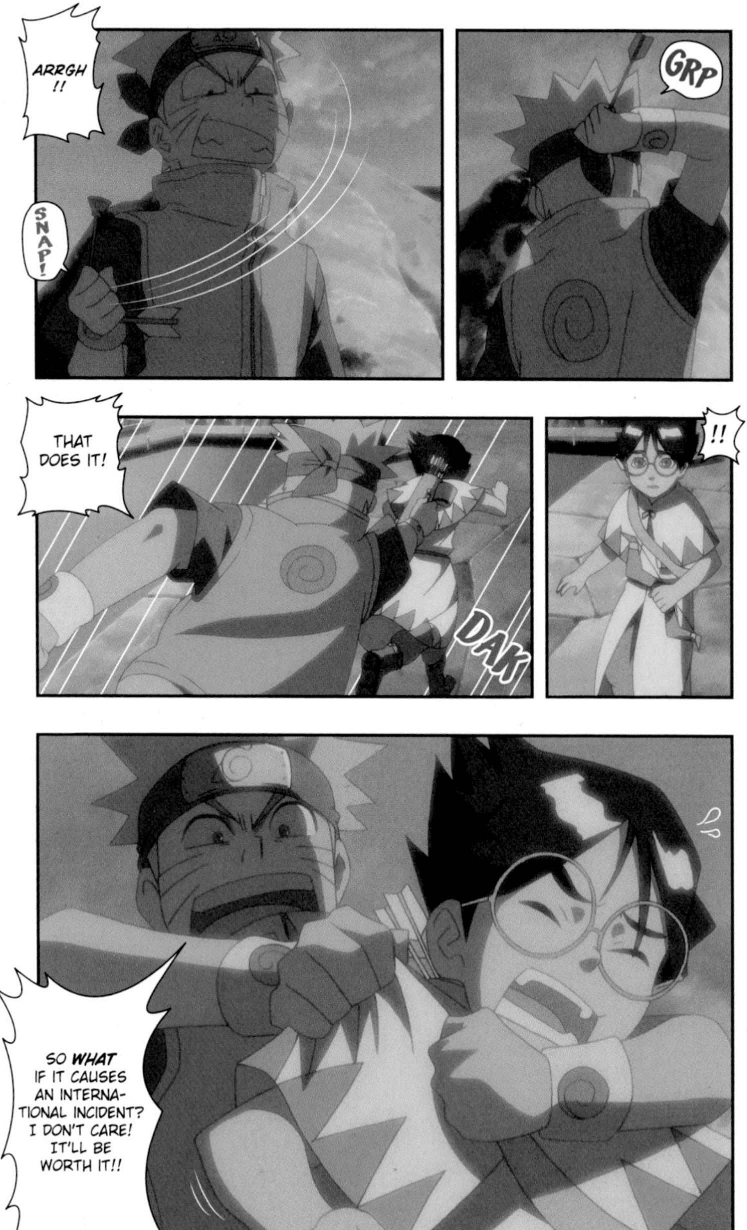
GRP
ARRGH !!
SNAP!
!!
THAT DOES IT!
DAK
SO WHAT IF IT CAUSES AN INTERNATIONAL INCIDENT? I DON'T CARE! IT'LL BE WORTH IT!!

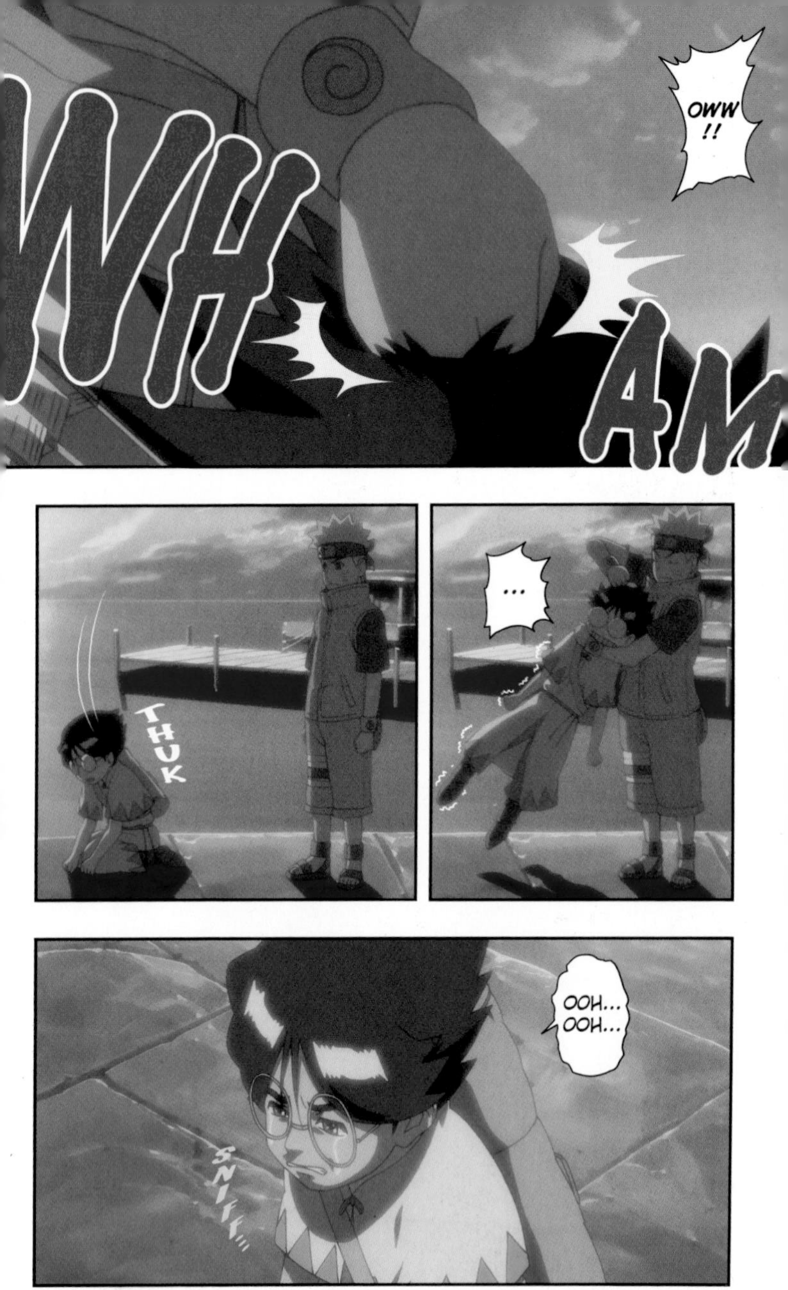
OWW !!
WHAM
...
THUK
OOH... OOH...
SNIFF...

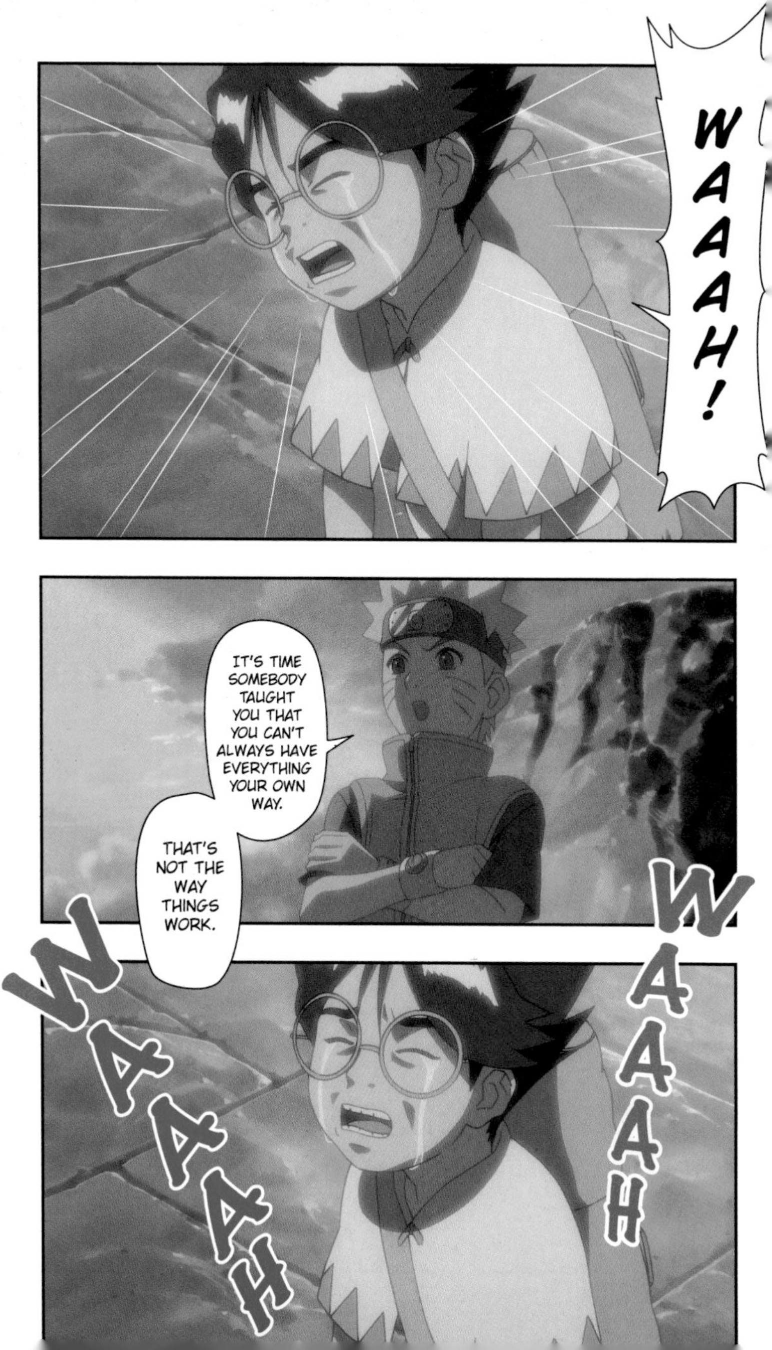
WAAAAH!
IT'S TIME SOMEBODY TAUGHT YOU THAT YOU CAN'T ALWAYS HAVE EVERYTHING YOUR OWN WAY.
THAT'S NOT THE WAY THINGS WORK.
WAAAAH
WAAAAH

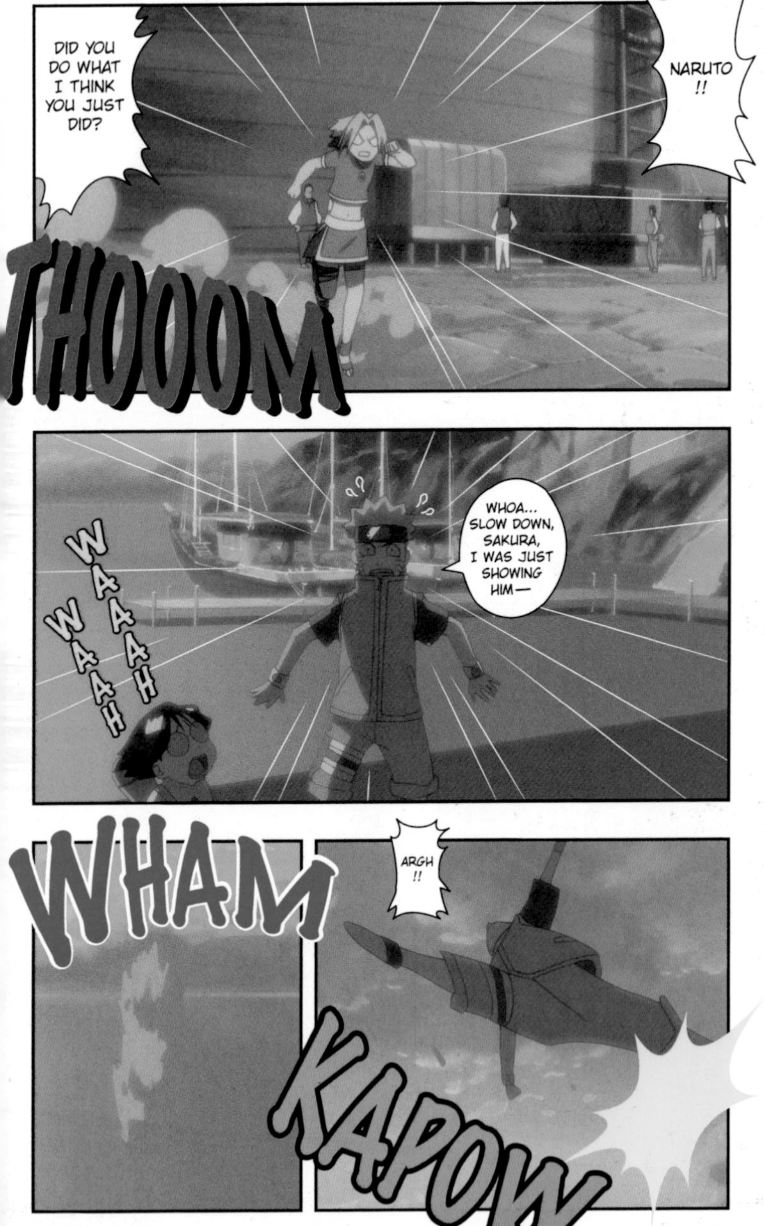
NARUTO !!
DID YOU DO WHAT I THINK YOU JUST DID?
THOOOM
WHOA... SLOW DOWN, SAKURA, I WAS JUST SHOWING HIM—
WAAAAH
WAAAH
ARGH !!
KAPOW
WHAM

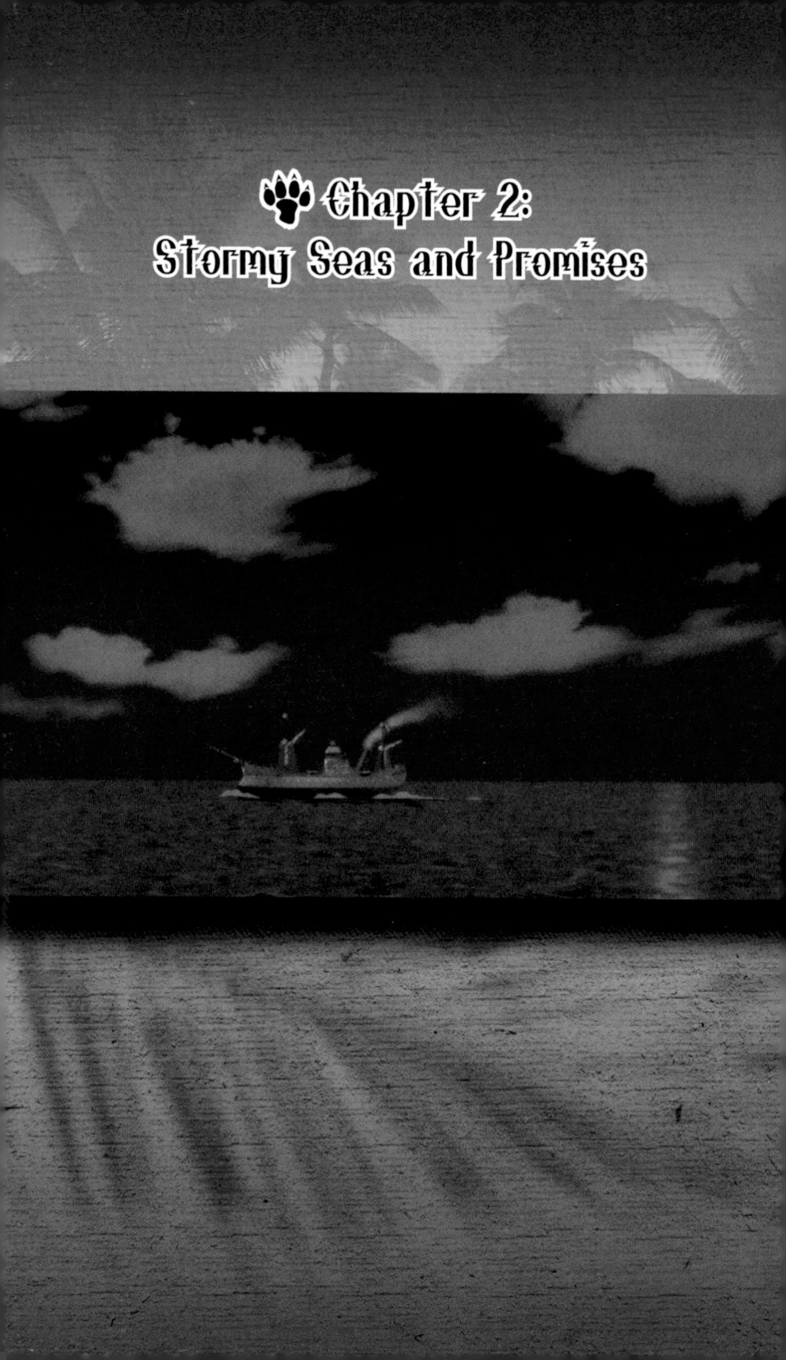
Chapter 2:
Stormy Seas and Promises

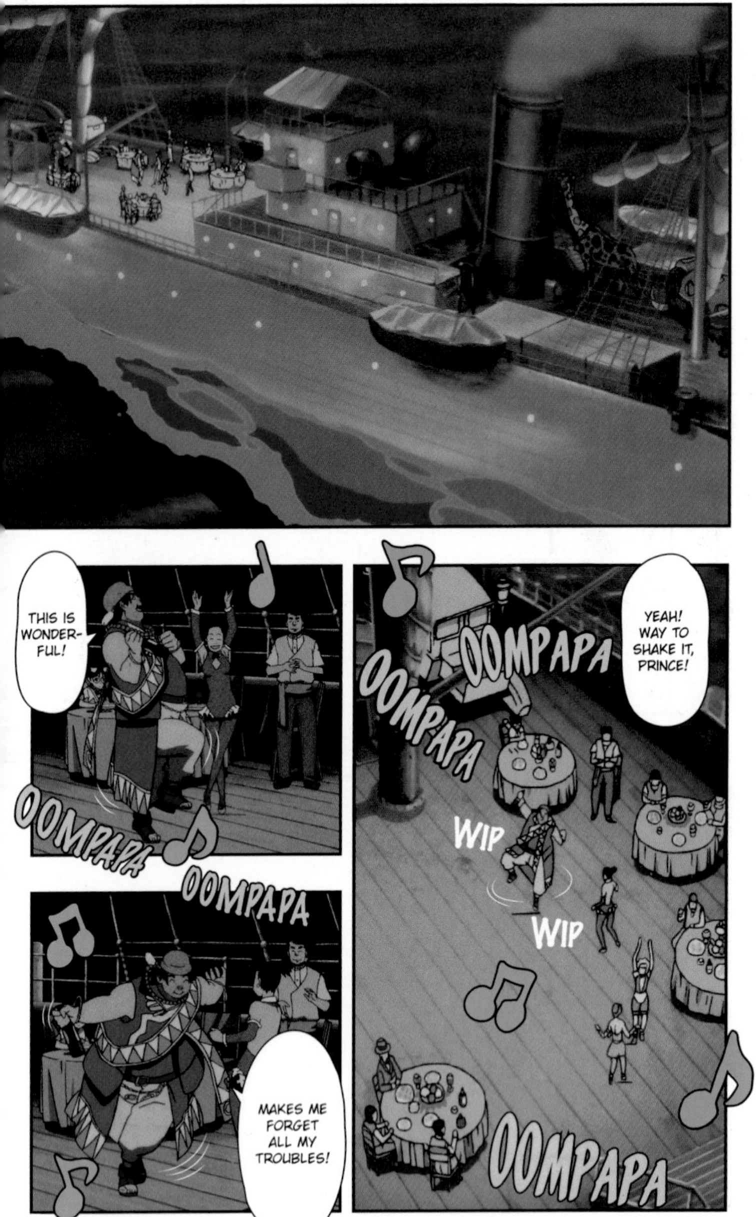
YEAH! WAY TO SHAKE IT, PRINCE!
OOMPAPA
OOMPAPA
WIP
WIP
OOMPAPA
THIS IS WONDER-FUL!
OOMPAPA
OOMPAPA
MAKES ME FORGET ALL MY TROUBLES!

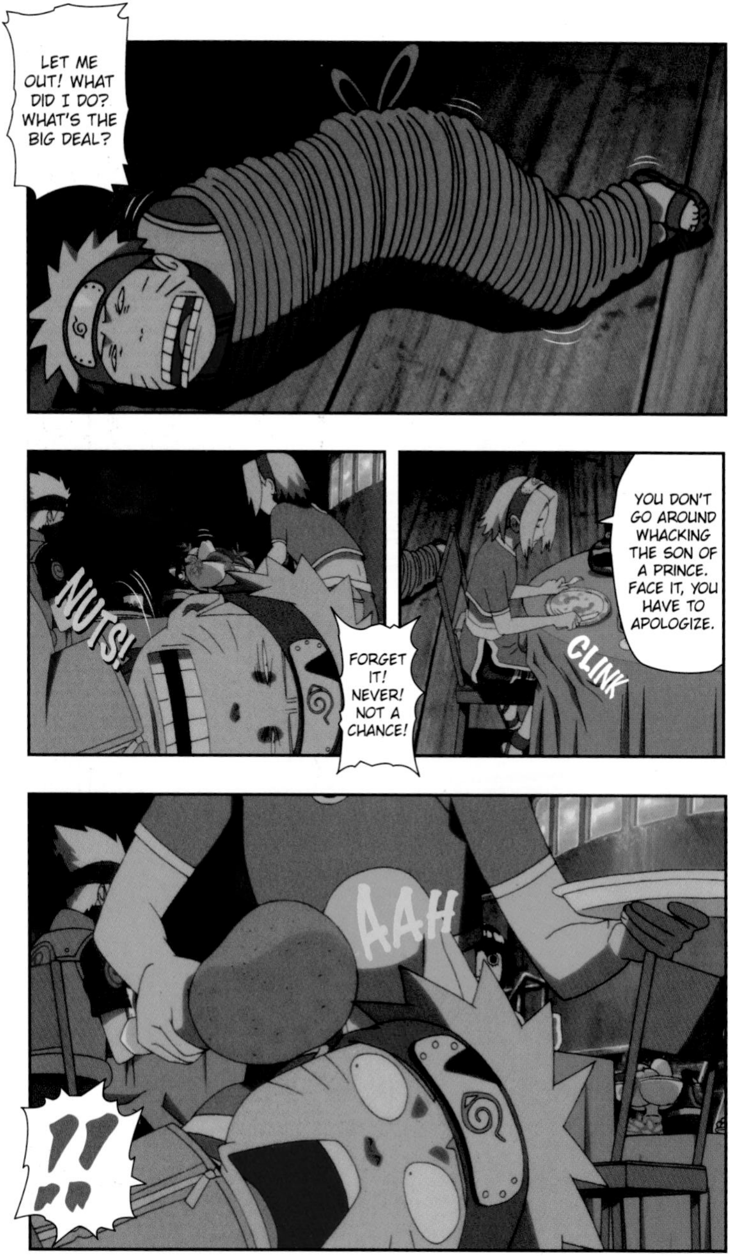
LET ME OUT! WHAT DID I DO? WHAT'S THE BIG DEAL?
YOU DON'T GO AROUND WHACKING THE SON OF A PRINCE. FACE IT, YOU HAVE TO APOLOGIZE.
CLINK
FORGET IT! NEVER! NOT A CHANCE!
NUTS!
AAH
!!

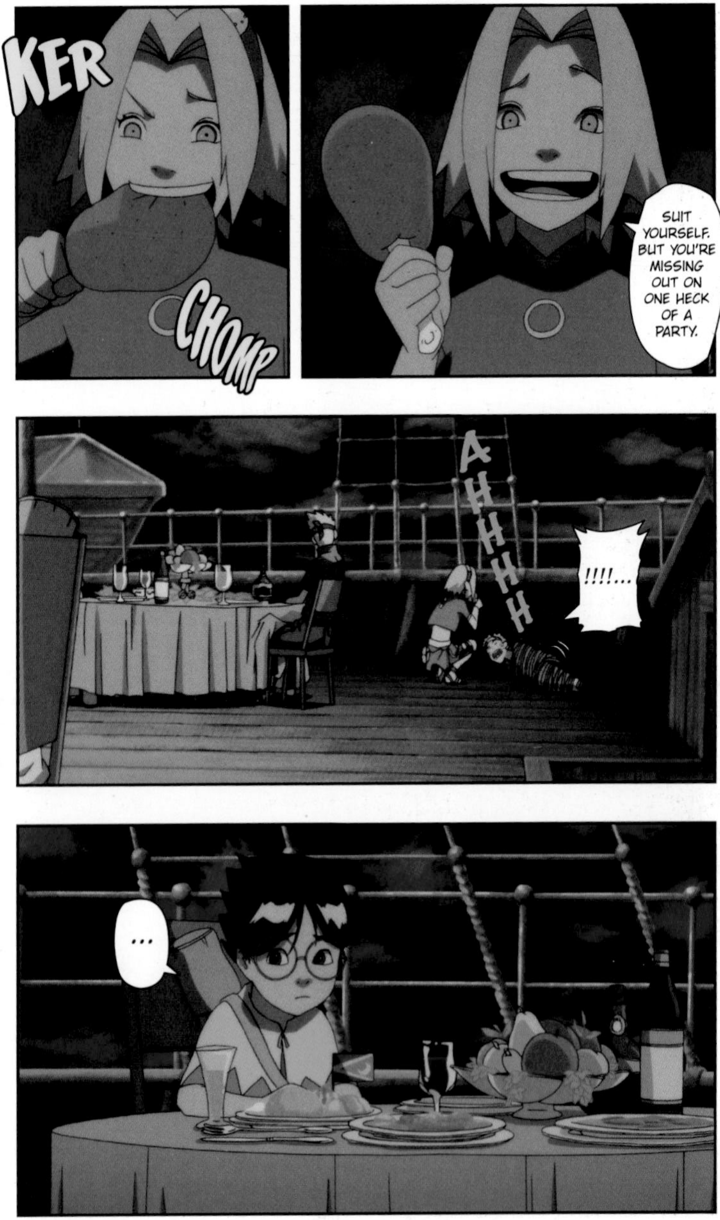
SUIT YOURSELF. BUT YOU'RE MISSING OUT ON ONE HECK OF A PARTY.
KER
CHOMP
!!!!...
AHHHH
...

WUB
WSHT
?
...
KI
KI

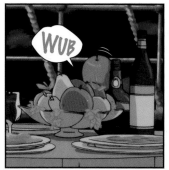

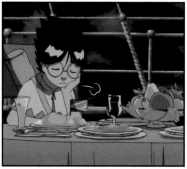

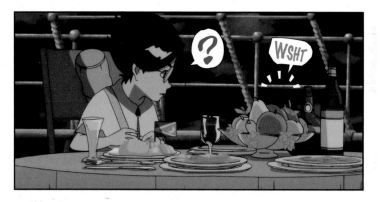

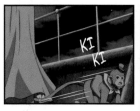

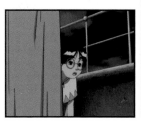

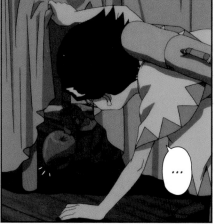

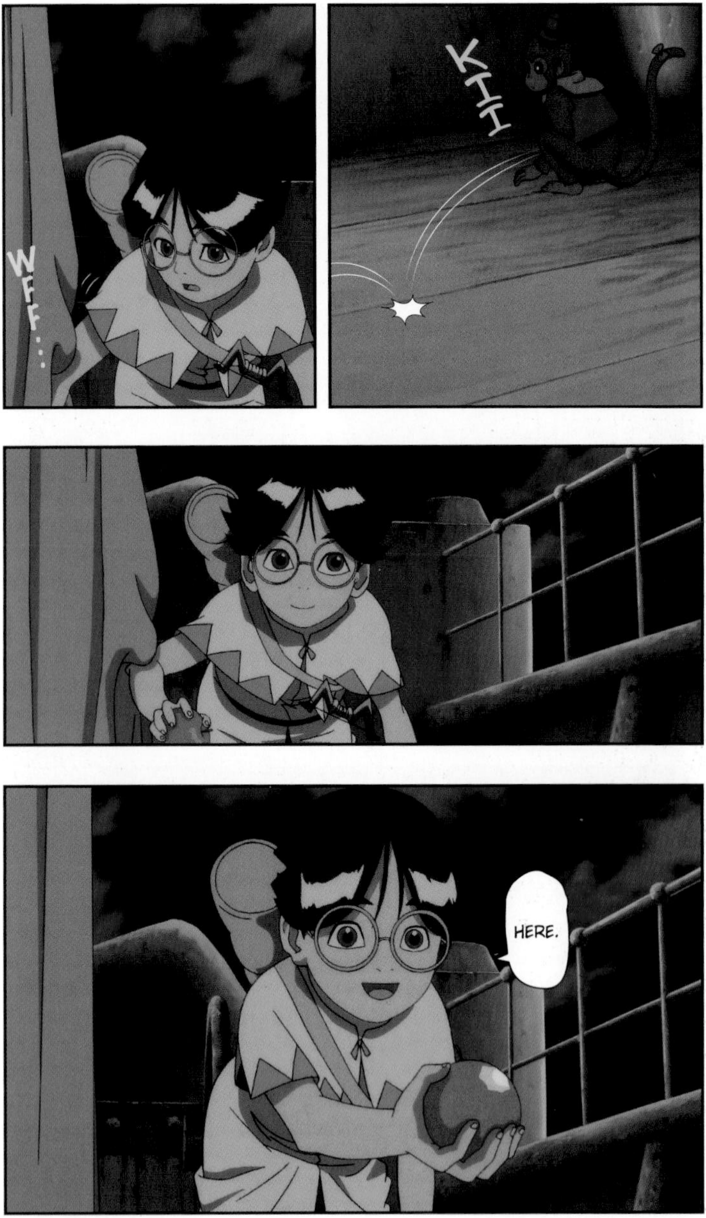
KIII
WFF...
HERE.

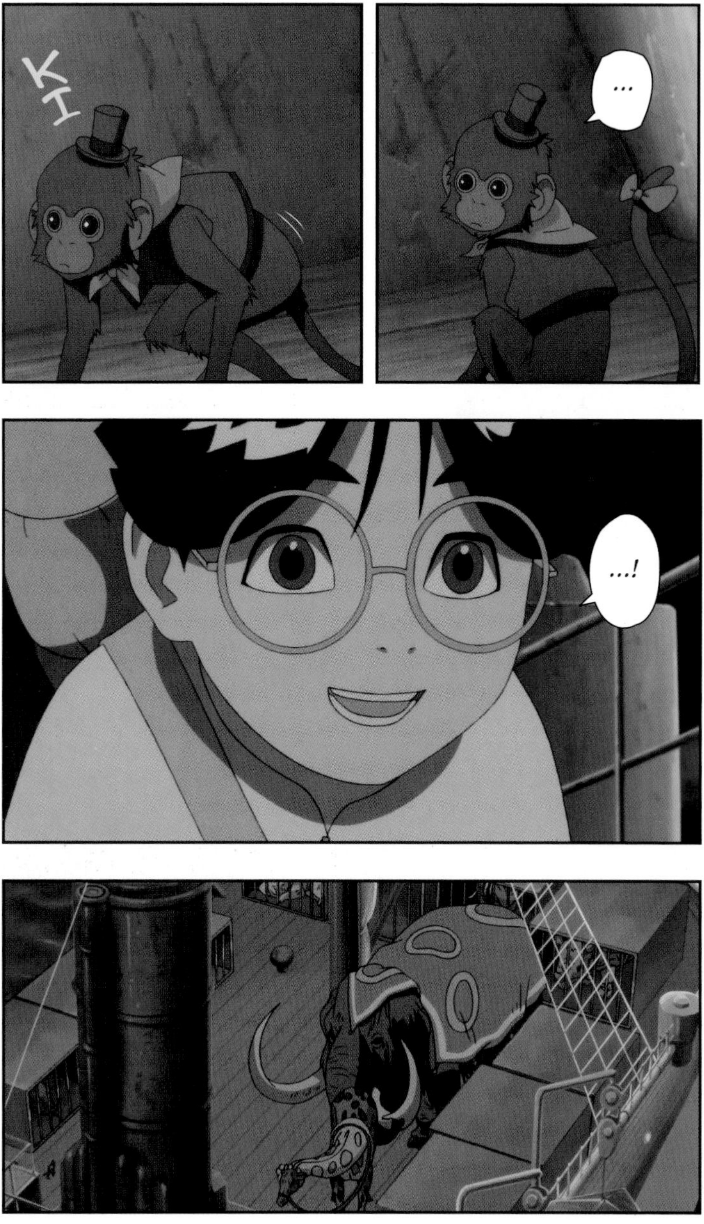
...
KI
...!

KI
GRRRR...

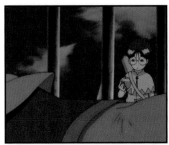

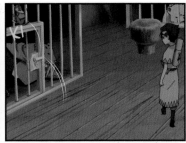

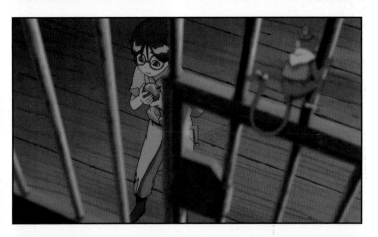

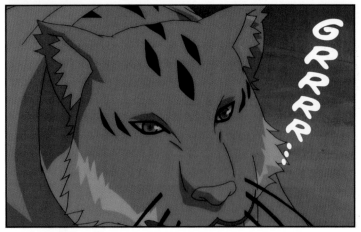

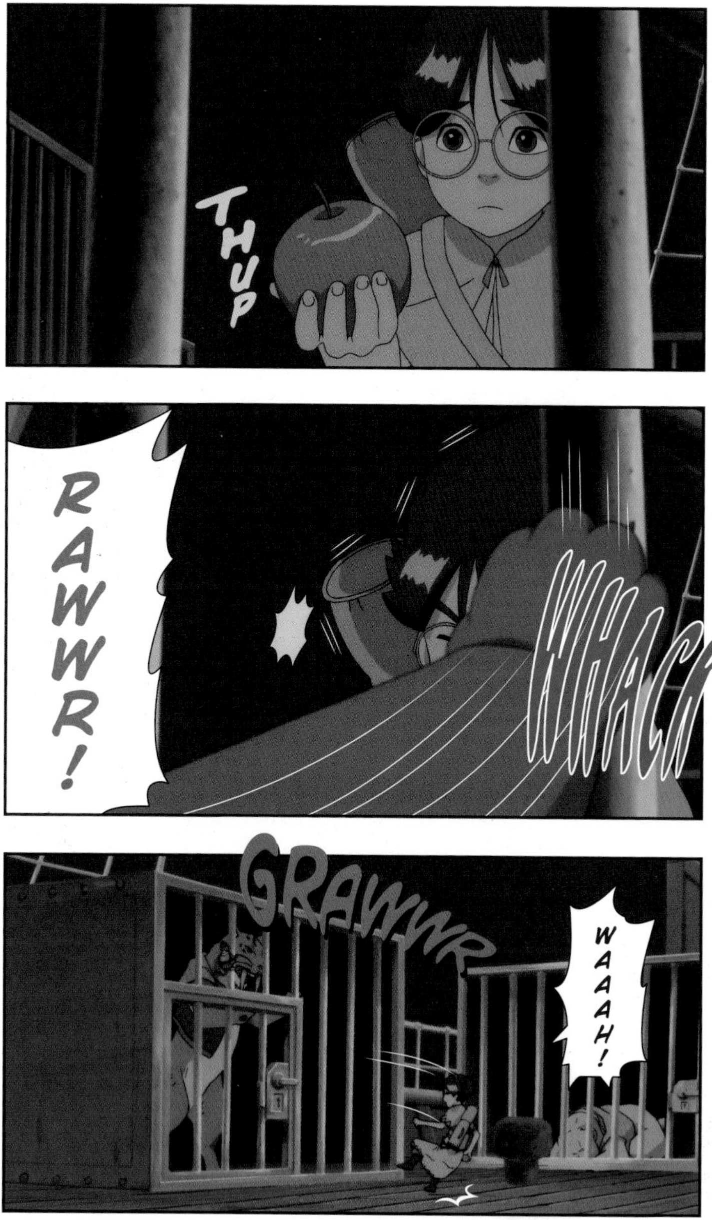
THUP
WHACK
RAWWR!
GRAWWR
WAAAAH!

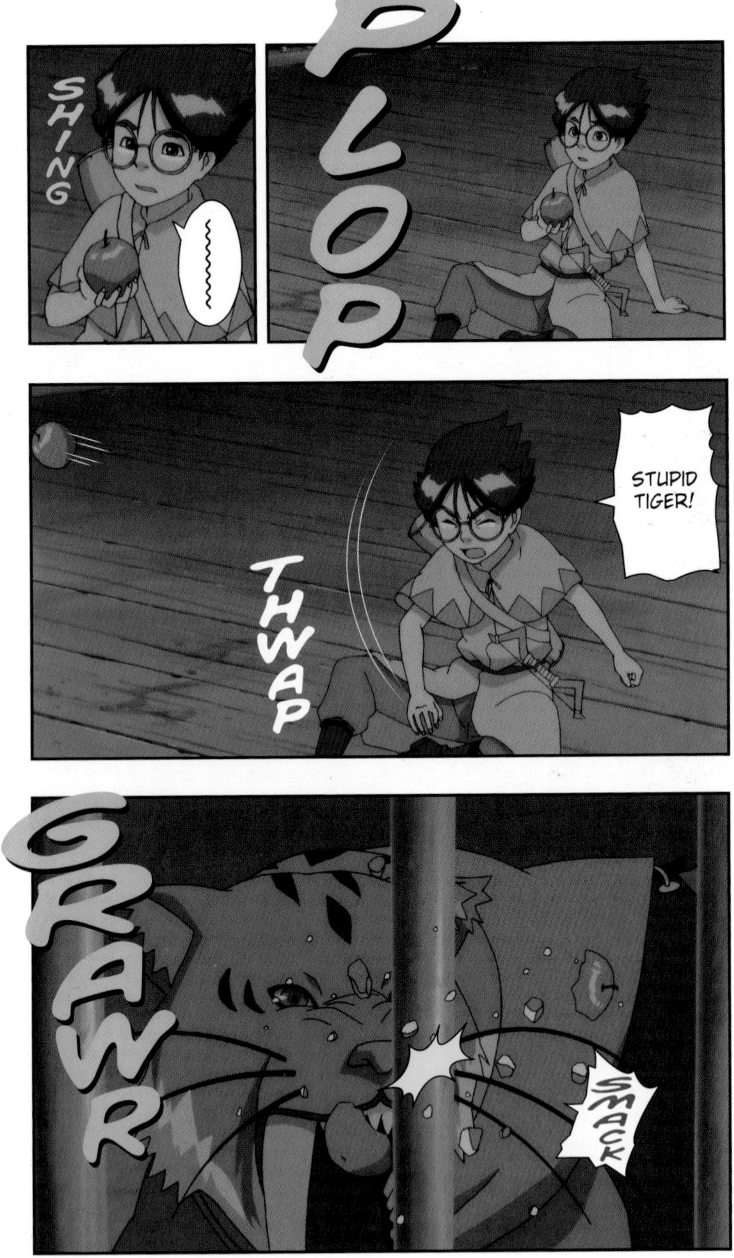
PLOP
SHING
STUPID TIGER!
THWAP
GRAWR
SMACK

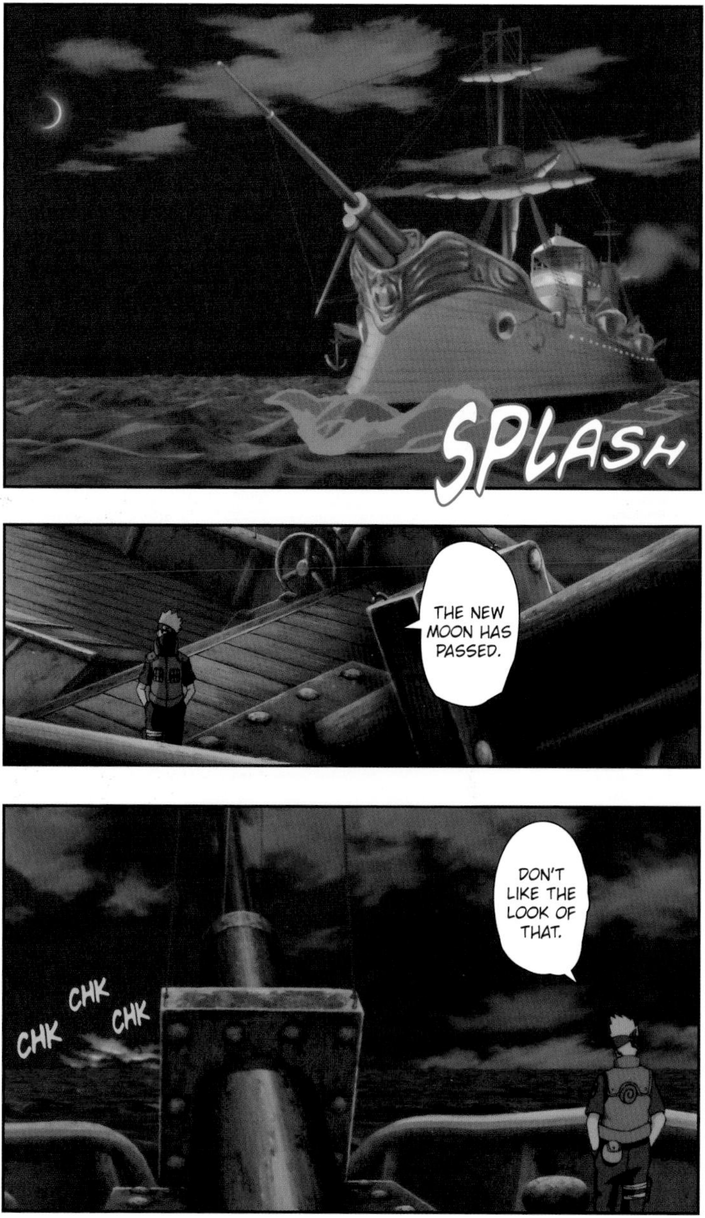
SPLASH
THE NEW MOON HAS PASSED.
DON'T LIKE THE LOOK OF THAT.
CHK
CHK
CHK

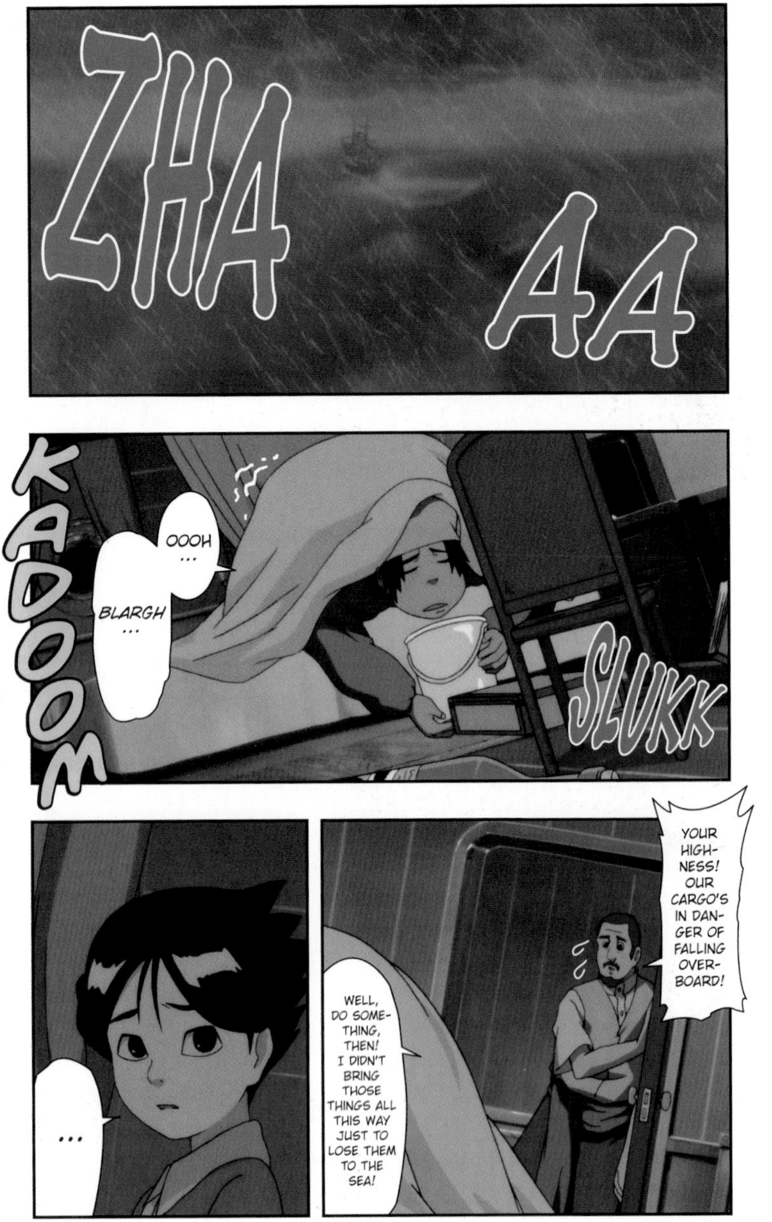
ZHA AA
SLUKK
OOOH...
BLARGH...
KADOOOM
YOUR HIGHNESS! OUR CARGO'S IN DANGER OF FALLING OVERBOARD!
WELL, DO SOMETHING, THEN! I DIDN'T BRING THOSE THINGS ALL THIS WAY JUST TO LOSE THEM TO THE SEA!
...

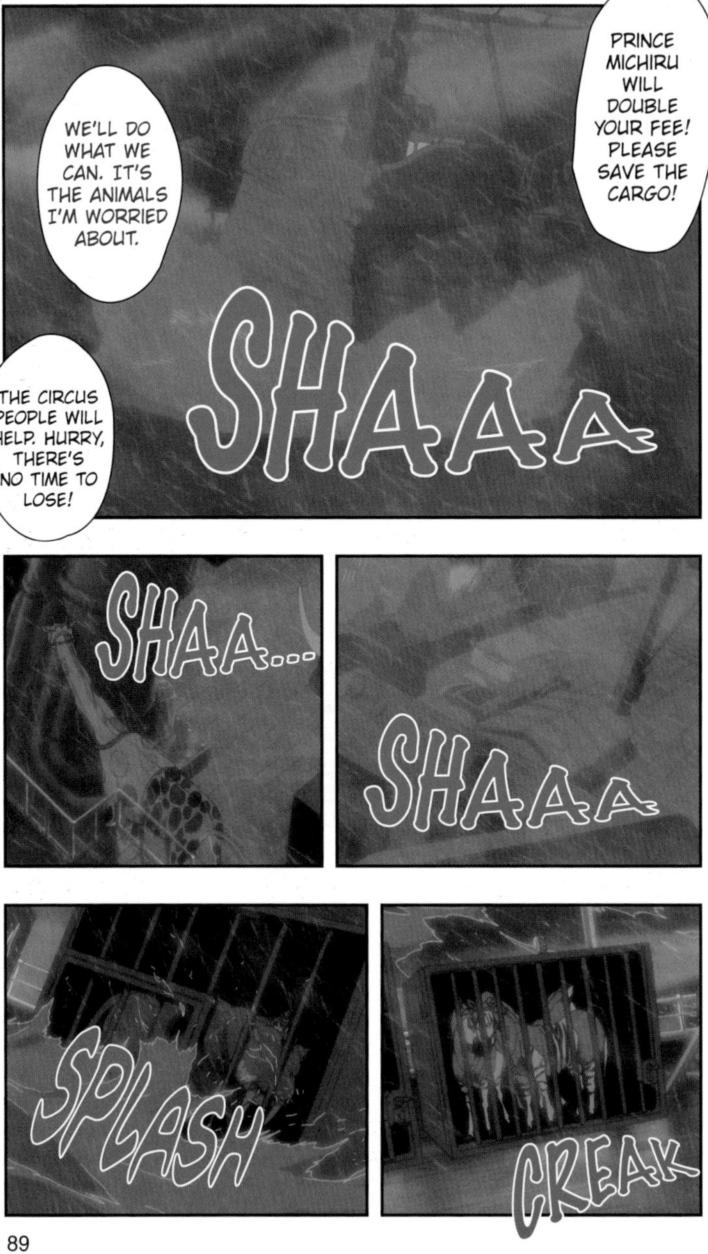
PRINCE MICHIRU WILL DOUBLE YOUR FEE! PLEASE SAVE THE CARGO!
WE'LL DO WHAT WE CAN. IT'S THE ANIMALS I'M WORRIED ABOUT.
THE CIRCUS PEOPLE WILL HELP. HURRY, THERE'S NO TIME TO LOSE!
SHAAAA
SHAAA
SHAA...
CREAK
SPLASH

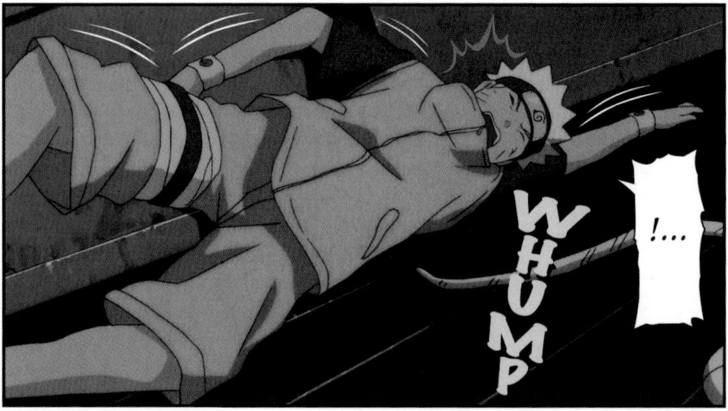
!...
WHUMP

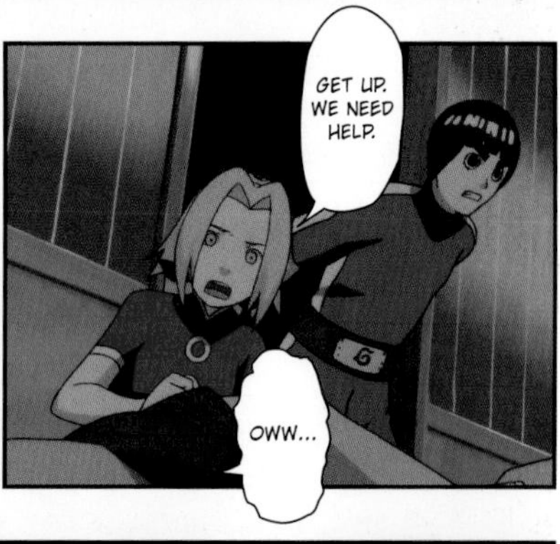
GET UP. WE NEED HELP.
OWW...

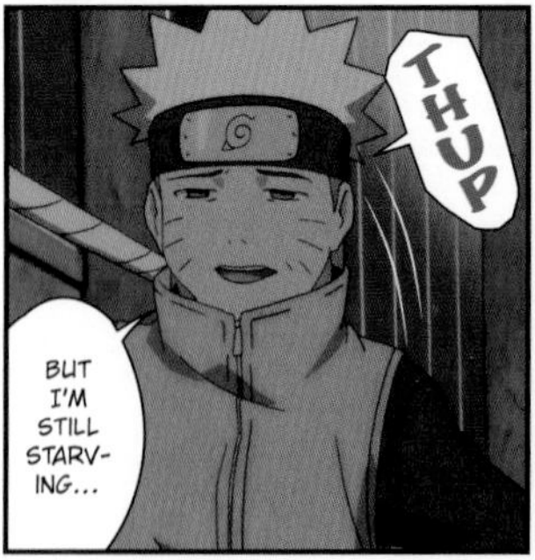
THUP
BUT I'M STILL STARV-ING...

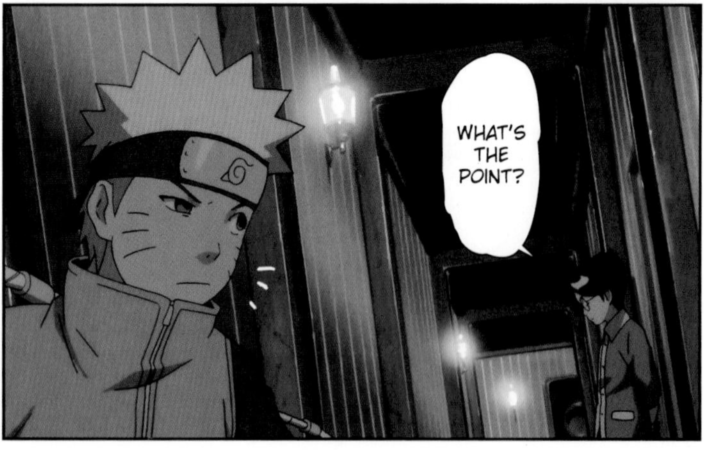
WHAT'S THE POINT?

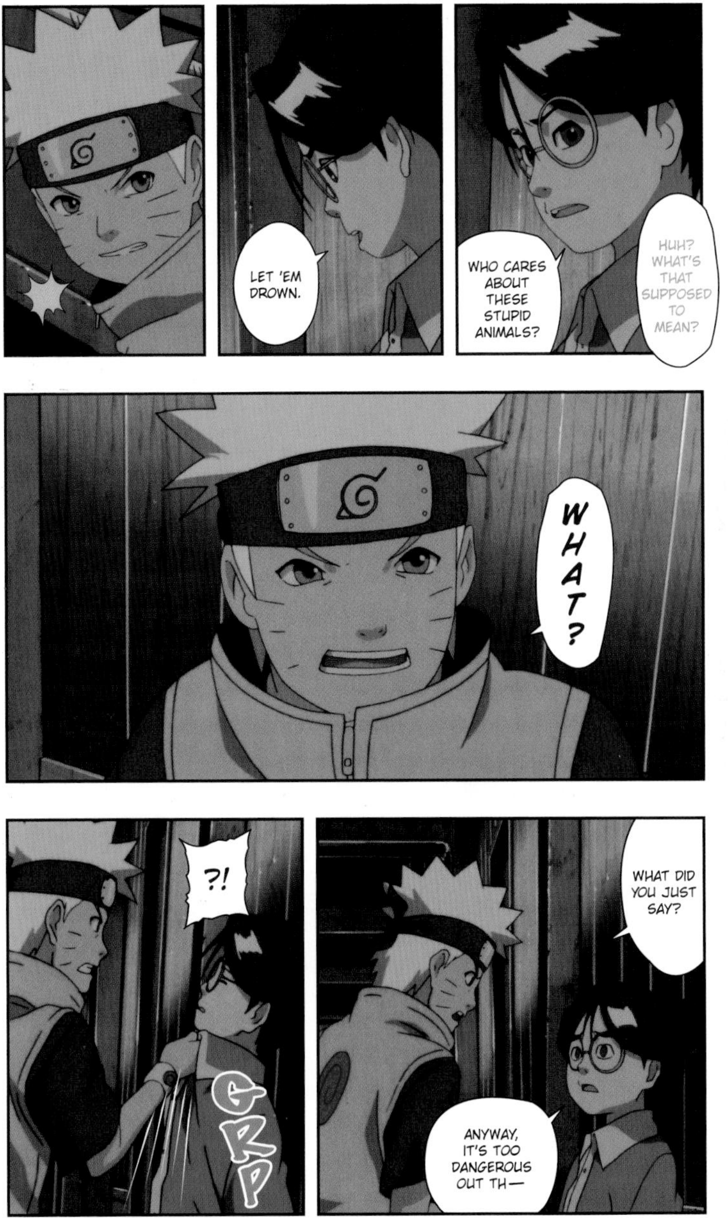
HUH? WHAT'S THAT SUPPOSED TO MEAN?
WHO CARES ABOUT THESE STUPID ANIMALS?
LET 'EM DROWN.
WHAT?
WHAT DID YOU JUST SAY?
ANYWAY, IT'S TOO DANGEROUS OUT TH—
?!
GRP

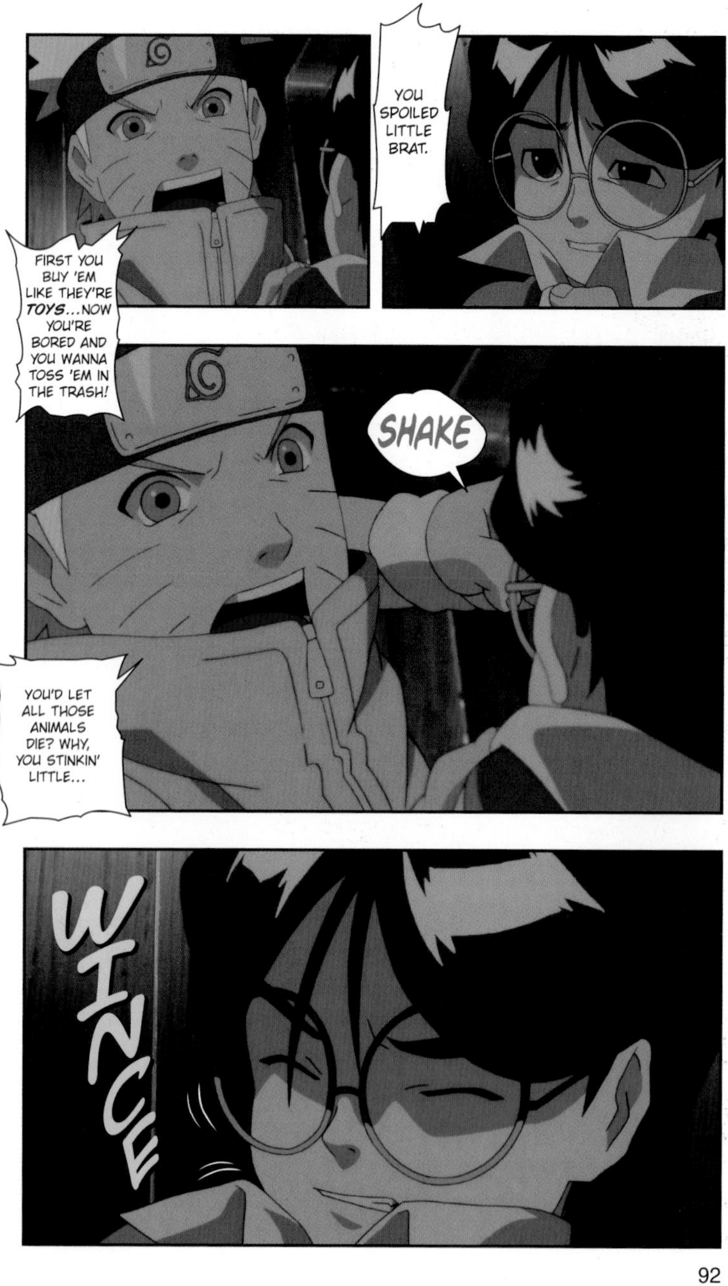
YOU SPOILED LITTLE BRAT.
FIRST YOU BUY 'EM LIKE THEY'RE ***TOYS***...NOW YOU'RE BORED AND YOU WANNA TOSS 'EM IN THE TRASH!
SHAKE
YOU'D LET ALL THOSE ANIMALS DIE? WHY, YOU STINKIN' LITTLE...
WINCE

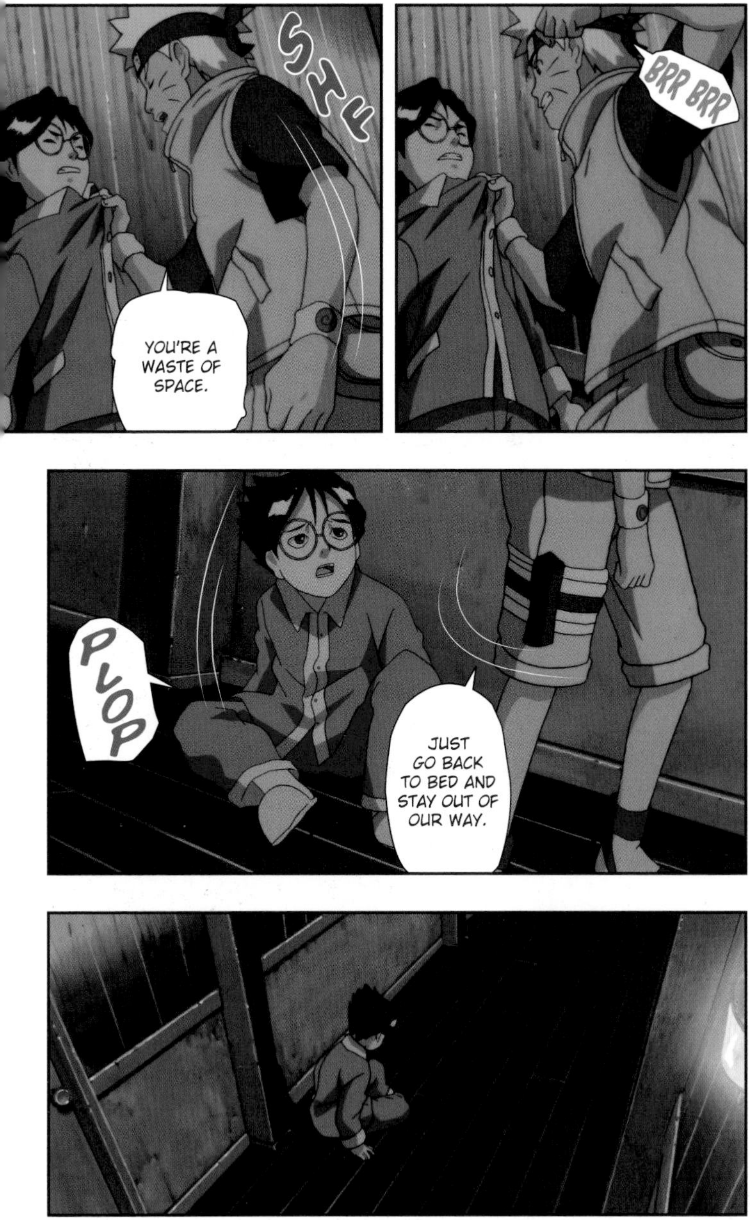
BRR BRR
SHF
YOU'RE A WASTE OF SPACE.
JUST GO BACK TO BED AND STAY OUT OF OUR WAY.
PLOP

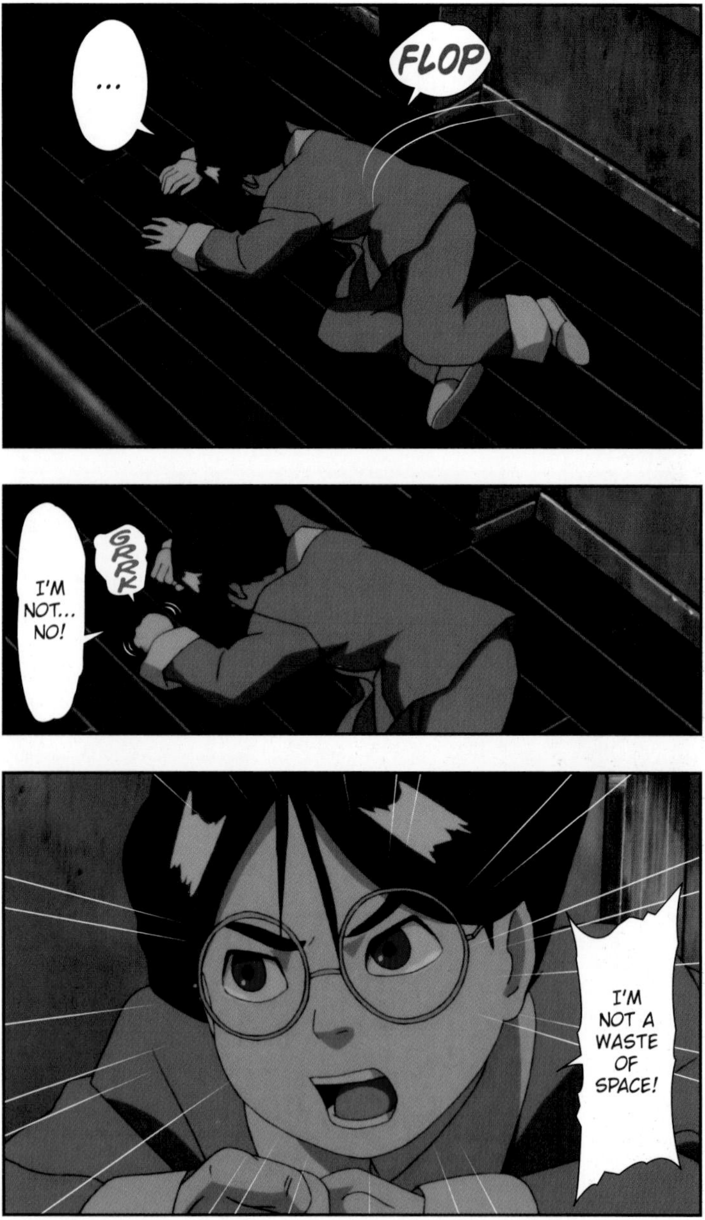
FLOP
...
GRRK
I'M NOT... NO!
I'M NOT A WASTE OF SPACE!

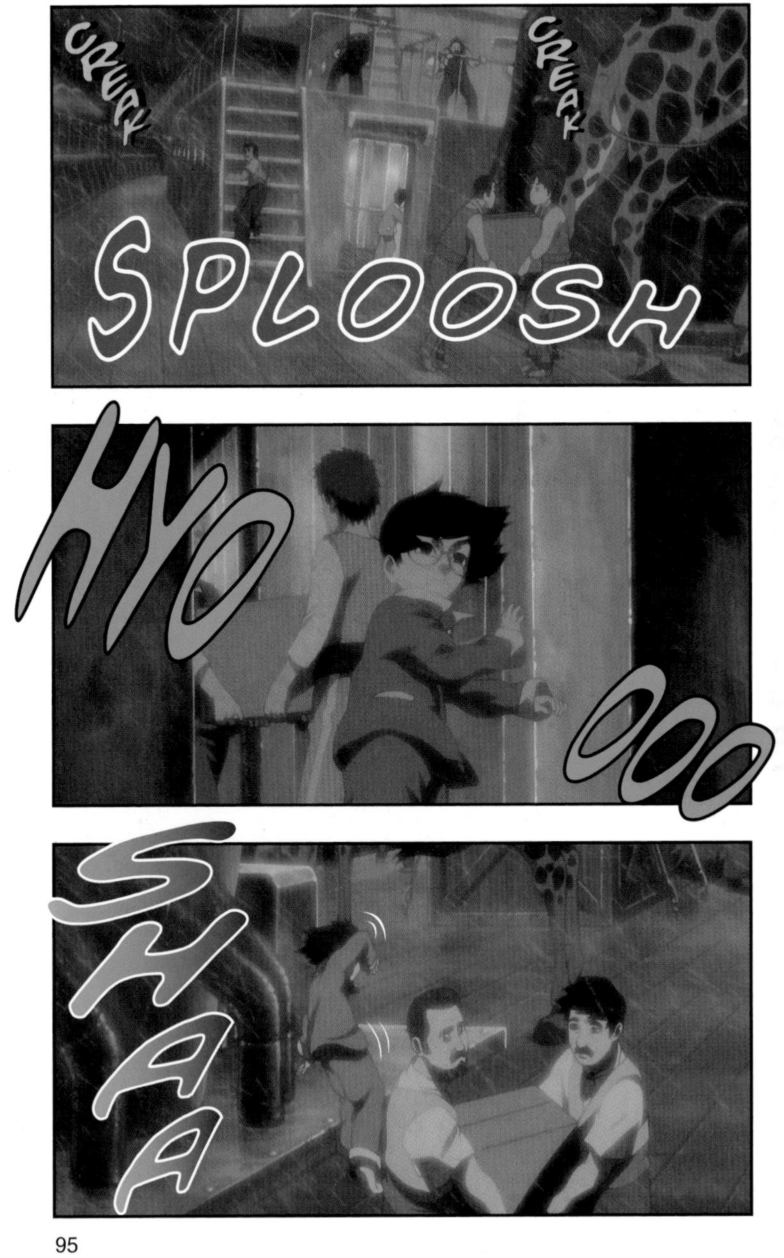
CREAK
CREAK
SPLOOSH
HYO
OOO
SHAA

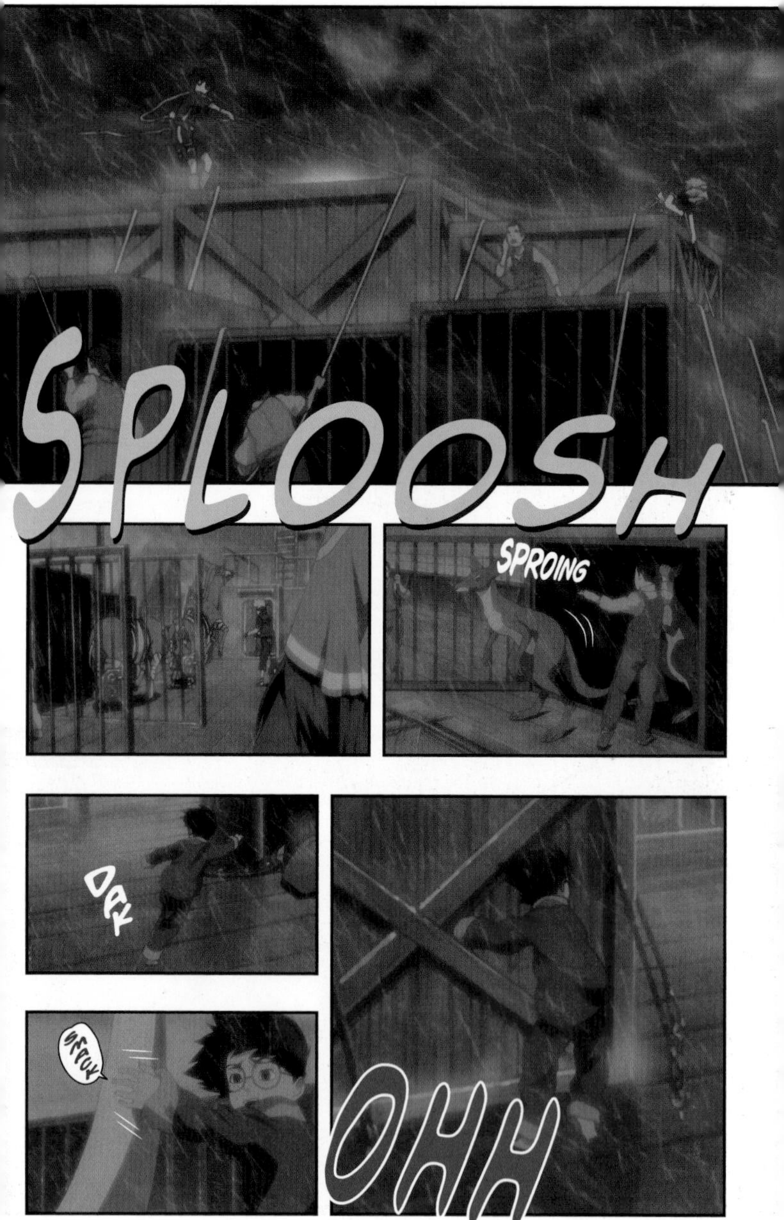
SPLOOSH
SPROING
OHH
DAK
SMACK

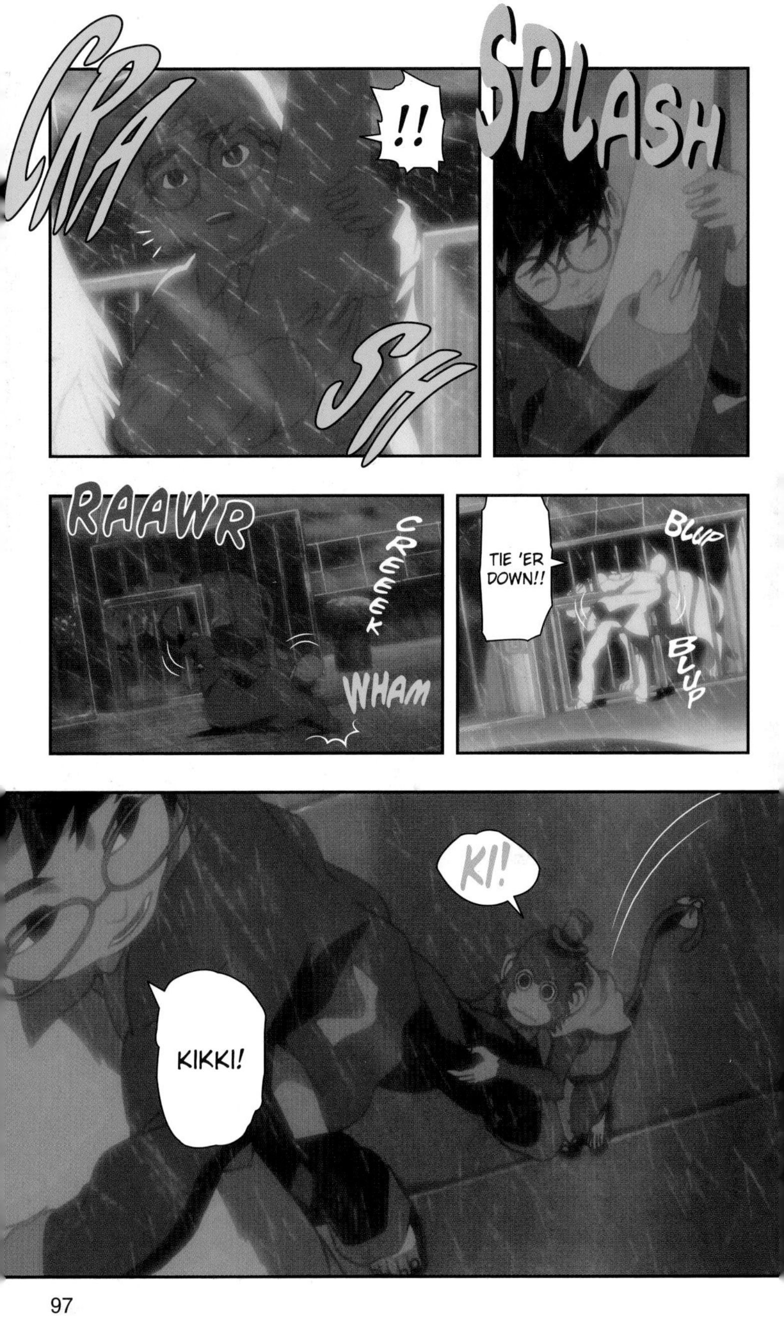
SPLASH
!!
CRA
SH
TIE 'ER DOWN!!
BLUP
BLUP
RAAWR
CREEEK
WHAM
KI!
KIKKI!

SPLO
OSH
SHA
CR
!!
SPLASH
SHAA
IT'S NO USE!

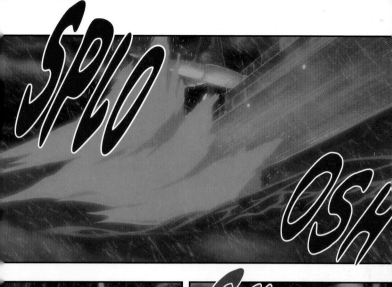

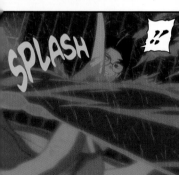

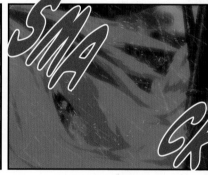

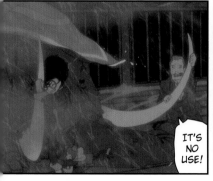

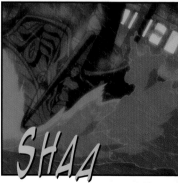

WHAM
WHAM
WHAM
WHAM
GRRR...
BRR BRR
...

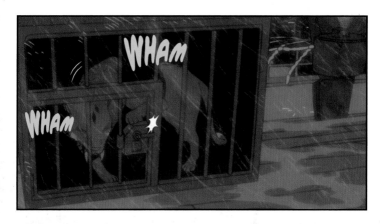

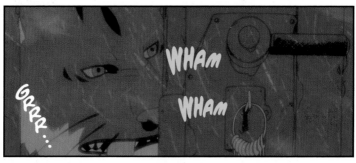

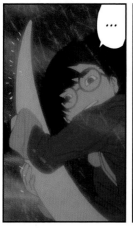

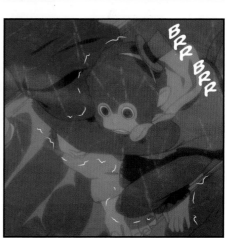

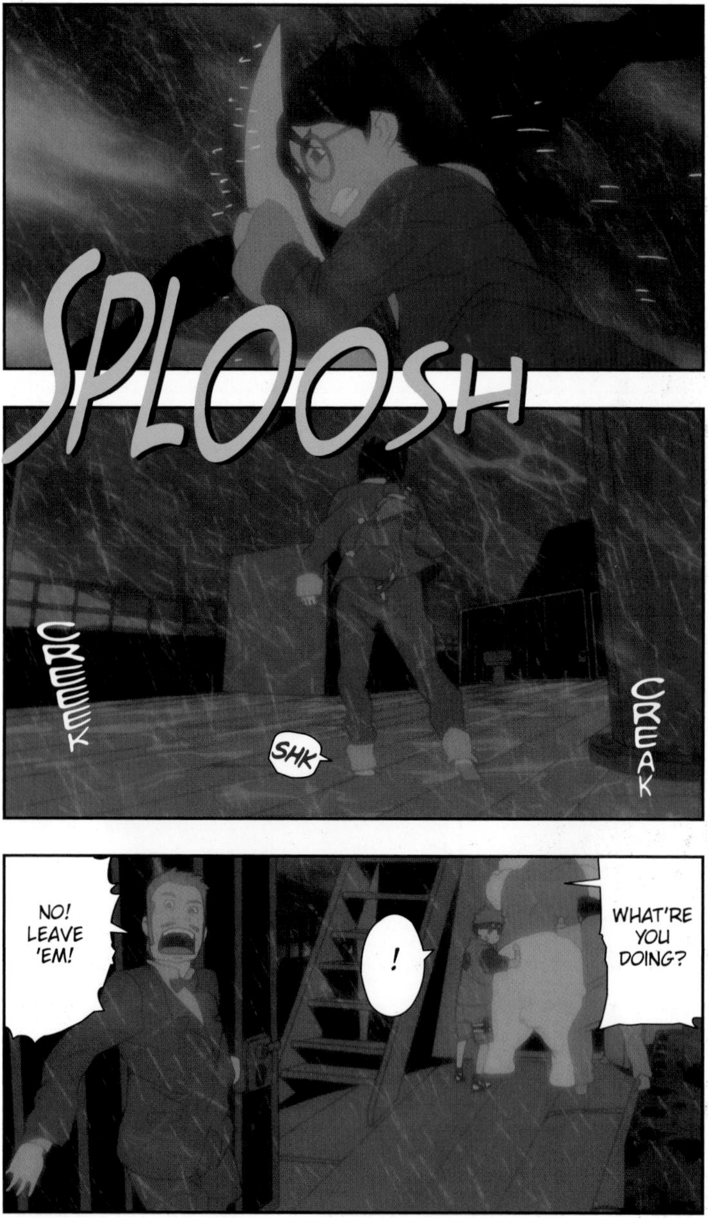
SPLOOSH
CREAK
SHK
CREEEK
WHAT'RE YOU DOING?
!
NO! LEAVE 'EM!

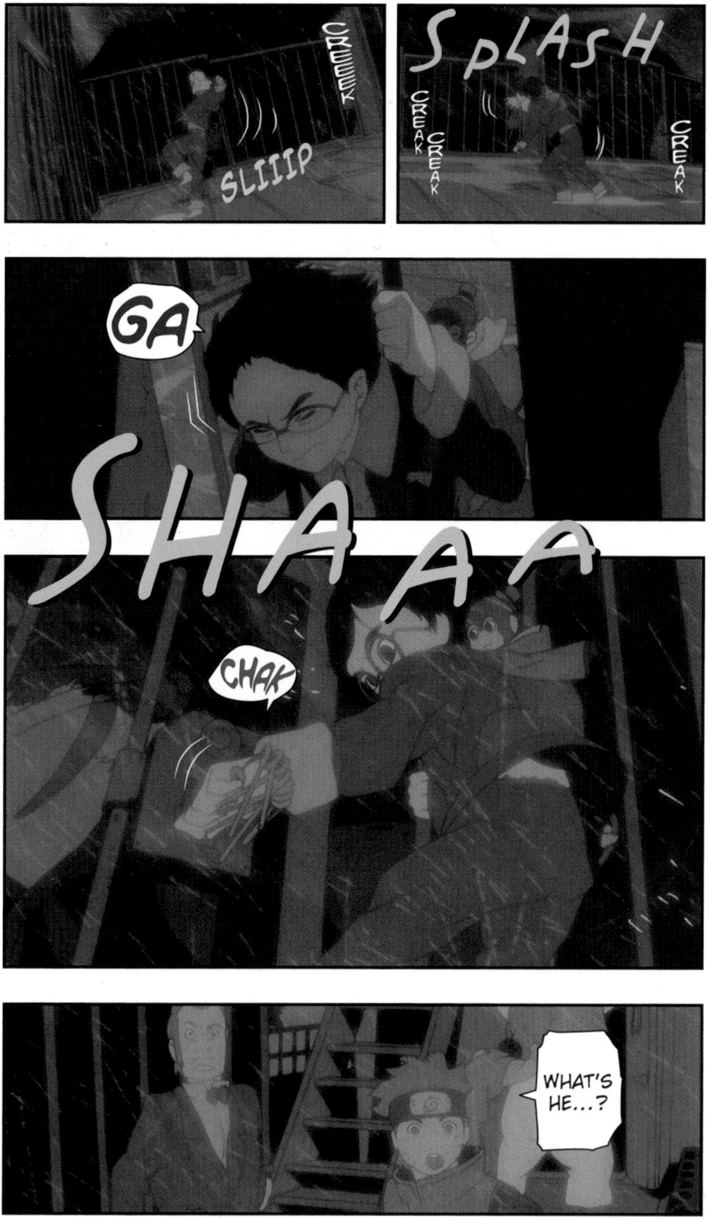
SPLASH
CREAK
CREAK
CREAK
CREEEK
SLIIIP
GA
SHAAAA
CHAK
WHAT'S HE...?

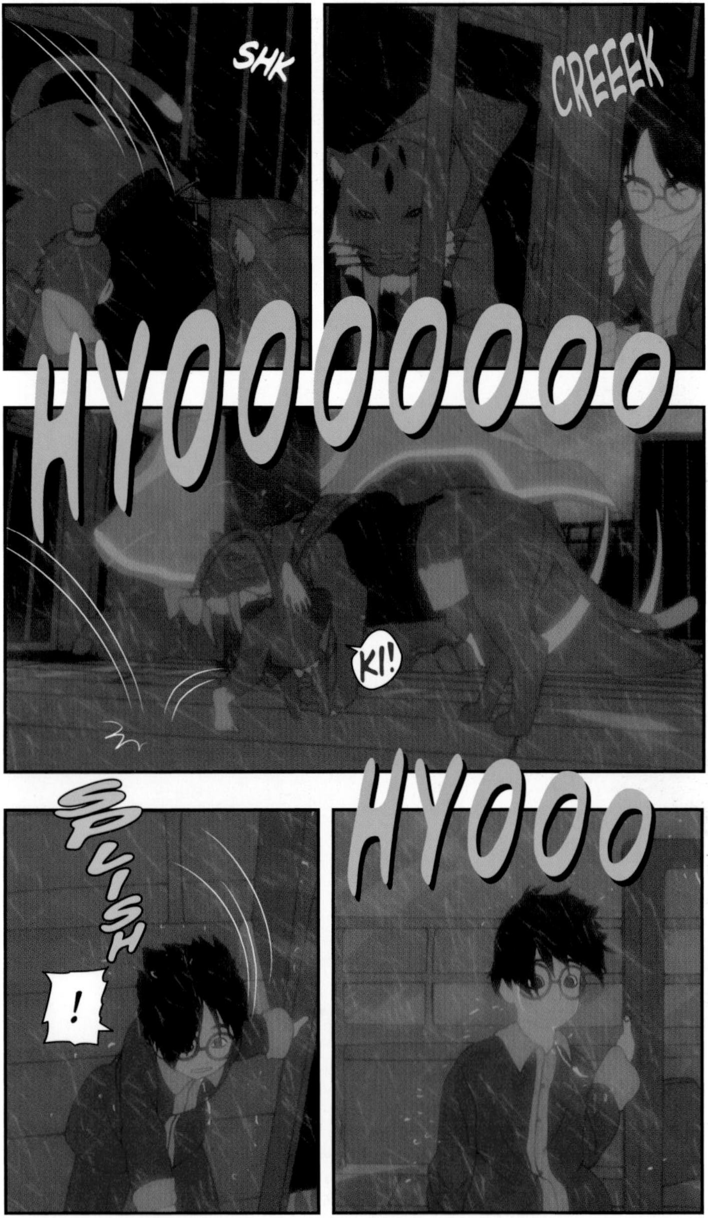
CREEEK
SHK
HYOOOOOOO
KI!
HYOOO
SPLISH
!

SPLO
OSH
FWOOM
!
KIII!
SWUP
KIKKI!
SLOSH
GRP

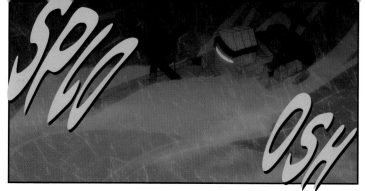

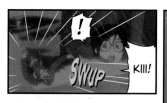

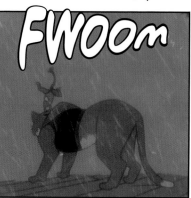

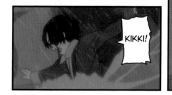

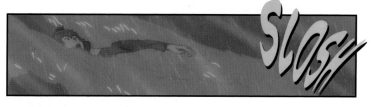

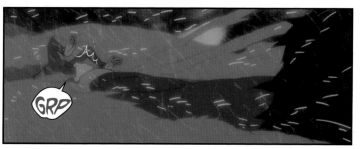

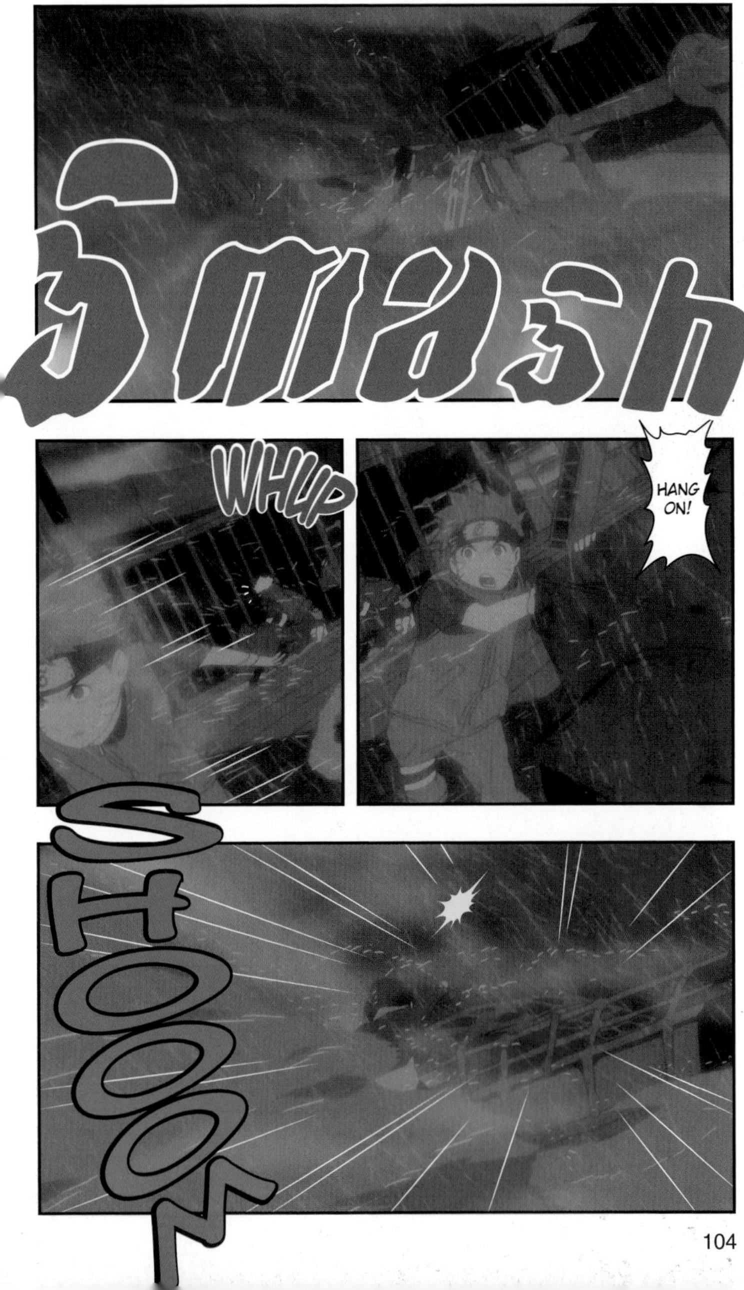
SMASH
HANG ON!
WHUP
SHOOOM

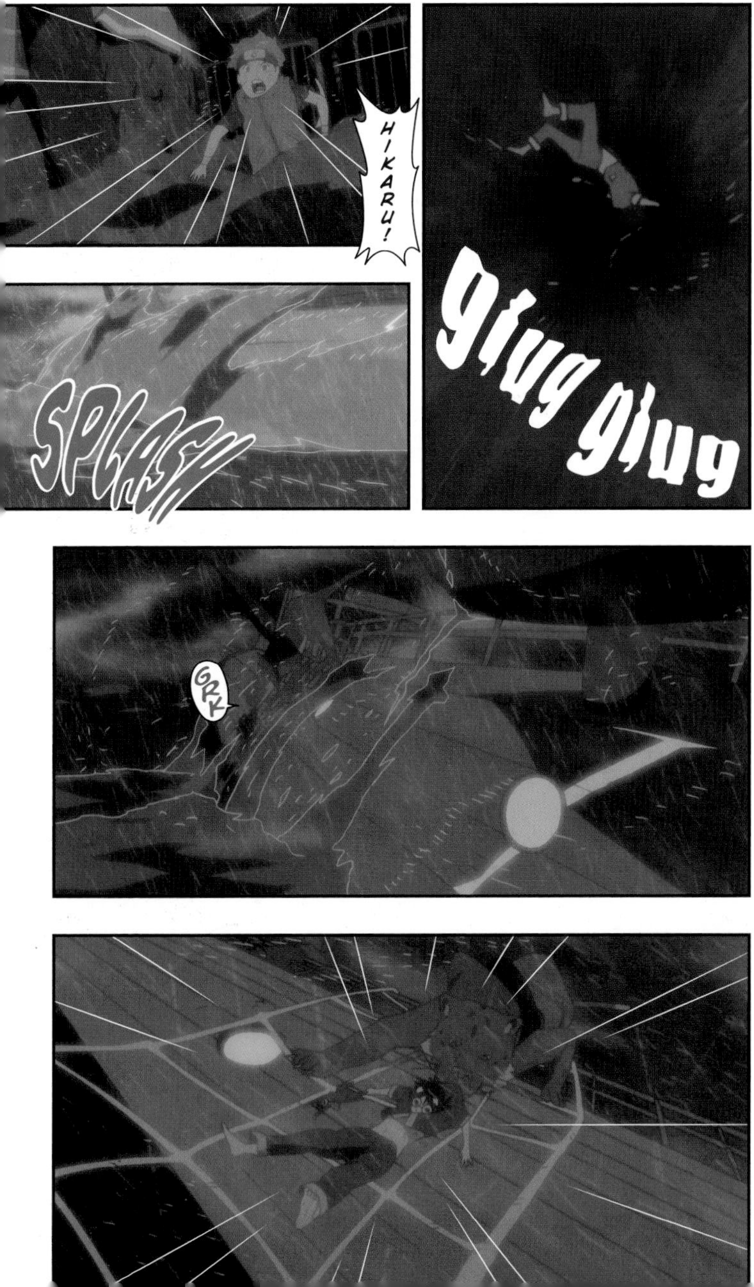
glug glug
HIKARU!
SPLASH
GRK

CREAK
CREAK
GRAB
GRRK
FWOOSH
SPLASH
POP
HIKARU!

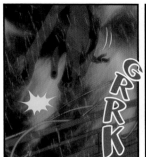

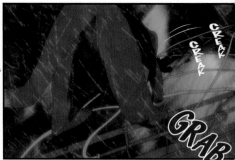

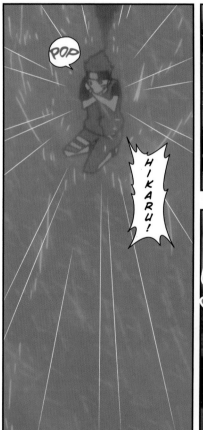

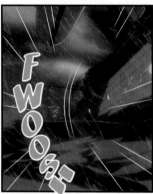

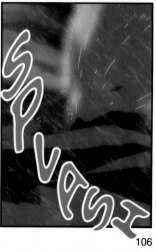

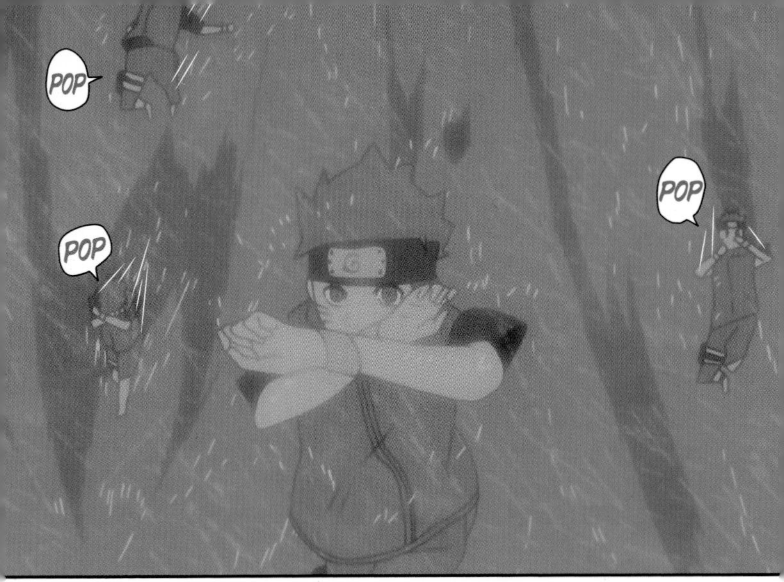
POP
POP
POP

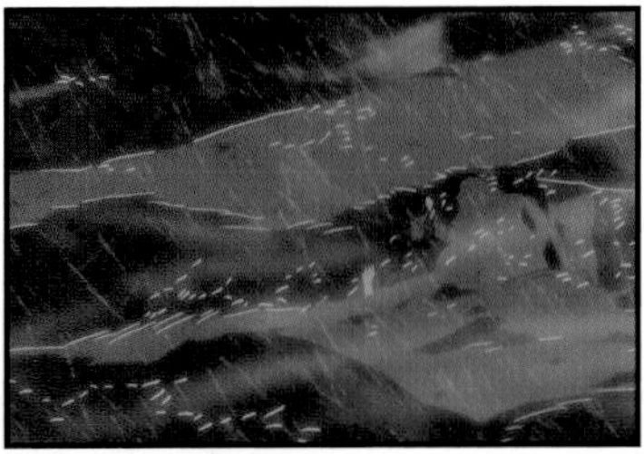

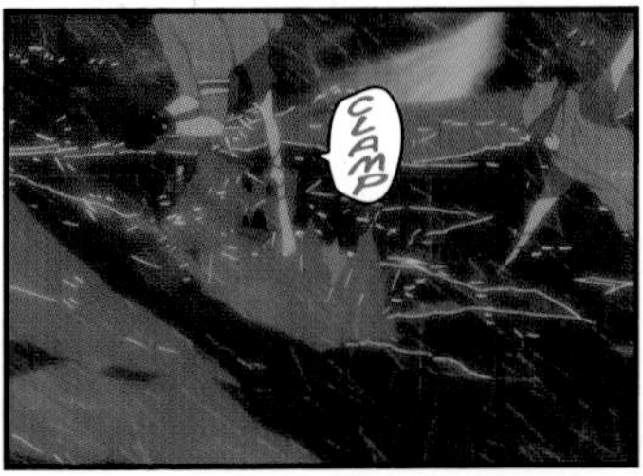
CLAMP

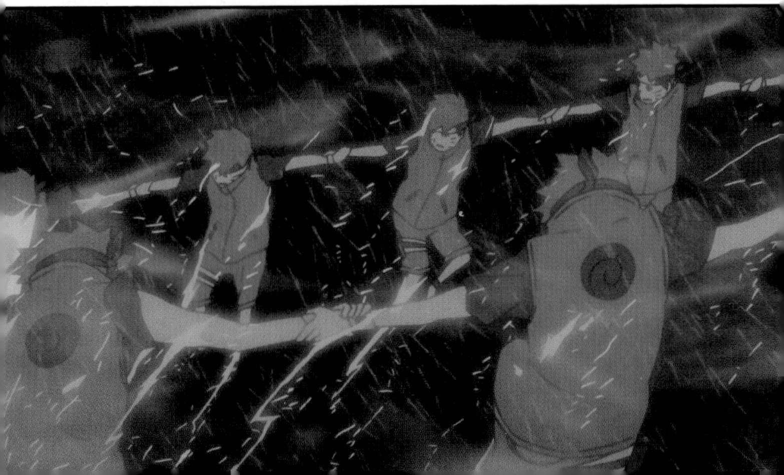

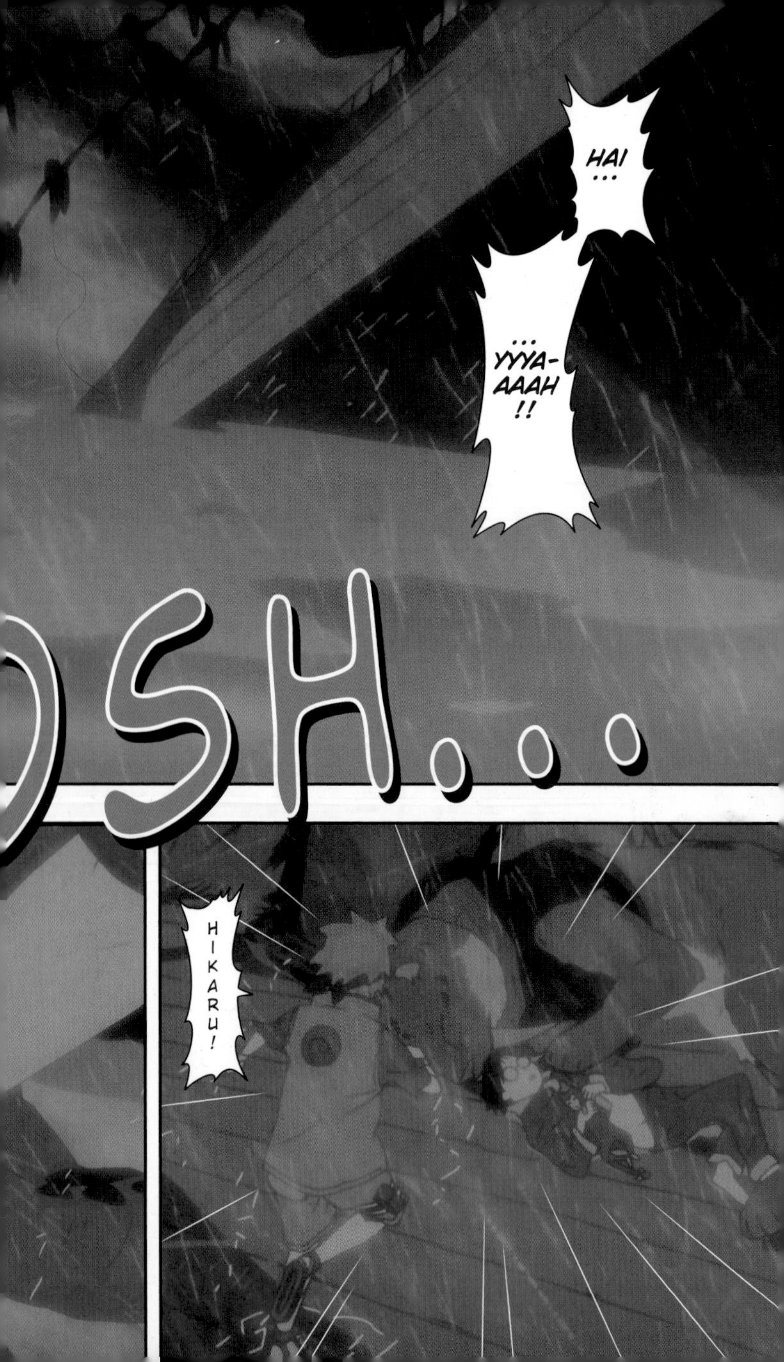
HAI! ...
... YYYA-AAAH!!
OSH...
HIKARU!

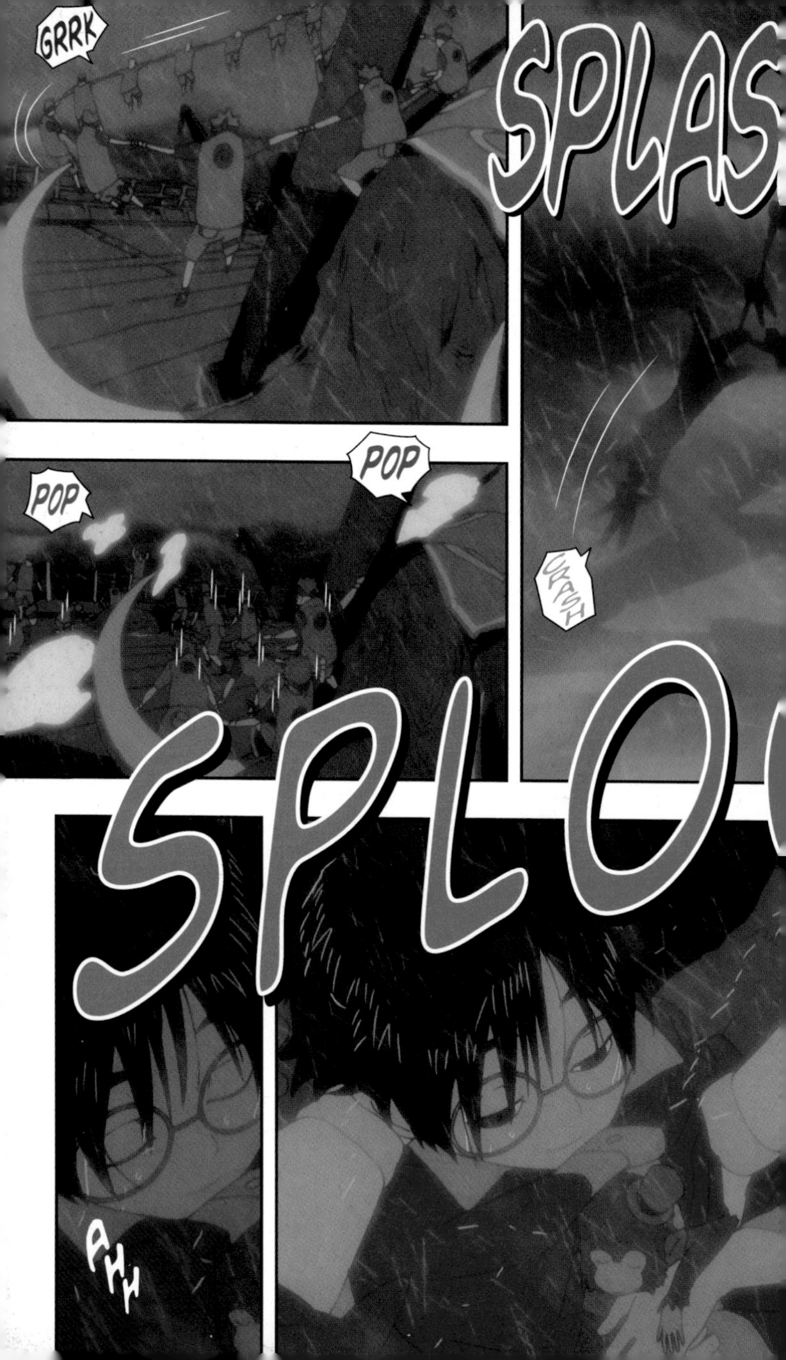
SPLAS
CRASH
GRRK
POP
POP
SPLO
AHH

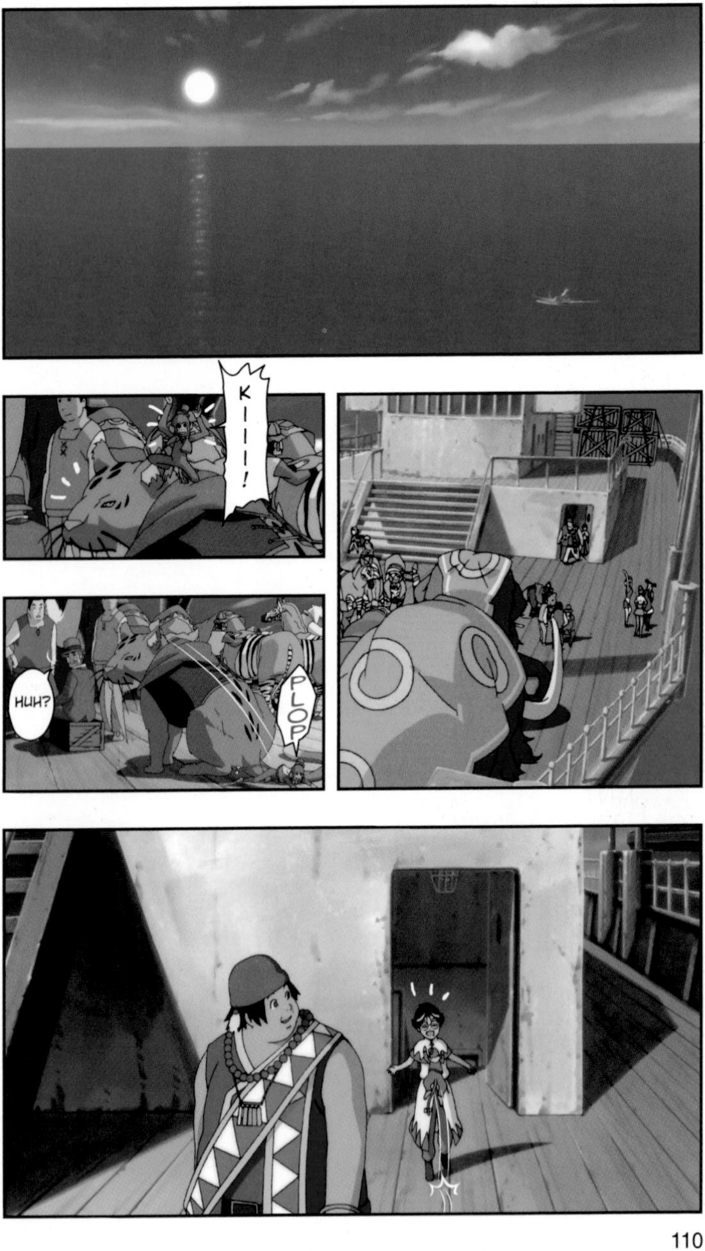
KIII!
PLOP
HUH?

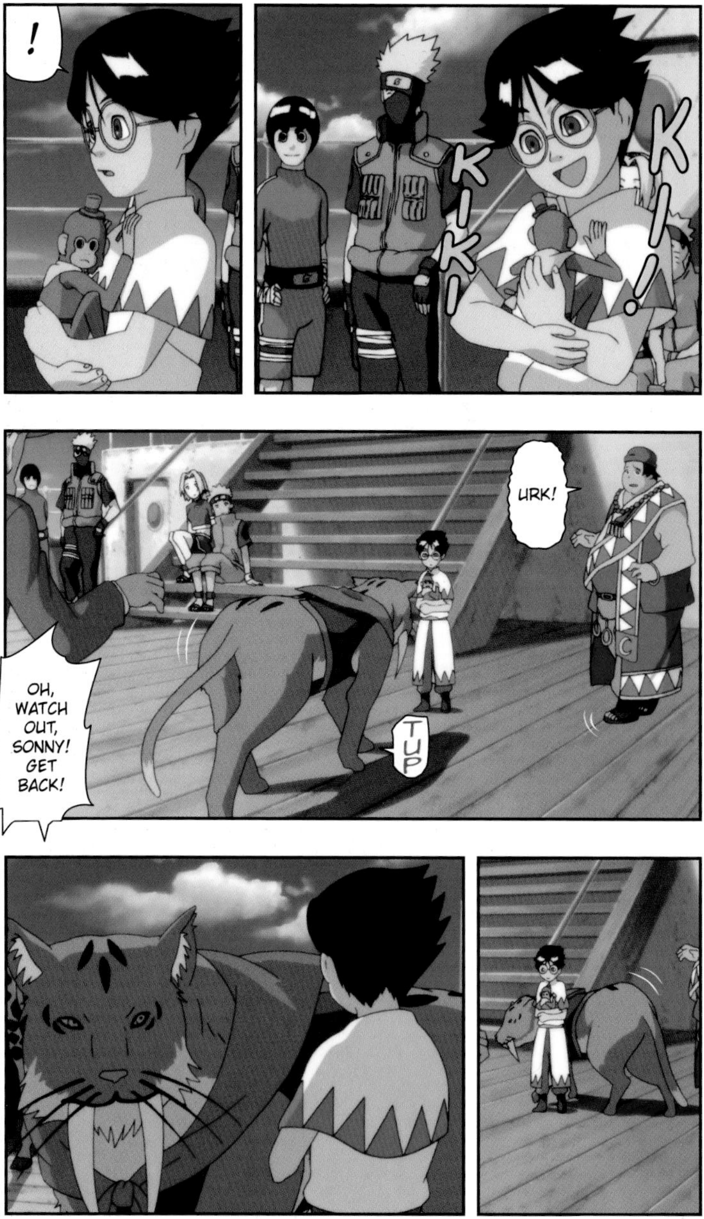
KI-!
KI-
!
URK!
OH, WATCH OUT, SONNY! GET BACK!
TUP

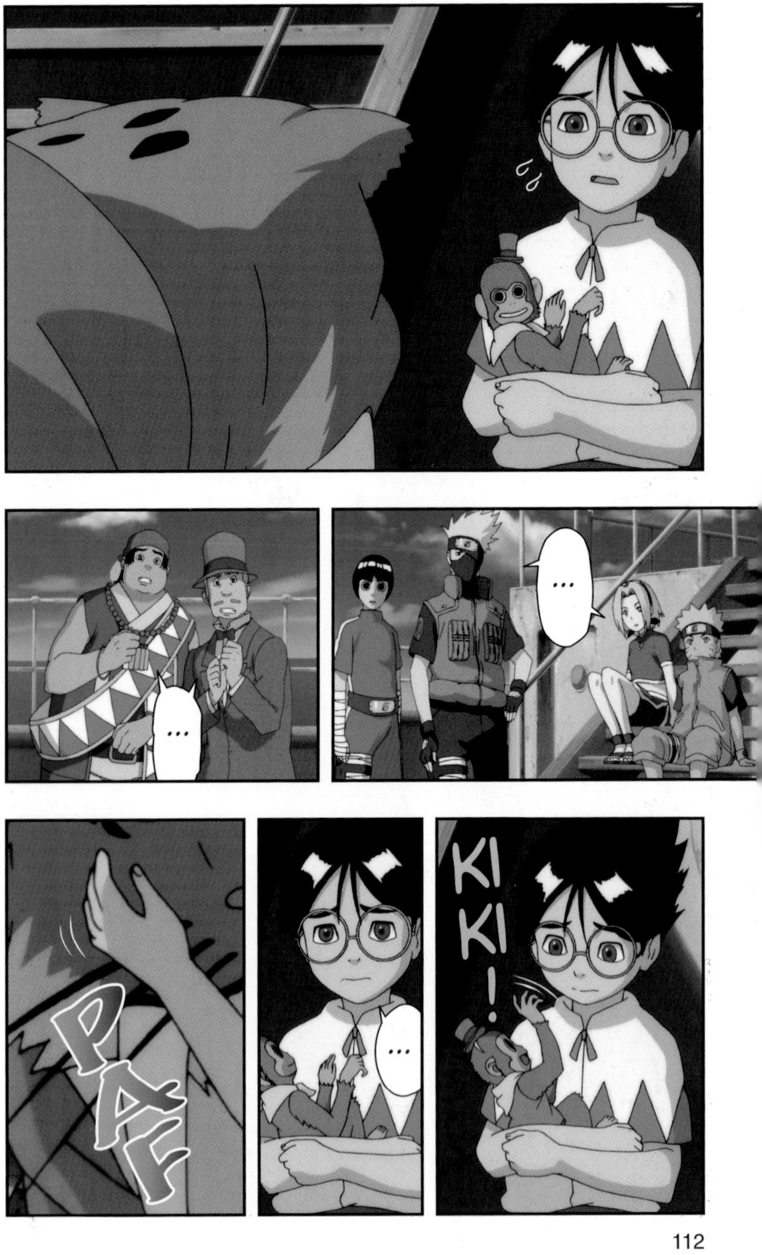
...
...
KI KI!
...
PAF

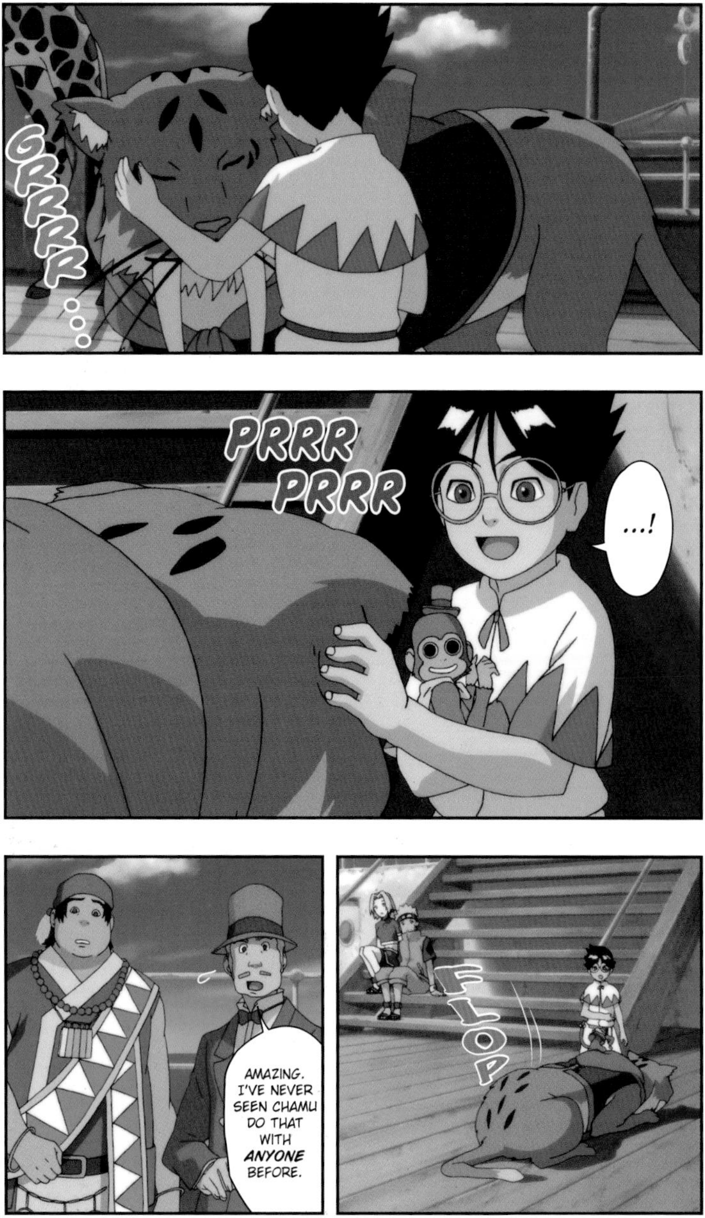
GRRRR...
PRRR PRRR
...!
FLOP
AMAZING. I'VE NEVER SEEN CHAMU DO THAT WITH ***ANYONE*** BEFORE.

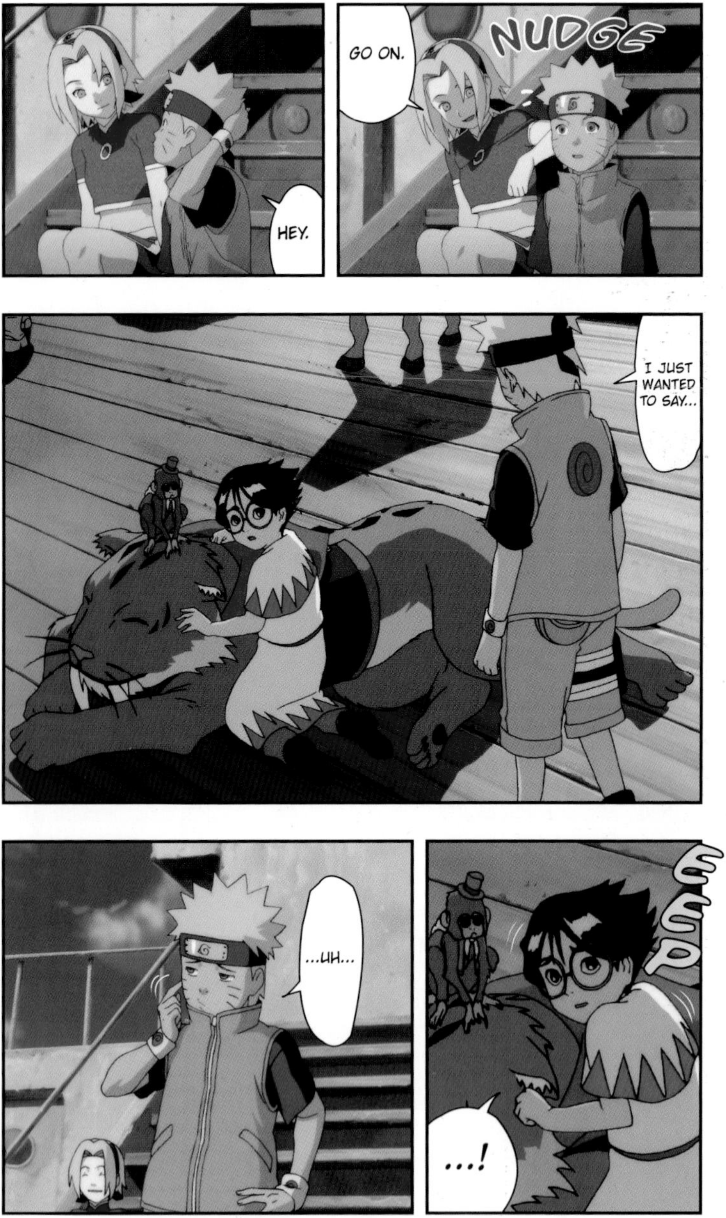
NUDGE
GO ON.
HEY.
I JUST WANTED TO SAY...
EEP
...!
...UH...

I SHOULDN'T HAVE WHACKED YOU AND I SHOULDN'T HAVE SAID THOSE THINGS, SO...I'M SORRY.

!

I'M SORRY!

MAN, YOU... YOU WERE *GREAT*.

MAYBE A LITTLE RECKLESS, BUT YOU SURE GET POINTS FOR GUTS.

...

AND I'M NOT THE ONLY ONE WHO KNOWS HOW BRAVE YOU WERE. THEY KNOW IT TOO.

SAME
HERE.

...

I'M SORRY
TOO. FOR
EVERYTHING
I DID AND
SAID.

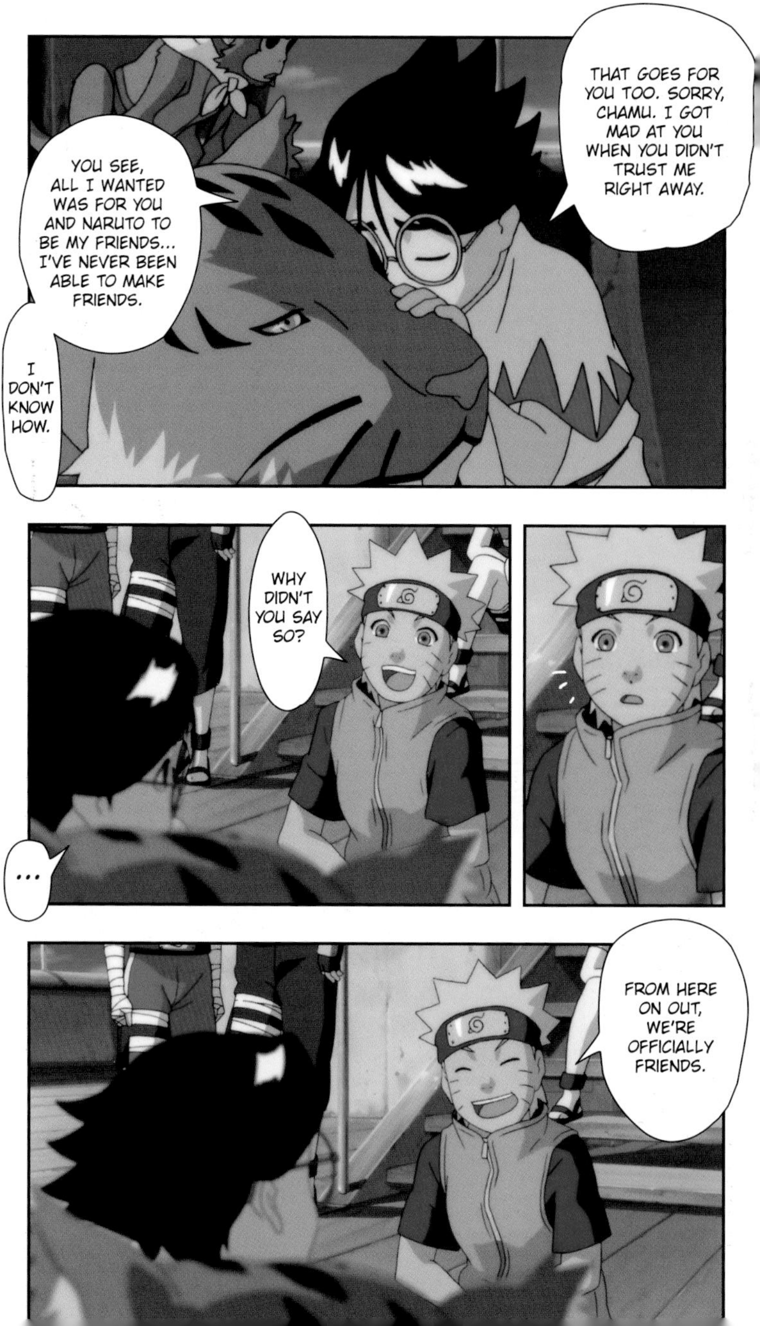
THAT GOES FOR YOU TOO. SORRY, CHAMU. I GOT MAD AT YOU WHEN YOU DIDN'T TRUST ME RIGHT AWAY.
YOU SEE, ALL I WANTED WAS FOR YOU AND NARUTO TO BE MY FRIENDS... I'VE NEVER BEEN ABLE TO MAKE FRIENDS.
I DON'T KNOW HOW.
WHY DIDN'T YOU SAY SO?
...
FROM HERE ON OUT, WE'RE OFFICIALLY FRIENDS.

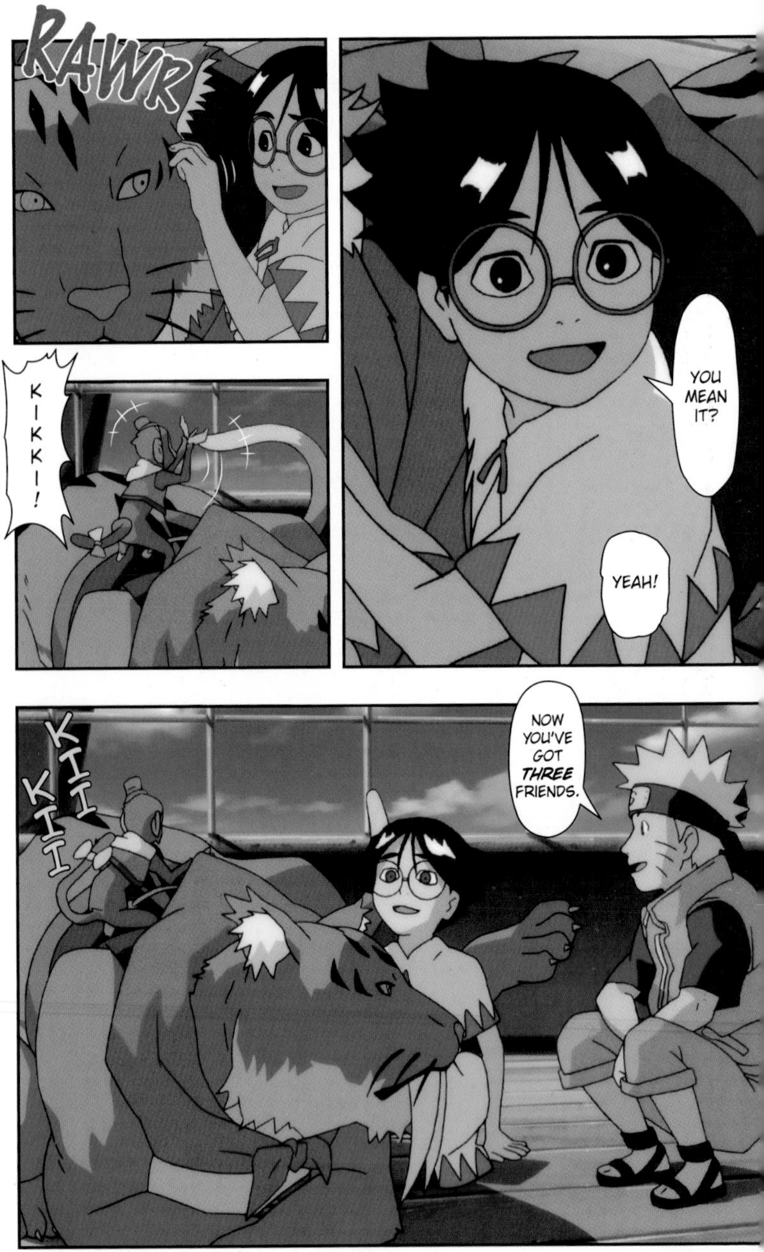
YOU MEAN IT?
YEAH!
RAWR
KIKKI!
NOW YOU'VE GOT ***THREE*** FRIENDS.
KIKIII

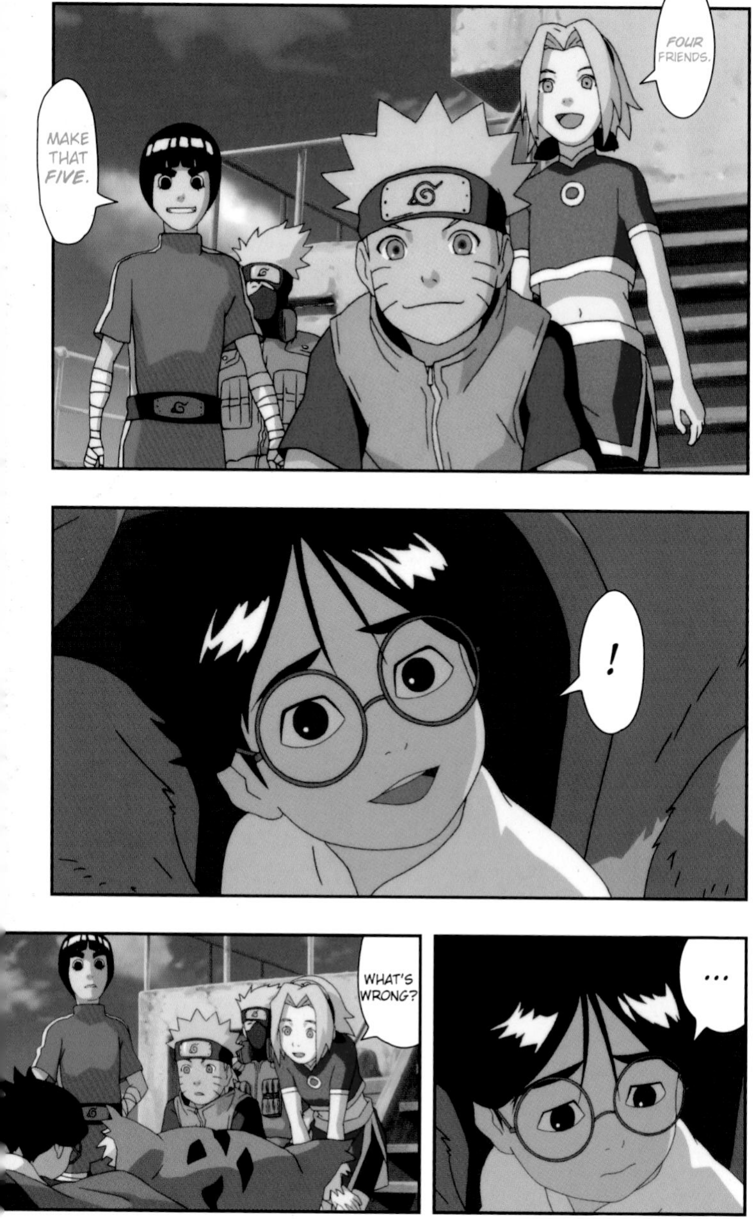
FOUR FRIENDS.
MAKE THAT FIVE.
!
...
WHAT'S WRONG?

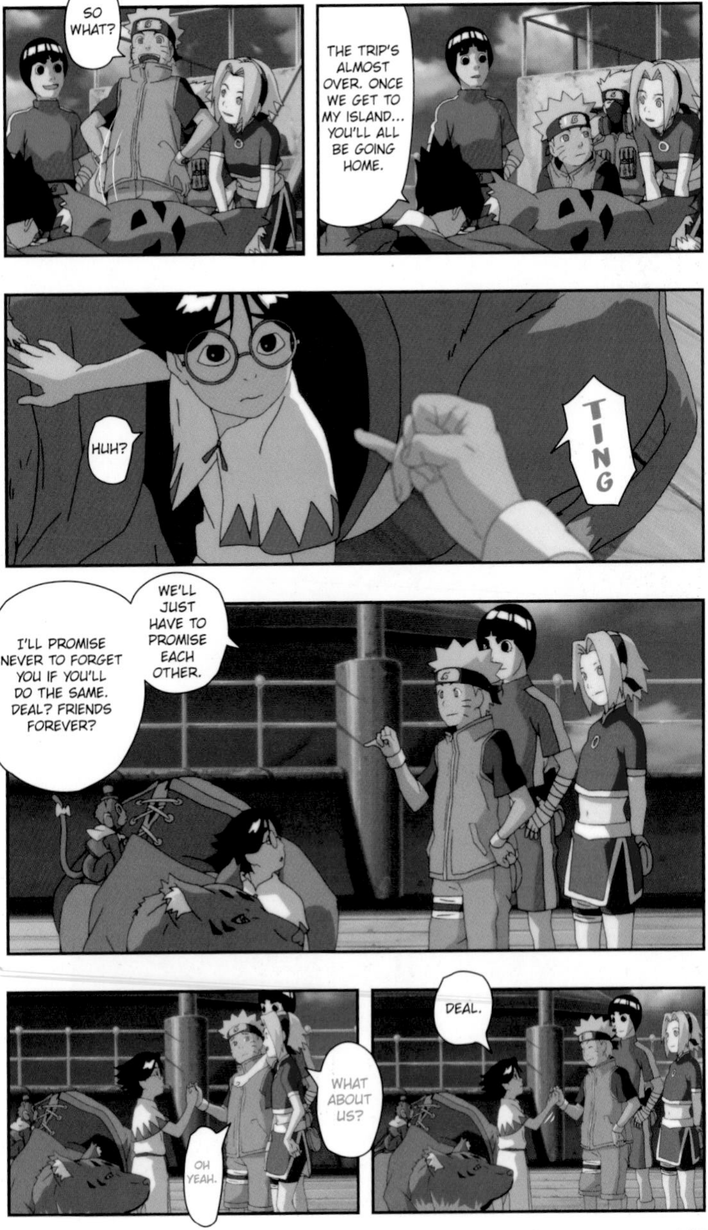
THE TRIP'S ALMOST OVER. ONCE WE GET TO MY ISLAND... YOU'LL ALL BE GOING HOME.
SO WHAT?
TING
HUH?
WE'LL JUST HAVE TO PROMISE EACH OTHER.
I'LL PROMISE NEVER TO FORGET YOU IF YOU'LL DO THE SAME. DEAL? FRIENDS FOREVER?
DEAL.
WHAT ABOUT US?
OH YEAH.

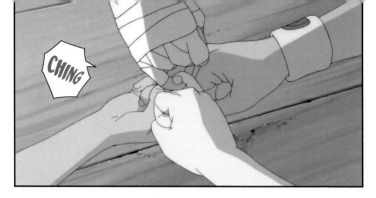

SO WE'RE — ALL OF US — FRIENDS FOREVER, RIGHT?

WHOA!!

RAA

WR

HA HA HA

HA HA HA

....!

FLOP

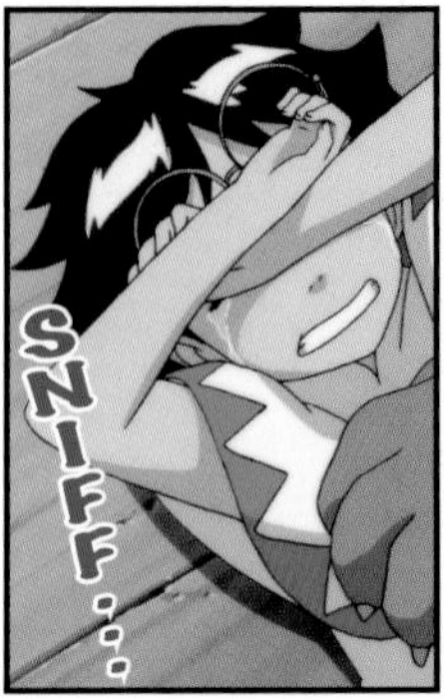
SNIFF...

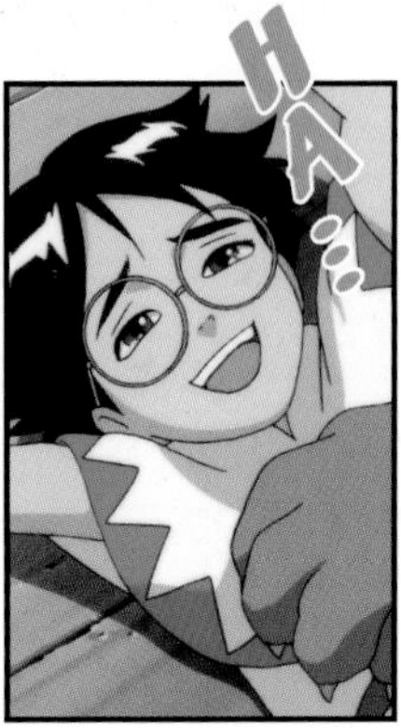
HA...

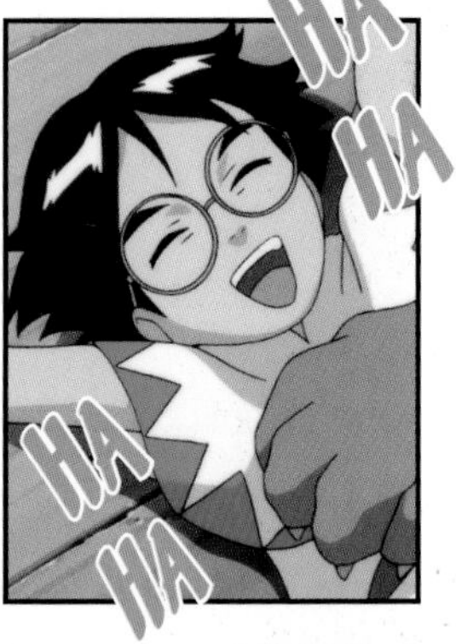
HA HA
HA HA

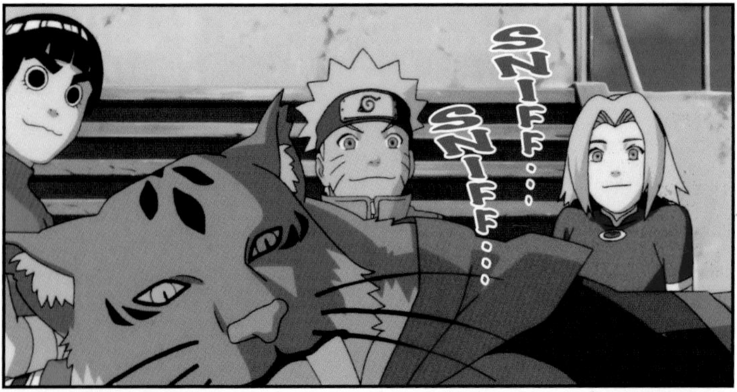
SNIFF...
SNIFF...

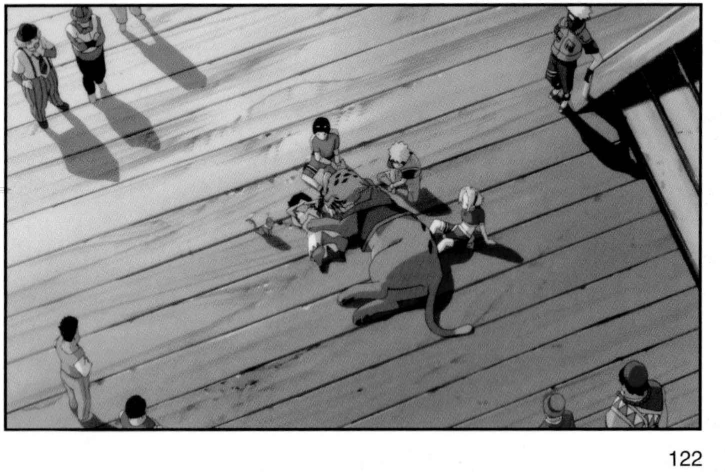

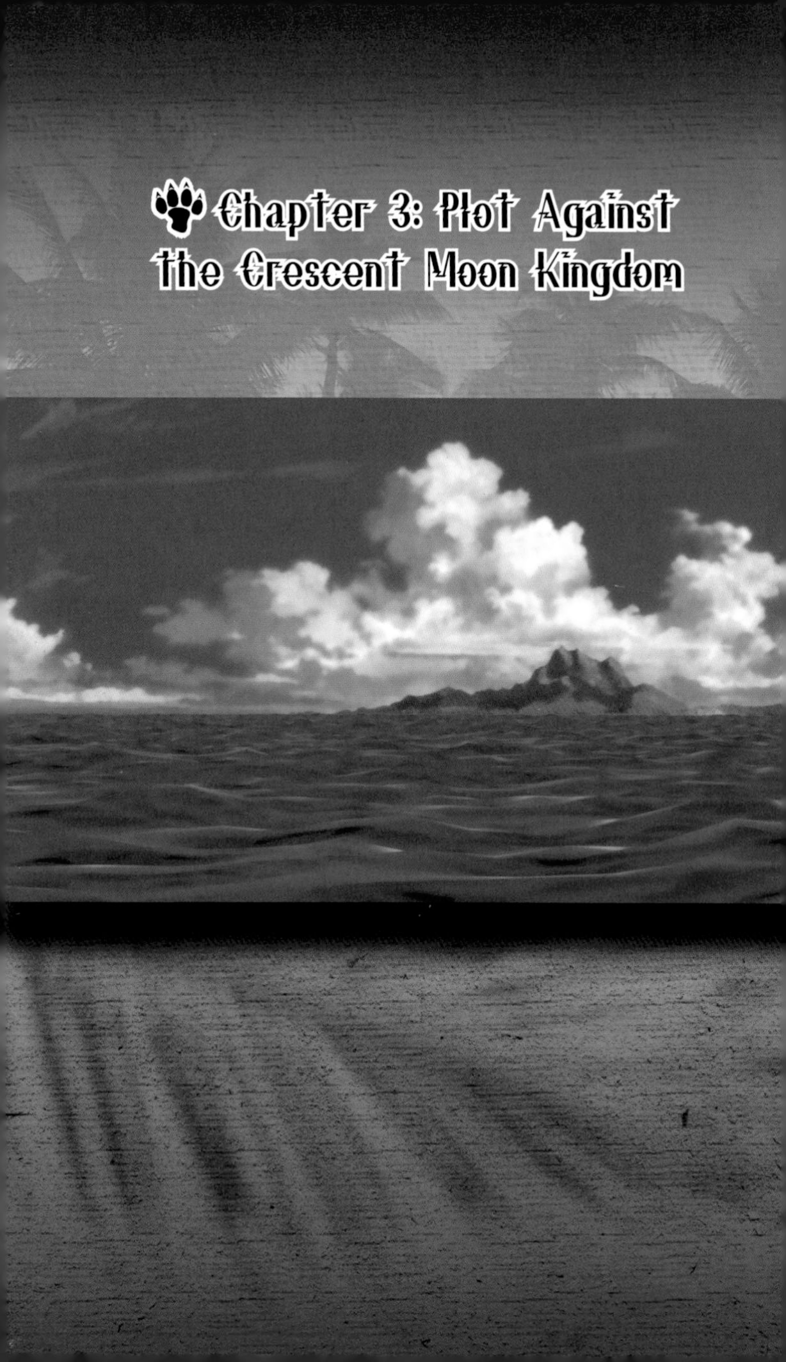
Chapter 3: Plot Against the Crescent Moon Kingdom

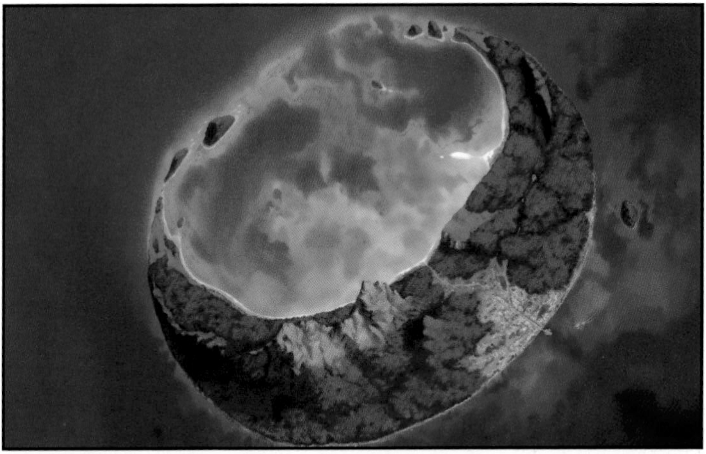

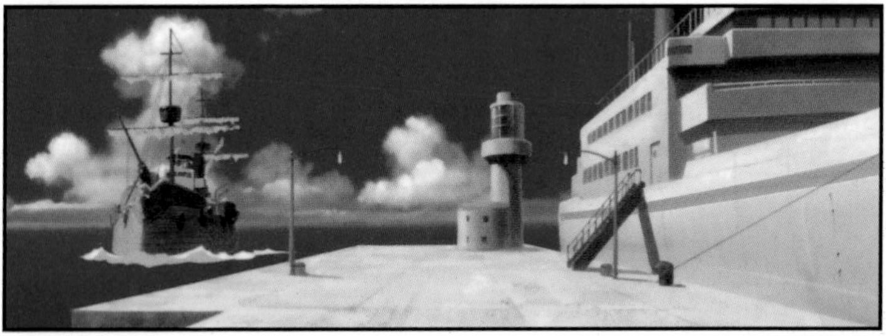

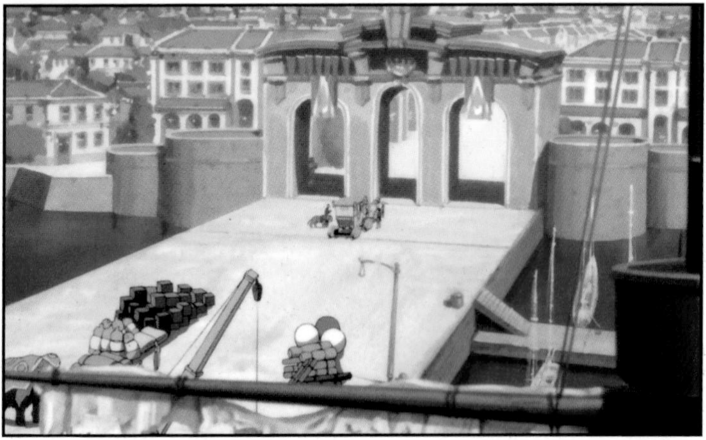

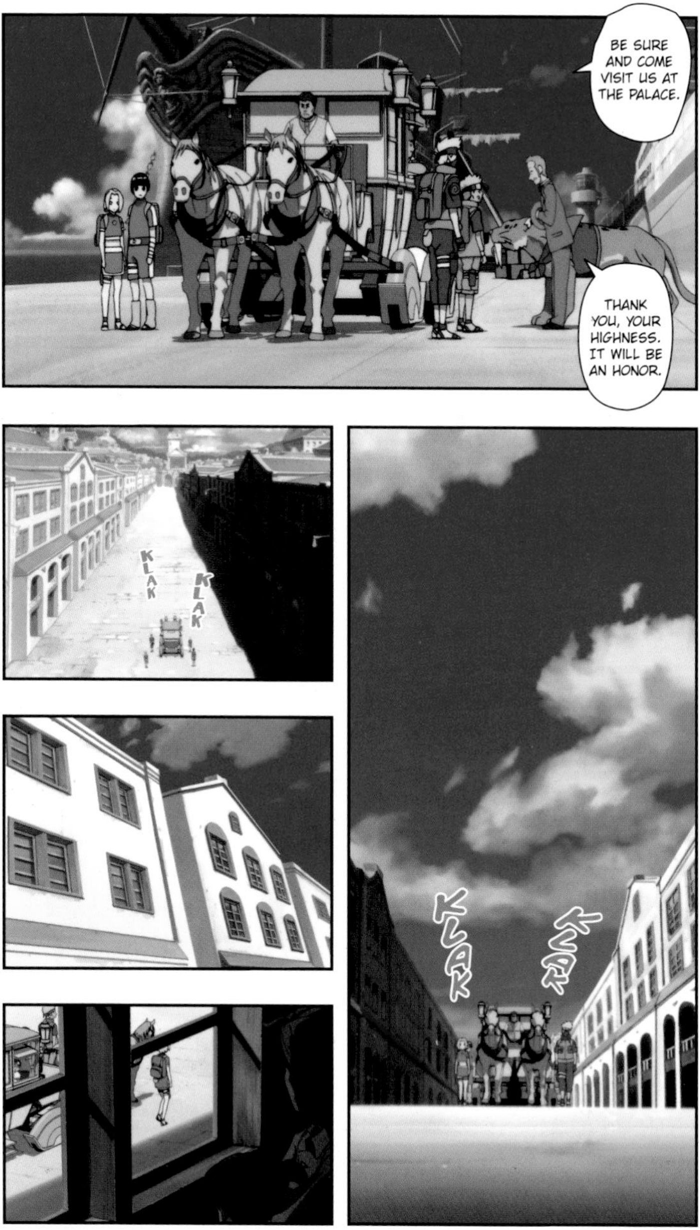
BE SURE AND COME VISIT US AT THE PALACE.
THANK YOU, YOUR HIGHNESS. IT WILL BE AN HONOR.
KLAK
KLAK
KLAK
KLAK

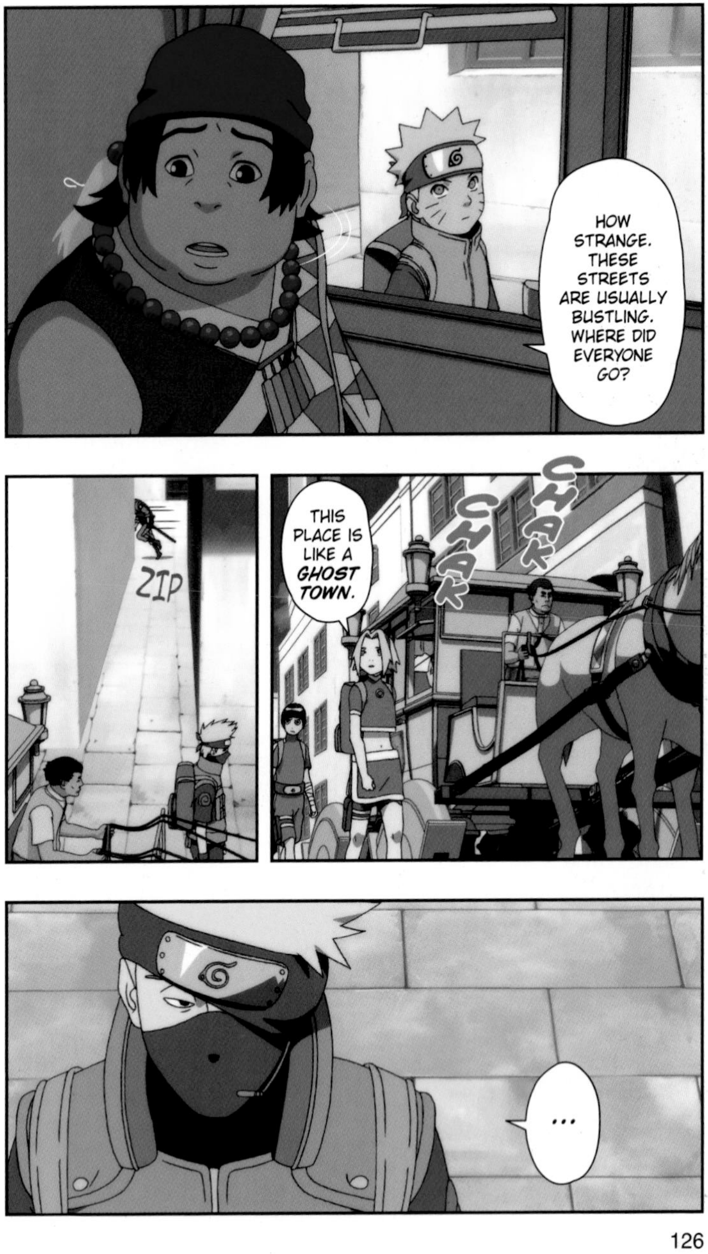
HOW STRANGE. THESE STREETS ARE USUALLY BUSTLING. WHERE DID EVERYONE GO?
CHAK CHAK
THIS PLACE IS LIKE A *GHOST TOWN.*
ZIP
...

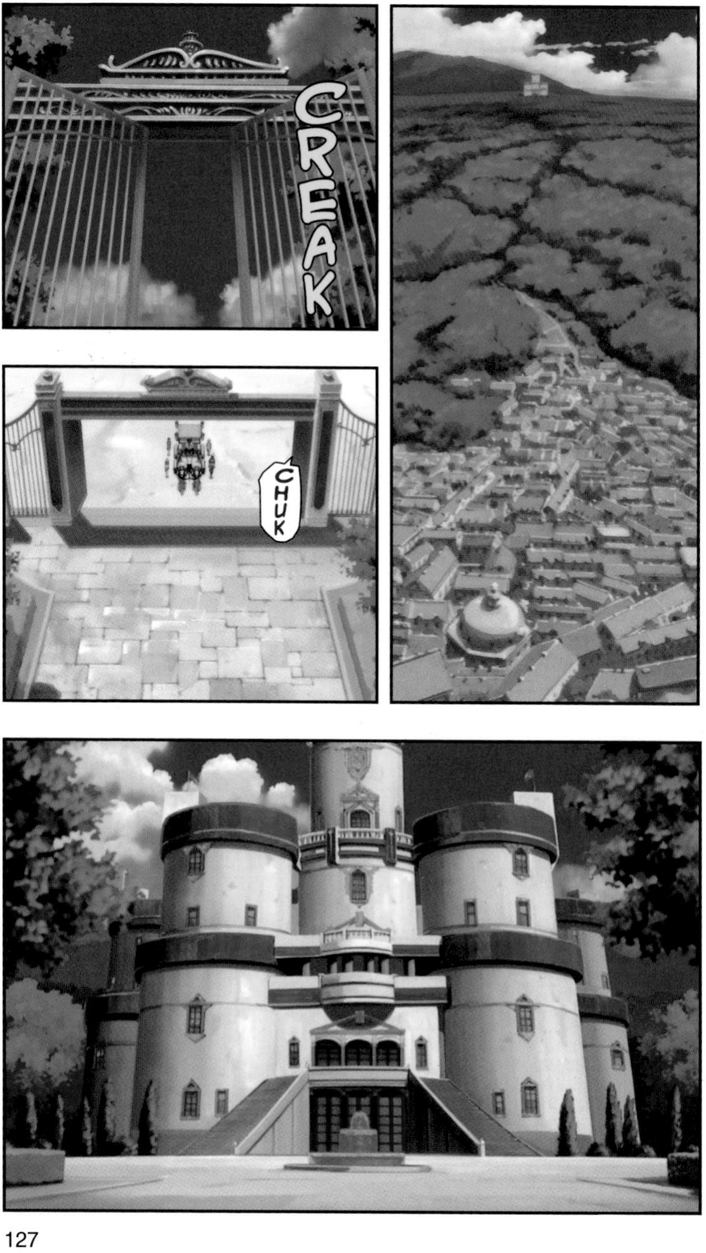
CREAK
CHUK

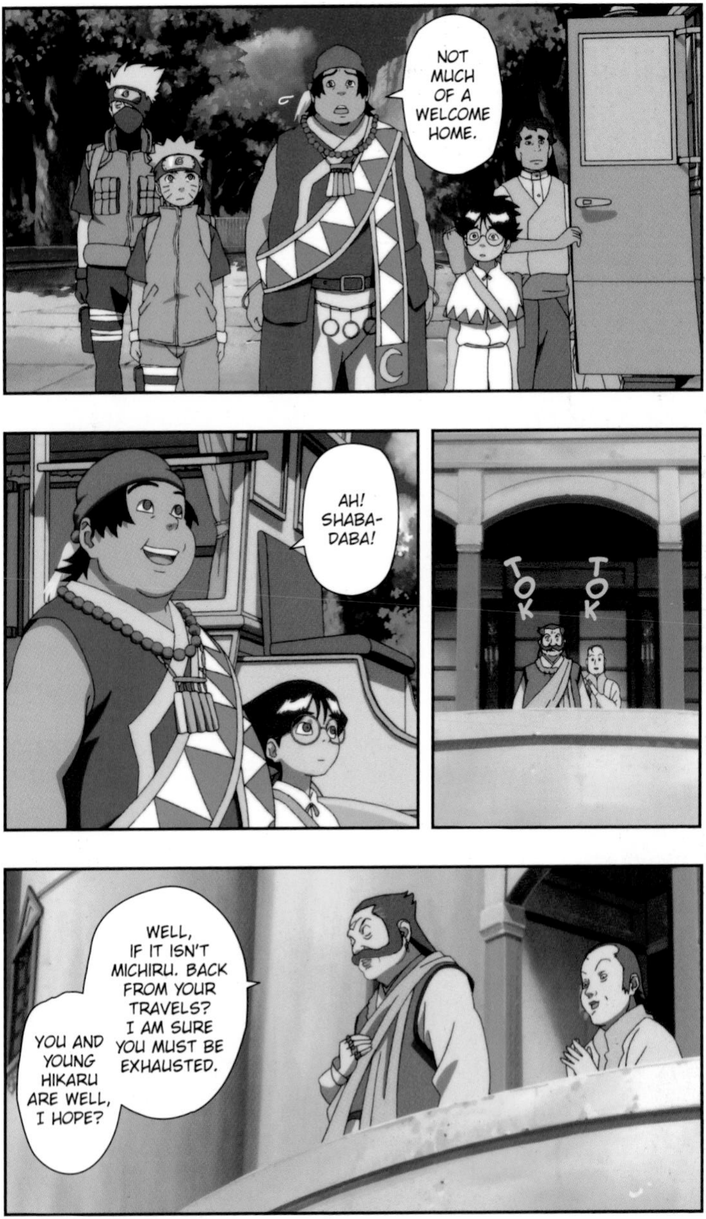
NOT MUCH OF A WELCOME HOME.
TOK TOK
AH! SHABA-DABA!
WELL, IF IT ISN'T MICHIRU. BACK FROM YOUR TRAVELS? I AM SURE YOU MUST BE EXHAUSTED.
YOU AND YOUNG HIKARU ARE WELL, I HOPE?

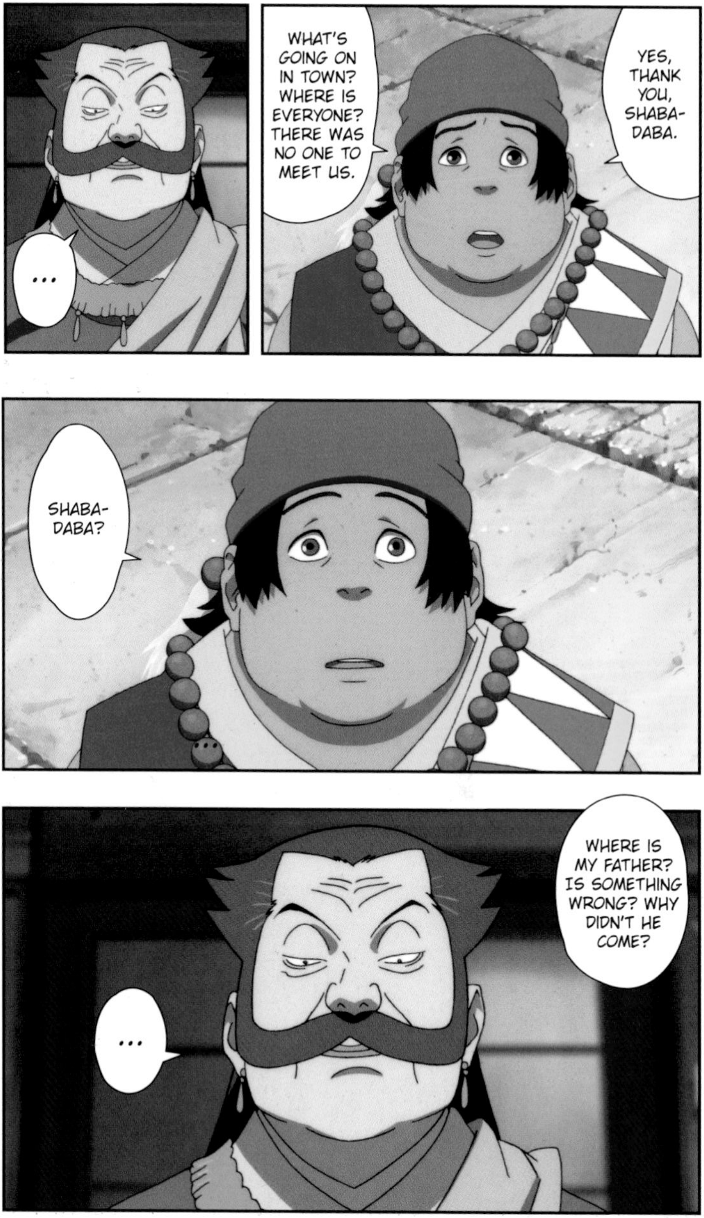
YES, THANK YOU, SHABA-DABA.
WHAT'S GOING ON IN TOWN? WHERE IS EVERYONE? THERE WAS NO ONE TO MEET US.
...
SHABA-DABA?
WHERE IS MY FATHER? IS SOMETHING WRONG? WHY DIDN'T HE COME?
...

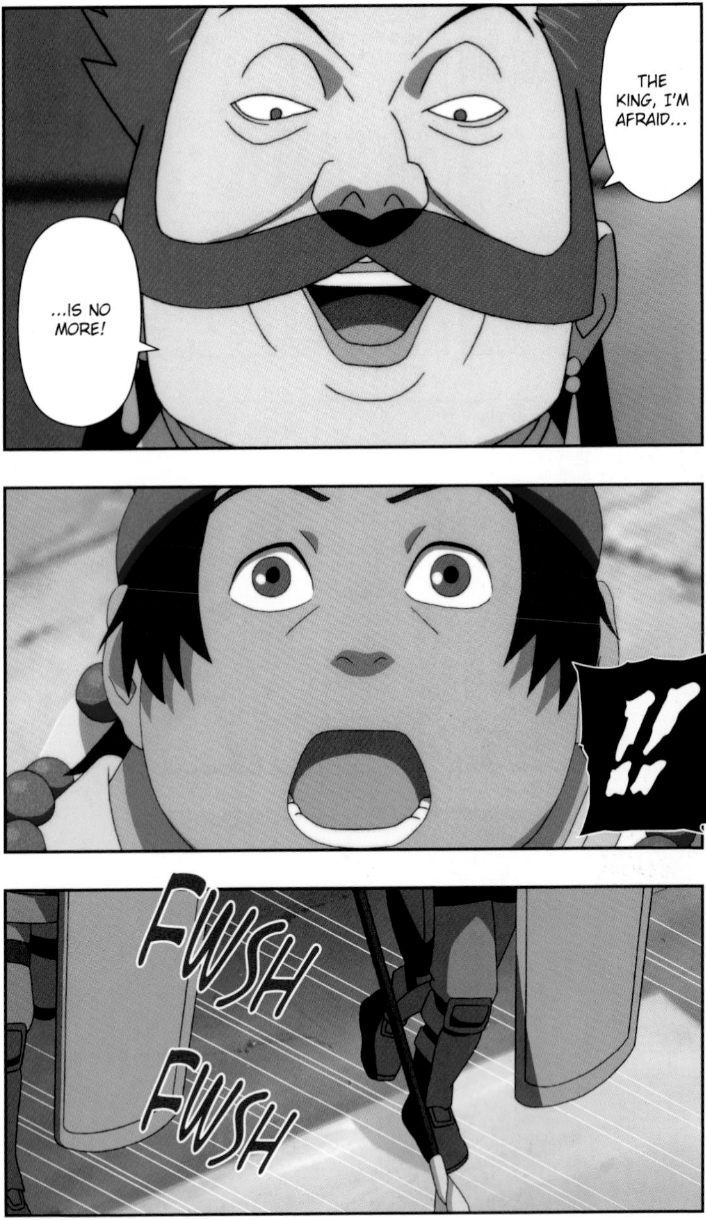
THE KING, I'M AFRAID...
...IS NO MORE!
!!
FWSH
FWSH

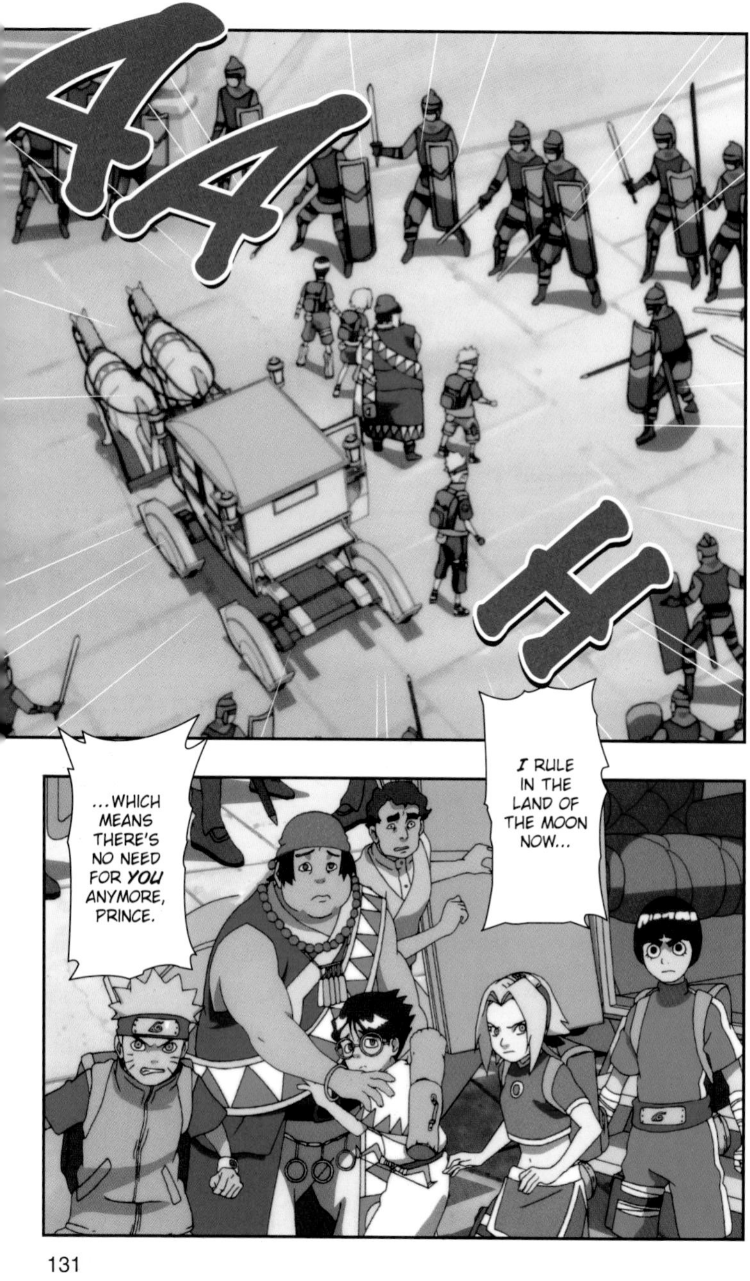
AAH
I RULE IN THE LAND OF THE MOON NOW...
...WHICH MEANS THERE'S NO NEED FOR YOU ANYMORE, PRINCE.

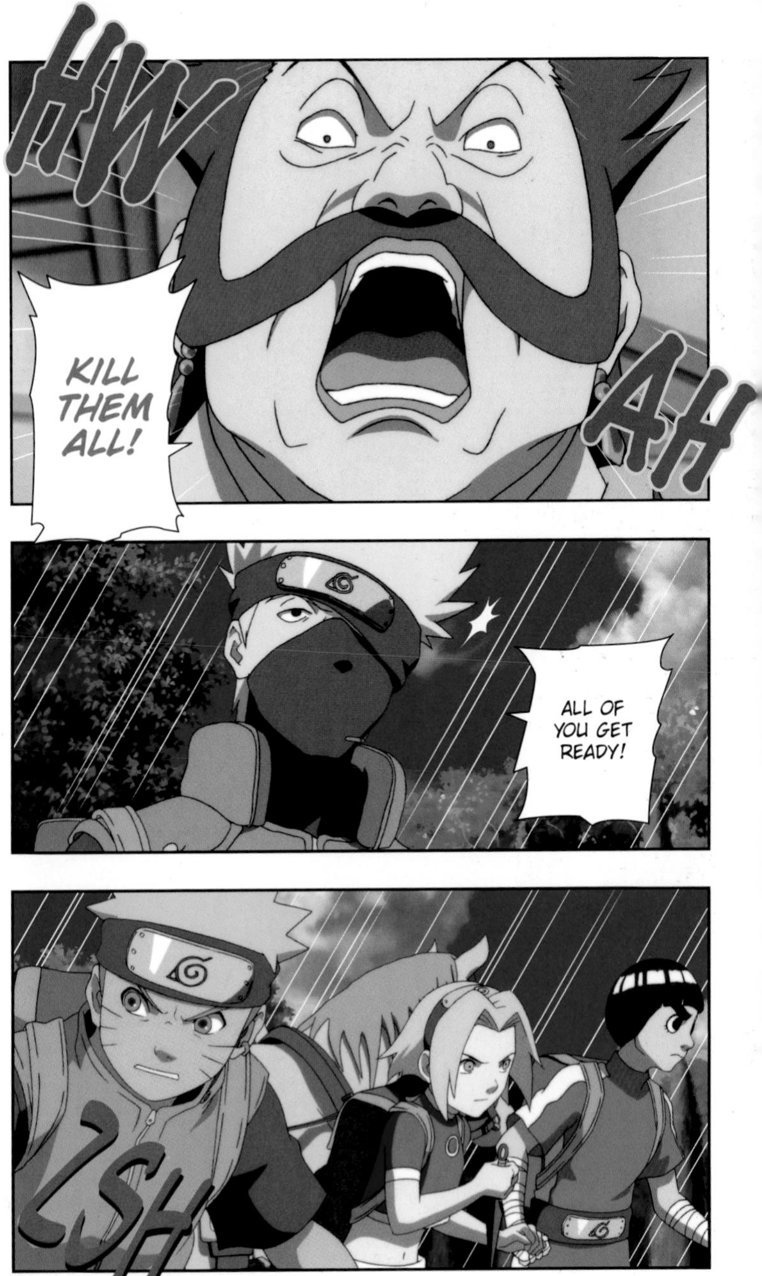
HW
AH
KILL THEM ALL!
ALL OF YOU GET READY!
CSH

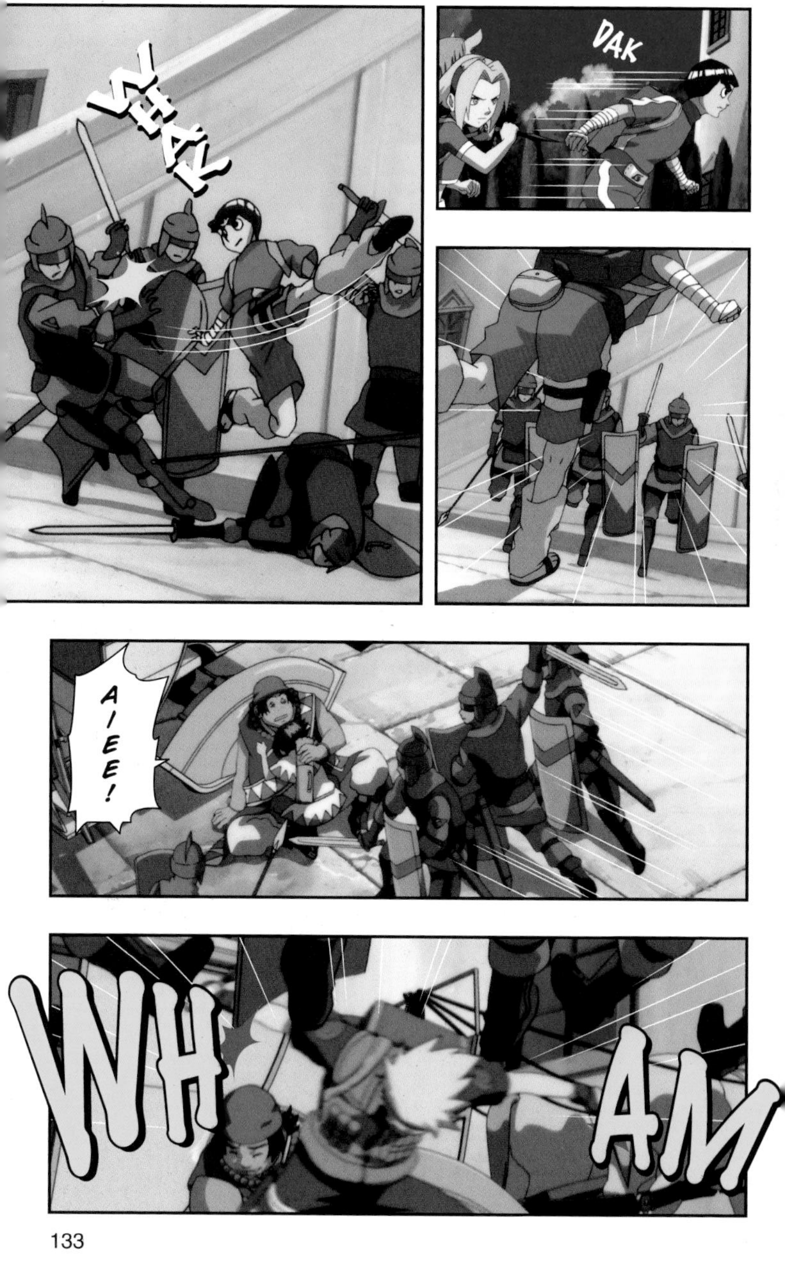
DAK
WHAK
AIEEE!
WH
AM

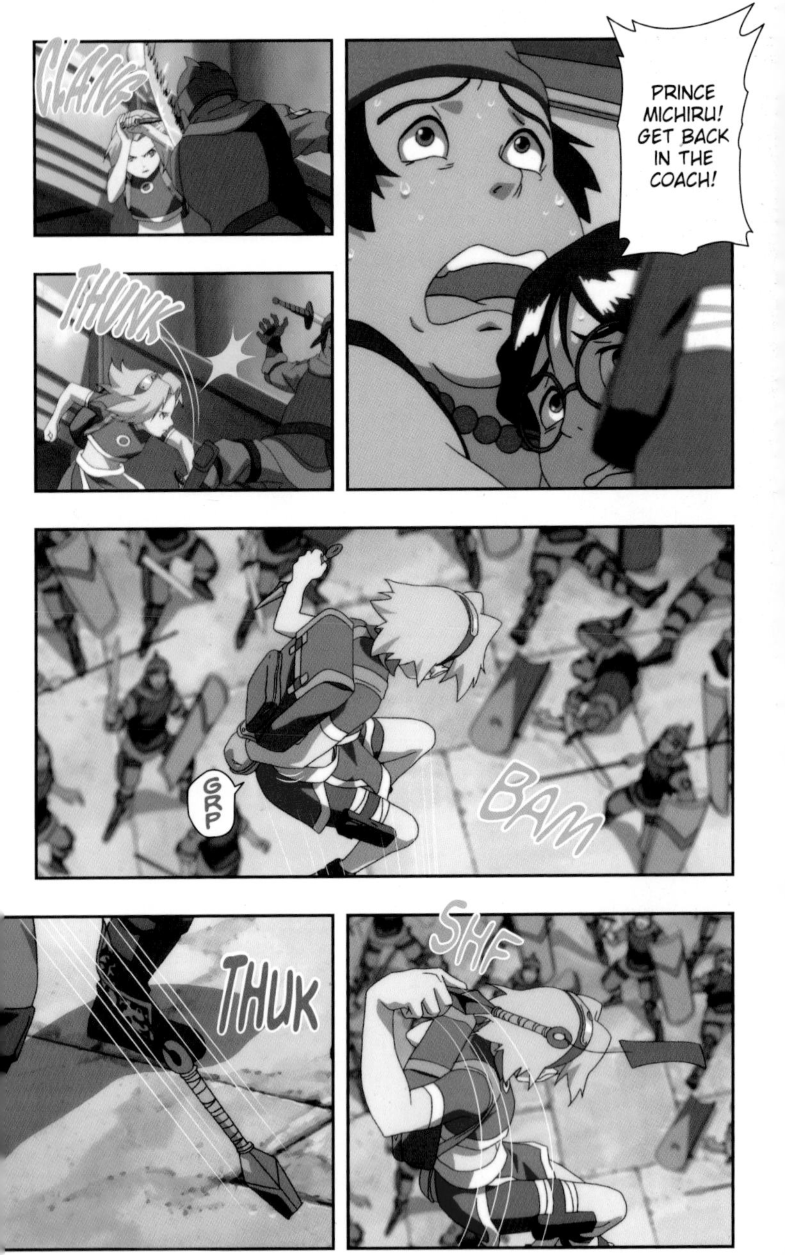
PRINCE MICHIRU! GET BACK IN THE COACH!
CLANG
THUNK
BAM
GRP
SHF
THUK

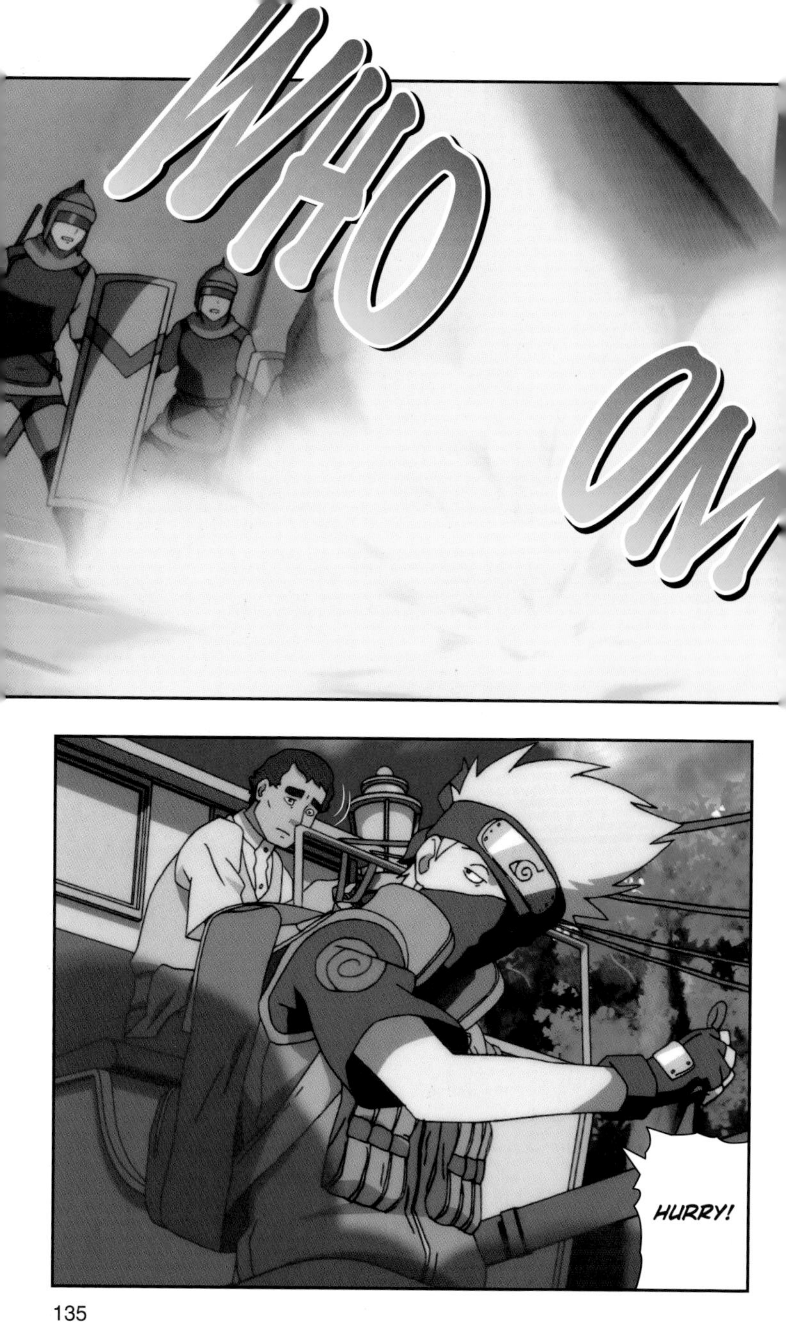
WHOOM
HURRY!

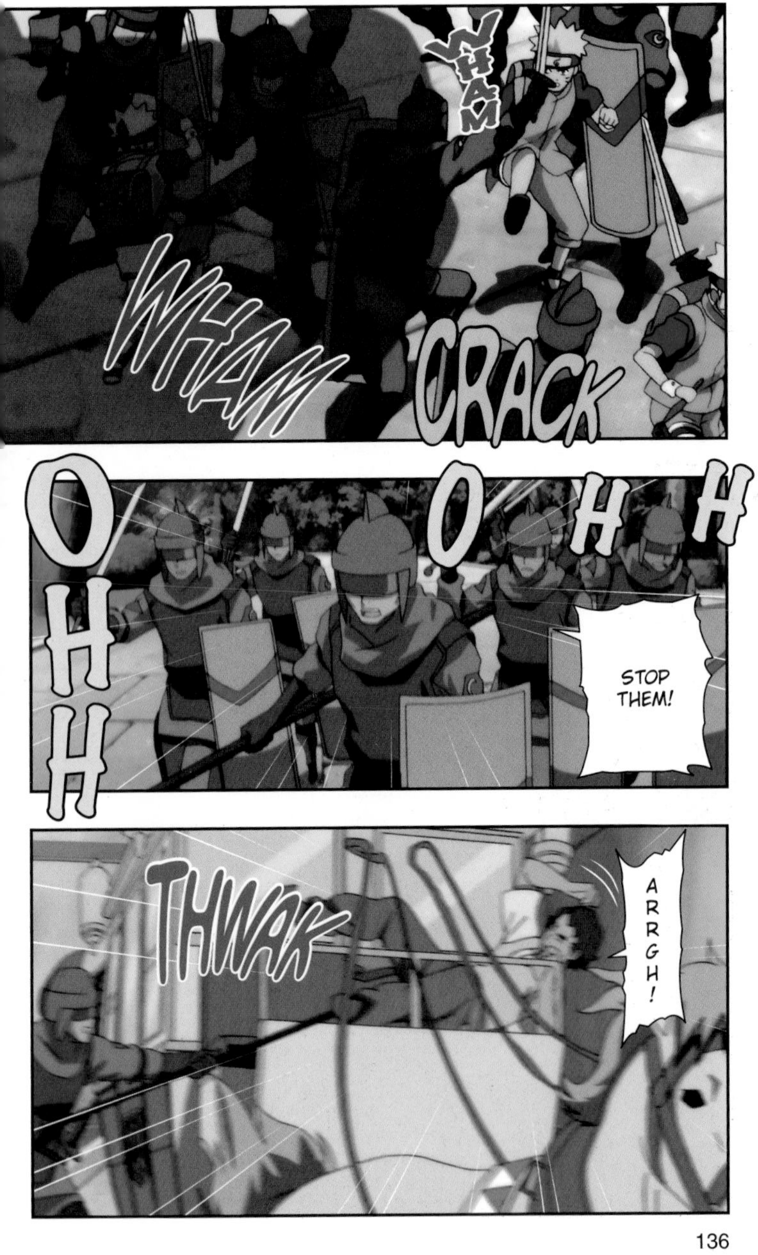
WHAM
CRACK
WHAM
OHH
OHHH
STOP THEM!
ARRGH!
THWAK

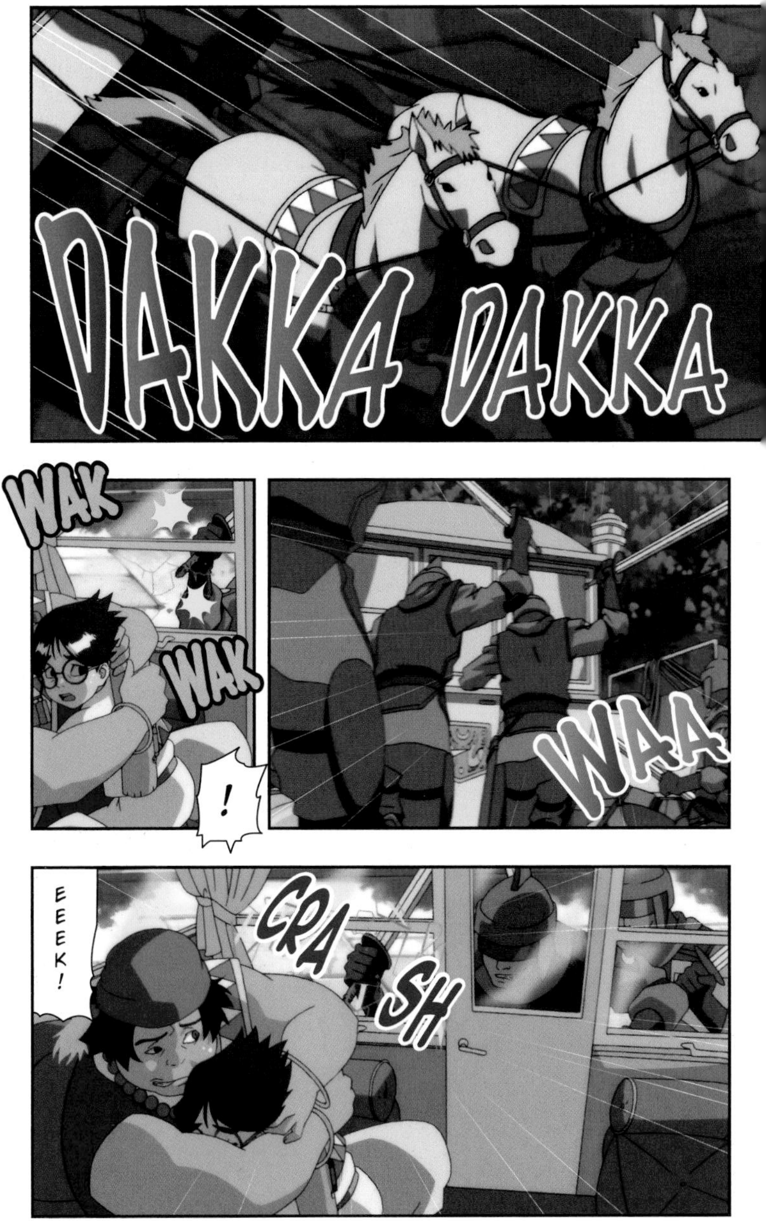
DAKKA DAKKA
WAA
WAK
WAK
!
CRASH
EEEEK!

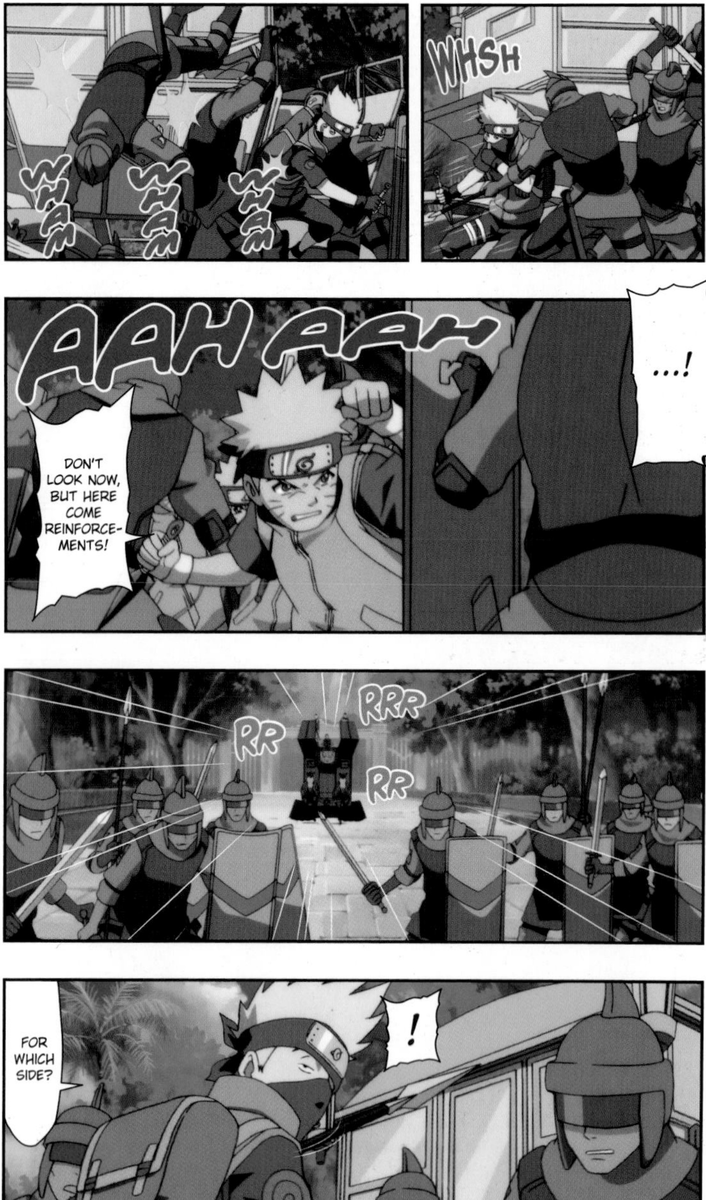
WHSH
WHAM
WHAM
WHAM
...!
AAH AAH
DON'T LOOK NOW, BUT HERE COME REINFORCEMENTS!
RRR
RR
RR
!
FOR WHICH SIDE?

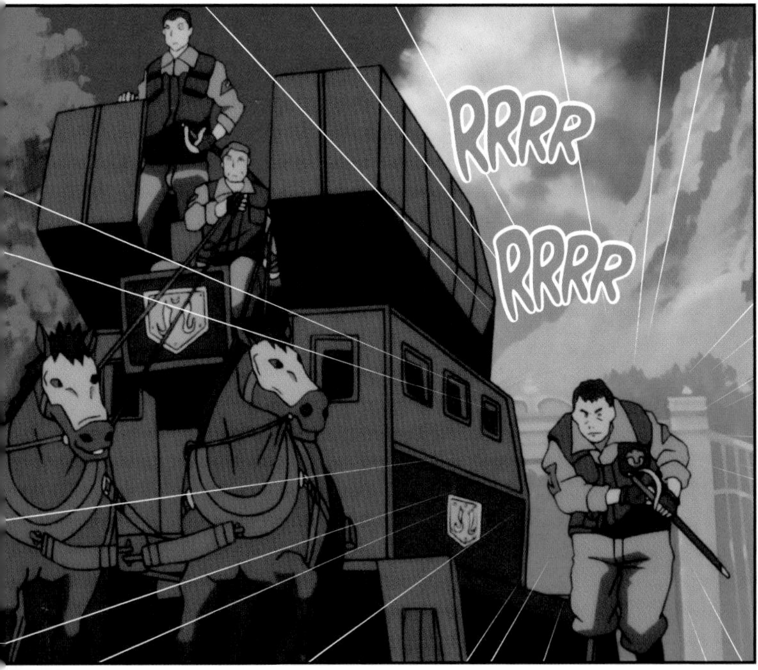
RRRR
RRRR

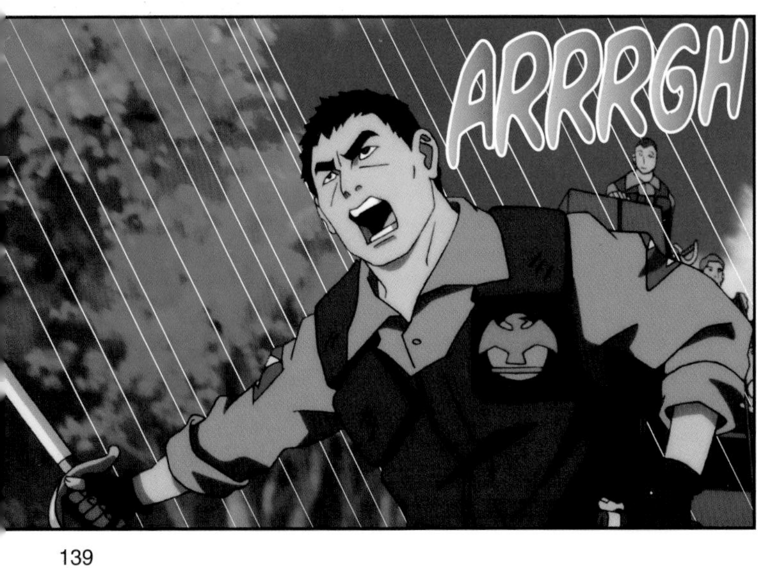
ARRRGH

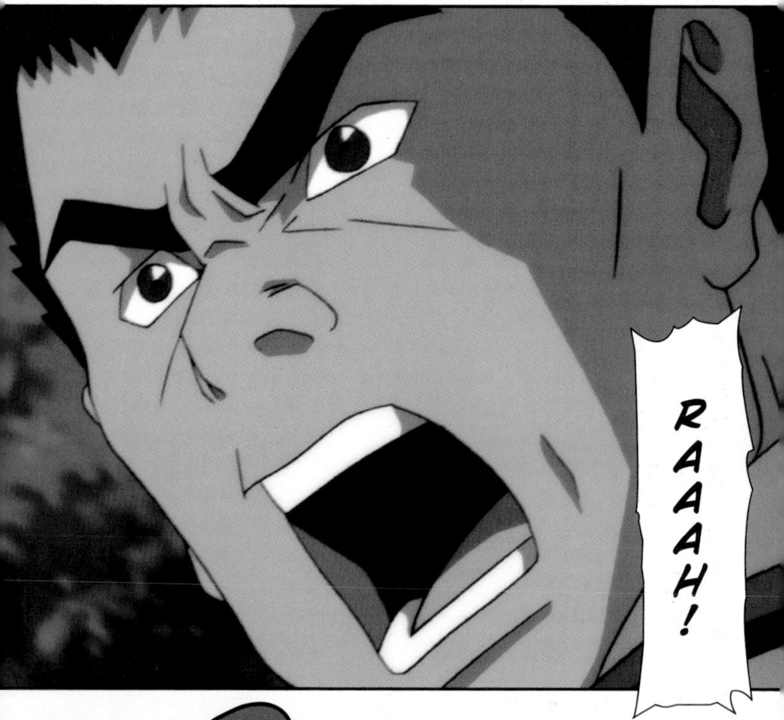
RAAAAH!
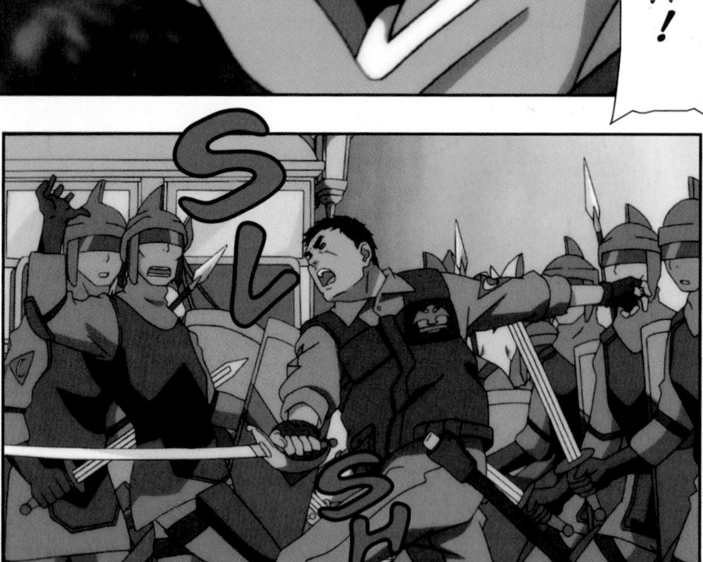
SLSH

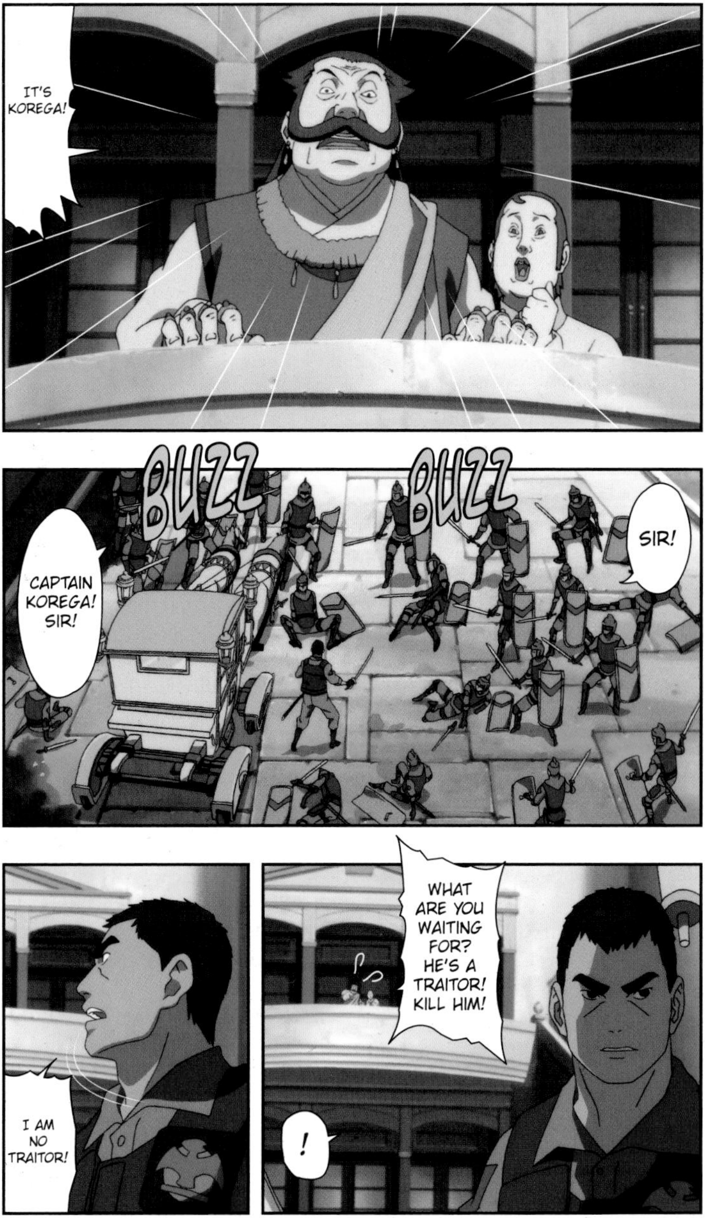

IT'S KOREGA!
BUZZ
BUZZ
SIR!
CAPTAIN KOREGA! SIR!
WHAT ARE YOU WAITING FOR? HE'S A TRAITOR! KILL HIM!
!
I AM NO TRAITOR!

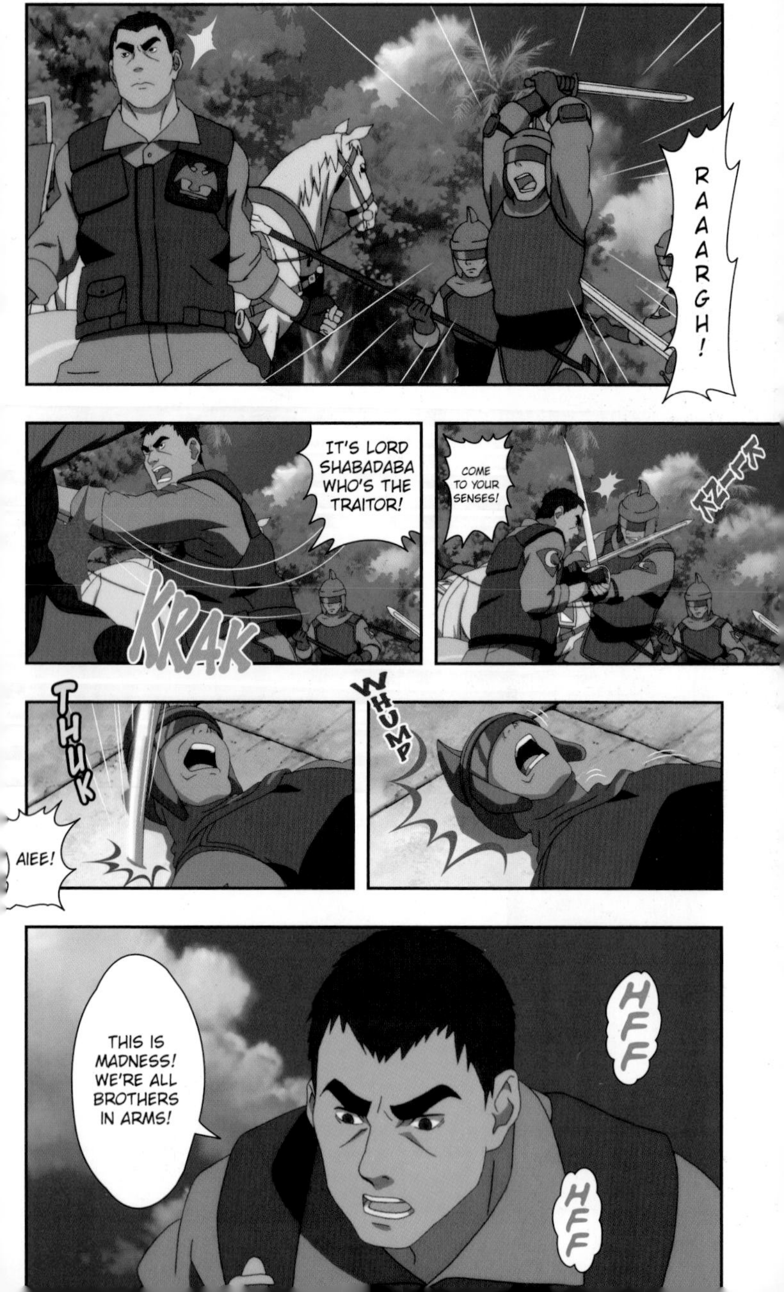
RAAAARGH!
IT'S LORD SHABADABA WHO'S THE TRAITOR!
KRAK
COME TO YOUR SENSES!
THUK
AIEE!
WHUMP
THIS IS MADNESS! WE'RE ALL BROTHERS IN ARMS!
HFF
HFF

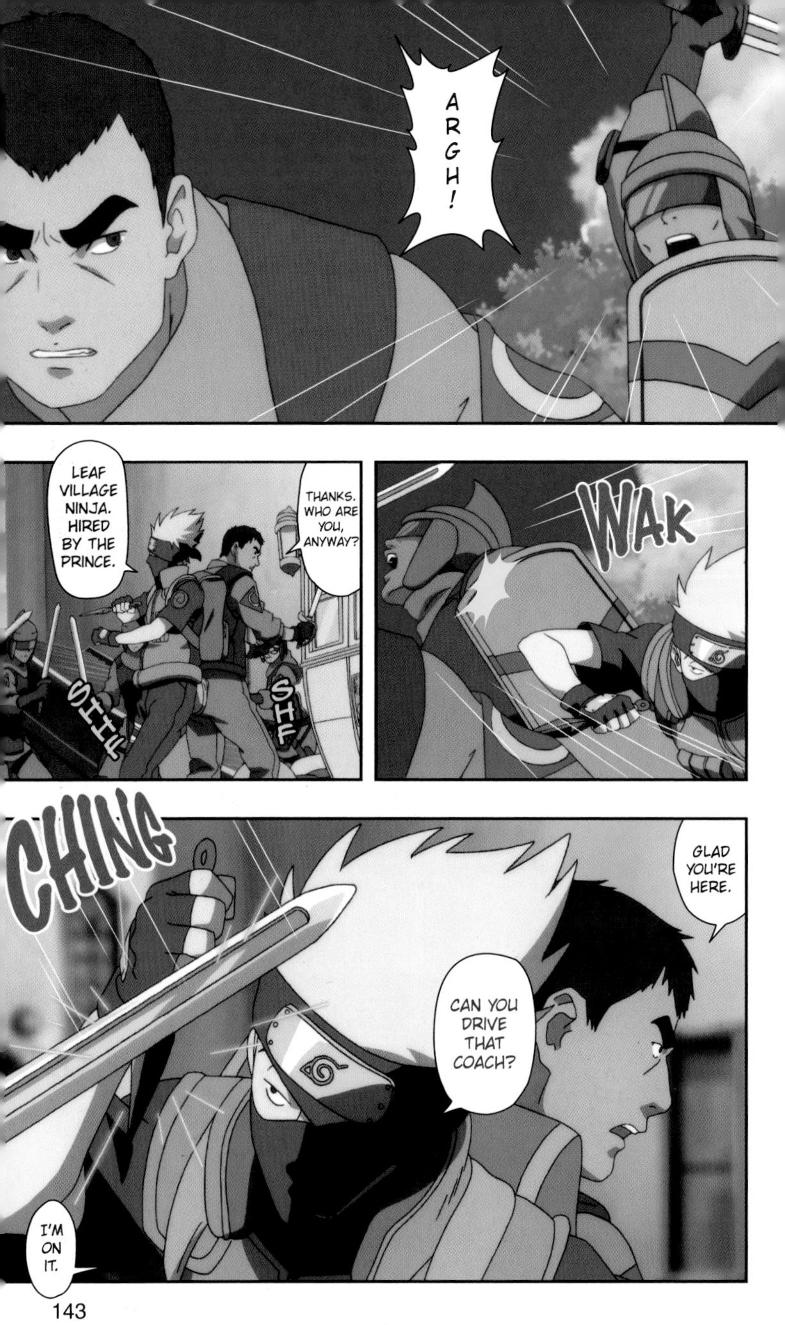
ARGH!
WAK
THANKS. WHO ARE YOU, ANYWAY?
LEAF VILLAGE NINJA. HIRED BY THE PRINCE.
SHF
SHF
GLAD YOU'RE HERE.
CAN YOU DRIVE THAT COACH?
CHING
I'M ON IT.

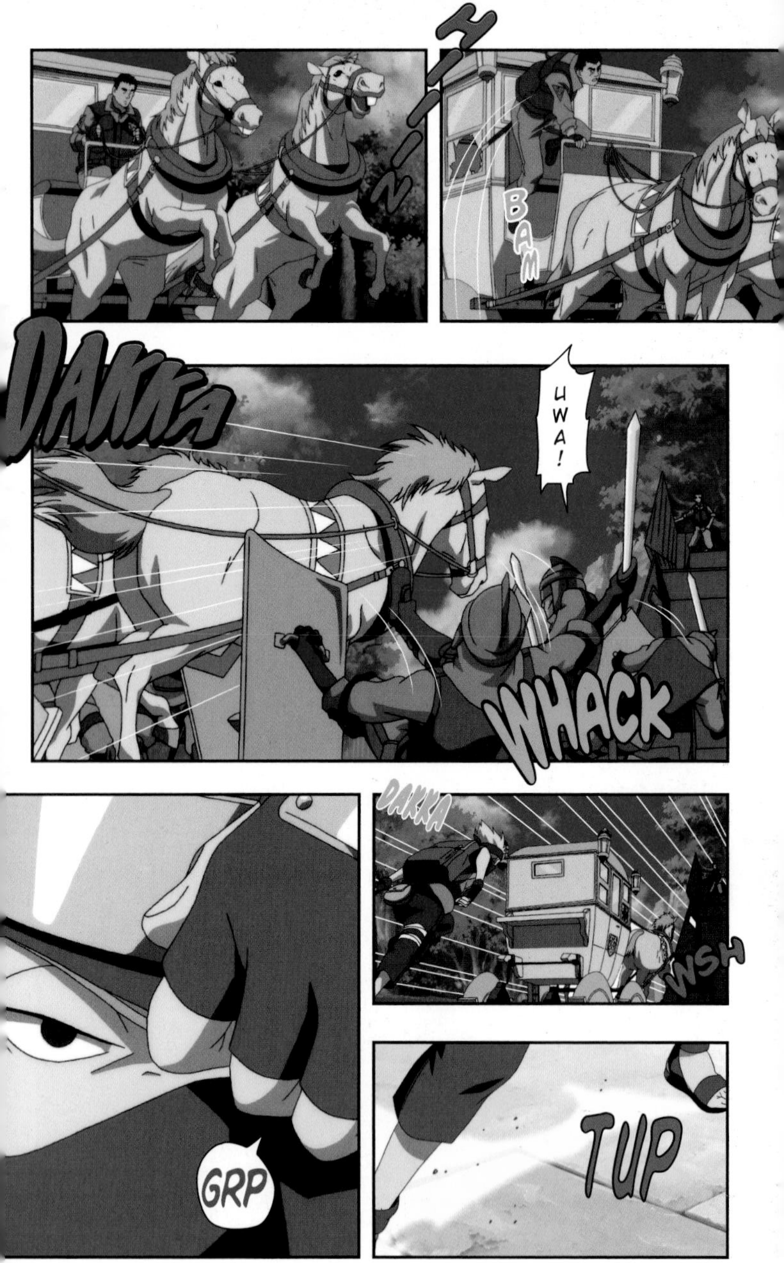
BAM
HIIIN
UWA!
WHACK
DAKKA
DAKKA
WSH
TUP
GRP

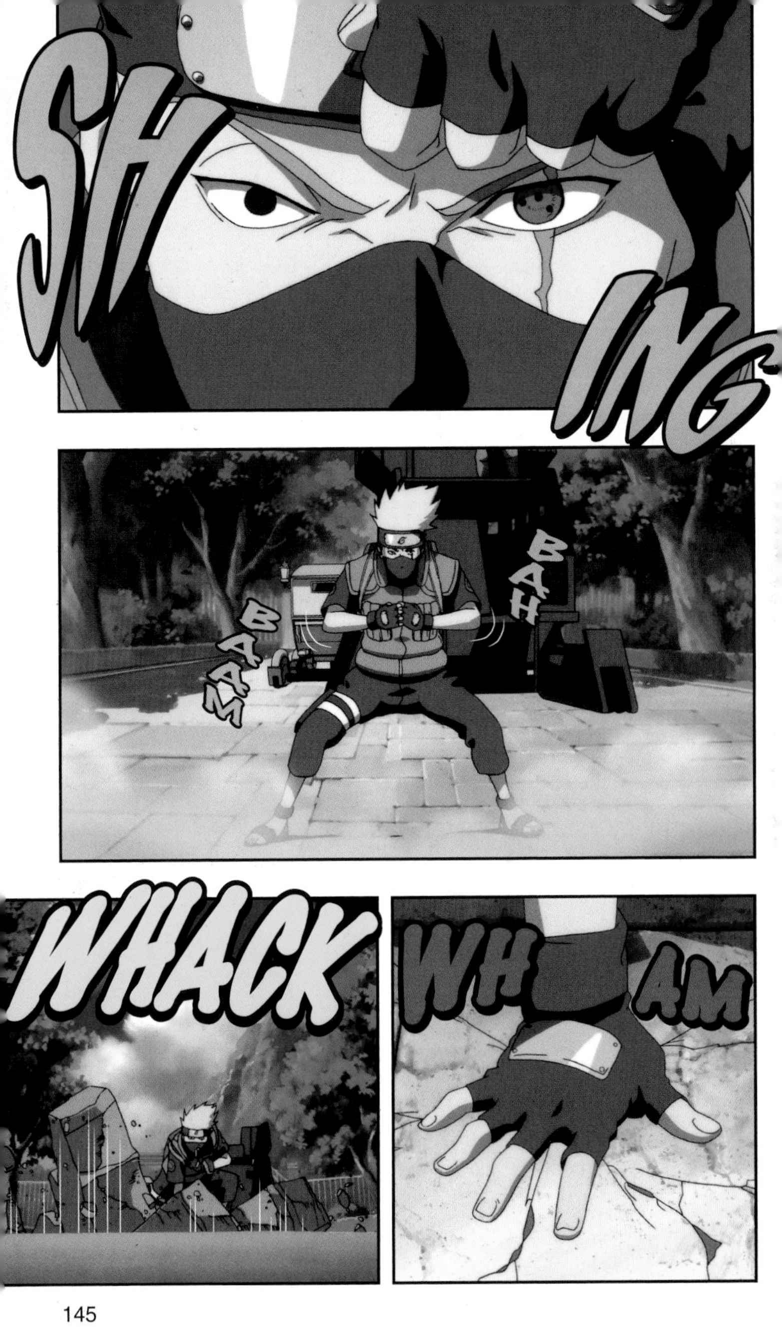
SHING
BAH
BAAM
WH AM
WHACK

GRRRRM

RRRM

ARRGH!

WHO *ARE* THOSE PEOPLE?

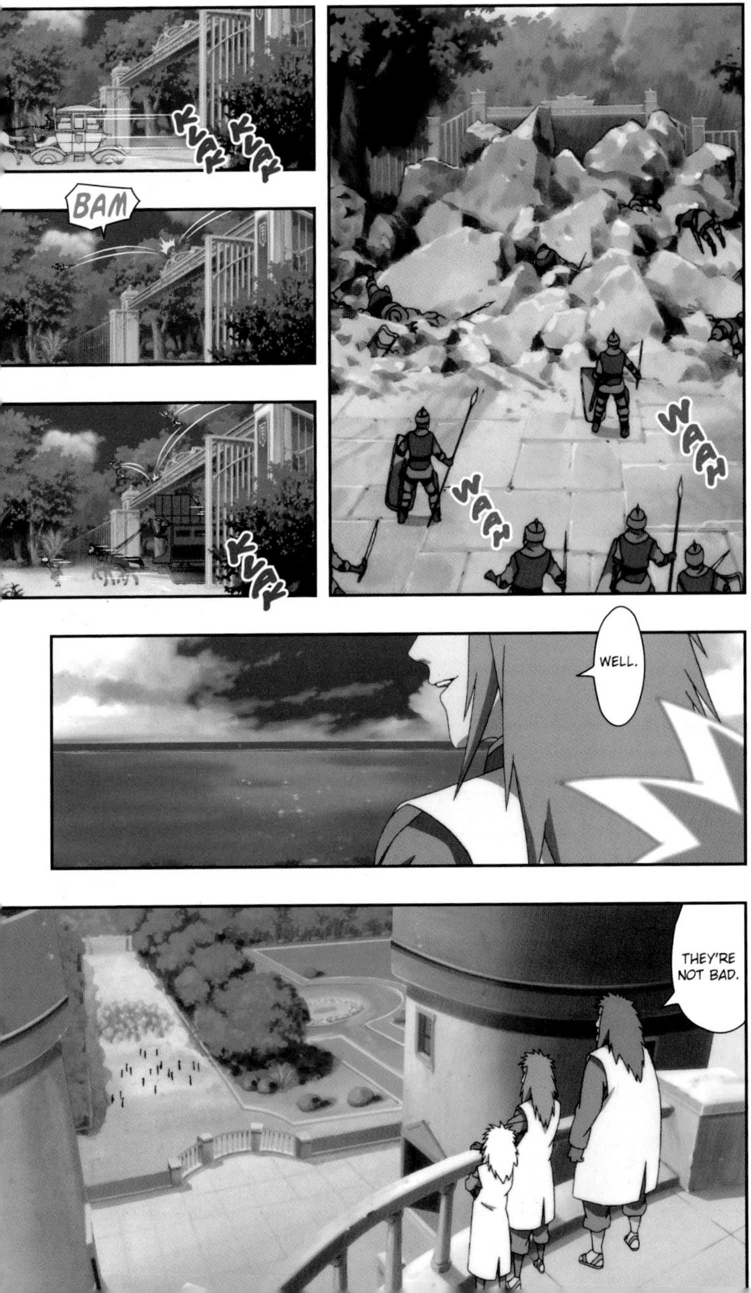
WAAH
WAAH
KVAK
KVAK
BAM
KVAK
WELL.
THEY'RE NOT BAD.

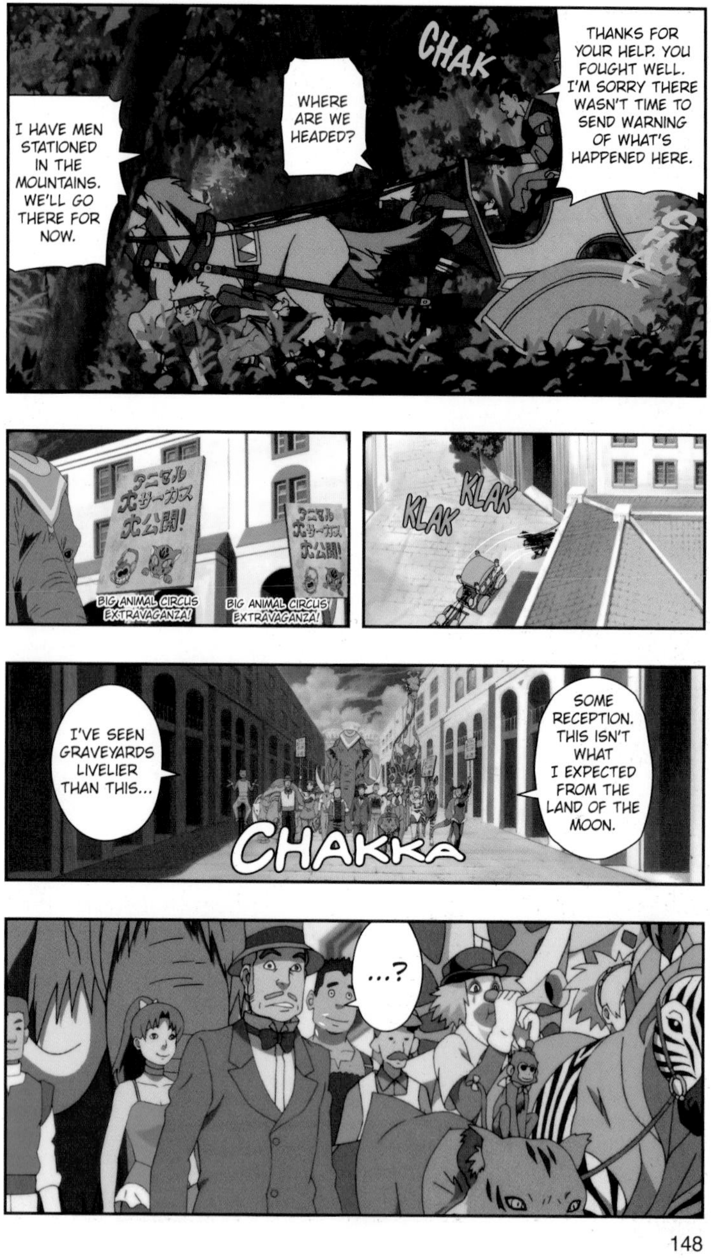
THANKS FOR YOUR HELP. YOU FOUGHT WELL. I'M SORRY THERE WASN'T TIME TO SEND WARNING OF WHAT'S HAPPENED HERE.
CHAK
WHERE ARE WE HEADED?
I HAVE MEN STATIONED IN THE MOUNTAINS. WE'LL GO THERE FOR NOW.
CHAK
KLAK
KLAK
アニマル 大サーカス 大公開!
BIG ANIMAL CIRCUS EXTRAVAGANZA!
アニマル 大サーカス 大公開!
BIG ANIMAL CIRCUS EXTRAVAGANZA!
SOME RECEPTION. THIS ISN'T WHAT I EXPECTED FROM THE LAND OF THE MOON.
CHAKKA
I'VE SEEN GRAVEYARDS LIVELIER THAN THIS...
...?

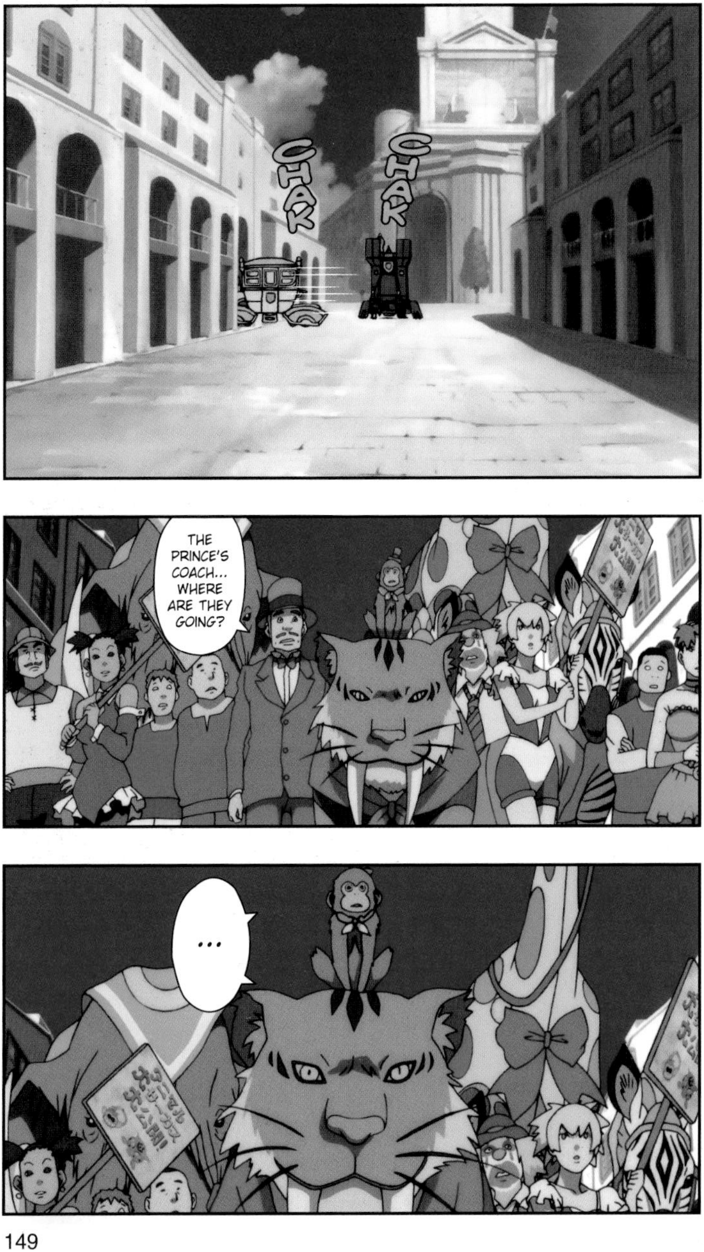
CHAK
CHAK
THE PRINCE'S COACH... WHERE ARE THEY GOING?
...

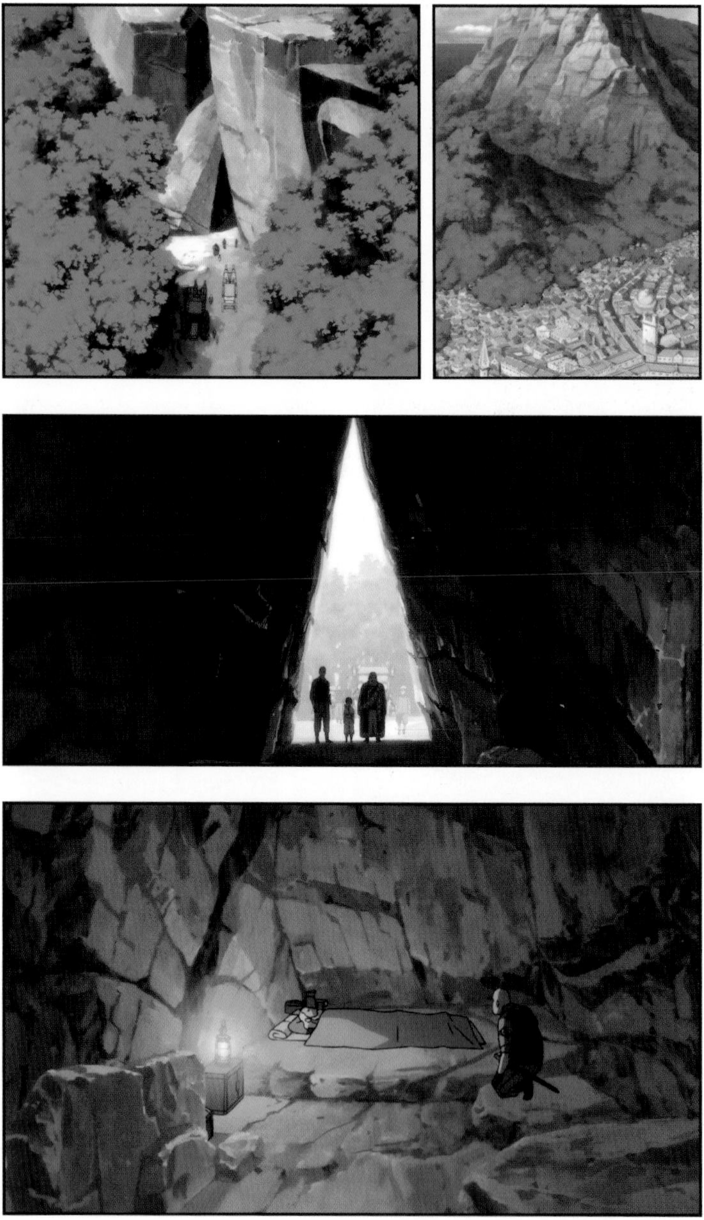

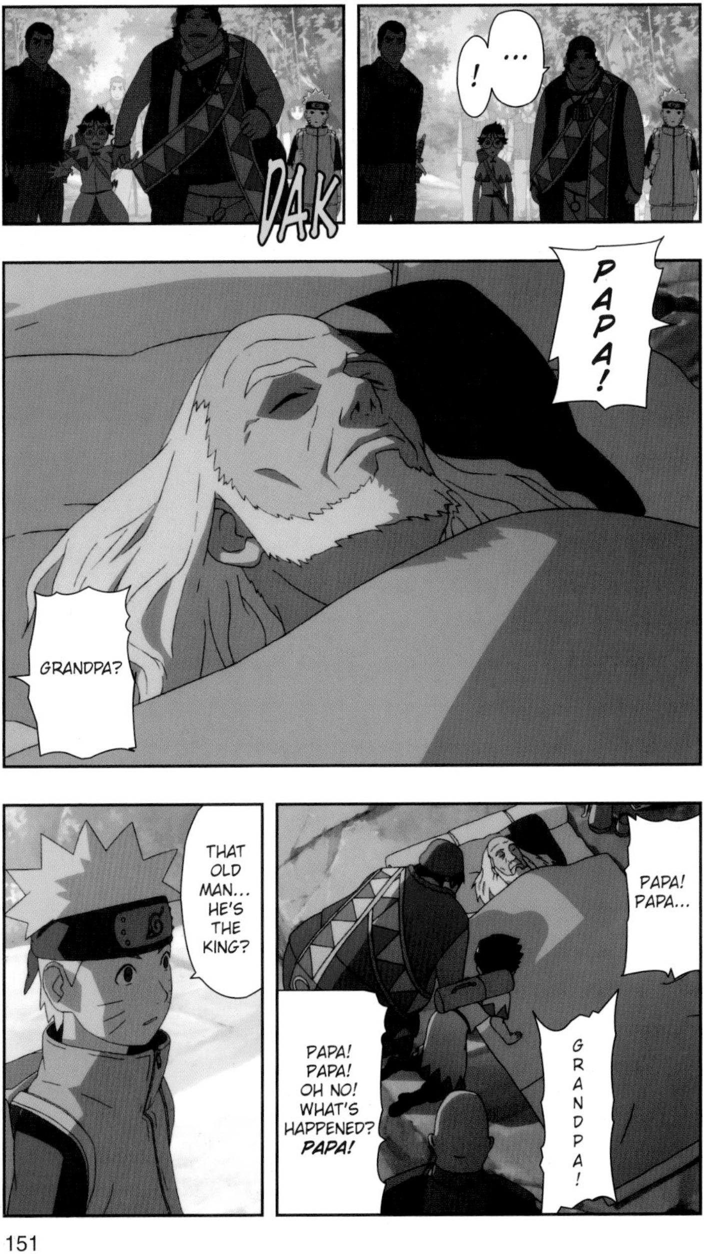
...
!
DAK
PAPA!
GRANDPA?
PAPA! PAPA...
GRANDPA!
PAPA! PAPA! OH NO! WHAT'S HAPPENED? **PAPA!**
THAT OLD MAN... HE'S THE KING?

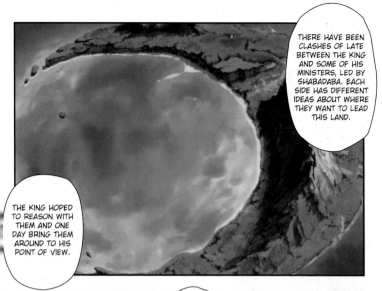

THERE HAVE BEEN CLASHES OF LATE BETWEEN THE KING AND SOME OF HIS MINISTERS, LED BY SHABADABA. EACH SIDE HAS DIFFERENT IDEAS ABOUT WHERE THEY WANT TO LEAD THIS LAND.

THE KING HOPED TO REASON WITH THEM AND ONE DAY BRING THEM AROUND TO HIS POINT OF VIEW.

BUT MEANWHILE SHABADABA TOOK MATTERS INTO HIS OWN HANDS. HE PLOTTED TO OVERTHROW THE KING.

BY CHANCE, WE DISCOVERED HIS PLOT IN TIME AND INFORMED HIS MAJESTY. HE REALIZED THE TIME HAD COME TO CONFRONT HIS MINISTERS.

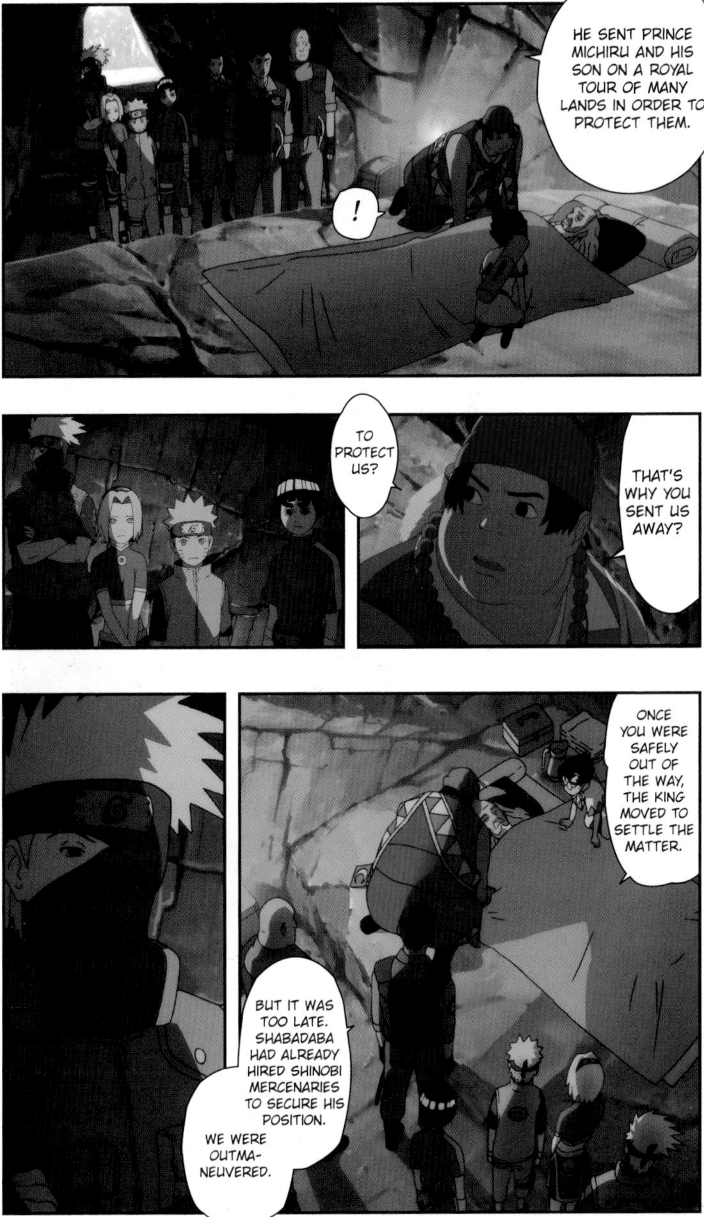
HE SENT PRINCE MICHIRU AND HIS SON ON A ROYAL TOUR OF MANY LANDS IN ORDER TO PROTECT THEM.
!
TO PROTECT US?
THAT'S WHY YOU SENT US AWAY?
ONCE YOU WERE SAFELY OUT OF THE WAY, THE KING MOVED TO SETTLE THE MATTER.
BUT IT WAS TOO LATE. SHABADABA HAD ALREADY HIRED SHINOBI MERCENARIES TO SECURE HIS POSITION.
WE WERE OUTMANEUVERED.

WE BARELY MANAGED TO ESCAPE IN THE NICK OF TIME.
BUT THE KING, TO MY SHAME, DID NOT.
!
!
GRANDPA...

LET ME TAKE A LOOK AT HIS INJURIES.

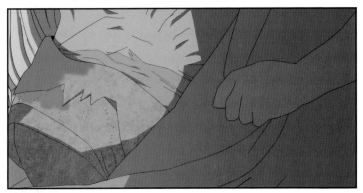

!

...

!

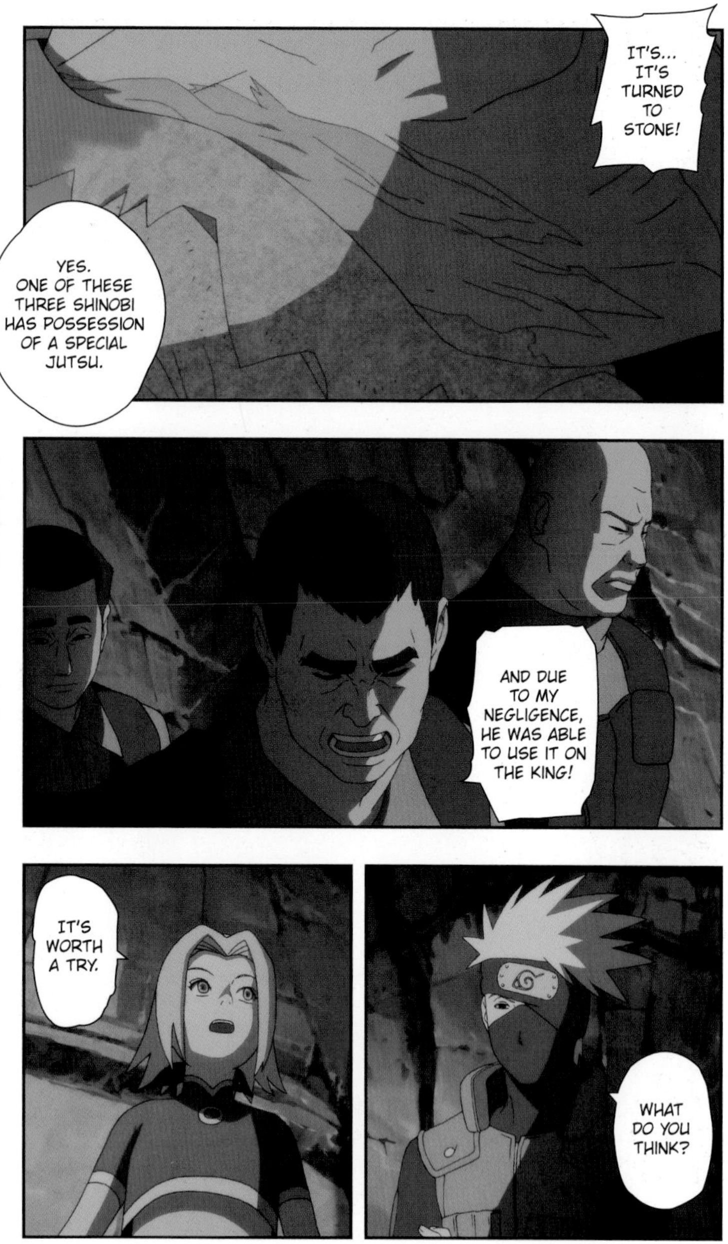
IT'S... IT'S TURNED TO STONE!
YES. ONE OF THESE THREE SHINOBI HAS POSSESSION OF A SPECIAL JUTSU.
AND DUE TO MY NEGLIGENCE, HE WAS ABLE TO USE IT ON THE KING!
WHAT DO YOU THINK?
IT'S WORTH A TRY.

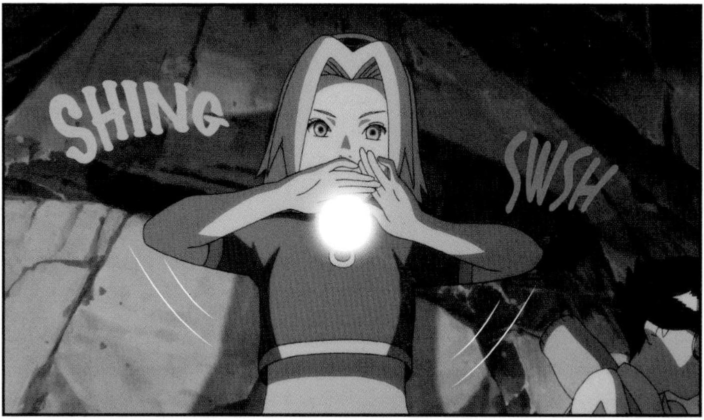
SWSH
SHING
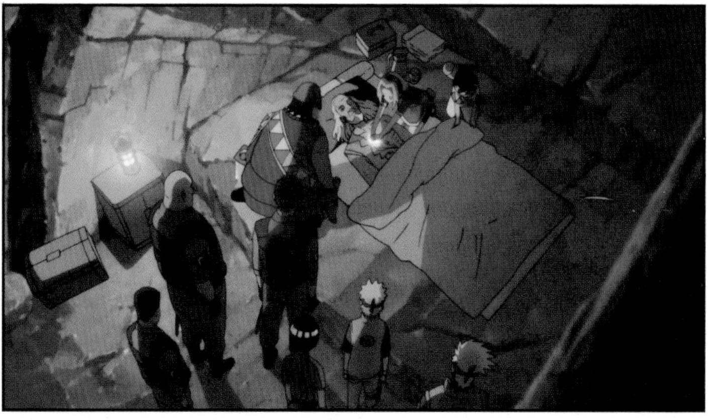
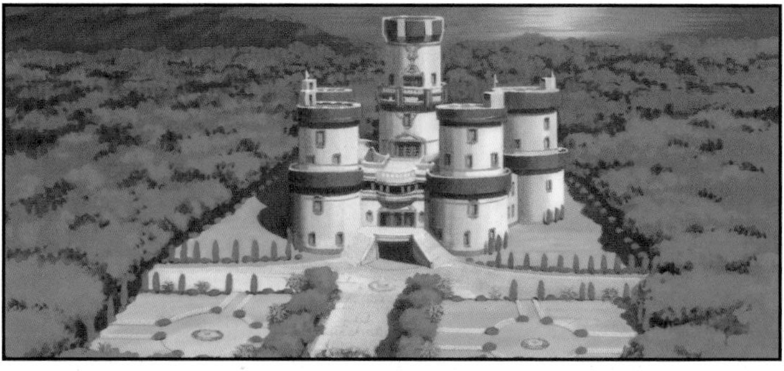

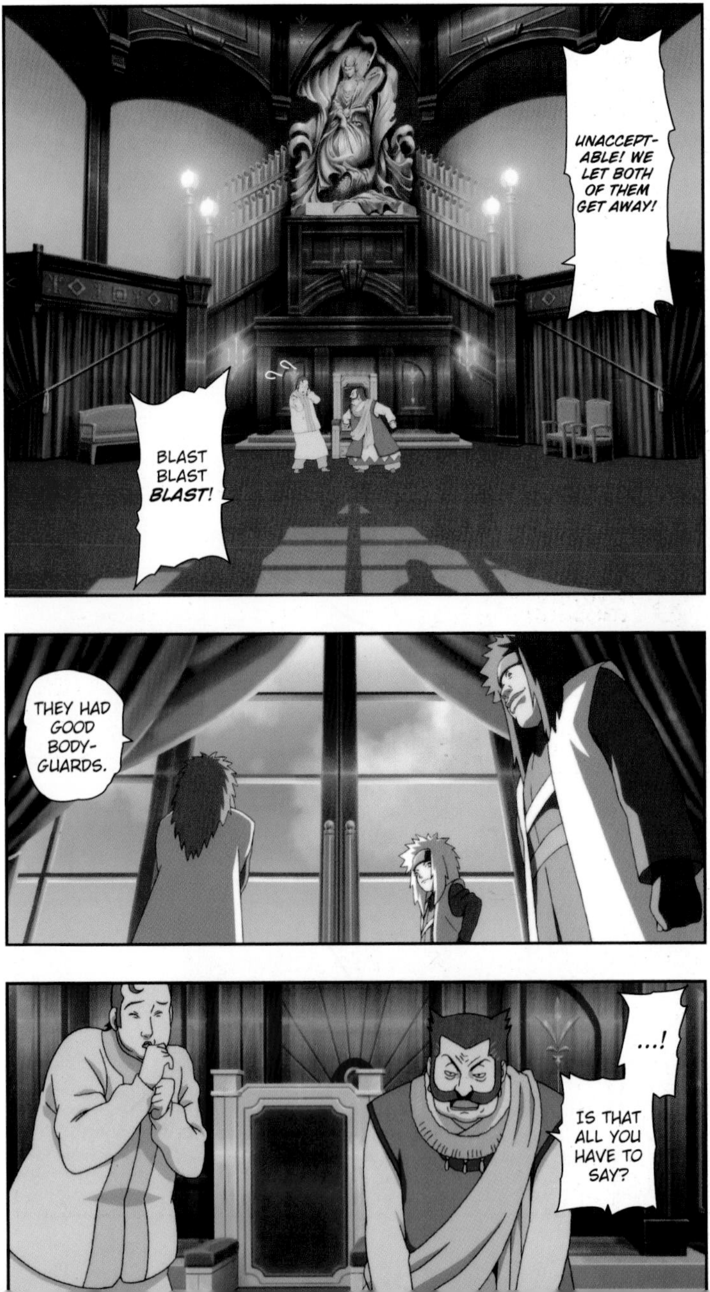
UNACCEPT-ABLE! WE LET BOTH OF THEM GET AWAY!
BLAST BLAST BLAST!
THEY HAD GOOD BODY-GUARDS.
...!
IS THAT ALL YOU HAVE TO SAY?

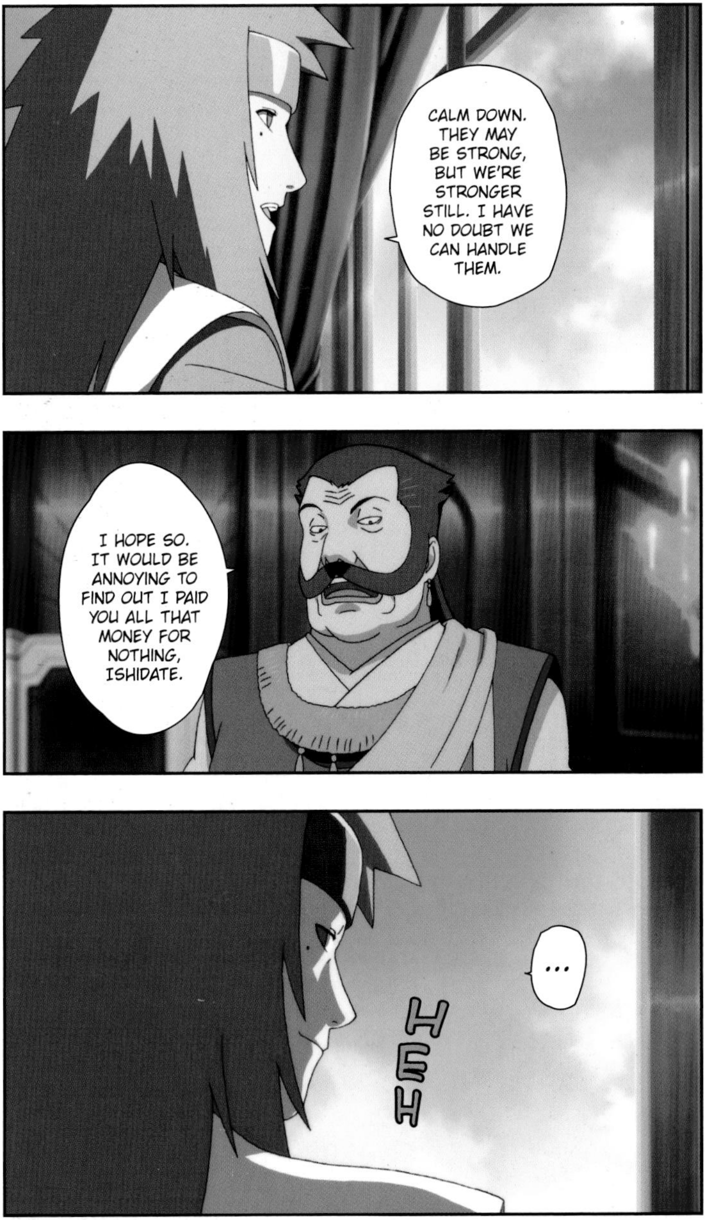
CALM DOWN. THEY MAY BE STRONG, BUT WE'RE STRONGER STILL. I HAVE NO DOUBT WE CAN HANDLE THEM.
I HOPE SO. IT WOULD BE ANNOYING TO FIND OUT I PAID YOU ALL THAT MONEY FOR NOTHING, ISHIDATE.
...
HEH HEH

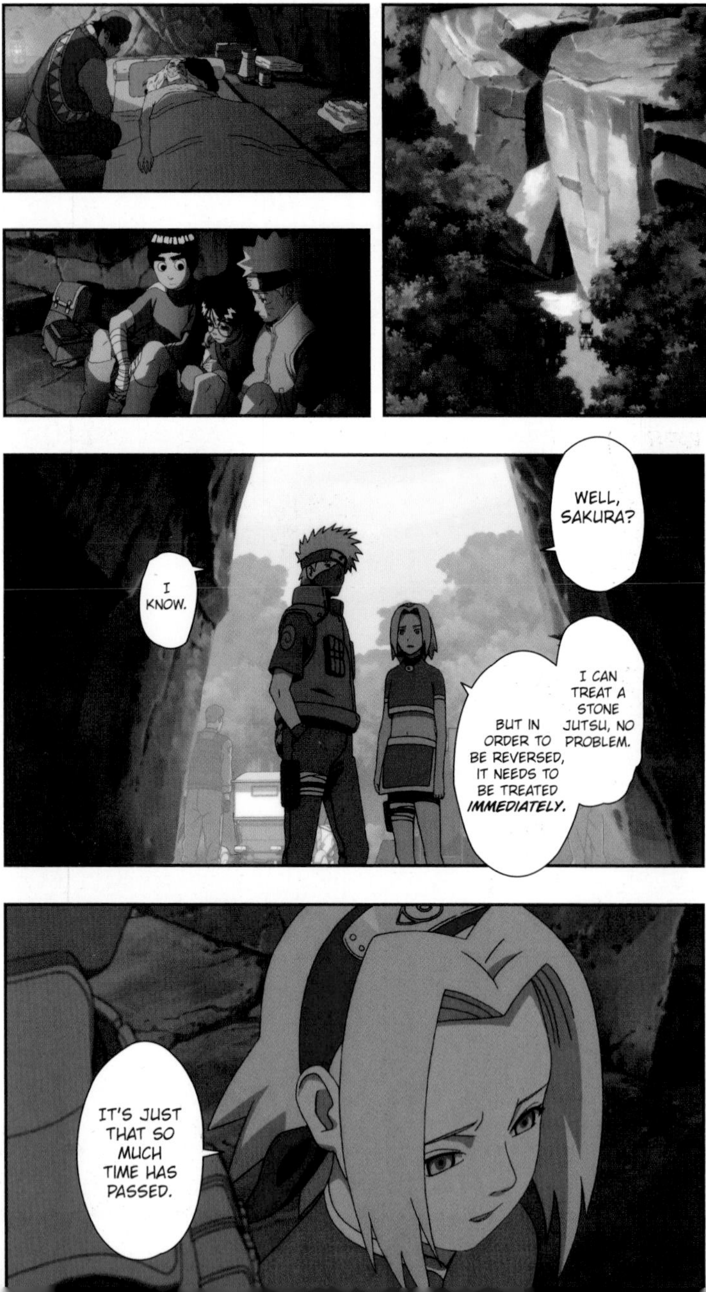
WELL, SAKURA?
I CAN TREAT A STONE JUTSU, NO PROBLEM.
BUT IN ORDER TO BE REVERSED, IT NEEDS TO BE TREATED *IMMEDIATELY*.
I KNOW.
IT'S JUST THAT SO MUCH TIME HAS PASSED.

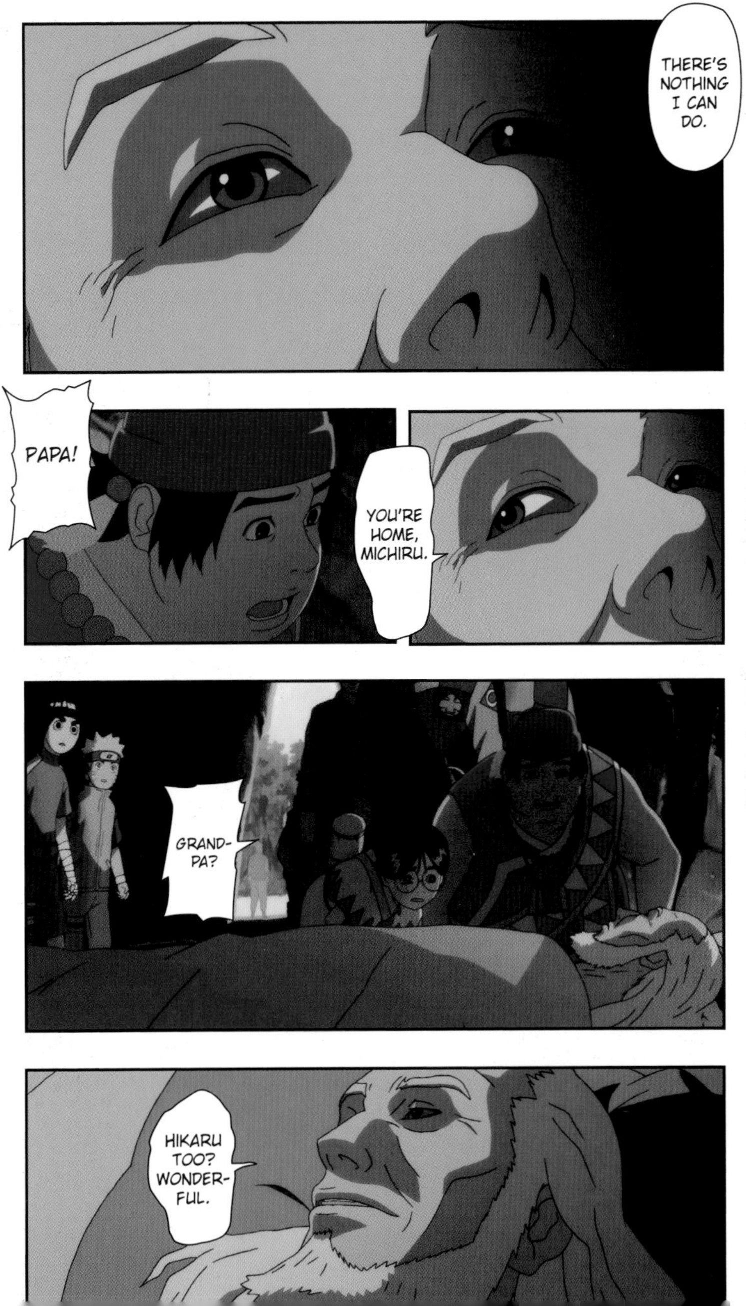
THERE'S NOTHING I CAN DO.
YOU'RE HOME, MICHIRU.
PAPA!
GRAND-PA?
HIKARU TOO? WONDER-FUL.

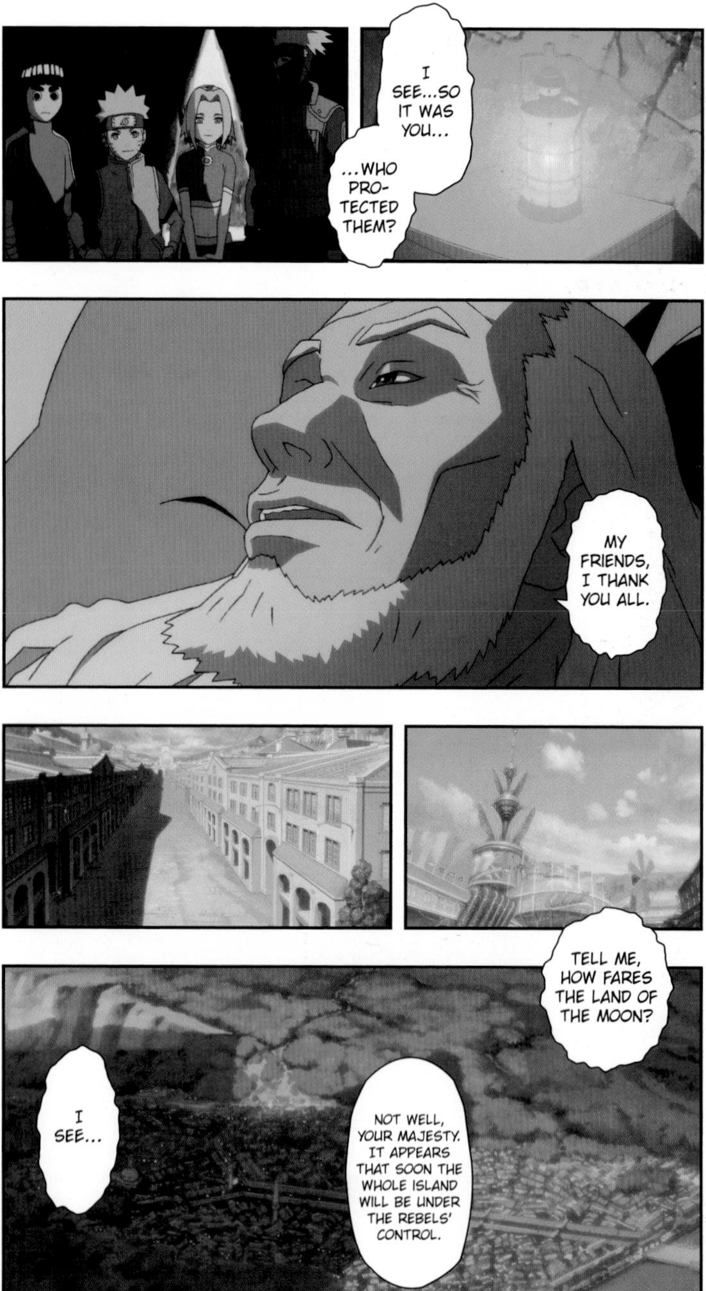
I SEE...SO IT WAS YOU...
...WHO PRO-TECTED THEM?
MY FRIENDS, I THANK YOU ALL.
TELL ME, HOW FARES THE LAND OF THE MOON?
NOT WELL, YOUR MAJESTY. IT APPEARS THAT SOON THE WHOLE ISLAND WILL BE UNDER THE REBELS' CONTROL.
I SEE...

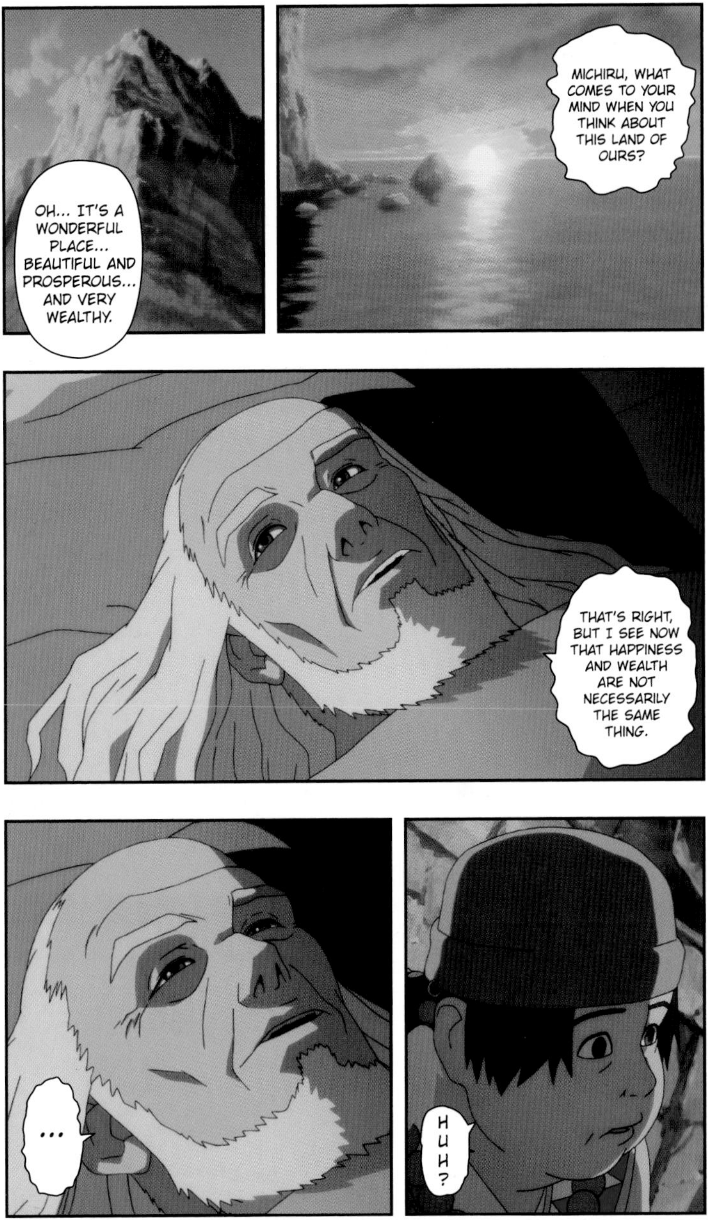
MICHIRU, WHAT COMES TO YOUR MIND WHEN YOU THINK ABOUT THIS LAND OF OURS?
OH... IT'S A WONDERFUL PLACE... BEAUTIFUL AND PROSPEROUS... AND VERY WEALTHY.
THAT'S RIGHT, BUT I SEE NOW THAT HAPPINESS AND WEALTH ARE NOT NECESSARILY THE SAME THING.
HUH?
...

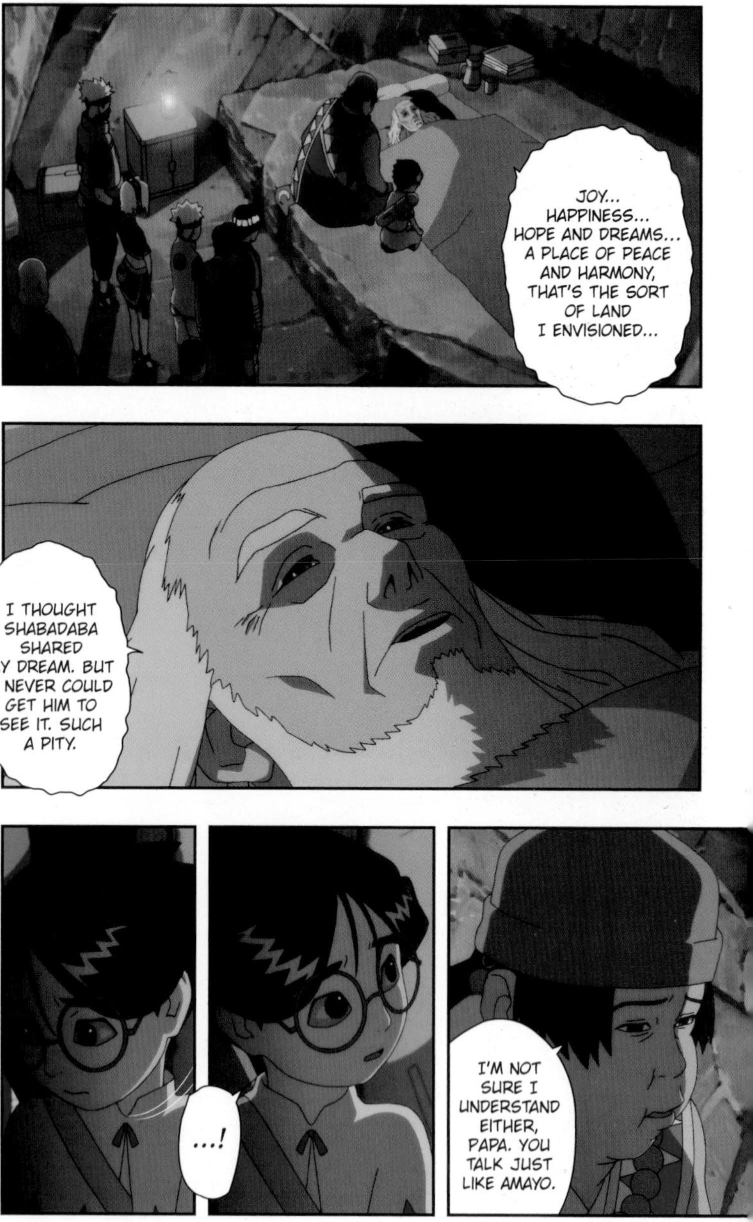
JOY... HAPPINESS... HOPE AND DREAMS... A PLACE OF PEACE AND HARMONY, THAT'S THE SORT OF LAND I ENVISIONED...
I THOUGHT SHABADABA SHARED MY DREAM. BUT I NEVER COULD GET HIM TO SEE IT. SUCH A PITY.
I'M NOT SURE I UNDERSTAND EITHER, PAPA. YOU TALK JUST LIKE AMAYO.
...!

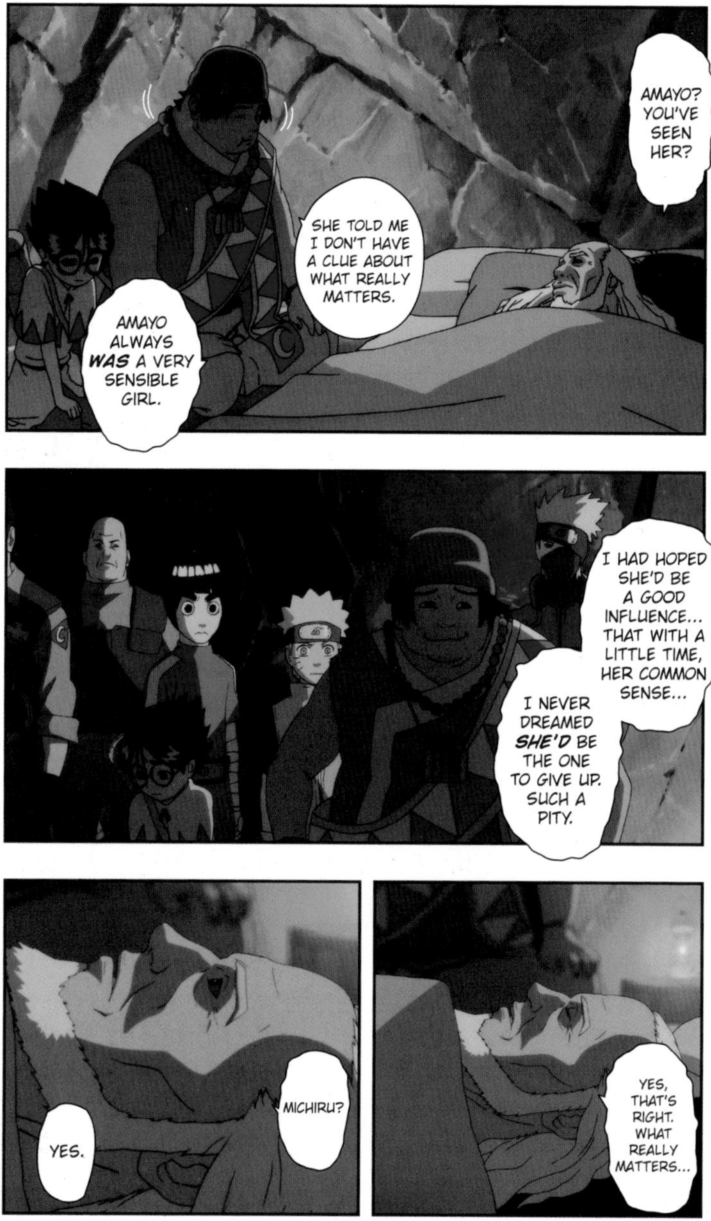
AMAYO? YOU'VE SEEN HER?
SHE TOLD ME I DON'T HAVE A CLUE ABOUT WHAT REALLY MATTERS.
AMAYO ALWAYS **WAS** A VERY SENSIBLE GIRL.
I HAD HOPED SHE'D BE A GOOD INFLUENCE... THAT WITH A LITTLE TIME, HER COMMON SENSE...
I NEVER DREAMED **SHE'D** BE THE ONE TO GIVE UP. SUCH A PITY.
YES, THAT'S RIGHT. WHAT REALLY MATTERS...
MICHIRU?
YES.

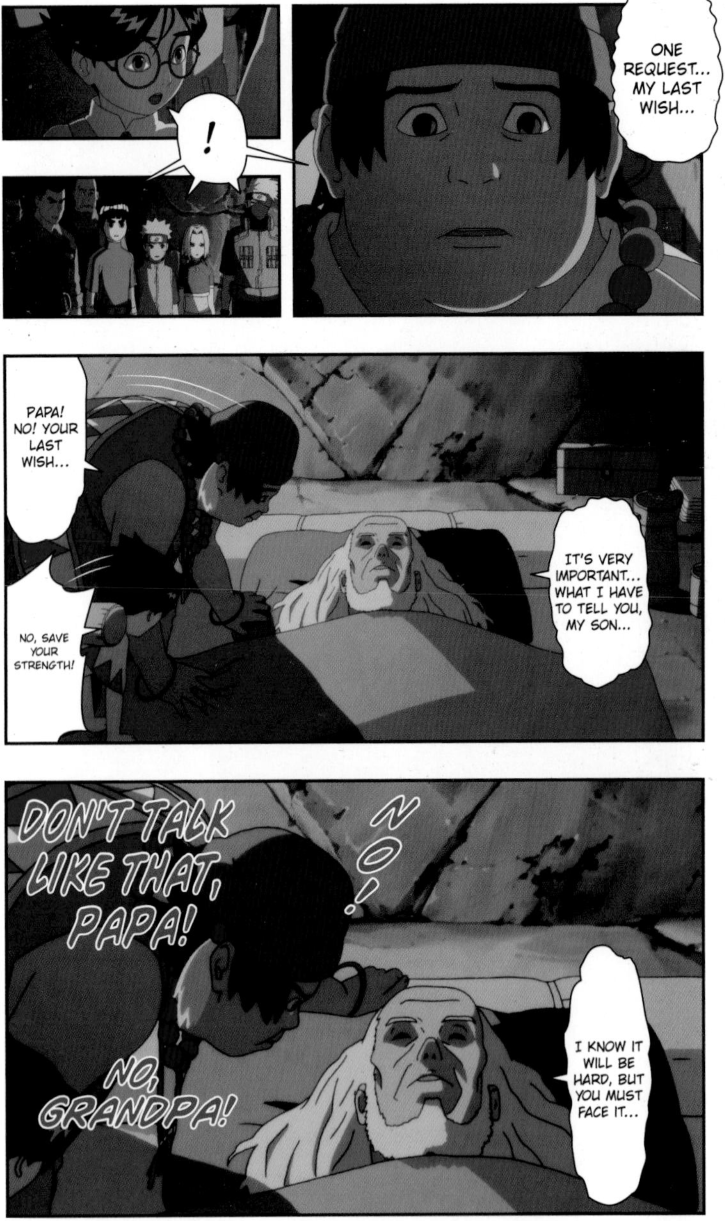
ONE REQUEST... MY LAST WISH...
!
PAPA! NO! YOUR LAST WISH...
IT'S VERY IMPORTANT... WHAT I HAVE TO TELL YOU, MY SON...
NO, SAVE YOUR STRENGTH!
NO!
DON'T TALK LIKE THAT, PAPA!
I KNOW IT WILL BE HARD, BUT YOU MUST FACE IT...
NO, GRANDPA!

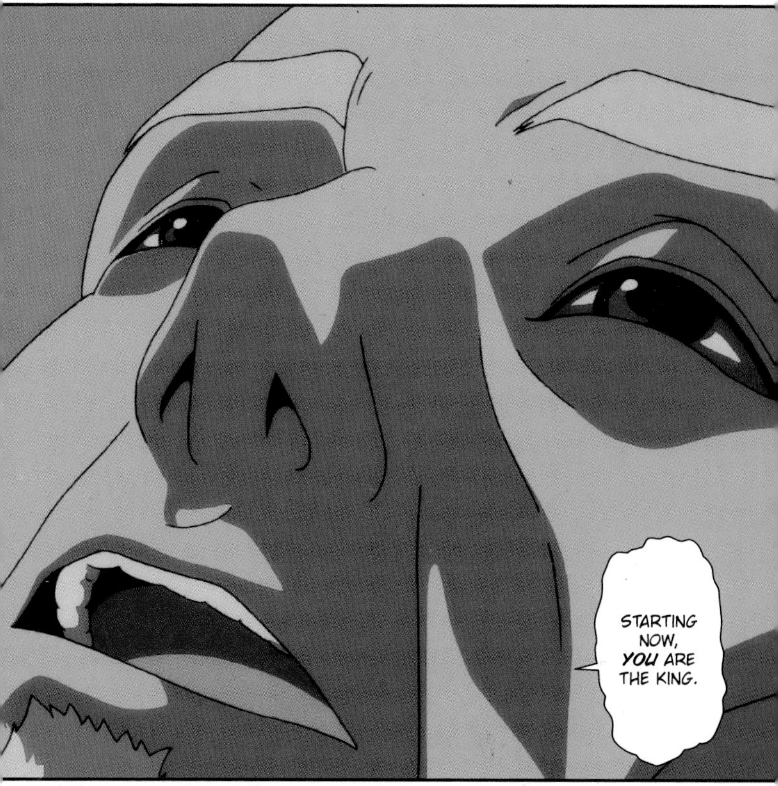
STARTING NOW, YOU ARE THE KING.

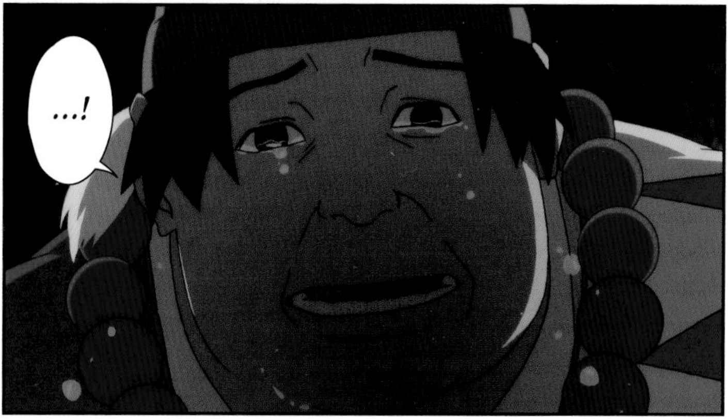
...!

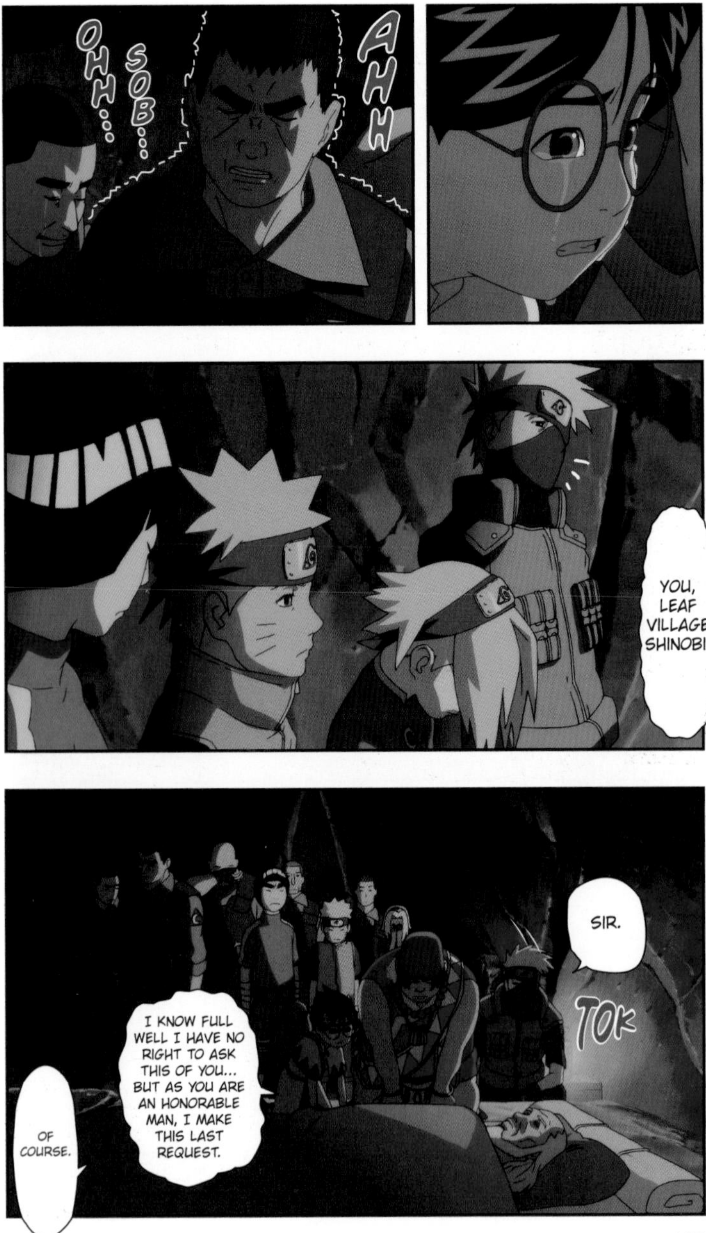
AHHH
SOB...
OHH...
YOU, LEAF VILLAGE SHINOBI.
SIR.
TOK
I KNOW FULL WELL I HAVE NO RIGHT TO ASK THIS OF YOU... BUT AS YOU ARE AN HONORABLE MAN, I MAKE THIS LAST REQUEST.
OF COURSE.

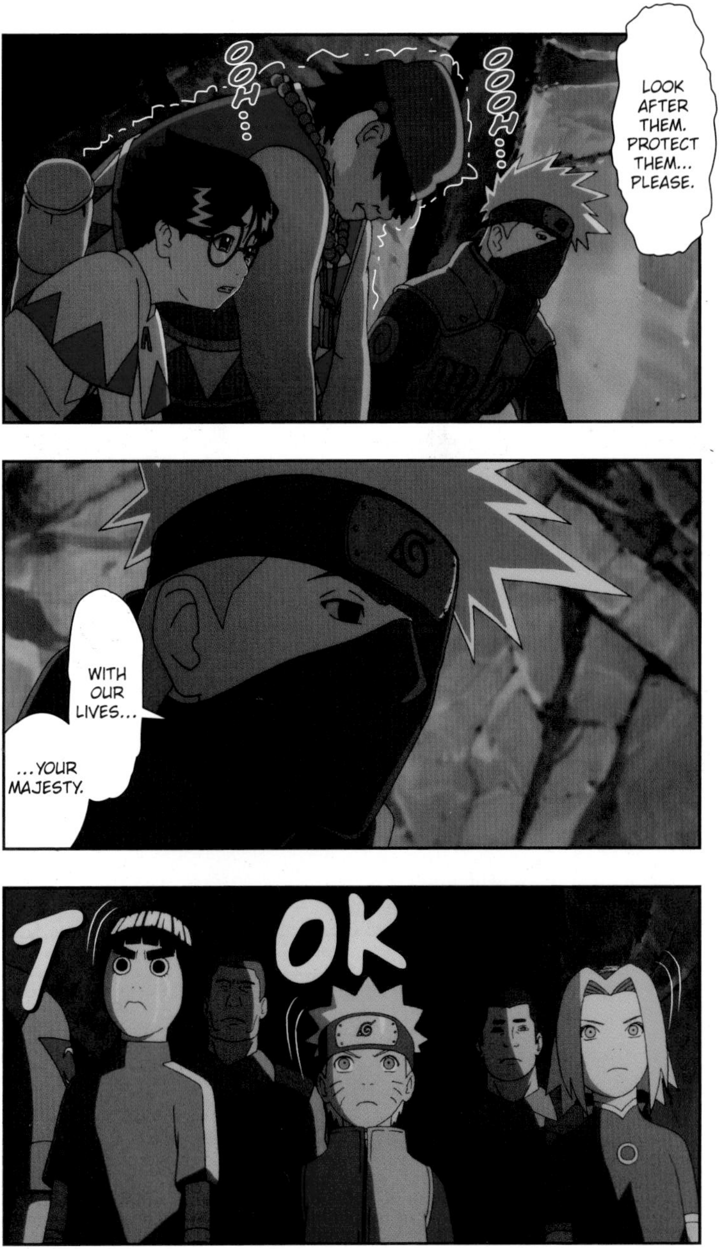

LOOK AFTER THEM. PROTECT THEM... PLEASE.
OOOH...
OOOH...
WITH OUR LIVES...
...YOUR MAJESTY.
TOK

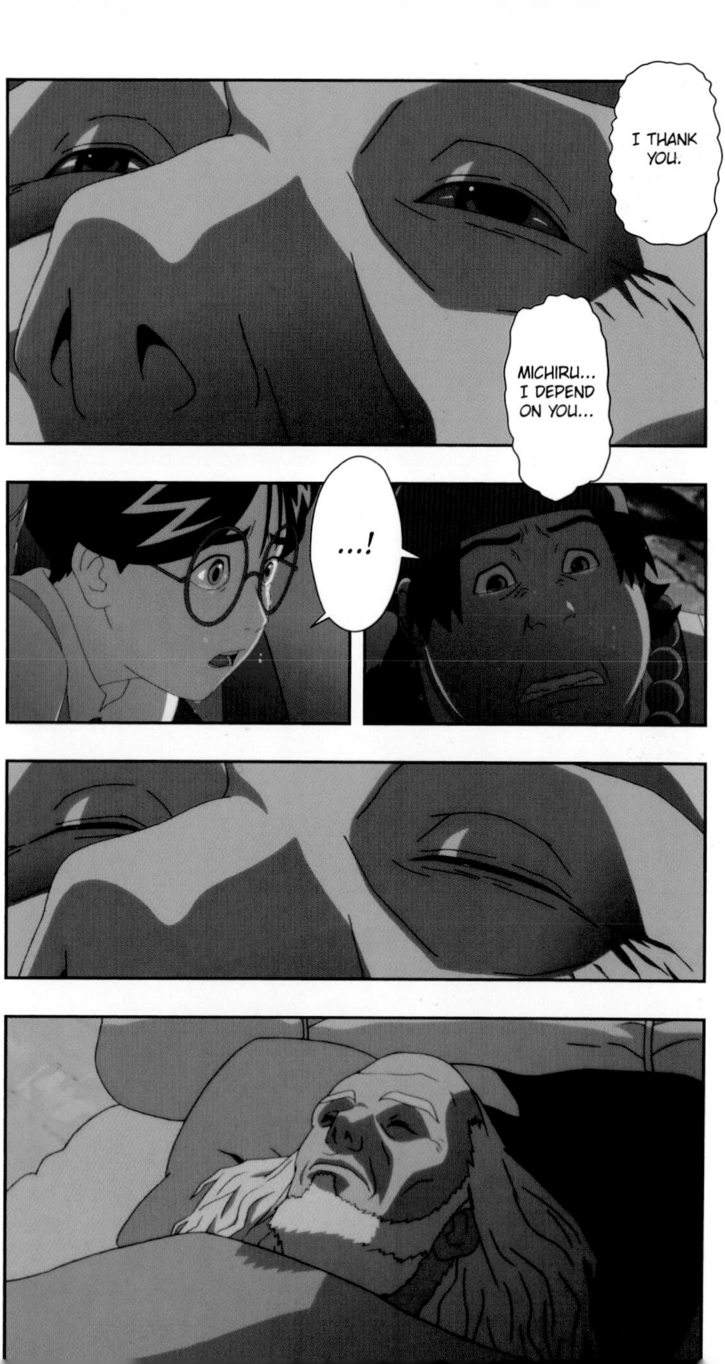
I THANK YOU.
MICHIRU... I DEPEND ON YOU...
...!

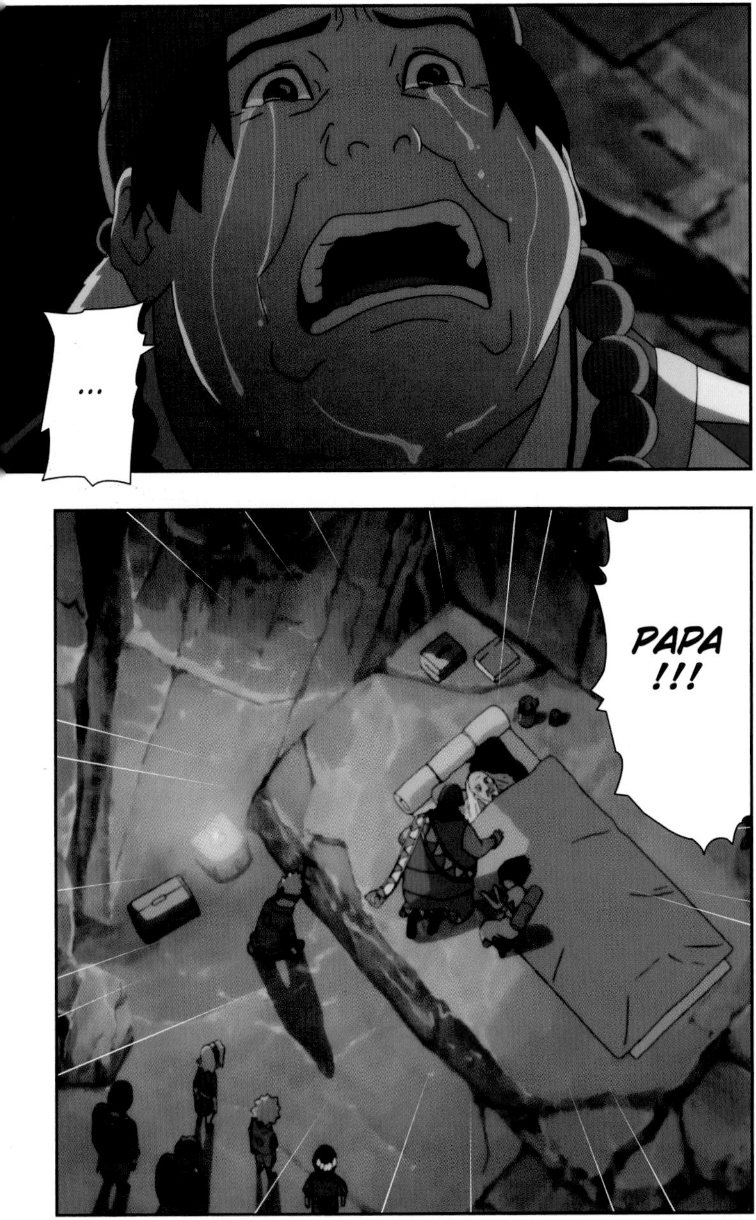
...
PAPA !!!

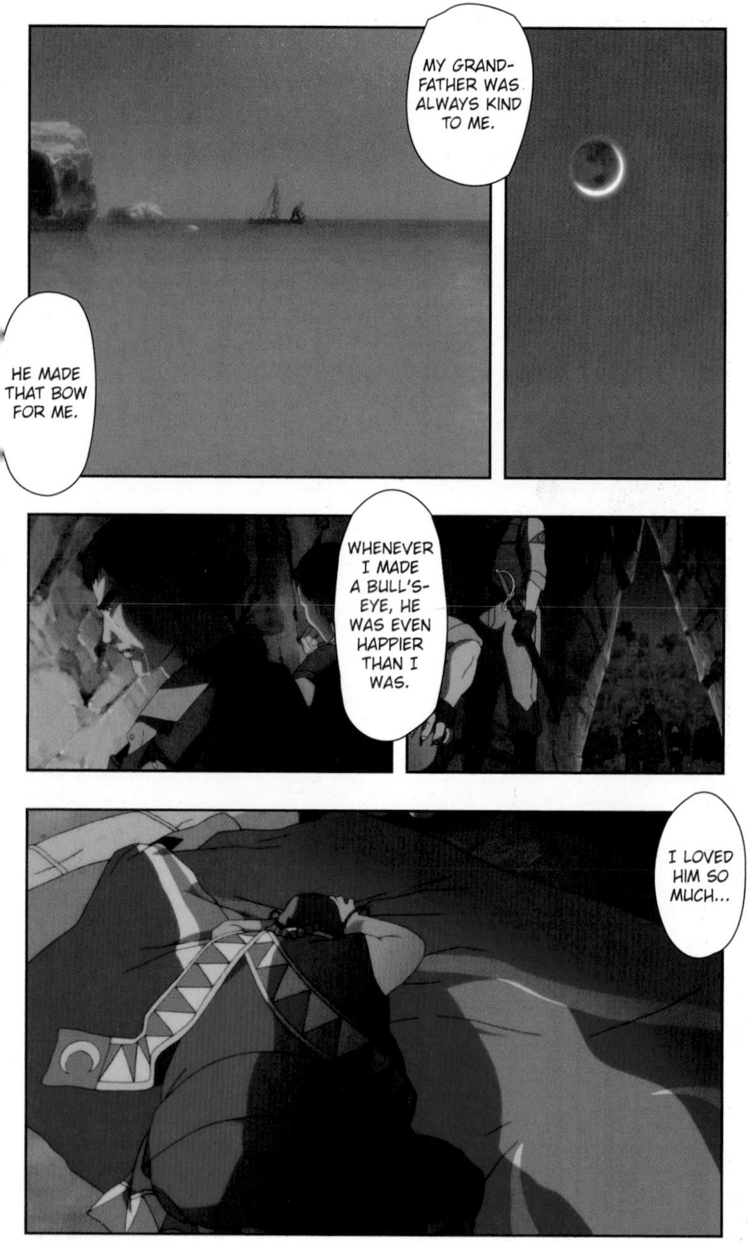
MY GRAND-FATHER WAS ALWAYS KIND TO ME.
HE MADE THAT BOW FOR ME.
WHENEVER I MADE A BULL'S-EYE, HE WAS EVEN HAPPIER THAN I WAS.
I LOVED HIM SO MUCH...

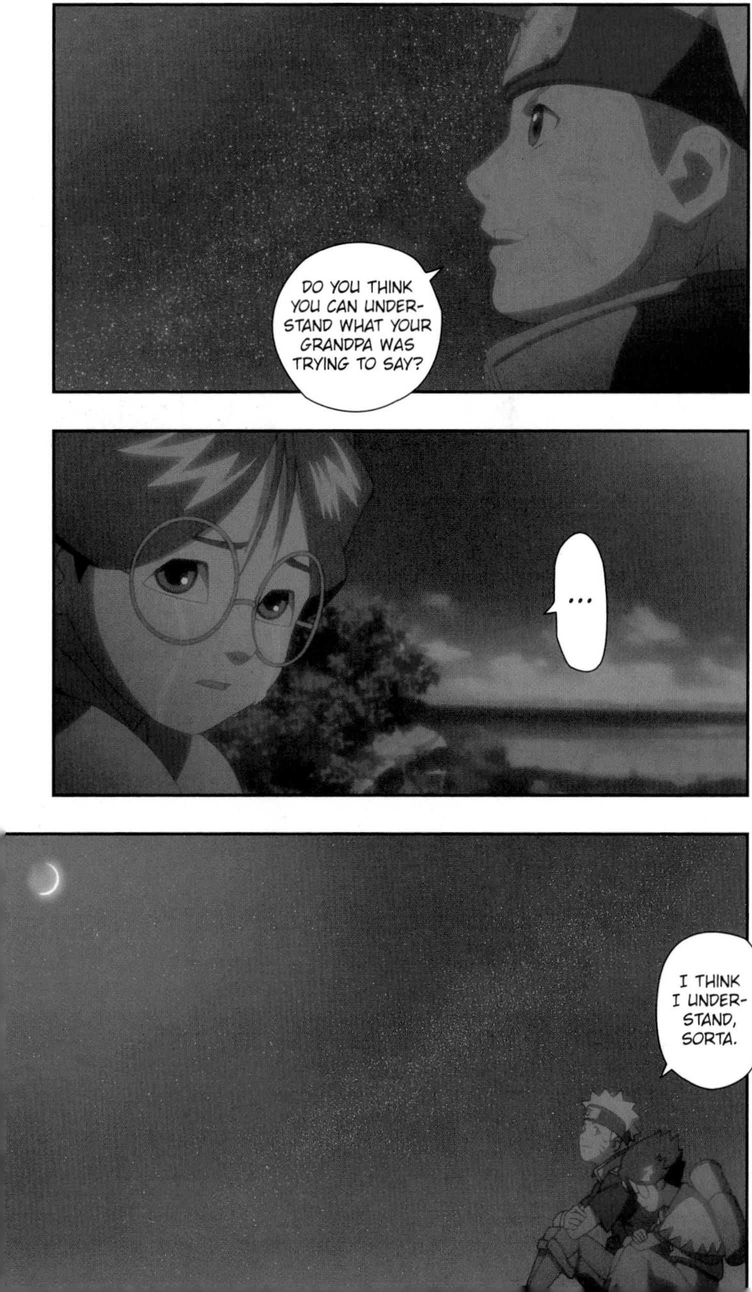
DO YOU THINK YOU CAN UNDER-STAND WHAT YOUR GRANDPA WAS TRYING TO SAY?
...
I THINK I UNDER-STAND, SORTA.

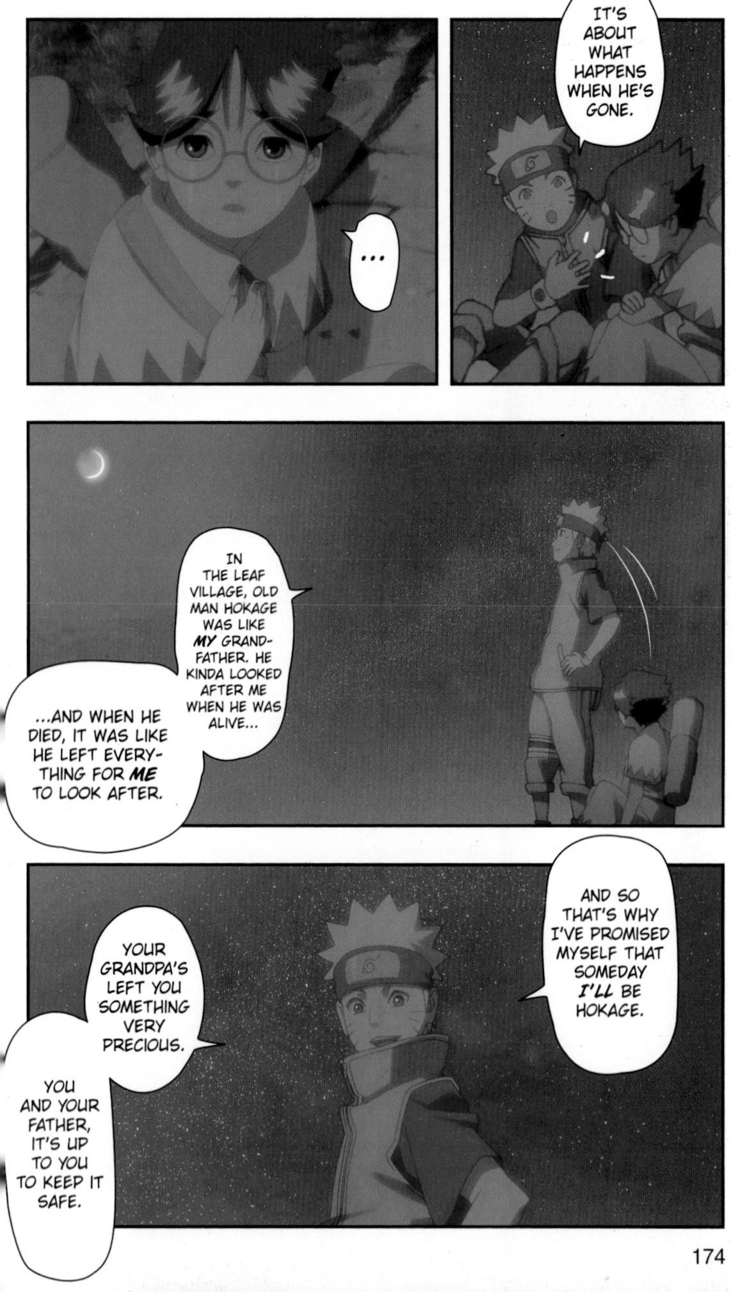
IT'S ABOUT WHAT HAPPENS WHEN HE'S GONE.
...
IN THE LEAF VILLAGE, OLD MAN HOKAGE WAS LIKE *MY* GRAND-FATHER. HE KINDA LOOKED AFTER ME WHEN HE WAS ALIVE...
...AND WHEN HE DIED, IT WAS LIKE HE LEFT EVERY-THING FOR *ME* TO LOOK AFTER.
AND SO THAT'S WHY I'VE PROMISED MYSELF THAT SOMEDAY *I'LL* BE HOKAGE.
YOUR GRANDPA'S LEFT YOU SOMETHING VERY PRECIOUS.
YOU AND YOUR FATHER, IT'S UP TO YOU TO KEEP IT SAFE.

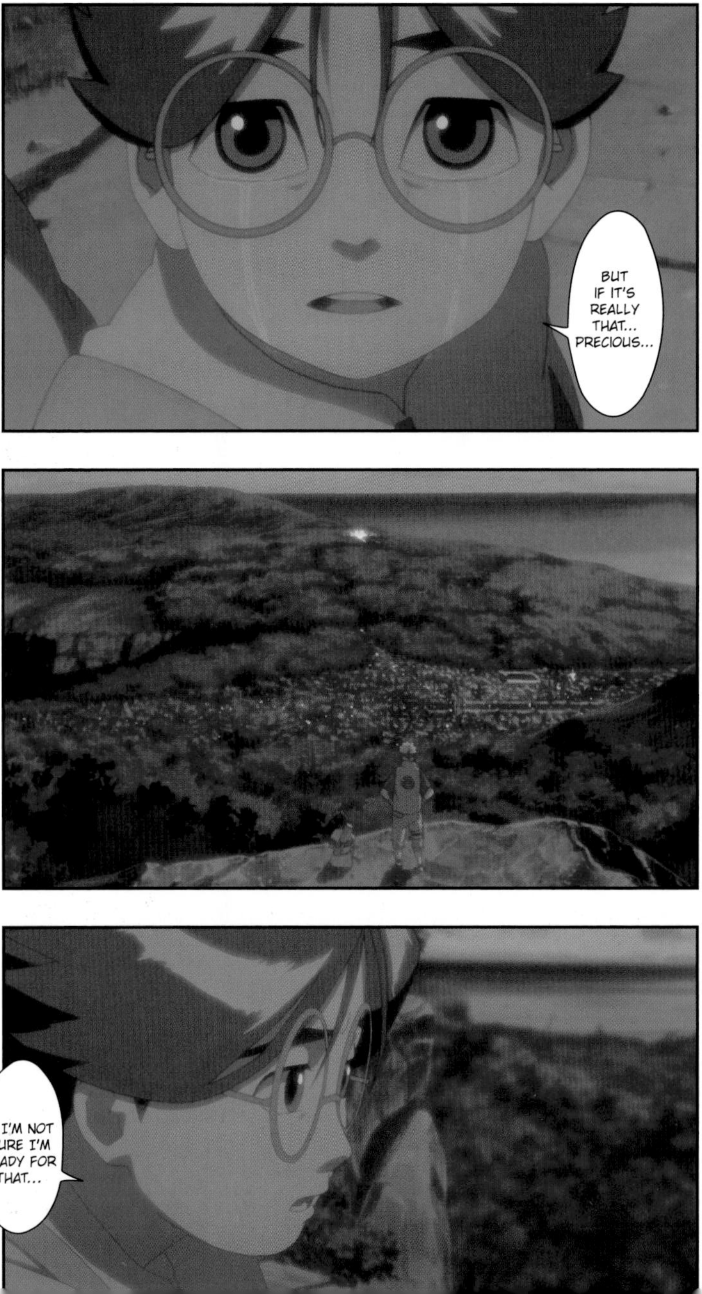
BUT IF IT'S REALLY THAT... PRECIOUS...
...I'M NOT SURE I'M READY FOR THAT...

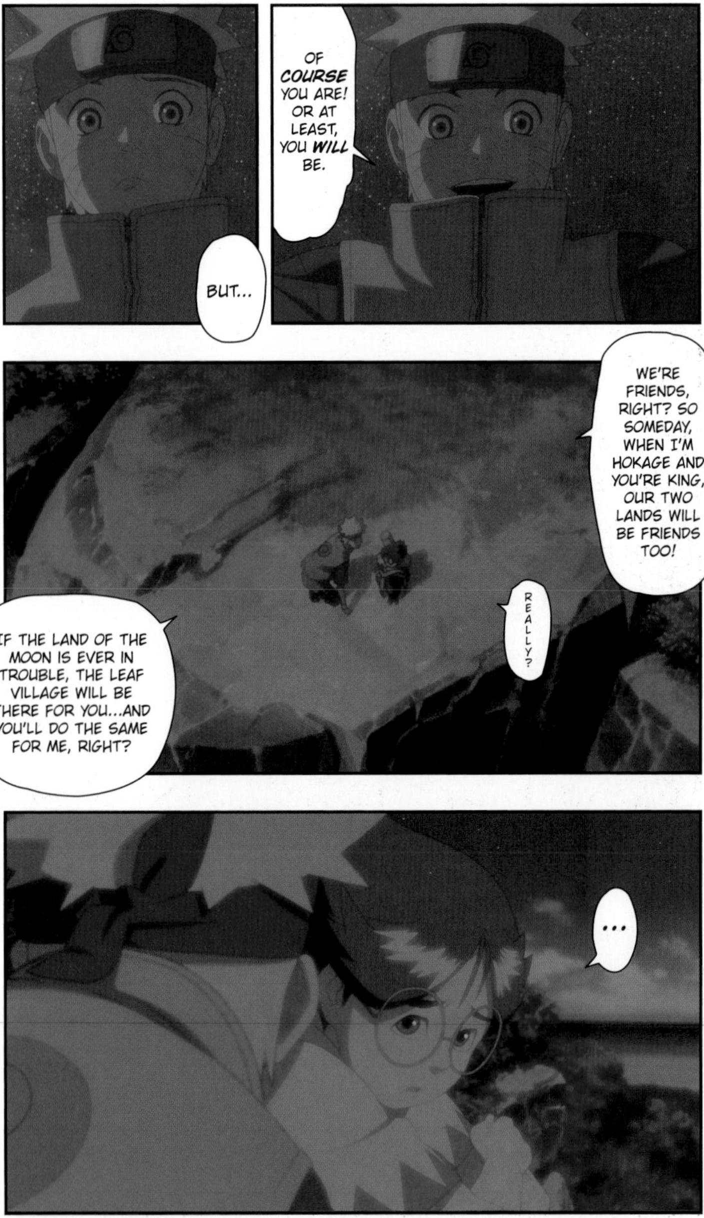
OF **COURSE** YOU ARE! OR AT LEAST, YOU **WILL** BE.
BUT...
WE'RE FRIENDS, RIGHT? SO SOMEDAY, WHEN I'M HOKAGE AND YOU'RE KING, OUR TWO LANDS WILL BE FRIENDS TOO!
REALLY?
IF THE LAND OF THE MOON IS EVER IN TROUBLE, THE LEAF VILLAGE WILL BE THERE FOR YOU...AND YOU'LL DO THE SAME FOR ME, RIGHT?
...

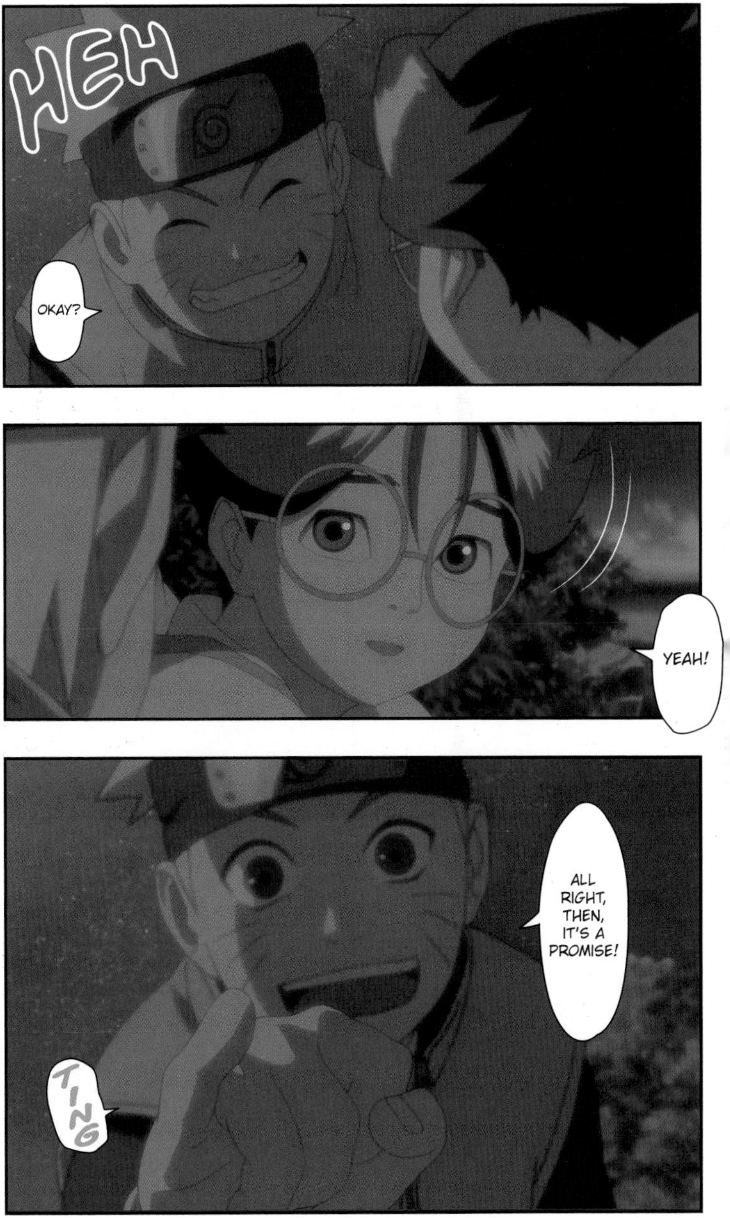
HEH
OKAY?
YEAH!
ALL RIGHT, THEN, IT'S A PROMISE!
TING

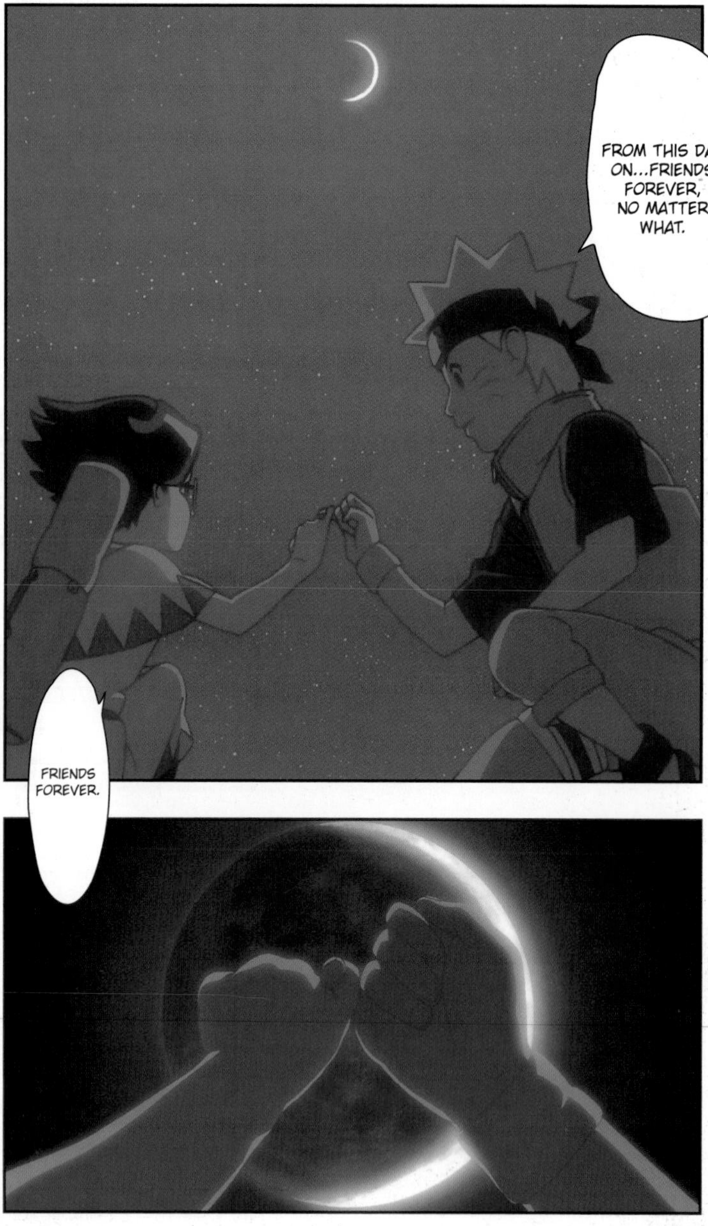
FROM THIS DAY ON...FRIENDS FOREVER, NO MATTER WHAT.
FRIENDS FOREVER.

Chapter 4: Three Shinobi

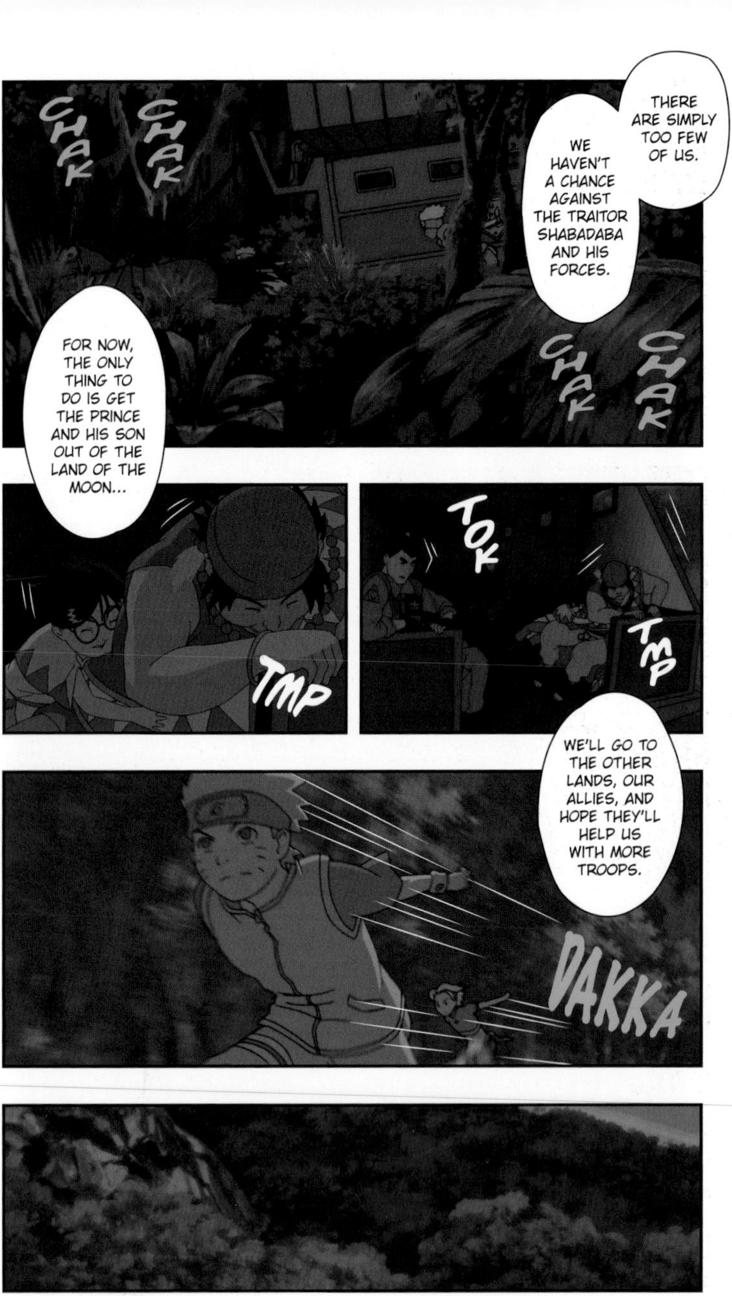
THERE ARE SIMPLY TOO FEW OF US.
WE HAVEN'T A CHANCE AGAINST THE TRAITOR SHABADABA AND HIS FORCES.
CHAK CHAK
CHAK CHAK
FOR NOW, THE ONLY THING TO DO IS GET THE PRINCE AND HIS SON OUT OF THE LAND OF THE MOON...
TOK
TMP
TMP
WE'LL GO TO THE OTHER LANDS, OUR ALLIES, AND HOPE THEY'LL HELP US WITH MORE TROOPS.
DAKKA

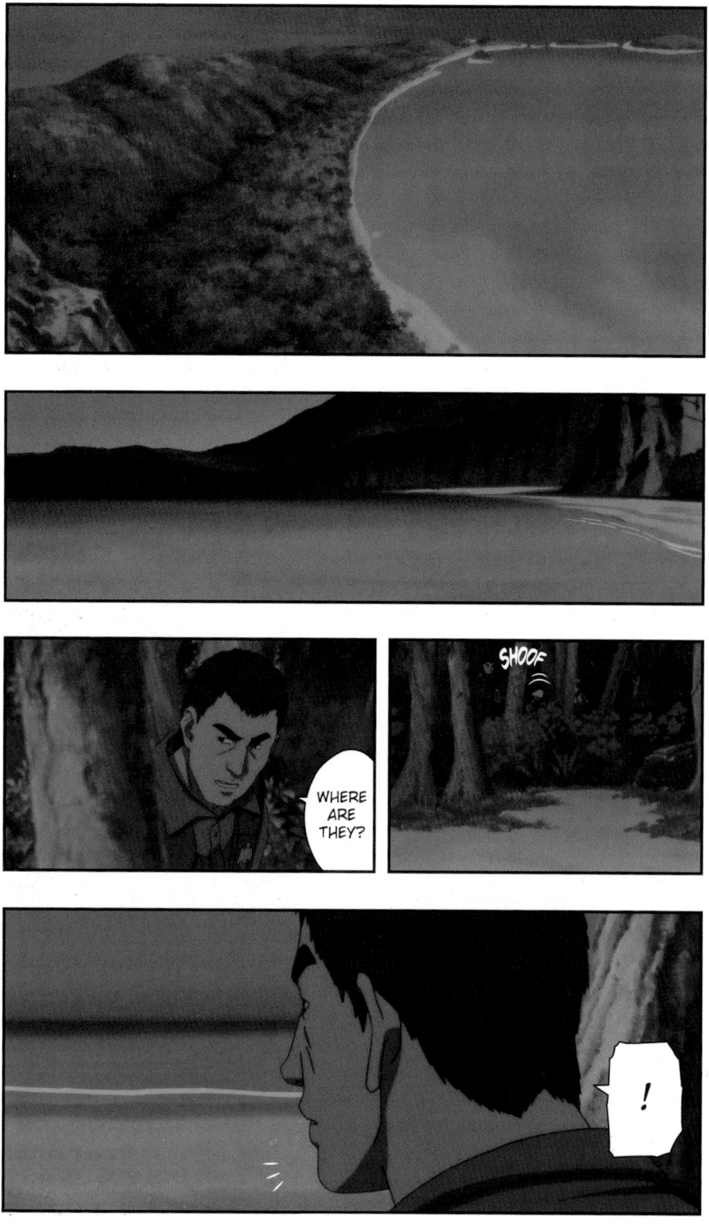
SHOOF
WHERE ARE THEY?
!

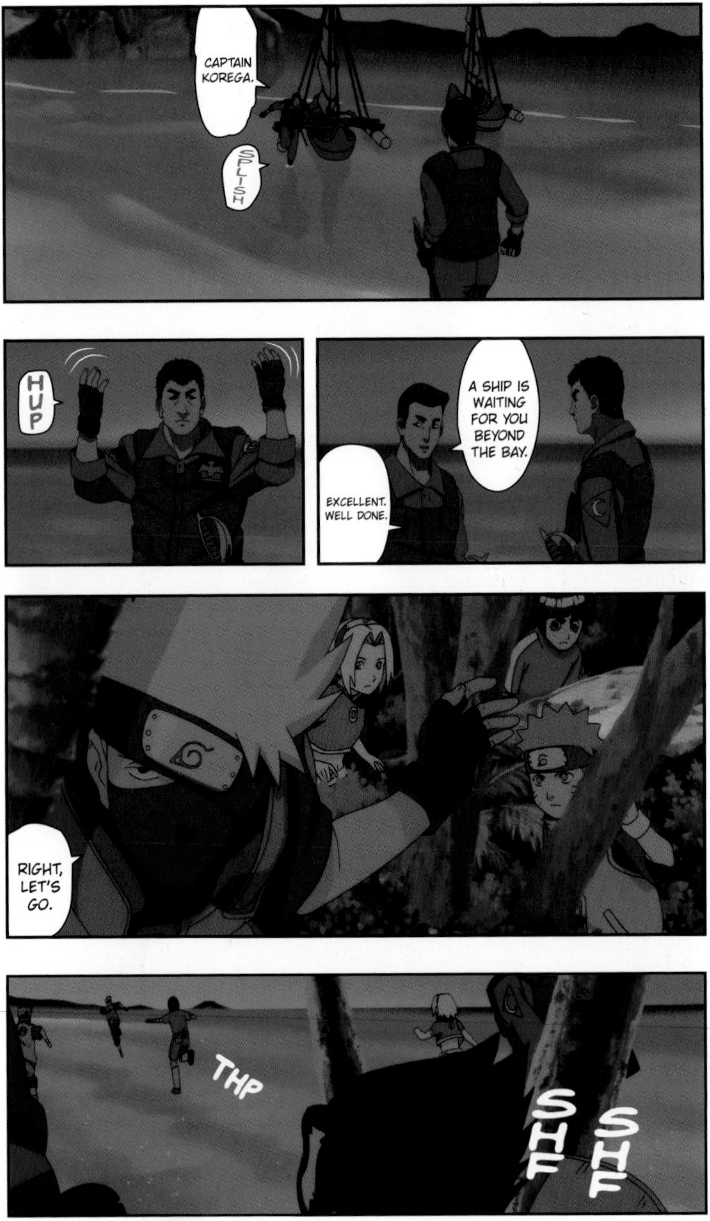
CAPTAIN KOREGA.
SPLISH
A SHIP IS WAITING FOR YOU BEYOND THE BAY.
EXCELLENT. WELL DONE.
HUP
RIGHT, LET'S GO.
SHF
SHF
THP

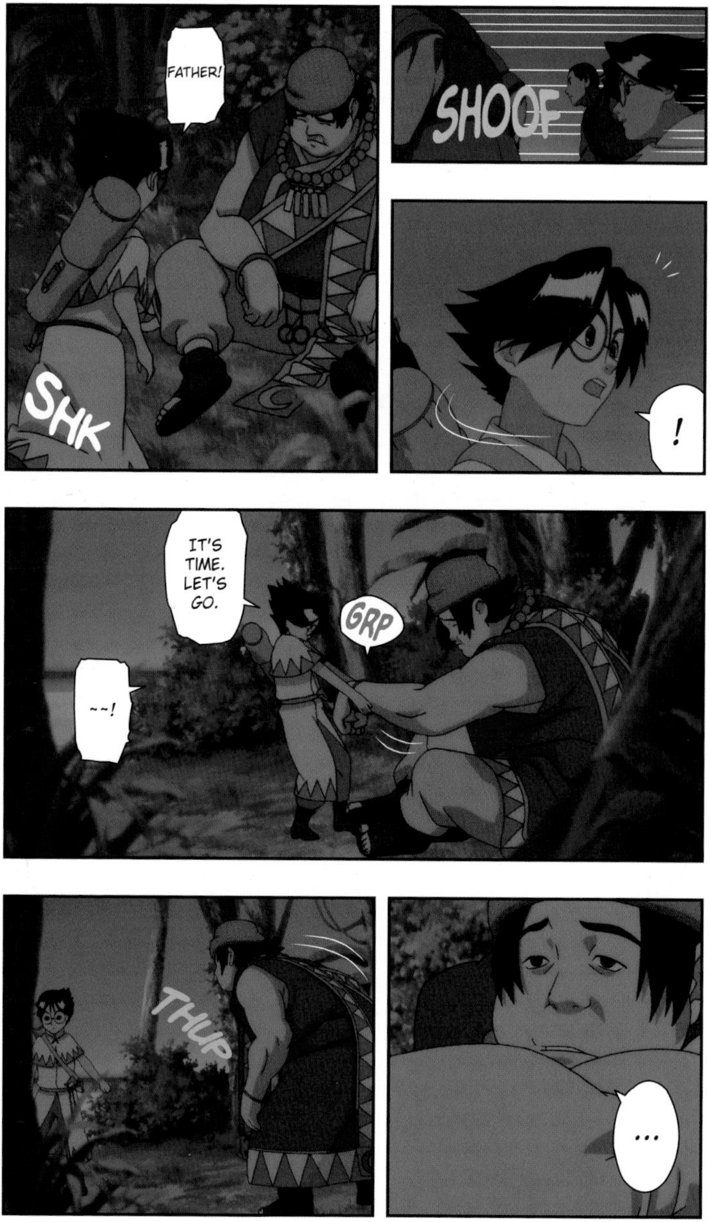
SHOOF
!
FATHER!
SHK
IT'S TIME. LET'S GO.
GRP
~~!
...
THUP

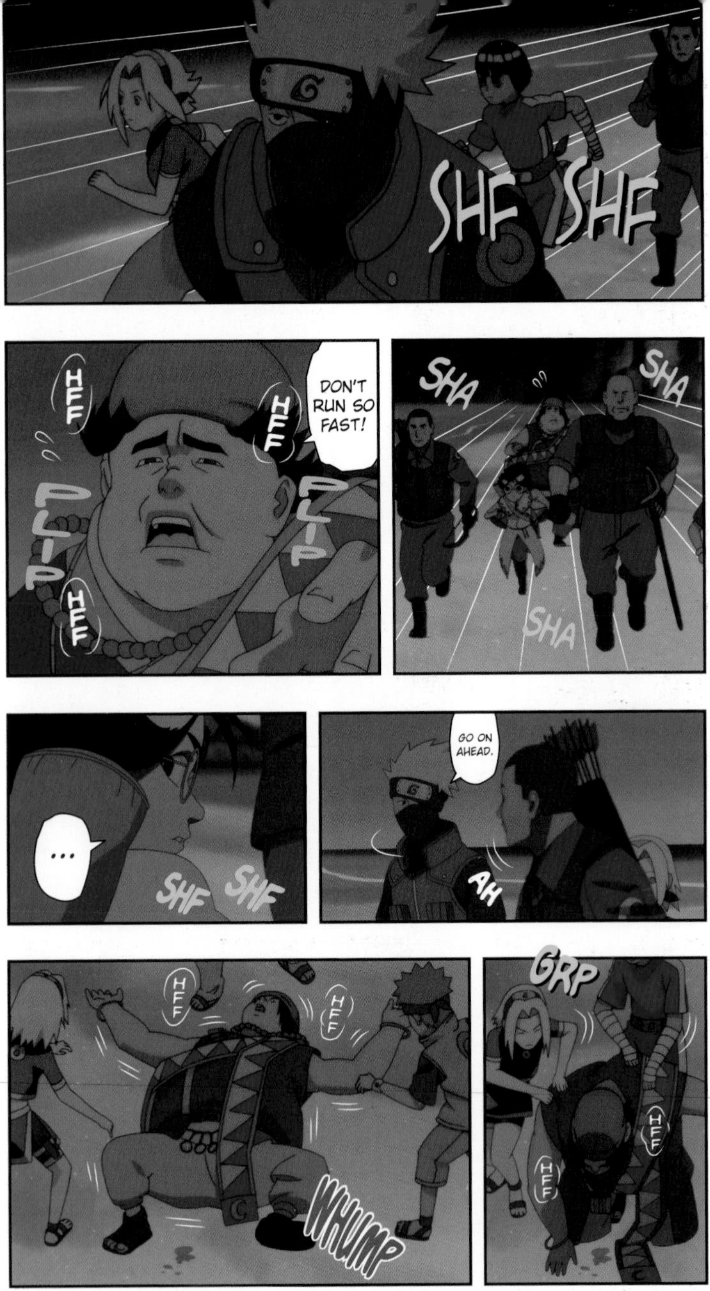
SHF SHF
SHA
SHA
SHA
HFF
DON'T RUN SO FAST!
HFF
PLIP
PLIP
HFF
GO ON AHEAD.
AH
...
SHF
SHF
GRP
HFF
HFF
HFF
HFF
WHUMP

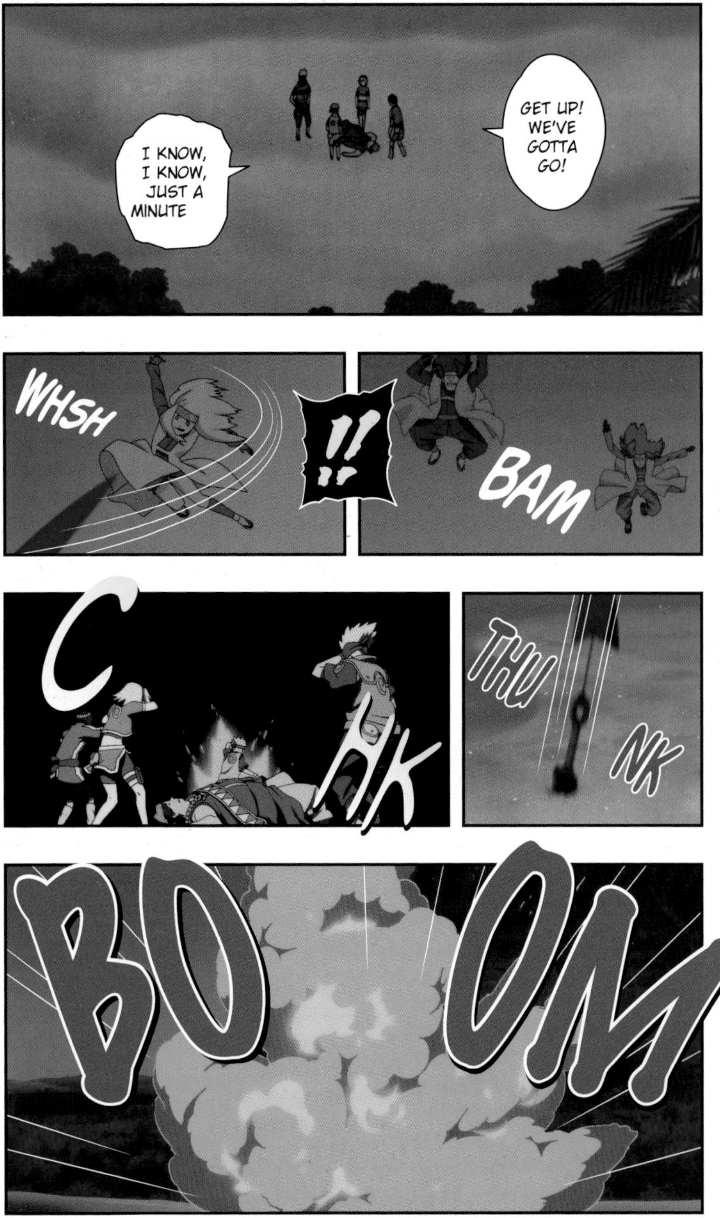
GET UP! WE'VE GOTTA GO!
I KNOW, I KNOW, JUST A MINUTE
BAM
!!
WHSH
THUNK
CHK
BOOM

FWOOSH

‼

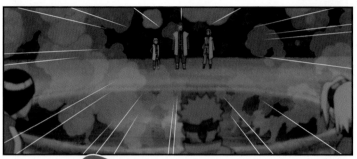

DOOM

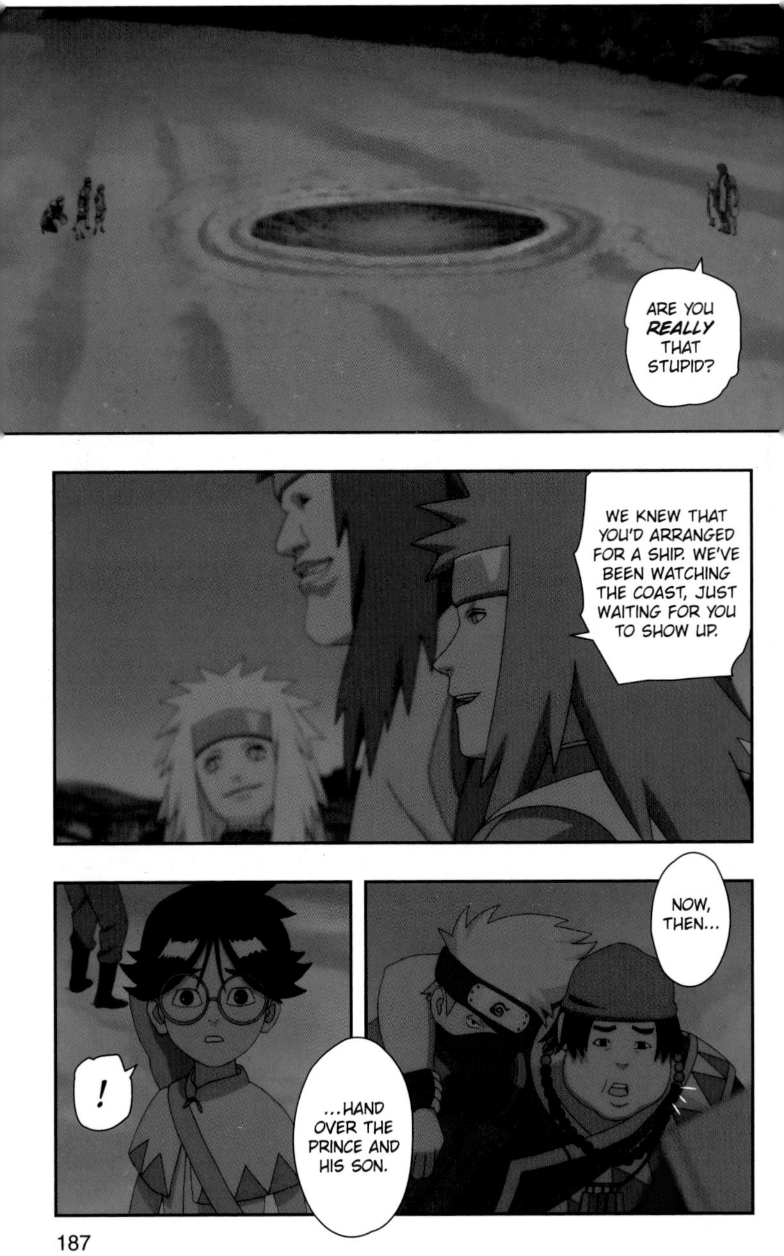
ARE YOU REALLY THAT STUPID?
WE KNEW THAT YOU'D ARRANGED FOR A SHIP. WE'VE BEEN WATCHING THE COAST, JUST WAITING FOR YOU TO SHOW UP.
NOW, THEN...
...HAND OVER THE PRINCE AND HIS SON.
!

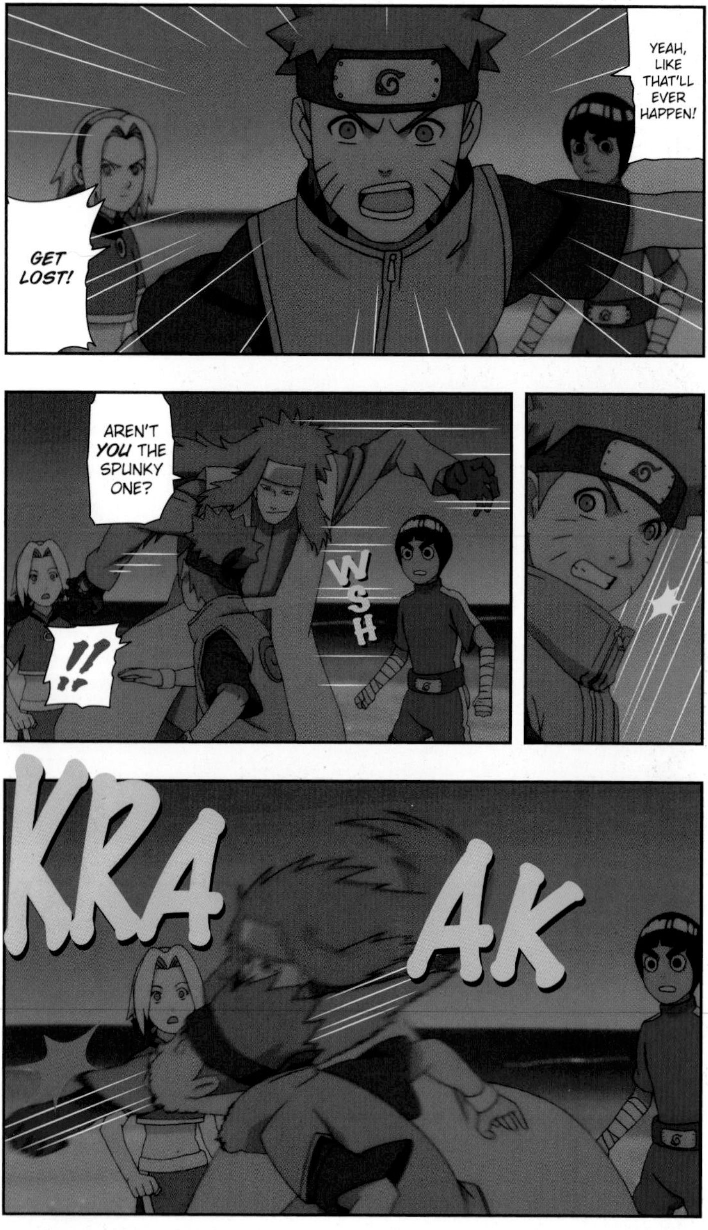

YEAH, LIKE THAT'LL EVER HAPPEN!
GET LOST!
AREN'T *YOU* THE SPUNKY ONE?
WSH
!!
KRA AK

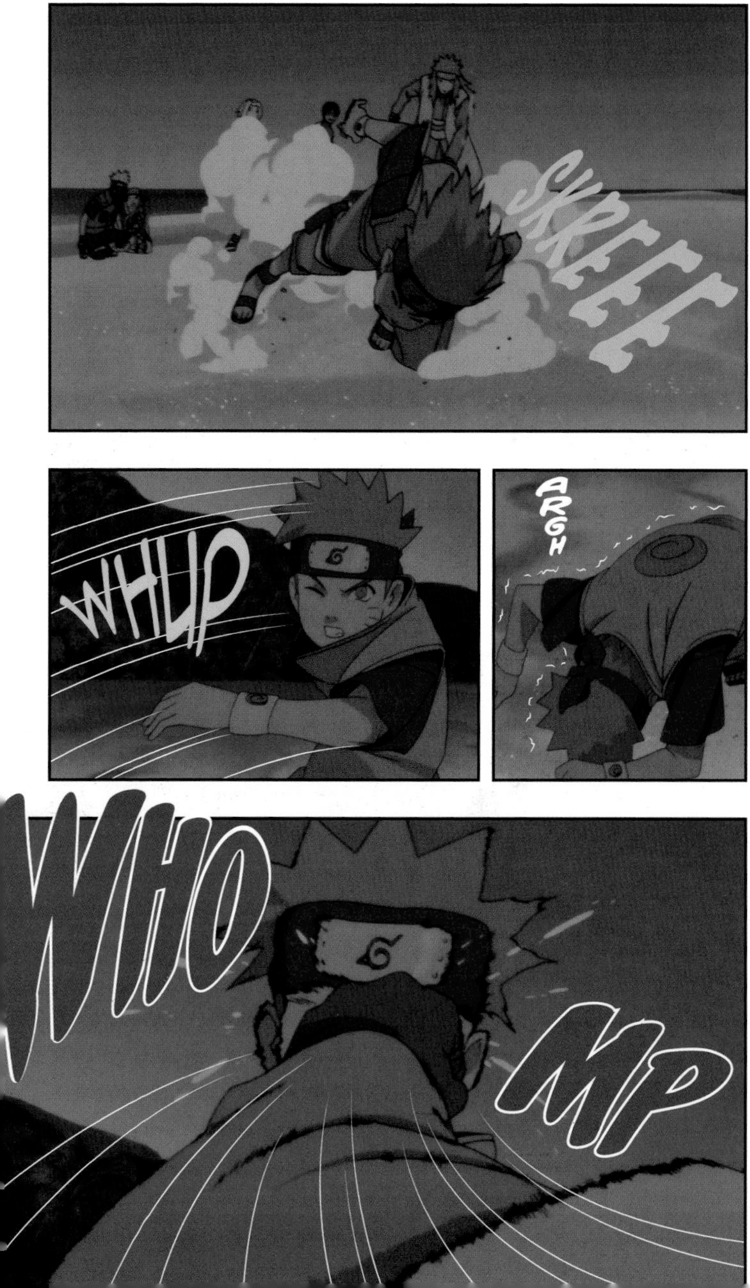
SKREEE
ARGH
WHUP
WHOMP

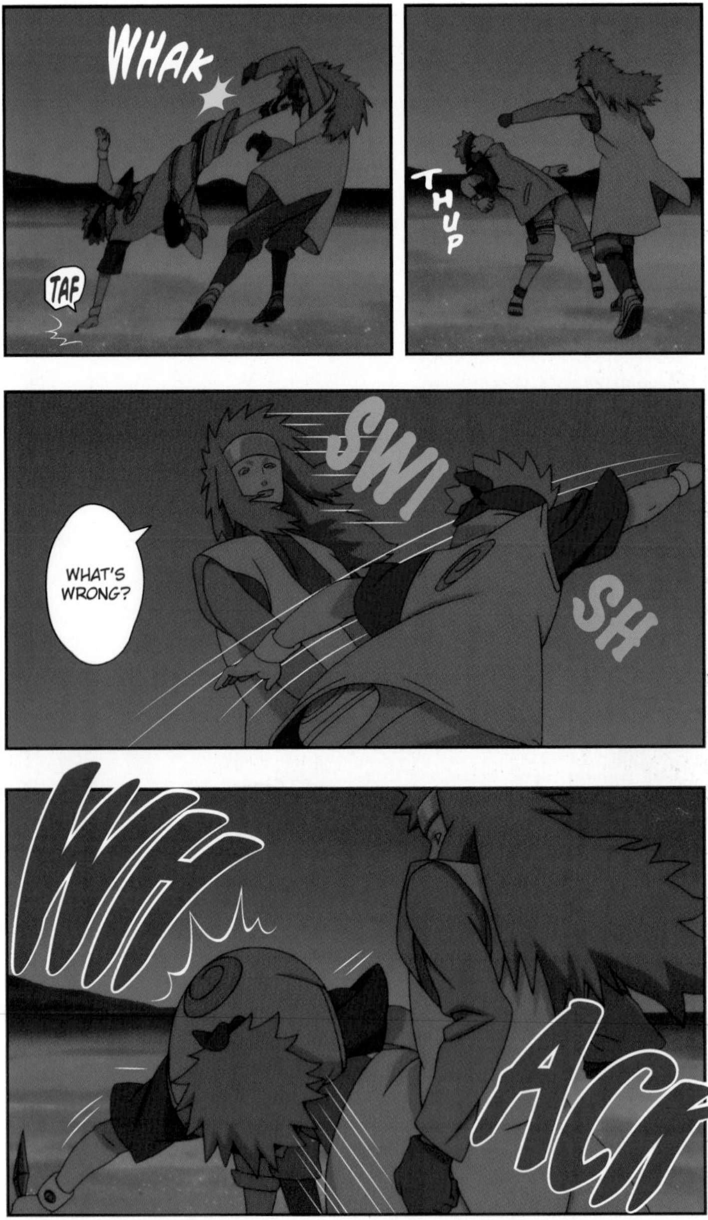
THUP
WHAK
TAF
SWISH
WHAT'S WRONG?
WHACK

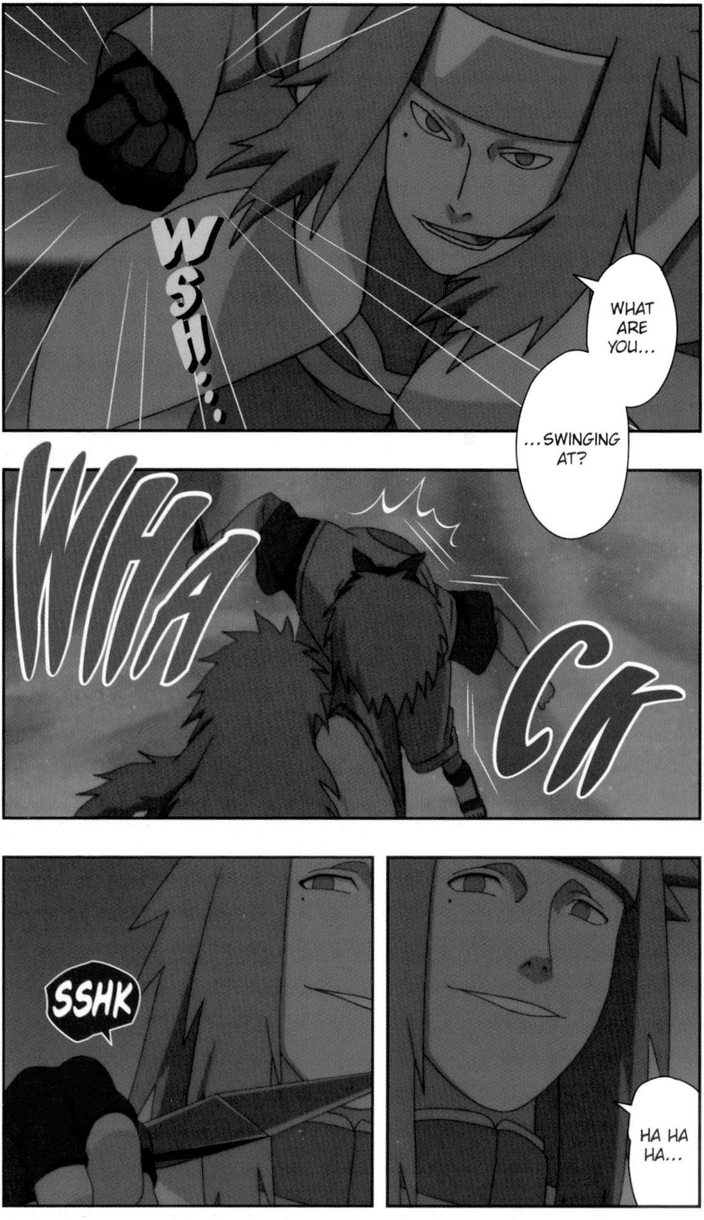
WHAT ARE YOU...
...SWINGING AT?
WSH...
WHACK
HA HA HA...
SSHK

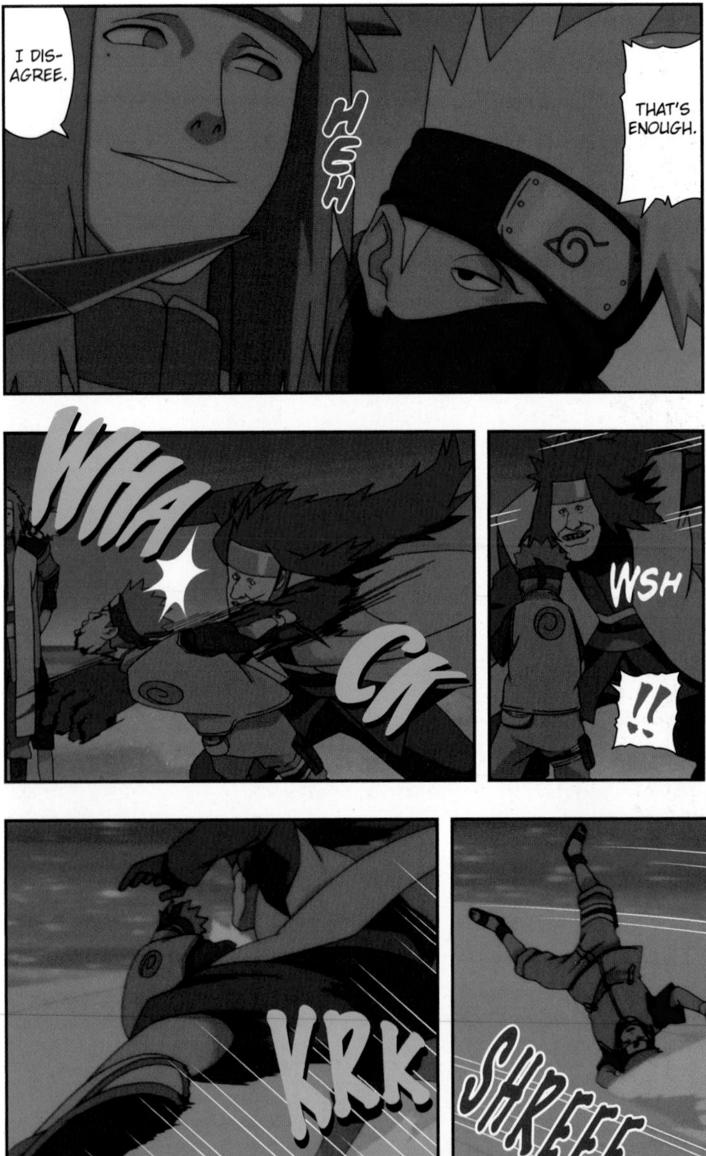
THAT'S ENOUGH.
HEH
I DIS-AGREE.
WSH
!!
WHACK
SHREEE
KRK

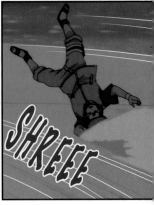

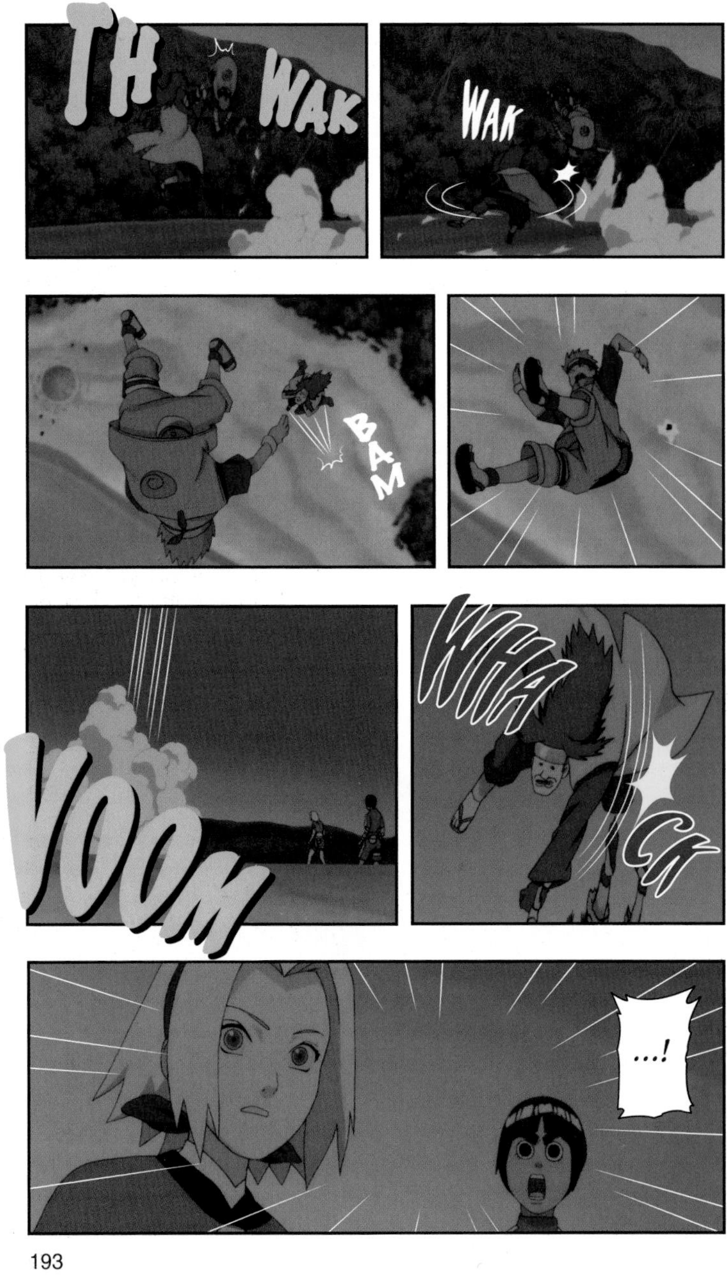
WAK
TH WAK
BAM
WHA CK
VOOM
...!

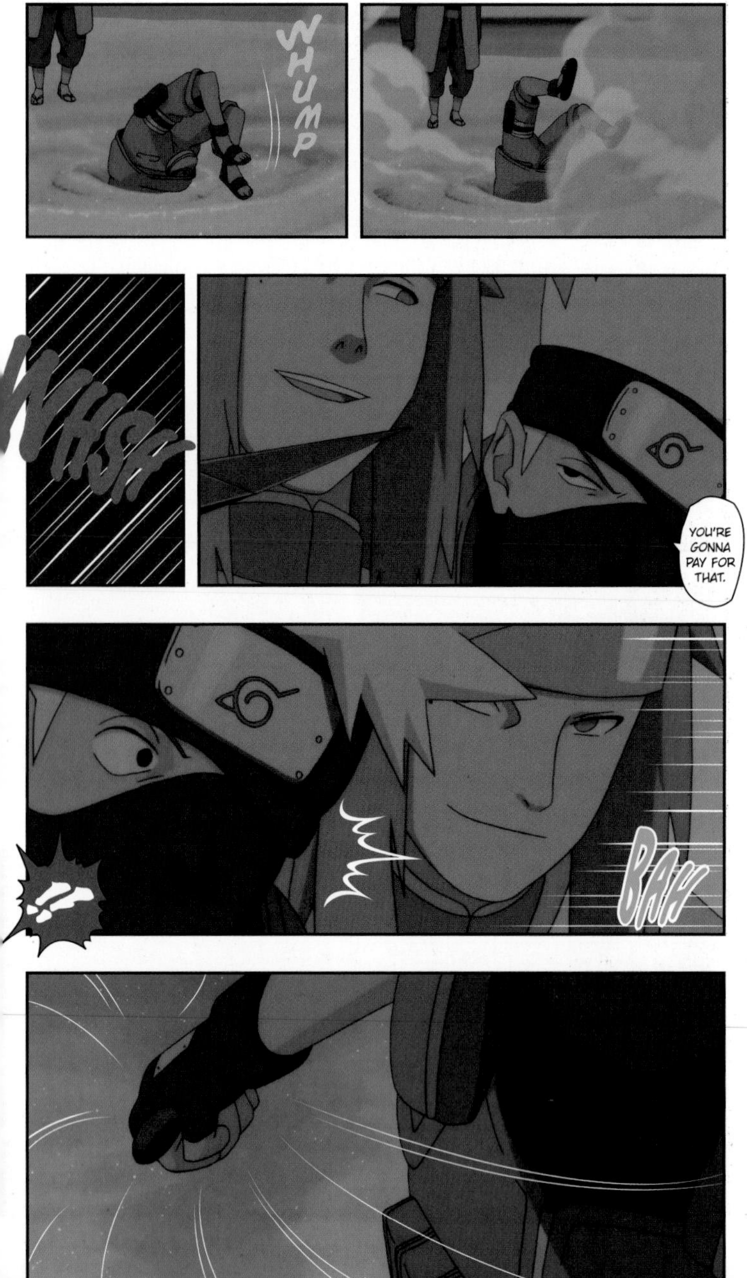
WHUMP
YOU'RE GONNA PAY FOR THAT.
WHSH
BAH
!!

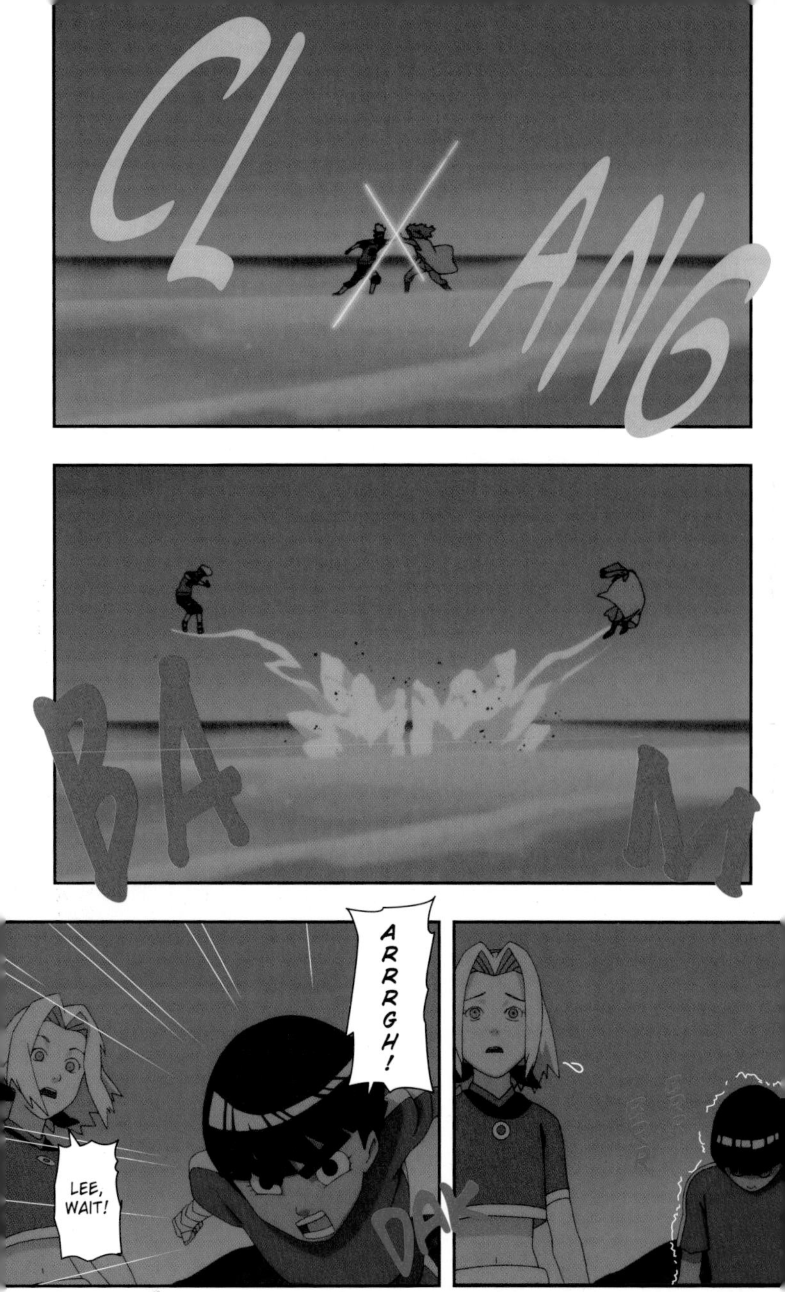
CLANG
BAM
ARRRGH!
LEE, WAIT!
DAK

HOW DARE YOU DO THAT TO NARUTO?

CRASH

DAK

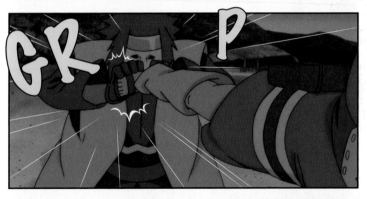

GR P

!

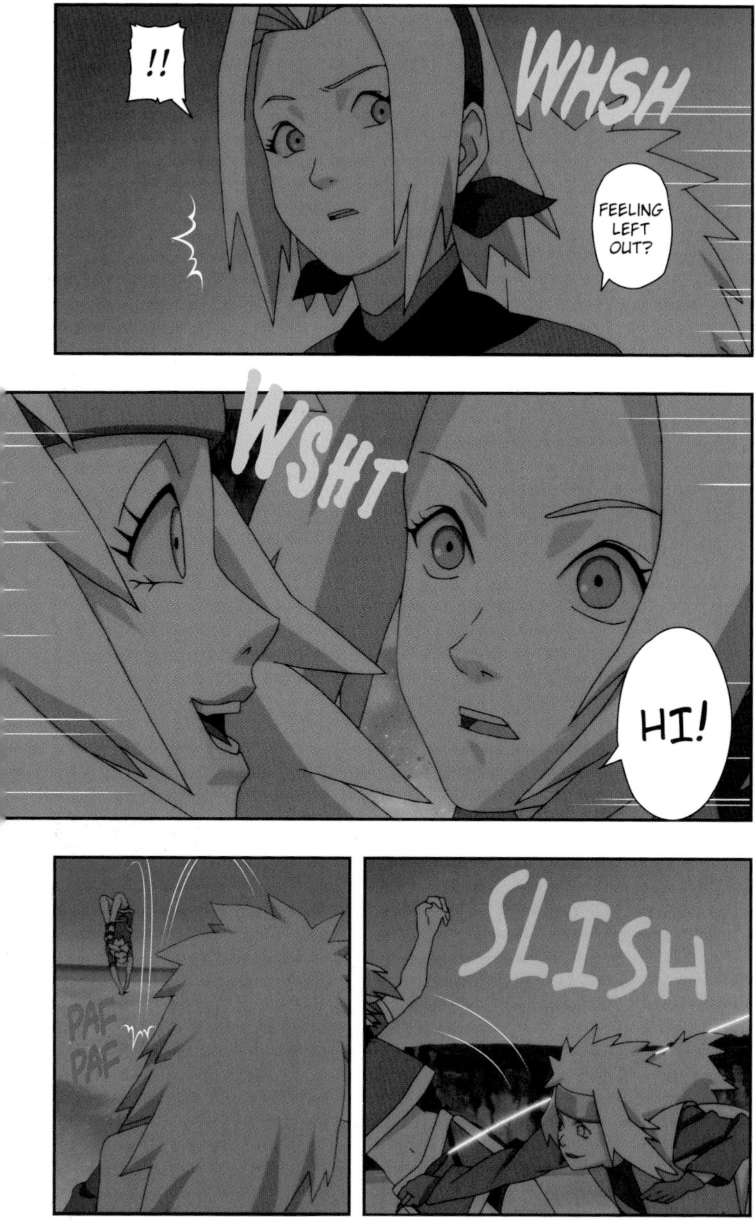
WHSH
FEELING LEFT OUT?
!!
WSHT
HI!
SLISH
PAF PAF

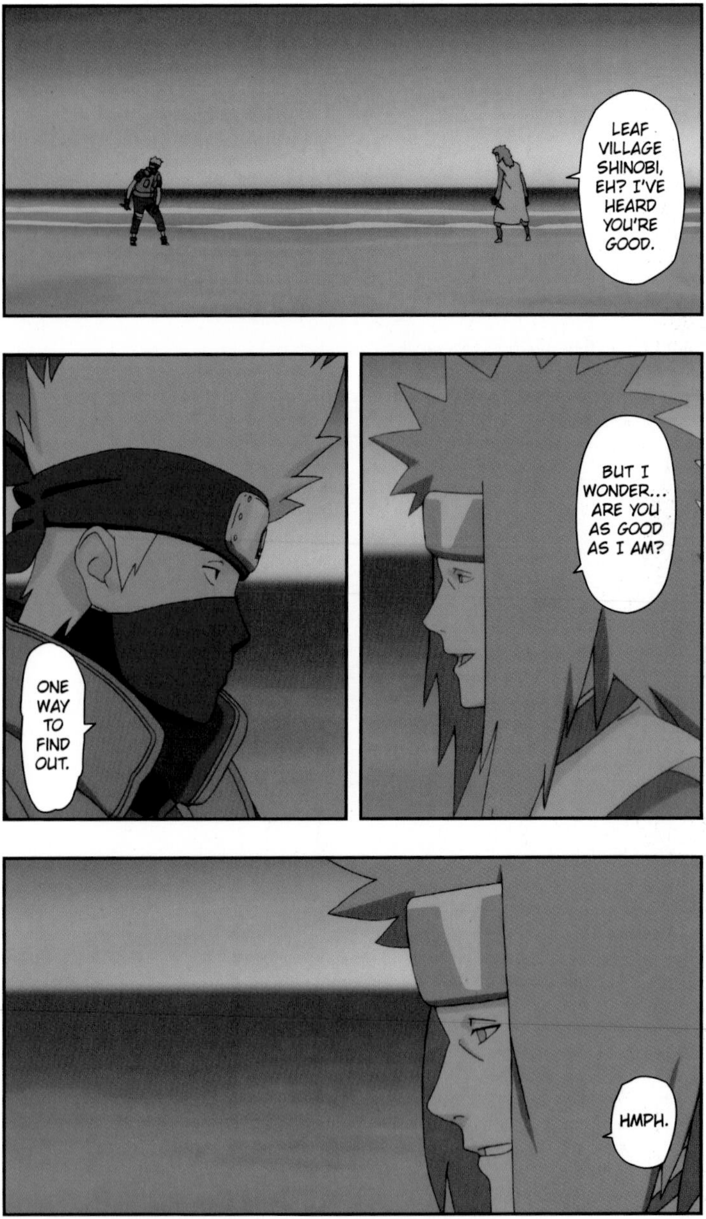
LEAF VILLAGE SHINOBI, EH? I'VE HEARD YOU'RE GOOD.
BUT I WONDER... ARE YOU AS GOOD AS I AM?
ONE WAY TO FIND OUT.
HMPH.

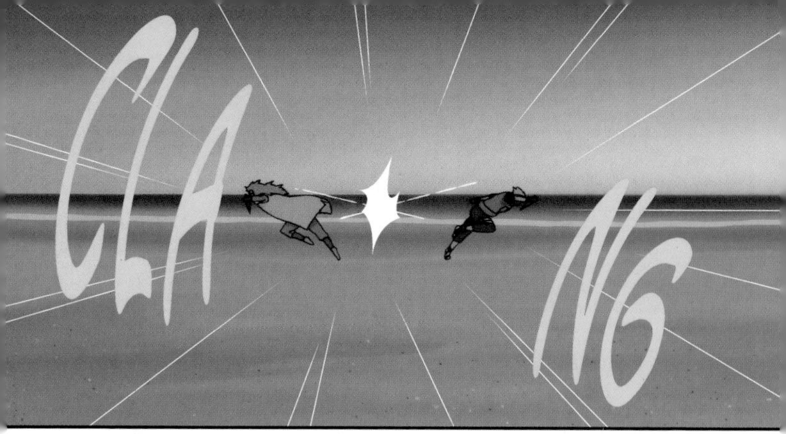
CLANG

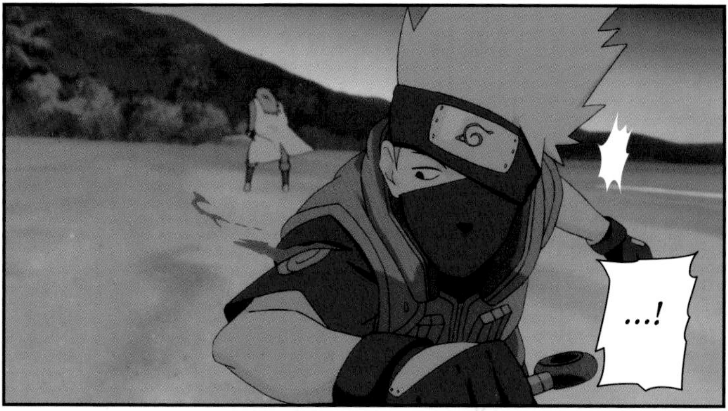
...!

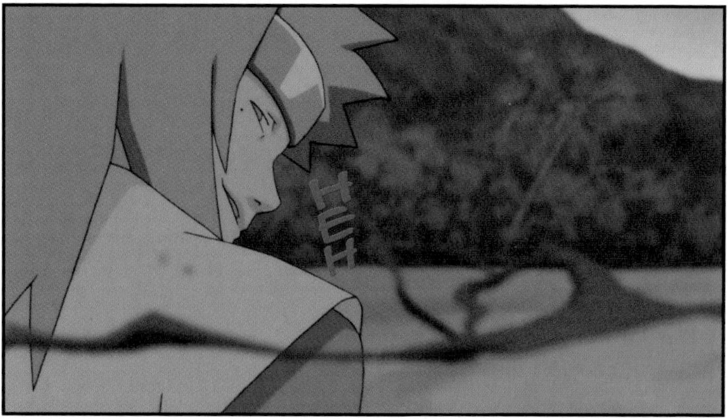
HEH

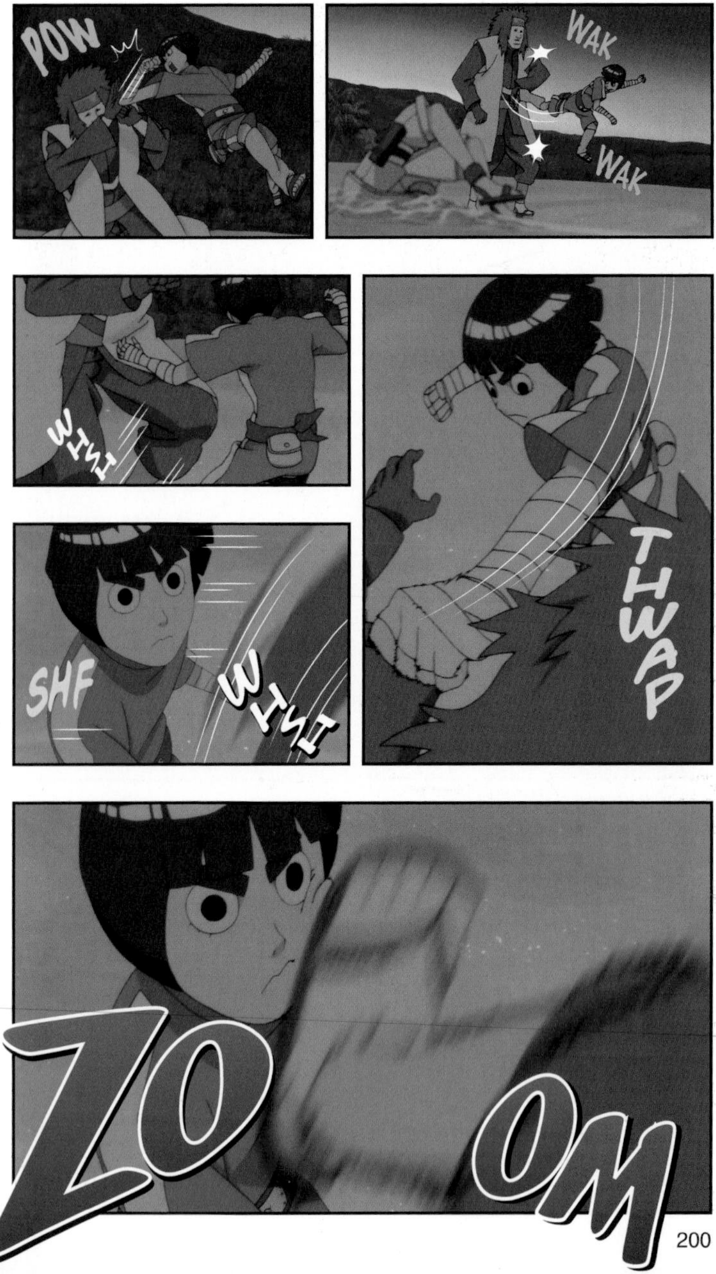
WAK
WAK
POW
THWAP
SHF
ZOOM

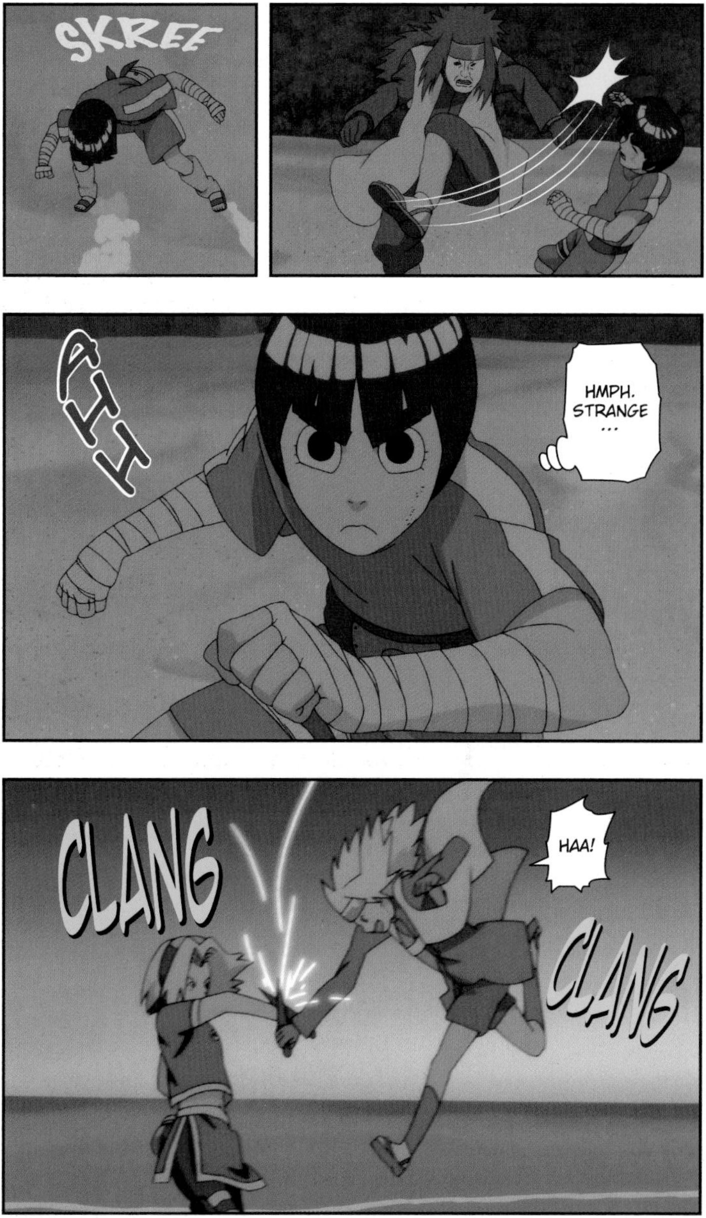
SKREE
HMPH. STRANGE ...
HAA!
CLANG
CLANG

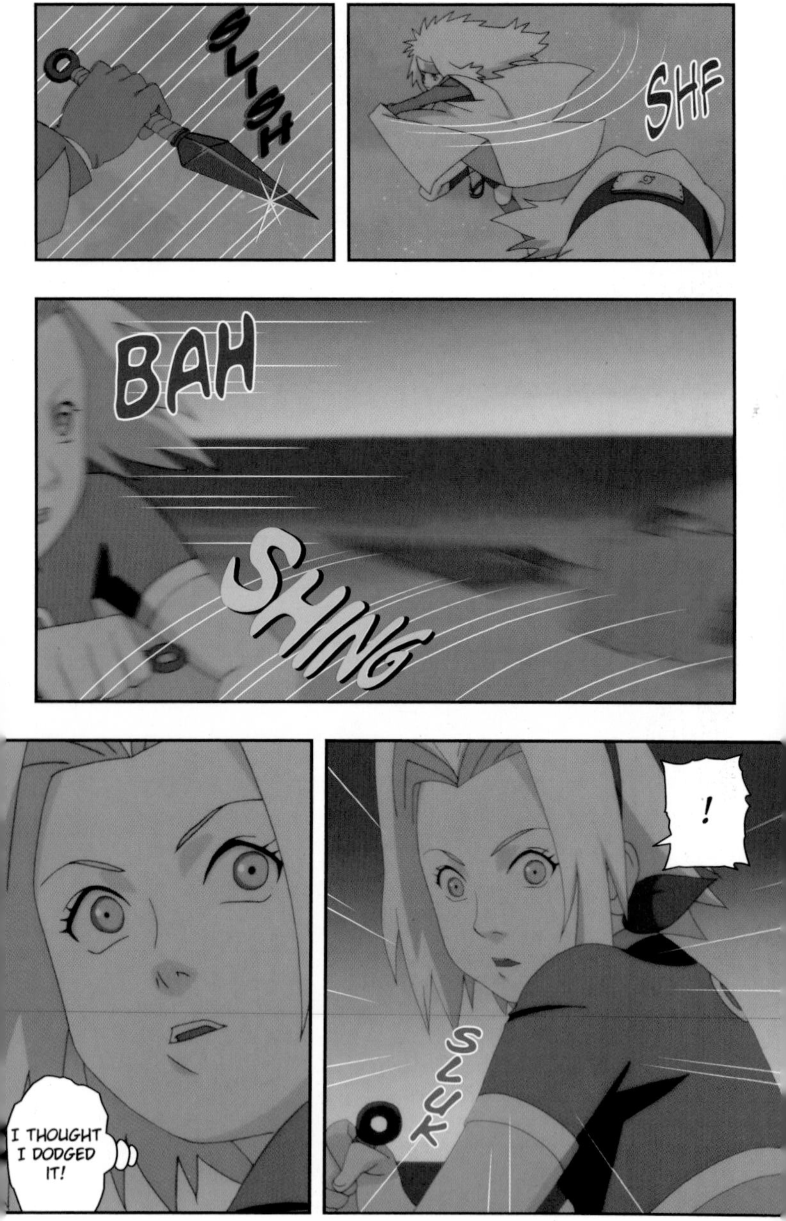
SHF
SLISH
BAH
SHING
!
SLUK
I THOUGHT I DODGED IT!

SKREEE

SOMETHING'S WRONG...

SPFUK

....!

EVERYTHING'S MOVING SO *SLOW.*

ARRRGH

ARRRGH

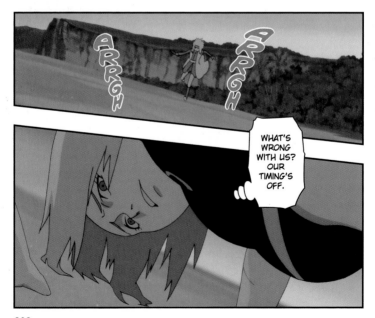

WHAT'S WRONG WITH US? OUR TIMING'S OFF.

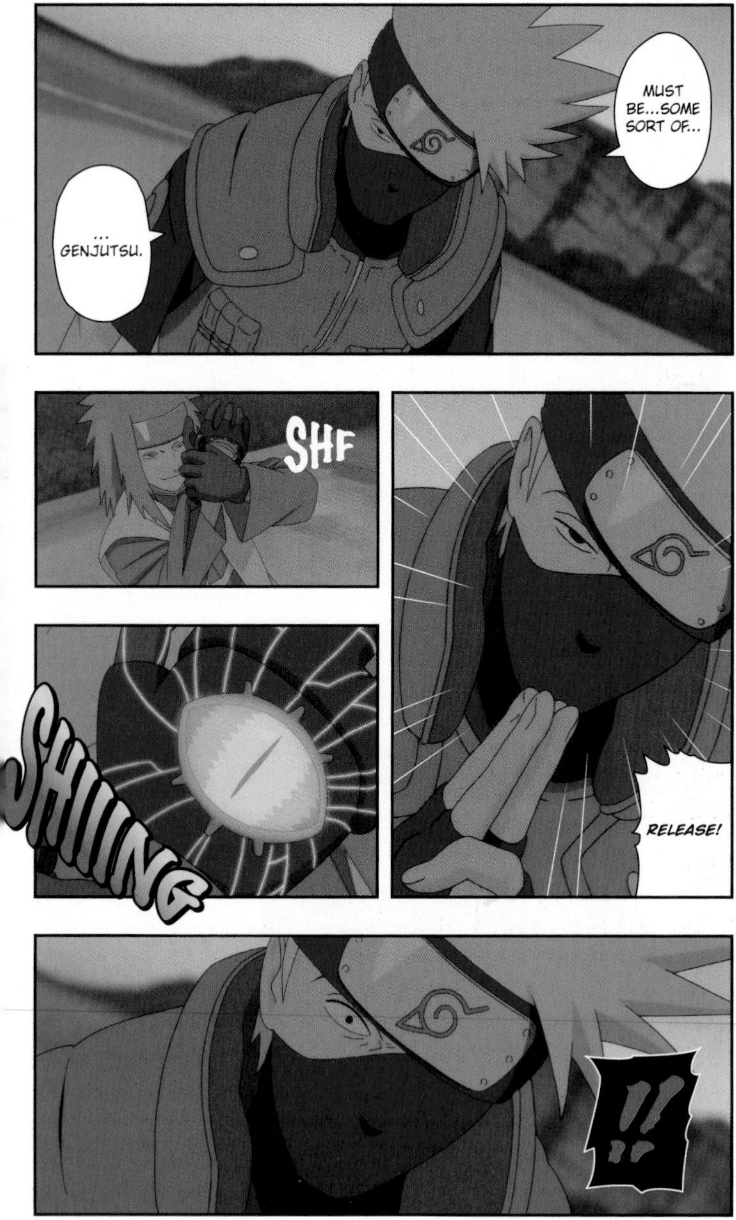
MUST BE...SOME SORT OF...
...GENJUTSU.
RELEASE!
SHF
SHIING
!!

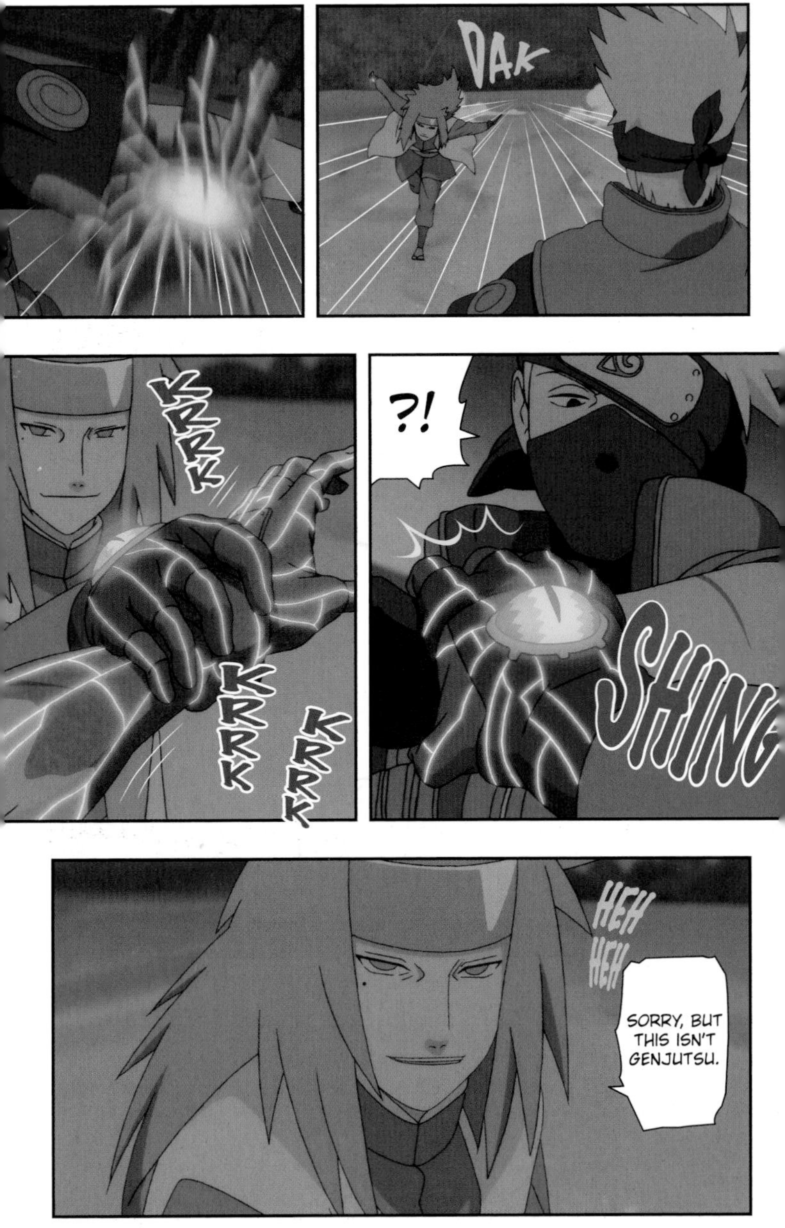
DAK
?!
SHING
KRRK
KRRK
KRRK
HEH HEH
SORRY, BUT THIS ISN'T GENJUTSU.

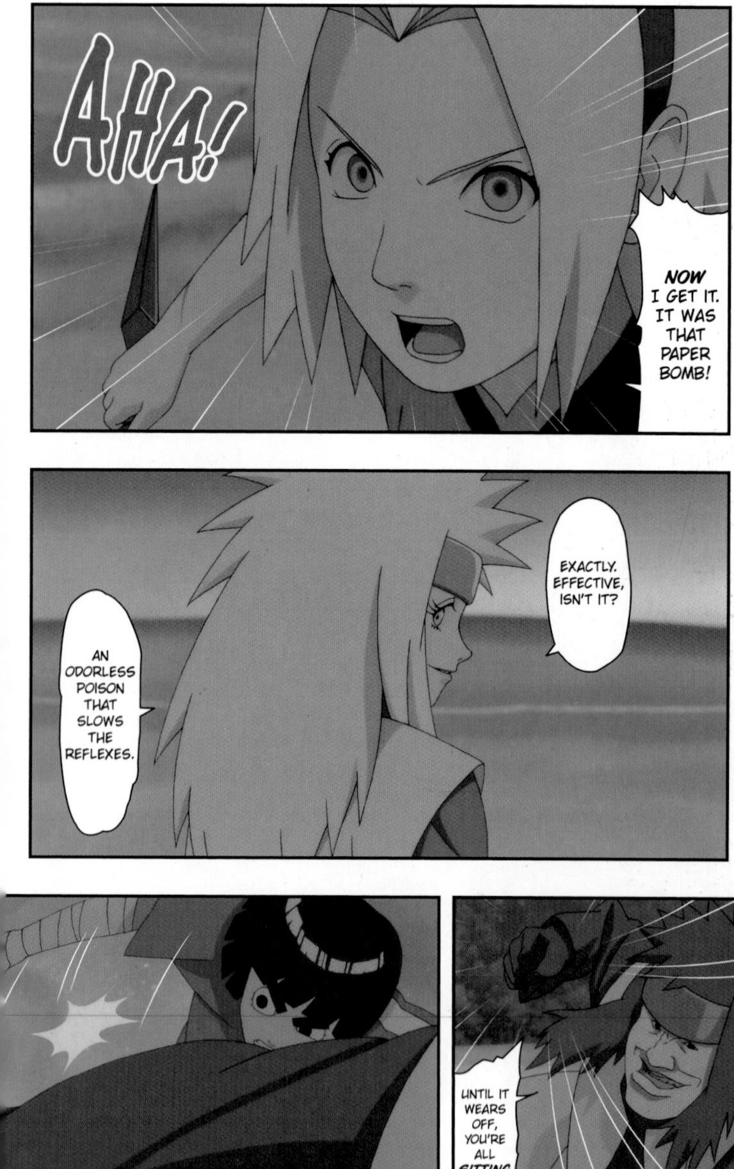
AHA!
NOW I GET IT. IT WAS THAT PAPER BOMB!
EXACTLY. EFFECTIVE, ISN'T IT?
AN ODORLESS POISON THAT SLOWS THE REFLEXES.
UNTIL IT WEARS OFF, YOU'RE ALL SITTING DUCKS.

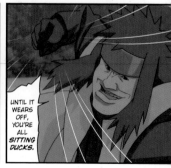

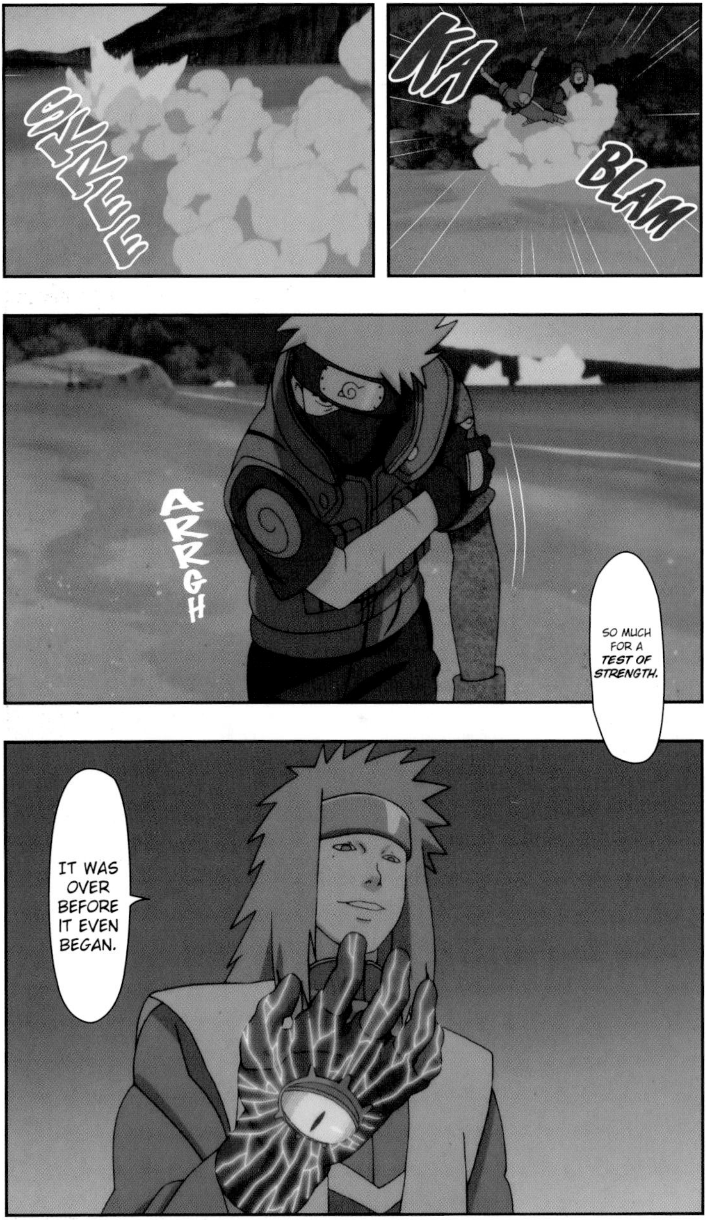
KA
BLAM
ARRGH
SO MUCH FOR A TEST OF STRENGTH.
IT WAS OVER BEFORE IT EVEN BEGAN.

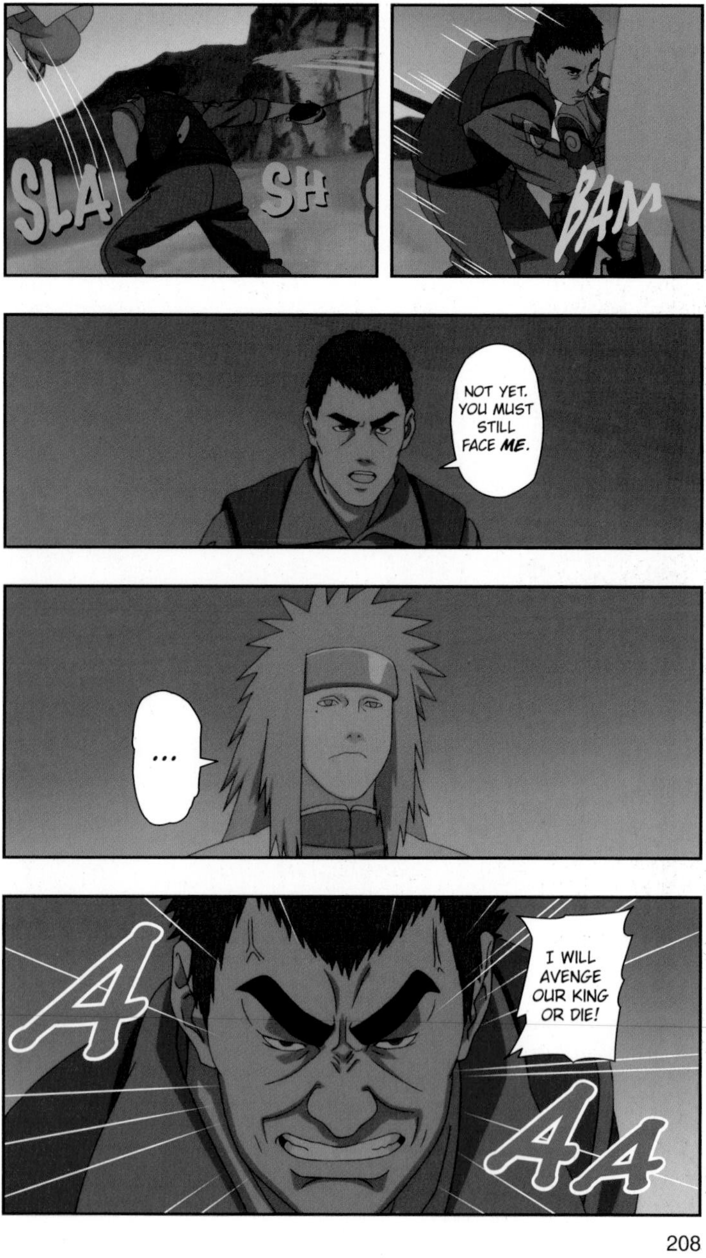
BAM
SLASH
NOT YET. YOU MUST STILL FACE *ME*.
...
I WILL AVENGE OUR KING OR DIE!
A
AA

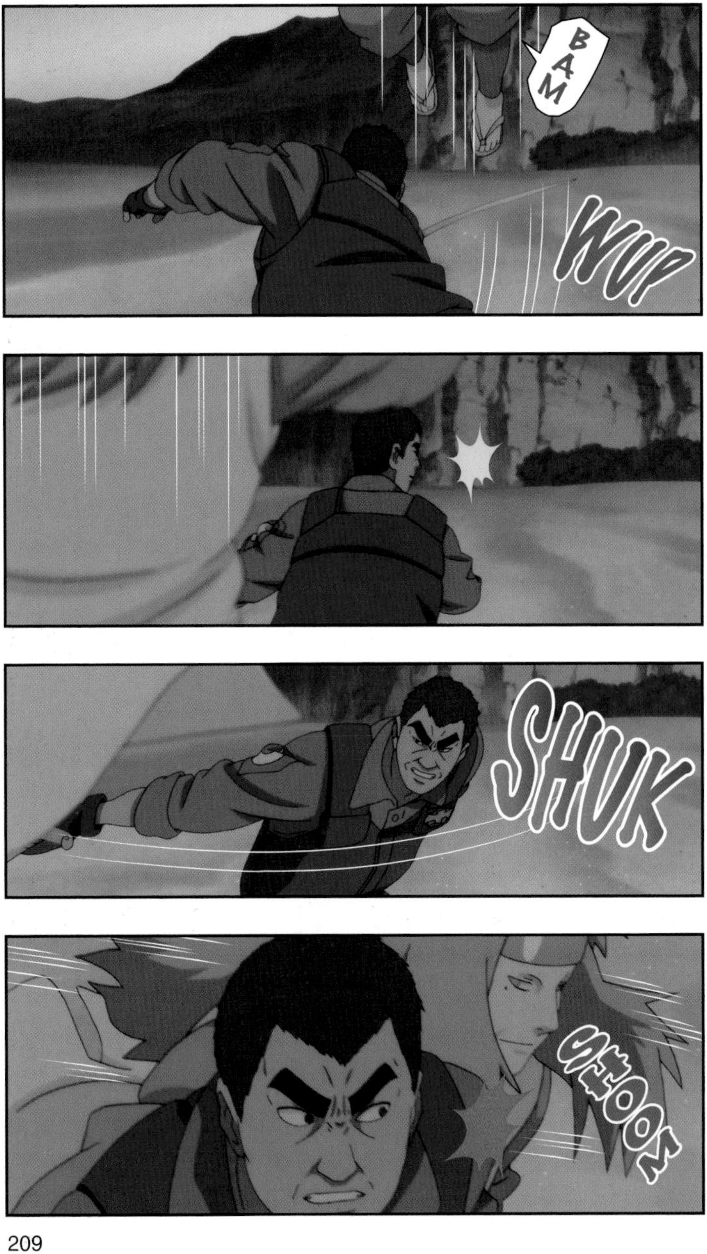
BAM
WUP
SHUK
SHOOM

ARGH
ARGH
HIIIIN
THEY'VE GOT ME SURROUNDED!!
PRINCE MICHIRU!
!!
WHAM
KRRK
KRRK

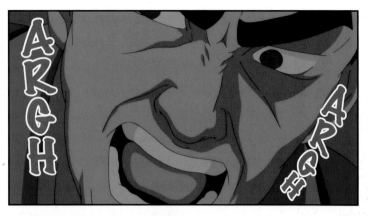

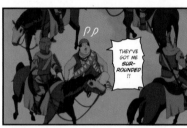

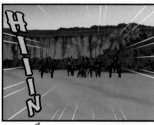

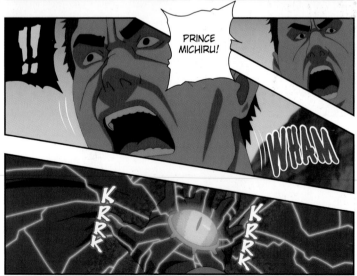

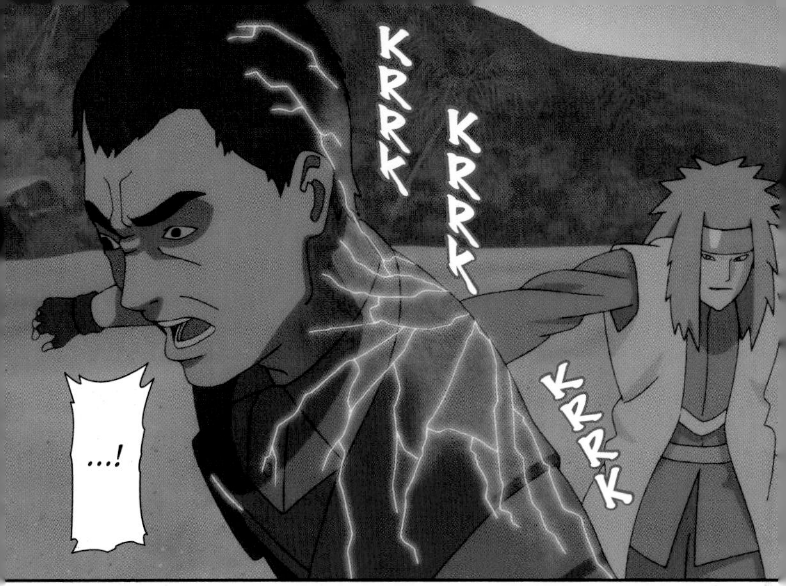
KRRK
KRRK
KRRK
...!

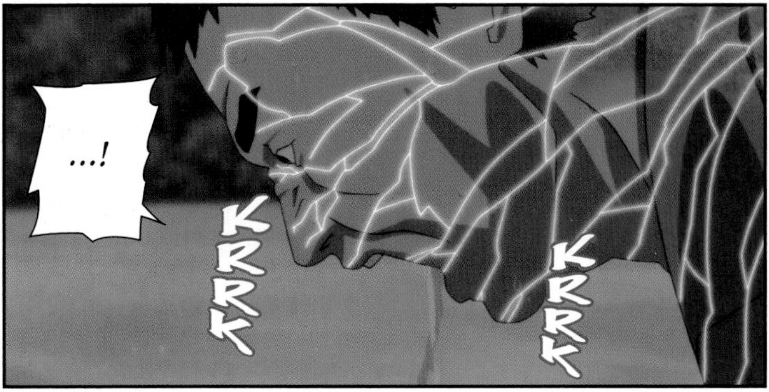
...!
KRRK
KRRK

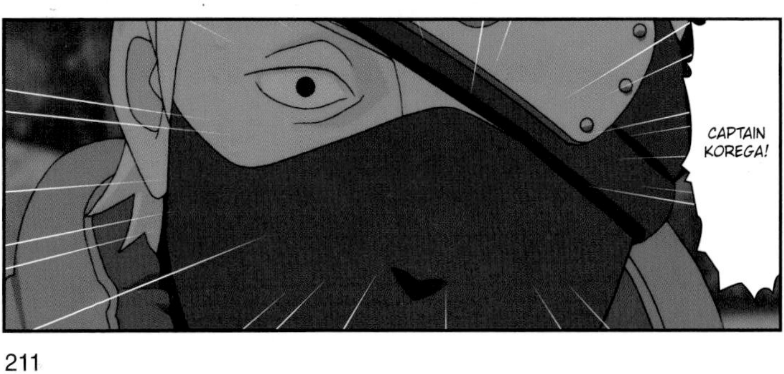
CAPTAIN KOREGA!

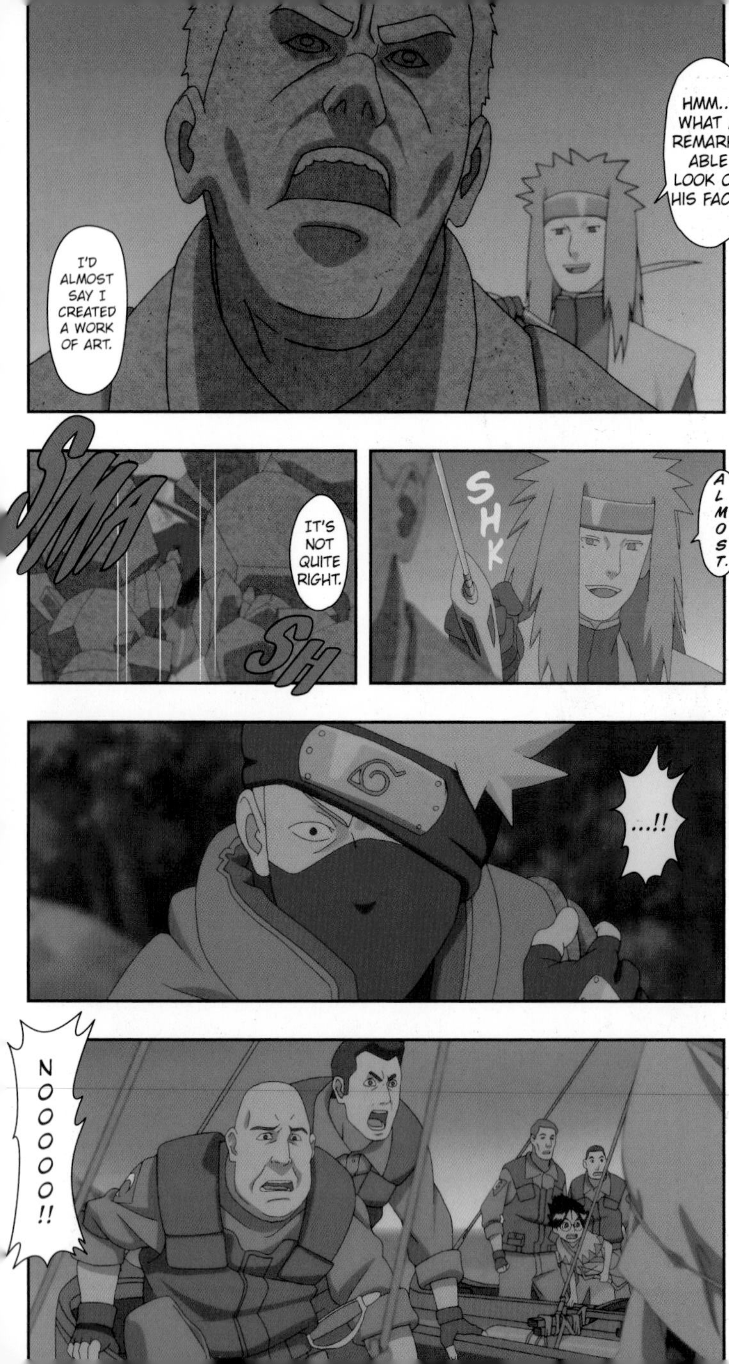
HMM... WHAT A REMARK-ABLE LOOK ON HIS FACE!
I'D ALMOST SAY I CREATED A WORK OF ART.
SHK
ALMOST.
IT'S NOT QUITE RIGHT.
SMA
SH
...!!
NOOOOOO!!

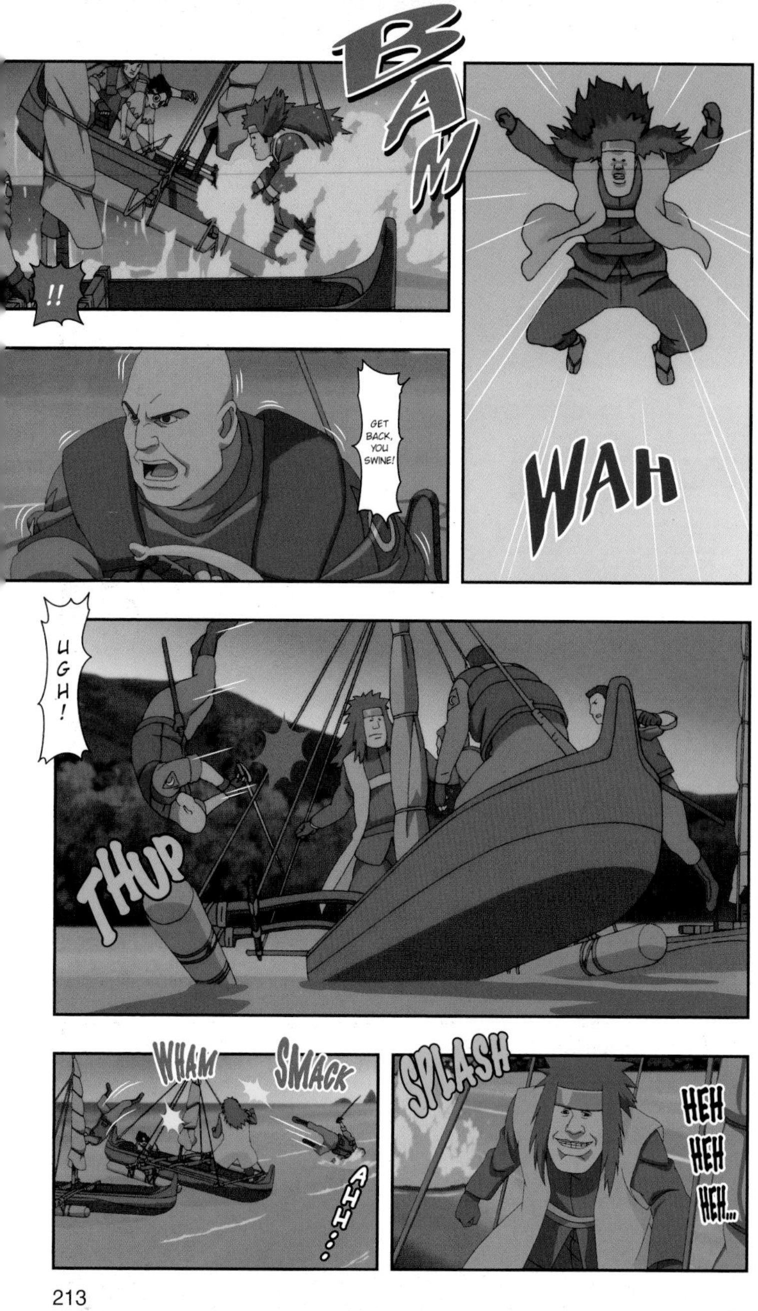
BAM
WAH
!!
GET BACK, YOU SWINE!
UGH!
THUP
SPLASH
HEH HEH HEH...
WHAM
SMACK
AHHH...

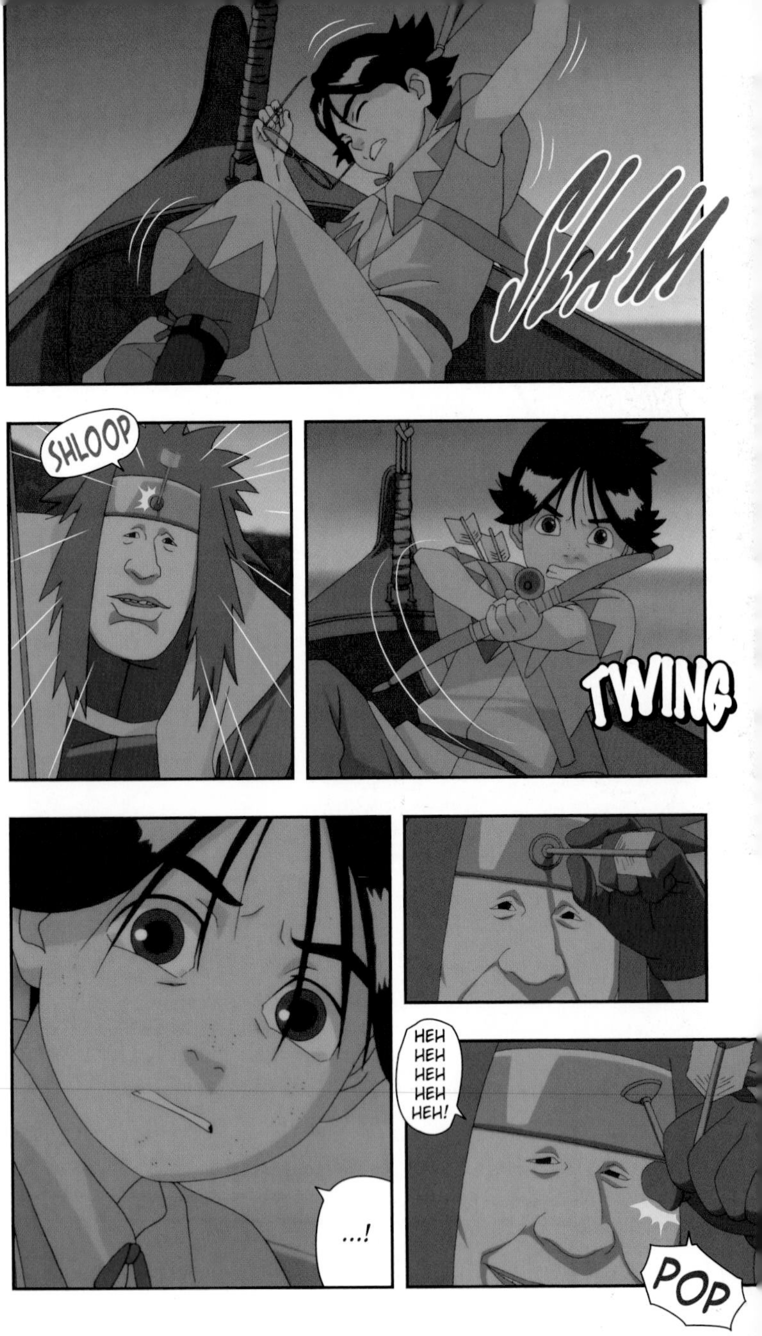
SLAM
TWING
SHLOOP
HEH HEH HEH HEH HEH!
POP
...!

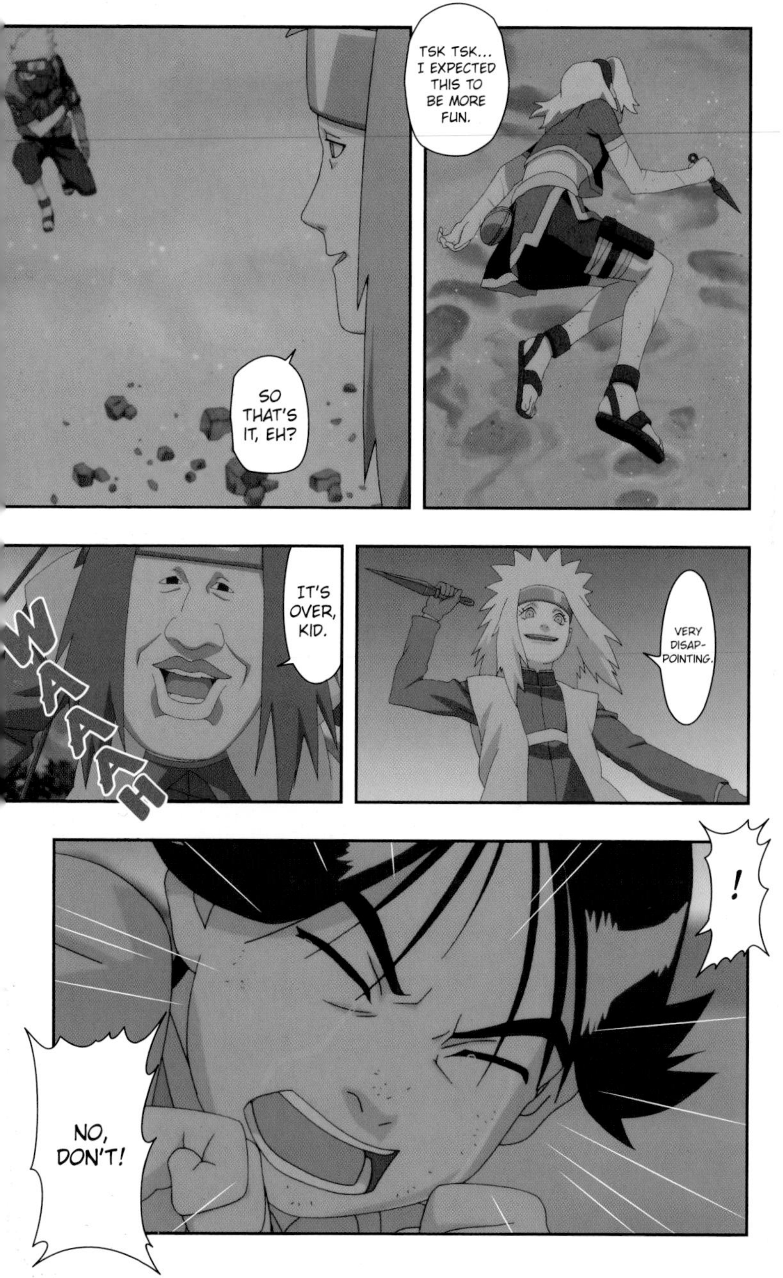
TSK TSK... I EXPECTED THIS TO BE MORE FUN.
SO THAT'S IT, EH?
VERY DISAP-POINTING.
IT'S OVER, KID.
WAAAAH
!
NO, DON'T!

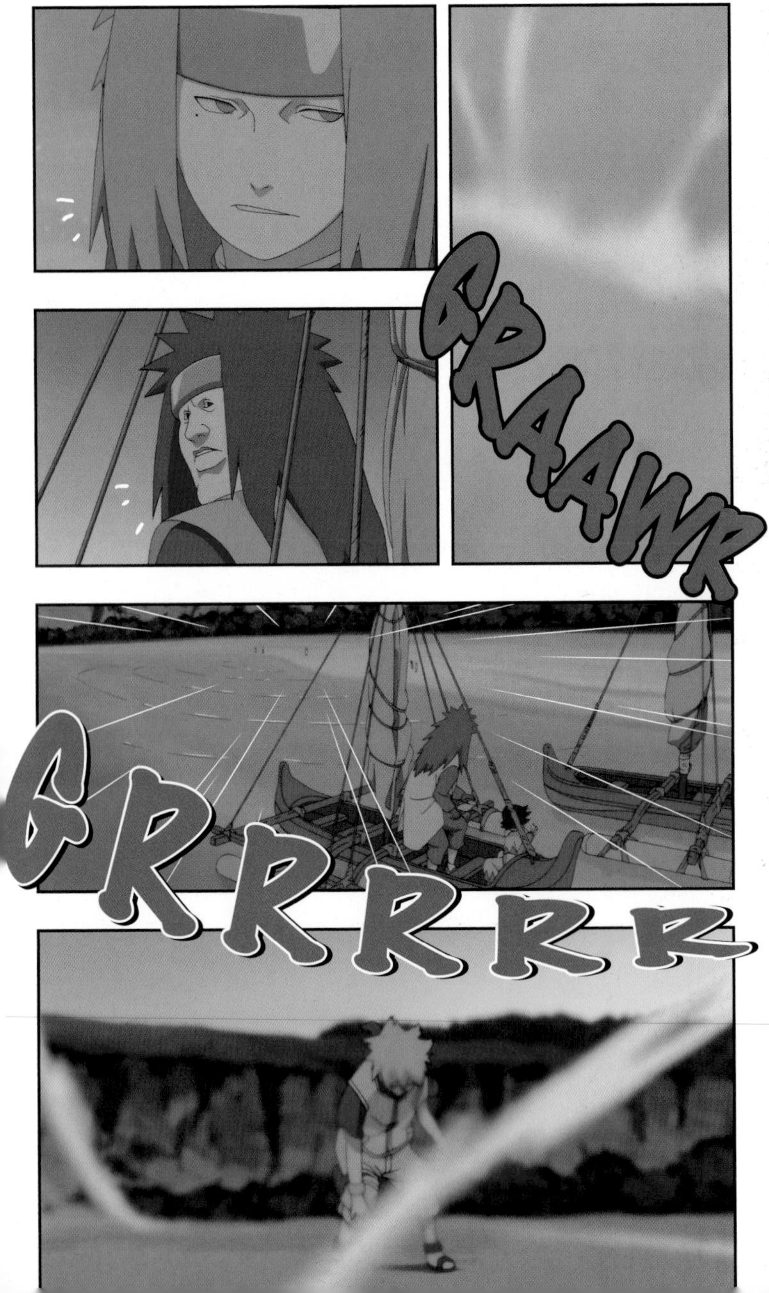
GRAAWR
GRRRRR

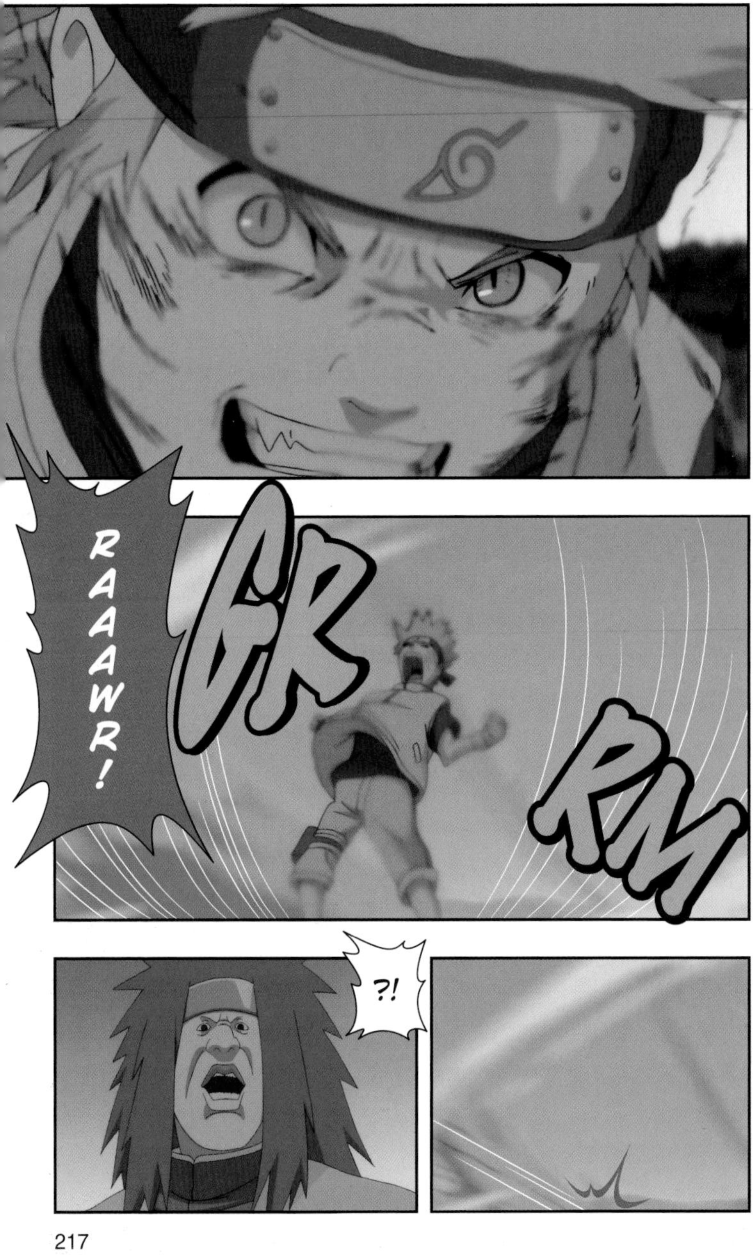
RAAAAWR!
GR
RM
?!

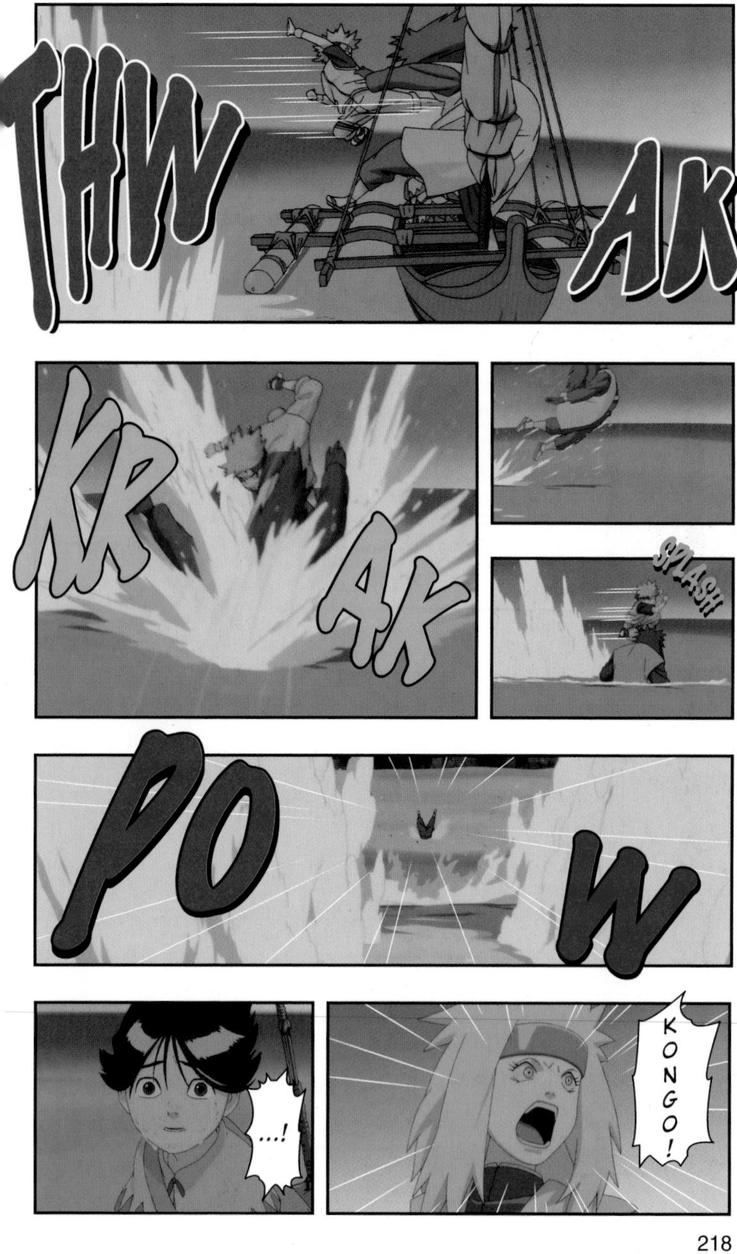
THWAK
SPLASH
KRAK
POW
KONGO!
...!

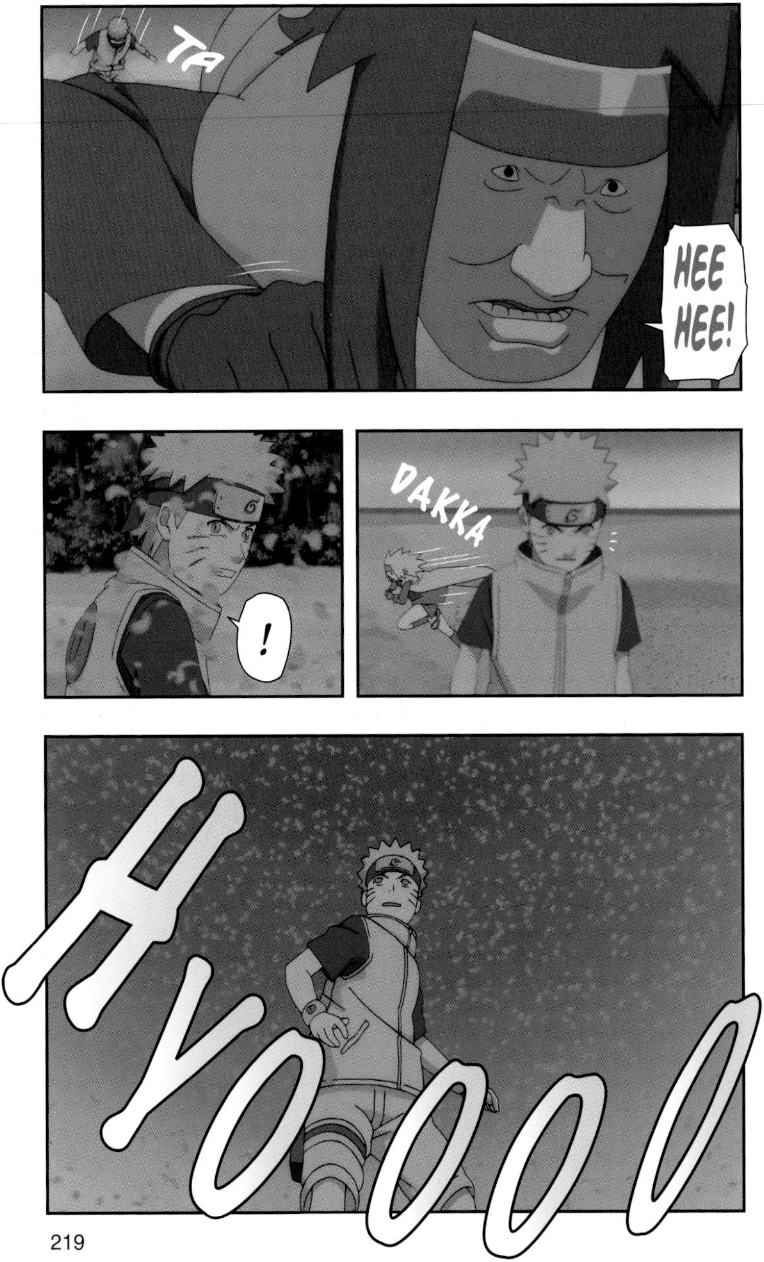
TA
HEE HEE!
DAKKA
!
HYOOOO

SNIK
SLA
SH
SLASH
SLASH
WSH
UNGH
SWIP

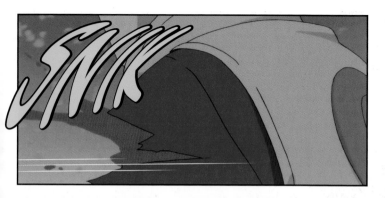

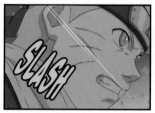

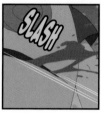

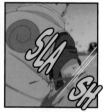

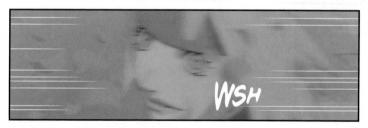

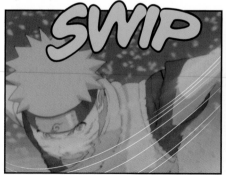

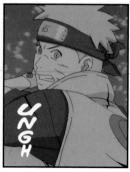

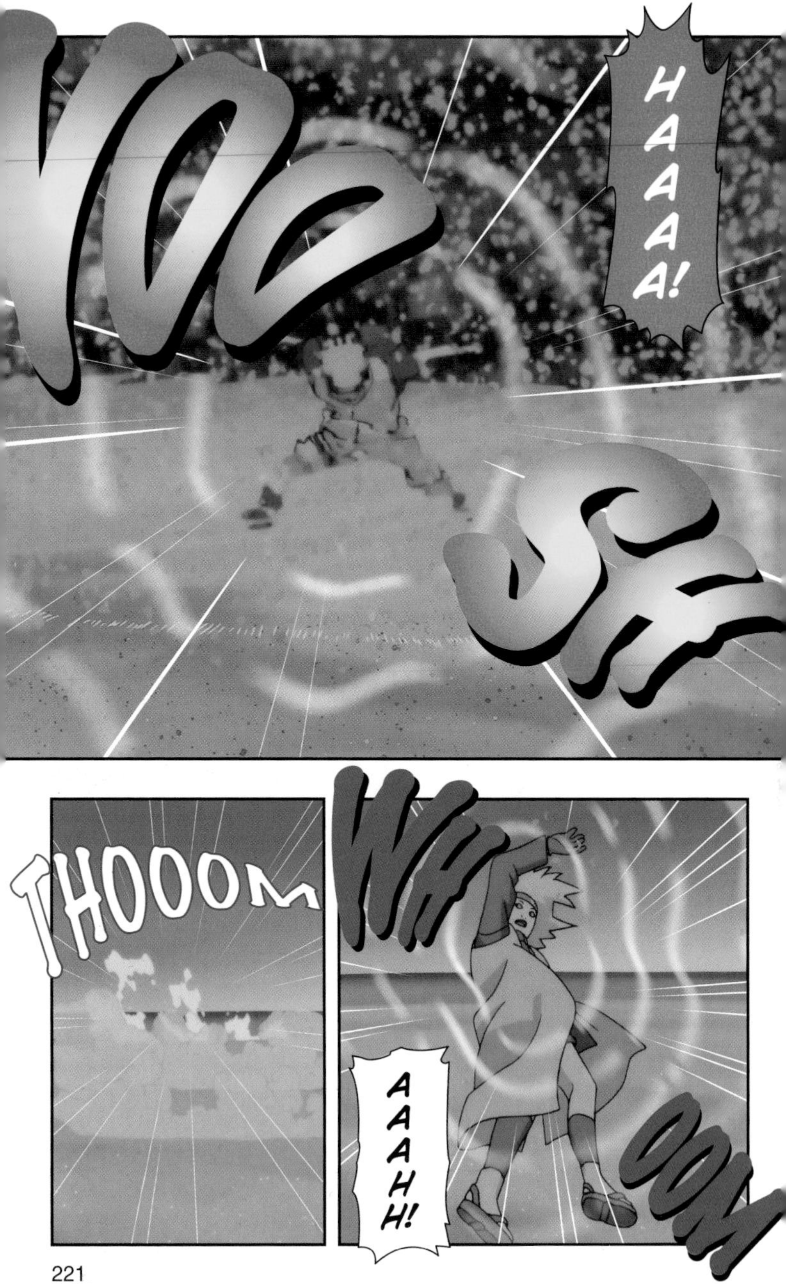
HAAAAA!
VOO
SH
WH
OOOM
AAAAHH!
THOOOM

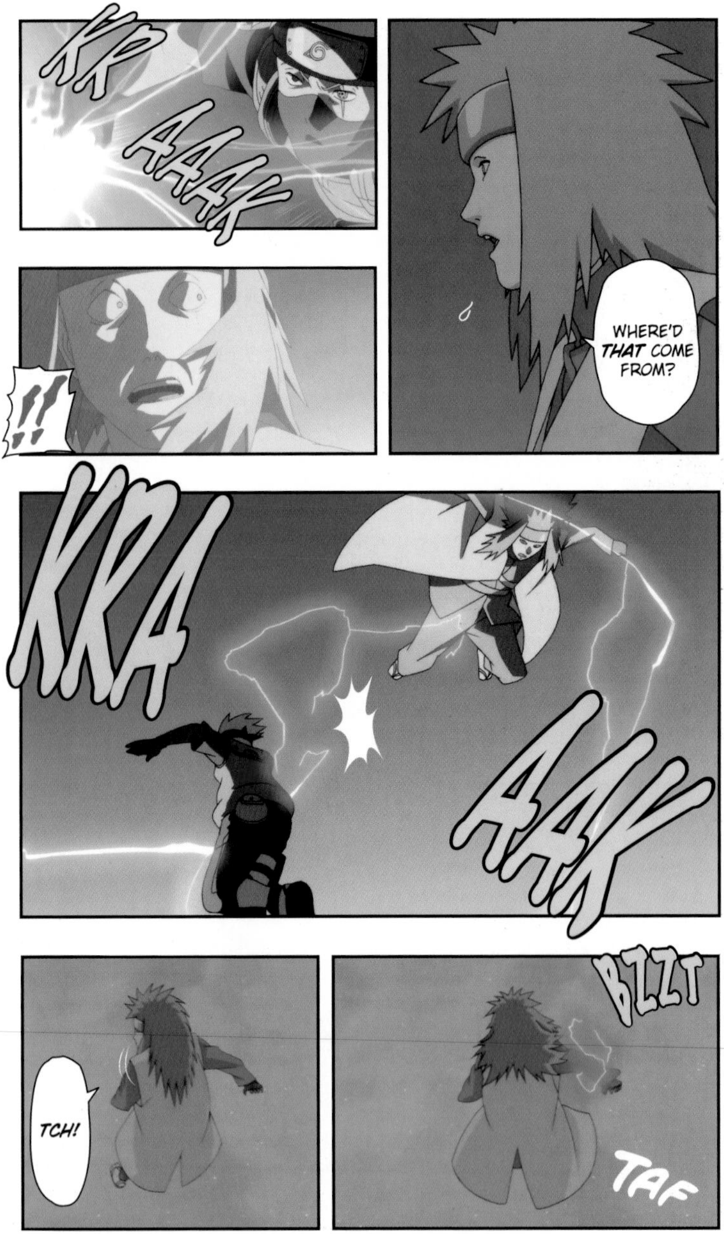
WHERE'D *THAT* COME FROM?
KRAAAK
!!
KRAAAK
BZZT
TAF
TCH!

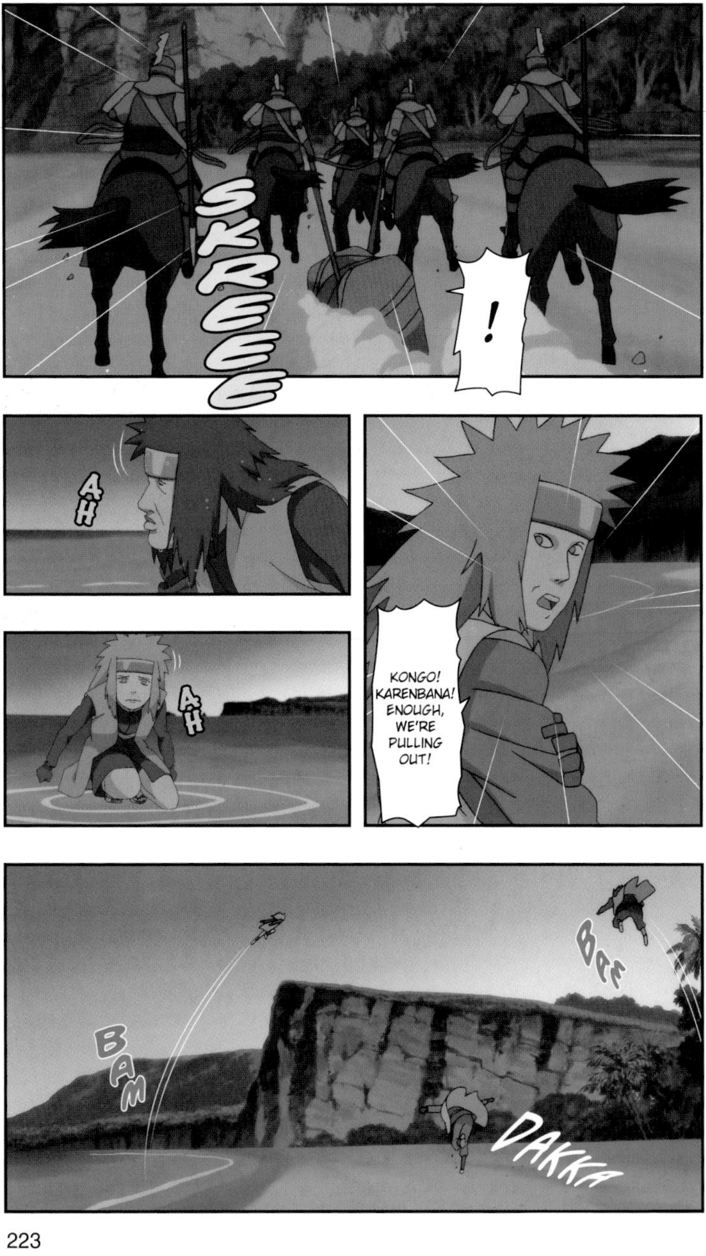
SKREEE
!
KONGO! KARENBANA! ENOUGH, WE'RE PULLING OUT!
AH
AH
BAM
BAM
DAKKA

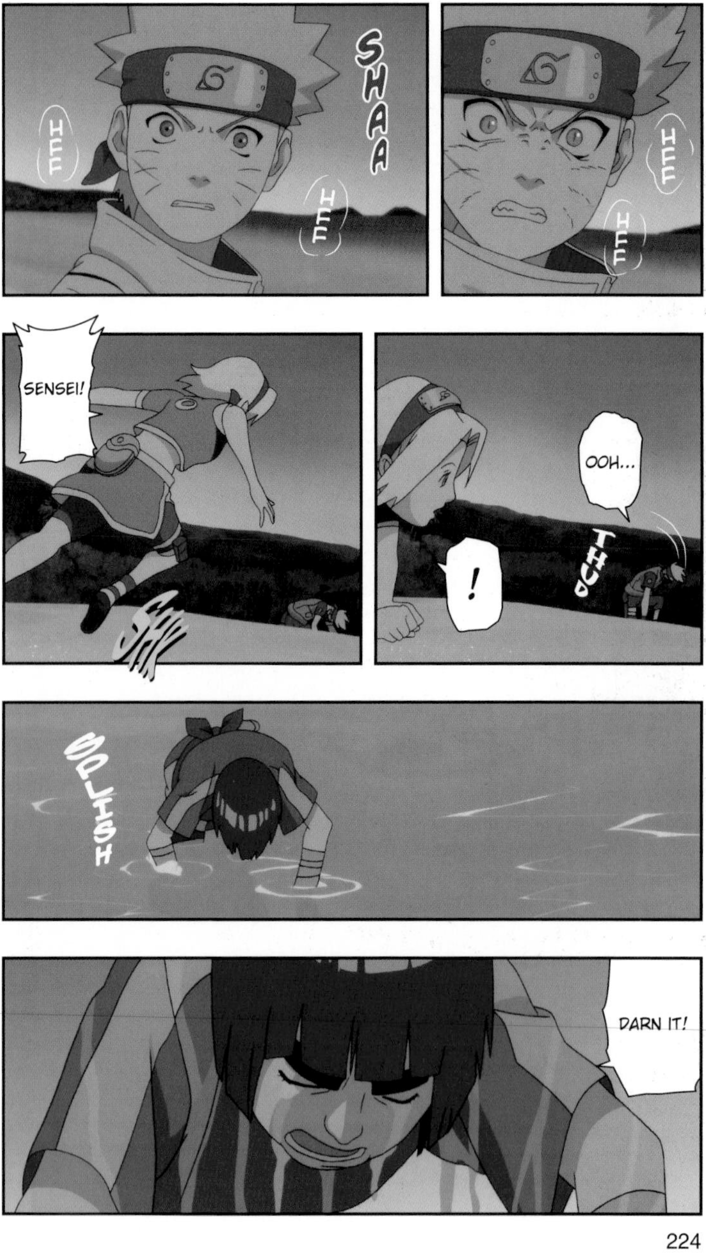
HFF
HFF
SHAA
HFF
HFF
OOH...
!
THUD
SENSEI!
SPLISH
DARN IT!

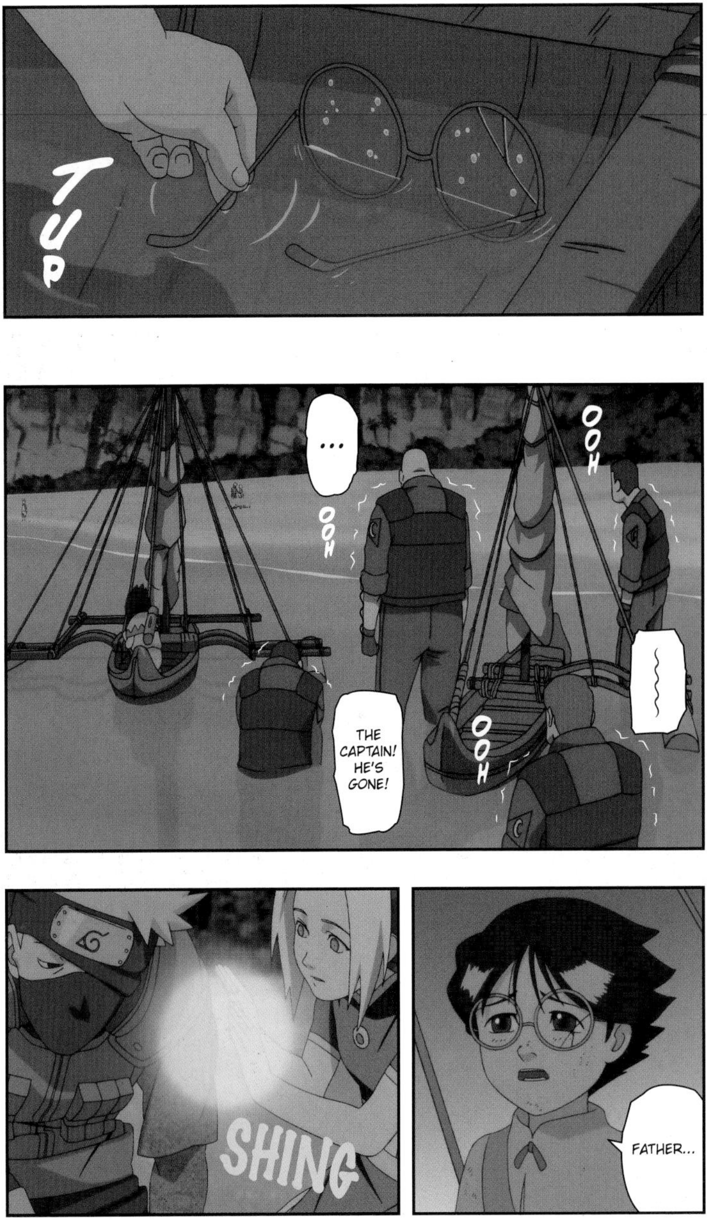
TUP
OOH
...
OOH
OOH
THE CAPTAIN! HE'S GONE!
FATHER...
SHING

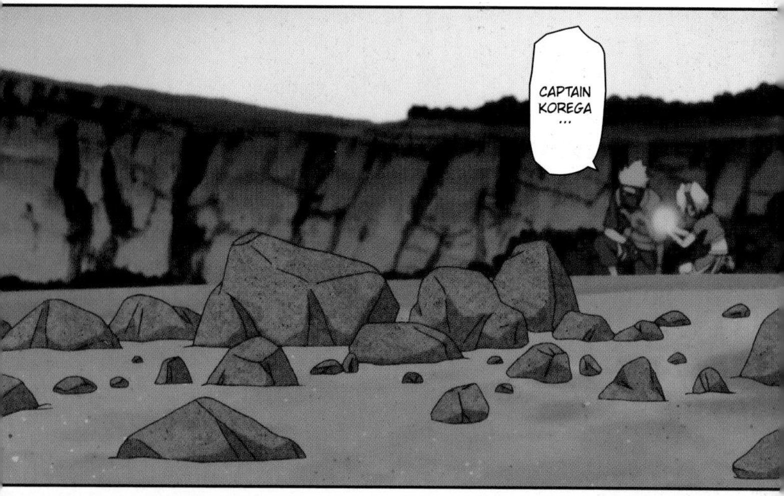
CAPTAIN KOREGA ...
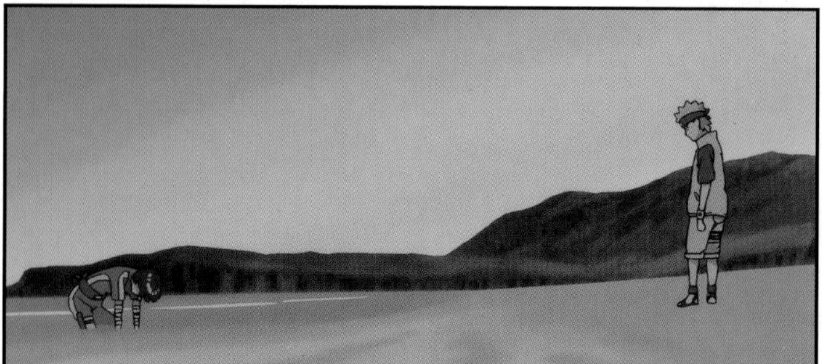
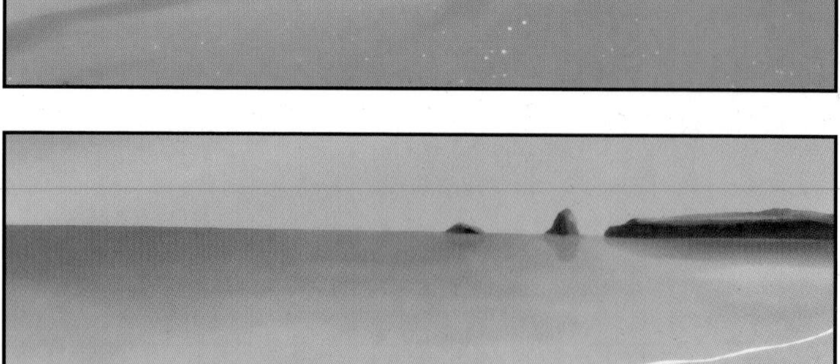

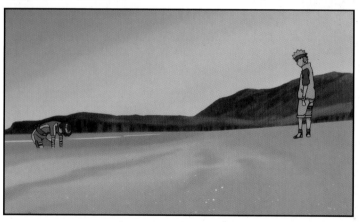

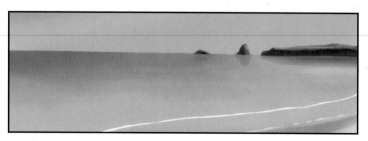

Chapter 5: Hikaru's Choice

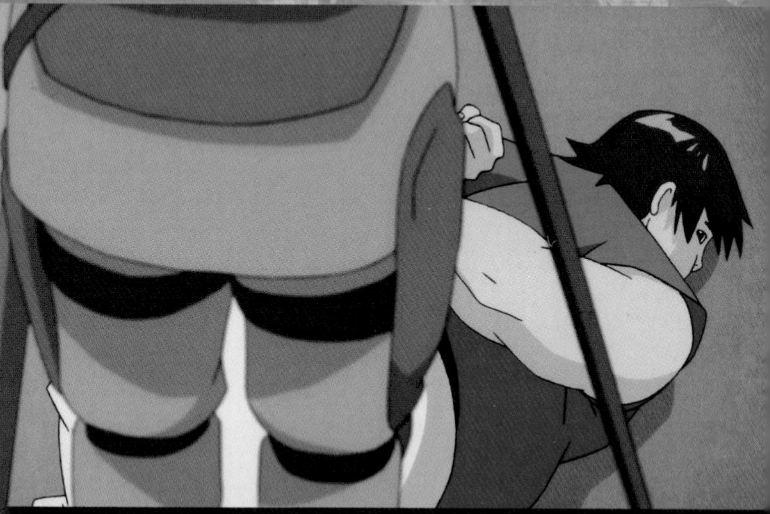

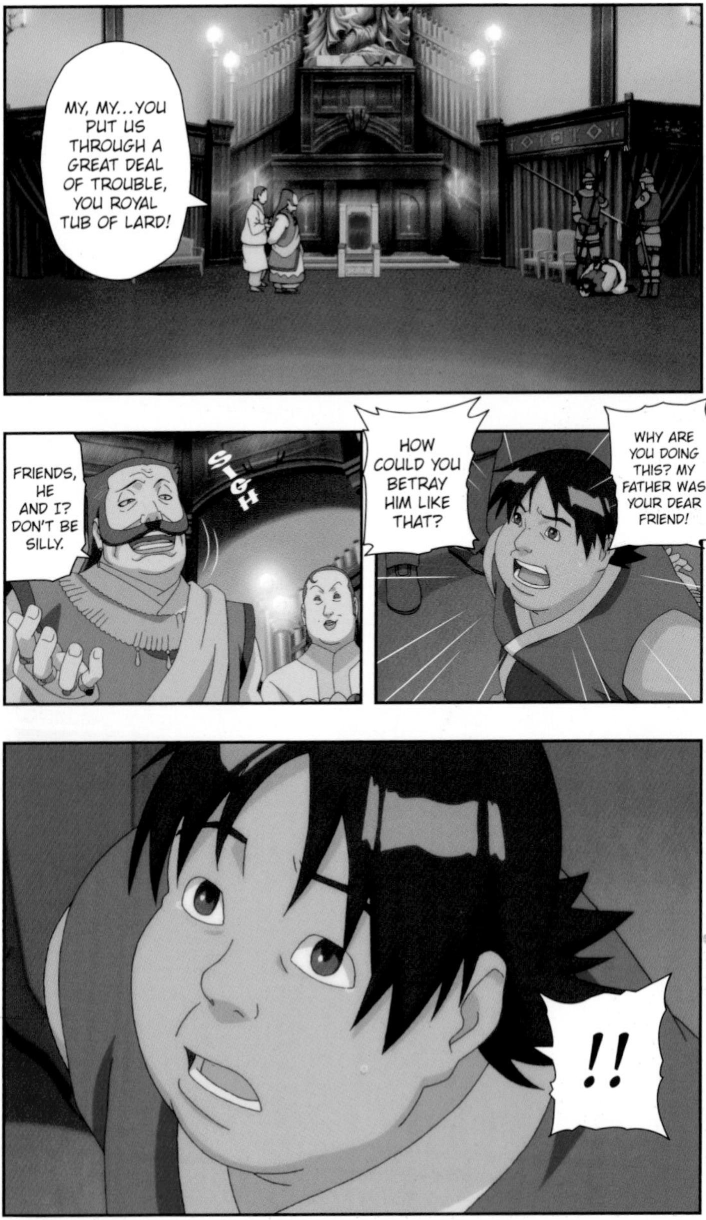
MY, MY...YOU PUT US THROUGH A GREAT DEAL OF TROUBLE, YOU ROYAL TUB OF LARD!
WHY ARE YOU DOING THIS? MY FATHER WAS YOUR DEAR FRIEND!
HOW COULD YOU BETRAY HIM LIKE THAT?
SIGH
FRIENDS, HE AND I? DON'T BE SILLY.
!!

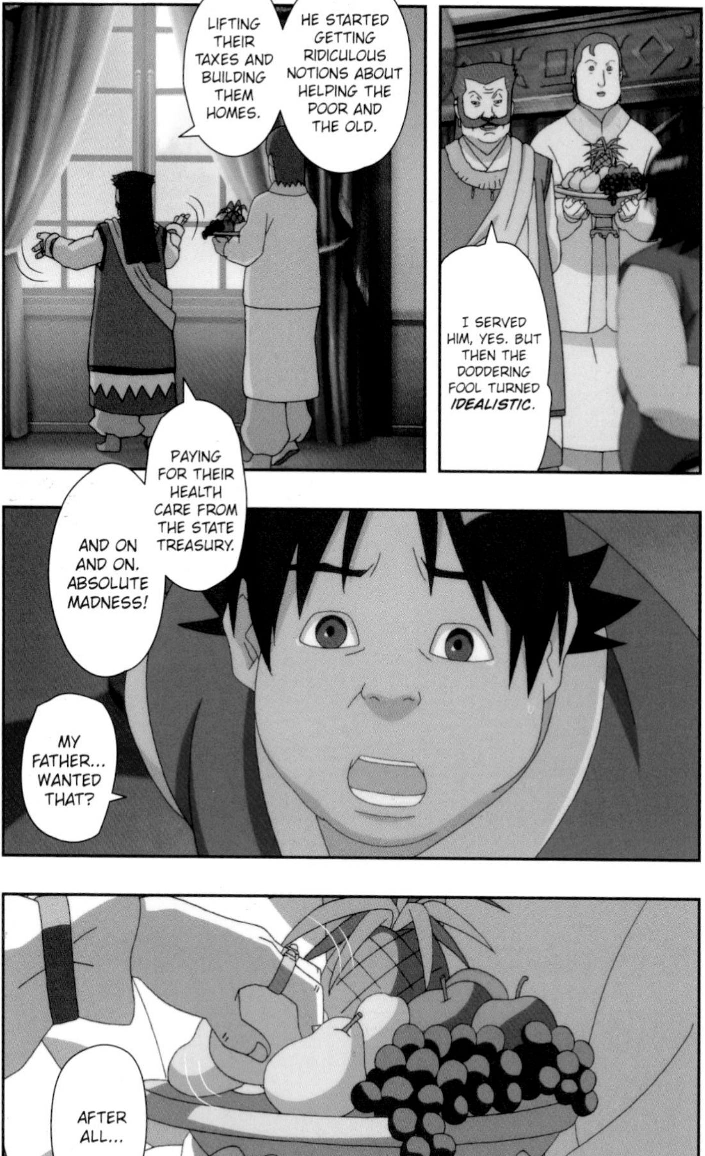
I SERVED HIM, YES. BUT THEN THE DODDERING FOOL TURNED *IDEALISTIC*.
HE STARTED GETTING RIDICULOUS NOTIONS ABOUT HELPING THE POOR AND THE OLD.
LIFTING THEIR TAXES AND BUILDING THEM HOMES.
PAYING FOR THEIR HEALTH CARE FROM THE STATE TREASURY.
AND ON AND ON. ABSOLUTE MADNESS!
MY FATHER... WANTED THAT?
AFTER ALL...

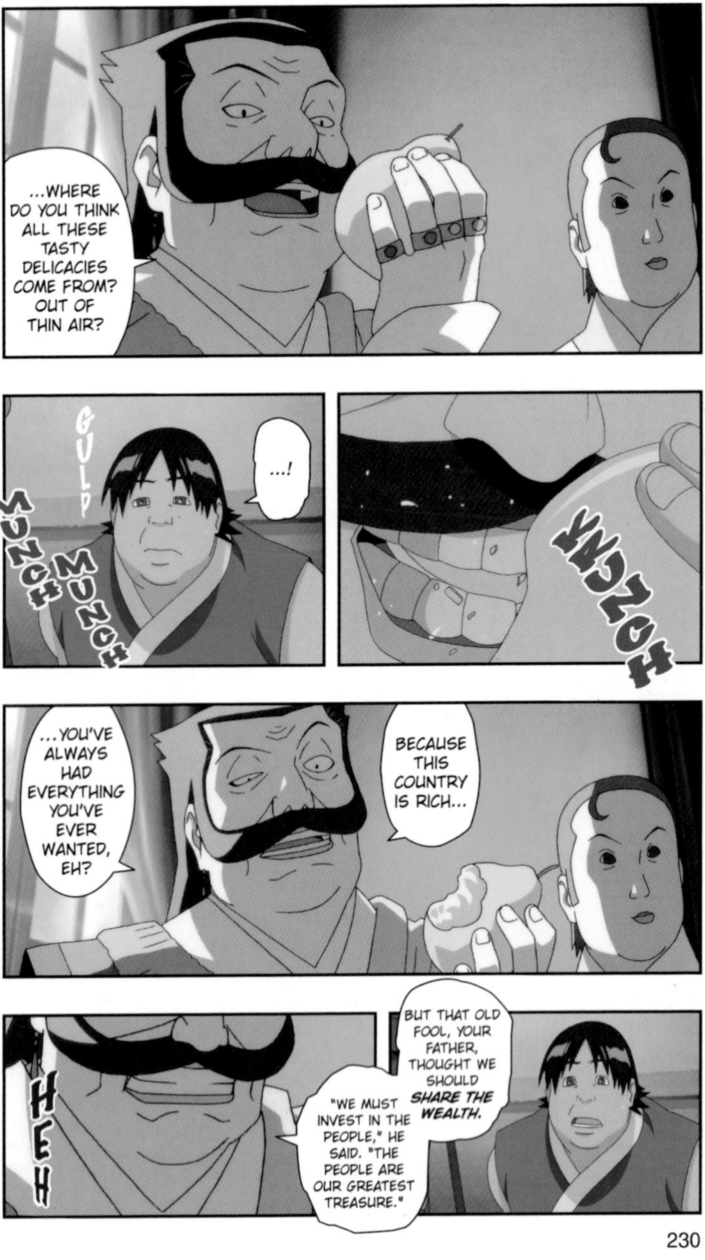
...WHERE DO YOU THINK ALL THESE TASTY DELICACIES COME FROM? OUT OF THIN AIR?
KRUNCH
...!
GULP
MUNCH MUNCH
BECAUSE THIS COUNTRY IS RICH...
...YOU'VE ALWAYS HAD EVERYTHING YOU'VE EVER WANTED, EH?
BUT THAT OLD FOOL, YOUR FATHER, THOUGHT WE SHOULD ***SHARE THE WEALTH.***
"WE MUST INVEST IN THE PEOPLE," HE SAID. "THE PEOPLE ARE OUR GREATEST TREASURE."
HEH

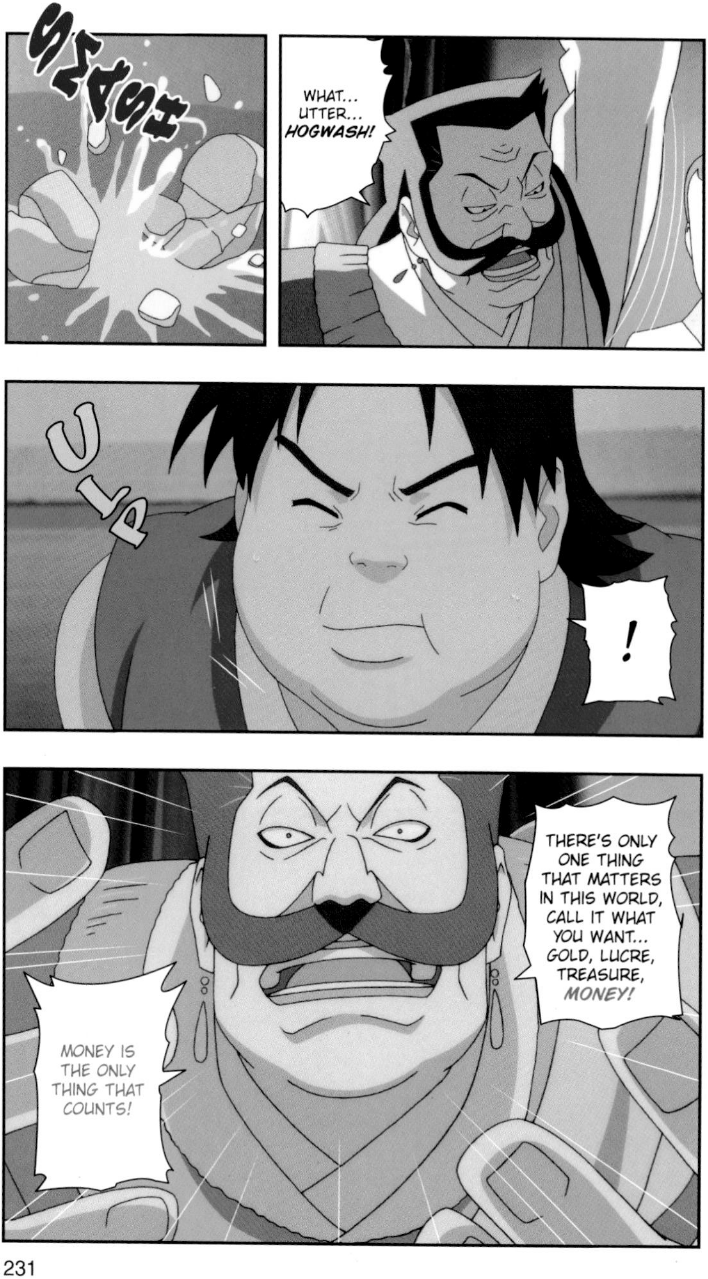
WHAT... UTTER... HOGWASH!
SMASH
!
THERE'S ONLY ONE THING THAT MATTERS IN THIS WORLD, CALL IT WHAT YOU WANT... GOLD, LUCRE, TREASURE, MONEY!
MONEY IS THE ONLY THING THAT COUNTS!

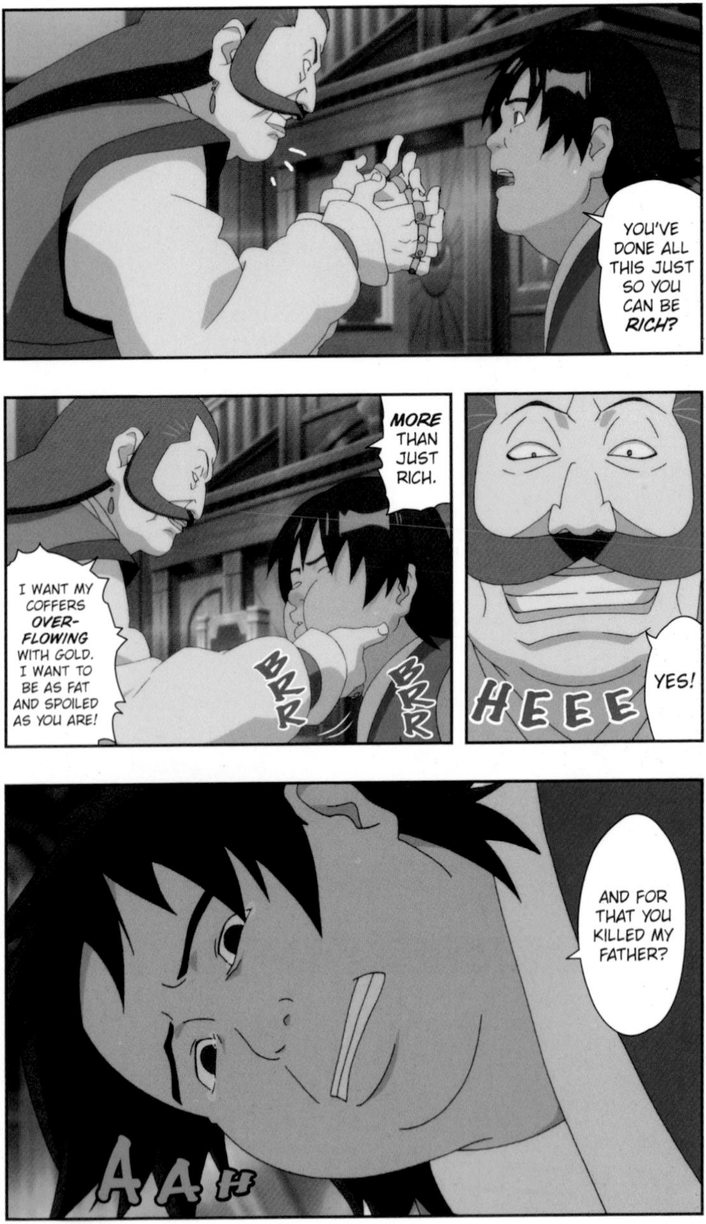
YOU'VE DONE ALL THIS JUST SO YOU CAN BE *RICH?*
YES!
HEEE
MORE THAN JUST RICH.
I WANT MY COFFERS *OVER-FLOWING* WITH GOLD. I WANT TO BE AS FAT AND SPOILED AS YOU ARE!
BRR
BRR
AND FOR THAT YOU KILLED MY FATHER?
AAH

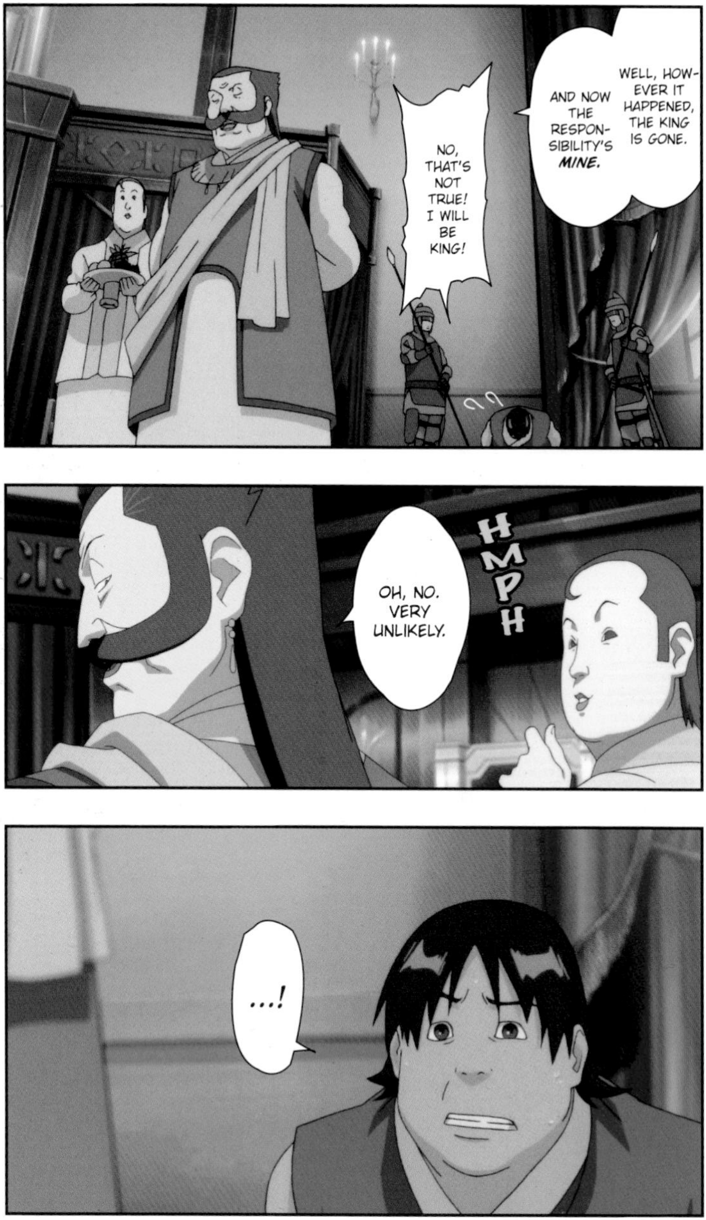
WELL, HOW-EVER IT HAPPENED, THE KING IS GONE.
AND NOW THE RESPON-SIBILITY'S ***MINE.***
NO, THAT'S NOT TRUE! I WILL BE KING!
HMPH
OH, NO. VERY UNLIKELY.
...!

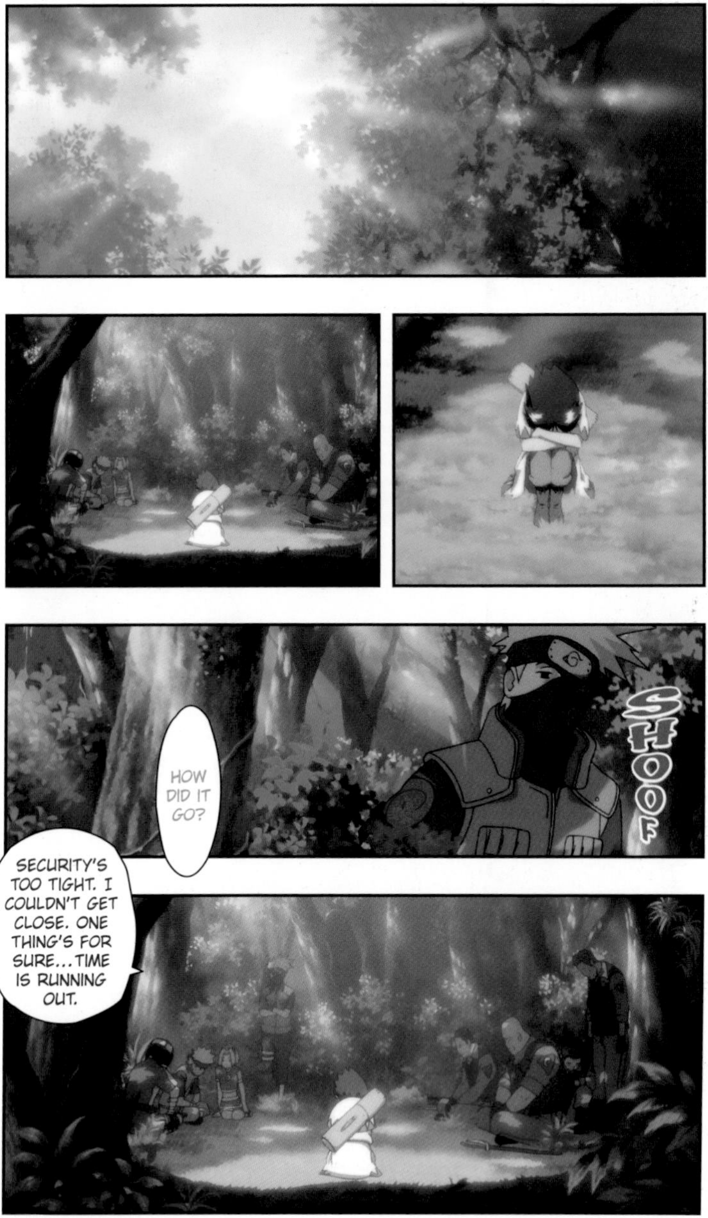
SHOOF
HOW DID IT GO?
SECURITY'S TOO TIGHT. I COULDN'T GET CLOSE. ONE THING'S FOR SURE...TIME IS RUNNING OUT.

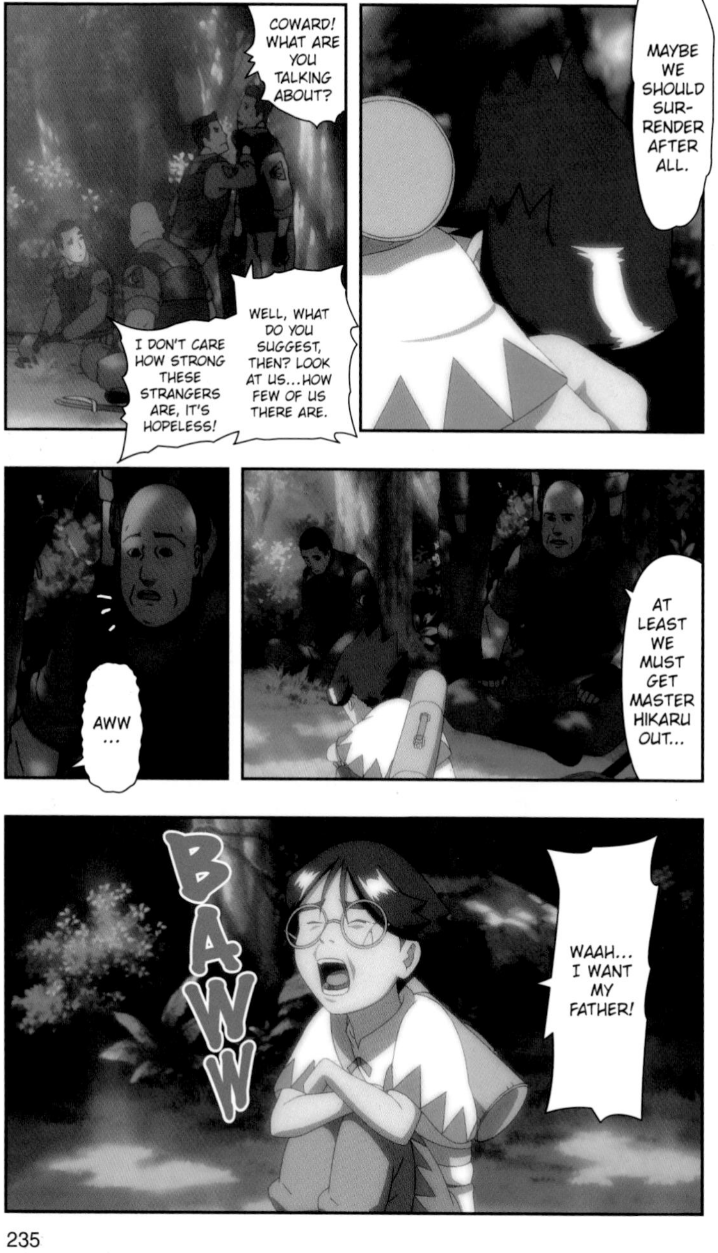
MAYBE WE SHOULD SURRENDER AFTER ALL.
COWARD! WHAT ARE YOU TALKING ABOUT?
WELL, WHAT DO YOU SUGGEST, THEN? LOOK AT US...HOW FEW OF US THERE ARE.
I DON'T CARE HOW STRONG THESE STRANGERS ARE, IT'S HOPELESS!
AT LEAST WE MUST GET MASTER HIKARU OUT...
AWW ...
WAAH... I WANT MY FATHER!
BAWW

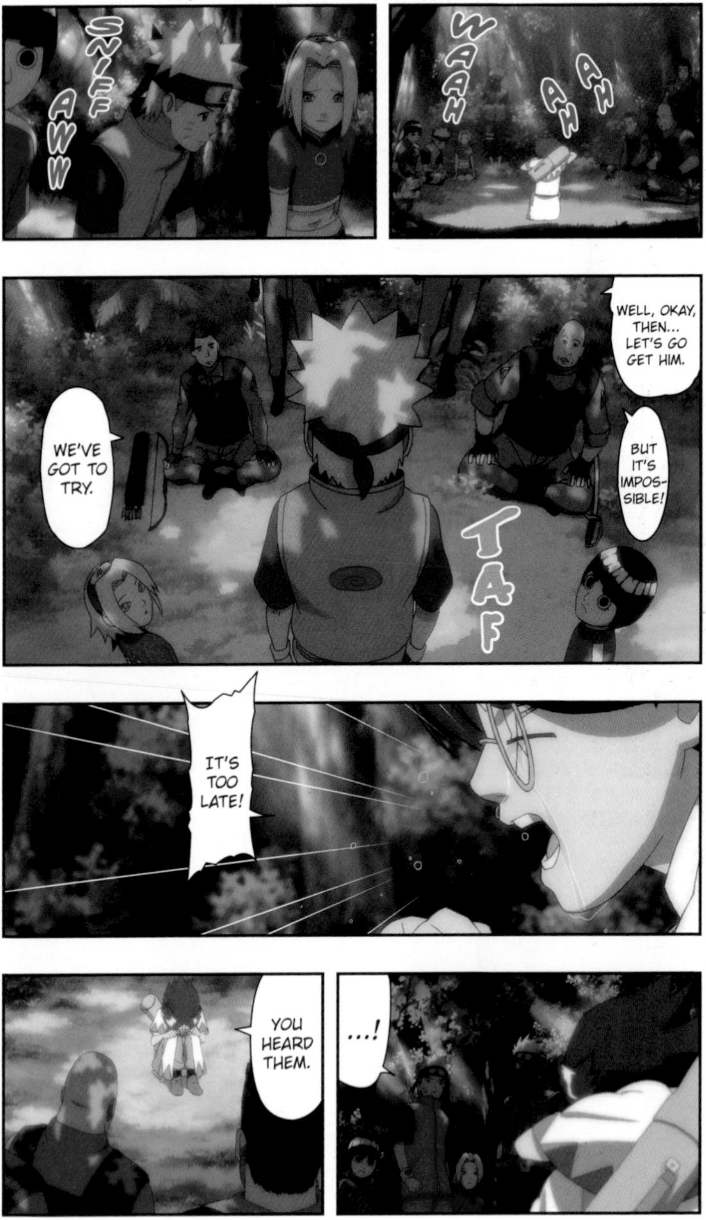
WAAAH
AH AH
SNIFF
AWWW
WELL, OKAY, THEN... LET'S GO GET HIM.
BUT IT'S IMPOS-SIBLE!
TAF
WE'VE GOT TO TRY.
IT'S TOO LATE!
...!
YOU HEARD THEM.

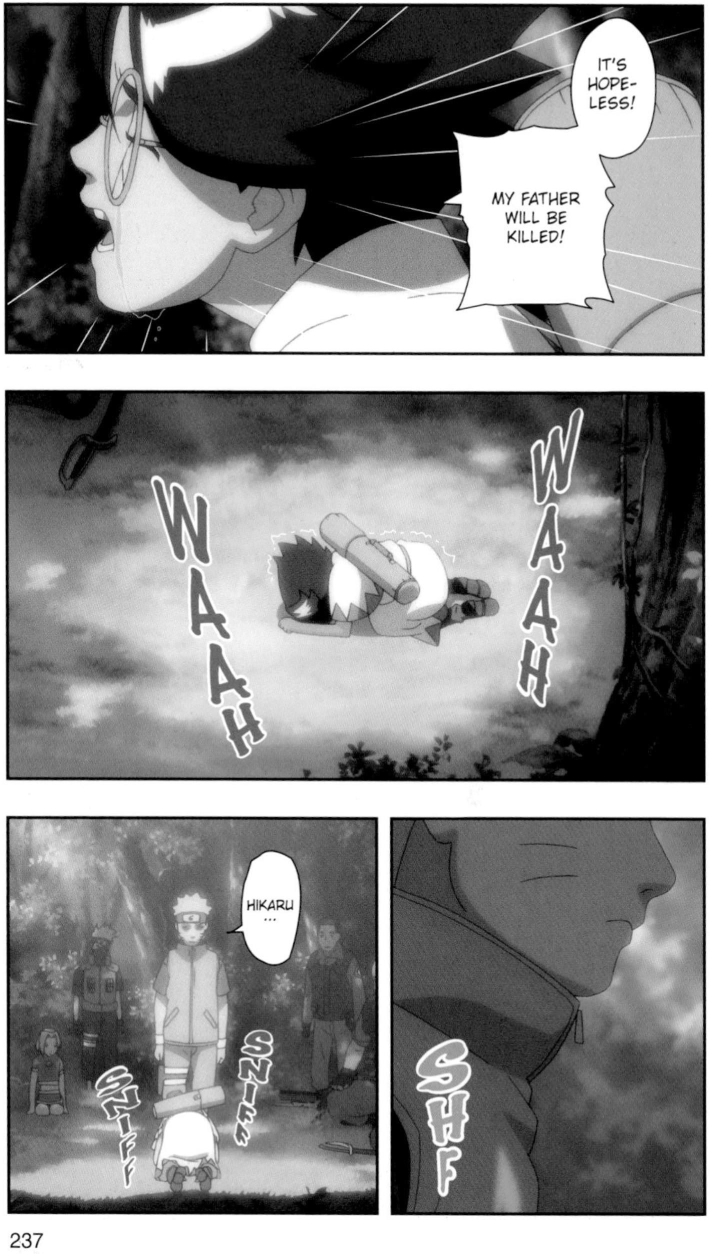
IT'S HOPE-LESS!
MY FATHER WILL BE KILLED!
WAAH
WAAH
SHF
HIKARU ...
SNIFF
SNIFF

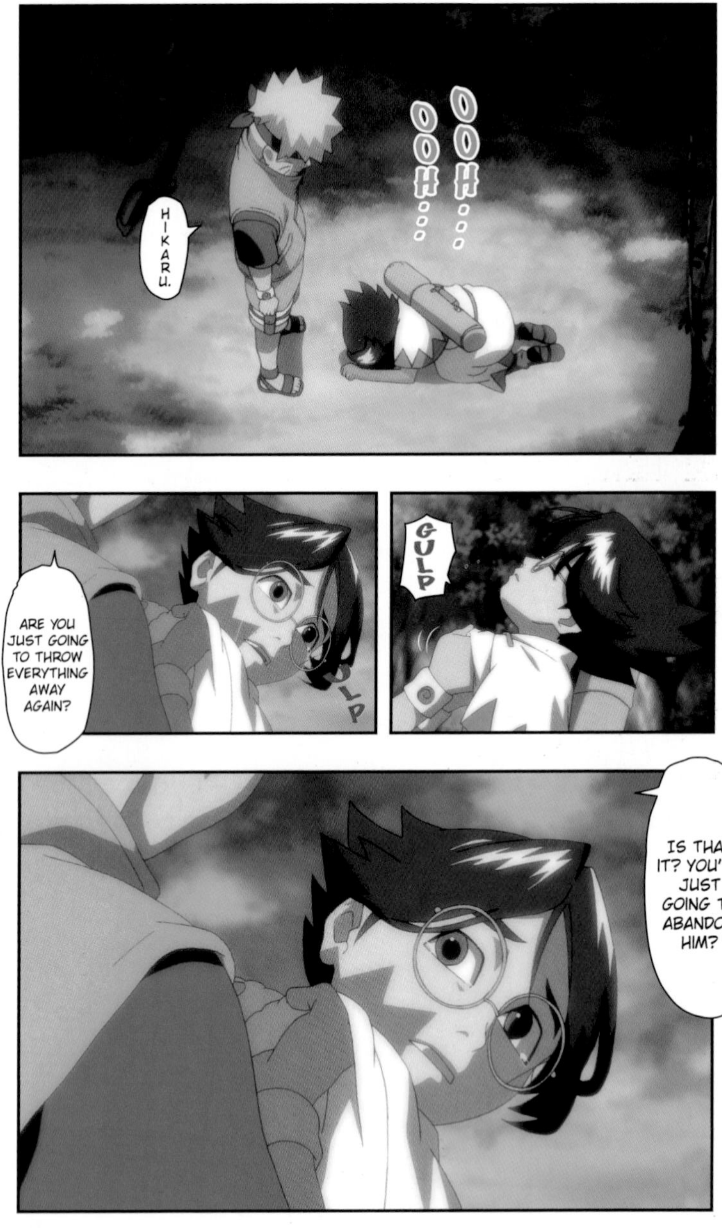
OOOH...
OOOH...
HIKARU.
GULP
ARE YOU JUST GOING TO THROW EVERYTHING AWAY AGAIN?
LP
IS THAT IT? YOU'RE JUST GOING TO ABANDON HIM?

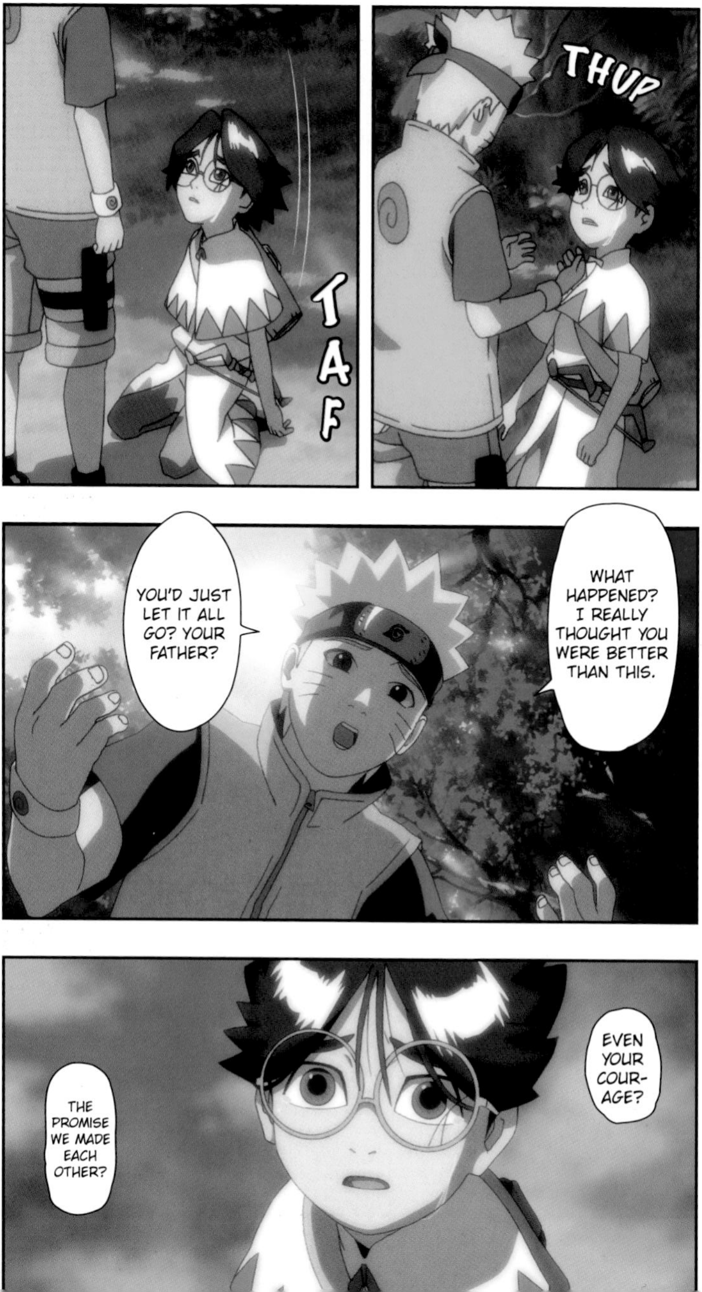
THUP
TAF
WHAT HAPPENED? I REALLY THOUGHT YOU WERE BETTER THAN THIS.
YOU'D JUST LET IT ALL GO? YOUR FATHER?
EVEN YOUR COUR-AGE?
THE PROMISE WE MADE EACH OTHER?

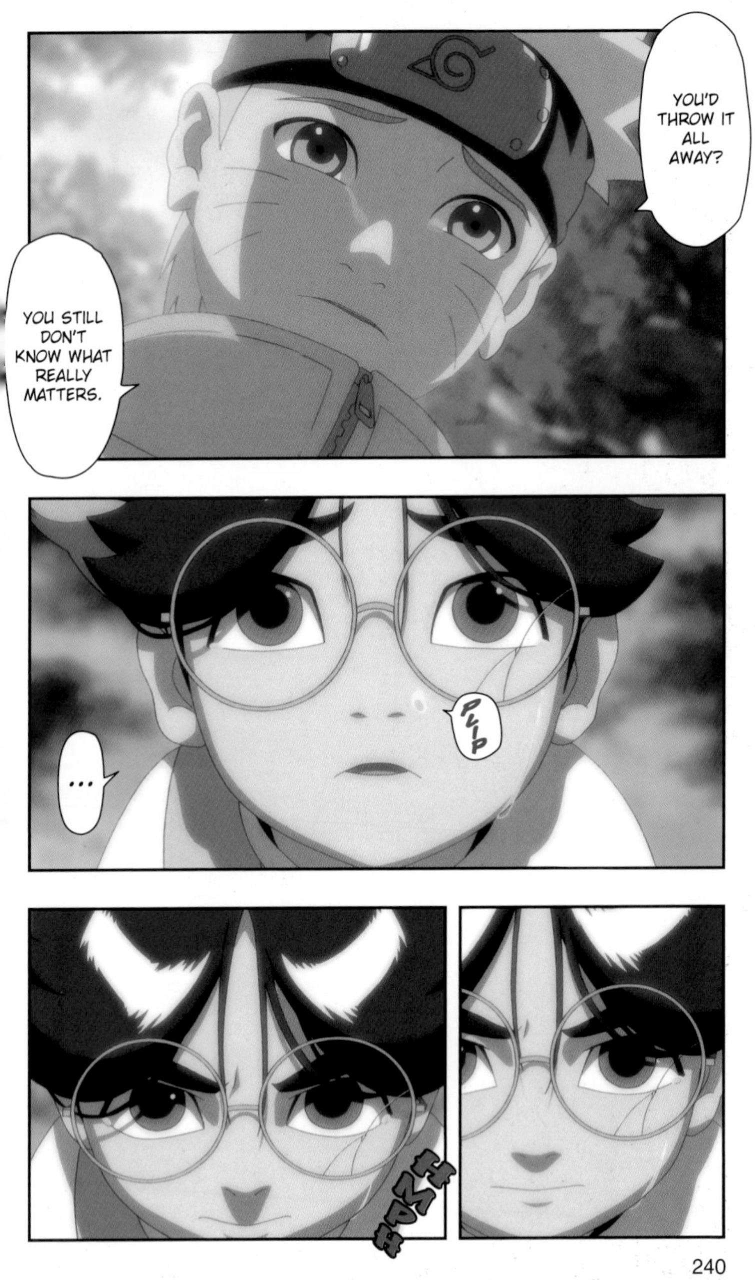
YOU'D THROW IT ALL AWAY?
YOU STILL DON'T KNOW WHAT REALLY MATTERS.
PLIP
...
HMPH

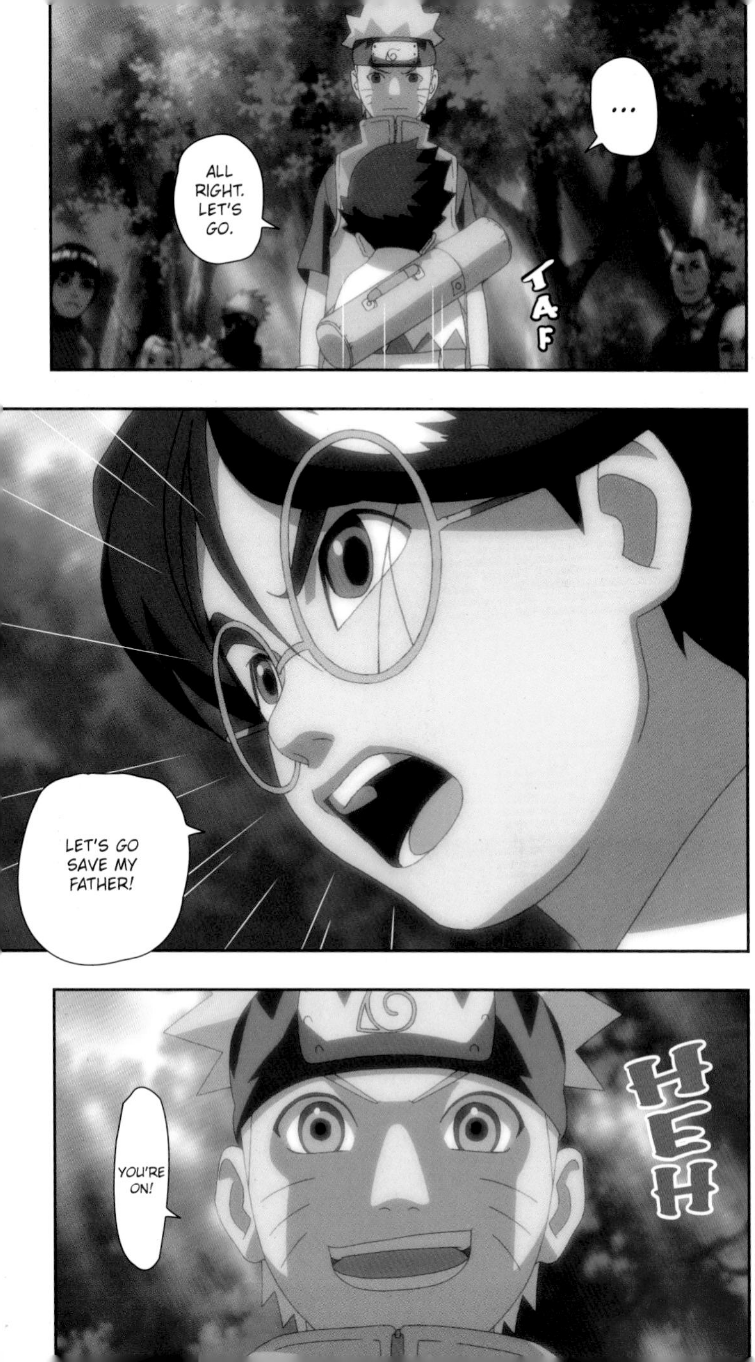
...
ALL RIGHT. LET'S GO.
TAF
LET'S GO SAVE MY FATHER!
HEH
YOU'RE ON!

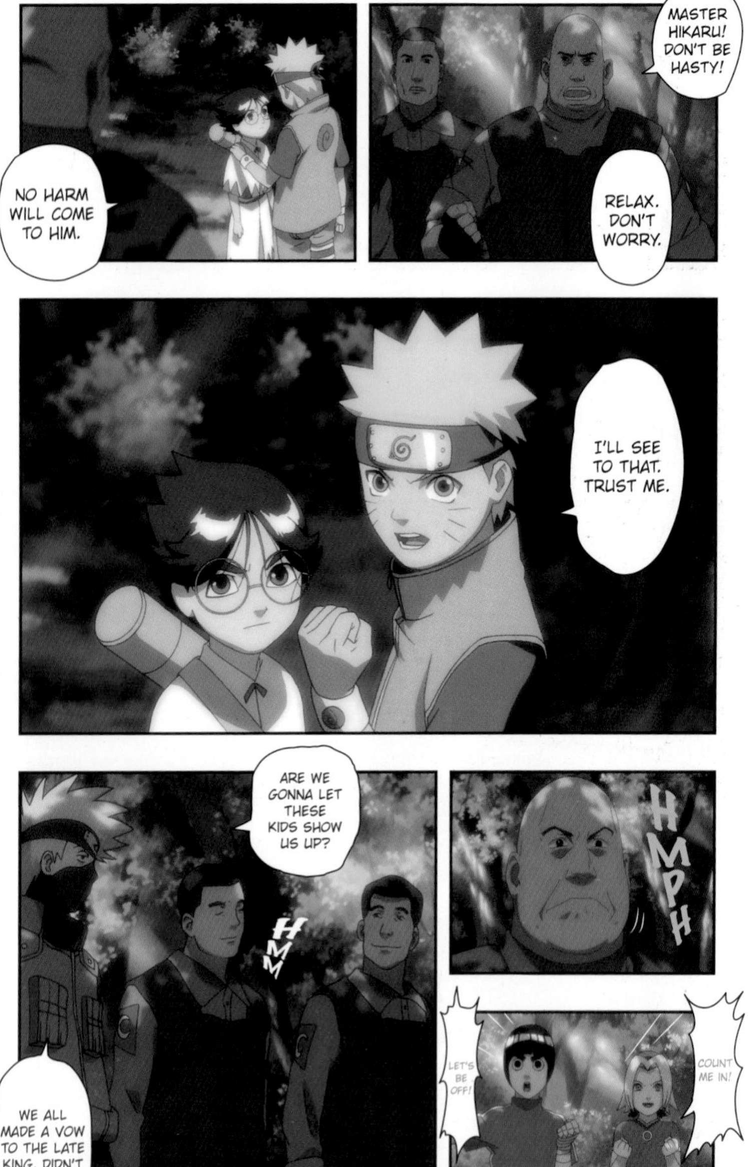
MASTER HIKARU! DON'T BE HASTY!
RELAX. DON'T WORRY.
NO HARM WILL COME TO HIM.
I'LL SEE TO THAT. TRUST ME.
HMPH
COUNT ME IN!
LET'S BE OFF!
ARE WE GONNA LET THESE KIDS SHOW US UP?
HMM
WE ALL MADE A VOW TO THE LATE KING, DIDN'T WE?

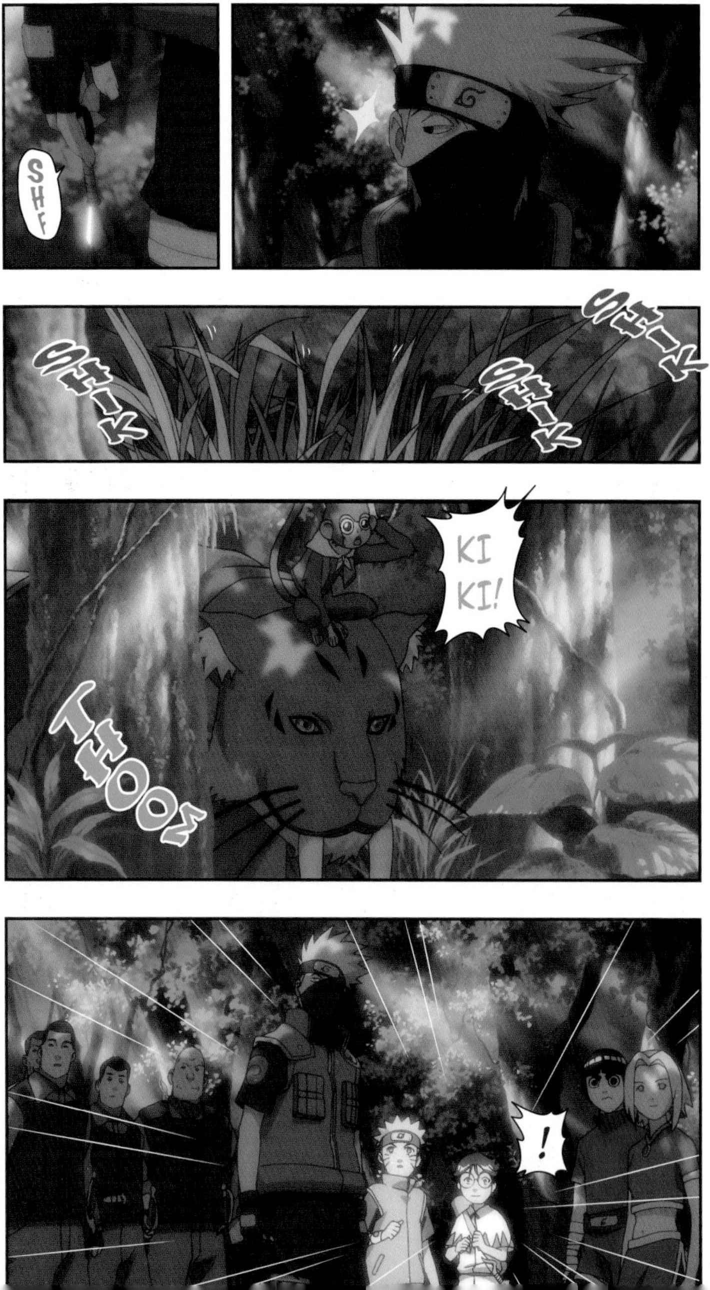
SHF
KI KI!
!

CHAMU!
KIKKI!
KI KI
AH HA HA HA HA
PURR PURR
HEY, CHAMU!
WHERE IS THAT CAT?
RUSTLE RUSTLE
!
WELL, WHADDYA KNOW... YOU GUYS.

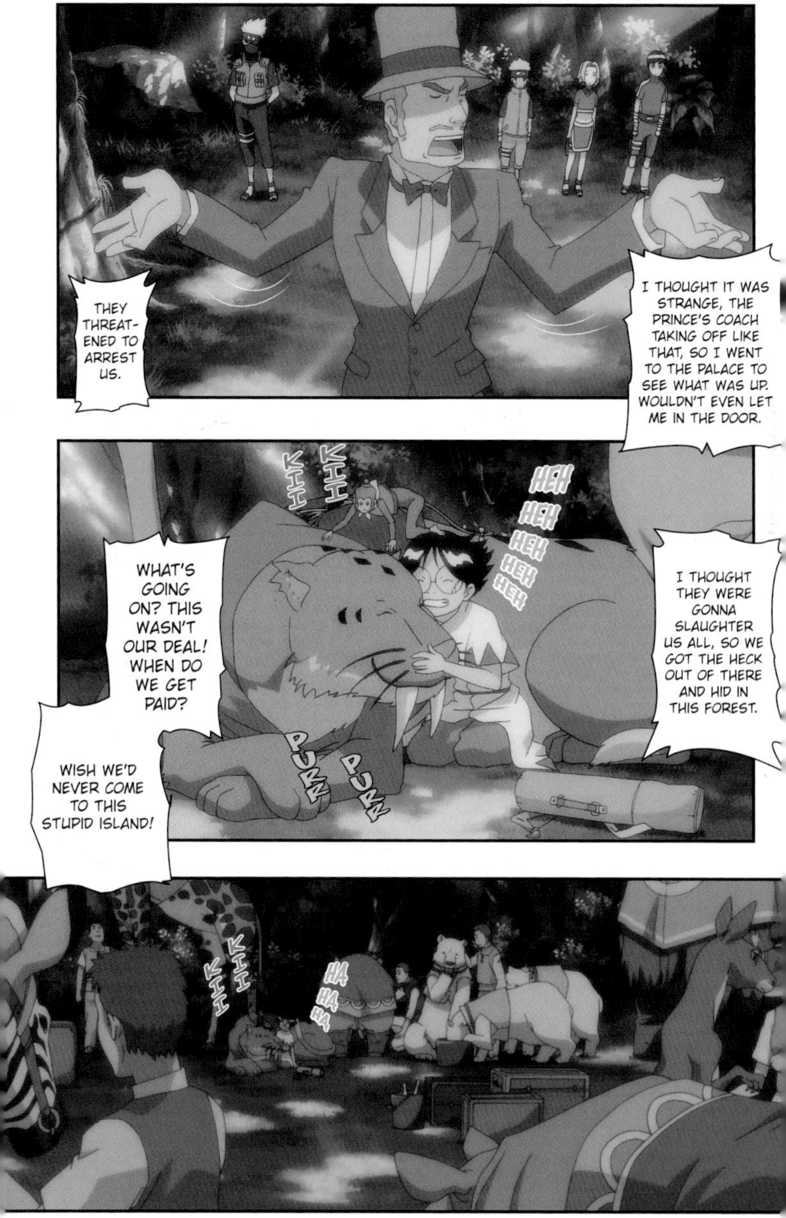
I THOUGHT IT WAS STRANGE, THE PRINCE'S COACH TAKING OFF LIKE THAT, SO I WENT TO THE PALACE TO SEE WHAT WAS UP. WOULDN'T EVEN LET ME IN THE DOOR.
THEY THREAT-ENED TO ARREST US.
I THOUGHT THEY WERE GONNA SLAUGHTER US ALL, SO WE GOT THE HECK OUT OF THERE AND HID IN THIS FOREST.
HEH HEH HEH HEH HEH
KII KII
WHAT'S GOING ON? THIS WASN'T OUR DEAL! WHEN DO WE GET PAID?
PURR PURR
WISH WE'D NEVER COME TO THIS STUPID ISLAND!
KII KII
HA HA HA

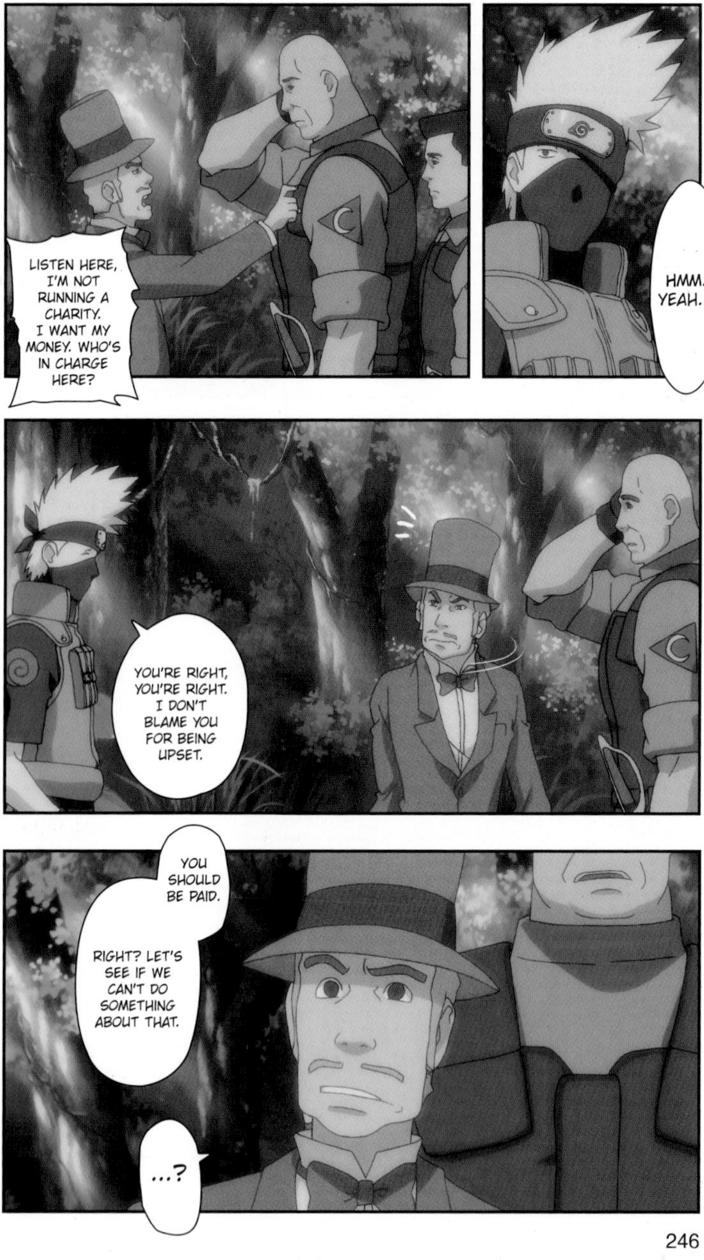
HMM. YEAH...
LISTEN HERE, I'M NOT RUNNING A CHARITY. I WANT MY MONEY. WHO'S IN CHARGE HERE?
YOU'RE RIGHT, YOU'RE RIGHT. I DON'T BLAME YOU FOR BEING UPSET.
YOU SHOULD BE PAID.
RIGHT? LET'S SEE IF WE CAN'T DO SOMETHING ABOUT THAT.
...?

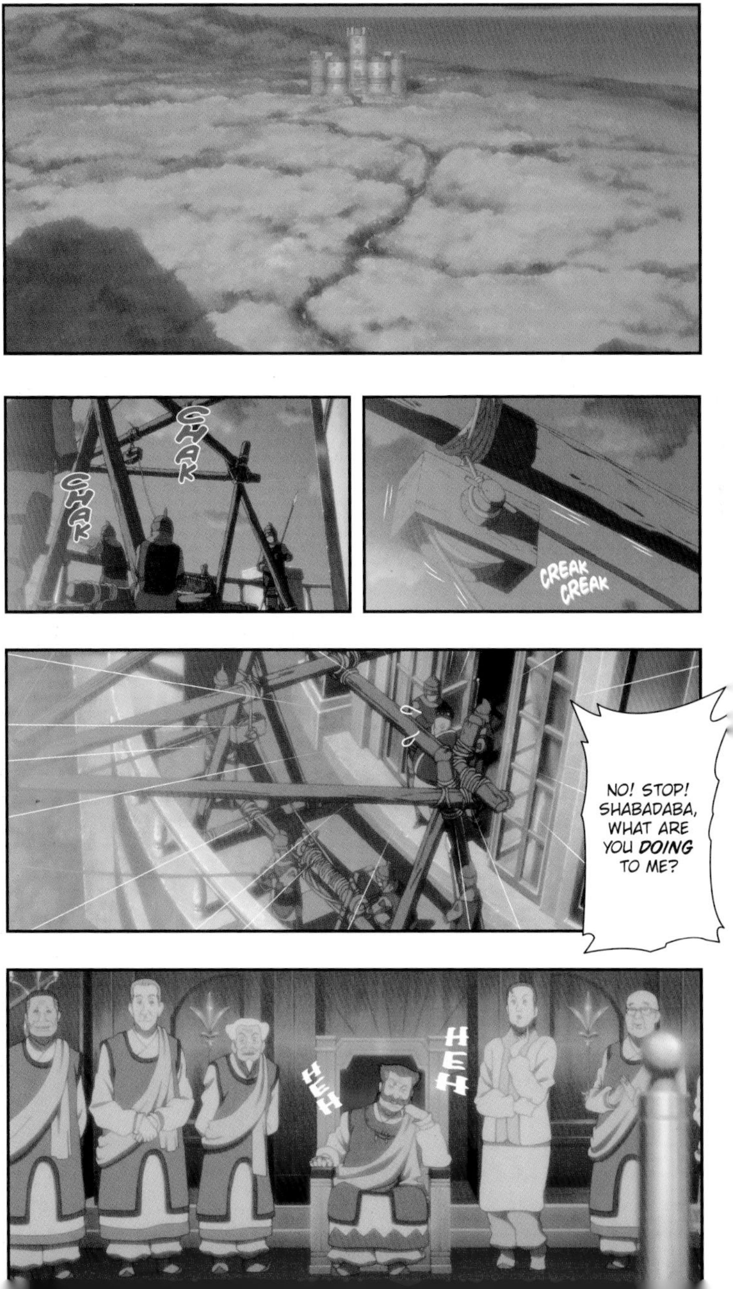
CREAK
CREAK
CHAK
CHAK
NO! STOP! SHABADABA, WHAT ARE YOU ***DOING*** TO ME?
HEH
HEH

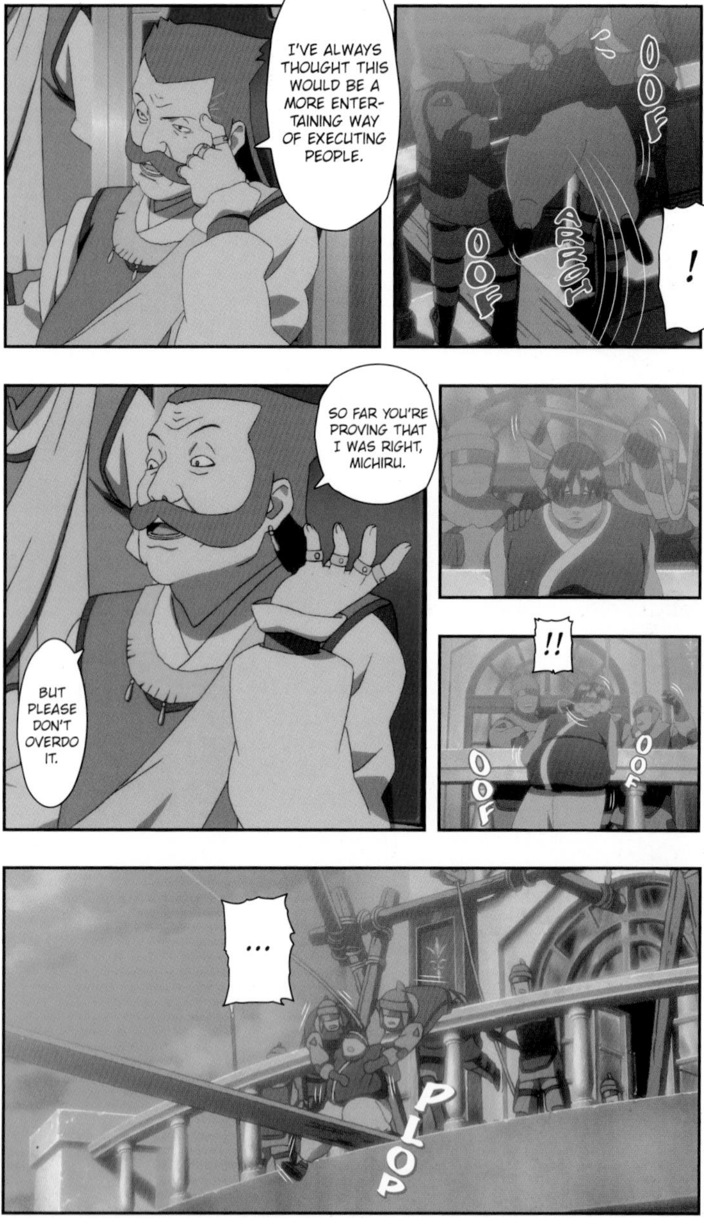

!
OOF
ARRGH
OOF
I'VE ALWAYS THOUGHT THIS WOULD BE A MORE ENTERTAINING WAY OF EXECUTING PEOPLE.
!!
OOF
OOF
SO FAR YOU'RE PROVING THAT I WAS RIGHT, MICHIRU.
BUT PLEASE DON'T OVERDO IT.
...
PLOP

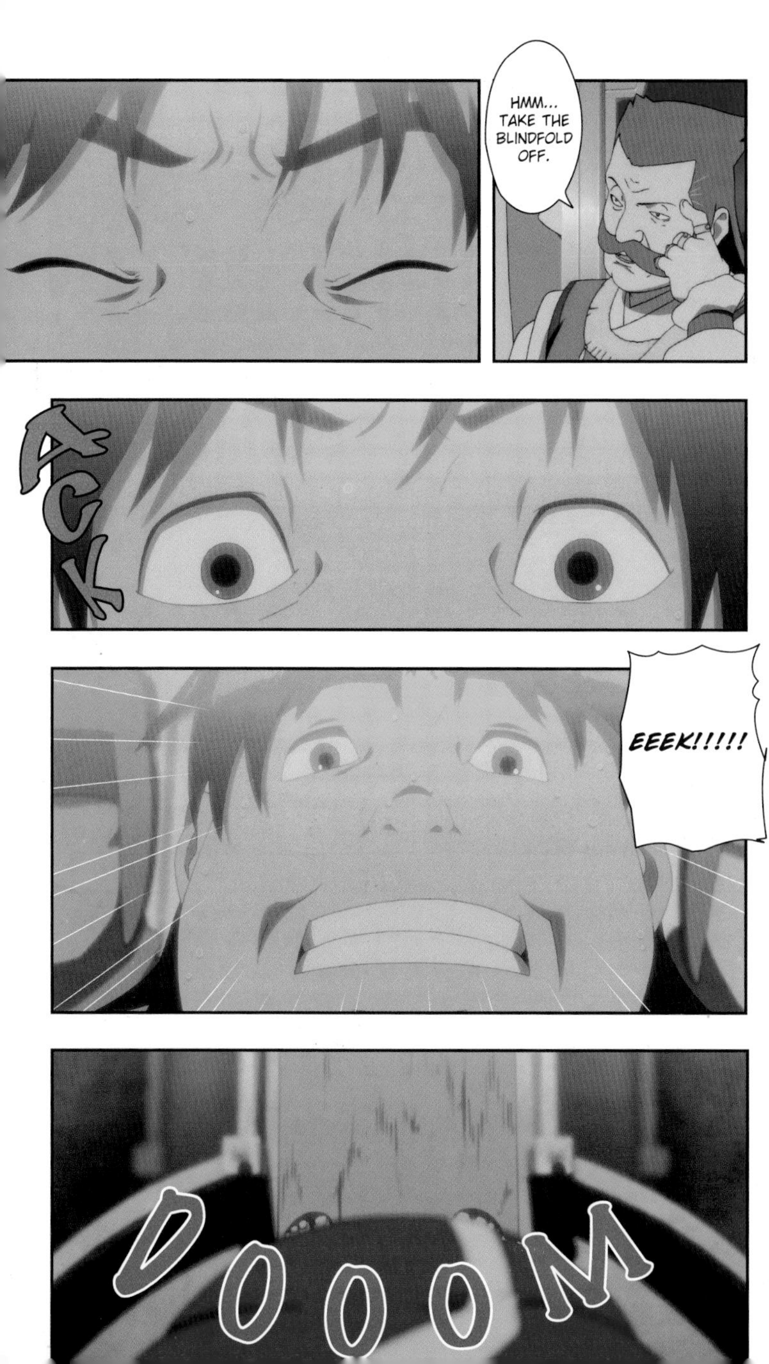
HMM... TAKE THE BLINDFOLD OFF.
ACK
EEEK!!!!!
DOOOM

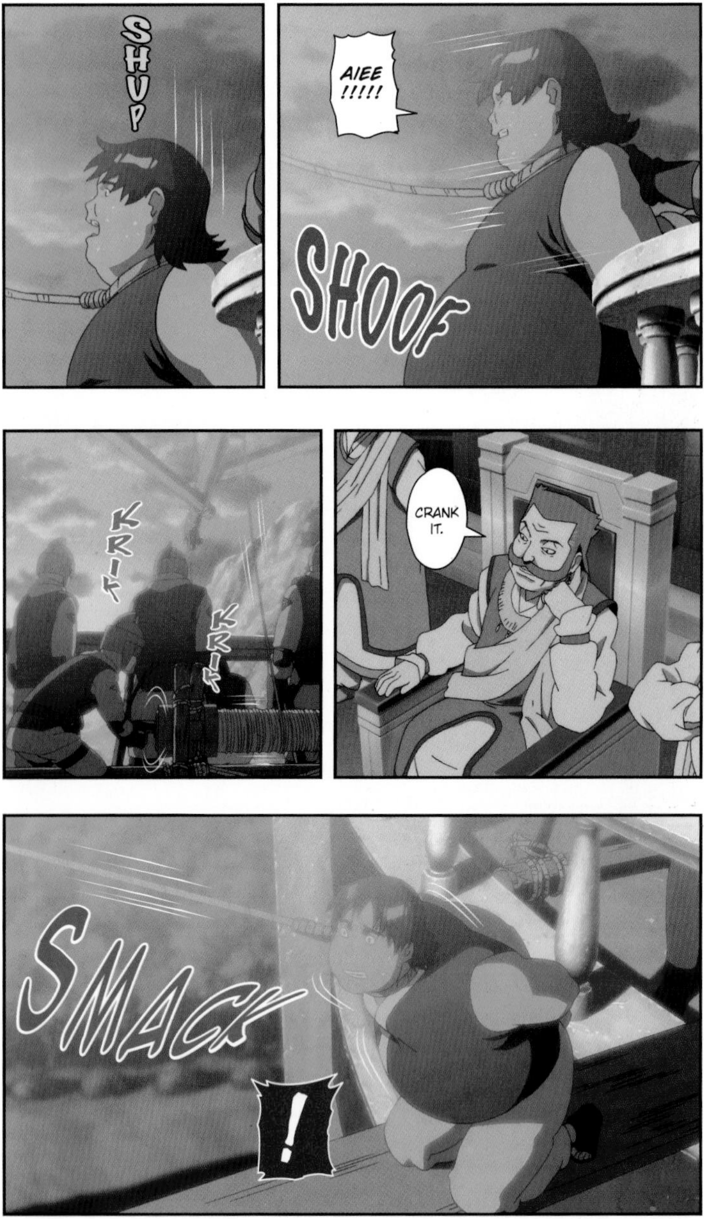
AIEE !!!!!
SHOOF
SHUP
CRANK IT.
KRIK
KRIK
SMACK
!

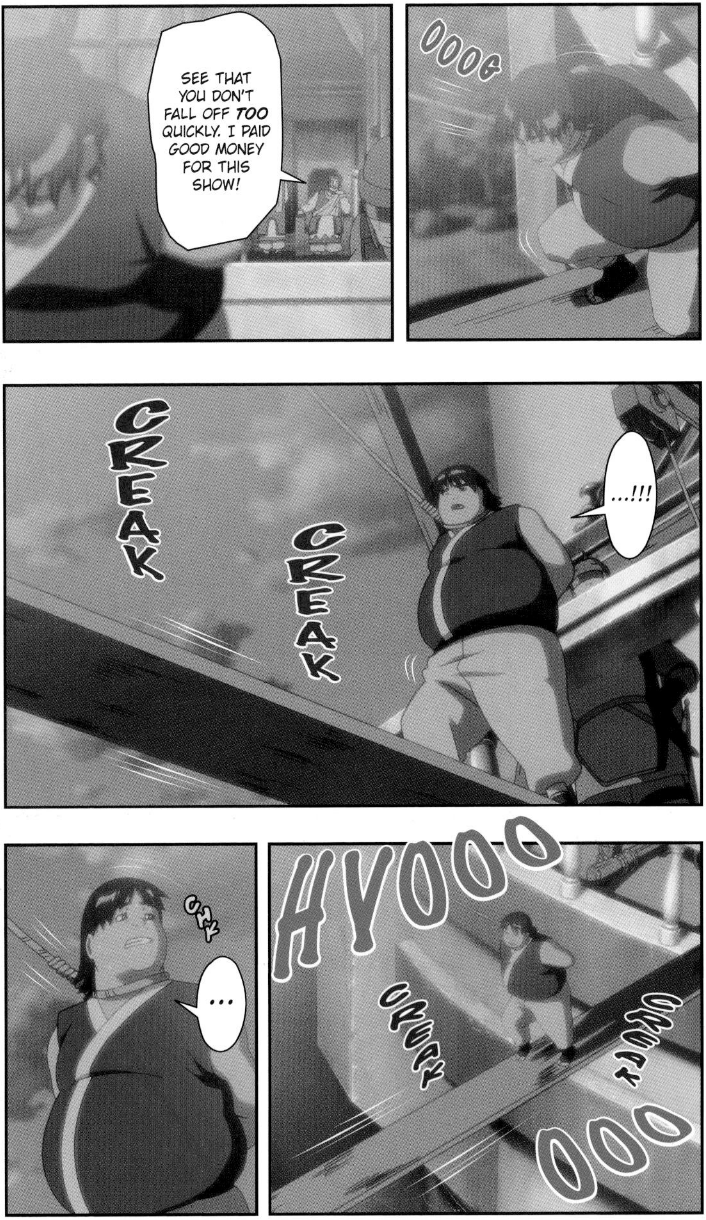
OOOG
SEE THAT YOU DON'T FALL OFF **TOO** QUICKLY. I PAID GOOD MONEY FOR THIS SHOW!
...!!!
CREAK
CREAK
HYOOOOOO
CREAK
CREAK
...

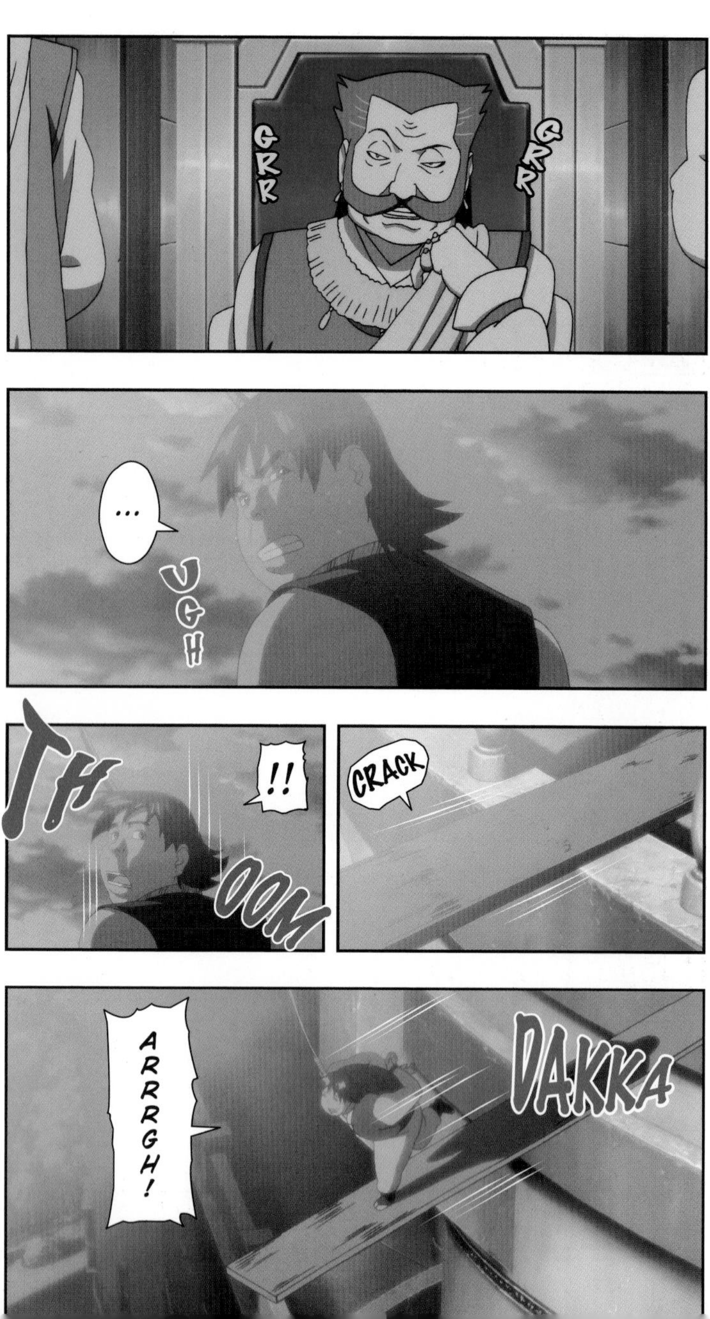
GRR
GRR
...
UGH
CRACK
!!
THOOM
DAKKA
ARRRGH!

...!
!
OOF
HM...

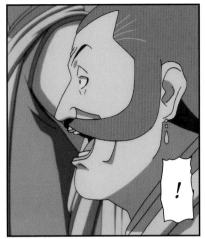

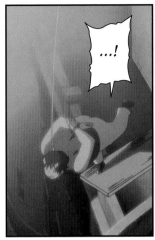

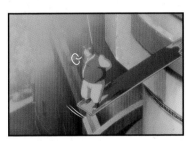

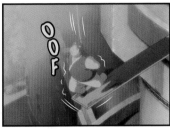

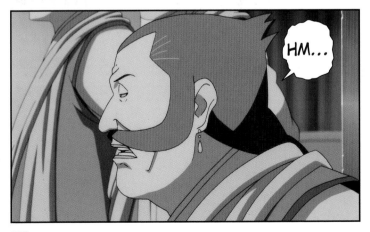

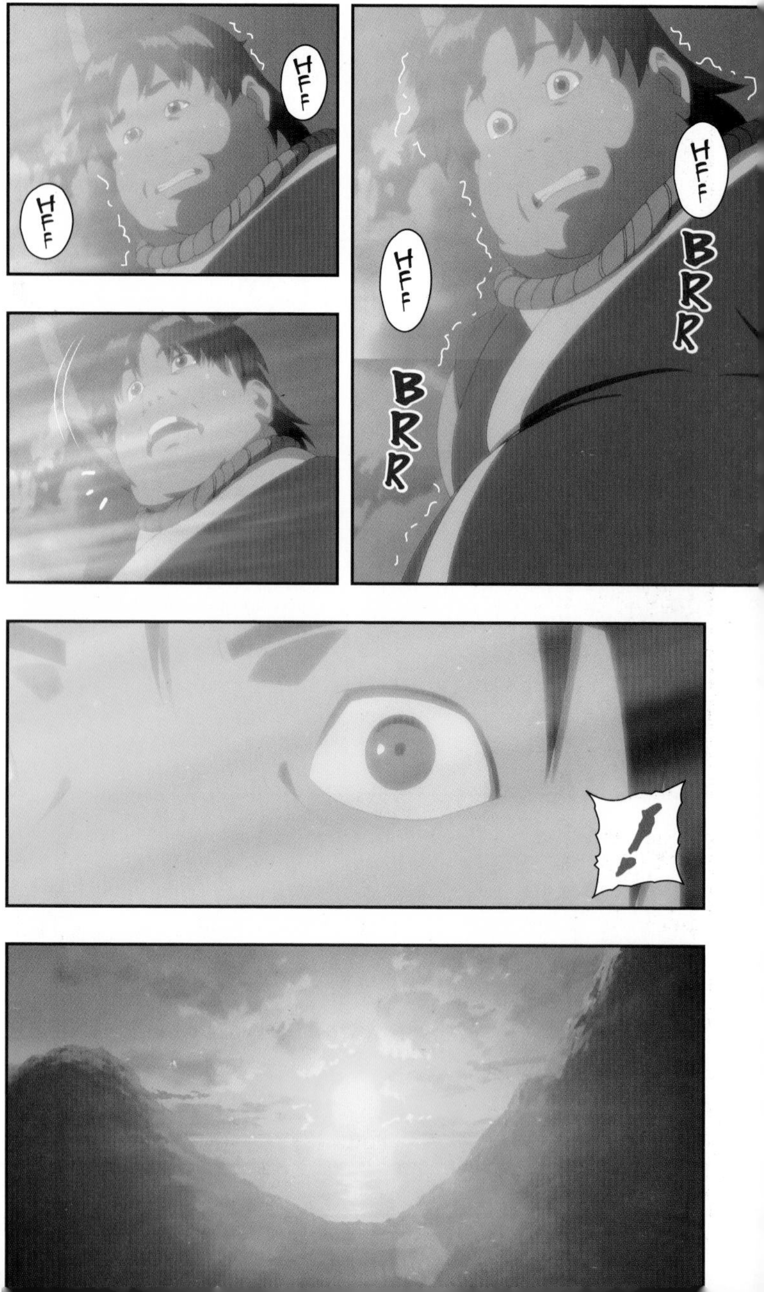
HFF
BRR
HFF
BRR
HFF
HFF
!

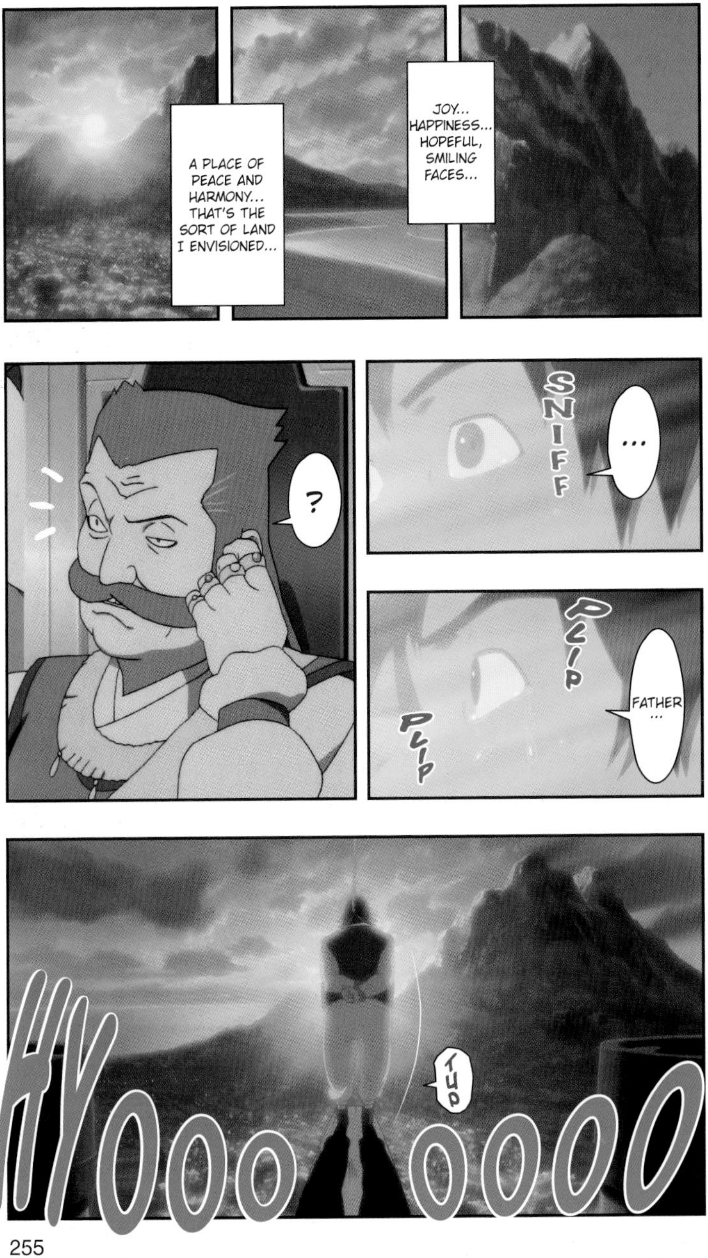
JOY... HAPPINESS... HOPEFUL, SMILING FACES...
A PLACE OF PEACE AND HARMONY... THAT'S THE SORT OF LAND I ENVISIONED...
SNIFF
...
PLIP
FATHER...
PLIP
?
TUP
HYOOOOOOOO

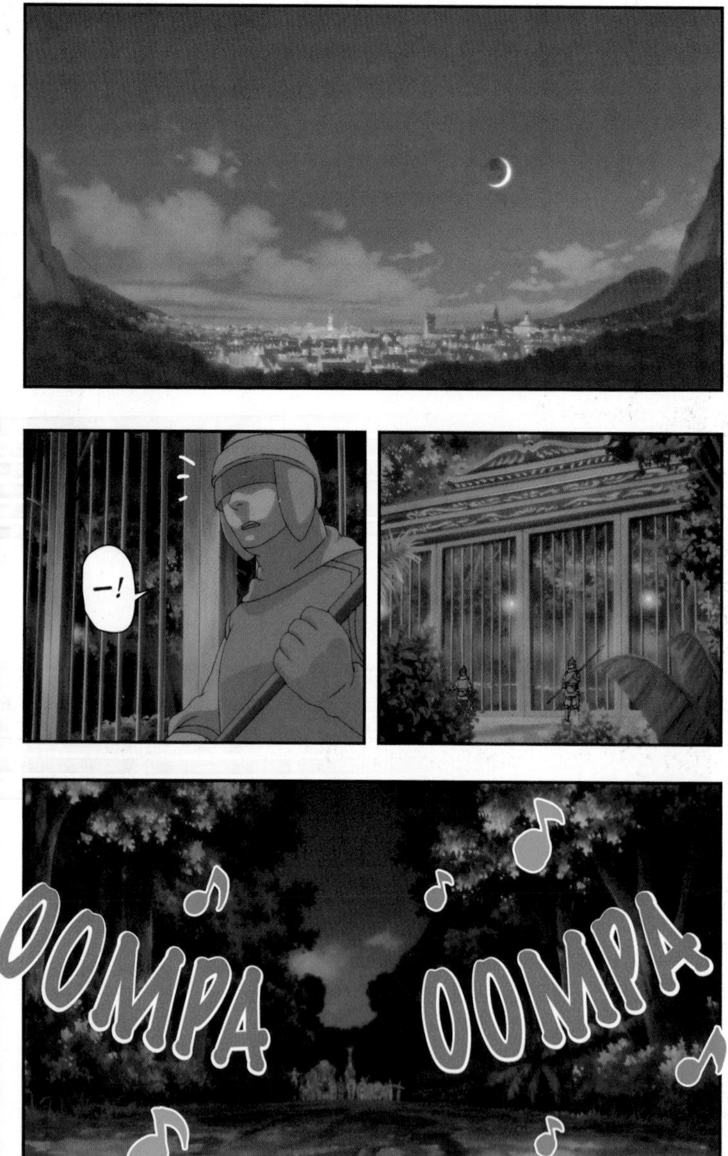
—!
OOMPA
OOMPA

🐾 Chapter 6: The Decisive Battle

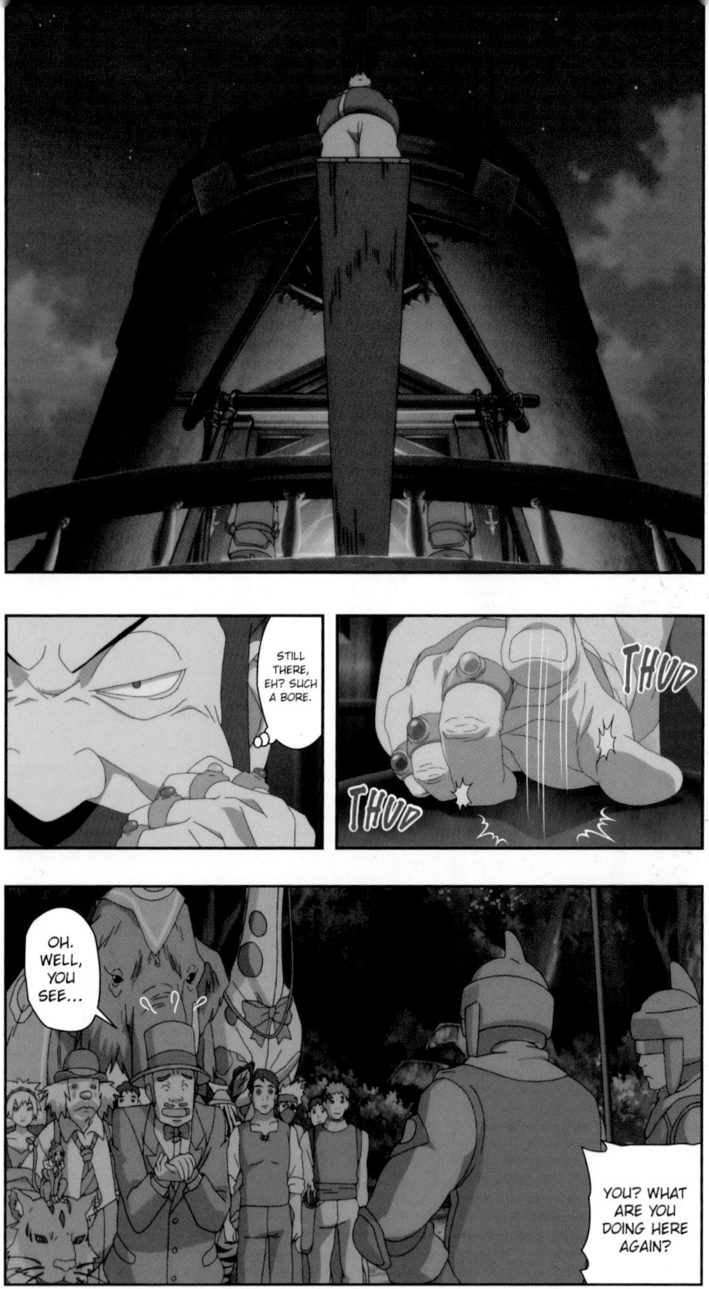
THUD
THUD
STILL THERE, EH? SUCH A BORE.
YOU? WHAT ARE YOU DOING HERE AGAIN?
OH. WELL, YOU SEE...

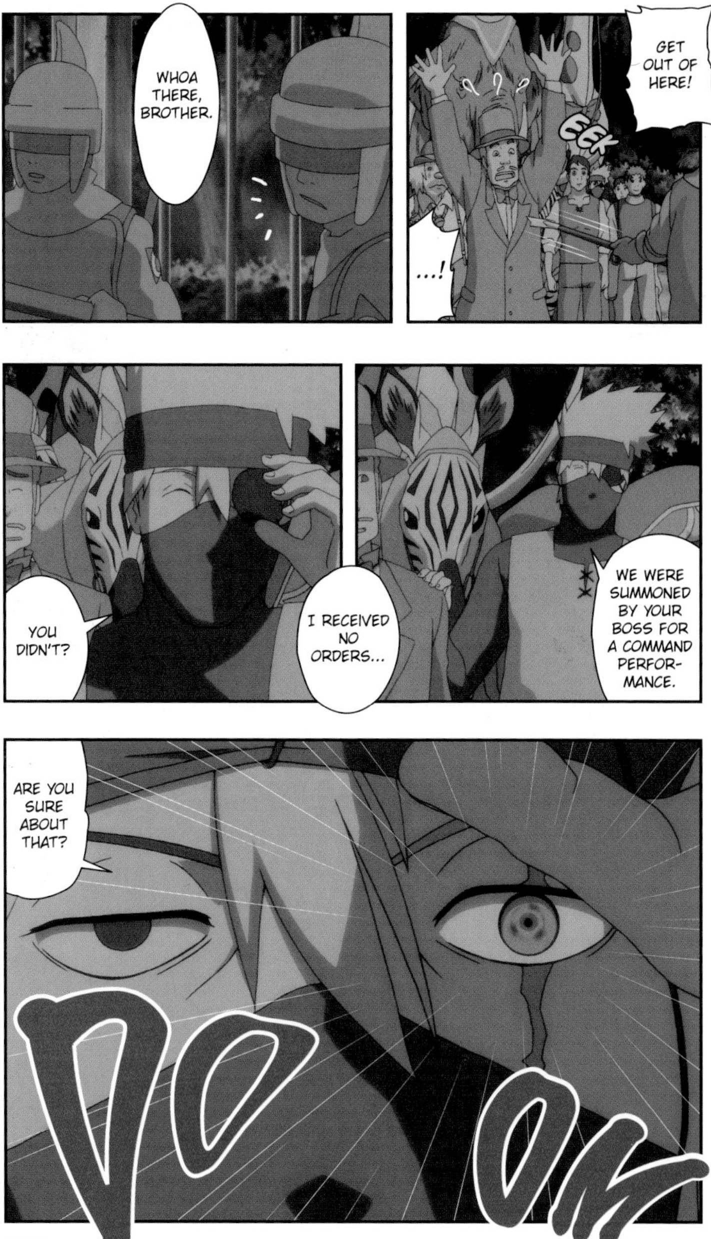
GET OUT OF HERE!
EEK
...!
WHOA THERE, BROTHER.
WE WERE SUMMONED BY YOUR BOSS FOR A COMMAND PERFORMANCE.
I RECEIVED NO ORDERS...
YOU DIDN'T?
ARE YOU SURE ABOUT THAT?
DOOM

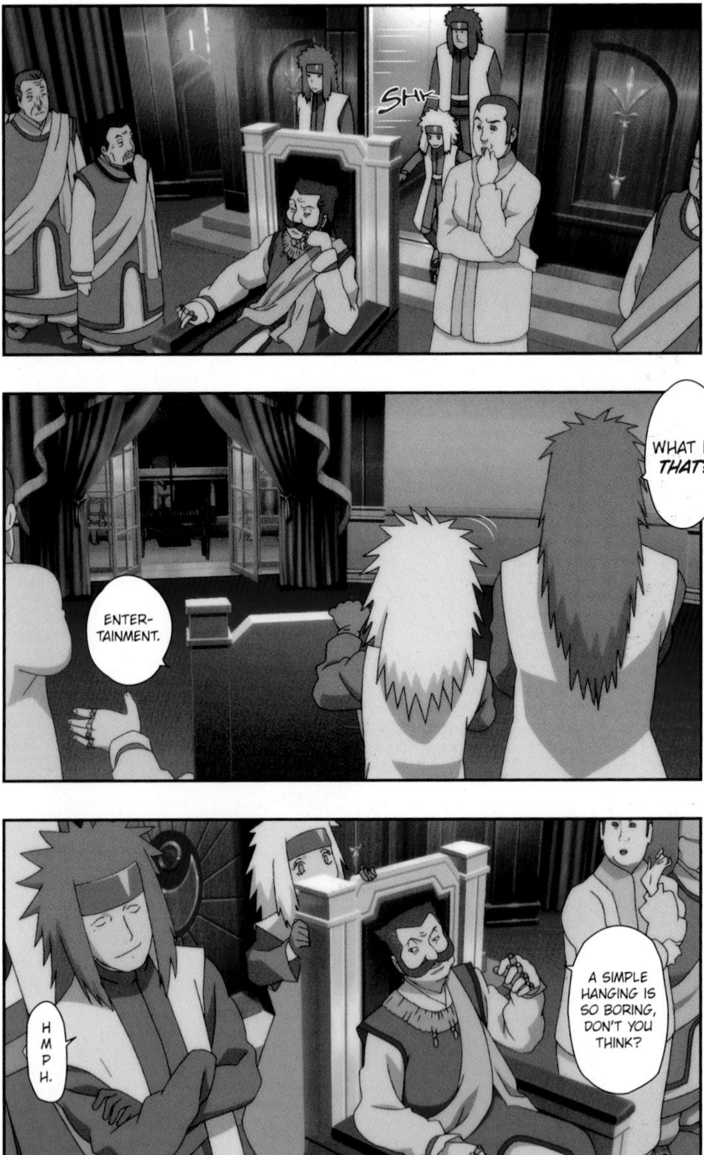
SHK
WHAT IS *THAT?*
ENTER-TAINMENT.
A SIMPLE HANGING IS SO BORING, DON'T YOU THINK?
HMPH.

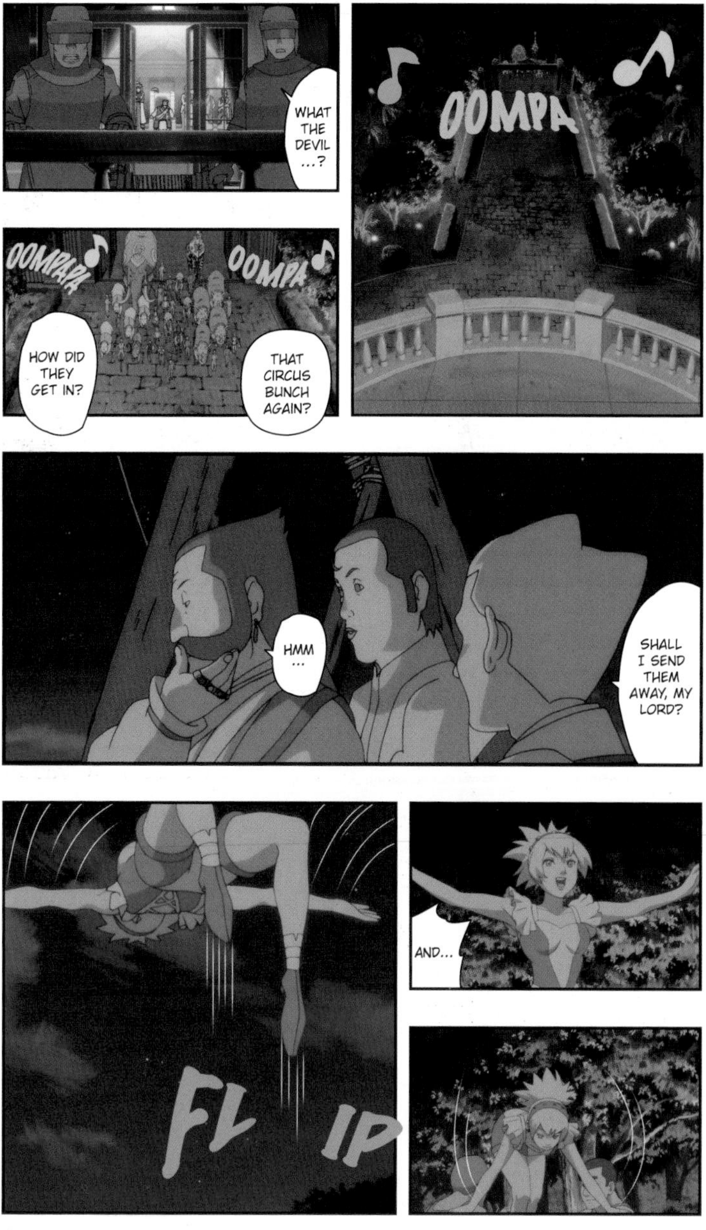
OOMPA
WHAT THE DEVIL ...?
OOMPA
OOMPAPA
THAT CIRCUS BUNCH AGAIN?
HOW DID THEY GET IN?
SHALL I SEND THEM AWAY, MY LORD?
HMM ...
AND...
FL IP

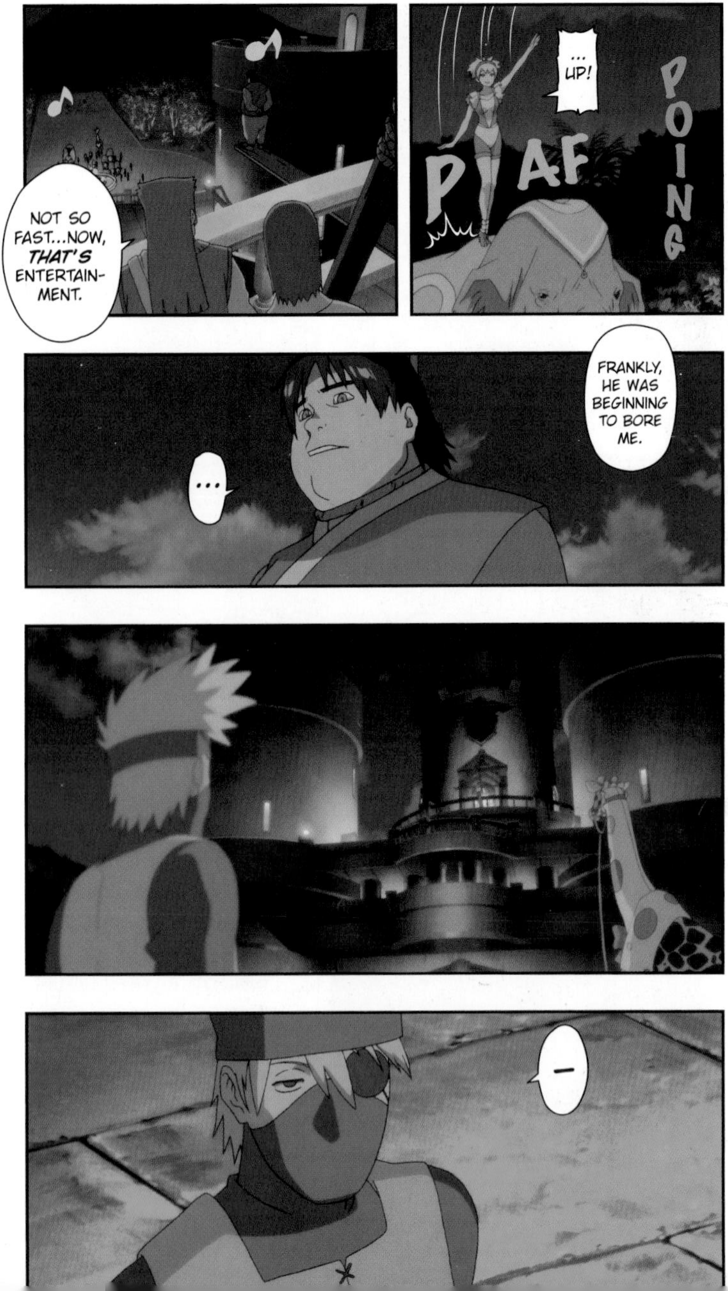
...UP!
PAF
POING
NOT SO FAST...NOW, ***THAT'S*** ENTERTAINMENT.
FRANKLY, HE WAS BEGINNING TO BORE ME.
...
—

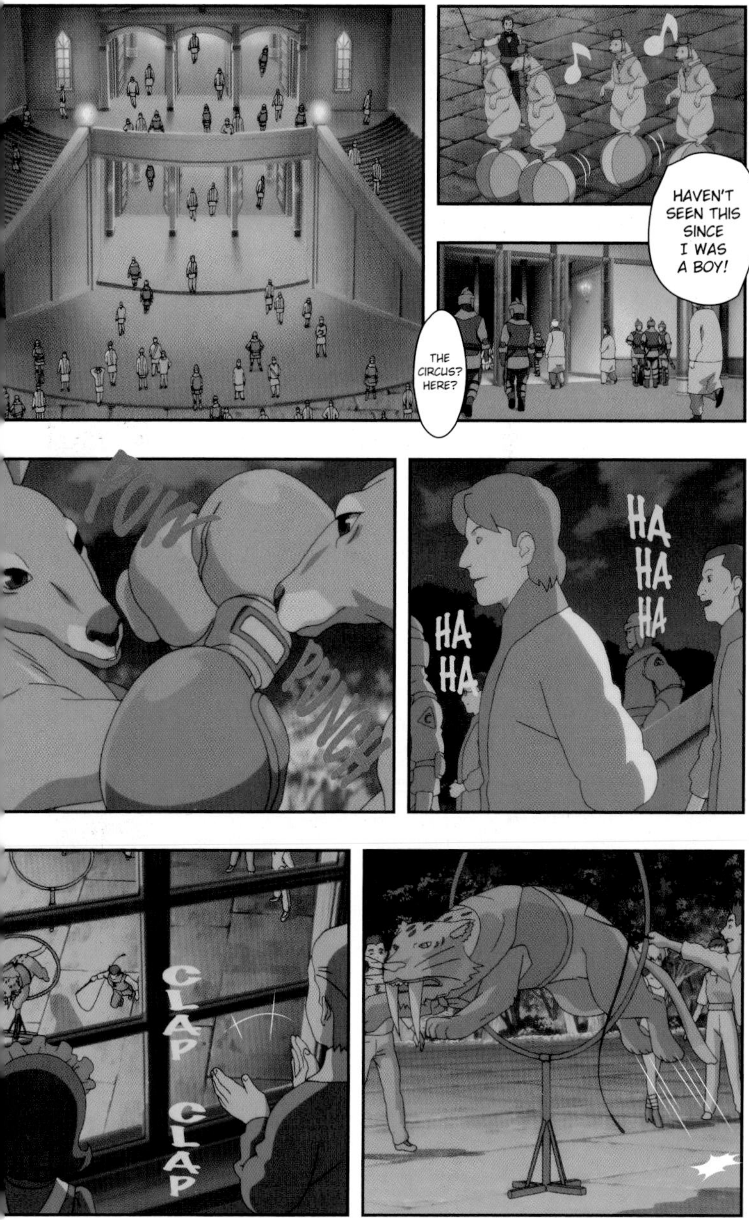
HAVEN'T SEEN THIS SINCE I WAS A BOY!
THE CIRCUS? HERE?
HA HA HA
HA HA
POW
PUNCH
CLAP CLAP

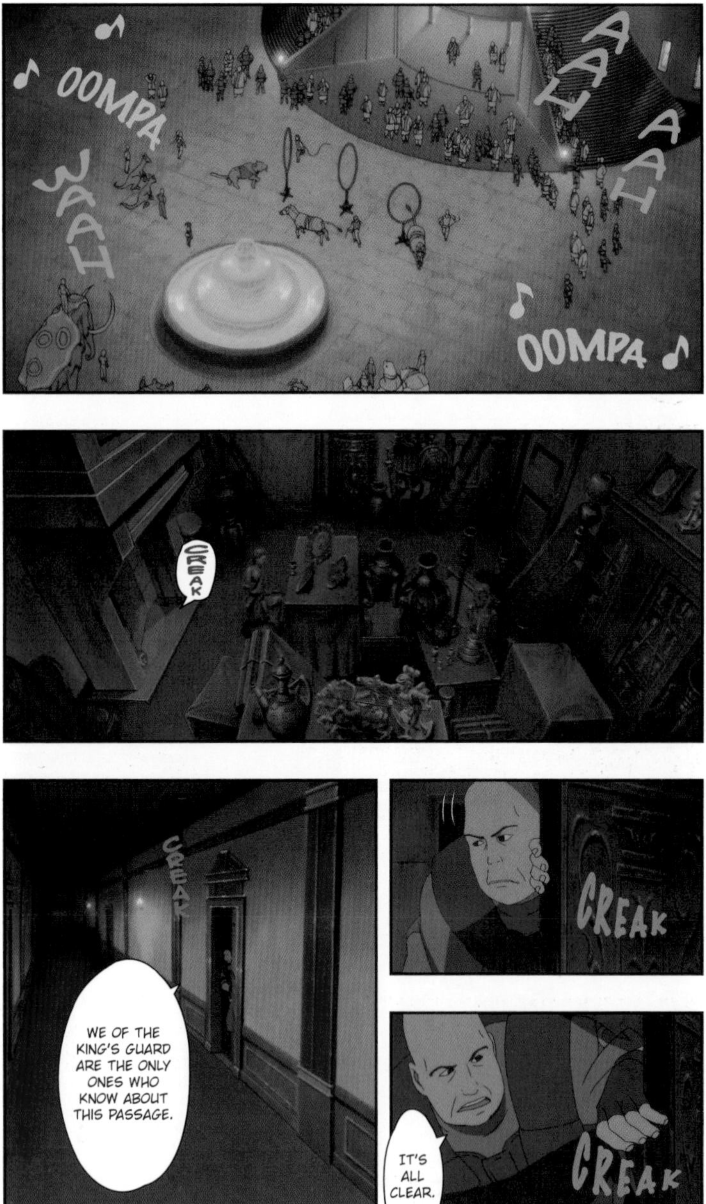
AAH
AAH
OOMPA
AAAH
OOMPA
CREAK
CREAK
IT'S ALL CLEAR.
CREAK
CREAK
WE OF THE KING'S GUARD ARE THE ONLY ONES WHO KNOW ABOUT THIS PASSAGE.

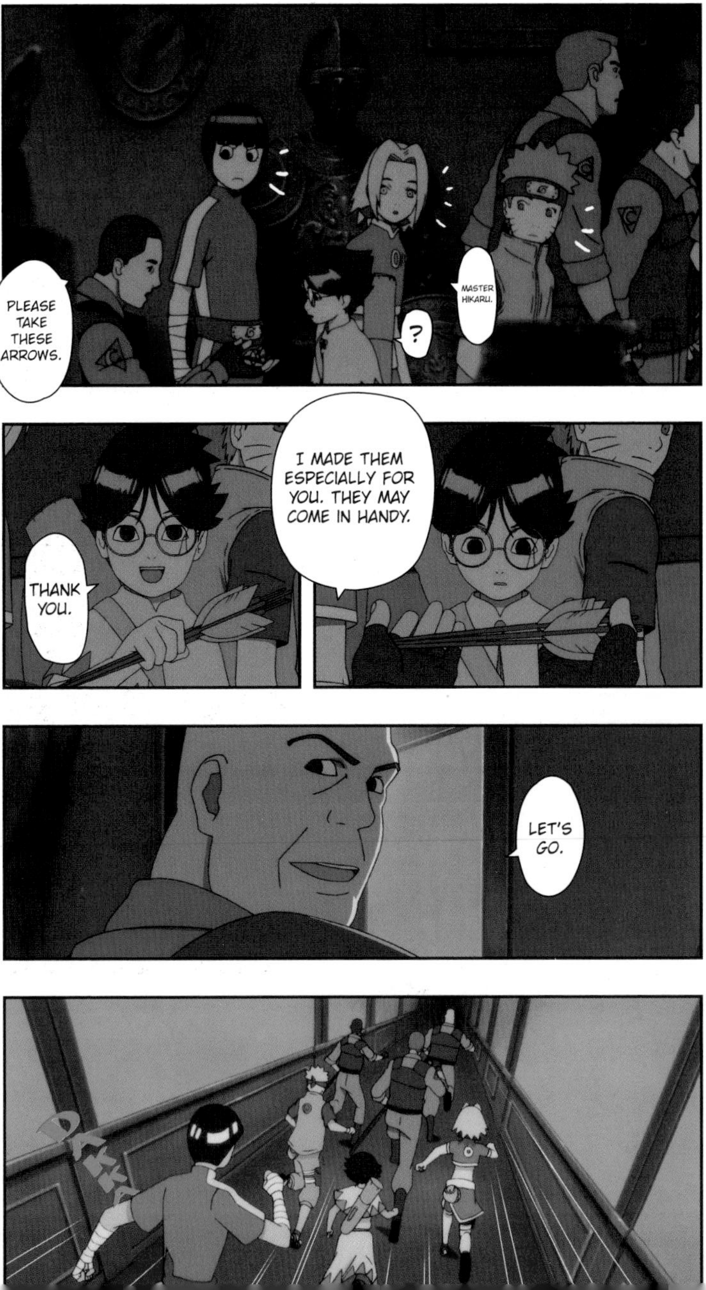
MASTER HIKARU.
?
PLEASE TAKE THESE ARROWS.
I MADE THEM ESPECIALLY FOR YOU. THEY MAY COME IN HANDY.
THANK YOU.
LET'S GO.

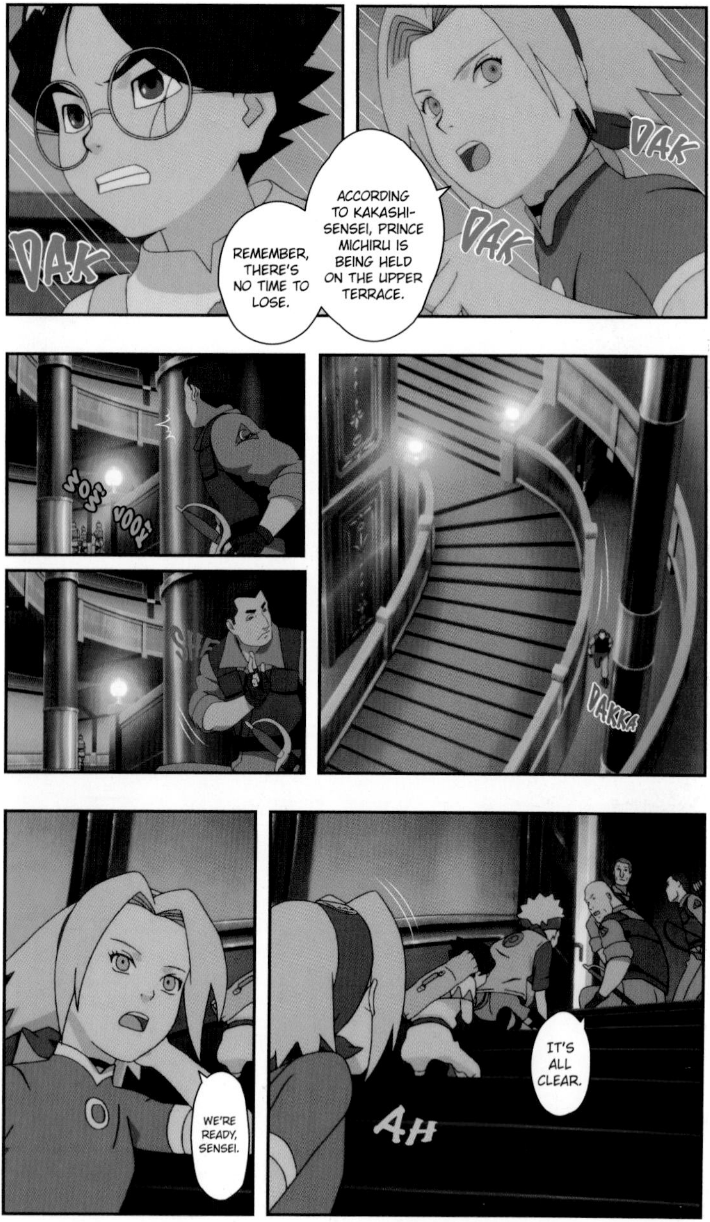
DAK
DAK
ACCORDING TO KAKASHI-SENSEI, PRINCE MICHIRU IS BEING HELD ON THE UPPER TERRACE.
REMEMBER, THERE'S NO TIME TO LOSE.
DAK
DAKKA
IT'S ALL CLEAR.
AH
WE'RE READY, SENSEI.

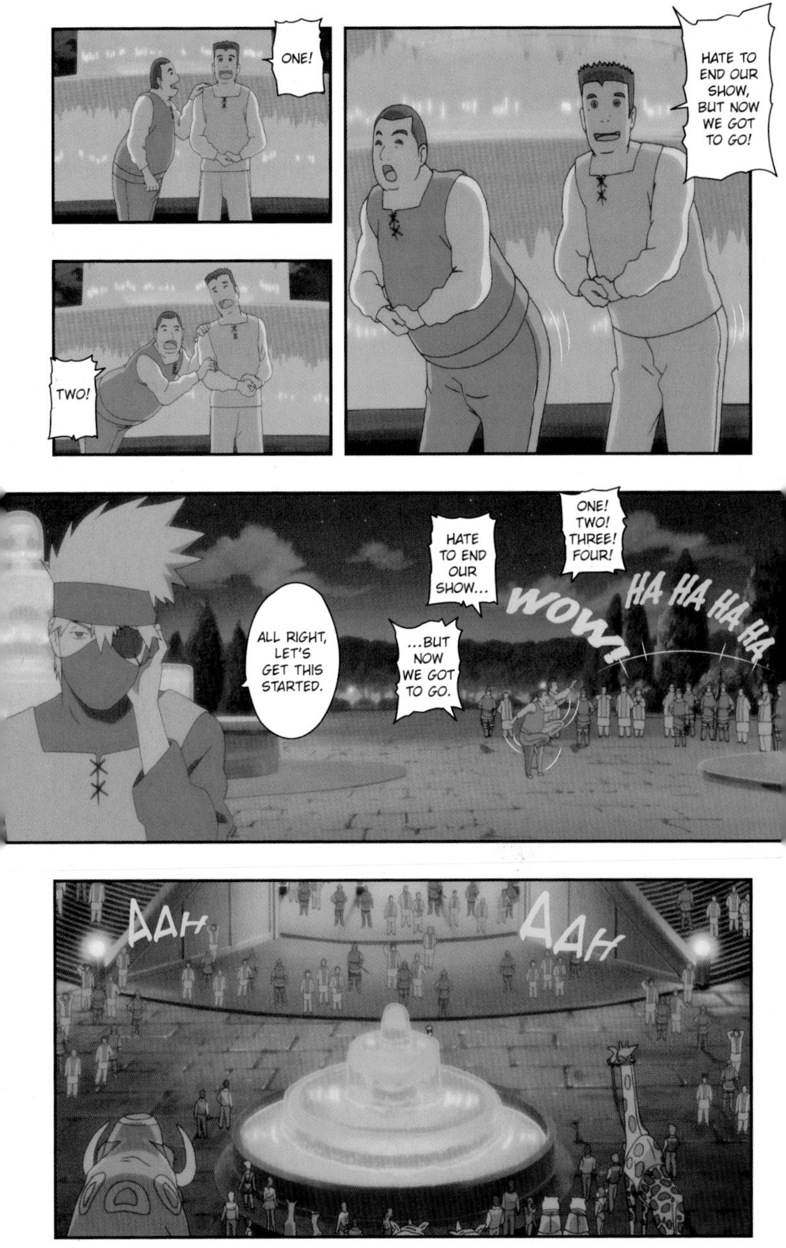
HATE TO END OUR SHOW, BUT NOW WE GOT TO GO!
ONE!
TWO!
ONE! TWO! THREE! FOUR!
HA HA HA HA
HATE TO END OUR SHOW...
WOW!
...BUT NOW WE GOT TO GO.
ALL RIGHT, LET'S GET THIS STARTED.
AAH
AAH

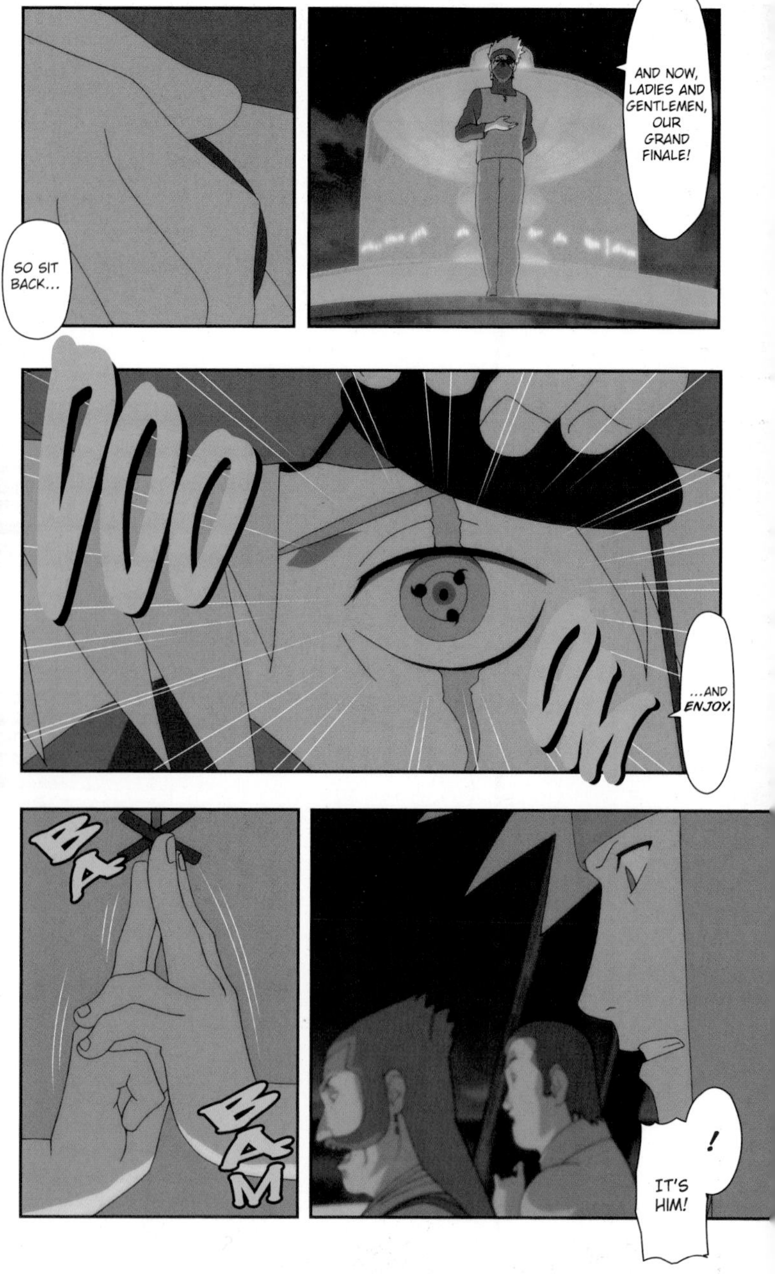
AND NOW, LADIES AND GENTLEMEN, OUR GRAND FINALE!
SO SIT BACK...
DOOOOM
...AND ENJOY.
!
IT'S HIM!
BA
BAM

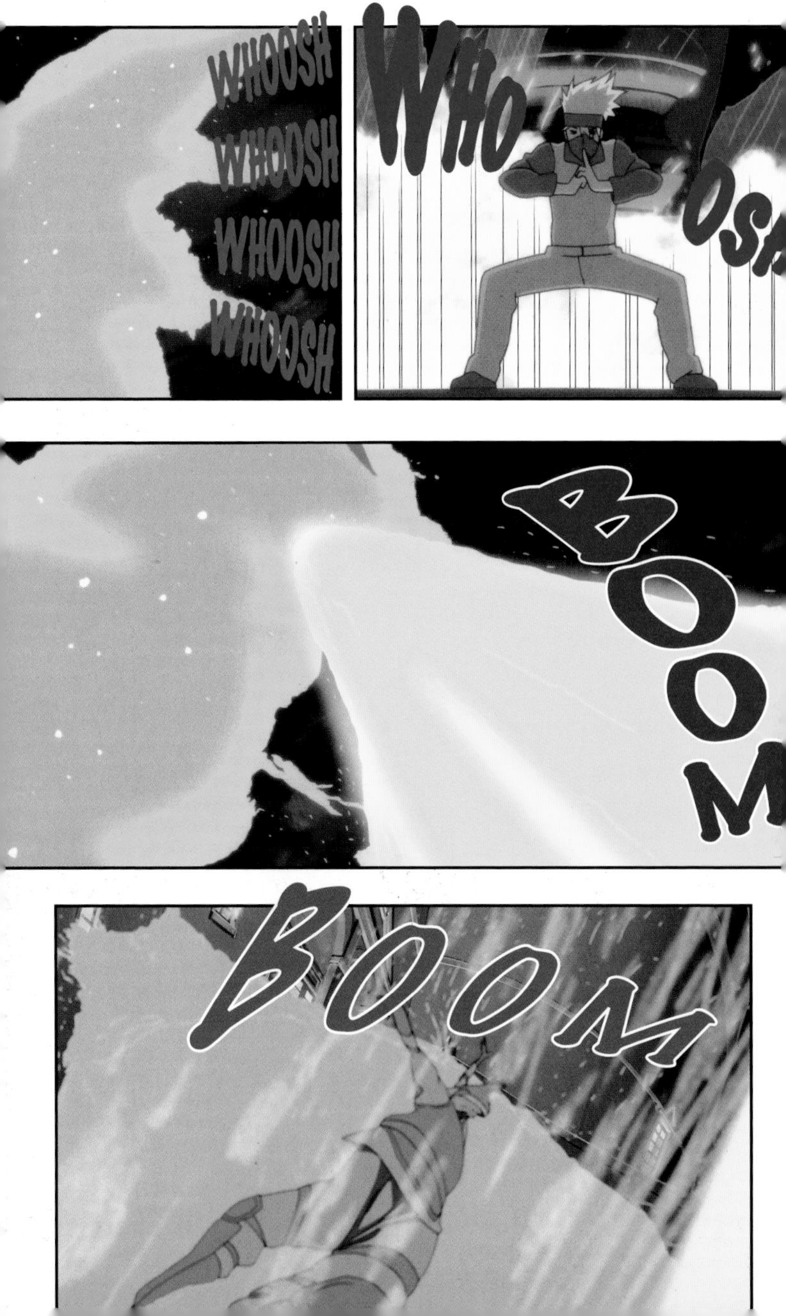
WHO OSH
WHOOSH
WHOOSH
WHOOSH
WHOOSH
BOOM
BOOM

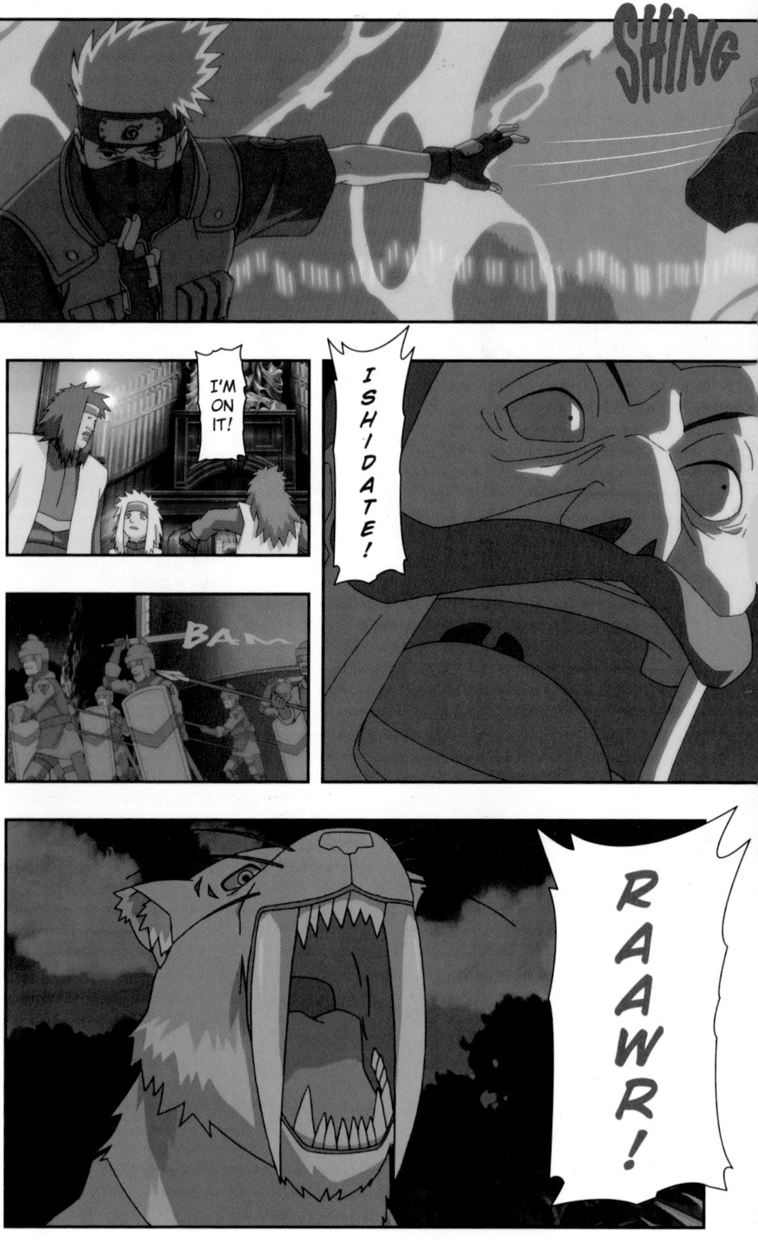
SHING
ISHIDATE!
I'M ON IT!
BAM
RAAWR!

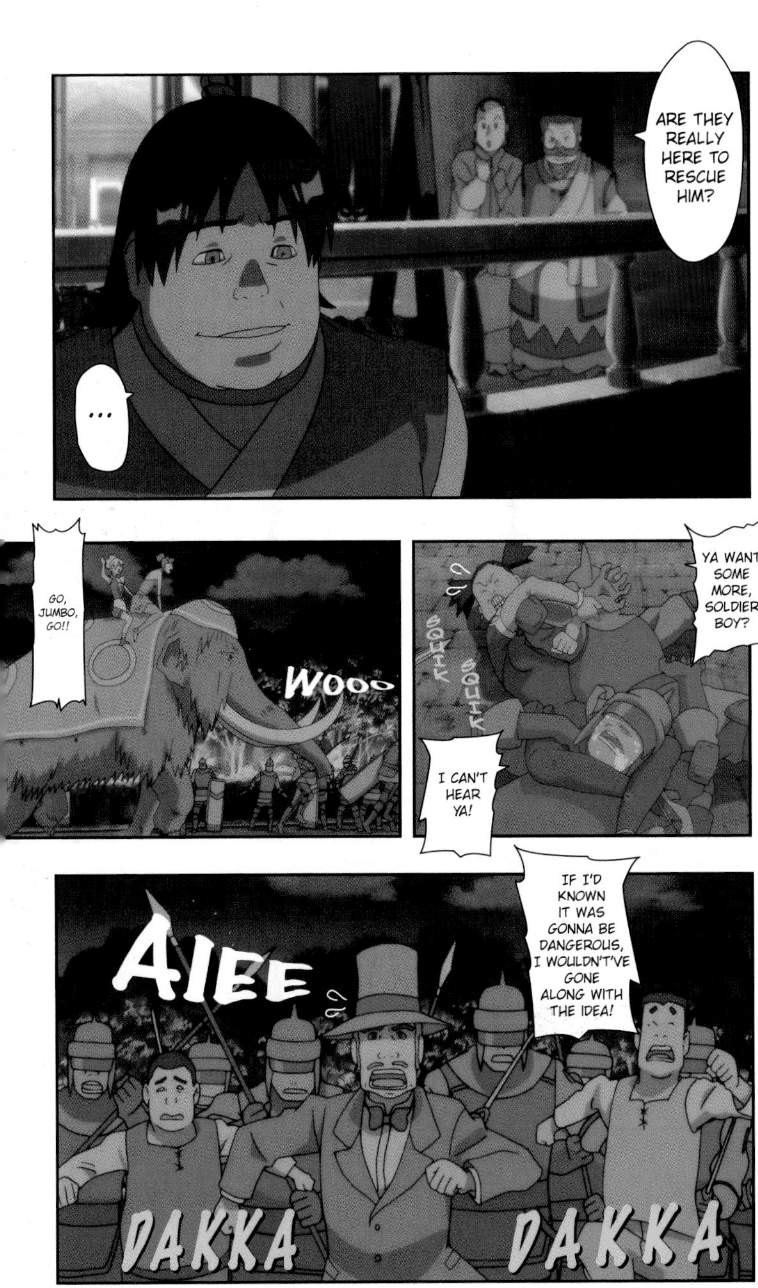
ARE THEY REALLY HERE TO RESCUE HIM?
...
YA WANT SOME MORE, SOLDIER BOY?
I CAN'T HEAR YA!
GO, JUMBO, GO!!
WOOO
IF I'D KNOWN IT WAS GONNA BE DANGEROUS, I WOULDN'T'VE GONE ALONG WITH THE IDEA!
AIEE
DAKKA
DAKKA

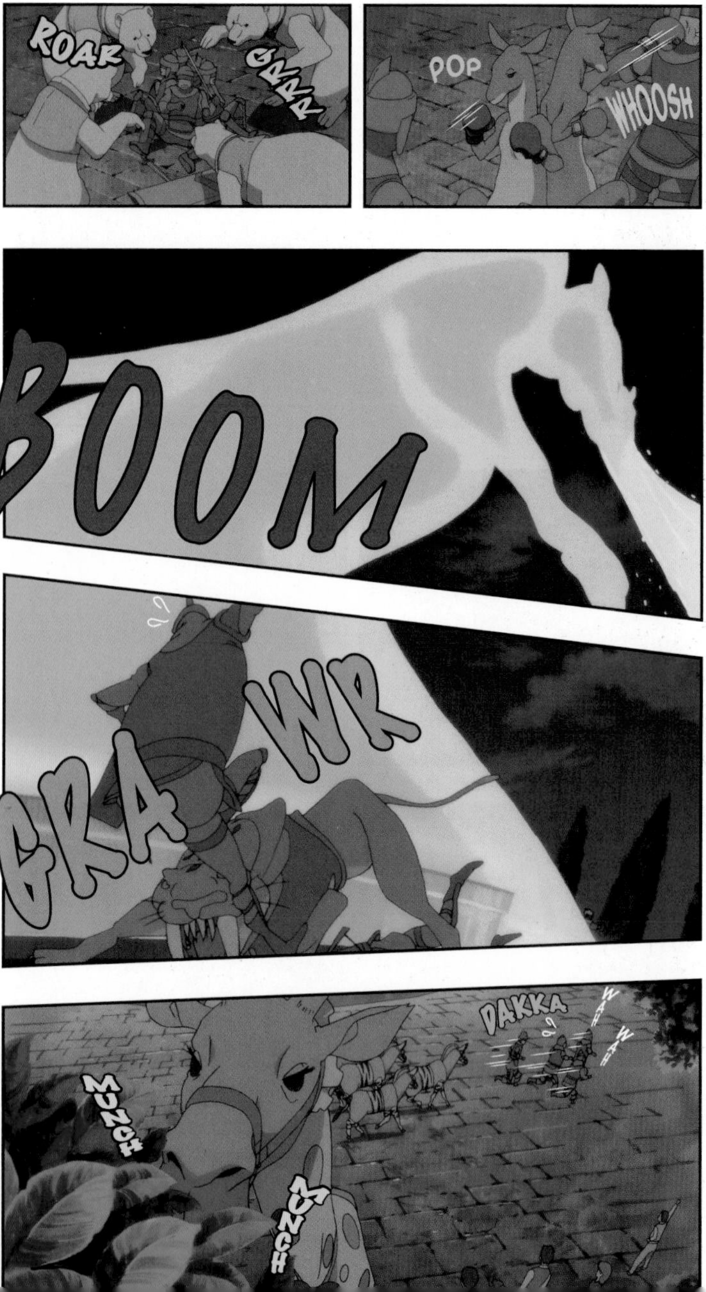
POP
WHOOSH
GRRR
ROAR
BOOM
GRAWR
WAH
WAH
DAKKA
MUNCH
MUNCH

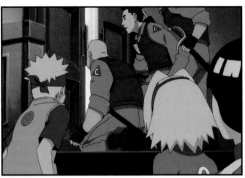

...

KRRK

YOU TRUST ME, RIGHT?

HIKARU.

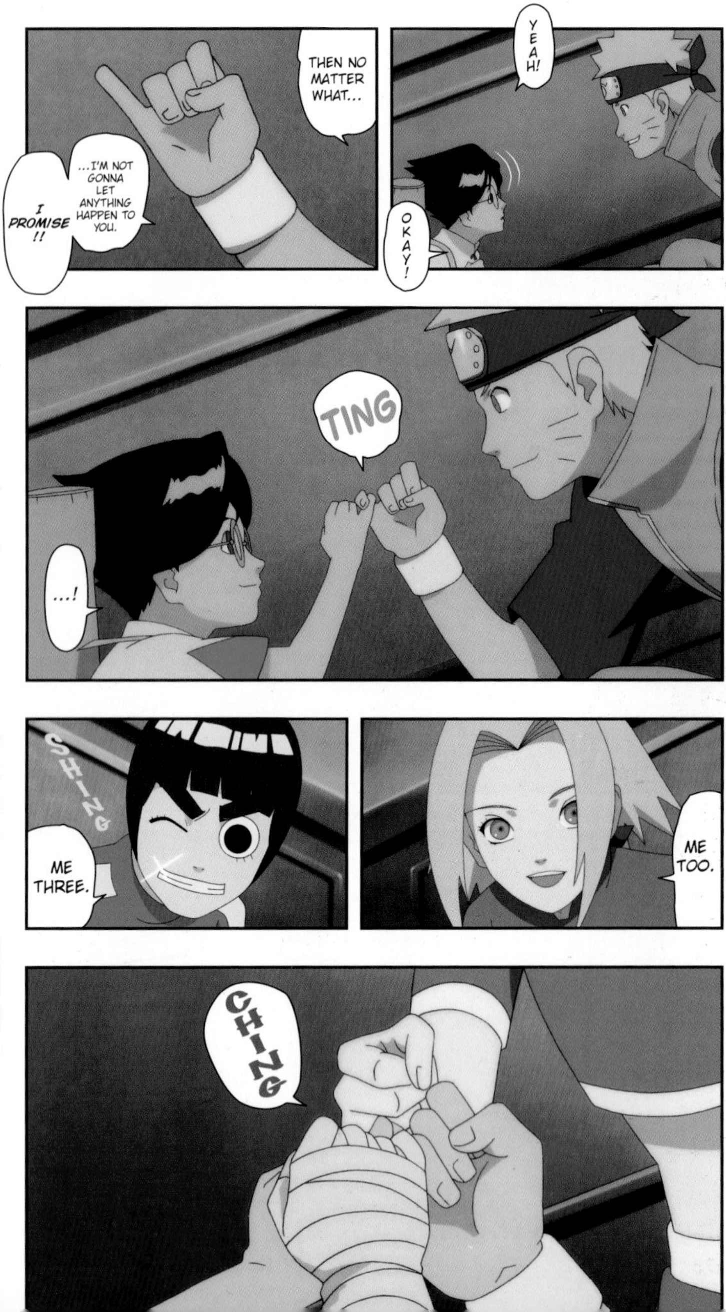
YEAH!
OKAY!
THEN NO MATTER WHAT...
...I'M NOT GONNA LET ANYTHING HAPPEN TO YOU.
I PROMISE!!
TING
...!
ME TOO.
SHING
ME THREE.
CHING

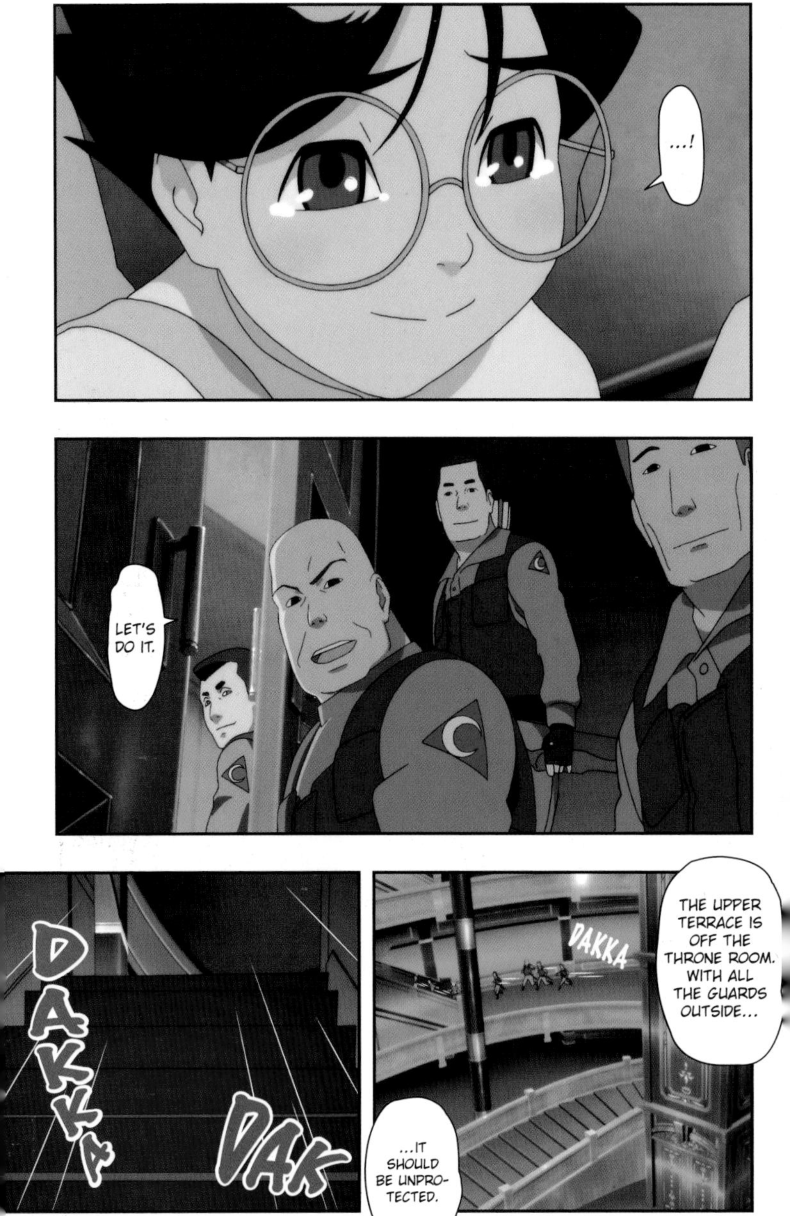
...!
LET'S DO IT.
THE UPPER TERRACE IS OFF THE THRONE ROOM. WITH ALL THE GUARDS OUTSIDE...
DAKKA
...IT SHOULD BE UNPROTECTED.
DAKKA
DAK

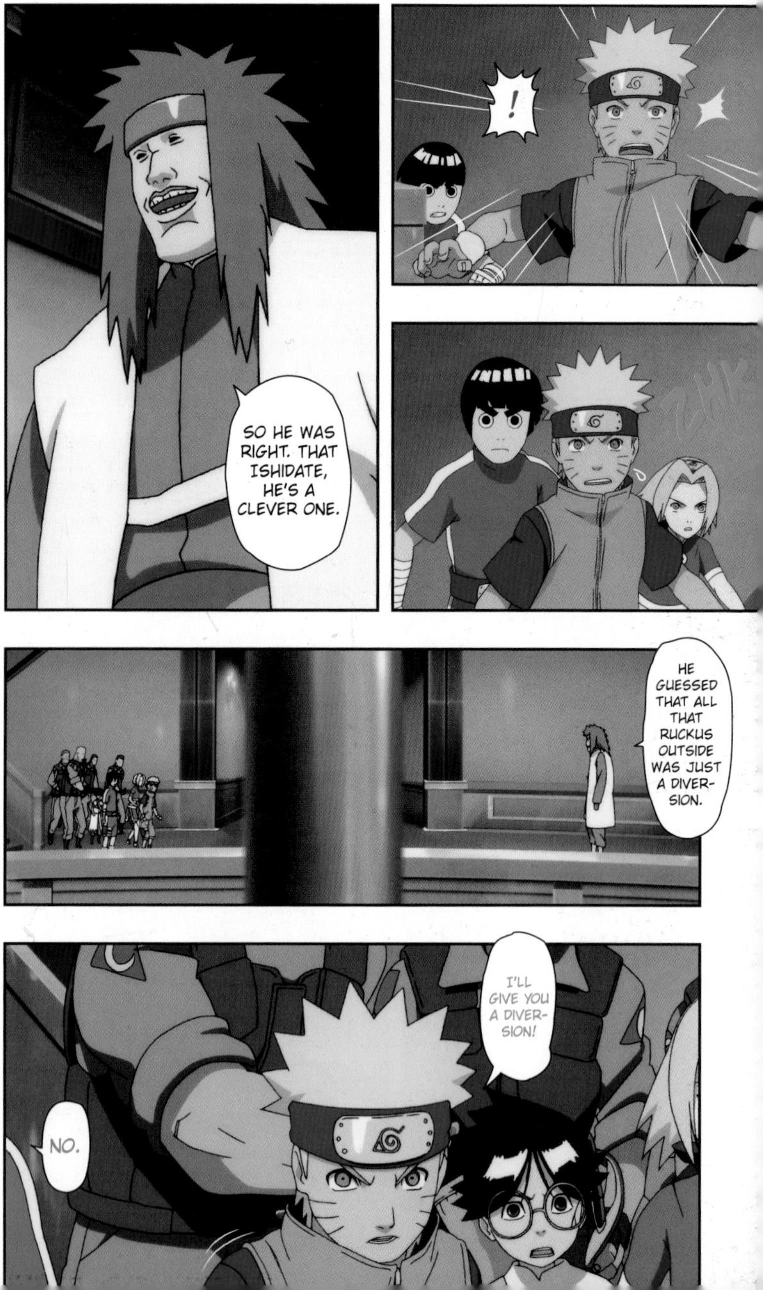
!
SO HE WAS RIGHT. THAT ISHIDATE, HE'S A CLEVER ONE.
HE GUESSED THAT ALL THAT RUCKUS OUTSIDE WAS JUST A DIVERSION.
I'LL GIVE YOU A DIVERSION!
NO.

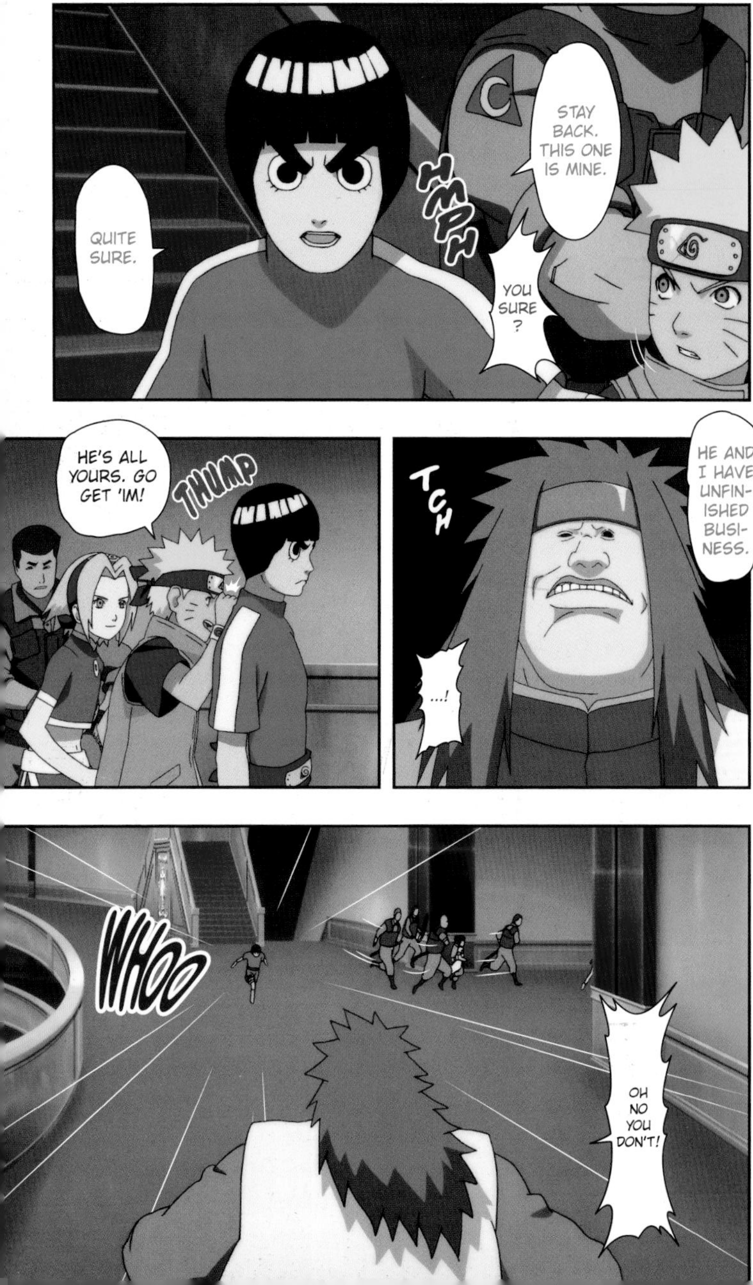
STAY BACK. THIS ONE IS MINE.
HMPH
YOU SURE?
QUITE SURE.
HE AND I HAVE UNFIN-ISHED BUSI-NESS.
TCH
...!
THUMP
HE'S ALL YOURS. GO GET 'IM!
WHOO
OH NO YOU DON'T!

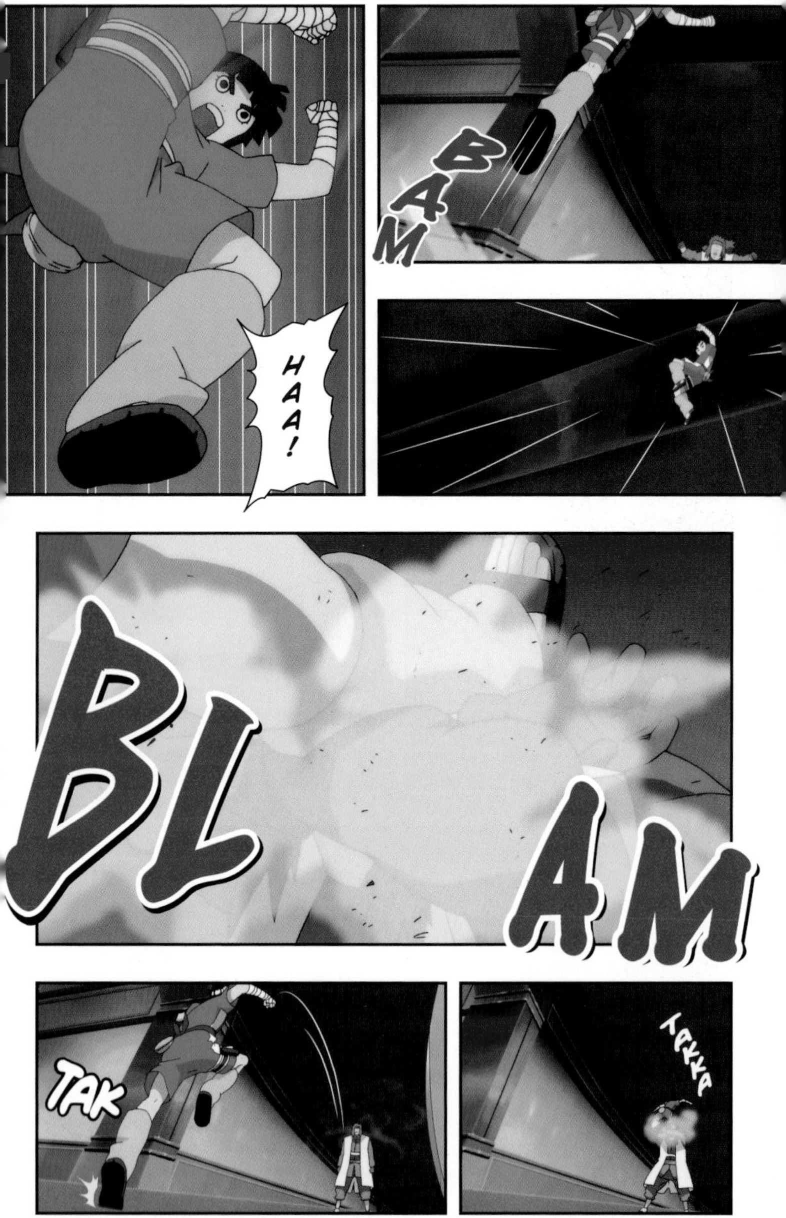
HAAA!
BAM
BLAM
TAK
TAKKA

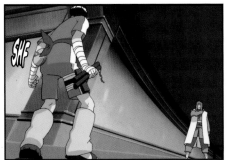

THIS TIME I WON'T GO EASY ON YOU.

I COULD SAY THE SAME!

SHF

KCK

WHSH

WOOOO
THOOM
DAK
DAK
SHK
FWIP
WHUK

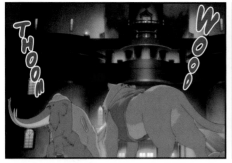

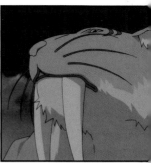

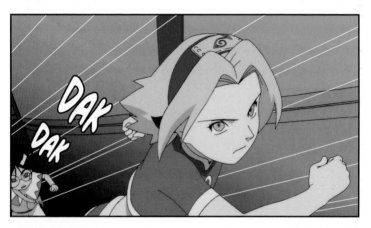

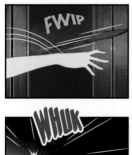

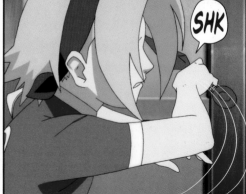

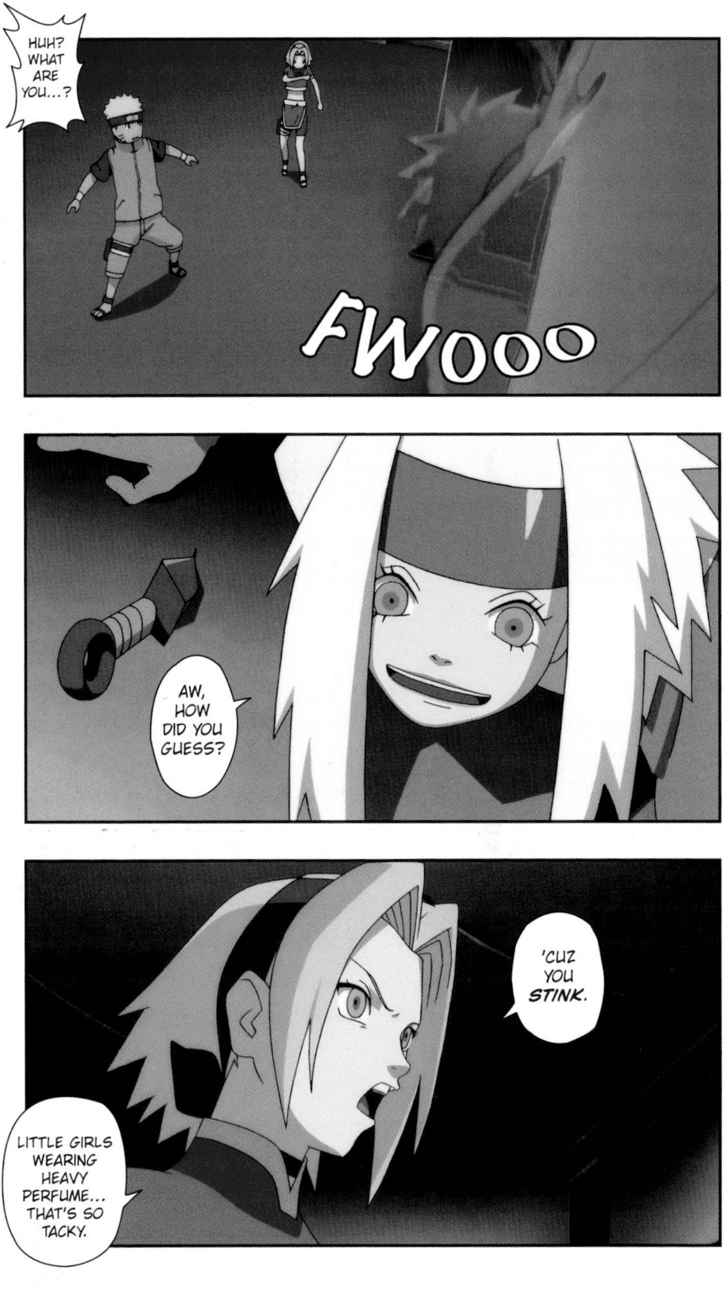
HUH? WHAT ARE YOU...?
FWOOO
AW, HOW DID YOU GUESS?
'CUZ YOU STINK.
LITTLE GIRLS WEARING HEAVY PERFUME... THAT'S SO TACKY.

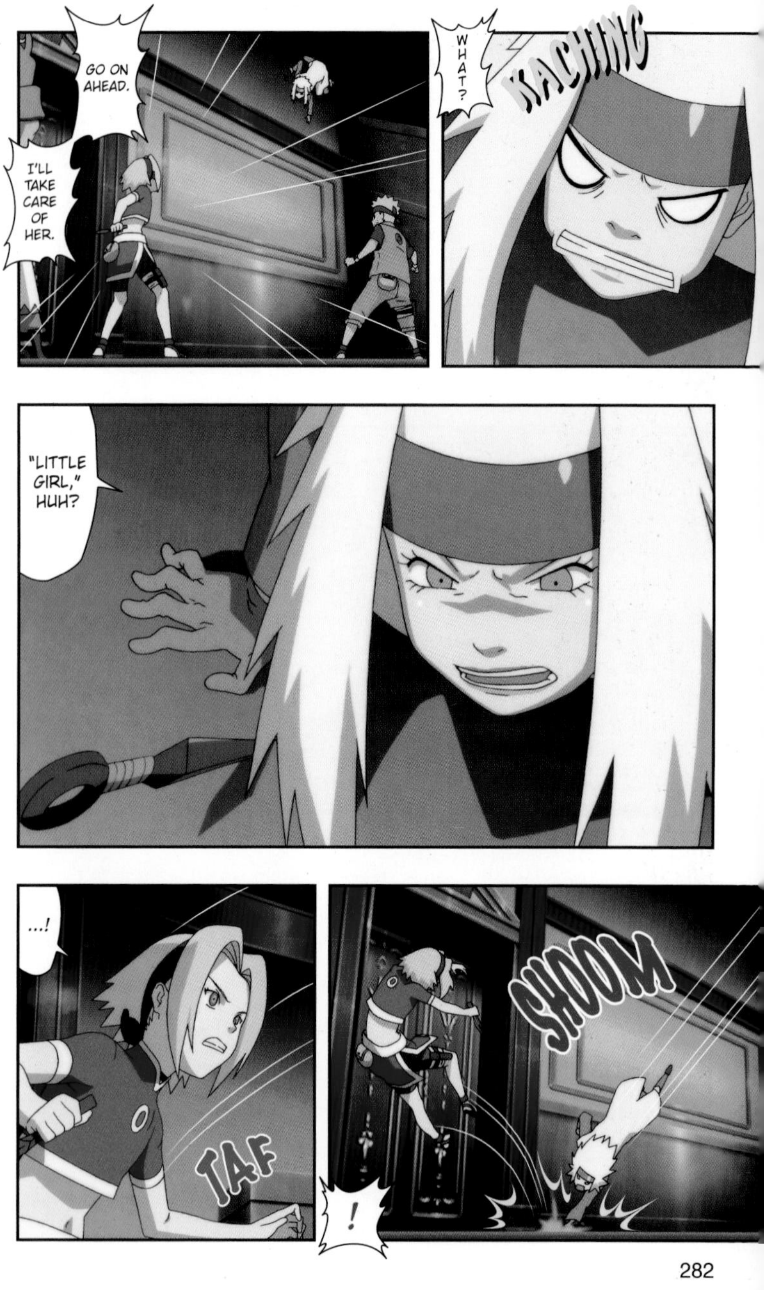
KACHING
WHAT?
GO ON AHEAD.
I'LL TAKE CARE OF HER.
"LITTLE GIRL," HUH?
SHOOM
!
...!
TAF

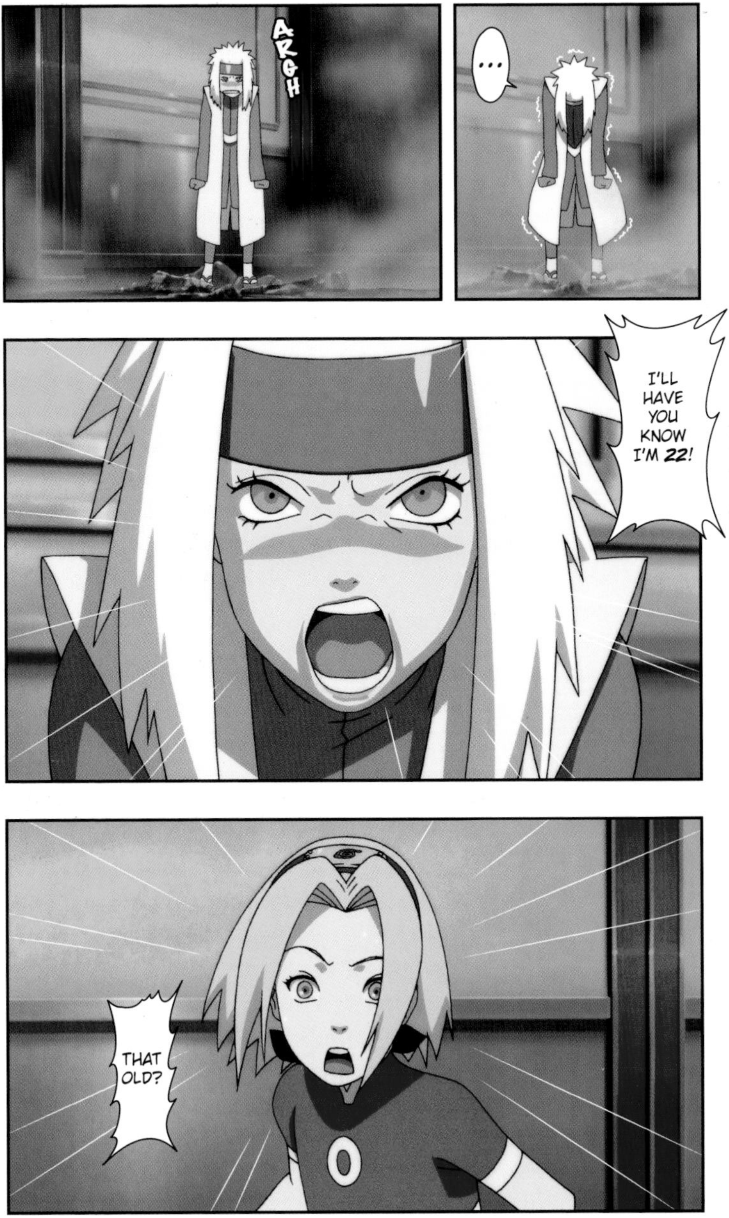
...
ARGH
I'LL HAVE YOU KNOW I'M **22**!
THAT OLD?

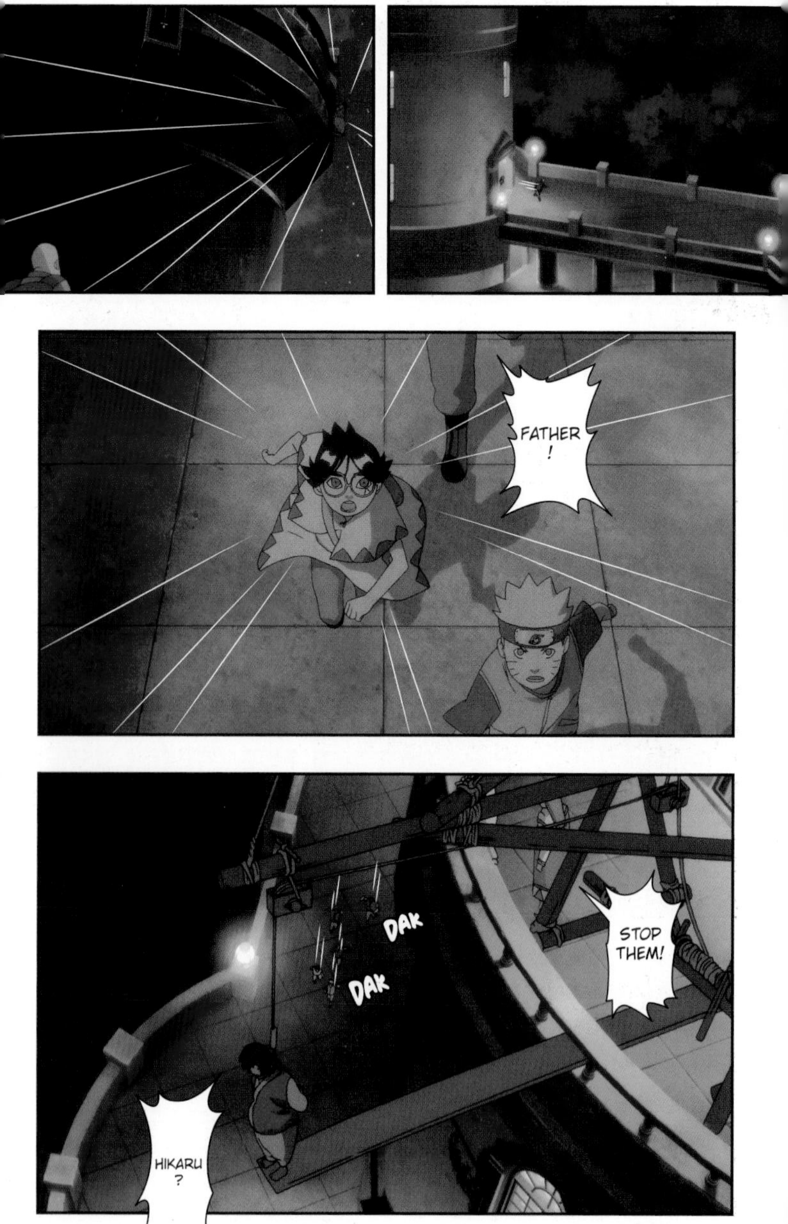
FATHER!
STOP THEM!
DAK
DAK
HIKARU?

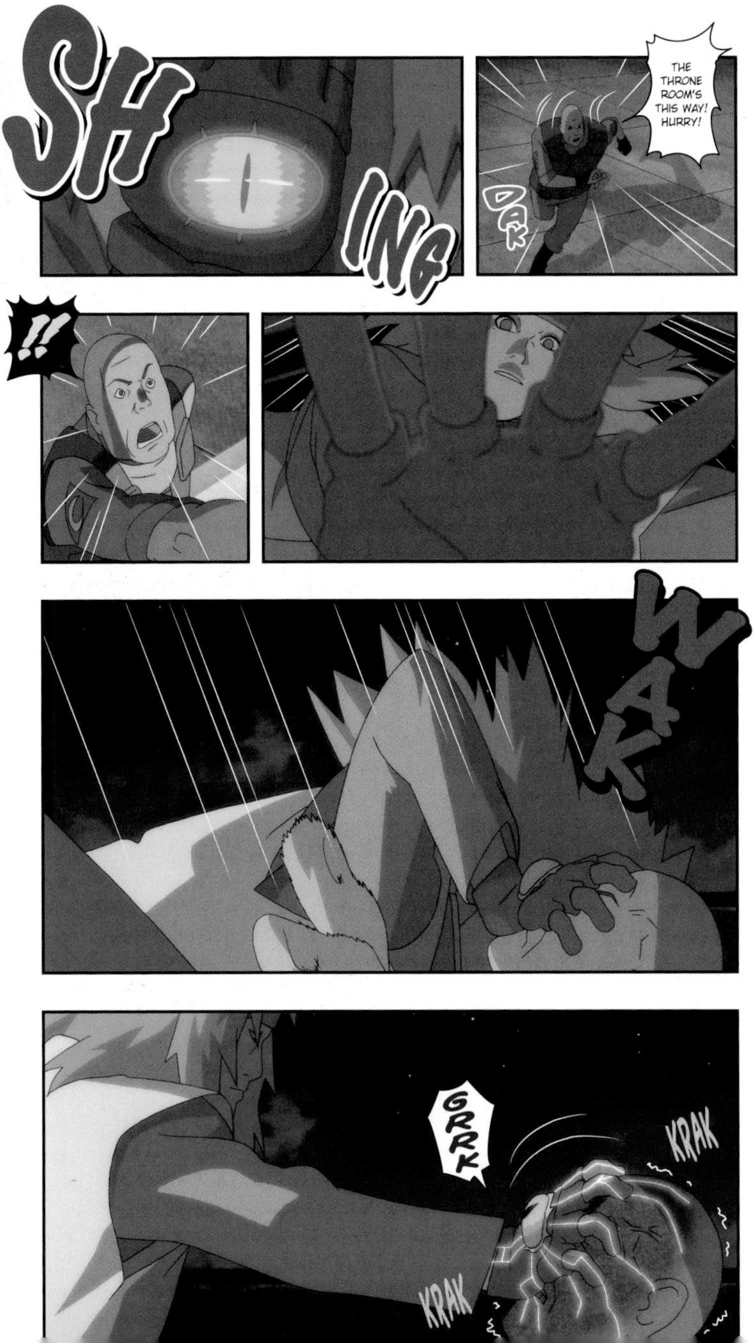
THE THRONE ROOM'S THIS WAY! HURRY!
DAK
SHING
!!
WAK
GRRK
KRAK
KRAK

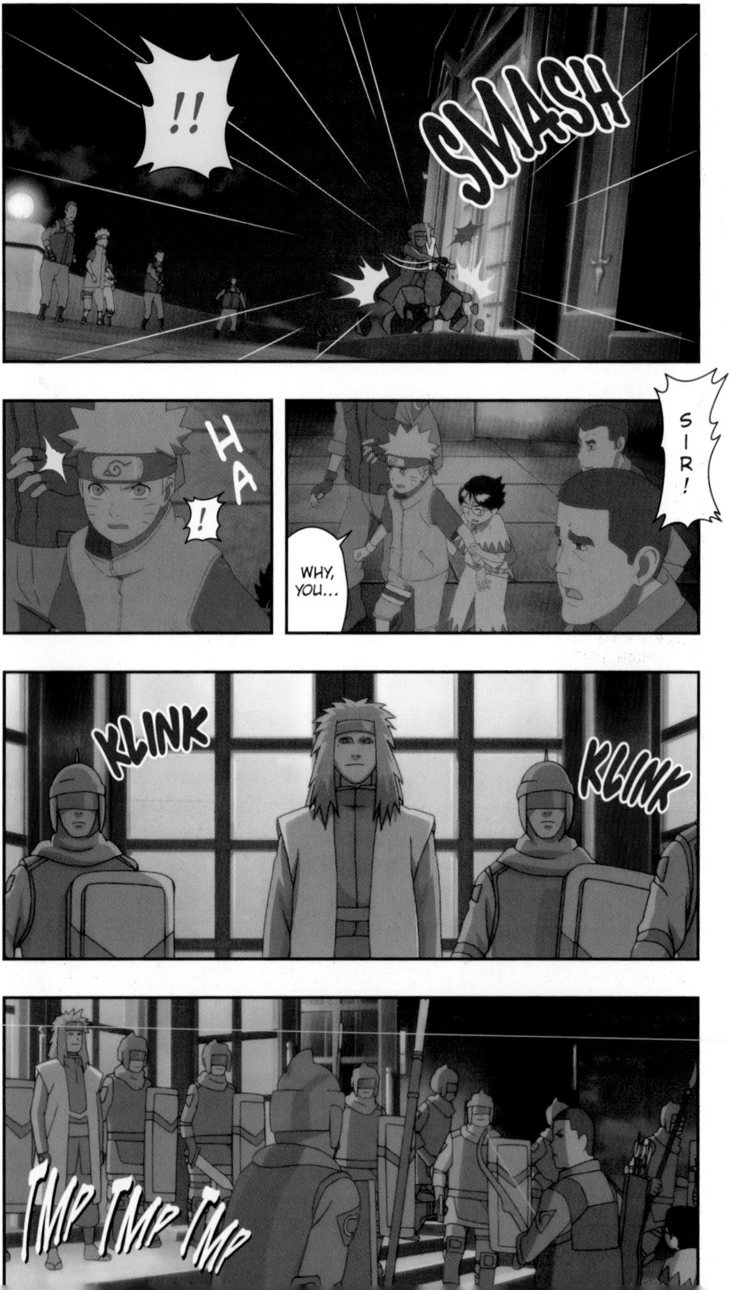
SMASH
!!
SIR!
WHY, YOU...
HA
!
KLINK
KLINK
TMP TMP TMP

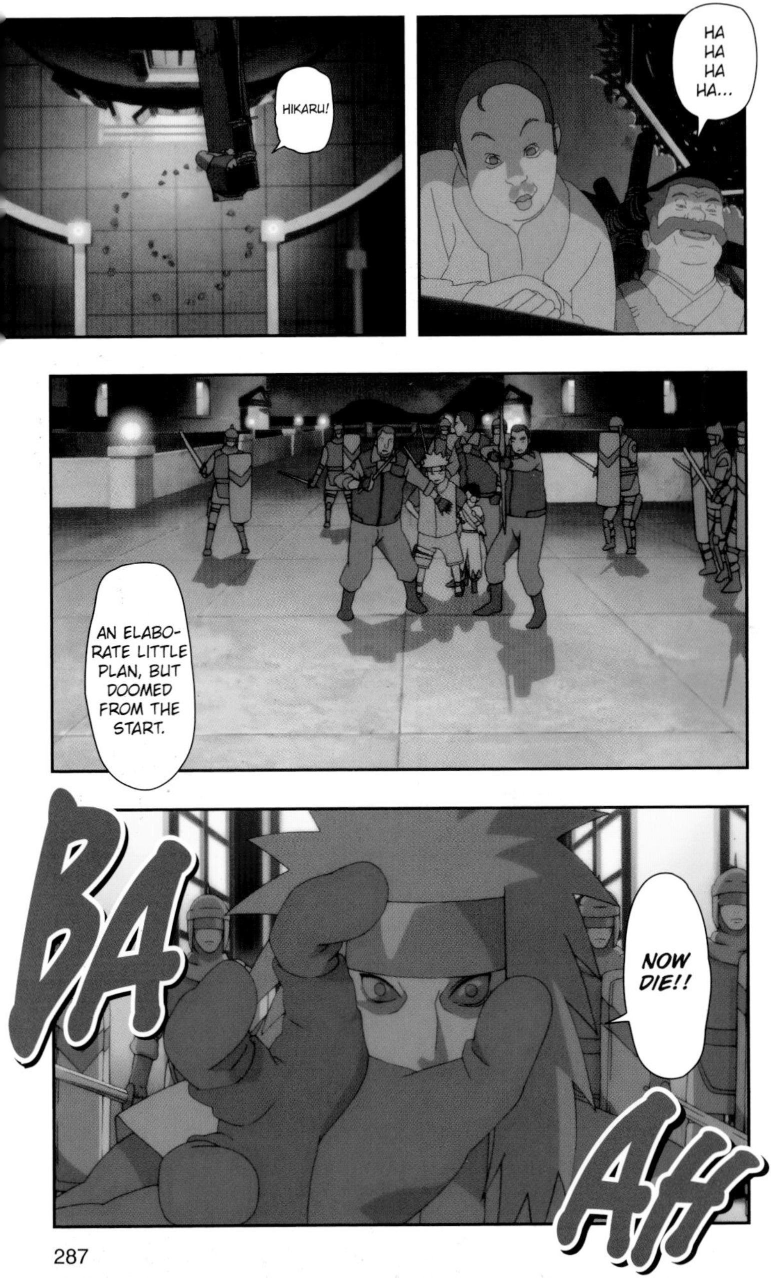
HA HA HA HA...
HIKARU!
AN ELABORATE LITTLE PLAN, BUT DOOMED FROM THE START.
BA
NOW DIE!!
AH

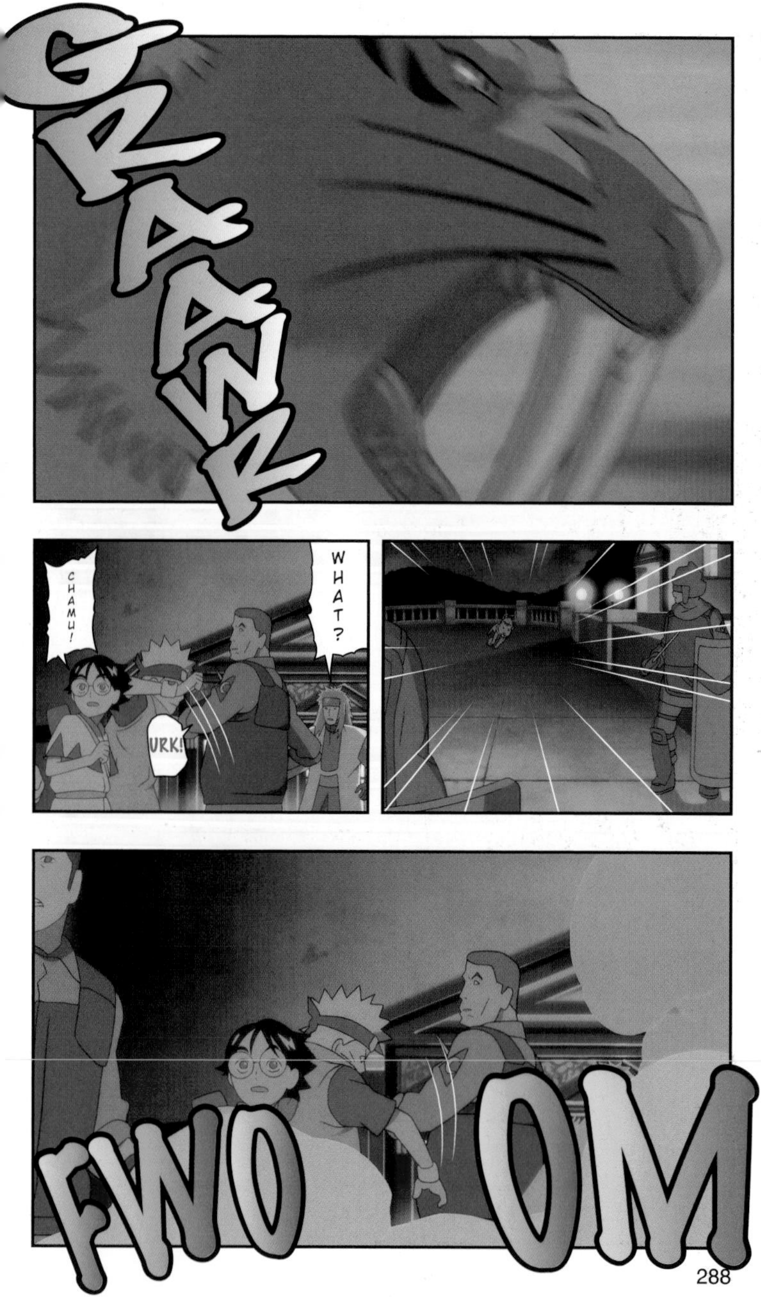
GRAWR
WHAT?
CHAMU!
URK!
FWOOM

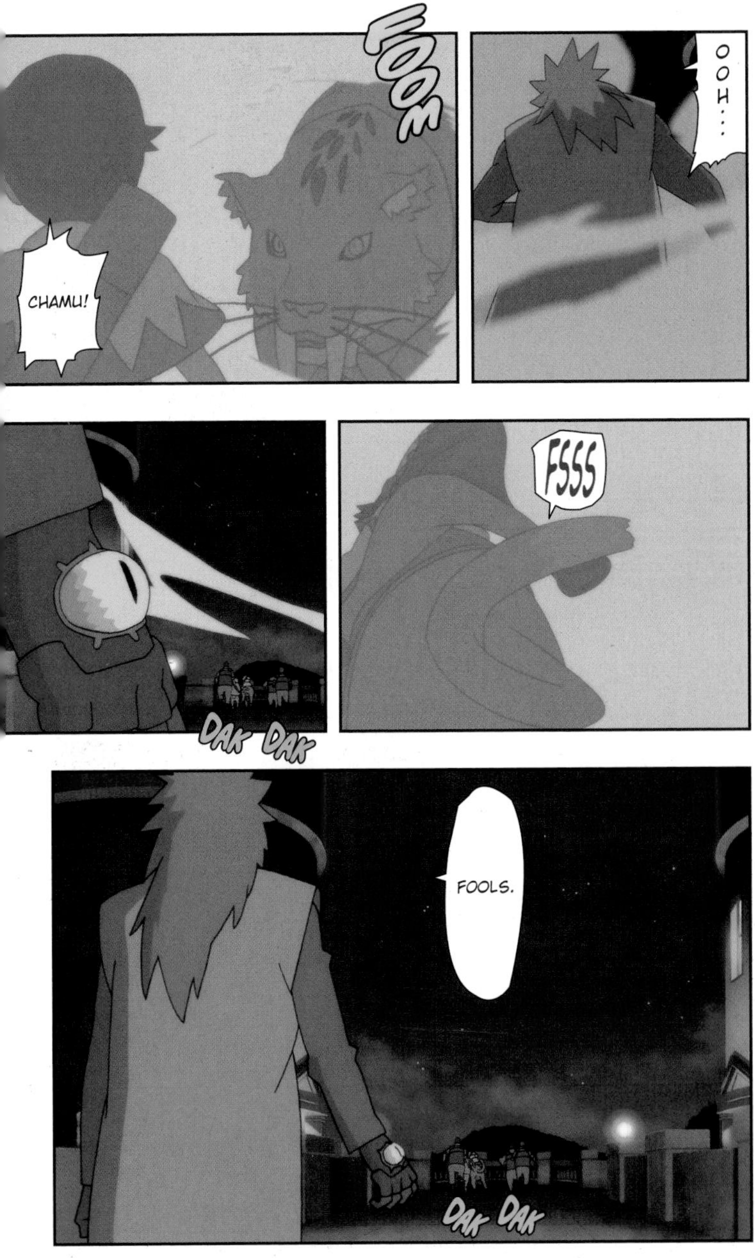
OOH...
FOOM
CHAMU!
FSSS
DAK DAK
FOOLS.
DAK DAK

WUP
WHUMP
SHF
SHO OM
WHU NK
KRRAK

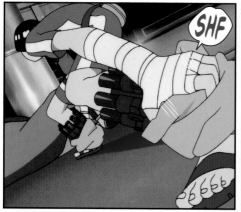

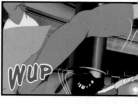

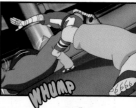

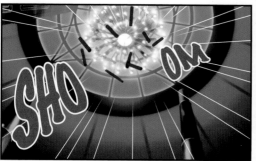

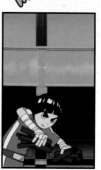

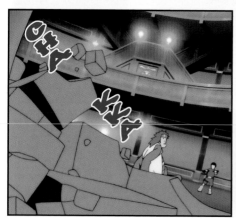

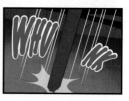

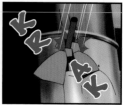

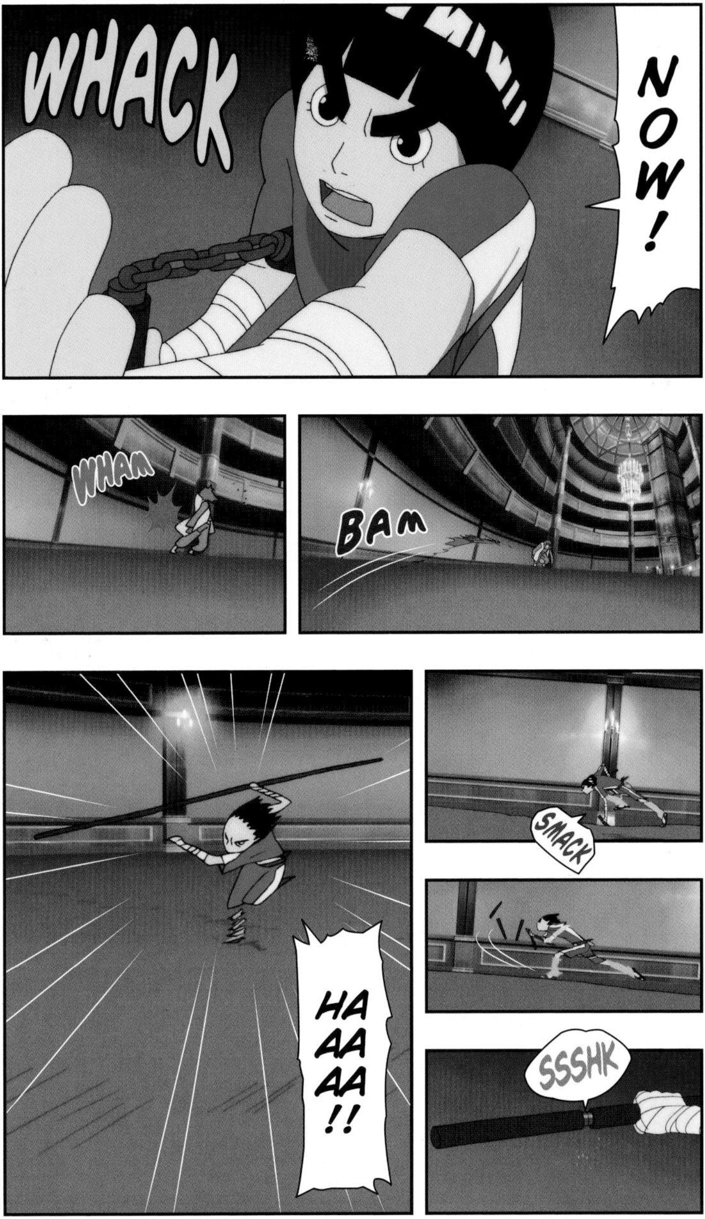
NOW!
WHACK
BAM
WHAM
SMACK
SSSHK
HAAAAAA!!

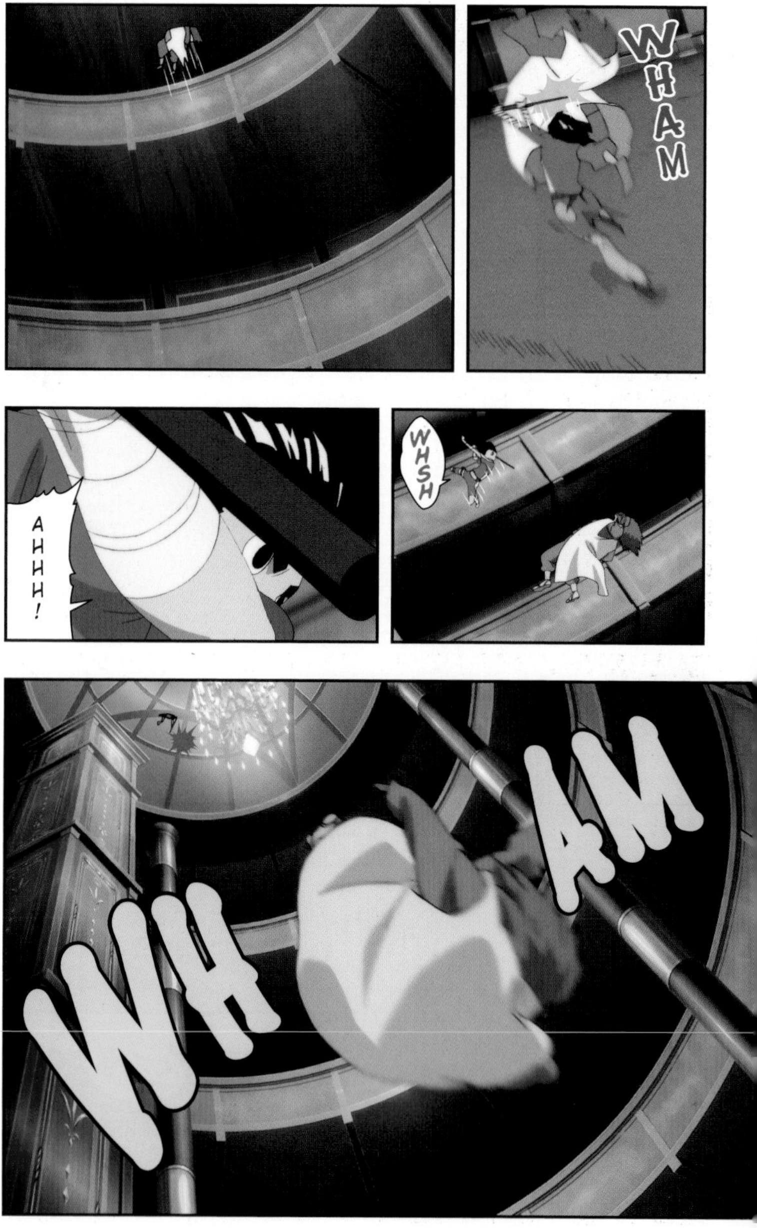
WHAM
WHSH
AHHHH!
WHAM

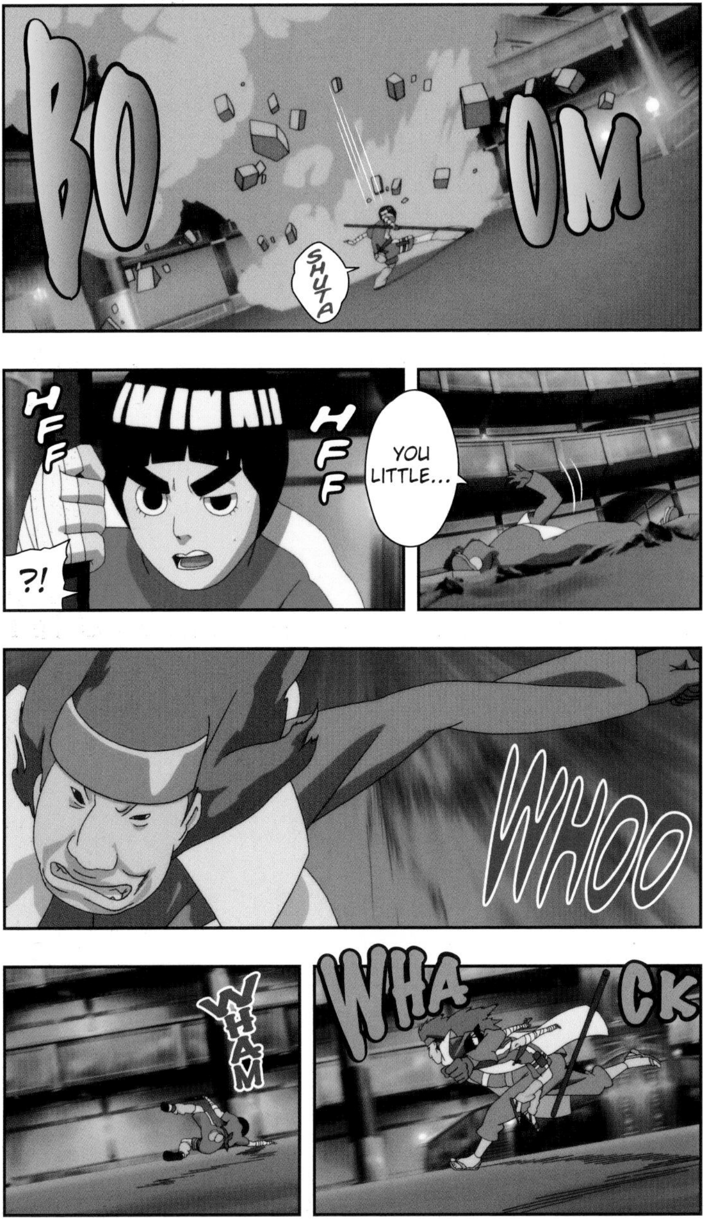
BOOM
SHUTA
YOU LITTLE...
HFF
HFF
?!
WHOO
WHACK
WHAM

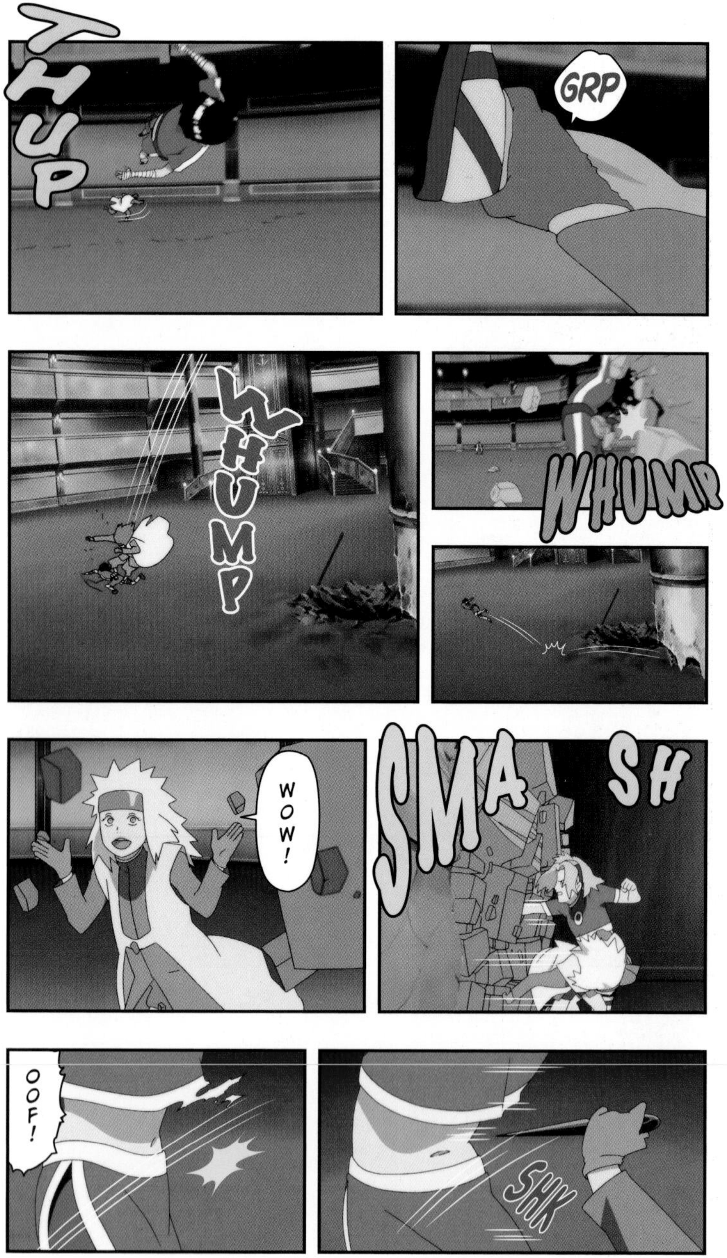
GRP
THUP
WHUMP
WHUMP
SMASH
WOW!
SHK
OOF!

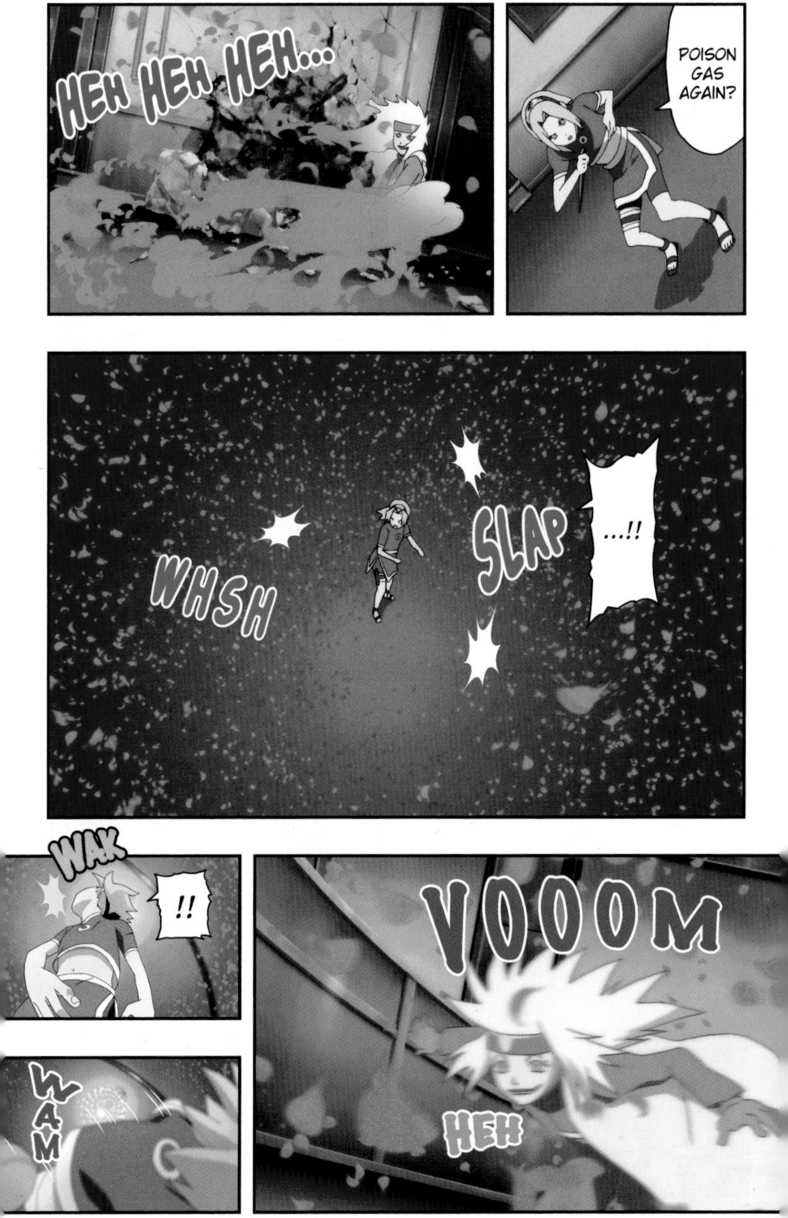
POISON GAS AGAIN?
HEH HEH HEH...
...!!
SLAP
WHSH
VOOOM
HEH
WAK
!!
WAM

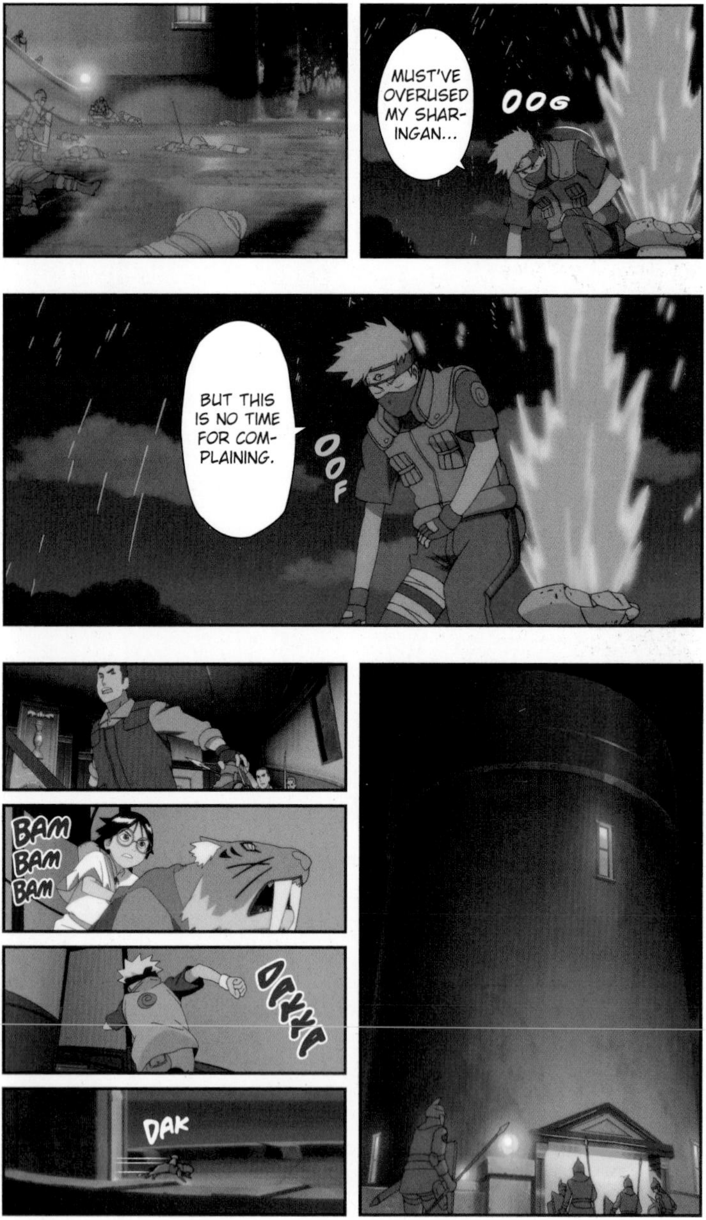
MUST'VE OVERUSED MY SHAR-INGAN...
OOG
BUT THIS IS NO TIME FOR COM-PLAINING.
OOF
BAM BAM BAM
DAKKA
DAK

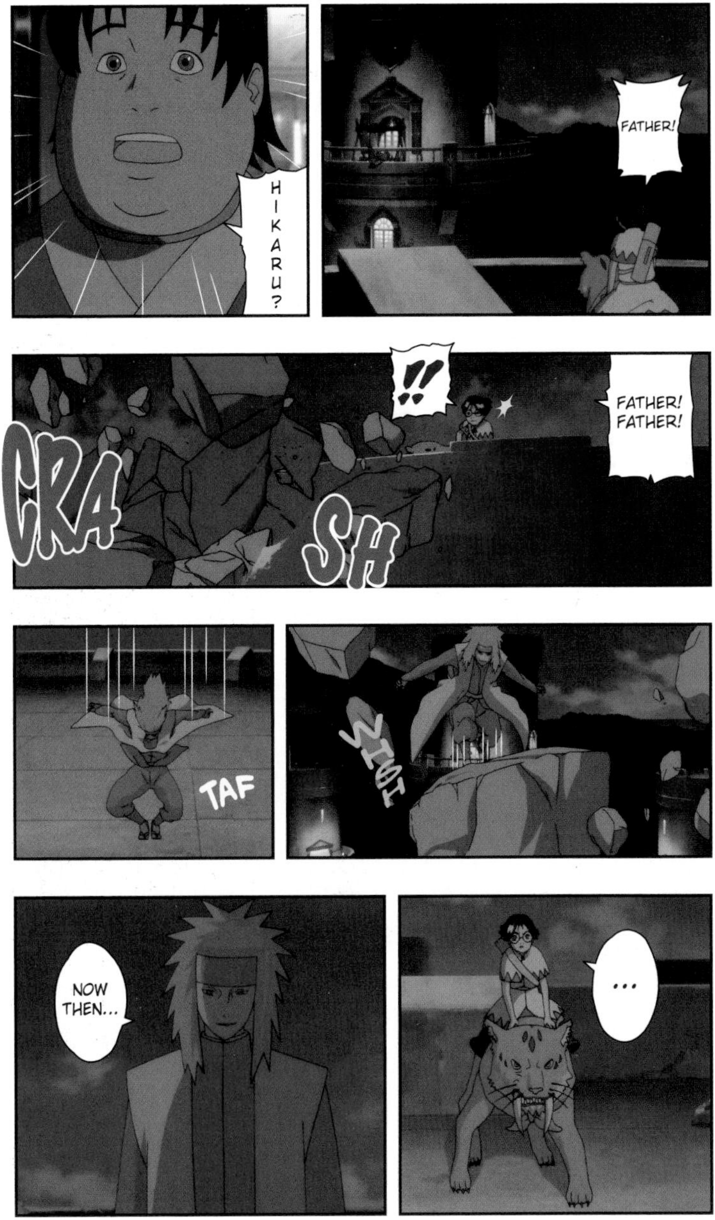
FATHER!
HIKARU?
FATHER! FATHER!
!!
CRASH
TAF
...
NOW THEN...

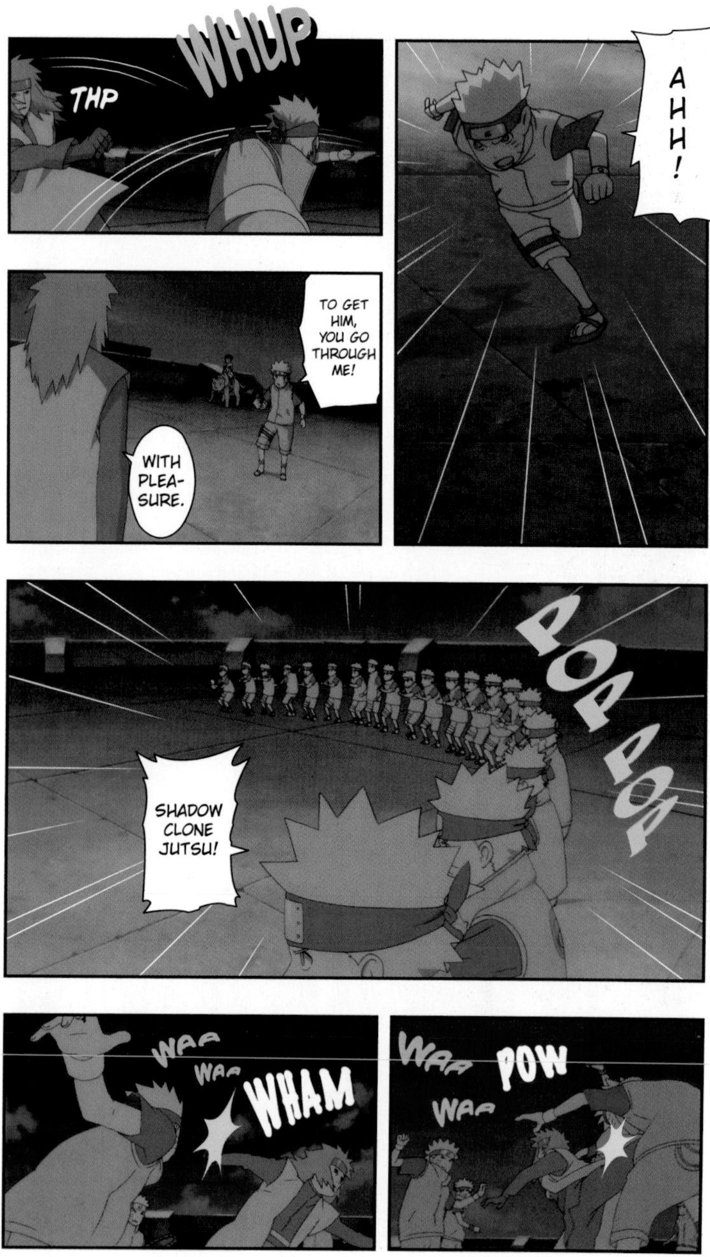
AHH!
WHUP
THP
TO GET HIM, YOU GO THROUGH ME!
WITH PLEA-SURE.
POP POP POP
SHADOW CLONE JUTSU!
WAA
POW
WAA
WAA
WAA
WHAM

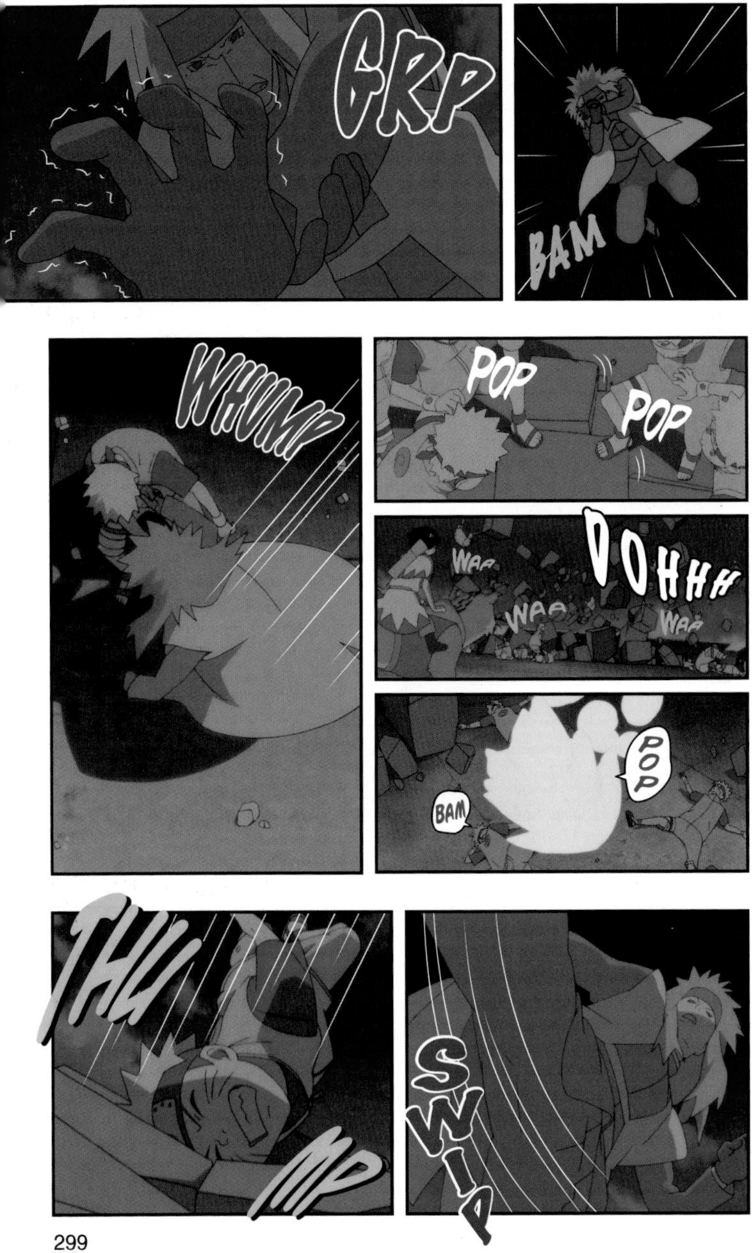

BAM
GRP
POP
POP
DOHHH
WAA
WAA
WAA
POP
BAM
WHUMP
SWIP
THUMP

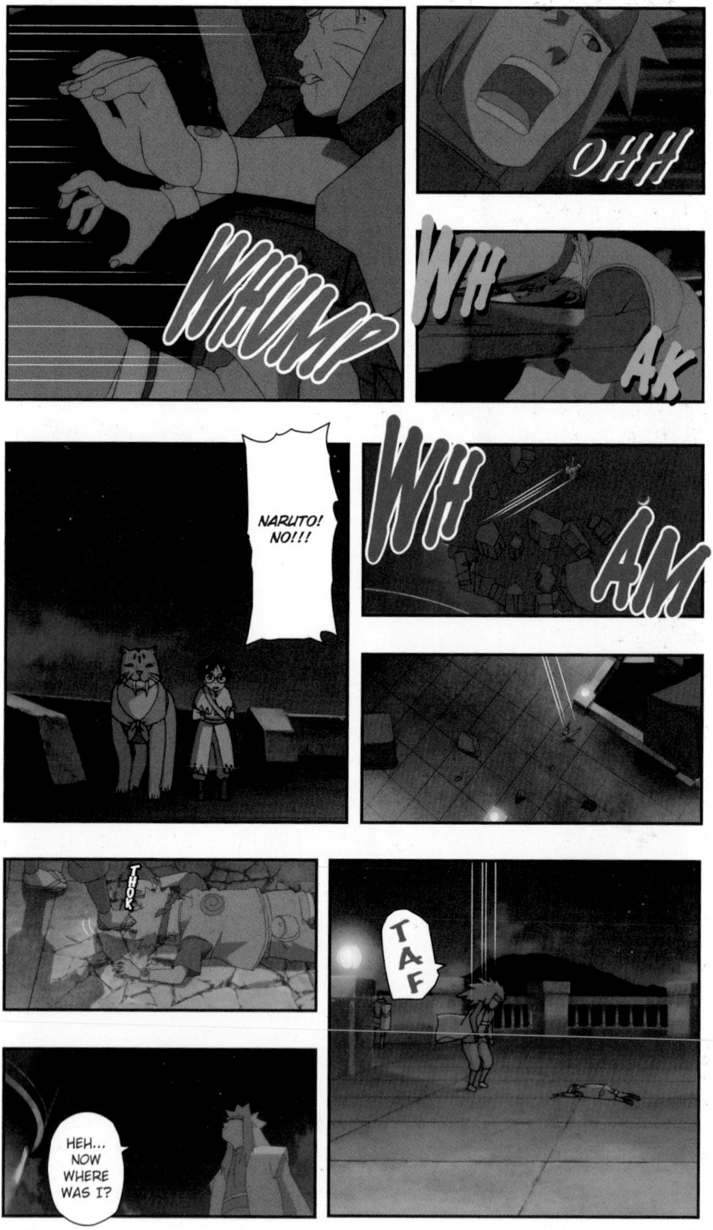
OHH
WH
AK
WHUMP
WH
AM
NARUTO! NO!!!
TAF
THOK
HEH... NOW WHERE WAS I?

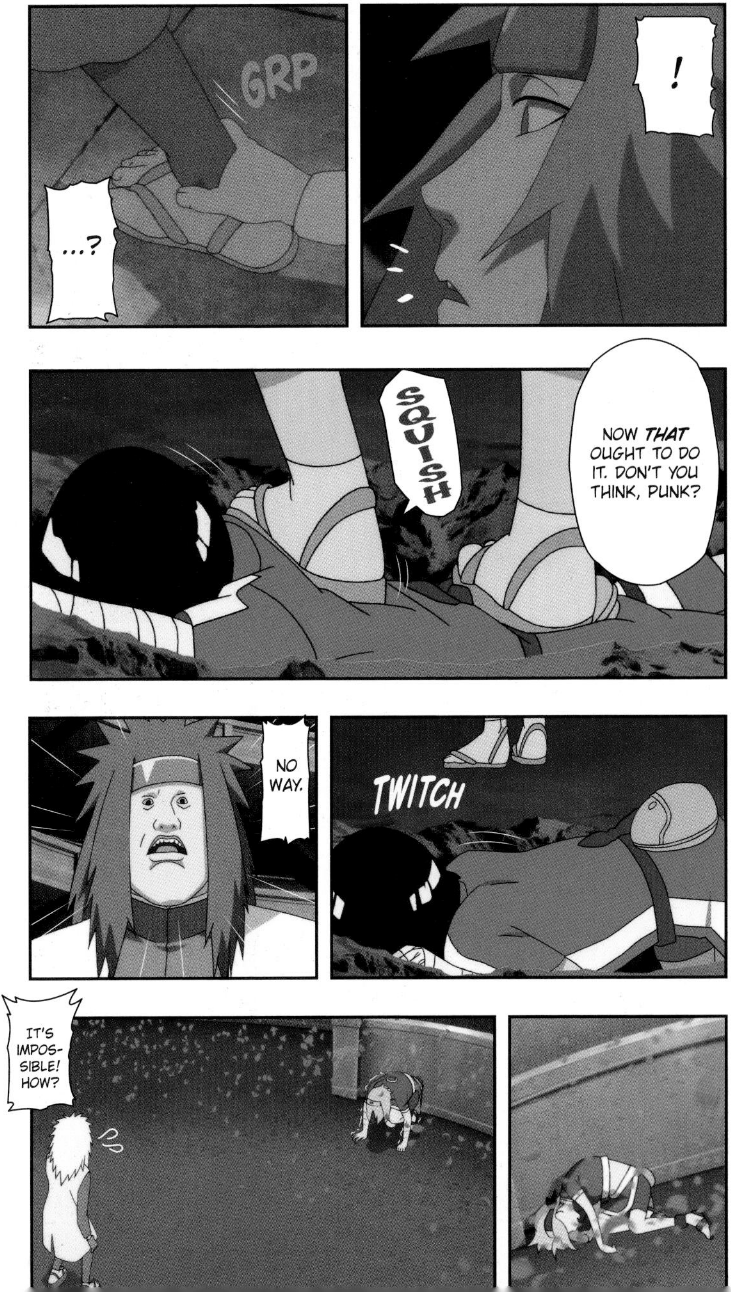
!
GRP
...?
NOW THAT OUGHT TO DO IT. DON'T YOU THINK, PUNK?
SQUISH
TWITCH
NO WAY.
IT'S IMPOS-SIBLE! HOW?

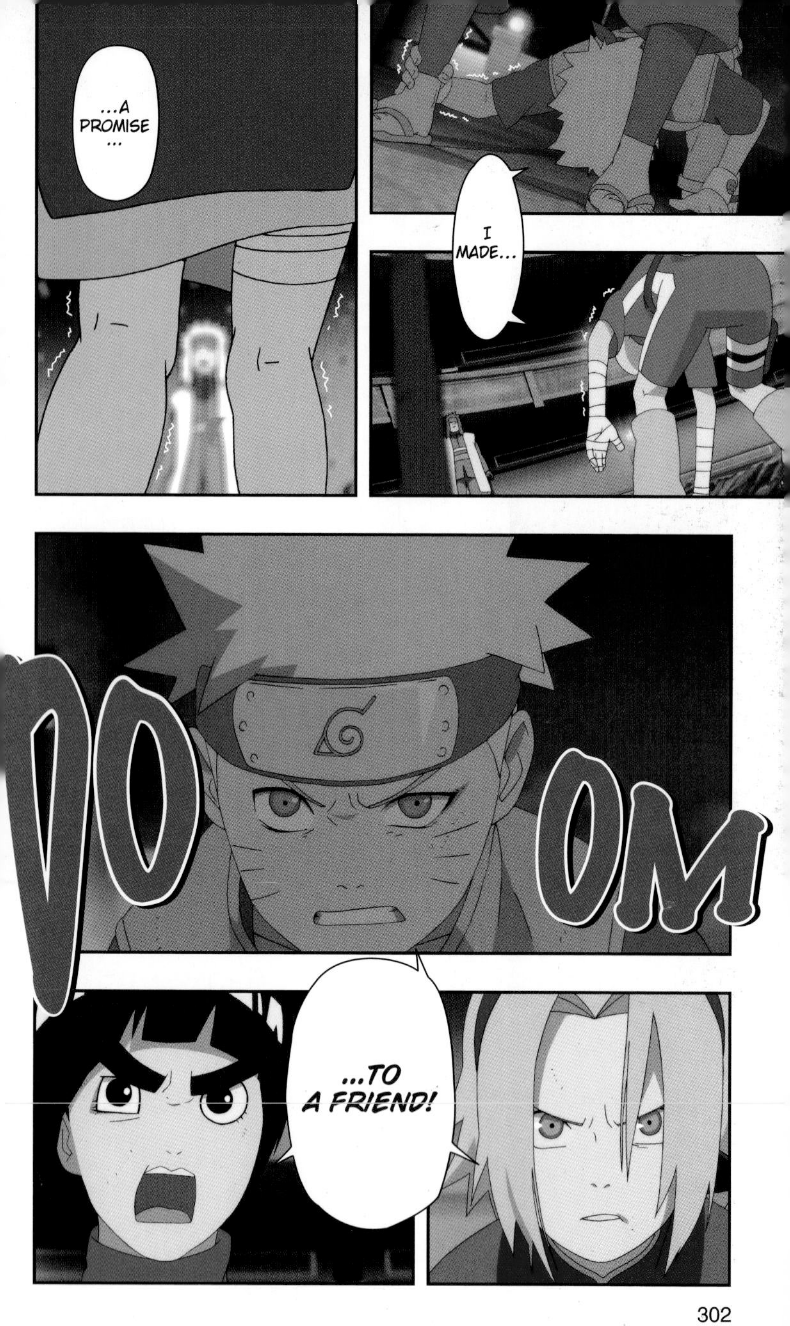
...A PROMISE ...
I MADE...
DOOM
...TO A FRIEND!

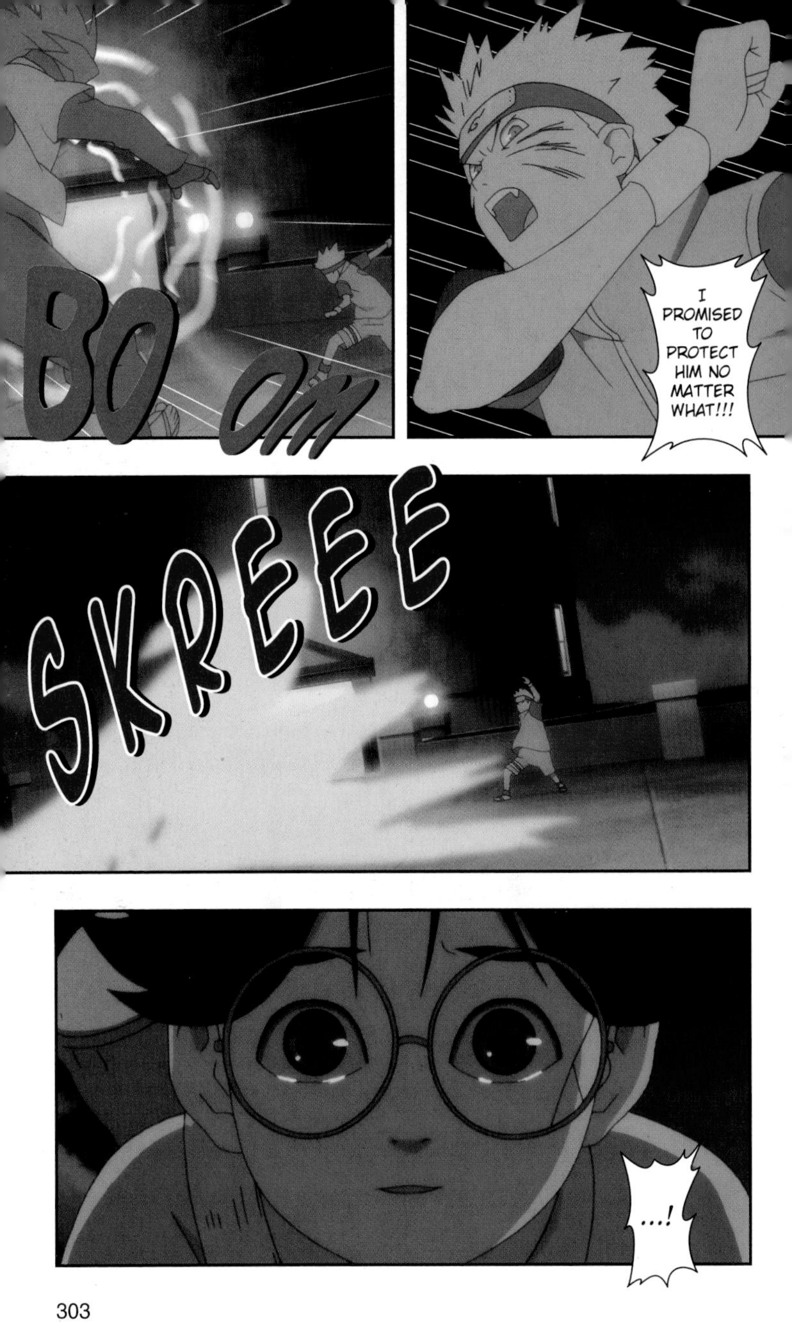
I PROMISED TO PROTECT HIM NO MATTER WHAT!!!
BOOM
SKREEE
...!

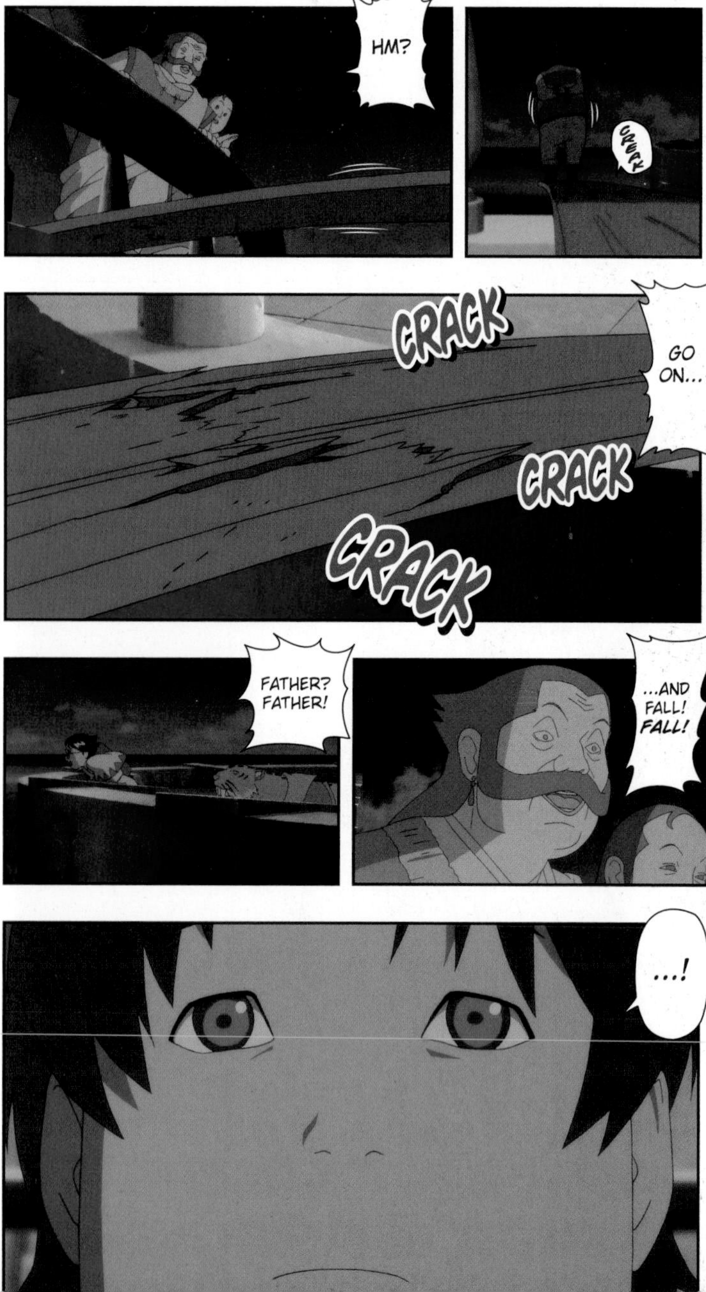
CREAK
HM?
GO ON...
CRACK
CRACK
CRACK
...AND FALL! FALL!
FATHER? FATHER!
...!

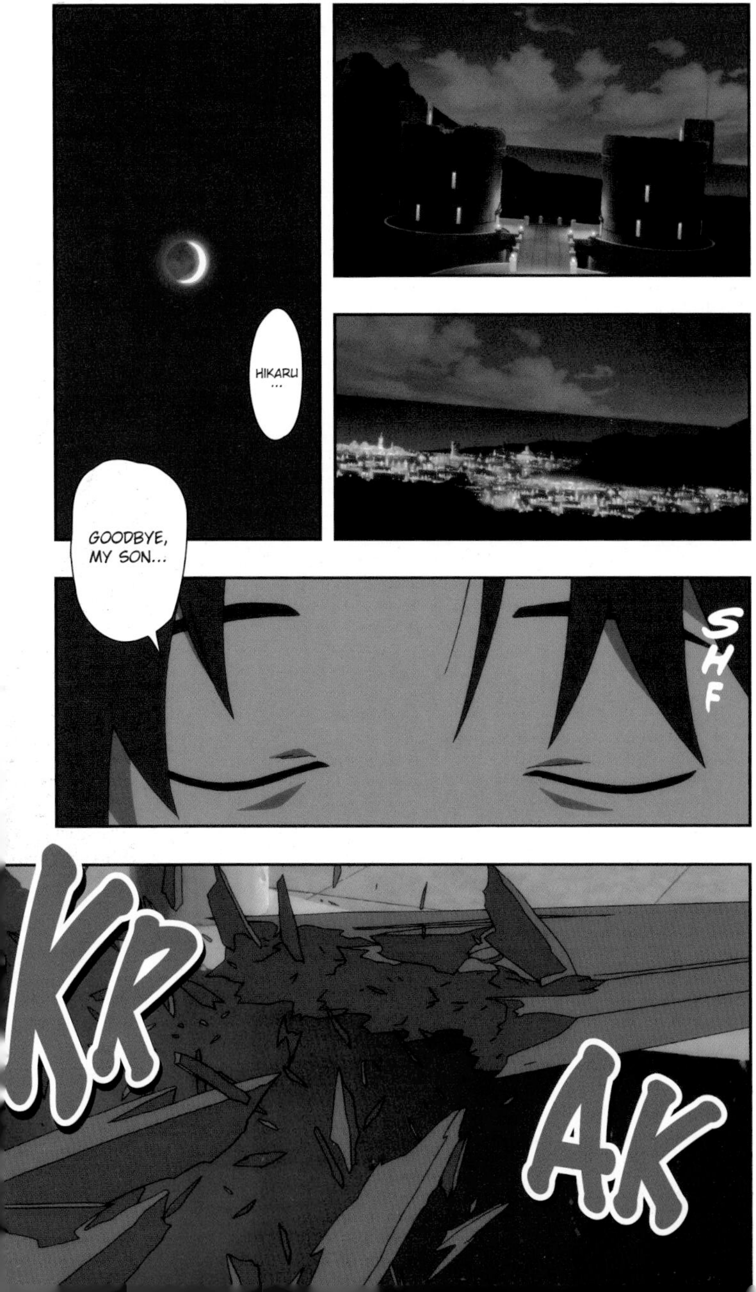
HIKARU...
GOODBYE, MY SON...
SHF
KRAK

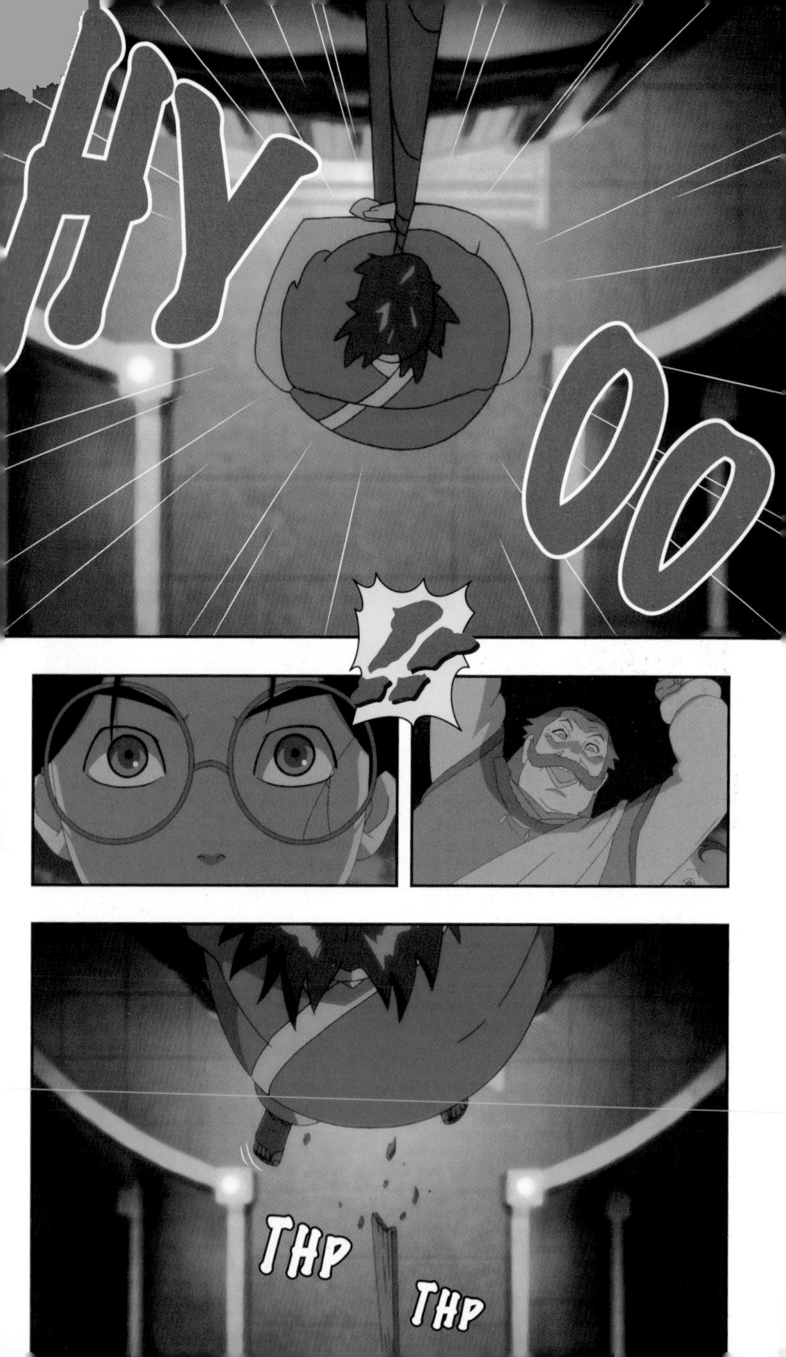
HYOO
THP
THP

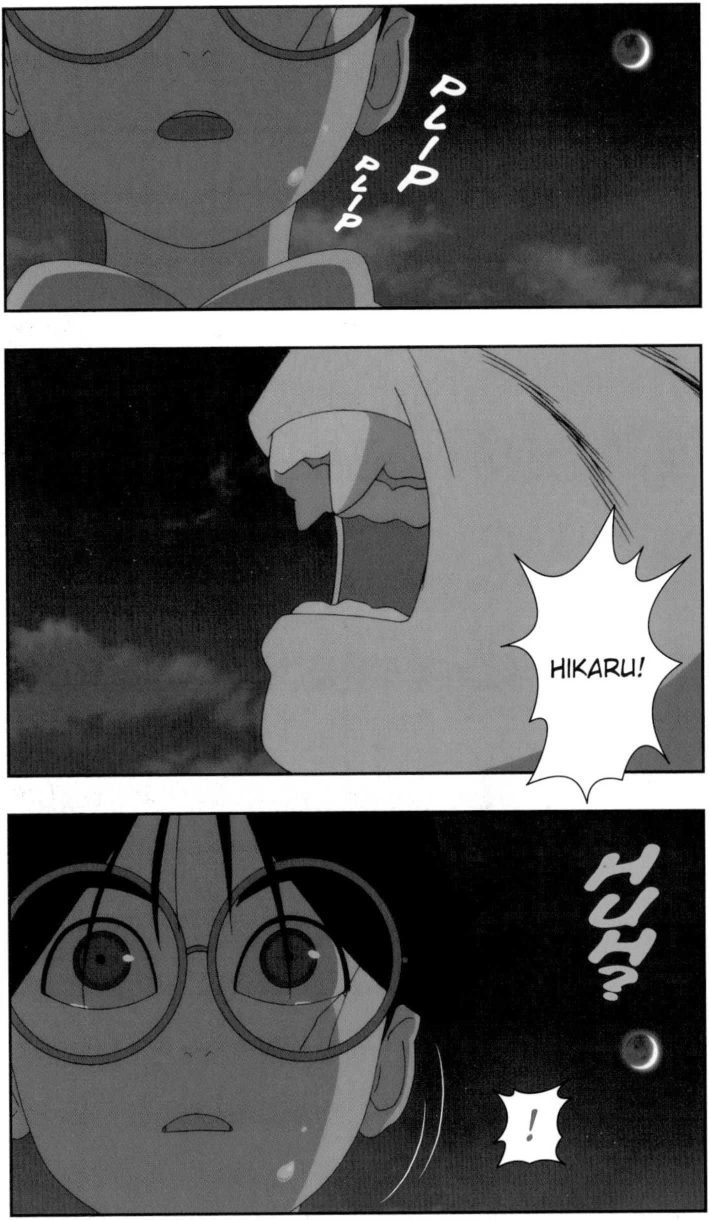
PLIP
PLIP
HIKARU!
HUH?
!

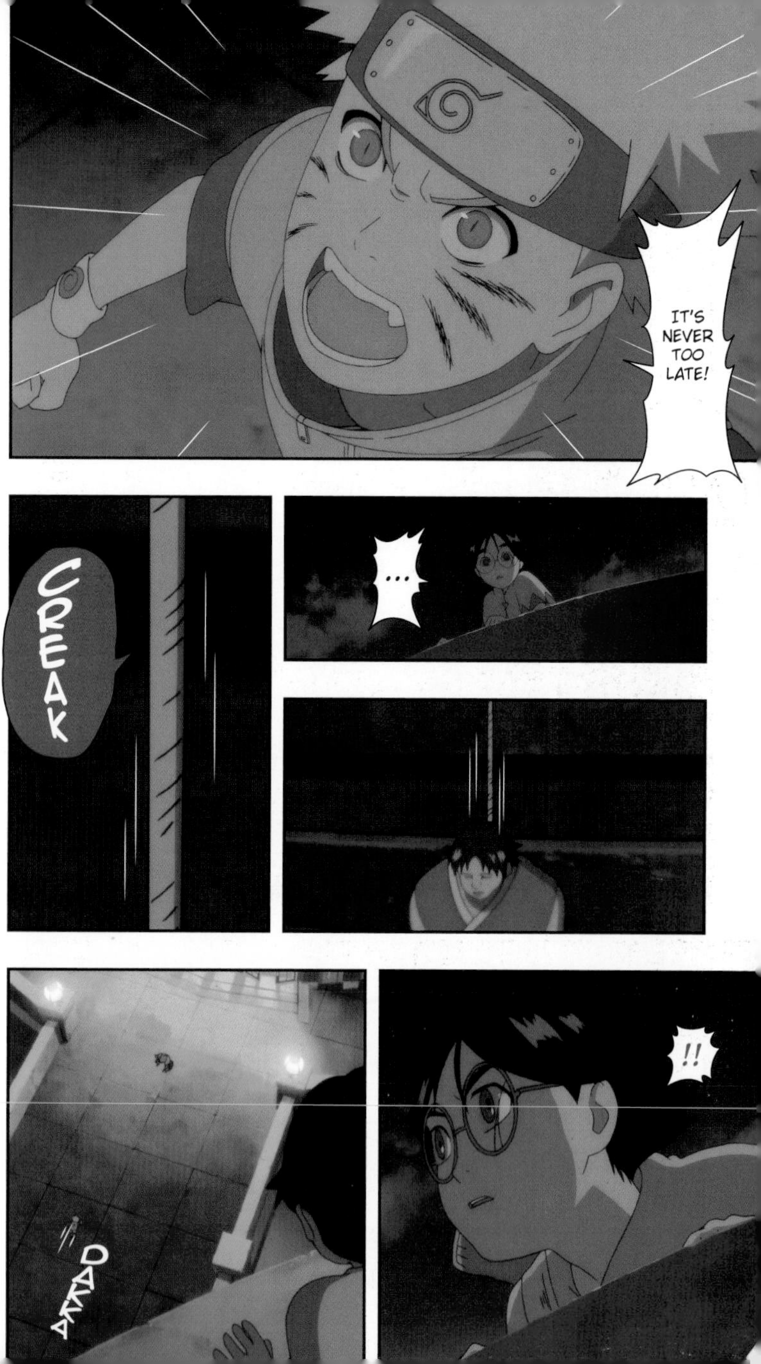
IT'S NEVER TOO LATE!
...
CREAK
!!
DAKA

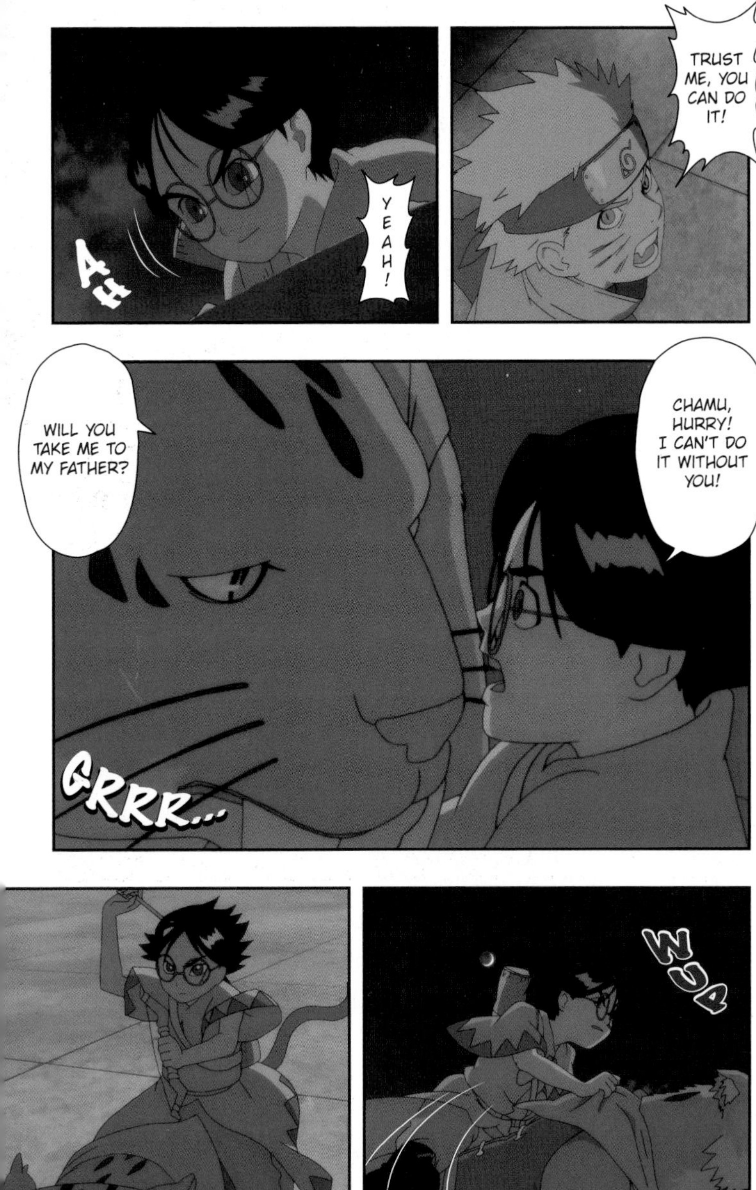
TRUST ME, YOU CAN DO IT!
YEAH!
AH
CHAMU, HURRY! I CAN'T DO IT WITHOUT YOU!
WILL YOU TAKE ME TO MY FATHER?
GRRR...
WUP

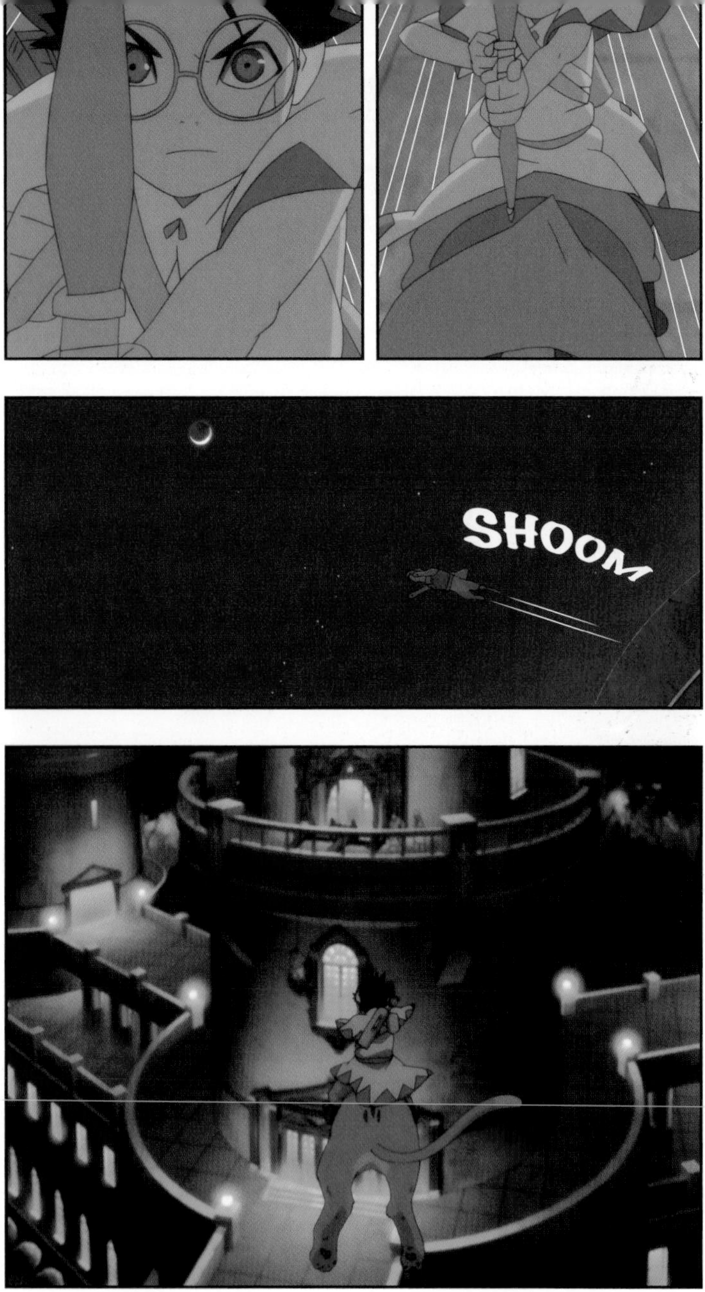
SHOOM

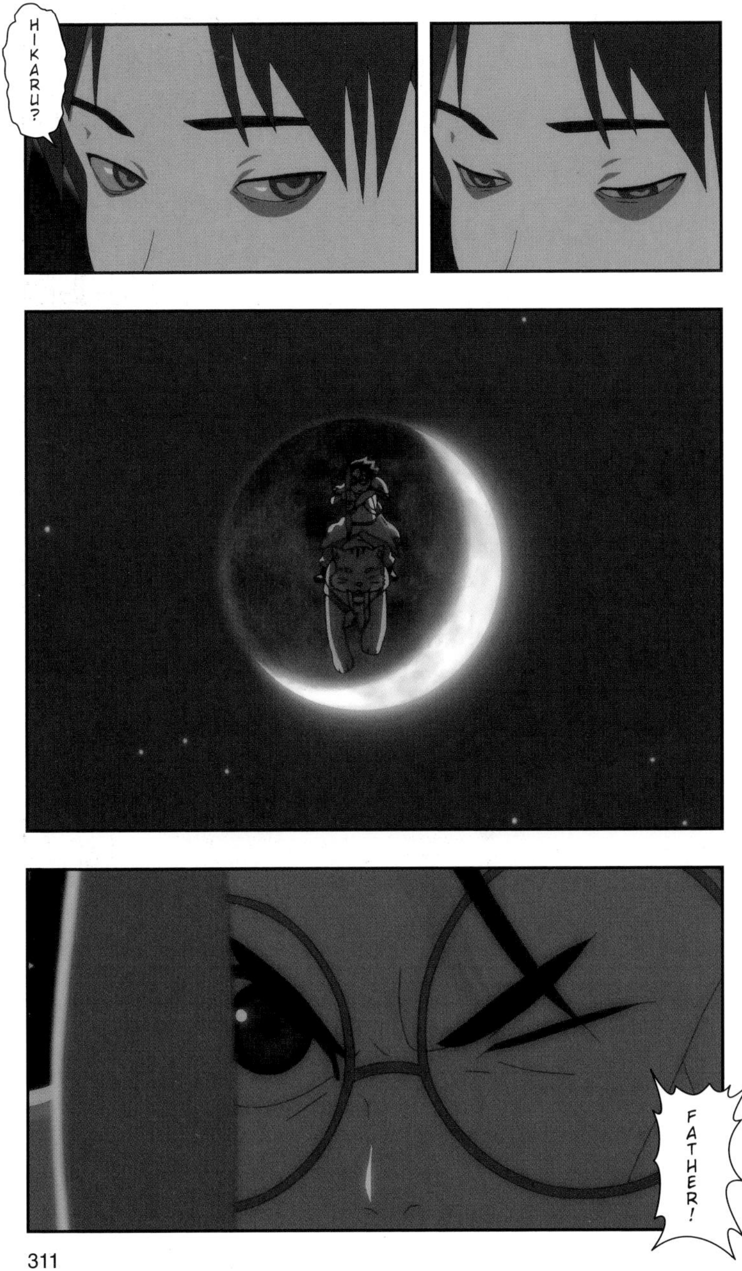
HIKARU?
FATHER!

WHSSH

KRRK

SNIP

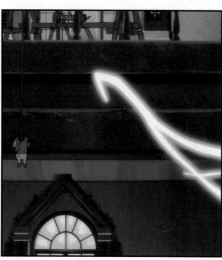

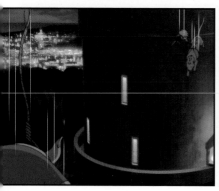

DAKKA

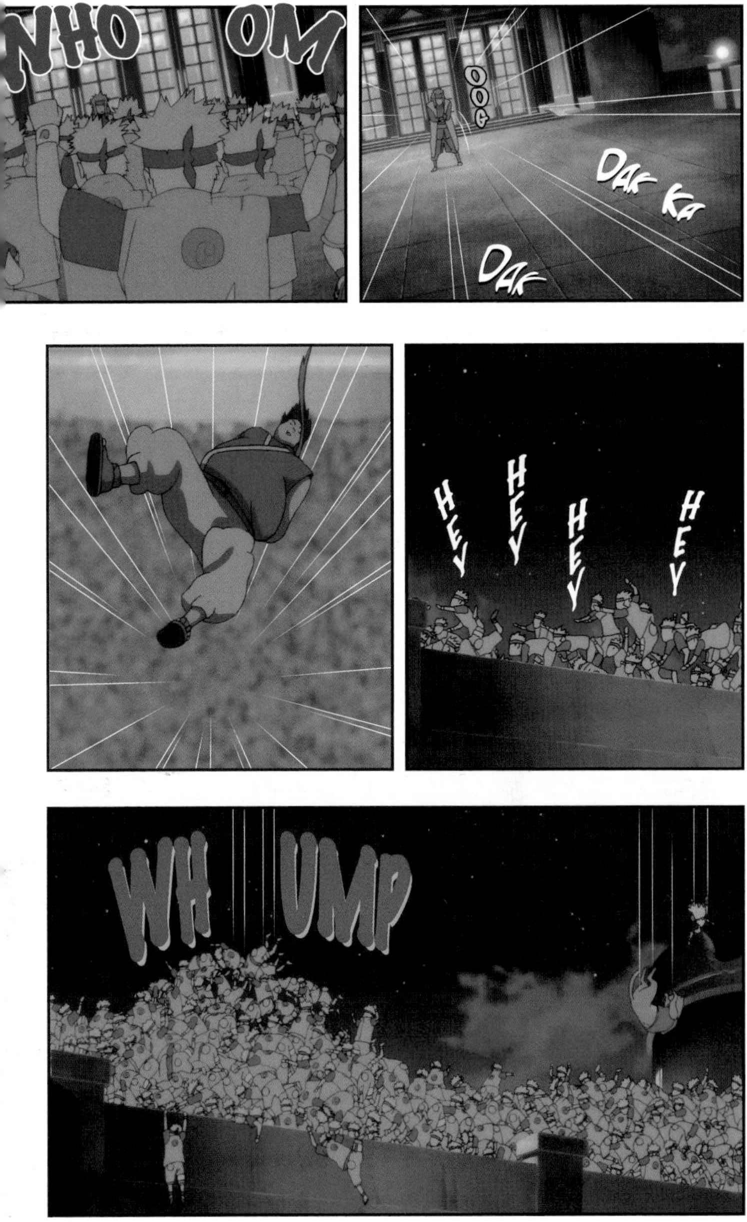
OOG
DAK KA
DAK
WHOOM
HEY
HEY
HEY
HEY
WHUMP

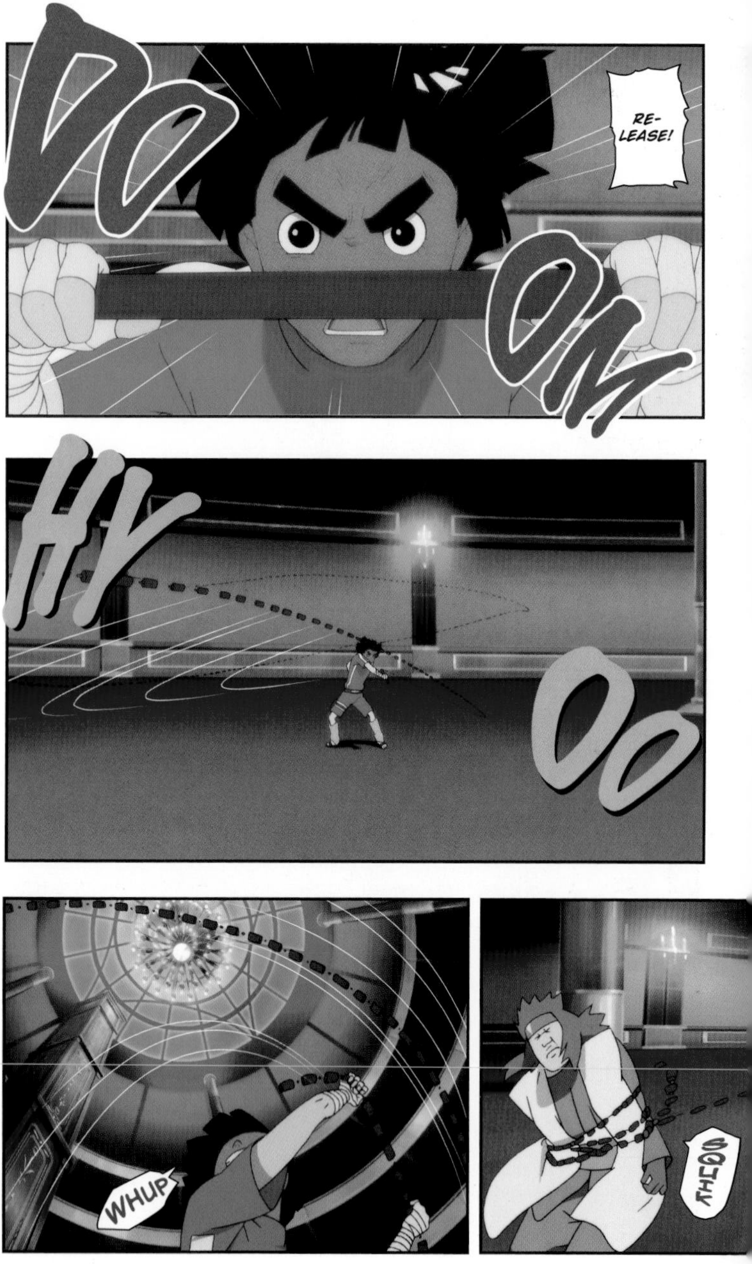
RE-
LEASE!
DOOOM
HYOO
SQUHK
WHUP

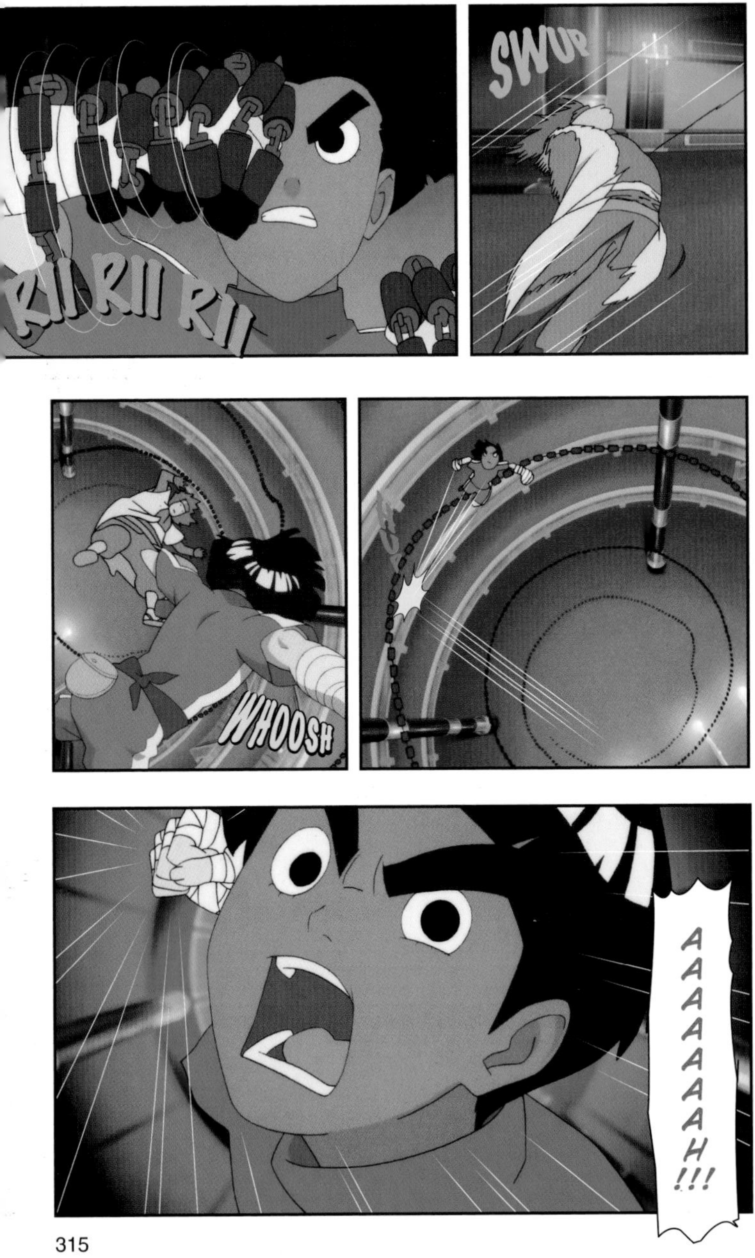
SWUP
RII RII RII
WHOOSH
AAAAAAAH!!!

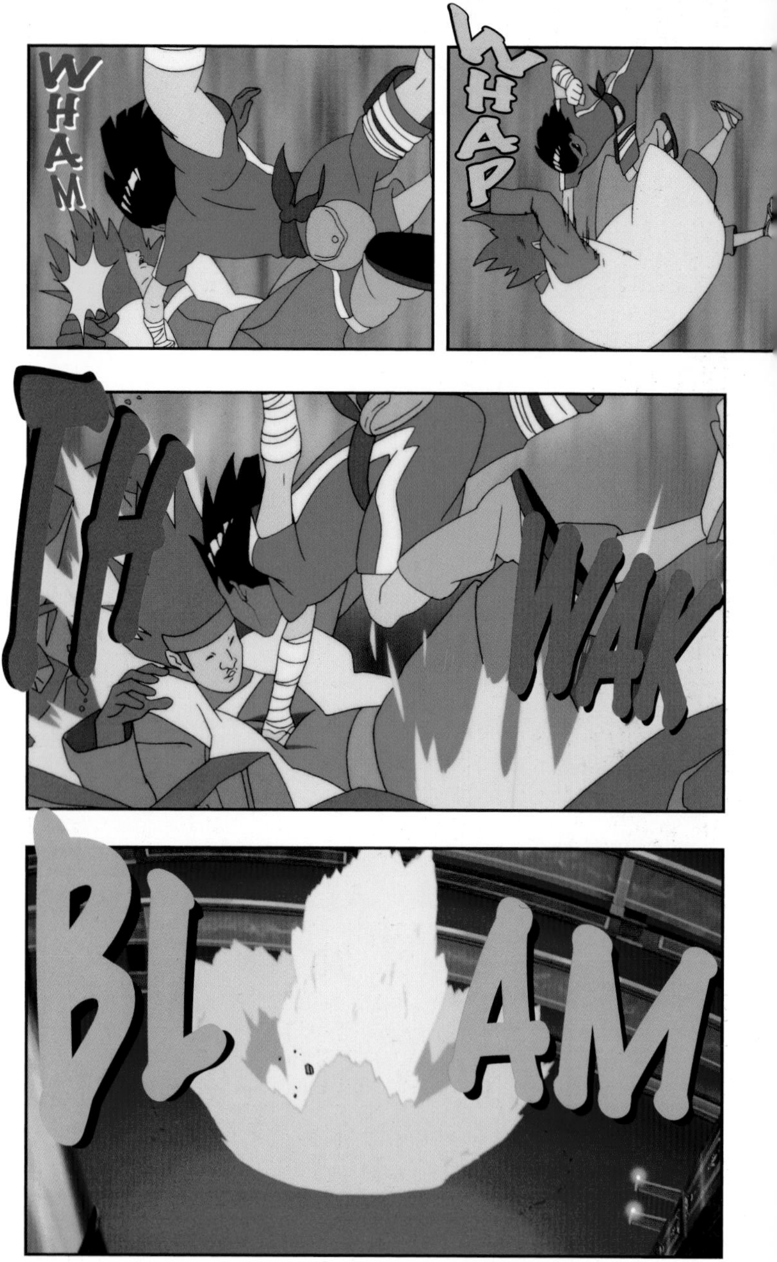
WHAP
WHAM
THWAK
BLAM

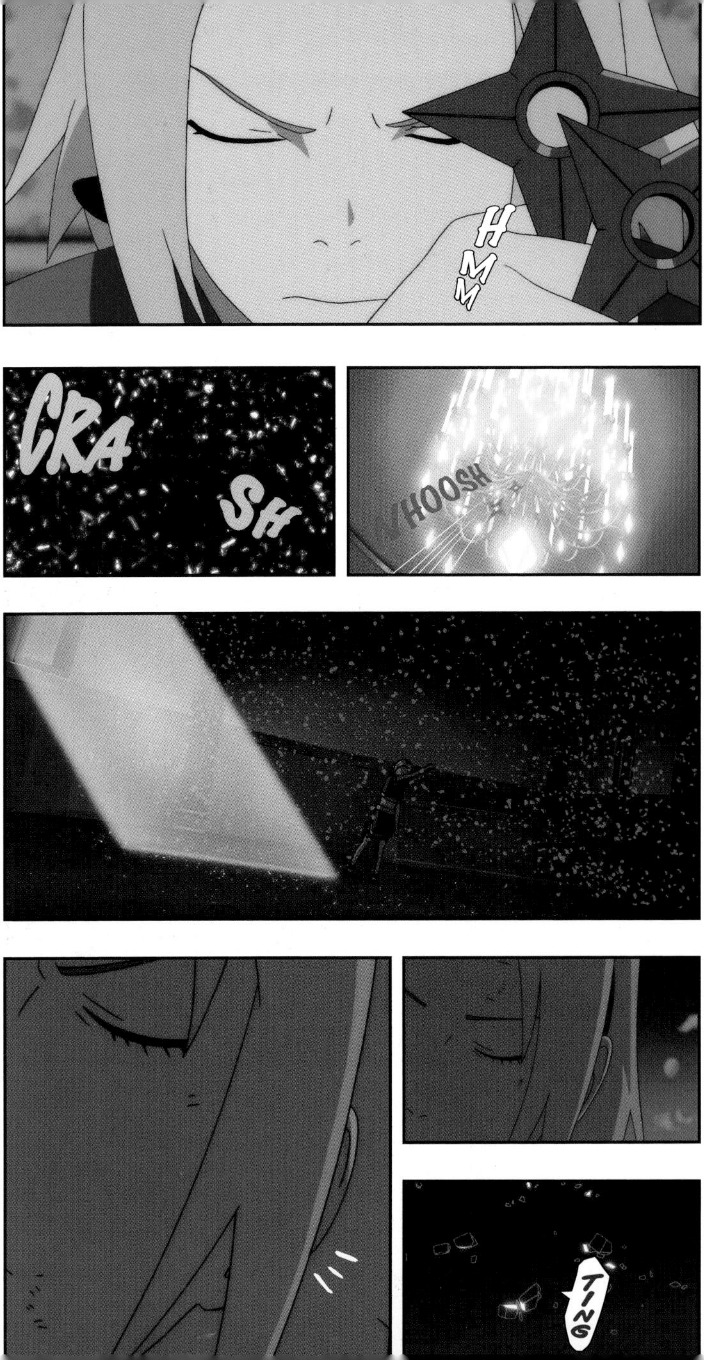
HMM
WHOOSH
CRASH
TING

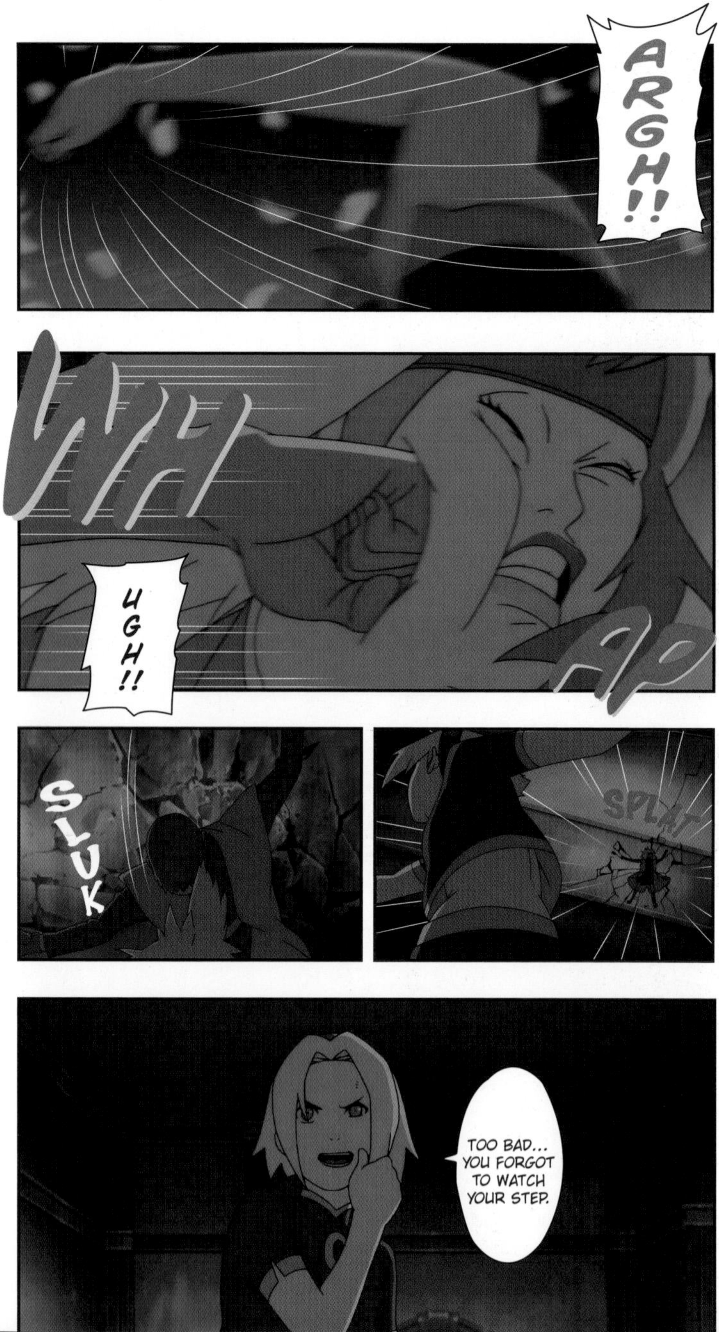
ARGH!!
UGH!!
SPLAT
SLUK
TOO BAD... YOU FORGOT TO WATCH YOUR STEP.

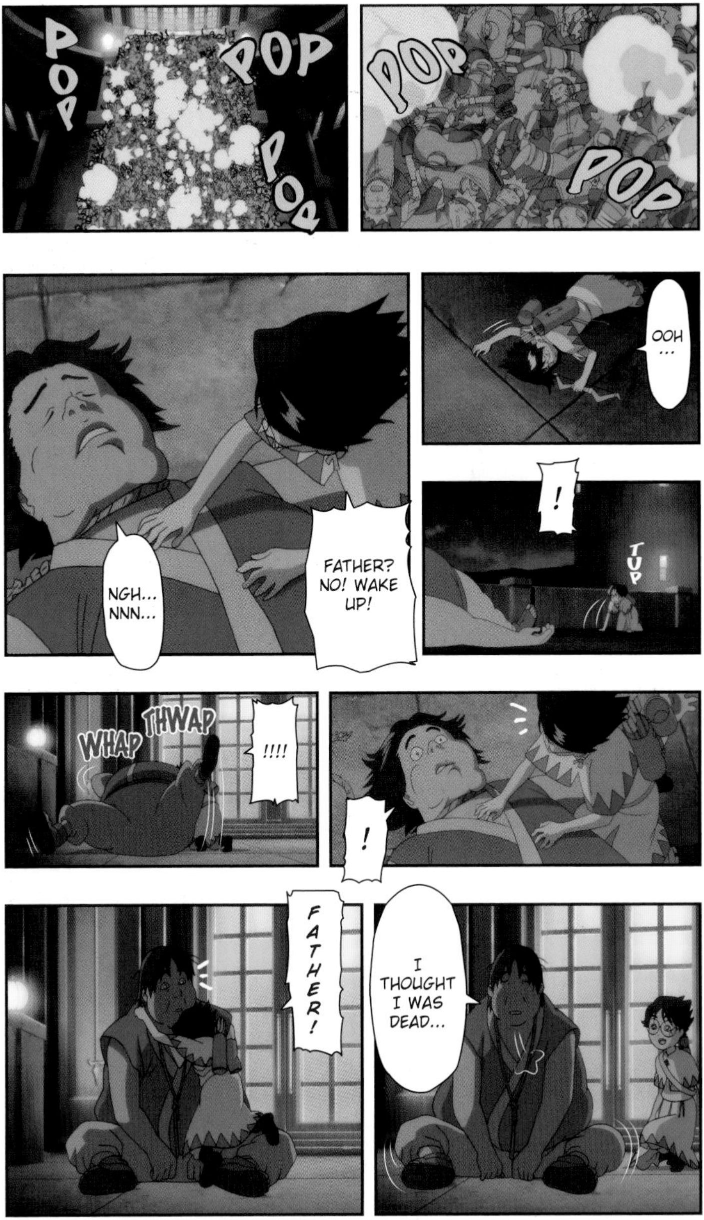
POP
POP
POP
POP
POP
POP
OOH ...
!
TUP
FATHER? NO! WAKE UP!
NGH... NNN...
!
!!!!
THWAP
WHAP
I THOUGHT I WAS DEAD...
FATHER!

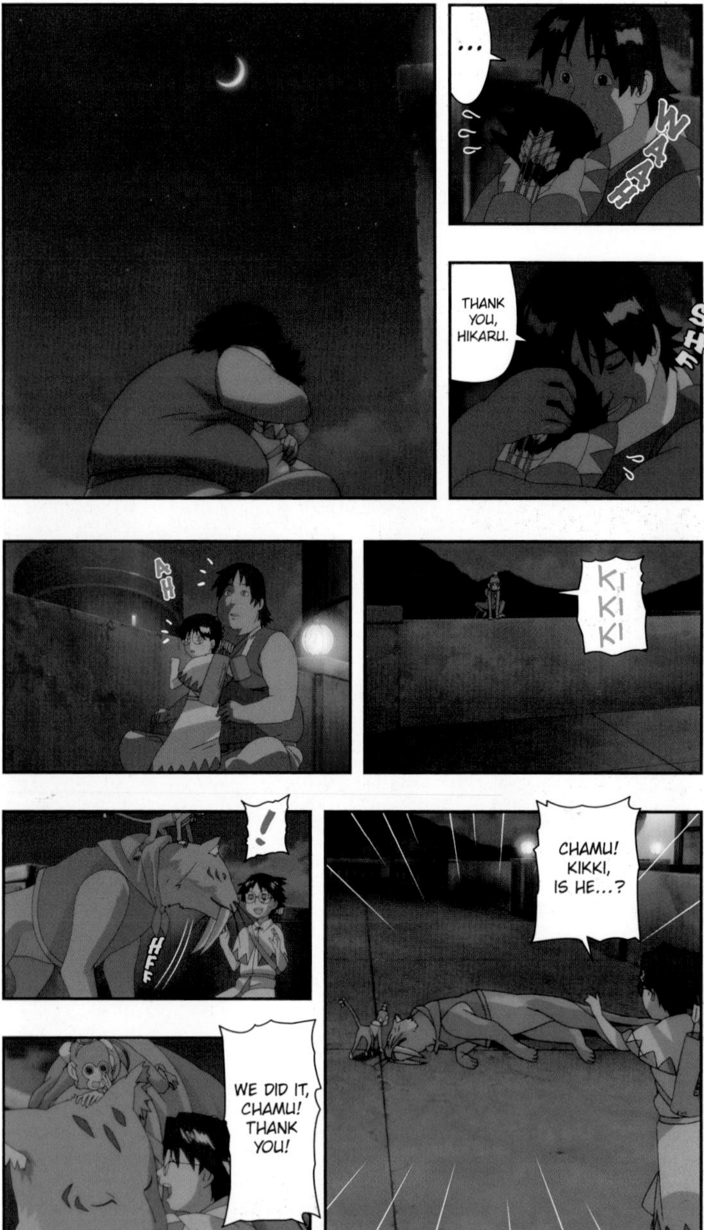
...
WAAH
THANK YOU, HIKARU.
SHF
KI KI KI
AH
CHAMU! KIKKI, IS HE...?
!
HFF
WE DID IT, CHAMU! THANK YOU!

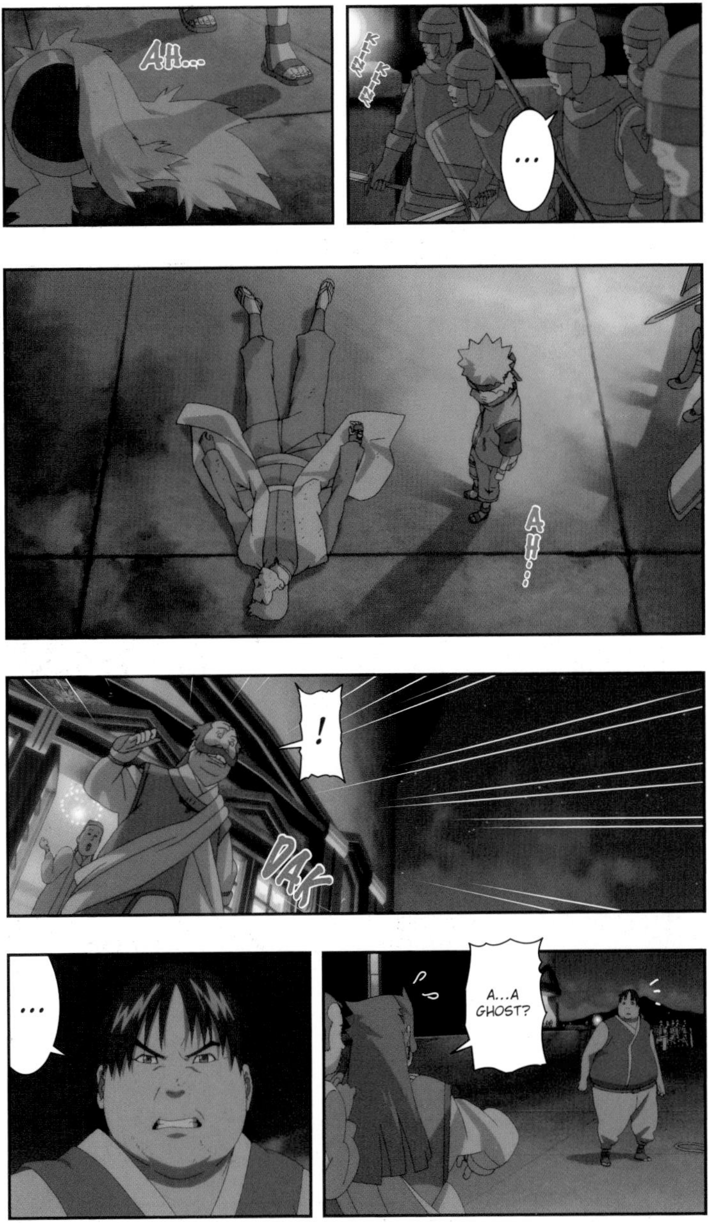
KLINK KLINK
...
AH...
AH...
!
DAK
A...A GHOST?
...

AHH!

*S
H
A
B
A
D
A
B
A
!!*

SO HE WAS THE ONE PULLING THE STRINGS, HUH?

WHY, YOU...

DAK

SH ING

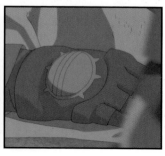

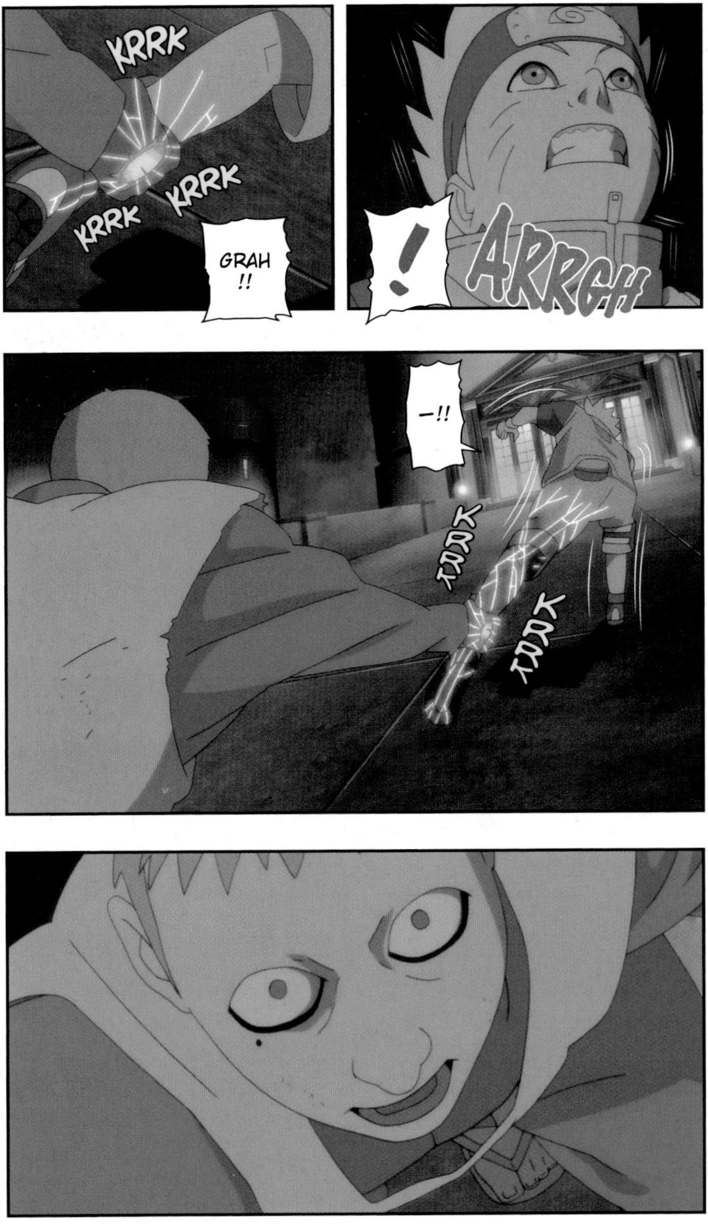
!
ARRGH
KRRK
KRRK
KRRK
GRAH !!
—!!
KRRK
KRRK

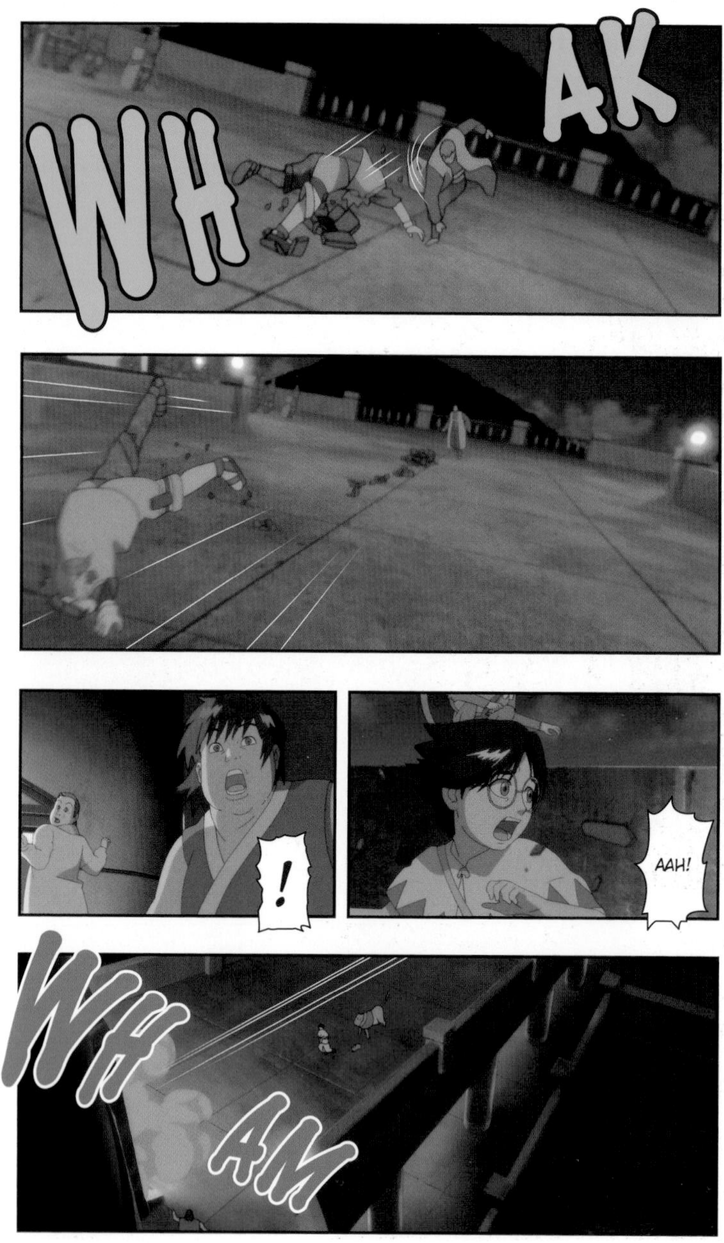
WHAK
AAH!
!
WHAM

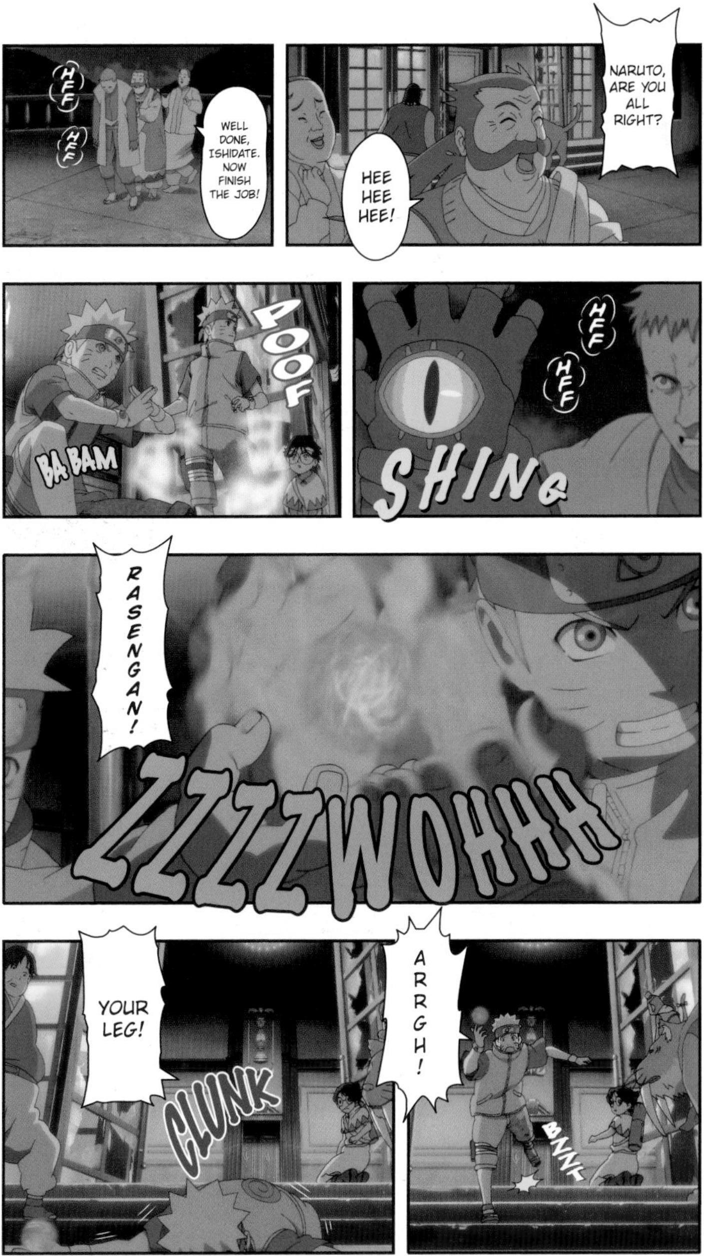
NARUTO, ARE YOU ALL RIGHT?
HEE HEE HEE!
HFF HFF
WELL DONE, ISHIDATE. NOW FINISH THE JOB!
HFF HFF
SHING
POOF
BA BAM
RASENGAN!
ZZZZWOHHH
ARRGH!
BZZZ
YOUR LEG!
CLUNK

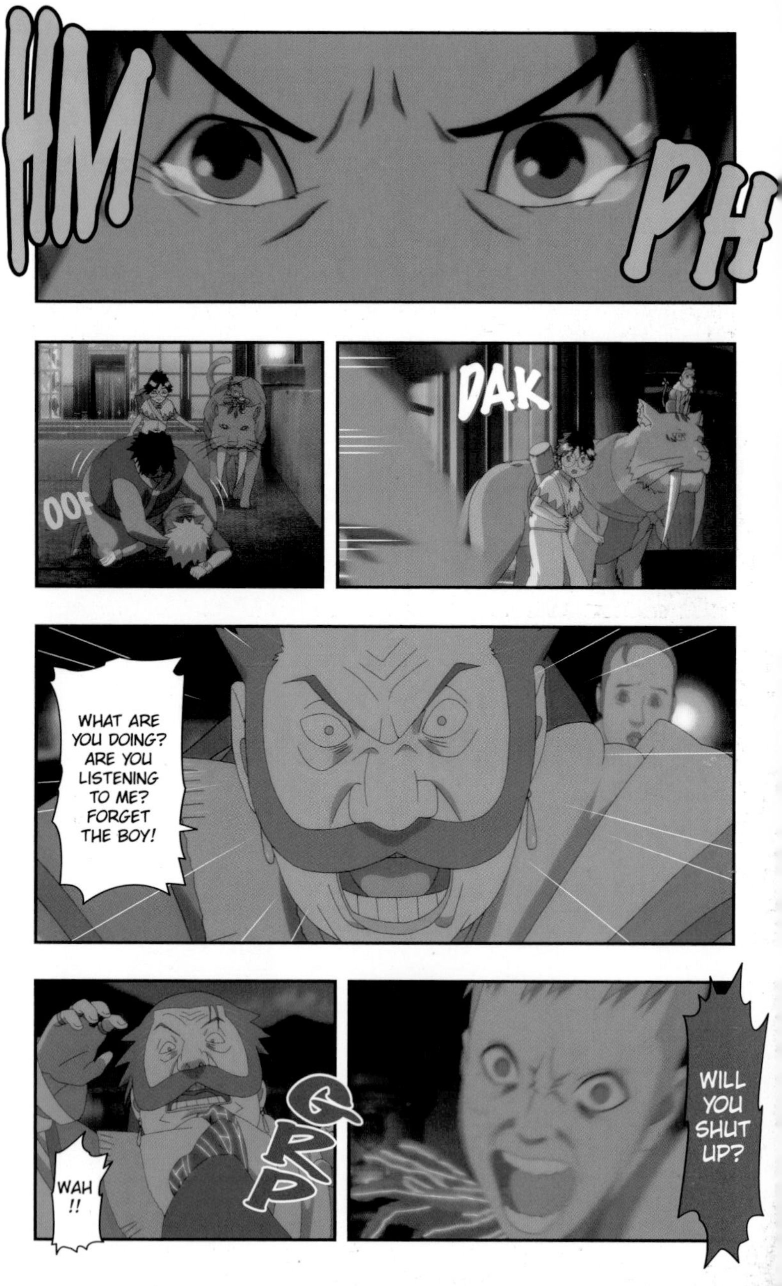
HMPH
DAK
OOF
WHAT ARE YOU DOING? ARE YOU LISTENING TO ME? FORGET THE BOY!
WILL YOU SHUT UP?
GRP
WAH !!

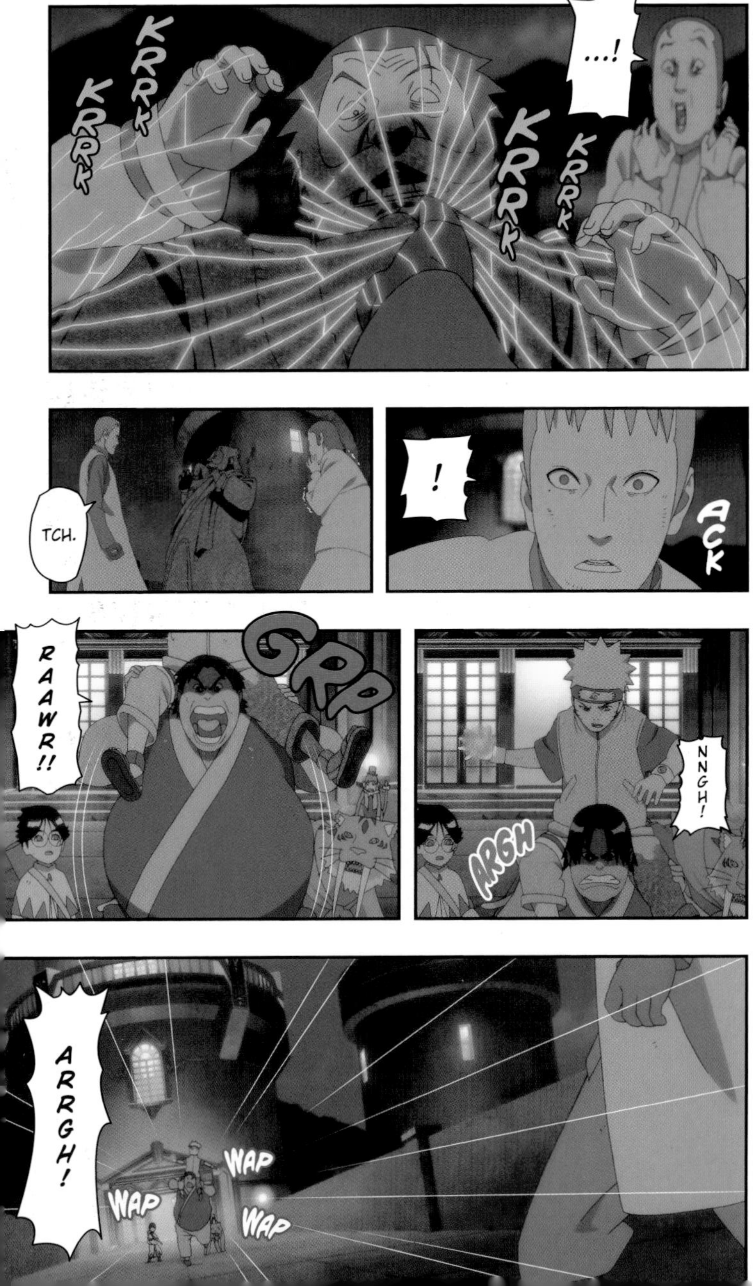
...!
KRRRK
KRRRK
KRRRK
KRRRK
!
ACK
TCH.
NNGH!
ARGH
GRP
RAAWR!!
ARRGH!
WAP
WAP
WAP

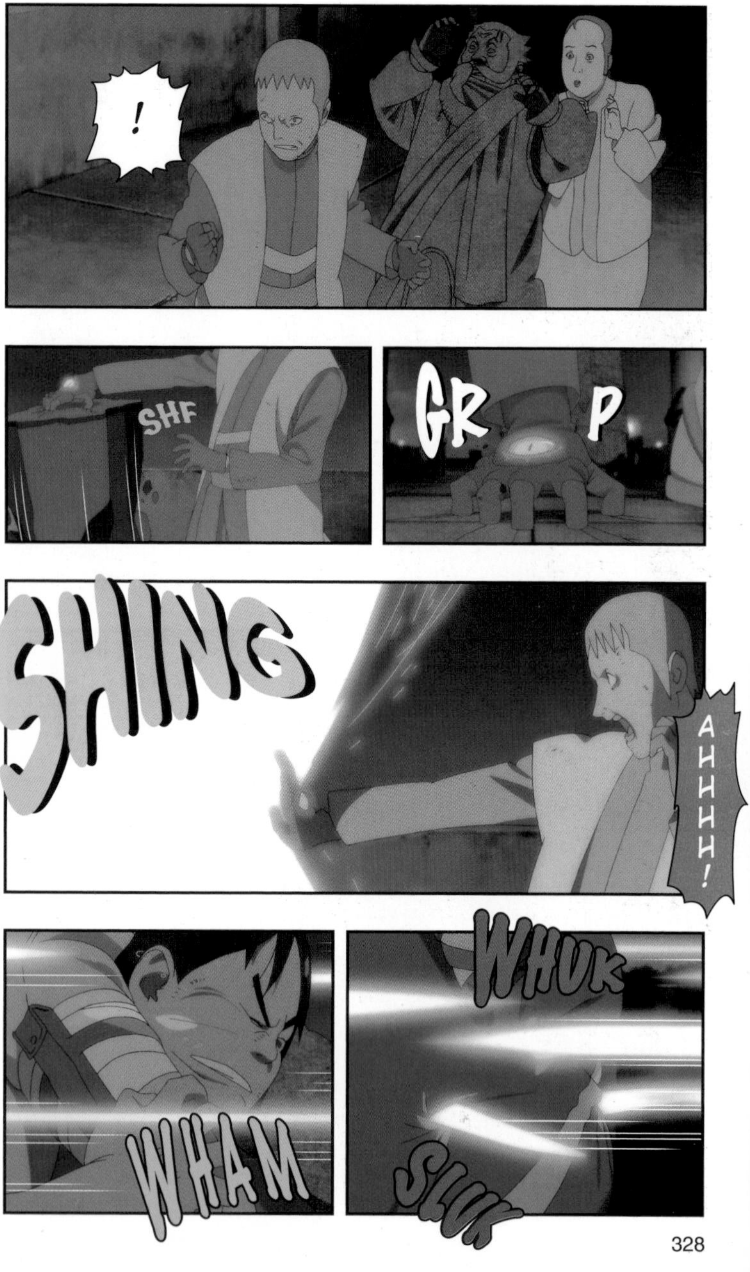
!
GR P
SHF
SHING
AHHHHH!
WHUK
SLUK
WHAM

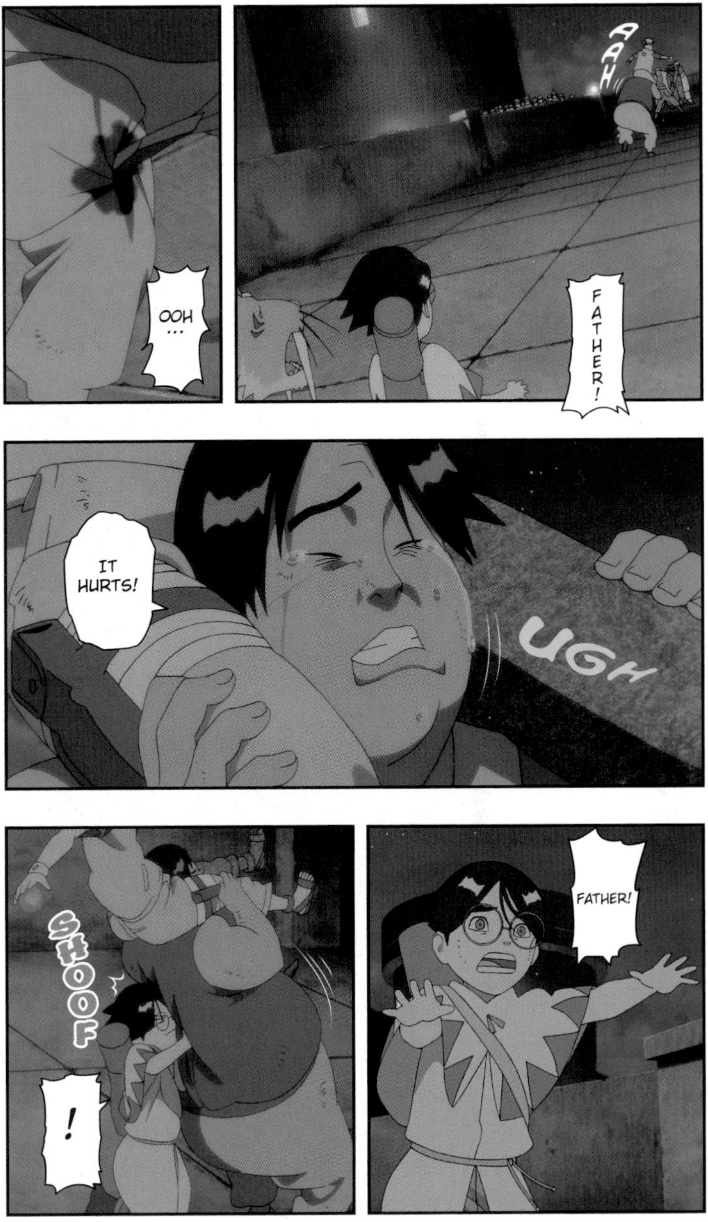
AAH
FATHER!
OOH...
IT HURTS!
UGH
FATHER!
SHOOF
!

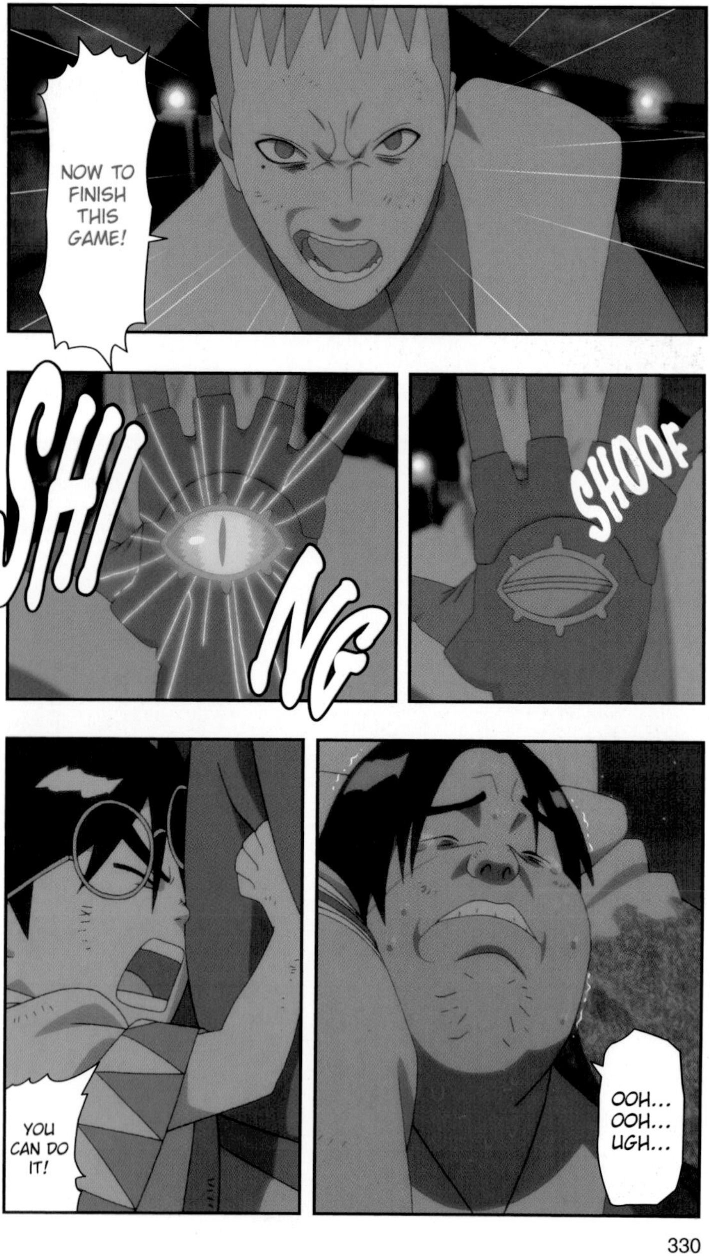
NOW TO FINISH THIS GAME!
SHOOF
SHING
OOH... OOH... UGH...
YOU CAN DO IT!

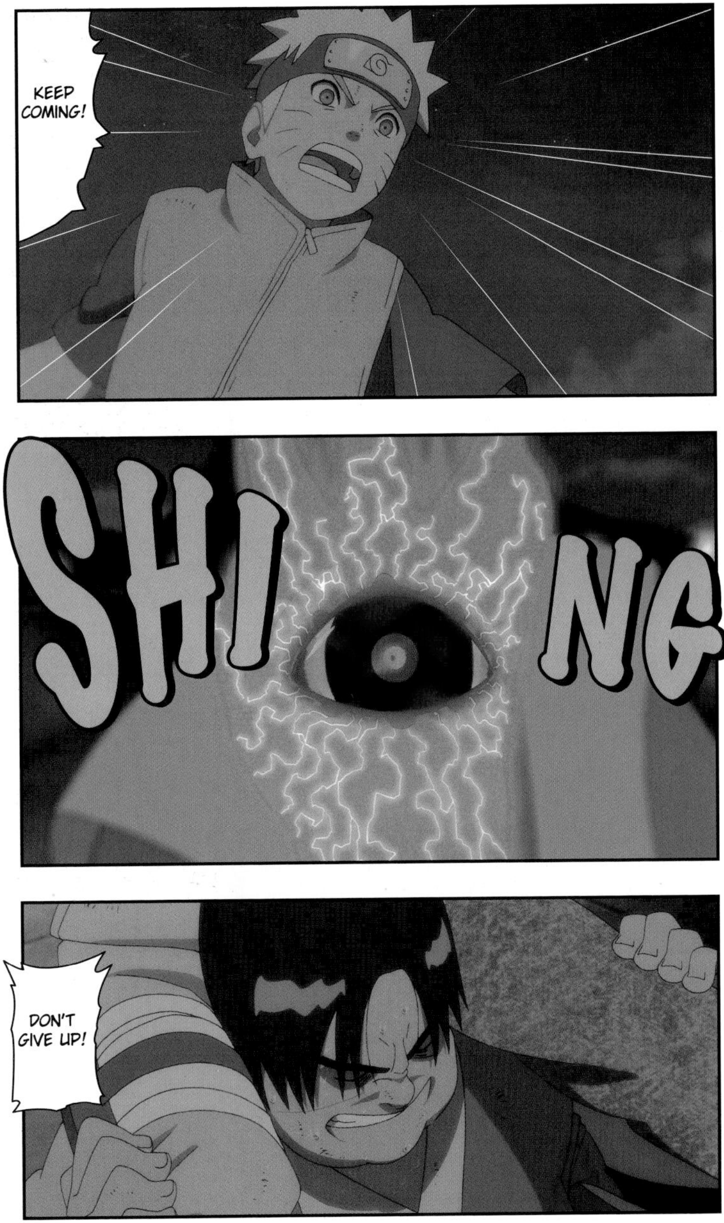
KEEP COMING!
SHI NG
DON'T GIVE UP!

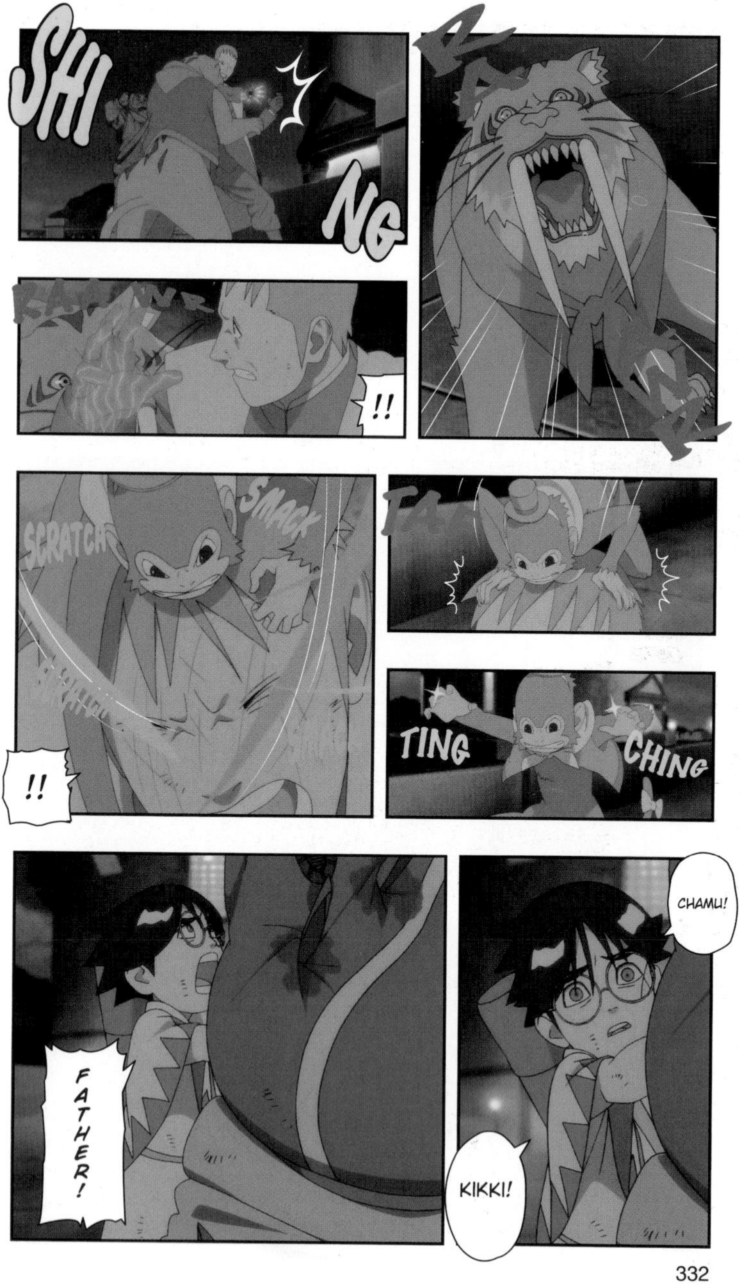
SHI
NG
!!
TING
CHING
SCRATCH
SMACK
!!
CHAMU!
KIKKI!
FATHER!

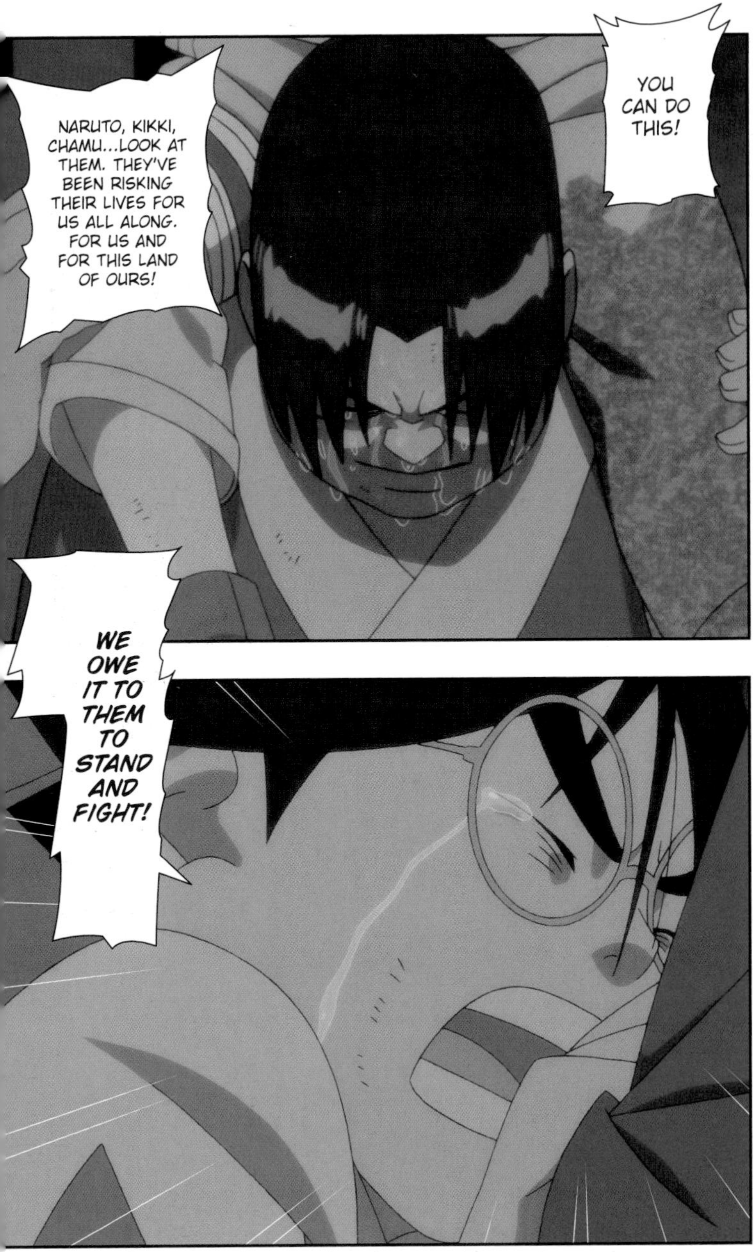
YOU CAN DO THIS!
NARUTO, KIKKI, CHAMU...LOOK AT THEM. THEY'VE BEEN RISKING THEIR LIVES FOR US ALL ALONG. FOR US AND FOR THIS LAND OF OURS!
WE OWE IT TO THEM TO STAND AND FIGHT!

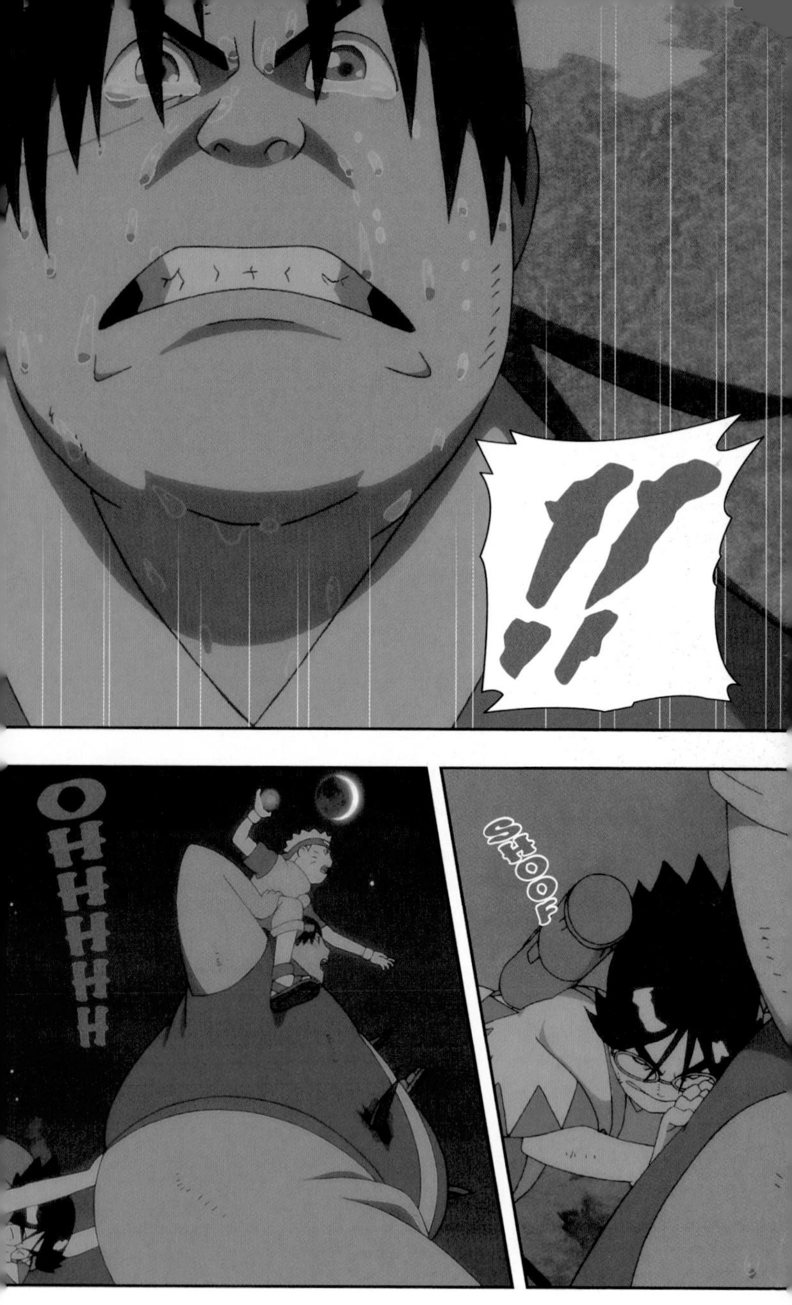
!!
SHOOF
OHHHHHHH

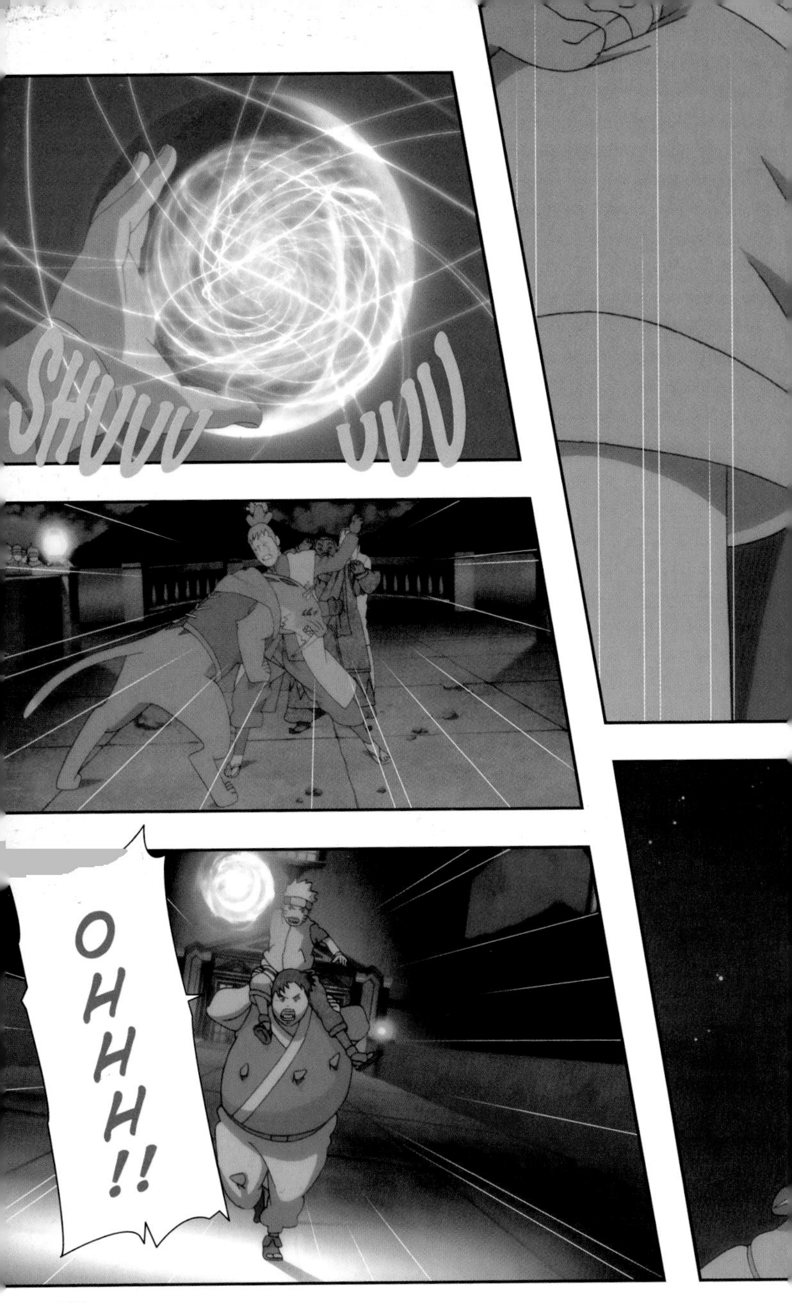
SHUUU UUU
OHHH!!

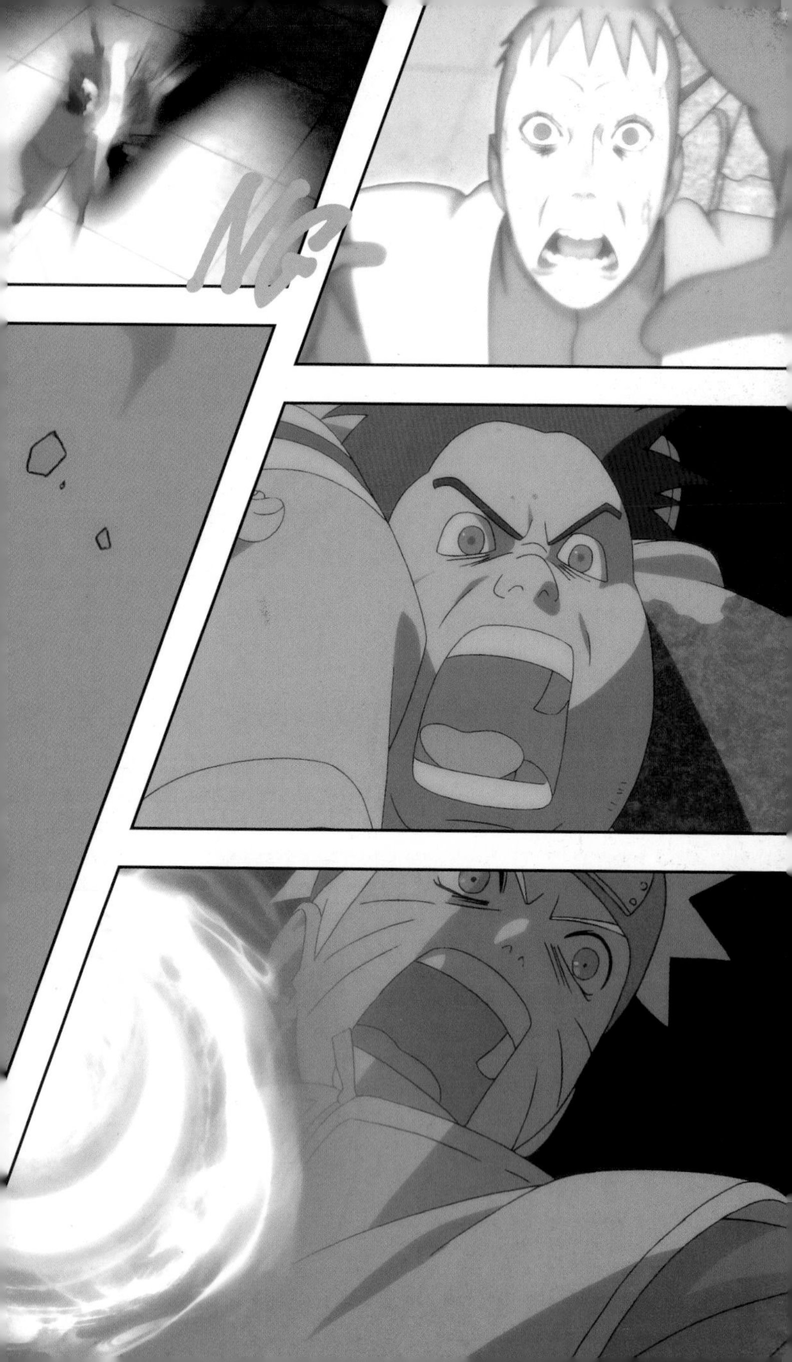

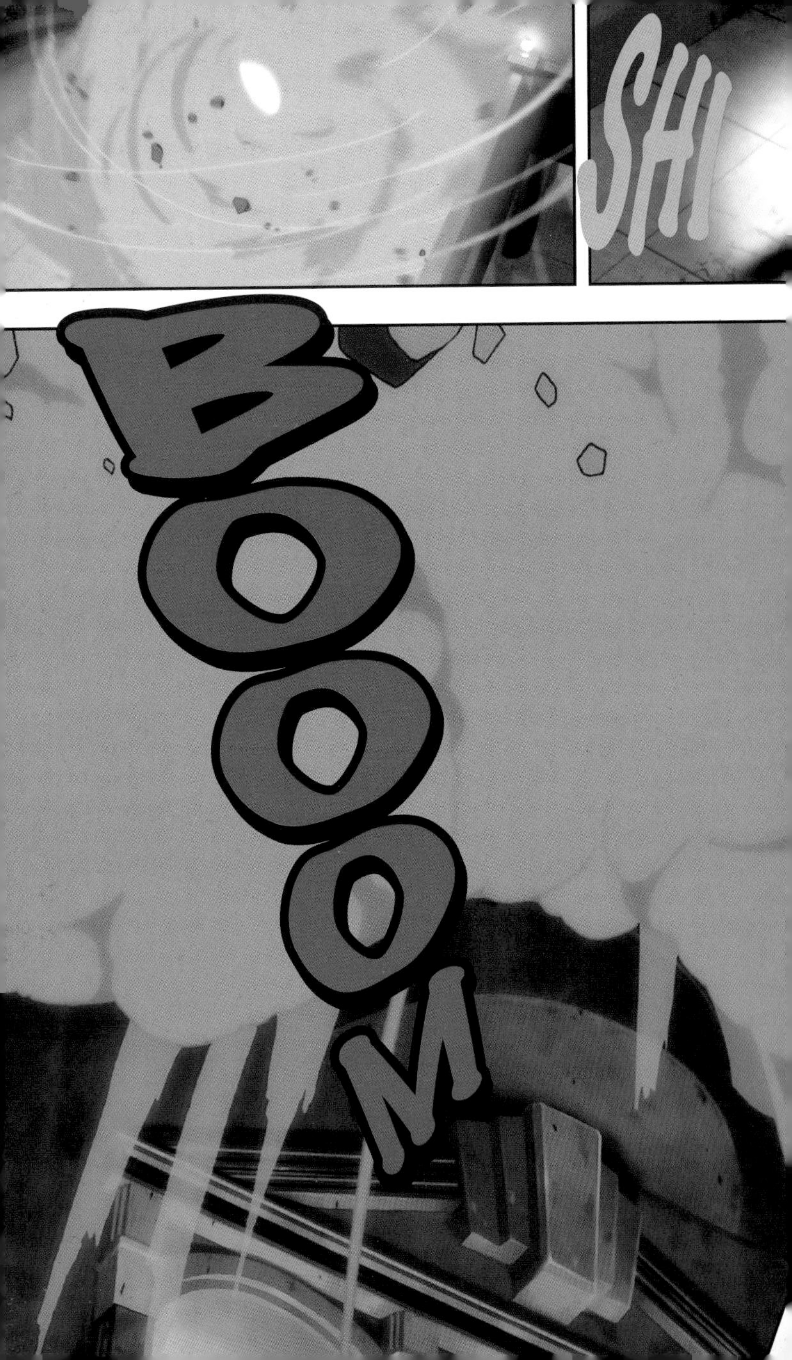
SHI
BOOOM

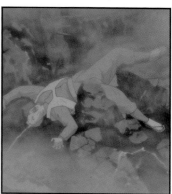
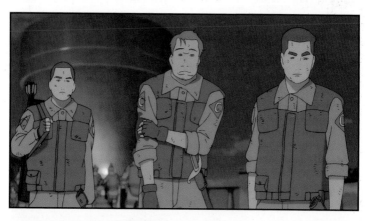

338

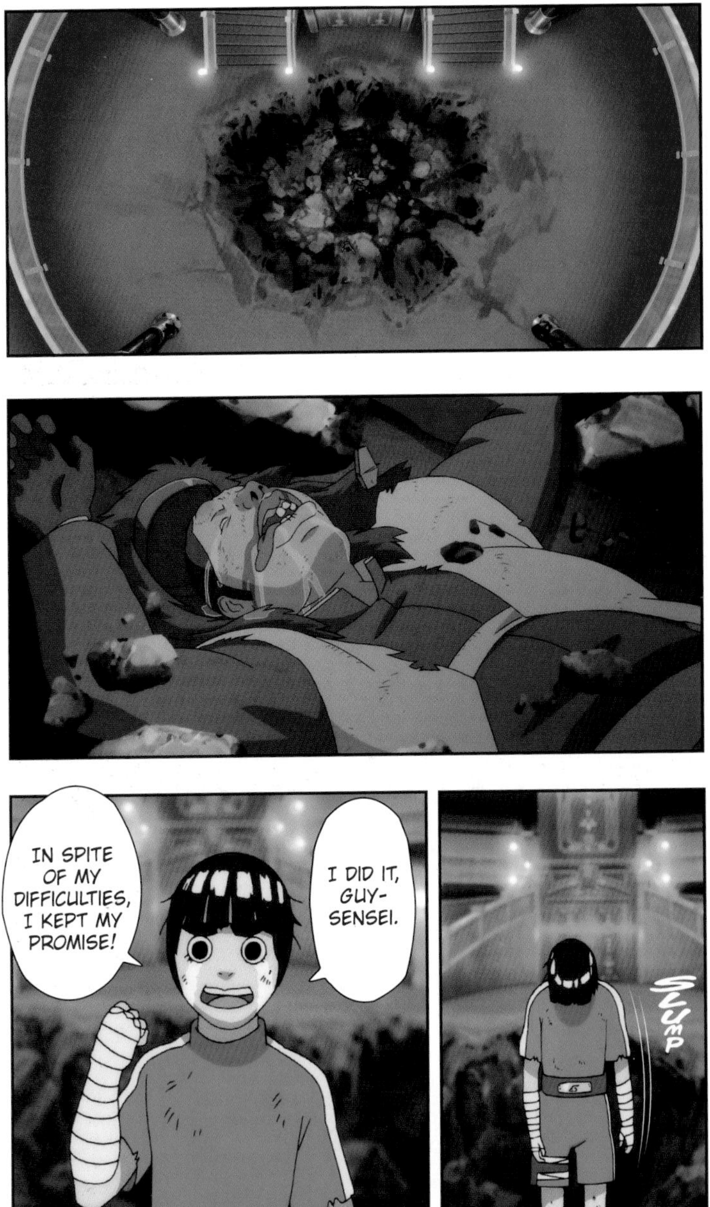
SLUMP
I DID IT, GUY-SENSEI.
IN SPITE OF MY DIFFICULTIES, I KEPT MY PROMISE!

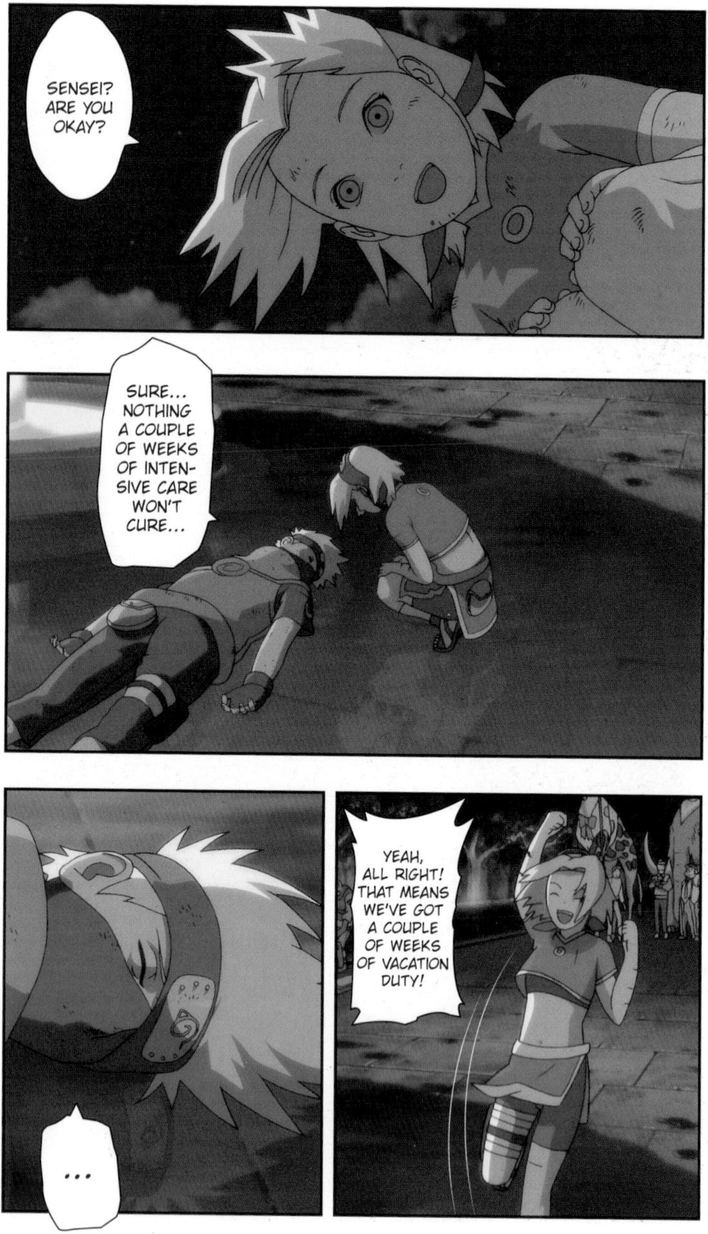
SENSEI? ARE YOU OKAY?
SURE... NOTHING A COUPLE OF WEEKS OF INTEN-SIVE CARE WON'T CURE...
YEAH, ALL RIGHT! THAT MEANS WE'VE GOT A COUPLE OF WEEKS OF VACATION DUTY!
...

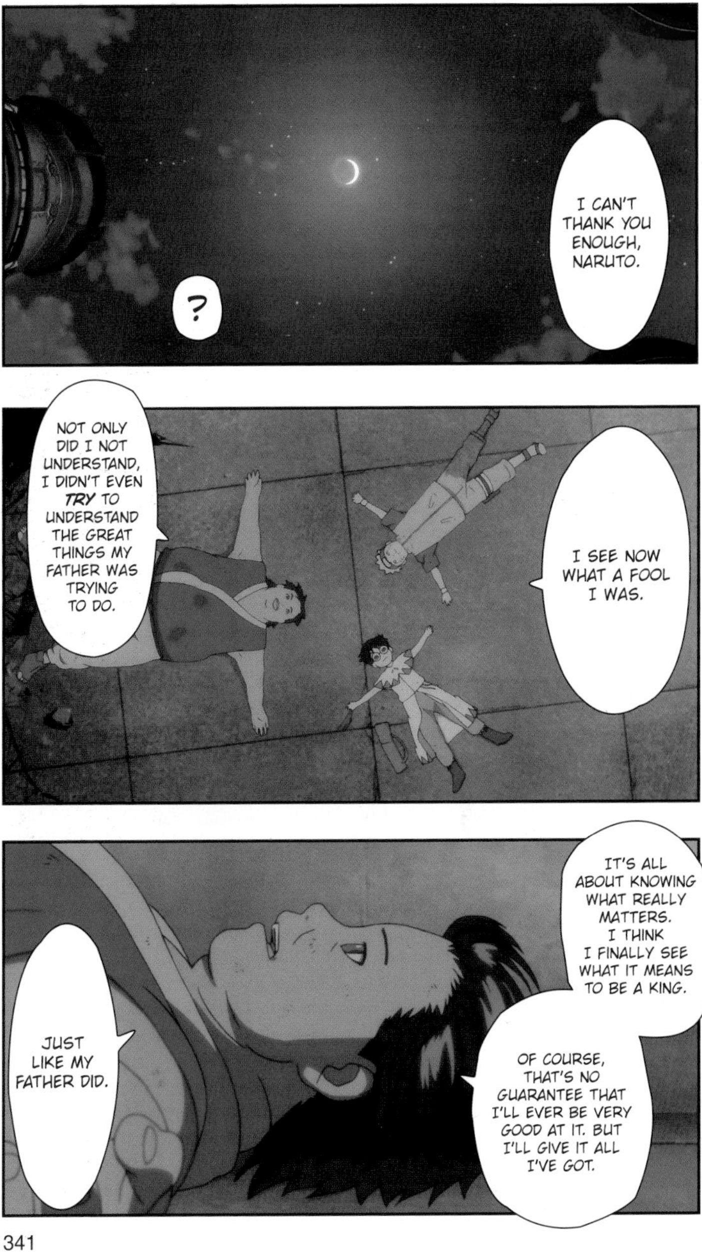
I CAN'T THANK YOU ENOUGH, NARUTO.
?
I SEE NOW WHAT A FOOL I WAS.
NOT ONLY DID I NOT UNDERSTAND, I DIDN'T EVEN ***TRY*** TO UNDERSTAND THE GREAT THINGS MY FATHER WAS TRYING TO DO.
IT'S ALL ABOUT KNOWING WHAT REALLY MATTERS. I THINK I FINALLY SEE WHAT IT MEANS TO BE A KING.
OF COURSE, THAT'S NO GUARANTEE THAT I'LL EVER BE VERY GOOD AT IT. BUT I'LL GIVE IT ALL I'VE GOT.
JUST LIKE MY FATHER DID.

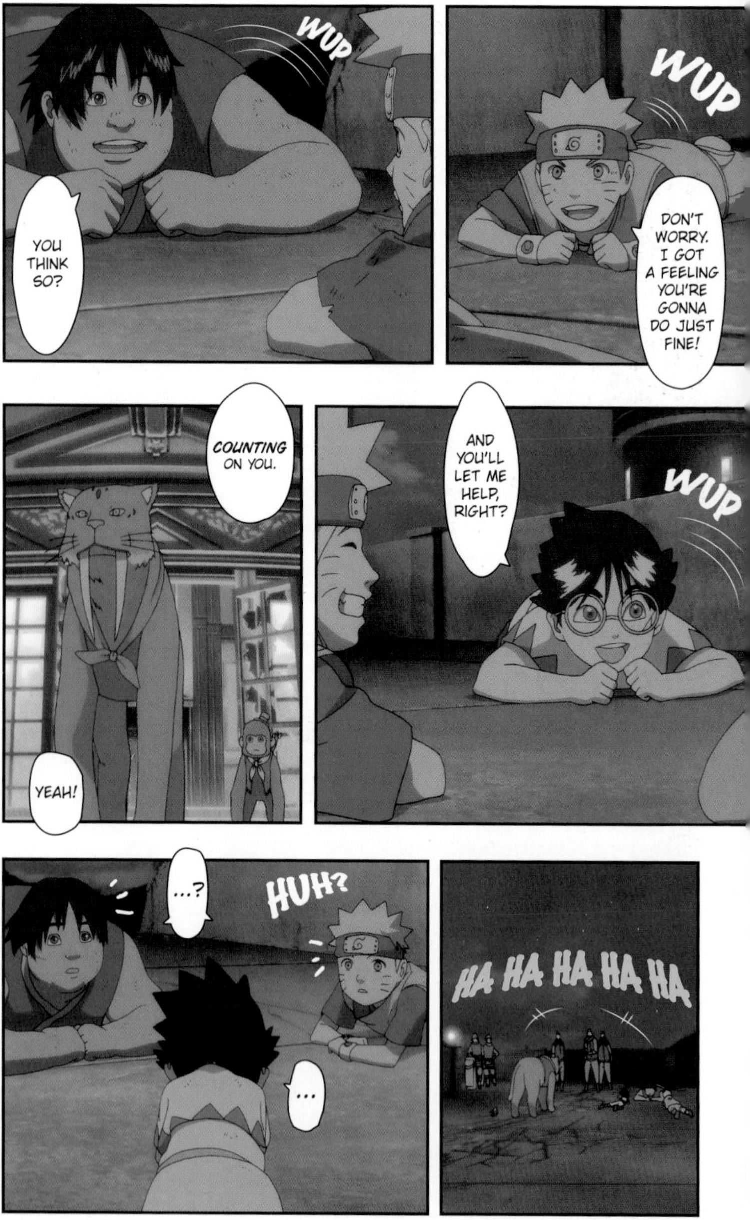
WUP
DON'T WORRY. I GOT A FEELING YOU'RE GONNA DO JUST FINE!
WUP
YOU THINK SO?
WUP
AND YOU'LL LET ME HELP, RIGHT?
COUNTING ON YOU.
YEAH!
HA HA HA HA HA
HUH?
...?
...

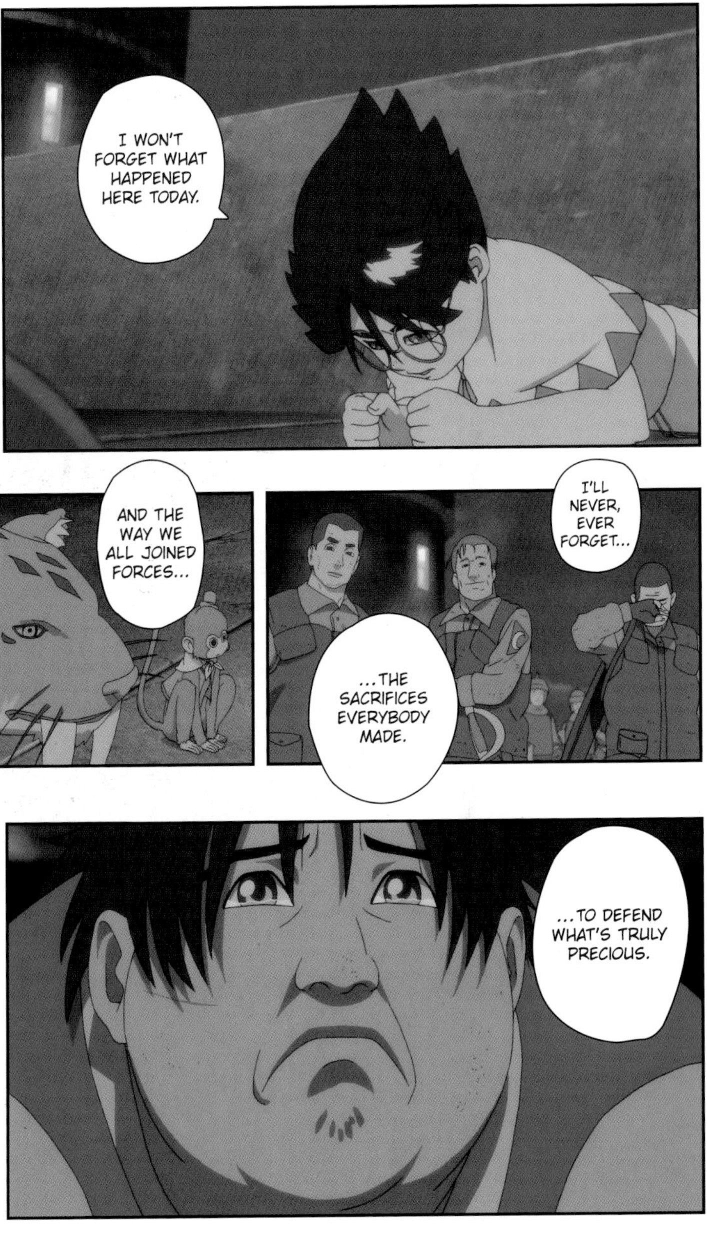
I WON'T FORGET WHAT HAPPENED HERE TODAY.
I'LL NEVER, EVER FORGET...
...THE SACRIFICES EVERYBODY MADE.
AND THE WAY WE ALL JOINED FORCES...
...TO DEFEND WHAT'S TRULY PRECIOUS.

BUT MOST OF ALL... I WON'T FORGET THE **FRIENDS** I'VE MADE.

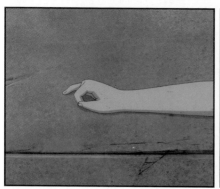

SHf

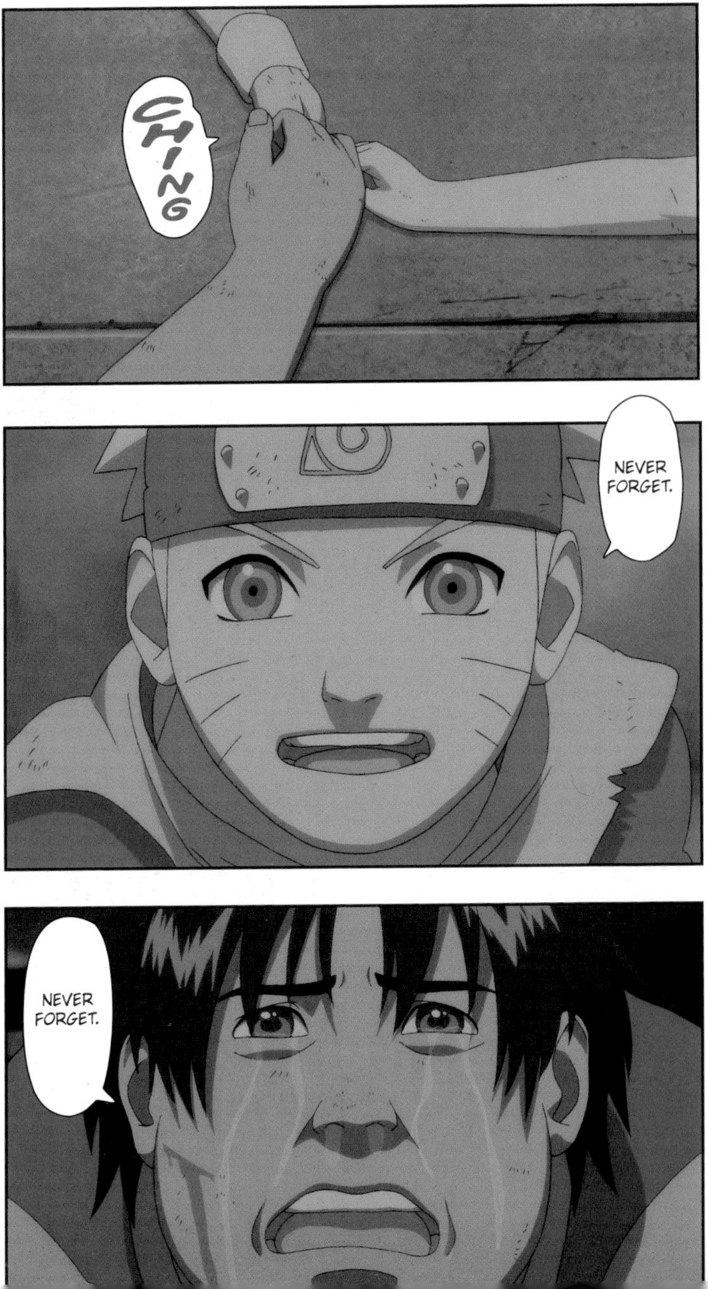
CHING
NEVER FORGET.
NEVER FORGET.

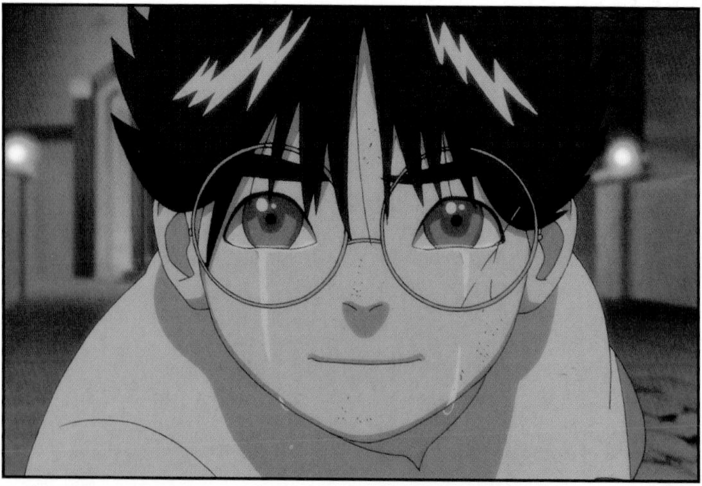

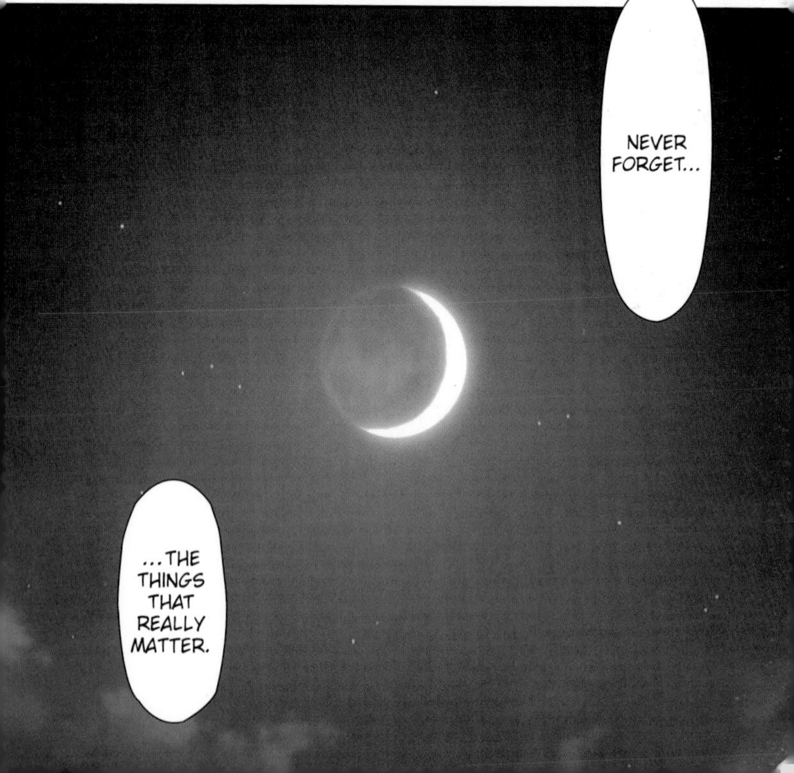
NEVER FORGET...
...THE THINGS THAT REALLY MATTER.

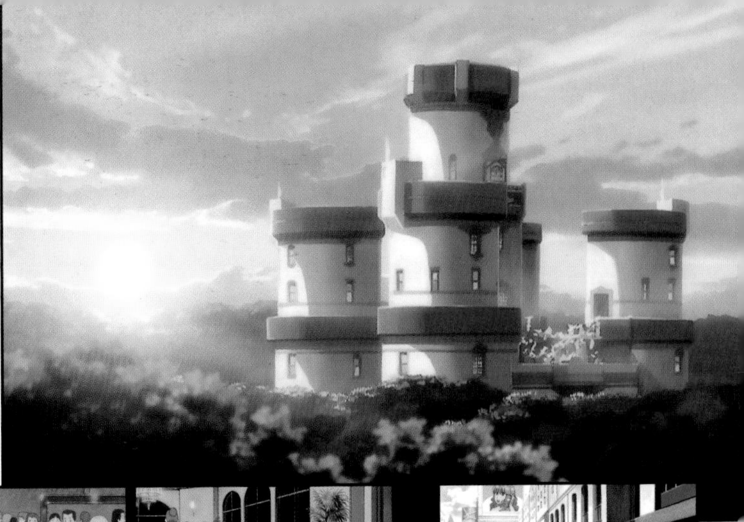

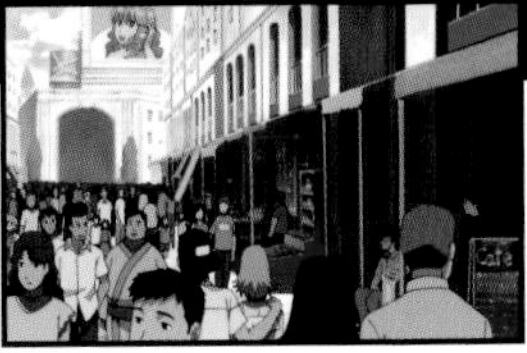
Cafe

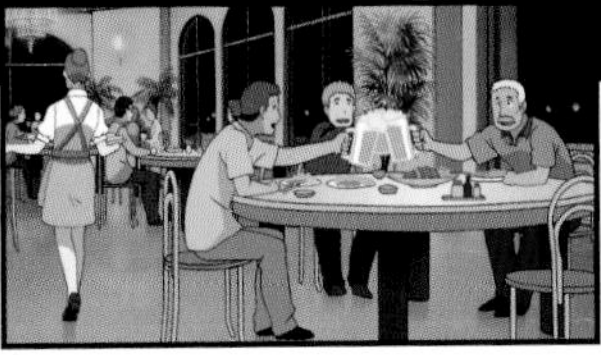

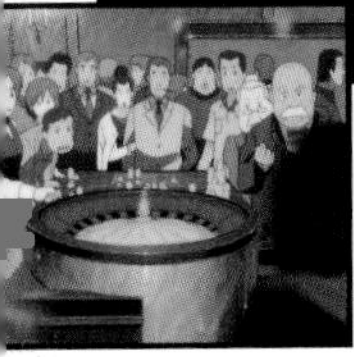

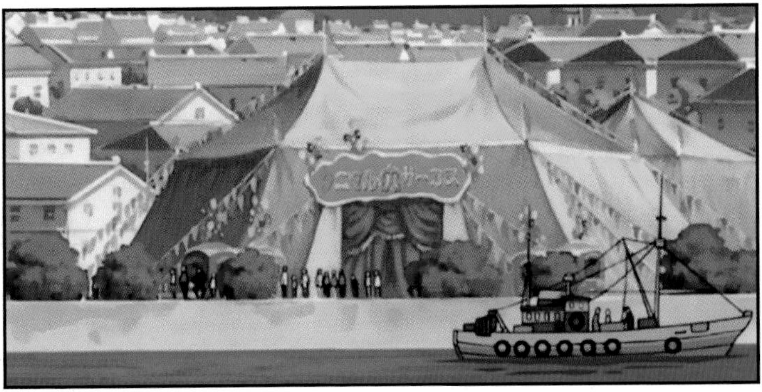

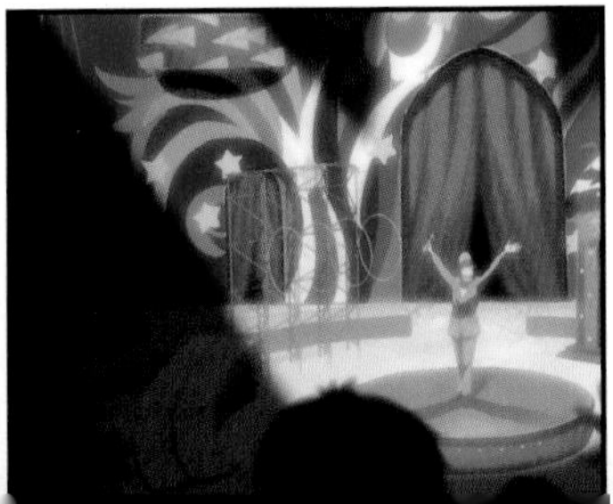

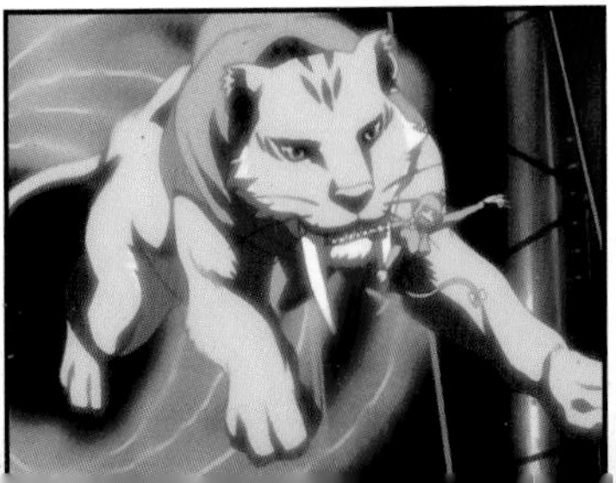

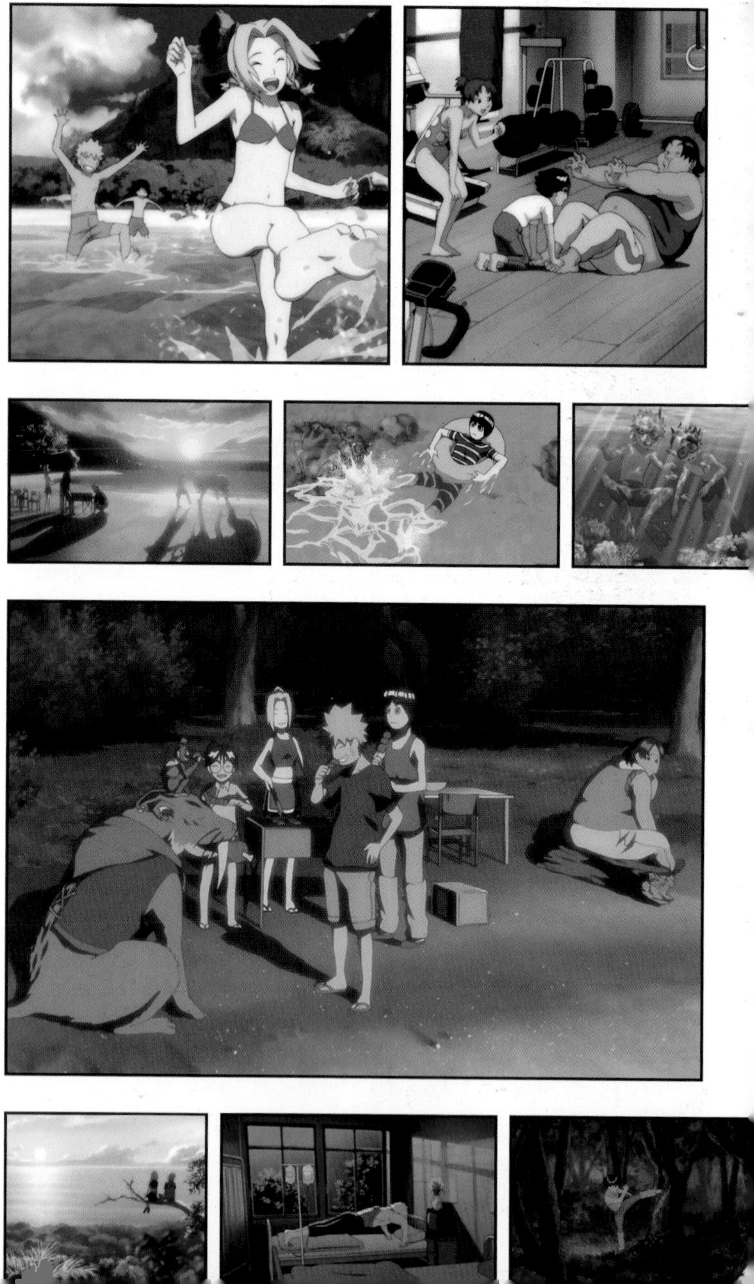

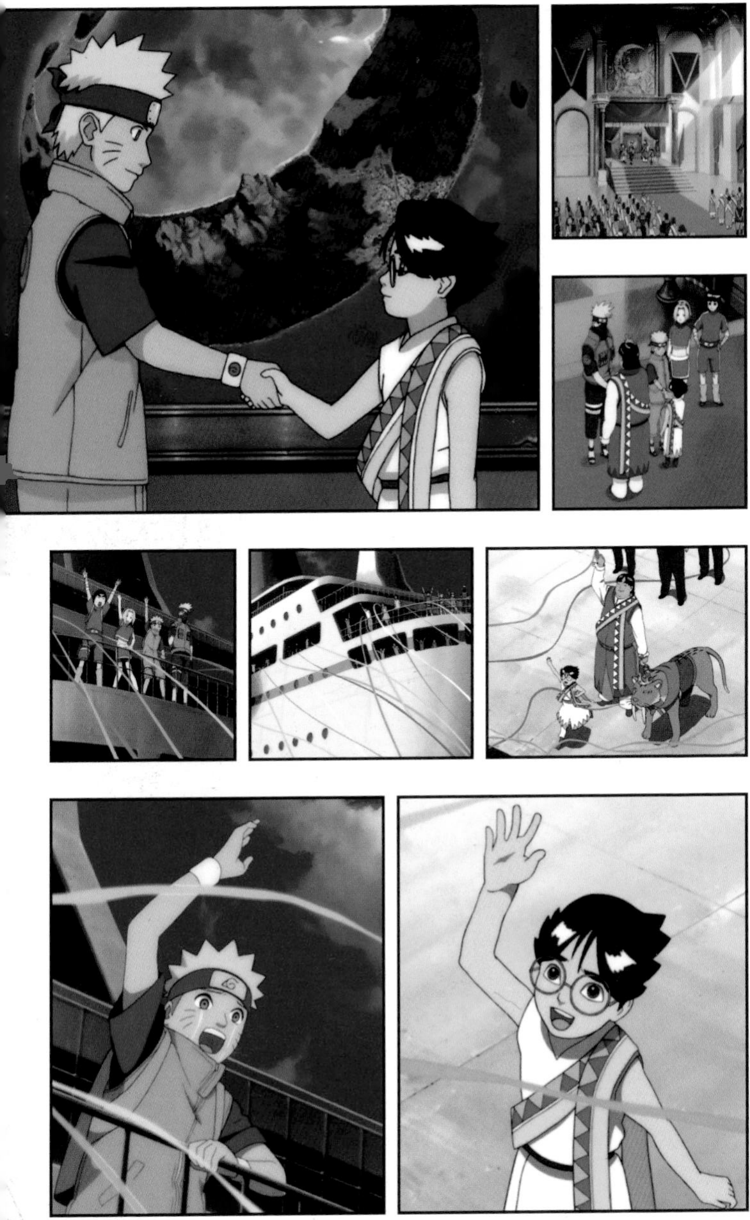

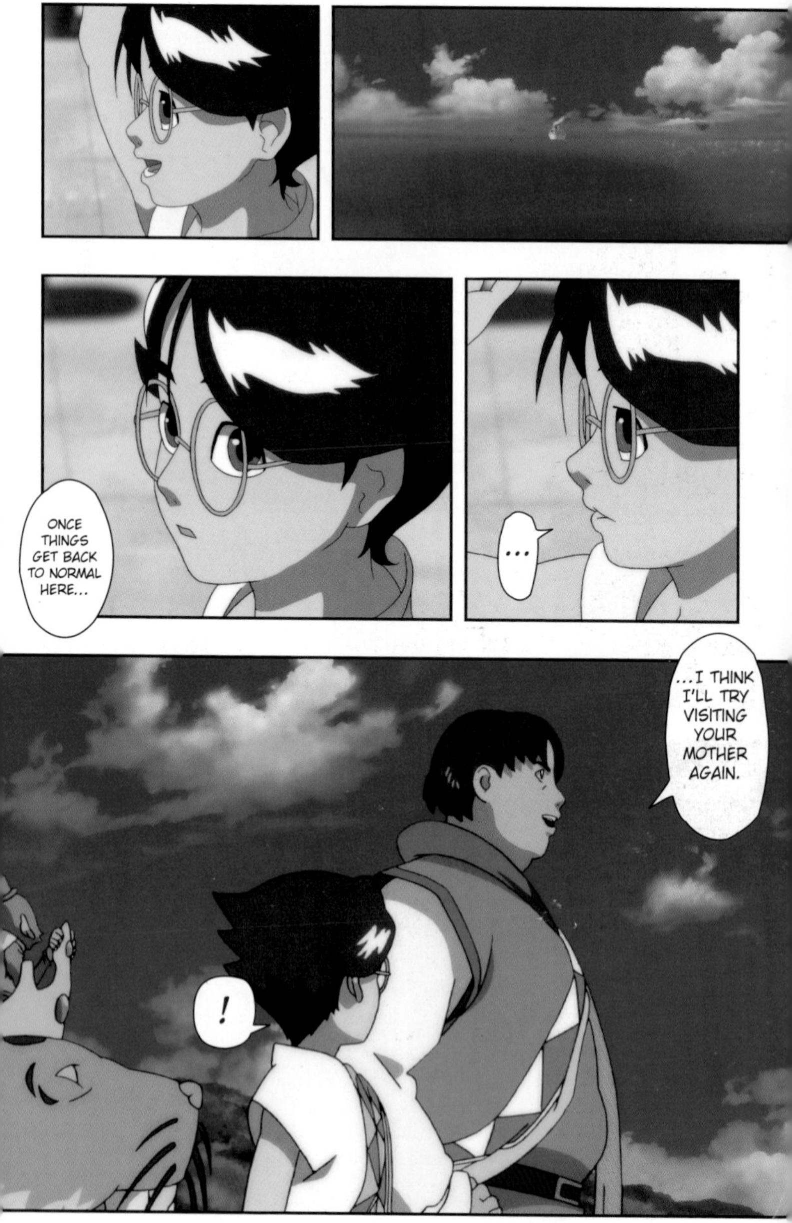
...
ONCE THINGS GET BACK TO NORMAL HERE...
...I THINK I'LL TRY VISITING YOUR MOTHER AGAIN.
!

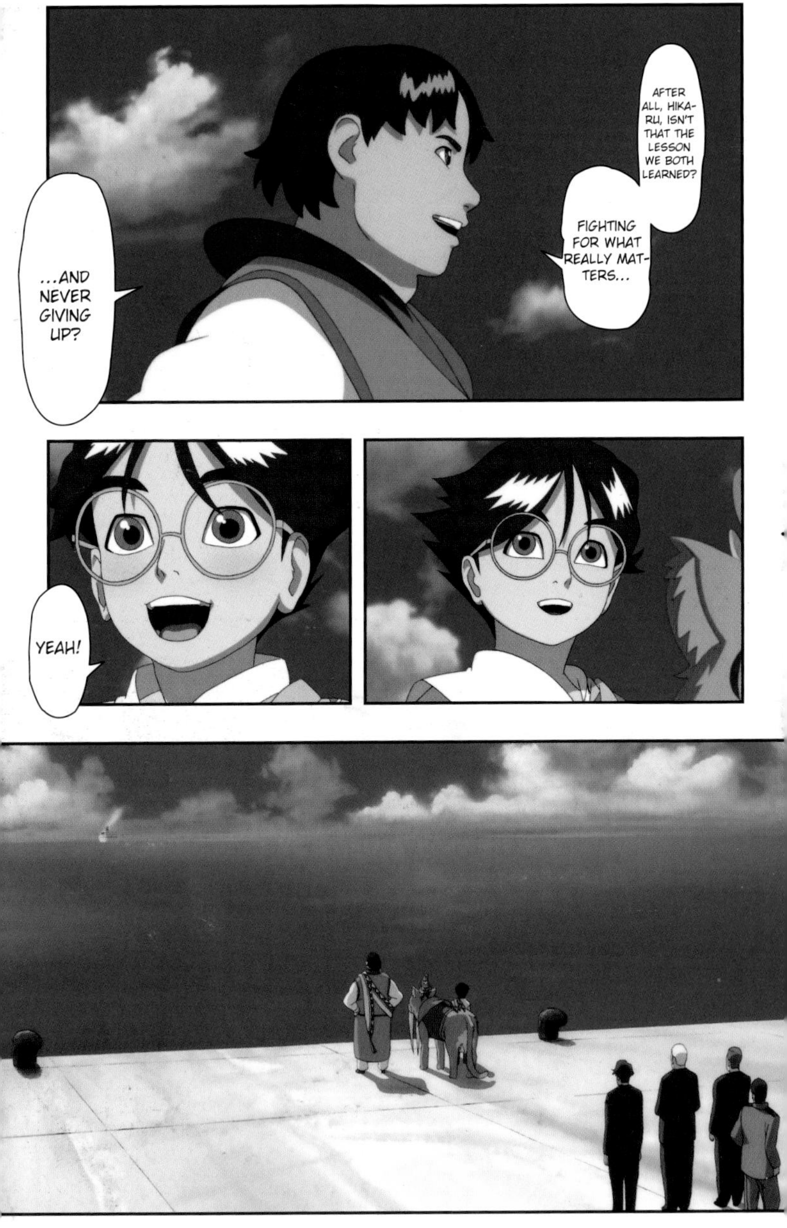
AFTER ALL, HIKA-RU, ISN'T THAT THE LESSON WE BOTH LEARNED?
FIGHTING FOR WHAT REALLY MAT-TERS...
...AND NEVER GIVING UP?
YEAH!

TOSHIO KAIDO
KUMIKO KIMURA
ANNA TORII
KAORI SAKAMOTO

Filming Cooperation
STUDIO COSMOS
DIGITAL FACTORY
Takahashi production,ltd./
T2studio

Paint Inspection
YOSHIKO SHIMIZU
KIMIKO KOJIMA
IZUMI MURASAKI
TOMOE IMAMURA
MAKIKO YAGIHASHI
YUKIE MATSUZAKI
HITOMI SHIMOGANNA
MAMI YARIWAKE
SHINNOSUKE NAGARE

Backgound Scanning
YURI SHIMIZU
RURIKO IKEJIRI
KAORU NAGASAWA
TOMOE MURAMATSU
SAEKO YUYAMA

Visual Art
RYUSUKE SHIINO

Background Retouching
SHINJI YAGINUMA
NAOMI WADA
NOBUO KIMURA
KAZUKO OYANAGI
KENJI IKEDA
YUMI MORITA
SHINYA ODA

System Management
TAKAKI OKUNAGA

3DCGI Director
XINHON WU

3DCGI
MIYUKI KOJIMA
KAZUYA SUGIYAMA
YOSHIHIRO YANAGIYA
WATARU SHIRAISHI
TAKAYUKI CHIBA
SHINSUKE OHSHIMA

3D Production
Cooperation
TETSUYA TABUCHI
TAKAYUKI INOUE
DAIKI UCHIDA
MAKIKO SAITO
MIO MATSUDA
MIHO HORA
FUMIROU SATO
FUKUTARO MIYAJI

HD24P Editing
TOMOMI TAKEMURA
KOHEI FUJIMORI
(Sony PCL)

HD Conversion
LEE JAEYOUNG
JUNICHI KATO
(Sony PCL)

HD Coordination
HIDEKI ITO
(Dinext)

CMS Technical Supervisor
HIDEO MORITA

CMS Supervisor
TADASHI NAKAMURA

CMS Technician
ATSUHIKO TANAKA

Film Recording
TOKYO LABORATORY LTD

Films
Kodak

Sound Effects
TAKUYA HASEGAWA
(SOUND BOX)

Sound Engineers
AKIRA NOGUCHI
(sound team • DON
JUAN)
OMNIBUS • JAPAN
KAZUTOSHI
YAMAMOTO
AKIRA SASAKI
The Tokyo Television
Center Co., Ltd.
EIJI HOTTA
MICHIHIKO IWANA
FUTOSHI UEDA

MA Studio
OMNIBUS • JAPAN
STUDIO GONG
The Tokyo Television
Center Co., Ltd.

Sound Production
RAKUONSHA

Sound Producer
MASAHIRO TSUKADA

Digital Recording Engineer
NOBORU NISHIO

Theme Song
"TSUBOMI" -BLOSSOM
BUDS-
Song by
MARIA
Lyrics by
MARIA
Composed by
TATTSU
Arranged by
HYOUE YASUHARA
Sony Music Records

Theme Song Promotion
TADAHITO KIMURA
YOSHIO KONNO
KAZUOMI KAJIHARA

Music Production

Music Producers
SHUICHI KURITA
MASAYUKI WATANABE
AI ABE

Recording & Surround
Mixing Engineer
HITOSHI HASHIMOTO

Assistant Mixing Engineers
TETSUYA KANESHIGE
YASUAKI SAKUMA

Production Assistant
TATSUYA IGARASHI

<MUSASHI Members>

Music Producers
KATSUNOSUKE
KOBARI
EMIKO OOIWA
TAKESHI FUJII

Japanese Drums
TAKARA OOTSUKA
Shamisen Guitar
HAJIME NISHI
Guitar
MASAAKI IIZUKA
Drums
TAKEKI MIYAUCHI
Shakuhachi, Noukan, Flute
KINOHACHI
6 String Bass Guitar
ISAMU TAKITA
Keyboards
YASUHARU TAKANASHI

Recording Studio
TOM • TOM STUDIO
AVACO CREATIVE
STUDIO

5.1 Mixing Studio
AVACO CREATIVE
STUDIO

Music Cooperation
TV Tokyo Music

Voice Directors
YU YAMASHITA
KOHJI ARITOMI

Voice Direction Support
KOJI MASUNARI

Assistant Animation
Producer
SYOJI MATSUI

Production Supervisor
SHIGEHIRO SUZUKI
Floor Coordinator
KUNIYUKI AOKI

Production Chiefs
ATSUSHI KAMIMURA
SHINYA KAWABATA

Production Coordinators
KOICHI MACHIYAMA
MIKI KUROSAKA
YUTA KIMURA
NANAKI SATO
YUUKO HATASAKO
YOSHIMI SATO

Production Staff
MAIKO ISOGAI
TOMOHIRO TAKAHASHI
NAOHIKO MATSUZAWA

General Manager
OHKI ASAKA

Production Cooperation
MADHOUSE
MASAO MOROSAWA
TORU UMEOKA
DOGA KOBO
TAZUKO FUKUDO
MOOK ANIMATION
ARMS
OSAMU SHIMIZU
SAE OHBA
MSJ
HIROKAZU NAGAOKA
JEONG HAENG GUEON
JOUNG SE KWON
JEONG GYUN JEONG
GUEY JY HWANG

Production
SYOHEI IZAWA
NORITAKA YAMAJI
YUJI NUNOKAWA
YOSHISHIGE SHIMATANI
NAOKI KITAGAWA
SOUICHI AKIYAMA
KAZUHIRO TAKENAKA

Project Cooperation
KEISUKE IWATA
KAZUHIKO TORISHIMA
MICHIYUKI HONMA
KEN HAGINO

Producers
NORIKO KOBAYASHI
KAZUTERU OSHIKIRI

Project Cooperation
SHUEISHA/SHONEN
JUMP
MASAHIKO IBARAKI
MASANA TAKAHASHI
KOSUKE YAHAGI

Associate Producers
YUKAKO MATSUSAKO
MUTSUKO KANADA
TAKUYUKI HIROBE
MASATO TAKAMI
KAZUMICHI UEDA
YUKIO YOSHIMURA

Marketing Producer
MASAKI NAKAYAMA

Marketing Coordinators
NOBUHIRO FUKUDA
CHIZUKO AGATSUMA
SAYAKA ONO

Movie Trailer Producer
MASAYUKI OHHIRA

Movie Trailer Director
DAISUKE FUKUNAGA

Naruto Movie Project
TV TOKYO
OSAMU OGAWA
REI ANAMI
HARUYUKI IGUCHI

SHUEISHA
TSUNEO OYAMA
KENICHIRO USHIKI

PIERROT
HIROMICHI UCHIDA
MIKIO IGARASHI
KOTA KITAMURA
EMIKO YAKAME
CHIAKI KAKUMA

TOHO
MINAMI ICHIKAWA
HIKARU ONODA
GENKI KAWAMURA

Aniplex
HIDEO KATSUMATA
OSAMU TAKESUE
KAZUKO YAMAMOTO
TAKAMITSU INOUE

dentsu
RIICHIRO NAKAMURA
ATSUSHI HIGASHIYAMA
AYA MIZOBUCHI

BANDAI
KEISUKE FURUSAWA
MASARU HISAMOTO

Sponsored by
TAKARATOMY
KEITA SATO
SHIRYO OKUAKI
WATARU KUBO
ENSKY
KOICHI SOMEYA
HIRONOBU KAMADA
SHOWA NOTE
SHIGERU KATAGISHI
TOMIO HIGANO
MAMIKO ABE

Movic
MASAKI YASUDA
TOSHIHIKO SUZUKI

Cooperation
FAMILYMART
famima.com

Animation Production
studioPIERROT

Distributed by
TOHO

Produced by
NARUTO Movie Project
TV TOKYO
SHUEISHA
PIERROT
TOHO
Aniplex
dentsu
BANDAI

Director
TOSHIYUKI TSURU

English Production by
VIZ Media, LLC

Executive Producers
HIDEMI FUKUHARA
AKIRA FUJITA

Producer
JAMIE SIMONE

Production Supervisors
ALVIN LU
WILLIAM GERMAIN

Co-Producers
JASON BERGENFELD
MIKI MACALUSO

Production Associate
MITSUKO KITAJIMA

Creative Consultant
JOEL ENOS

Distributed by
VIZ Media, LLC

Casting by
JAMIE SIMONE

Voice Director
MARY ELIZABETH
MCGLYNN

Cast:
MAILE FLANAGAN
KATE HIGGINS
ROGER CRAIG SMITH
STEVE BLUM
KEITH SILVERSTEIN
KARI WAHLGREN
SAM RIEGEL
WILLIAM GERMAIN
BRIAN DONOVAN
BRIDGET HOFFMAN
CHRIS SMITH
CINDY ROBINSON
DAVE WITTENBERG
DEBI MAE WEST
JAMIESON PRICE
KIRK THORTON
MARY ELIZABETH
MCGLYNN
MICHAEL FORREST
MICHAEL SORICH
ROGER ROSE
WALLY WINGERT
TERRY STONE

Post Production
Supervisor
DENNY DENSMORE

Video Editors
TERRY MARLIN
LINDSEY MYERS

Additional Video
Compositing
HARLIN T. HARRIS
DAVID BUTTERWORTH

Recording Engineers
MICHAEL CLARK
DAVID W. BARR

English Adaptation by
ARDWIGHT
CHAMBERLAIN

Re-Recording Mixer
MARK ETTLE

Production Manager
LAURA LOPEZ

Production Coordinators
SEAN KELLEY
JESSICA RENSLOW

Produced at
STUDIOPOLIS, INC.

Distributed by
VIZ Media, LLC

Original Author
MASASHI KISHIMOTO
SHUEISHA/SHONEN JUMP

Screenplay
TOSHIYUKI TSURU

Continuity
KOJI MASUNARI
NORIO MASAMOTO
TOKUYUKI MATSUTAKE
YU YAMASHITA
JUNICHI TAKAOKA
YUZO SATO
KOHJI ARITOMI
TOSHIYUKI TSURU

Character Design
TETSUYA NISHIO
HIROFUMI SUZUKI

Property Design
HIROTO TANAKA
KEIKO SHIMIZU
HIROFUMI MASUDA

Visual Layout
HIROTO TANAKA

Animation Directors
HIROFUMI SUZUKI
HIROTO TANAKA
TSUGUYUKI KUBO
KEIKO SHIMIZU
CHIKARA SAKURAI
YUICHI ENDO
HIROFUMI MASUDA
HIROKI TAKAGI

Effect Animation Director
HIROFUMI MASUDA

Art Director
HITOSHI NAGASAKI

Color Design
YUKO SATO

Director of Cinematography
ATSUO MATSUMOTO

Editors
YUKIE OIKAWA
SEIJI MORITA

Recording Director
CHIHARU KAMIO

Sound Director
YASUNORI EBINA

Music
TOSHIO MASUDA &
MUSASHI PROJECT

CAST
Naruto Uzumaki
JUNKO TAKEUCHI
Sakura Haruno
CHIE NAKAMURA
Rock Lee
YOICHI MASUKAWA
Kakashi Hatake
KAZUHIKO INOUE
Michiru Tsuki
AKIO OHTSUKA
Hikaru Tsuki
KYOUSUKE IKEDA
Amayo
MARIKA HAYASHI
Shabadaba
UMEJI SASAKI
Ishidate
MASASHI SUGAWARA
Kongo
HISAO EGAWA
Karenbana
HARUHI TERADA
Korega
KENJI HAMADA
Guards
SHIGENORI SOYA
MASAYUKI KATO
DAI MATSUMOTO
KEIGO SUZUKI

Circus Ring Master
TOMOMICHI NISHIMURA
(Special Appearance)
Mammoth
ANIMAL HAMAGUCHI
Circus Dancer
KYOKO HAMAGUCHI
Circus Member Matsumoto
KOTA MATSUMOTO
Circus Member Nishikawa
AKIHIRO NISHIKAWA
Circus Audience
MARIA
Circus Members
EIJI YANAGISAWA
MASATO FUNAKI
ERIKO KIGAWA
WAKANA SUBE

**Voice Cooperation for
"People of Crescent
Moon Island"**
B-BOY

Kakeru Tsuki
ROKURO NAYA
Fifth Hokage Tsunade
MASAKO KATSUKI

Key Animation
NORIO MATSUMOTO
AKIKO YAMAGUCHI
MAMORU SASAKI
HUTOSHI SUZUKI
JUN ISHIKAWA
KATSUHIRO NAKATSURU
TADASHI MATSUZAKI
SHIGERU KIMIJIMA
MIWA SASAKI
MASAHARU TADA
TADAKATSU YOSHIDA
FUMIYO KIMURA
KAZUNOBU HOSHI
MASAYUKI YOSHIKI
HIROFUMI MASUDA
CHIKARA SAKURAI
HIROKI TAKAGI
YU YAMASHITA
HIROFUMI SUZUKI
TSUGUYUKI KUBO
HIROTO TANAKA
TAKAHIRO KISHIDA
HIDEKI HAMASU
MASARU YONEZAWA
RYOCHIMO
KENICHI KUTSUNA
ATSUKO NOZAKI
YOSHIHARU SHIMIZU
YUKI HAYASHI
KENJI HACHIZAKI
AYUMU KOTAKE
SHIRO KIKI
YUZO SATO
TOSHIHIKO MASUDA
YUICHI ENDO
ATSUKO OHTANI
MASAHIRO NERIKI
TOSHIHARU SUGIE
KENICHI KONISHI
MAYUMI ODA
SHO SUGAI
KAZUYA HAYASHI
JUN UEMURA
YOKO ONO
MAMIKO NAKANISHI
RYOTARO MAKIHARA
TOMOHISA SHIMOYAMA
TAKAYUKI URAGAMI
KUMIKO HORIKOSHI
TADASHI FUKUDA
NOBUHIRO OHSUGI
HARUO OOKAWASE
KEIICHI ISHIKAWA
KAZUYA SAITO
NAOKO IKEUCHI
MIKA NAIKI
ICHIRO UNO
HIDEKI NAGAMACHI
TAKAO SANO
SATOSHI HATTORI
TOMOHIRO KISHI
SATOMI HIGUCHI
YOSHIYUKI KISHI
MIEKO HOSOI
MINAKO SHIBA
CHIKASHI KUBOTA

SHOTA YANUMA
YOKO SUZUKI
KAZUYA MIYOSHI
HIROOMI YAMAKAWA
ICHIRO KAMEOKA
YASUYUKI KAI
SAYURI SUGITO
NORIKO OHTAKE
HIROTAKA KINOSHITA
MASAKI ENDO
HIROTSUGU KAWASAKI
SHINJI HASHIMOTO
KOJI YABUNO
TAKAHIRO CHIBA
TSUNEO NINOMIYA
TETSUYA NISHIO

Animation Director Assistants
HUTOSHI SUZUKI
JUN ISHIKAWA
KOJI YABUNO
HIDEKI NAGAMACHI
SHINGO KURAKARI
HIROYUKI OGURA
MASAYA OHNISHI
NORIKO OHTAKE
TOKUYUKI MATSUTAKE
SAYURI SUGITO

Second Key Animation
RYUTA YANAGI
MASAYUKI KOUDA
KIM BOMIN
HIDEHIKO OKANO
MIKI KATO
HIDEHITO TANAKA
TAKASHI TANAZAWA
KAYOKO SUZUKI
KASUMI WADA
JUNICHI TAKADATE
TOMOKO MURAKAMI
SHIGEKI KAWAI
RETSU OOKAWARA
CHIE HASHIMOTO
NOZOMI FUJII
RYOJI IKEMATSU
MASAYUKI KATO
RIE NAKANISHI
MIHO INOUE
MANABU NII
MIFUMI TOMITA
DOGA KOBO
MICHIKO TAKEGAMI
OSAMU MIWA
NOBUSHIGE ISHITA
NARA ANIMATION STUDIO
DR MOVIE
HANJIN ANIMATION

Assistant Art Dirctor
NORIHIKO YOKOMATSU

Backgrounds Studio Wyeth
YUKO KATAYAMA
MAYU USUI
SHIHO YANASE
MAYUKO MORI
MICHIKO TANIGUCHI
RIEKO OOIWA
STUDIO EASTER
JUNICHI HIGASHI
SHINIICHI TANIMURA
HIDENORI SANO
ERI NAKAMURA
YUKIE ABE
KOJI MIZUGUCHI
AKIRA ITOMITSU
TSUTOMU MOMOUCHI
MIYUKI ONODERA
KENTA SHIMIZU
JUNKO SHIMIZU
TAKAFUMI SUZUKI
SHINJI TAKASUGA
KUSANAGI
TOSHIKI NISHI
HIROSHI ITO
ANNA OHIZUMI
SADAHIKO TANAKA
DR MOVIE
STUDIO RAIN
STUDIO LOFT
KAZUHIKO SUZUKI
TOSHIKO ABE
TETSUHIRO SHIMIZU
TSUYOSHI FUKUMOTO
MISUMI AIZAWA

SEOUL LOFT
KLAS
YOSHIHITO WATANABE
TOSHIHIDE KAWANA
TAKIMI ECHIZEN
TATSURO IZERI
TOMOKO SASAKI

3D Backgrounds
STUDIO EASTER
HIDENORI SANO
TAKAHIRO MIZUGUCHI
ERI NAKAMURA
TSUTOMU MOMOUCHI

Layout Cooperation
SHIGENORI TAKADA
SHINJI SUGIYAMA

Overseas Contact
MOON SONHO

Background Supervisor
MINORU NAKAMURA

In-between Animation
PIERROT
RINAKO J. NISHIHARA
DAISUKE IRIE
CHIE OHTSUKI
YASUKO SHII
IKUMI OKA
NATSUKI KOJIMA
NAMI MIYANOGAWA
PIERROT FUKUOKA
MIKA OOKUBO
ETSUKO KIMURA
EMI KIRIKIHIRA
FUMIE KANEKO
YOKO TAKAYANAGI
HIROMI JO
OH PRODUCTION
MIHOKO UDA
MINAKO SEKIHARA
ASAMI TAKANO
SHINICHI KUNIYASU
MISUZU ICHINOSE
PRODUCTION IG
MASATSUGU NISHIDA
KOTOE SAITO
HARUYO NEBU
HISAKO SHIMOTSUMA
YUKI SATO
MARIKO ISHIKAWA
KIM YUNJI
KATSURA TSUSHIMA
DAIKI NISHIKAWA
YUKIKO WATABE
YASUKO TAKAHASHI
ASAMI MANNEN
TAKESHI ISHIZUKA
NARA ANIMATION STUDIO
WHANG JI NA
PARK EUN JU
CHOI DO YOUNG
SUNG JI YOUNG
LEE SUN MI
YI DO RUEM
AN HI GYEONG
YUN JOUNG HYE
CHO HYE JUNG
YOUN EUN JU
SEONG BO YANG HAENG
BAE YONG OH
PAK EUN AH
SONG HYUN JU
JO HYUN MI
YM GAB SOOK
MIN HO JEONG
JEON EUN KYUNG
LEE SE YUN
DR MOVIE
KIM MIN KYOUNG
BYUN EUN SOON
SONG NA AE
LEE EUN KYUNGA
HONG SEUNG HEE
HWANG MI SUN
BUSAN DR
MONSTER
HYOIN
MSJ
HAYASHI Co., Ltd.
Triple A
HANJIN ANIMATION
JIWOO ANIMATION
KYONGNAN ANIMATION
FAR EASTERN ANIMATION
LIMITED
MADHOUSE

KYONGAN ANIMATION
FAR EASTERN ANIMATION
LIMITED
MADHOUSE
MAYUMI SUZUKI

Animation Inspection
HIROKO TEZUKA
KUMIKO KAWASHIMA
YASUHITO NISHIKATA
ERIKO MURAKAMI
MITSUKO TOSHIMA
TAKAAKI KOMORI

Color Correction
YUKI KASE
YASUKO SUENAGA
MAYUMI NAGASHIMA

Digital Painting
PIERROT FUKUOKA
YUKIE MATSUZAKI
YUKIKO TANISHIMA
SHINNOSUKE NAGARE
HITOMI SHIMOGANNA
MAMI YARIWAKE
STUDIO KILLY
TOSHIHO IWAKIRI
NAOMI TAKAHASHI
SAYURI TAKAGI
MIYOKO YOSHIDA
KAORI ISHIKAWA
HIROMI TSUCHIYA
MICHIKO IKUSHIMA
YOSHIE IWAKIRI
STUDIO TARGE
SHUJI TSUCHIYA
NAOKO MIYAHARA
KAZUMI HOSOKAWA
TOSHIYUKI ITO
NATSUKO INOHARA
RYUSUKE MINAMI
SAYURI MISEZAKI
HISASHI KOYANAGI
KOTOMI IYAMURA
AYAE OGASAWARA
YOSHIHIRO NAKAKAWA
AKIYUKI HATANAKA
SAYURI SUZUKI
KUMIKO AKAHORI
KOJI USUI
YUKIE MAEHARA SEONG
BO YANG HAENG
GEON OH SOOK
HAE YN HWA
YU HYE JEONG
SEO KYUNG HWA
KIM JEONG HWA
YM MAE YL
GOOK GYU SEON
NA HYE JEONG
NARA ANIMATION STUDIO
CHOI SEONG SOOK
CHUN HYUN JOO
O YOUNG SOOK
JEONG JI HYON
SON EUN SUK
KIM MI JUNG
HAN MYUNG SUN
PARK KYUNG SUK
DR MOVIE
CHOI SOON LEE
JEON SO RA
JUN MYOUNG HEE
JUNG SU HYUN
KANG NAM LEE
KIM A JIN
LEE JEONG EUN
PARK YUN HEE
BUSANDR
MONSTER
HYOIN
MSJ
HAYASHI Co., Ltd.
Triple A
HANJIN ANIMATION
JIWOO ANIMATION
KYONGNAN ANIMATION
FAR EASTERN ANIMATION
LIMITED
MADHOUSE

Filming
KAORI KAWASHIMA
YUKA NAKAYA
MAI UEMATSU

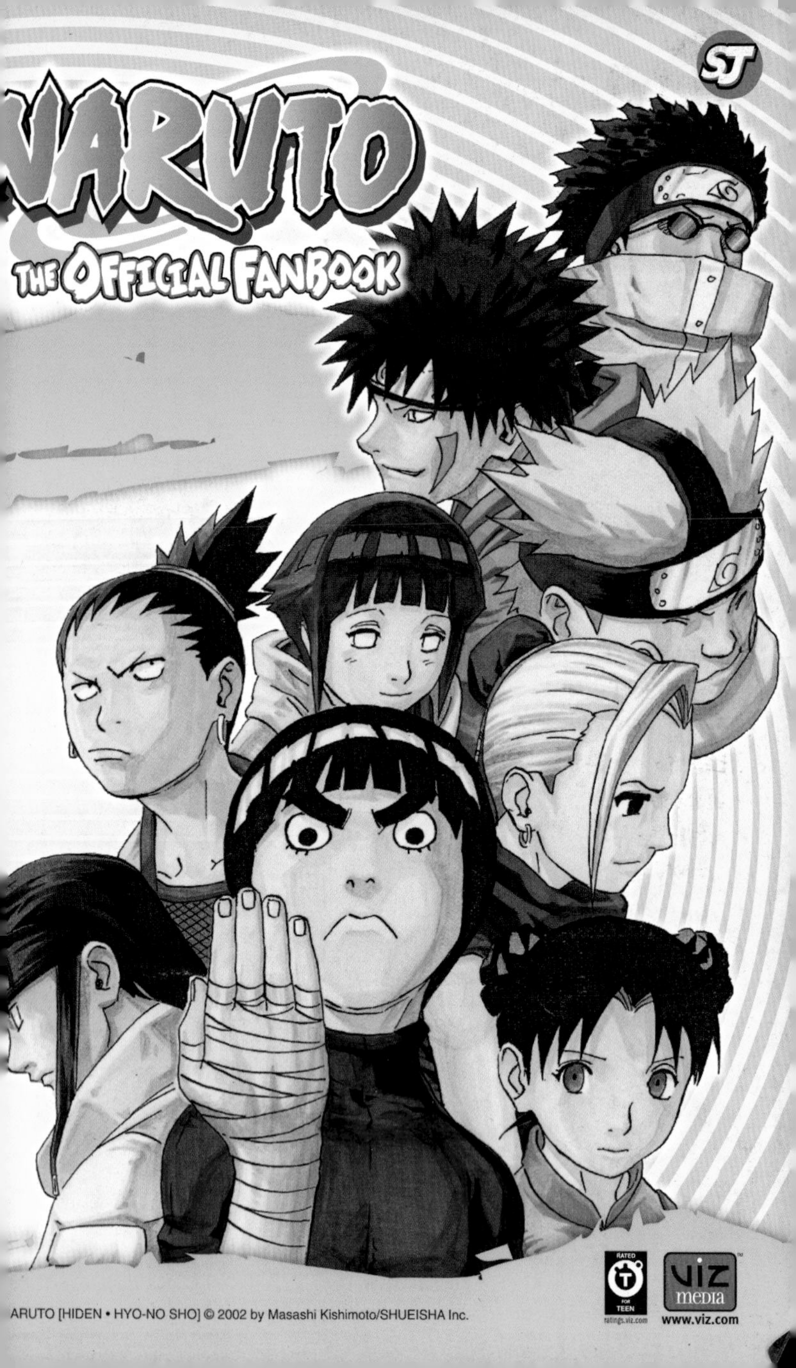

SJ
NARUTO
THE OFFICIAL FANBOOK
RATED T FOR TEEN
ratings.viz.com
VIZ media
www.viz.com
ARUTO [HIDEN • HYO-NO SHO] © 2002 by Masashi Kishimoto/SHUEISHA Inc.

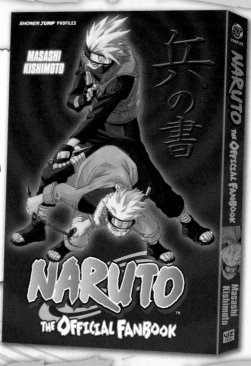

When a dream of utopia becomes a **NIGHTMARE**, it'll take a ninja to set things right!

SHONEN JUMP™
NARUTO
THE MOVIE
LEGEND of the STONE GELEL

2 DISC SET
SHONEN JUMP
NARUTO
THE MOVIE
LEGEND of the STONE GELEL

NARUTO The Movie 2:
Legend of the Stone of Gelel
NOW ON DVD!

GET THE COMPLETE
NARUTO COLLECTION
OF BOOKS, MAGAZINES AND DVDS

ON SALE AT NARUTO.VIZ.COM
ALSO AVAILABLE AT YOUR LOCAL BOOKSTORE AND COMIC STORE

RATED
FOR TEEN
ratingjsl.viz.com

www.viz.com